# The Management of Marine Regions:
## The North Pacific

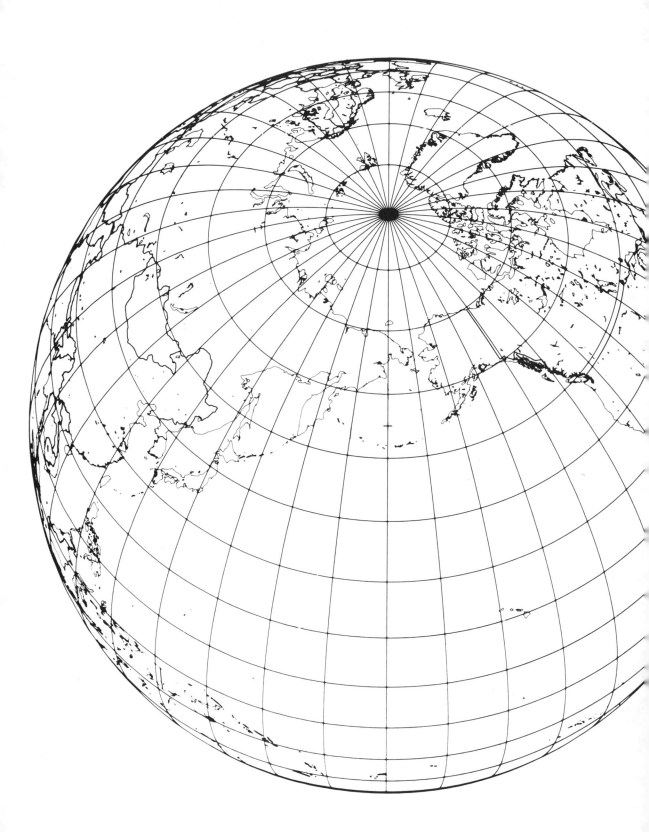

# The Management of Marine Regions: The North Pacific

An Analysis of Issues Relating to Fisheries, Marine
Transportation, Marine Scientific Research, and Multiple Use
Conditions and Conflicts

EDWARD MILES, STEPHEN GIBBS, DAVID FLUHARTY,
CHRISTINE DAWSON, AND DAVID TEETER

with

WILLIAM BURKE, WLODZIMIERZ KACZYNSKI, AND
WARREN WOOSTER

UNIVERSITY OF CALIFORNIA PRESS

BERKELEY   LOS ANGELES   LONDON

NORTHWEST COMMUNITY
COLLEGE

UNIVERSITY OF CALIFORNIA PRESS
Berkeley and Los Angeles, California


UNIVERSITY OF CALIFORNIA PRESS, LTD.
London, England

**Library of Congress Cataloging in Publication Data**

Main entry under title:

The Management of marine regions.

    Includes bibliographical references and index.
    1. Fishery management, International—North Pacific
Ocean. 2. Marine resources and state—North Pacific Ocean.
3. Shipping—North Pacific Ocean—Government policy.
4. Marine sciences—Research—North Pacific Ocean—
Government policy. 5. Fishery policy—North Pacific Ocean.
6. Maritime law—North Pacific Ocean. I. Miles, Edward L.
SH214.2.M36    333.91′64′091644    81-19657
ISBN  0-520-04458-4              AACR2


PRINTED IN THE UNITED STATES OF AMERICA


1 2 3 4 5 6 7 8 9

For the late Donald L. McKernan, the Faculty, and Students of the Institute for Marine Studies, University of Washington

# Contents

## PART III: Marine Scientific Research in the North Pacific

PART V: **Conclusions**

**Appendixes**

# Tables

# Appendixes

# Figures

**Appendix A**

# Abbreviations

| | |
|---|---|
| ABC | allowable biological catch |
| ACFM | Advisory Committee on Fishery Management |
| AEC | Atomic Energy Commission |
| AJIL | American Journal of International Law |
| AR | American Tanker Rate Schedule |
| ATRS | American Tanker Rate Schedule |
| CBR | Committee on Biology and Research |
| CBT | clean ballast tanks |
| CCMP | Advisory Committee on Marine Pollution (Russia) |
| CCOP | Committee for Coordination of Joint Prospecting for Mineral Resources in Asian Offshore Areas (UN Economic and Social Council) |
| CEPEX | Controlled Ecosystem Pollution Experiment |
| CFRWP | Commission for Fisheries Research in the Western Pacific |
| CINECA | Cooperative Investigation of the Northeast Central Atlantic |
| COLREG | collision regulations |
| COW | crude oil washing |
| CPUE | catch per unit effort |
| CS | Coastal States |
| CSK | Cooperative Studies of Kuroshio and Adjacent Areas |
| DAH | domestic annual harvest |
| DB | double bottom |
| DPRK | Democratic People's Republic of Korea |
| DWT | dead weight tons |
| ECOSOC | Economic and Social Council of the United Nations |
| EEC | European Economic Community |
| EEZ | exclusive economic zone |
| EIS | Environmental Impact Statement |
| EY | equilibrium yield |
| FAC | foreign allowable catch |
| FAO | Food and Agriculture Organization |
| FCMA | Fisheries Conservation and Management Act |
| FCZ | fisheries conservation zone |
| FESCO | Far Eastern Shipping Company |

| MSY | maximum sustained yield |
| NAFO | Northwest Atlantic Fisheries Organization |
| NAS | National Academy of Sciences |
| NEAFC | North East Atlantic Fisheries Commission |
| NMFS | National Marine Fisheries Service |
| NOAA | National Oceanic and Atmospheric Administration |
| NORPAX | North Pacific Climate Study |
| NPFSC | North Pacific Fur Seal Commission |
| OBO | combined carrier |
| OCIMF | Oil Companies International Marine Forum |
| OCS | outer continental shelf |
| OCS O&G | outer continental shelf oil and gas |
| ODS | operating differential subsidies |
| OECD | Organization for Economic Cooperation and Development |
| OY | optimum yield |
| PICES | Pacific International Council for the Exploration of the Sea |
| PMP | Preliminary Management Plan |
| PRC | People's Republic of China |
| PS | Port State |
| PWSA | Ports and Waterways Safety Act |
| ROK | Republic of Korea |
| RSW | refrigerated seawater |
| SBT | segregated ballast tanks |
| SC | Scientific Council |
| SCOR | Scientific Committee on Oceanic Research |
| SOLAS | International Convention for the Safety of Life at Sea |
| TAC | total allowable catch |
| TALFF | total allowable level of foreign fishing |
| TAPS | Trans-Alaskan Pipeline Act |
| TIAS | Treaties and International Agreements Series (post 1945), United Nations |
| TINRO | Pacific laboratory of the Ministry of Fisheries in Vladivostok, Russia |
| TS | territorial sea |
| TSPP | Tanker Safety and Pollution Prevention |
| TSS | traffic separation scheme |
| UJNER | United States–Japan Conference on Natural Resources Development |
| UNCTAD | United Nations Conference on Trade and Development |
| UNCLOS III | Third United Nations Conference on the Law of the Sea |
| UNLS | United Nations Legislative Series |
| UNTS | United Nations Treaty Series |
| U.S.C. | United States Code |
| USCG | U.S. Coast Guard |

| USFDA | United States Food and Drug Administration |
| USGS | U.S. Geological Survey |
| USNH | U.S. Gulf of Mexico to north of Cape Hatteras (route) |
| VLCC | very large crude carriers |
| VNIRO | Laboratory of the Ministry of Fisheries in Moscow, Russia |
| VTS | vessel traffic systems |
| WESTPAC | Western Pacific Investigations (IOC) |
| WMO | World Meteorological Organization |

| dwt | deadweight tons |
| dm | moulded draft amidships |
| MT | metric tons |
| mMT | million metric tons |
| ppb | parts per billion |
| ppm | parts per million |
| psi | pounds per square inch |

# Preface

The North Pacific Project was established at the Institute for Marine Studies, University of Washington, in September 1976, and was funded by the Rockefeller Foundation. This funding eventually covered the period September 1, 1976 to August 31, 1980.

The Project seeks to identify and describe in detail the major marine policy problems of the North Pacific region. This book and its accompanying Atlas complete the first phase. In future volumes the Project will attempt to formulate and evaluate alternative policies, organizational networks, and criteria for achieving optimal management of the following activities, singly and in combination: conservation and exploitation of living and nonliving (hydrocarbon) resources, marine transportation, scientific research, and control of marine pollution.

The basic Project team at the Institute of Marine Studies consists of Edward Miles as Principal Investigator, Stephen Gibbs, David Fluharty, and Wlodzimierz Kaczynski; the team was assisted by two graduate students each year. In addition, the team's cartographer is John Sherman of the Department of Geography, University of Washington. Oversight is provided by the Faculty Review Board of the North Pacific Project, currently chaired by Warren S. Wooster, Director, Institute for Marine Studies. Until his death on May 9, 1979, the Board was chaired by Donald L. McKernan. The Board consists of the following individuals: Dayton L. Alverson (fisheries), Donald E. Bevan (fisheries), Lewis J. Bledsoe (mathematics and fisheries), William T. Burke (law), James C. Crutchfield (economics), Richard H. Fleming (oceanography), Marc J. Hershman (law), Thane H. McCulloh (oceanography), Dean A. McManus (oceanography), and Robert L. Stokes (economics).

Phase I of the Project (this book and the Atlas) was completed primarily by the Seattle team with some collaboration with scholars in Japan and Canada. Phase II (the second book) was fully collaborative. The Japanese team consisted of an integrated fisheries group and individuals participating on marine transportation and marine pollution. The fisheries group was chaired by Shoichi Tanaka (Ocean Research Institute, University of Tokyo) and consisted of Akira Hasegawa (Tokyo Fisheries University), Tetsuya Hirano (Ocean Research Institute, University of Tokyo), Yutaka Hirasawa (Tokyo Fisheries University), Tsuyoshi Kawasaki (Tohuku University), and Kazuo Sumi (Yokohama City University). Individual participation on marine transportation problems was by Masao Oda (Tokyo University of Mercantile Marine). Individual participation on marine pollution was by Makato Shimizu (Ocean Research Institute, University of Tokyo).

Canadian participation in the Project (through August 1980) was by individual faculty members at the University of British Columbia, led by Mark Zacher, Director, Institute of International Relations. It involved, on fisheries, Gordon Munro (economics); on marine transportation, Trevor Heaver, George Gorelik, and William Waters (business), with the assistance of research fellows Earl Hedlund (U.S.), John Taplin (Australia), and Viktor Tikhonov (USSR); on Canadian interests and policies on the West Coast tanker trade, Mark Zacher and one research fellow; on Canadian–U.S. boundary conflicts in the Northeast Pacific, Donald McRae (law) and one research assistant.

The substantive focus in this volume is on the following issues:

1.  Fisheries
2.  Marine transportation
3.  Marine scientific research
4.  Multiple use conditions and conflicts
    (a)  offshore oil development
    (b)  problems of marine pollution
    (c)  multiple use interactions and conflicts

This focus excludes a large number of other issues from consideration, most notably those relating to military uses, recreational uses, and unconventional energy sources of the North Pacific region. There are several reasons for this choice. Primarily, we wanted to focus on the current major policy problems of using the resources of the North Pacific Ocean or of using the ocean as a medium for transportation. Furthermore, we wanted to look at the regional context in the sense that these issues are not fully contained within the boundaries of a single country. By these criteria, we excluded all policy issues of purely coastal significance (i.e., within twelve miles) and dealt with major issues falling outside the territorial seas of the countries concerned. This decision immediately excluded recreational issues.

We excluded any consideration of unconventional energy sources because the potential of the North Pacific (north of 30° north latitude) is not significant, and therefore this is not a major current or potential policy problem for the region. We excluded military uses because they fall solely within national control and, more importantly, are of such great sensitivity that access to detailed information would be severely constrained. We included problems of marine scientific research because adequate management of resources and the protection of the marine environment require that more systematic attention be paid to arrangements for improving the stock of available knowledge. This is beyond the capability of any single coastal state in the region to produce by itself and problems of cooperation are paramount.

Having "cleared the ground" with this volume and the accompanying Atlas, it is our intention to produce a future series of detailed policy studies on the most important marine policy problems of the North Pacific to which authoritative decision makers can have continuing reference.

We are aware that policy innovation in the marine area will not take place in a vacuum. The larger context consists of the current characteristics of the international system as a whole and the general foreign policy interests, objectives, and actions of the nation-states of the North Pacific region. Some major convention-breaking events have recently occurred within this region, both with respect to extended zones of national jurisdiction, the China–

Japan Treaty of Friendship, and the new demarche of the Chinese People's Republic toward the outside world. Moreover, developments relating to the joint exploration and exploitation of outer continental shelf hydrocarbons, involving Japan and the USSR in North Sakhalin and discussions between Japan and China relative to exploiting hydrocarbon resources in Po Hai Bay, are added complications. So are the proposed withdrawal of the U.S. from the Republic of Korea and the continuing territorial conflicts of the Northwest Pacific. The possible links between developments in regional marine policy and these events will have to be taken into account.

It seems particularly appropriate that scholars in Japan, Canada, and the United States cooperate at this time of radical change in the customary law of the sea; they must try to work out desirable new policies and institutional arrangements that can facilitate adaptation to the changes and forge new bonds of cooperation across the North Pacific Ocean.

# Acknowledgments

Since this is a large project we are indebted to many people in three countries for advice and assistance. It is a pleasure to acknowledge these debts publicly.

We are, first of all, grateful to the Rockefeller Foundation for four years of generous support for the North Pacific Project. Although the Foundation should in no way be held responsible for views expressed herein, the consideration and assistance we have received from our project officers since the Project began in September 1976 has been outstanding. Accordingly, we would like to express our gratitude to Elmore Jackson, Ralph Richardson, John Stremlau, Gary Toeniessen, and Mason Willrich.

We relied very heavily on the Faculty Review Board for the North Pacific Project for advice, criticism and many other forms of assistance. These individuals responded unstintingly to innumerable calls from us and helped in many more ways than we have space to specify. Several of them spent much time going over all or portions of this very large manuscript. We therefore say a special thank you to Dayton L. Alverson, William T. Burke, James A. Crutchfield, Richard H. Fleming, Thane McCulloh, the late Donald L. McKernan, and Warren S. Wooster. We are happy that Burke and Wooster were persuaded to contribute chapters to this volume in addition to providing trenchant critical review of other portions of the manuscript. We are also delighted to record our indebtedness to George Harry, Deputy-Director, Marine Mammal Laboratory, National Marine Fisheries Service, for providing us an evaluation of the work of the North Pacific Fur Seal Commission, which we include in this volume. Similarly, Frank Langdon, Department of Political Science, University of British Columbia, provided us the benefit of his expertise on marine resource conflicts in the Northwest Pacific. His analysis was incorporated in chapter 6 of this book.

We owe an enormous debt of gratitude to James Johnson, then U.S. Fisheries Attaché in Tokyo, and his assistant, Yoshio Nasaka. The extent of our debt is clear from statistical data on fisheries in Part I of this book. Similarly, we are indebted to Marilyn Myers, then Transportation Officer, U.S. Embassy, Tokyo, for facilitating our access to many important Departments and Divisions of the Japanese Ministry of Transportation.

A large number of colleagues and interested parties have responded to repeated requests for information and/or have read all or portions of this manuscript and given us the benefit of their counsel. We would like to mention Choon-ho Park, Douglas Johnston, Douglas Fleming, William Waters, Trevor Heaver, Mark Zacher, Gordon Munro, Parzival Copes, Masao Oda, Shoichi Tanaka, Kazuo Sumi, William Gray, Donald Roseman, Daniel

Sheehan, Robert Stewart, Stephen Kinnaman, the late Eldon Opheim, Richard Storch, and Lawrence Glosten.

It is a pleasure to record our very considerable gratitude to many government agencies and several private companies or industry associations in the United States, Canada, and Japan for providing us information on a wide variety of subjects. In the United States, we would like to mention the National Marine Fisheries Service, especially the Northwest and Alaska Fisheries Center and the Office of the Regional Director, Seattle; the U.S. Coast Guard, 14th District; the Department of State, Office of Oceans and Fisheries Affairs and Office of the Geographer; and the North Pacific and Pacific Fishery Management Councils. In Canada, we are indebted to the Fisheries Research Board of Canada, Nanaimo Station and Vancouver office, and to Michael Waldichuk of the Pacific Environment Institute, Vancouver.

In Japan, we are indebted to officials of the Japan Fisheries Agency, Ministry of Agriculture, Forestry and Fisheries; the Japan Fisheries Association; the Malacca Straits Council; Ocean Routes, Inc. of Monterey, California and Tokyo; the Marine Geology Division of the Geological Survey Institute of Japan; the Japan Hydrographic Service; the Japanese Maritime Safety Agency; the Japanese Ministry of Transportation, International Division, Traffic Safety and Environmental Pollution Control Division, Overseas Routes Division, and the Bureau of Ports and Harbors; the Japan Maritime Research Institute; and the Japan Shipowners Association. In Japan we are also indebted to Masayoshi Fumoto and Kiyofumi Nakauchi, who helped guide our introduction to the Japanese marine affairs community during the first two years of the Project.

A research project of this magnitude depends to a great extent on the assistance of expert librarians. We are therefore considerably indebted to Yasukot Fukano and her staff at the Fisheries and Oceanography Library, University of Washington. We are also indebted to the staffs of the Science, East Asia, Government Documents, and Engineering Libraries at the University of Washington.

We are pleased to acknowledge with gratitude the major contributions made to the North Pacific Project by our two budget managers, Martha Allison and Ora Chapman. By saying a public thank you to the Project's secretary, Irene Novak, we can only hint at the extent to which we depended on her truly phenomenal capabilities and her rapid and accurate typing of several versions of a dauntingly large manuscript.

Since a large number of individuals were involved in the production of this book, it is appropriate to identify their contributions. Chapters 1, 3, 4, 6, and 15 were written by Edward Miles; chapters 2, 4, and 14 by David Fluharty; chapters 3 and 12 by William Burke; chapters 5 and 6 by Christine Dawson; chapter 7 by Wlodzimierz Kaczynski; chapters 8 and 11 by Stephen Gibbs; chapters 9 and 10 by David Teeter; and chapter 13 by Warren Wooster.

# 1

# Introduction

The management of the world ocean is characterized by a haphazard quilt of global, regional, bilateral, and national arrangements differentiated by activity and ocean, but without effective mechanisms for achieving coordination across either activities or oceans. This fragmentation creates occasions for significant conflict and interferes with productive use of the oceans to a noticeable degree. As new technologies increasingly permit a variety of uses of ocean space, policies designed to achieve coordinated management of the oceans are required if conflict is to be avoided, and if human use of the marine environment is to be less wasteful. Such policies necessarily transcend national jurisdictional zones and are therefore beyond the capability of individual nation-states, irrespective of their level of development.

The emergence of a 200-mile economic zone (or other variously defined extended zones of national jurisdiction), in which the coastal state exercises exclusive control over marine resources, scientific research, and acts of pollution, has produced two immediate and interacting effects. The first places great stress on national institutions and requires the formulation of new national and international policies for management of ocean resources and ocean space. The second, significantly affected by the first, intensifies the need for increased bilateral and multilateral consultations, and a new level of coordination to cope with impending changes in the patterns of use. The second anticipated effect is the major impetus for this book because recent demands for expanded jurisdiction have seldom included consideration of the policies and organizational networks implied by the need for coordinated management and conflict resolution on the regional or subregional level. Accordingly, we address the need for a policy-oriented approach to management of human use of the oceans in the new regime by dividing the world ocean into a series of marine regions. For this purpose, a marine region is defined as a marine area in which the pattern of management problems posed by different activities is at least analytically separable from the rest of the world ocean.

It is important to realize that the interaction of technological advance and jurisdictional change produces significantly altered contexts for the management of ocean-related

1

activities. Since 1960, major advances have been made in vessel size and capabilities, the implantation of artificial islands and other installations in the ocean, and the capacity to exploit the ocean at greater depths than previously. Most of these advances result in increasing the density of ocean-related activities within neritic zones relatively near the shore; it is highly probable that resolving the conflicts of multiple use of the ocean in these zones will be one of the most important marine policy problems of the future.

Superimposed on the technological dimension lie a series of crucial jurisdictional changes that have crystallized in the establishment of exclusive economic zones. Article 56 of the Draft Convention on the Law of the Sea[1] defines the "Rights, jurisdiction and duties of the coastal state in the exclusive economic zone." In an area extending 188 miles beyond a 12-mile territorial sea,[2] the coastal state possesses:

(a)  sovereign rights for the purpose of exploring and exploiting, conserving and managing the natural resources, whether living or non-living, of the bed and subsoil and the superjacent waters and with regard to other activities for the economic exploitation and exploration of the zone, such as the production of energy from the water, currents and winds;
(b)  jurisdiction as provided for in the relevant provisions of the present Convention with regard to:
   (i)   the establishment and use of artificial islands, installations and structures;
   (ii)  marine scientific research;
   (iii) the preservation of the marine environment;
(c)  other rights and duties provided for in the present Convention.

It is clear that the economic zone will be a multipurpose zone. Not only more ocean space but many more types of activities will be controlled by the coastal state than ever before. This further implies the capacity to determine "net benefit" on the part of the management agency. Most coastal states, developed as well as developing, currently lack the capacity to make these determinations. One of our objectives, therefore, is to begin to fill this gap by using the North Pacific Ocean as an example for developing approaches that can be adapted to other parts of the world.

## REGIONS, REGIONALISM, AND APPLICATIONS TO OCEAN MANAGEMENT

A fairly extensive literature deals with political and economic dimensions of regionalism and regional integration.[3] There is no need to summarize this literature here, though it is necessary to dispose of the basic definitional problem before making extensions to the ocean environment.

There are essentially two choices for defining a region. The first is to use location or contiguity as the determining criterion, and infer that there is a direct causal relationship between this characteristic and the pattern of activities and policy problems dealt with. This turns out to be an excessively limiting approach since countries are often more tightly connected in terms of their transactions with countries outside the region than within. The second choice, and the one utilized in this book, is to treat location as being secondary, and to focus instead on the *pattern of activities and perceived policy problems* that should be at least analytically separable from the rest of the world. A policy problem is defined as the perception by some actor of the need to choose between different objectives or courses of action. The notion of choice reflects concern with both the processes of decision and of implementation.

The perspective outlined above requires that we focus on specific contexts, and that we identify (a) the countries involved, (b) the ways in which their interests are defined, (c) the ways in which capabilities are distributed, (d) the ways in which benefits and costs are seen to be divided up on the various issues of significance, (e) existing organizational arrangements and their relative effectiveness, (f) definitions of alternative strategies for dealing with policy problems, and (g) the impact on behavior of extraregional concerns and involvements.

Because this approach emphasizes the primacy of some specific context, we need to define more carefully what our expectations are when we claim that analyses of one situation can be used fruitfully in dealing with other situations in the world. We do not mean that the organizational arrangements and substantive policies adopted or recommended for one region can be automatically transferred elsewhere, irrespective of the diversity of conditions. We do contend, however, that *analytic perspectives* are more easily and usefully transferred, even though, here too, adaptation is necessary.

## THE NORTH PACIFIC AS A MARINE REGION

The North Pacific presents a likely starting point because it is an area of intense usage and clear importance, with a history of cooperation manifested through an existing network of international organizations. Only a small number of highly industrialized actors are involved who, despite differences in size and in political and economic systems, possess the scientific and technological capabilities essential to rational management, and an apparent will to achieve such a level of performance.

The North Pacific is here operationally defined as the north temperate zone of the Pacific Ocean, ranging from about 30° north latitude to the northern extremity of the Bering Strait, and bounded by the coasts of East Asia and North America. The region delimited thereby is marked by similar geological, physical, and biological parameters and a well-demarcated current system.[4]

This definition excludes the subtropical areas of the Pacific Ocean, which exhibit substantially different environmental conditions, resources, and patterns of use. The 30° N boundary roughly approximates the northern limit of the equatorial current and faunal systems. Since the majority of commercially valuable manganese nodule deposits are located south of the 30° N line, deep seabed mining activities are considered only as they affect other uses within the North Pacific area. So delimited, the North Pacific region is both analytically distinct and manageable for a pragmatic approach to the design of marine policy alternatives.

Since our focus is on the pattern of activities, we wish to avoid excessive rigidity in the application of the southern boundary of 30° N. Our concern is with activities related to fishing, shipping, petroleum production from the outer continental shelf (OCS), scientific research, and oil pollution. These activities represent a fairly discrete network of problems that involve the countries on the rim, primarily with each other. The choice of 30° N was made deliberately to exclude both the manganese nodule issue and the tuna issue. These are problems of near global dimension. Fisheries activities in the Northwest Pacific, however, require us to be concerned with what happens as far south as 20° N. Similarly, oil tanker movements take us even further south, to Malacca Strait and the Lombok–Makasar Channel; and in the Northeast the Panama Canal is significant for a variety of shipping movements.

The criteria guiding our choice of activities are: (a) that the activities involve countries from the region primarily with each other; and (b) that the policy problems to which these activities give rise are regarded by relevant actors, or the research team, as being of immediate significance and some urgency. Let us therefore describe the links between the issues and actors in more detail.

## Fisheries

Compared to most of the world ocean, the stakes in fisheries are very high in the North Pacific. The area produces more than one quarter (27.6% in 1975) of the total world production of fish and shellfish. The seven nation-states of the region—Canada, Chinese People's Republic (CPR), Democratic People's Republic of Korea (DPRK), Japan, Republic of Korea (ROK), USSR and U.S.—together produce almost 50 percent of the total world catch, and Japan and the USSR are the dominant distant-water fishing countries of the world.

Table 1.1 shows the importance of the North Pacific for the national catches of these seven states.

### TABLE 1.1

NORTH PACIFIC STATE CATCHES AS PERCENT OF NATIONAL CATCH

| North Pacific State | % of national catch (1975) |
|---|---|
| Canada | 13 |
| CPR | 100 |
| DPRK | 100 |
| Japan | 91.2 |
| ROK | 89.9 |
| USSR | 33.3 |
| U.S. | 12.5 |

Source: Chapter 2, table 2.3, this volume.

Only Japan, the ROK and the USSR fish throughout the region. Canada, the CPR, the DPRK, and the U.S. maintain primarily localized, coastal efforts and the CPR catch comes predominantly from inland waters. The change in regime, therefore, is most destabilizing for Japan, the ROK, and the USSR—particularly for the ROK. The USSR, however, does have a considerable capacity to compensate for its losses elsewhere in the world by drastically reducing the catches of Japan and the ROK in its exclusive fisheries zone. For Japan, this action places the greatest burden on its offshore fleet rather than on the coastal or long-distance fleets.

Kasahara and Burke have characterized the major problems of the traditional regime as being:

(a)   The lack of comprehensiveness in regulatory arrangements resulting in a complex network of *ad hoc* bilateral and trilateral agreements covering different species.

(b)   The arrangements are inflexible with respect to new entrants.

(c)   This patchwork quilt of agreements drastically increases the costs of administration and yields a limited monitoring capacity so that issues are usually not dealt with until they become serious.

(d)   There does not exist a uniform system of data collection and analysis. While each country carries on research, the information gained is not generally accessible.[5]

The traditional regime governing fisheries exploitation in the North Pacific was based on the open-access criterion, and the region experienced a much slower rate of extensions of national jurisdiction than in other regions of the world ocean. This is not surprising, since the mix of distant-water fishing interests and the broader security interests of the U.S., USSR, and Japan emphasized the necessity of keeping coastal state constraints on navigation to a minimum. Moreover, the principal states of the Northeast Pacific had no major long-distance fisheries operating in the region.

Consequently, a very complicated patchwork quilt of regional arrangements developed, including bilateral and multilateral agreements, which often established very weak commissions. Most stocks were in fact not regulated at all, and the system was increasingly inefficient and ineffective in resolving the intensifying conflicts that have emerged from about the mid-1960s. The early extensions of coastal state jurisdiction in the Northeast (and later in the Northwest) Pacific occurred with respect to continental shelf living resources, mainly crab. But there was growing domestic pressure in Canada and the U.S. to extend national jurisdiction over all fisheries, first to twelve miles and then beyond. These pressures grew as a result of the intensification of fishing effort by Japan and the USSR, which occurred after 1959 and multiplied the points of conflict between the coastal and distant-water fisheries. These points of conflict included gear conflicts, increasing incidental catch of species preferred by the North American coastal fisheries, increasing density of foreign fishing efforts encroaching on traditional fishing grounds of the North Americans, and more recently, the export and import imbalance in fisheries products.

Domestic pressures for extending national jurisdiction in the Northeast Pacific increased as the global move toward 200-mile exclusive economic zones gained momentum in the Third United Nations Conference on the Law of the Sea (UNCLOS III) after 1972. The U.S. government, however, in an attempt to balance a variety of sometimes conflicting interests, sought to deflect these pressures by seeking preferential (not exclusive) rights for the coastal state over fisheries, but this was not enough. Once the U.S. had accepted coastal state sovereignty over resources in the exclusive economic zone in 1974 as the major price for protecting its navigational interests, particularly passage through straits used for international navigation, the U.S. government had lost the fight vis-à-vis its domestic constituencies seeking to extend national jurisdiction over fisheries—hence, Public Law 94-265, the Fisheries Conservation and Management Act (the FCMA) in 1976.

Extensions of coastal state jurisdiction in the Northeast Pacific in 1976, combined with a variety of other actions being taken globally—especially for the USSR in the North Atlantic—triggered a rapid transformation of the regime for fisheries in the North Pacific as a whole, though the effects of that transformation were more drastic in the Northwest than in the Northeast Pacific.

In the Northeast Pacific the most dramatic change has affected the groundfish resources, where *all* species have for the first time come under the management authority of two coastal states. The terms of foreign access to the surpluses in these stocks are defined in the relevant domestic legislation and regulations of the U.S. and Canada. However, since by far the larger share of resources falls within the U.S. zone, the terms of access for most stocks are described in the Governing International Fishery Agreements (GIFAs) as required by FCMA.

This left only three major issues for which the transitional period would be somewhat more prolonged: (1) the renegotiation of arrangements relative to distribution of the salmon catch between the U.S. and Canada; (2) the renegotiation of the International North Pacific Fisheries Commission (INPFC) between the U.S., Canada, and Japan, and affecting primarily the Japanese high-seas salmon fishery; and (3) the renegotiation of the International Pacific Halibut Commission (IPHC) between the U.S. and Canada. This last issue also tangentially involved terms of access for U.S. groundfish fishermen for resources off the coast of British Columbia.

The U.S.−Canada salmon negotiations present perhaps the most complicated set of problems. The component issues involve such complex fisheries as the Yukon River fisheries of the North, with important components originating in the Yukon Territory of Canada and migrating through hundreds of miles of U.S. territory in Alaska to the Bering Sea. Other salmon issues involve salmon originating in the Columbia River of the U.S. and migrating through Canadian waters in British Columbia, and subject to varied domestic fisheries of both countries. Still other issues involve the Fraser River and the International Pacific Salmon Fisheries Commission (IPSFC), the ocean salmon fishery in general, and the boundary problems between the U.S. and Canada in two areas: first, between British Columbia and the U.S. off the Strait of Juan de Fuca; and, second, in waters between Canada and Alaska (Dixon Entrance).

While the major problems in fisheries management under "freedom of fishing" arrangements were the absence of central management authority and the inflexibility of the management mechanism created, these problems have for the most part been solved. There may, of course, still be serious problems of conservation, but these will clearly be the result of policies followed deliberately or inadvertently by one or the other, or both, of the coastal states involved. The major problems of the future appear to be: (1) specific foreign allocations, and the tensions between determinations of the surplus and strategies for the development of domestic fisheries; (2) competition for markets; (3) jurisdiction over shared stocks, as between the U.S. and Canada, and to a lesser extent between the U.S. and the USSR; and (4) arrangements concerning scientific research and standardization of data.

In the Northwest Pacific, the situation is much more complicated and considerably more difficult. In the first place, since 1956 there have been organic links between some of the management approaches adopted on both sides of the North Pacific. In 1953 the INPFC adopted the line of 175° W longitude as the "provisional abstention line." This line was intended to be flexible by the United States, especially since, at the time, it was not clear how far west salmon of North American origin migrated. As more detailed knowledge accumulated, the U.S. wished the line moved further west because in its interpretation the abstention line was to be placed so that no salmon of North American origin could be taken by the Japanese. The Japanese, however, claimed that the line should be moved further east, since more salmon of Asian origin moved nearer the U.S. and Canadian coasts and the abstention line was intended to divide the stocks equitably. This problem could not be resolved because the Convention required unanimity for decision. In addition, a further development in 1956 added to the inflexibility of the 175° W longitude boundary. This line was made the easternmost boundary of the Japan—USSR agreement and the Japanese salmon quota in the Soviet area would have been adversely affected had the line been moved further west.

With respect to the USSR, access to fisheries resources of the Northeast Pacific is also an important issue since in recent years Soviet fishermen have been taking 400,000—500,000 metric tons annually. However, the fact that the U.S. and Canada proposed to extend their jurisdiction in the Northwest Atlantic as well was a very significant factor for the Soviet Union. Equally significant was the fact that the members of the European Economic Community proposed to extend their jurisdiction as a group in the Northeast Atlantic. Faced with these two major perturbations, and seeing the chainlike reaction of extensions globally in connection with UNCLOS III, the Soviets decided to reserve most of the resources within their 200-mile zone in the Pacific for themselves. This resulted in the complete exclusion of the Republic of Korea, whose representatives sought to redress the balance in the Northeast Pacific at the expense of both the Japanese and the Soviets, and in the unexpectedly drastic curtailment of Japanese fishing in Soviet waters during their bilateral negotiations in May 1977.

All of these events, but particularly the enactment of the Soviet 200-mile zone, led Japan reluctantly to introduce its own extended fisheries zone in July 1977. North Korea has also extended its jurisdiction, but it is not clear at this time whether (and if so, when) China and South Korea will extend theirs. This means that the major fisheries problems of the future for the Northwest Pacific are: (1) how many and which economic zones will be extended, with the attendant problems of delimitation; (2) the problem of satisfying growing domestic demands for fish as a source of animal protein; and (3) joint management of shared stocks. These problems will be accentuated by the degree to which external political issues impinge upon fisheries conflicts. These are: (1) the problem of delimitation of the continental shelf in the East China and Yellow seas; (2) territorial conflicts (e.g., the Japan—USSR conflict over the northern Kurils); (3) the conflict between China and the USSR; (4) the broader game of coalition politics involving Japan, China, the U.S., and the USSR; and (5) the problem of the two Koreas.

It remains to be seen whether national control will turn out in fact to be a more efficient and effective regime for managing fisheries than the open-access regimes of the past. Theoretically, of course, national control gives the coastal state an opportunity to eliminate high levels of biological and economic waste if it wishes, but the interests of different fisheries often conflict and considerable disparity may exist between regional and national perceptions of utility. In the U.S., Canada, and Japan, internal regional pressures can and do exert great effect on national responses, and it is not always clear that the claims of special interests can be justified on the basis of more objective criteria for reducing biological and economic waste in the management of fisheries. The question of whether national regimes are more effective than open-access regimes is still to be decided.

Meanwhile, the change in regime has resulted in a marked shift in patterns of fishing, and in a massive shift on the substantive issues of international fisheries politics. No longer is the extent of national control a major issue, except in the case of transboundary stocks, which is more of a problem in the Northeast than in the Northwest Pacific. This decline in the intensity of conflicting claims to prescribe for management has been accompanied by a major increase in the significance and intensity of conflicting claims to regulate fishing practices. In addition, in the Northeast Pacific, there has been a significant increase in the salience of conflicting claims over access to markets, and this also is tangentially related to conflicts over national policies governing joint venture arrangements.

It appears that in the Northeast Pacific generally, we are in a transition period with respect to fisheries; this poses two major long-run questions: (1) What will be the rate of foreign phase-out from traditional fisheries and, correspondingly, how fast can and will domestic fishing effort be developed to replace the foreigners? There will be several answers to these questions and they will vary by fishery and market. (2) Who will set the rules within which the market for fisheries products will function in the future? Japan, of course, is the predominant influence here, but there is an increasing challenge from both the USSR and the U.S. It is not at all clear at the moment what the future holds in this respect beyond a steady rise in prices for consumers everywhere in the region.

## Marine Transportation

Japan dominates the trade of the North Pacific with the U.S. following a far second (Japan leads by a ratio of almost five to one). However, the Japan—U.S. connection is the dominant trade relationship in the region. About 45 percent of total exports (tonnage) out of the U.S. West Coast ports goes to Japan, and about 15 percent of imports come from Japan. The annual rate of increase of U.S. West Coast trade (primarily with Japan) is growing about 10 percent faster, in tonnage and value, than U.S. East Coast trade with Europe and other areas. It has been noted that if this trend continues, there will be a shift in the relative importance of the North Pacific as compared to the North Atlantic for maritime trade.

The Japanese pattern of trade is also very significant since most of its imports consist of low value, high tonnage basic commodities, while most exports consist of high value, low tonnage, finished goods. Japan imports a large tonnage from Southeast Asia and the Middle East, consisting primarily of crude petroleum, which has experienced sharp increases in value since 1973.

The growth of the Soviet flag fleet has been another significant recent trend in North Pacific maritime trade. In particular, the Soviet Far Eastern Shipping Company (FESCO) has introduced a large number of new break and bulk carriers in the general cargo trade, which have operated outside the traditional conference system. These carriers provide significant competition for liner conferences serving the North Pacific, particularly on the U.S. West Coast to Japan route. The Soviet rates have been generally 10 to 30 percent lower than the conference rates, but it is not clear whether the Soviets wish to maintain this competition indefinitely, or if they wish to use it primarily as a means of negotiating entry to particular conferences on favorable terms.

Japan's extensive reliance on maritime trade results in considerable congestion of shipping lanes and ports in and around Japan. For instance, a large proportion of Japanese maritime trade (44.6 percent) is concentrated in seventeen major ports. Twelve of these ports are located in three areas: the Bay of Tokyo, Bay of Ise, and the Seto Inland Sea. These three areas account for 14.1 percent of all ships calling at all Japanese ports, but 55.6 percent of the total number of ocean-going ships.[6] The total number of ships calling at the seventeen ports annually is 1,068,172, of which the total number of ocean-going ships was 55,536, with the rest being coast-wise vessels. In terms of scale, there is no other country in the world that has a comparable problem of congestion for its deep sea trades.

This extremely high density of marine traffic is a problem in itself, as well as for other uses of the coastal areas of Japan, in particular for fisheries. Most of this traffic must go through several narrow straits. Data for 1974, as shown in table 1.2, provide a measure of scale.

The rate of marine accidents is quite high. In 1971, 1,413 merchant ships of 1,827,670 gross tons were involved in accidents; in 1974, the numbers had changed to 1,368 ships of

TABLE 1.2

PASSAGE OF SHIPS THROUGH MAJOR NARROW STRAITS, JAPAN, 1974

| Strait | Average no. ships per day |
|---|---|
| Uraga Channel | 794 |
| Irako Strait | 1174 |
| Akashi Passage | 1981 |
| E. Bisan Passage | 1751 |
| W. Bisan Passage | 1022 |
| Kurushima Passage | 1260 |

Source: From Masao Oda, ''Marine Transportation of Japanese Seaborne Trade and Related Laws and Regulations'' in Christine L. Dawson, ed., *The North Pacific Project* (Seattle: Institute for Marine Studies, University of Washington, 1977), figure 4, p. 531.

2,053,549 gross tons, reflecting a shift to larger vessels.[7] For the same period, 1,187 fishing boats of 83,461 gross tons were involved in accidents during 1971; the number for 1974 was 1,121 fishing boats of 102,551 gross tons.

Most of the accidents occurred less than three nautical miles from port, followed by those occurring in port, followed by those occurring between three to fifty nautical miles from port. Navigation in the three areas has been strictly regulated since 1972 under the Maritime Traffic Safety Law, and the so-called fishery right fisheries have been preempted, though partially compensated.

With respect to other countries in the region, Vancouver is the only major Canadian port on the Pacific. It specializes in the export trade (84 percent of total tonnage in 1975) with emphasis on grain (to Japan and China) and coal (to Japan). Japan is Canada's most important trading partner in the Pacific, and is also the most important trading partner for the ROK and, we suspect, will soon be for China, if this is not already the case. Japan, therefore, is simply the focus of most North Pacific trade, with traffic density being generally higher in the Northwest Pacific than in the Northeast. But there is also a growing traffic density problem involving tankers off Los Angeles and Long Beach, and a potential problem arising from increased tanker traffic, and increased size of tankers, operating from Valdez, Alaska to Puget Sound, especially through Rosario Strait. The most important commodity groups of North Pacific trade are containerized general cargo, noncontainerizable general cargo, and petroleum.

It is worth emphasizing that tanker-generated oil pollution has been much less of a problem in the North Pacific region than elsewhere in the world, not only because of the vast area involved but also because the average annual input seems to be considerably below the world average. Accidental spills from tankers have not been a major problem so far. The largest spill occurred in 1975 but amounted to only 5,000 metric tons (MT). The normal range (1967−1976) is 1,345−2,851 MT, with no secular trend evident.[8]

With respect to oil input to the North Pacific via normal ship operations, the heaviest traffic occurs on the Middle East−Japan route via the Strait of Malacca and the Lombok−Makasar Channel. This amounts to about 19 percent of the total world petroleum trade, but much less than 19 percent of the estimated annual oil spillage goes into the North Pacific for two reasons: (1) on a ton-mile basis, a much smaller percentage of the world petroleum trade actually occurs in the North Pacific; and (2) concerted efforts are being made in Japan to reduce operational discharge. This results in less than the expected input, the best estimate being about 71,500 MT annually, or about .4 percent of the estimated world total.

The major potential challenges to the marine transportation system of the North Pacific are: (1) the implications of the United Nations Conference on Trade and Development (UNCTAD) Code of Conduct for Liner Conferences; (2) Soviet competition as represented by the growth of FESCO; (3) increasing domestic demands for more stringent port state regulation of tanker traffic, especially in Canada and the U.S.; (4) increasing domestic demands for more stringent strait state regulation of tanker traffic, and the Malacca Straits Council arrangement, which provides significant benefits to Singapore and Indonesia but less to Malaysia.

## Marine Scientific Research

The North Pacific is connected in a variety of ways in the conduct of marine scientific research, but the research system, as is usually the case, is largely decentralized. As shown by the analysis in chapter 12, no adequate mechanism for the facilitation of marine scientific research exists for the North Pacific as a whole. Even with respect to fisheries, existing arrangements exhibit piecemeal and nonadditive approaches to research, and bilateral arrangements do not yield studies that are comparable on both sides of the ocean. Moreover, no comprehensive work is currently being done on a regional basis concerning the budget of all important pollutants introduced into the North Pacific. We have no means of systematically comparing the results of investigations on the coastal areas around the Northeast and Northwest Pacific because there is virtually no standardization of measurements and intercalibration of instruments. ''While the general features of North Pacific circulation, flora and fauna, and sea bed characteristics are reasonably well known, the picture is inadequate in detail, and little is known about the pattern of variability.''[9]

As a result of these deficiencies, in chapter 13 we make the following case for the creation of an International Council for Scientific Investigation of the North Pacific, consisting of Canada, Japan, the USSR, and the U.S. as initial members:

1. Management decisions on the multiple use of the ocean and its resources should be based on adequate scientific understanding of ocean processes and phenomena in the region.

2. Despite the extensions of national jurisdiction now taking place or likely to take place in the North Pacfic, conflicts in use of living resources, both within and beyond the limits of national jurisdiction, are bound to increase.

3. Although several international bodies exist for the management of specific fishery resources in the region, there is no overall mechanism for the exchange of data and information on the status of stocks on which national and international decisions on resource management can be based.

4. Increasing uses of ocean resources, the transport of petroleum and other potentially toxic products, and industrial activities around the margins of the North Pacific represent intensifying threats to the health of the marine environment. No mechanism exists for pooling efforts to understand and to monitor these threats.

5. The role of the ocean in modulating weather and climate is now evident. An improved mechanism is required for the development and coordination of investigations of ocean-atmosphere interaction that will enhance the possibility of predicting weather and climate.

6. Scientific investigations are conducted in the North Pacific under the auspices of several governments, including those of the U.S., the USSR, Canada, and Japan. These investigations fall within all fields of marine science and its applications. Some are multiinstitutional and include arrangements for interinstitutional coordination; others are the efforts of single institutions. No general mechanism exists for the initiation,

planning, and coordination of multinational oceanographic and fishery research programs in the region.

7. Data resulting from these investigations, in part at least, eventually find their way into
   the world data exchange system. However, there is no mechanism for the orderly and
   timely exchange of data and information between governments and institutions engaged
   in the research, for improving the quality and intercomparability of measurements, or
   for selecting common statistical areas and bases.

The purpose of the proposed organization would be:

To promote the development of cooperative research activities and the exchange of
information concerning (1) the North Pacific marine environment and its interactions with
land and atmosphere; (2) uses of the North Pacific and its living and nonliving resources; and
(3) the effects of man's activities on the quality of the marine environment.

To achieve this purpose, the organization would engage in activities related to marine
science, fisheries, and quality of the marine environment, and to other marine fields as
appropriate, such as the following: (1) exchange of data and information; (2) review of
research plans, programs, and progress; (3) identification of critical research programs and
of methods appropriate for their solution; (4) planning development, and coordination of
cooperative investigations, of problems of common interest; and (5) evaluation and interpretation of available data and information from the scientific point of view.

## Multiple Use Conditions and Conflicts

We began this book by arguing that the management of human use of the world ocean is
characterized by a haphazard quilt of global, regional (international), bilateral (non-
regional), and national arrangements differentiated by activity and ocean, but without
effective mechanisms for achieving coordination across either oceans or activities. We think
the traditional sectoral approach to management is inadequate for the future, given the
pattern of technological advance and the revolution that has occurred in the world ocean
regime. The fact is that the economic zone is a multipurpose zone, and coastal states will
increasingly feel the necessity of making decisions affecting its multiple use in a far more
coordinated fashion than hitherto. This is very difficult to do for both practical and
conceptual reasons.

It is difficult for practical reasons because different patterns of ocean use exhibit
different patterns of institutionalization. They differ in the types of technologies utilized, the
interests perceived and pursued, the ways in which benefits are distributed, and the
composition of their national, transnational and intergovernmental constituencies. This high
level of decentralization is almost perfectly mirrored in the patterns of national organization
related to ocean management. Achieving coordinated management of ocean use, therefore,
involves transforming the structure and mode of operation of the entire national, transnational, and intergovernmental range of systems, in which perhaps the national dimension
may well be the most important. This is a Herculean task indeed!

But it seems to us that the conceptual task is almost as difficult as the practical one. The
taxonomic problem must be solved first for the world ocean as a whole. We think that the

starting point for taxonomies should be the two-dimensional problem of accommodating multiple uses of ocean space. This implies the need to construct two types of n-dimensional matrices that relate use against use and use against environmental conditions. It is difficult to fill in the cells of these matrices for specific locations in the world ocean because the data have not been collected in that fashion; nation-states are only now beginning to realize the need for more systematic treatment of the problem.

Once past the taxonomic problem, the measurement problem must be solved, and this may be insurmountable. Each pattern of use must be decomposed into several dimensions that reflect location, scale of operations, impacts on ocean space (type, time, and scope), impacts on other activities (degrees of compatibility and conflict), impacts on the ocean environment (degrees of compatibility and conflict), and value. The last dimension is critical for attempting to derive some criteria for determining economic optimality, but it may be a search for the Holy Grail since no common metric exists. The notion of value presupposes that for each cell in each matrix we find some way of dealing quantitatively with the trends relative to location, magnitude and intensity of effort, time, and appropriate discount rates. This is similar to attempts to develop a social welfare function in economics, which have not met with notable success.

We are therefore forced to rely on a qualitative cataloging of the conditions and conflicts of multiple uses of ocean space in specific marine regions of the world ocean.[10] These, in time, should lead to more comprehensive national data collection efforts and, we hope, to a greater degree of experimentation with approaches to their management. The aim that we had in mind for the North Pacific in this book was to facilitate systematic attempts to accommodate multiple uses of ocean space and to evaluate proposed solutions to policy problems in terms of their impacts on the interconnectedness of activities, in addition to other more familiar criteria. However, given the difficult theoretical and methodological problems identified above, we limited ourselves to the question whether in fact multiple use problems in the North Pacific are of sufficient regional scope to require deliberate attempts to manage them. Our investigations have shown that except in a few localized areas, most especially in the coastal waters of Japan, the management of multiple use conflicts is *not* a major problem for the North Pacific region as a whole and is not likely to be so for the foreseeable future.

## PLAN OF THE BOOK

The book is divided into five parts. Part I deals with fisheries in terms of five characteristics. First, the major living resources of the Northeast and Northwest Pacific are identified and the fisheries that have grown to depend upon them are briefly described. Second, the traditional regime for international fisheries management in the North Pacific is described. A considerable amount of unpublished material written previously by Professor William T. Burke is included at the end of chapter 3. Third, the major international conflicts that have emerged over the past two decades are summarized and the trends leading to unilateral extensions of coastal state jurisdiction in 1976 and 1977 are analyzed. Fourth, a detailed comparative analysis of the coastal state acts is presented. Fifth, the major international fisheries policy problems generated by extended jurisdiction in the North Pacific are analyzed in some detail and an assessment of their short- and long-term implications is provided. In this section, Professor Frank Langdon's analysis of some of the special problems of the Northwest Pacific is included as part of chapter 6.

Part II deals with the system for marine transportation as it operates in the North Pacific. It describes, in general fashion, the existing marine transportation system in terms of price levels and vessel supply, major ports and the volume and value of tonnage through-put, the major trade routes by cargo and vessel type, and the influence of climate on vessel routing. The Project Team also summarizes a variety of studies that attempt to forecast future developments in technology, in particular technology relating to control of ship-generated oil pollution.

In addition to the technical and economic dimensions of the marine transportation system, Part II also deals with existing regulatory arrangements, and assesses the implications for the North Pacific of changes in the law of the sea, demands by coastal and port-states for greater protection against oil pollution hazards, and the UNCTAD Code of Conduct for Liner Conferences.

In comparing the fisheries and marine transportation sections, it is apparent that in the North Pacific, fisheries really constitute *the* major *regional* problem. Marine transportation constitutes a very important dimension of the marine activities in the region but the system is driven by global rather than primarily regional dynamics. Consequently, a certain awkwardness is incurred by adopting a regional focus to marine transportation problems. We have done so because the subject is simply too important to be left out of the book.

There are differences in the level of detail in the treatment accorded each section. It is not possible to achieve the same level of detail for the marine transportation section as we have done for the fisheries section because the former issue has not been the subject of public regulation in the region to the extent that the latter has been. Less documentation is therefore available.

Part III provides an analysis of international arrangements affecting marine research in the North Pacific, and makes a case for the establishment of a new international organization concerned with scientific investigation of the North Pacific Ocean.

Part IV deals with problems of multiple use conditions and conflicts by focusing on the exploitation of oil, gas and other minerals, problems of marine pollution, and specific problems of conflicts between oil and gas production and fisheries activities in the United States and Japan. These problems are all of local rather than regional scale and the available information on pollution is skimpy and not systematic for the region as a whole.

Part V concludes the book. It deals primarily with policy problems that remain unsolved and specifies the additional research and analyses that appear to be necessary in the future.

# PART I

# Living Resources in the North Pacific

# 2

# Development of Living Resources Under the Regime of the High Seas

The North Pacific Ocean is a major world source of marine organisms; harvests of these organisms play an important role in the economic and international relations of the bordering nations. Study of the rapid development of the fishery resources of the North Pacific and its increasingly international character is essential to understanding the conflicts that have developed there, the attempts to create an international regime for fisheries management, and the potential for further development of the fishery resources in light of extended national jurisdiction over fisheries. It is impossible to deal effectively with all the relevant aspects of fisheries development in the North Pacific in a single chapter. Therefore, the approach here focuses on the international context and major trends in fisheries development. The aspects can be grouped into three broad categories: (1) the biological and environmental conditions affecting the distribution of the fishery resources; (2) the development of fish harvesting by North Pacific nations, with special attention given to fish stocks where more than one nation is involved in exploitation; and (3) the role that fisheries play in the economic and social life of the nations in the region. With respect to the third category, attention is given to fisheries as a source of employment, an investment opportunity measured in size of the fishing fleet, a component of international trade, and a supplier of food for human consumption.

## DISTRIBUTION OF LIVING RESOURCES

This section deals with the environmental conditions that influence the distribution of living resources in the North Pacific, and with the distribution patterns of major commercial species according to ecological and taxonomic groupings. It is important to note at the outset that, while the North Pacific is defined as a region for this study, the patterns of trade, fishing, and even environmental conditions, are not homogeneous throughout the area. An understanding of the diversity of the region is a key to comprehending the region as a whole. The region itself extends from the near-tropical waters off southern Japan to the arctic waters of the Bering Sea. The Bering Sea contains one of the largest and most productive areas of continental shelf in the world ocean, while the continental shelves along the Pacific coast of Japan and the United States are relatively narrow and productivity is variable. Typhoons of tropical origin can make fisheries operations hazardous in the southwestern part of the region, while ice can form quickly from spray blown on the rigging and overburden and capsize fishing vessels off the coasts of the Soviet Union and Alaska.

## ENVIRONMENTAL CONDITIONS

Many oceanographic phenomena interact to influence the productivity of the various subregions of the North Pacific. Among the most important are the bathymetry (or configuration) of the ocean bottom, the system of ocean currents, and the water temperature. Differential solar heating of the earth's surface influences water temperature and ocean currents, which in turn are affected by the shape of the ocean basins and other factors. Ocean currents and surface temperature regimes influence the world weather system.

In terms of the bathymetry, the North Pacific might be characterized as a steep-sided, half-moon shaped pan. It has a narrow rim of continental shelf (usually less than 150– 180 meters deep) which extends outward from the shore a distance that seldom exceeds 50–60 kilometers except in the marginal seas and the Gulf of Alaska. In the eastern Bering Sea, the continental shelf is nearly 700 km wide. The continental slope constitutes a relatively sharp transition zone between the edge of the continental shelf and the 4,000– 7,000 meter deep abyssal plain of the Pacific. In addition, there are five marginal seas surrounding the North Pacific—the Bering Sea, Sea of Japan, Okhotsk Sea, Yellow Sea and East China Sea. Together, these seas constitute an area exceeding all the other marginal seas of the world's oceans.

Comparison of bathymetry of the North Pacific and marginal seas in table 2.1 shows considerable variation in the amount of continental shelf, slope, and ocean basin. The North Pacific has a continental shelf that occupies less than 2 percent of its total area, while the continental shelves of the Yellow and East China seas underlie almost the entire sea area. The Sea of Japan contains little continental shelf and, for the most part, is extremely deep. Similarly, the Bering Sea shows a sharp division between the continental shelf and the deep basin areas. The Okhotsk Sea has a much larger continental slope area than the other seas. The Yellow Sea has an area of approximately 40,000 km² and an average depth of only 50 meters.[1]

The shallow continental shelf and upper continental slope areas are important because most of the fish production and harvest in the North Pacific is in the upper 300 to 500 meters of the water column;[2,3] the richest areas of fish production are located on or near the continental shelf. This is probably because the shallower bottom topography traps nutrient-rich materials and keeps them available in the ecosystem rather than being lost in the deep ocean basins, and because light is available for photosynthesis.[4] Other reasons are that the shelf serves as a physical barrier to wider spatial distribution, shallow areas are enriched by nutrients supplied by land or coastal upwelling, and the richer coastal waters are favorable

## TABLE 2.1

### BATHYMETRY OF THE NORTH PACIFIC AND ADJACENT SEAS

| | Pacific Ocean[a] | Bering Sea | Sea of Okhotsk | Sea of Japan | Yellow and East China seas[a] |
|---|---|---|---|---|---|
| Area | 22,000,000 km²[b] | 2,261,000 km²[b] | 1,392,000 km²[b] | 1,013,000 km²[b] | 1,202,000 km²[b] |
| Mean Depth | 4,188 m. | 1,492 m. | 973 m. | 1,667 m. | 272 m. |
| Volume | 92,180,000 km³[c] | 3,373,000 km³[c] | 1,354,000 km³[c] | 1,690,000 km³[c] | 327,000 km³[c] |
| Continental Shelf Area (0–200 m) | 1.6%[d] | 46.4% | 26.5% | 23.5% | 81.3% |
| Continental Slope Area (200–1000 m) | 2.6% | 6.0% | 39.5% | 15.2% | 11.4% |
| Deep Basin Area | 95.8% | 47.6% | 44.0% | 61.3% | 7.3% |

Source: Calculated on the basis of H. W. Menard and S. M. Smith, "Hypsometry of Ocean Basin Provinces" in *Journal of Geophysics* (Sept–Oct, 1966), tables 3 and 4b, 77:4305-4323.

[a]Includes only portions north of 30° N latitude.

[b]Calculated by 2 degree squares and estimates of partial squares using a Lamberts Conformal Projection and oceanographic tables from E. C. Lafond, *Processing Oceanographic Data*, U.S. Navy Hydrographic Office (Washington, D.C.: G.P.O., 1951). This represents 13.3% of the total Pacific Ocean area of 166,241,000 km² as calculated by Menard and Smith above.

[c]Assuming that the mean depth for the Pacific Ocean is the same as the mean depth for the study area and using 22,000,000 km² as the area north of 30° N latitude.

[d]This figure is calculated by Menard and Smith for the total Pacific Ocean.

habitats for reproduction and fish growth.[5] Therefore, the approximately 1.6 percent of the North Pacific and marginal sea areas defined as continental shelf constitute an extremely valuable area with respect to production of fish.

The surface waters over deep ocean areas are not biological deserts, however, since considerable quantities of various plankton and other organisms are produced there. The concentration of plankton is sufficient to support only small populations of pelagic fish, most of which are commercially unattractive at the present time. At least one Soviet expert argues that there are commercially exploitable fish stocks at depths of from 5,000 to 7,000 meters in the world oceans,[6] some of which are located in the North Pacific.

Not all areas of the shelf and upper slope are uniformly productive. Temperature differences associated with ocean currents and flow of rivers from the continent can have profound impacts on fish production in various areas. As one example of this situation, Kasahara cites the case of the eastern Okhotsk Sea where extremely cold water temperatures prevail in areas of the continental shelf even during the summer. These areas would probably be productive under a warmer temperature regime.[7] In contrast, on the western side of the Okhotsk Sea, a portion of the slightly warmer waters from the Sea of Japan are carried into the region by currents, and raise the temperature enough to permit a very productive fishery. It should be noted that "differences in productivity are reflected, in a general way, in the standing crops of phytoplankton and zooplankton, abundance of fish and other animals, and finally in catches of commercial fisheries, although the relationships are never direct or clearcut."[8] Furthermore, the seasonal fluctuations in productivity have significant effects on distribution of fish populations and fish behavior. Lack of available food during the winter months, for example, forces some fish into dormancy or forces them to migrate.

As briefly indicated, the current system in the North Pacific can have a decided influence upon fish distribution. Detailed descriptions of the current systems in the region are contained in two excellent studies. The first deals with the oceanography of the subarctic Pacific region, and the second describes the interrelationship of living resources with environmental conditions.[9] In general, the circulation in the North Pacific is clockwise, so that waters warmed in the southern region flow northward along the Asian continent. Cooling gradually, the watermass swings eastward of northern Japan into the Gulf of Alaska. From there, it divides; part of the current flows south as a cold current down the coast of British Columbia and the United States, and part of it swings anticlockwise through the Gulf of Alaska and westwardly along the Aleutian Islands chain. A circuit around the Pacific Rim is thought to take from six to eight years.

Within this general circulation pattern, researchers have identified many subcurrent systems. In the Bering Sea alone, there are 21 different named currents, and in the Sea of Okhotsk, 20 others.[10] One of the most noteworthy features of the currents is the confluence of the Kuroshio and Oyashio off northern Japan. The Kuroshio is a warm current, which trends northward off the coast of Japan; and the Oyashio is a cold current, which flows southward along the coast of Asia. Where these currents meet and mix off the coast of Japan, favorable conditions are produced for very high productivity, and commercial fish catches in the area reflect this. There are seasonal shifts in the location of the confluence of these currents.

Probably the most noticeable zoogeographic phenomenon associated with the current systems is the influence they have on fish migration patterns. On the Asian side, fish migrate northward during the summer, following the warm current as it penetrates the winter chilled northern waters. The process is reversed in winter as the cooled waters drive temperature-sensitive fish southward. Along the North American continent, the fluctuations in temperature are less pronounced and do not produce as extensive migrations. In the winter on the Asian side, the 0° and 16°C. isotherms are separated by only 10 degrees of latitude, while on the eastern side of the Pacific, the zone is 30 degrees wide. Similarly, the difference between the 10 and 26°C. isotherms on the western side is 15 degrees of latitude in summer, and on the eastern side of the Pacific off the United States the width of the zone is 40 degrees.[11] Temperature fluctuations, however, are not the only influence on fish migration. Extensive counternatant migration by Pacific hake, sardines, sablefish, and halibut are known to occur. Seasonal movements onshore during the summer and offshore during the winter are also common in many species of commercially important fish.

Currents can play an important part in the success or failure of spawning and feeding. Fluctuations in the course of a current may reduce or increase the productivity at a given place, and affect the availability of appropriate food for fish and fish larvae at various stages of growth.

In summary, while the diversity of the subregions of the North Pacific discourages attempts to generalize on the interaction of environmental conditions and fish production, certain broad features are apparent. First is the correlation between fish production and the shallower areas of the continental shelf and slopes. Second is the sensitivity of fish production to changes in current patterns, temperature regimes, and the quantities and time sequence of food production. Third is the relatively low basic productivity associated with the open ocean areas over deep basins.

## DISTRIBUTION OF MAJOR COMMERCIAL SPECIES

There are over 2,000 species of fish in the North Pacific, of which approximately 80 species are of commercial significance.[12] Species of international commercial importance or potential importance, which are representative of general ecological or taxonomic groups for which a sizeable scientific literature exists, are examined in this chapter. As Alverson points out, many species do not fit neatly into categories, since they may have different behaviors at various times of the year and at various periods in their life cycles.[13] There seems to be general agreement about the grouping of most species in the publications of the International North Pacific Fisheries Commission (INPFC) and the National Marine Fisheries Service (NMFS), and these are followed here. The categories used in this examination are demersal, pelagic, and anadromous for fish species, and crustaceans, cephalopods, marine mammals, seabirds, and seaweeds for other oganisms. Focus on the commercially utilized species disregards the importance of other species in the food webs of the targeted species. Unfortunately, this omission cannot be avoided if this study is to remain within reasonable bounds.

Emphasis in this section is on distribution and migration of the species related to issues of international management. Summary accounts of many of the species described have been previously published.[14] These accounts include a more complete life history and other information. Reference to the scientific literature for each species can be found on the individual fish pages of the *Atlas of Marine Use in the North Pacific Region.*

Demersal species occupy the bottom layers of the ocean and constitute the largest biomass of commercially harvested fish in the North Pacific. Many pelagic species are not associated with the continental shelf areas and are pronounced in oceanic areas where there are divergent or other nutrient removal processes. Anadromous species have both a neritic and oceanic distribution, and are distinguished by spawning in rivers and lakes and spending part of their early life in freshwater. Crustaceans in the North Pacific are generally found on or in association with the continental shelf. They include crabs and shrimp. Cephalopods, members of the mollusk family, may lead either pelagic or demersal lives and are known to be abundant on both the continental shelf and slope, and in oceanic areas. Marine mammals are warm-blooded, air-breathing animals found in the sea, and include seals, whales, and walruses.

There are over 150 species of seabirds in the North Pacific area, and many species of seaweeds are found in local concentrations in coastal areas, both in natural populations and under mariculture.

The common names of the fish species or other animal species are used in the text, with the scientific names given the first time the species is mentioned. Maps of the distribution of the species can be found in the *Atlas of Marine Use in the North Pacific Region.*

## Demersal Species

Species that are considered here are walleye pollock (*Theragra chalcograma*), Pacific cod (*Gadus macrocephalus*), Pacific halibut (*Hippoglossus stenolepis*), yellowfin sole (*Limanda aspera*), Pacific hake (*Merluccius productus*), and sablefish (*Anoplopoma fimbria*).

Walleye pollock have wide distribution around the entire North Pacific rim and appear in great abundance in the northern areas, except the extreme northern parts of the Bering Sea and Okhotsk Sea where temperatures are very low. They account for over 25 percent of the commercial catch of all species in the area. Pollock are most in evidence at the edge of the continental shelf regions of the Bering Sea but are found as far south as central California on the eastern side, and as far south as northern Honshu and the eastern coast of Korea on the Asian side. Pollock migrate into deeper waters during winter and, as waters warm up, move back into shallower waters in the spring and summer months. Pollock feed largely on small crustaceans and squid; adult pollock are known to cannibalize other fish. Young pollock are an important constituent in the diet of salmon at certain times of the year. The largest catch of pollock occurs near the Kamchatka Peninsula, and the period of heaviest fishing is January to April in that area.[15]

Pacific cod have a distribution similar to walleye pollock except for a small isolated population in the Yellow Sea.[16] They are not caught in as great a quantity as pollock. The major fishing grounds are near the Kamchatka Peninsula, the Kuril Islands, northern Japan, the east coast of the Korean Peninsula, and the Aleutian Islands. Cod have seasonal onshore and offshore migrations related to water temperature. They feed on a few species of fish including pollock, sand lance, large crustaceans in their soft molting stages, flounders, salmon, squid, and octopus, depending on the seasonal abundance of these fish in their habitat.

Pacific halibut are found on the continental shelf and upper slope in the North Pacific from central California to Nome in Alaska, and from the Gulf of Anadyr in the Soviet Union to Hokkaido, the northern island of Japan. Adult halibut migrate offshore into deeper water in winter and onshore in summer. They also migrate from spawning grounds to feeding grounds over distances of several hundred kilometers. Some halibut are known to have migrated considerable distances in tagging experiments; one fish tagged in Asiatic waters was recovered near Shumagin island in Alaska.[17] Halibut are more abundant on the North American side than on the Asian side owing to more favorable temperature and spawning conditions.[18] Halibut are long-lived fish and grow to a large size on a diet of other fish such as pollock and herring, and on crustaceans, such as tanner crab.[19]

Yellowfin sole on the Asiatic side are found as far south as southeastern Korea and western Hokkaido on the Japan Sea coast, and along the continental shelf to the Bering Strait. On the North American side, the range of distribution extends from the Bering Sea as far south as the coasts of Washington and Oregon. Areas of greatest concentration are in the middle parts of the range[20] and in the southeastern Bering Sea.[21] Their migrations tend to be somewhat more restricted than those of halibut, and they are generally found at depths of 180−250 meters, although juvenile fish can be found in quite shallow water.[22] Yellowfin sole feed on small benthic forms like crustacea and mollusks. The distribution of other flounders follows that of sole and halibut, although their ranges are generally more restricted and they are not as numerous. A convenient reference for the depth distribution of various species of demersal fish is available.[23]

Pacific hake are found at intermediate depths in waters over the continental shelf and slope from the Gulf of Alaska to the Gulf of California, with greatest commercial aggregations off Washington, Oregon and California.[24] Due to the lack of evidence of any spawning activity in the northern portions of the range, it appears that hake spawn primarily in the deep waters along the continental shelf of California in winter months. Northern stocks are thought to migrate southward to spawn. The pelagic eggs and larvae have been sampled as far as 260 miles offshore.[25] After a period of one to two years of pelagic existence, the juvenile hake are thought to settle on the bottom with the older fish. Hake feed nocturnally in surface waters on various euphausiids and return to deeper waters along the bottom during the day.

Sablefish are found along the coasts of North America and at least as far south as the Kamchatka Peninsula on the Asian side.[26] The area of greatest abundance appears to be in the Gulf of Alaska; stocks in Asian waters are relatively scarce. Although most adult sablefish are found on the outer continental shelf and upper slope at depths of from 200 to 700 m, some have been found at depths of over 1200 m. Sablefish are known to migrate over considerable distances; interchange of stocks has occurred between the Bering Sea and the west coast of Canada and the state of Washington. Still, most of the stocks appear to be rather sedentary and move only locally, if at all. Sablefish feed on a wide variety of marine organisms depending on the season, availability of food species, and daily movements.[27]

A large number of other species of demersal fish are found in the warmer waters of the East China and Yellow seas, but the proportion of total catch of any one species is less than in more northern waters, where as few as 10 species make up 80 percent of the catch.[28] Yellow croaker (*Pseudosciaena manchurica*), hairtail (*Trichiurus lepturus*), the conger pike eel (*Muraenesox cinereus*), and various species of rockfish, for example, kichiji (*Sebastolobus macrochir*), constitute the most important species caught by Japan in that area. Yellow croaker, hairtail, and conger eels are caught in the East China Sea and Yellow Sea.[29]

## Pelagic Species

The pelagic species in the North Pacific considered here are Pacific herring (*Clupea harengus pallasi*), anchovy (*Engraulis japonica*), sardine (*Sardinops melanosticta*), chub mackerel (*Scomber japonicus*), and Pacific saury (*Cololabis saira*).

Herring occur from the Arctic to as far south as Korea and northern Japan in Asia, and to San Diego Bay on the North American side. Herring conduct seasonal migrations from feeding to spawning grounds. Many Pacific herring spawn in the spring in shallow coastal areas that are somewhat diluted by freshwater from continental rivers, and may even return to the same area each year. Stocks of herring show extreme unexplained variations in abundance over a period of years; these fluctuations make it difficult to predict the size of stocks, and therefore to manage the species along conventional lines.[30]

Sardines and anchovies are similar to herring in that they are subject to large fluctuations in population size and location. Sardines have a more southerly distribution than herring, extending only as far north as the southern Kamchatka Peninsula in the west, and the southeastern Gulf of Alaska in the east. Their southerly range is the northern tip of the Ryukyu Islands on the west, and Baja California on the east.[31] They are generally caught in littoral zones.[32] Anchovies are found both in coastal areas and bays and on the high seas. They both feed on zooplankton.

Chub mackerel are found in greatest concentration in the temperate and tropical coastal waters off both the eastern and western Pacific coasts. On the eastern side, they occur from Baja to southern Alaska; in Asia their northern limit is the southern tip of Sakhalin Island, and they are found along the coasts of Japan and in the East China Sea. Their migration pattern, which is similar to herring, sardine, and anchovy stocks, is highly seasonal and temperature-dependent, although local conditions in some areas constitute exceptions.[33]

In the Northwest Pacific, the population fluctuations of the four species result in a rather unpredictable large-scale fishery for any one species, but the fishery for the various species combined has yielded a fairly stable production of pelagic fish for food and industrial purposes.

Pacific saury is a species with trans-Pacific distribution in the area between 25 and 50 degrees north latitude. It is fished commercially in the Sea of Japan, Okhotsk Sea, and East China Sea, predominantly for industrial reduction for fish meal.[34] Relatively little is known about the eastern Pacific stocks and they are lightly exploited.[35]

## Anadromous Species

Pacific salmon is the main anadromous stock for quantity and value of catch. Five species of salmon are widely distributed in the North Pacific and spawn in rivers along the coasts of Asia and North America. They are chinook salmon (*Oncorhynchus tshawytscha*), coho salmon (*O. kisutch*), pink salmon (*O. gorbuscha*), sockeye salmon (*O. nerka*), and chum salmon (*O. keta*). A sixth species, the masu salmon (*O. masou*), found mostly off the Japanese coast and southern USSR, is of comparatively minor importance and is not considered here.

Salmon species have similar ranges of total distribution, but distribution of stocks from specific rivers may vary considerably.[36] Chum salmon are found as far south as the Korean peninsula, and pink salmon are found in the northern Sea of Japan. Sockeye salmon are most abundant from the rivers of the Kamchatka Peninsula, the Bristol Bay region, and the Fraser River. Pink salmon are found mostly in central Alaska and British Columbia, and are very abundant in Asia. Chum salmon are largely of Asian origin, while coho originate predominantly from North American rivers, those of British Columbia, Washington and Oregon in particular. Chinook are many times more abundant in North American catches than in Asian catches.[37].

All species of salmon have extensive migration patterns during their long growth period in marine waters. Tagging studies, incidental catches in trawls, and the Japanese high-seas salmon fisheries have provided some indications of the migration routes of the different species from various spawning locations, but in general the routes are not well-defined. The area between 175 degrees west longitude and 175 degrees east longitude is an area where the distribution of migrating stocks of Asian and North American origin overlap, and the difficulty in distinguishing between stocks that spawn in different rivers has been a major source of conflict in the management of salmon fisheries in the North Pacific. It should also be noted that stocks originating in the rivers of the nations of Asia intermingle with other stocks of Asian and North American origin and vice versa. Thus, high-seas fishing and, to some extent, even coastal fishing can occasion significant interception of stocks. Salmon feed on large zooplankton and small fishlike lanternfish.[38]

## Crustaceans

The major species of crustaceans subject to international commercial exploitation are king crab (*Paralithodes camtschatica*), tanner crab (*Chionoecetes bairdi* and *C. opilio*), pink shrimp (*Pandalus borealis* and *P. jordani*), and several species of sea snails including *Neptunia lyrata*. Many other crustaceans, especially crabs, are exploited in Northwest Pacific waters.

King crab is a cold water species with a northern limit of commercial distribution in Bristol Bay on the east and northern Kamchatka on the west. In Asia, king crab are found as far south as Korea, but in the northeastern Pacific their southern commercial limit is northern British Columbia. The major fishing grounds are Bristol Bay and Prince William Sound in North America,[39] and the west coast of Kamchatka, around Sakhalin Island, Hokkaido, and the Japan Sea coast of USSR in Asia.[40] Adult king crab do not conduct long migrations as a general rule, but in the larval stages may be carried considerable distances by the currents.

Tanner crab distribution extends along the continental shelf further south than king crab and further to the northwest in the Bering Sea. Its southern range extends as far south as Oregon on the North American side.[41] Tanner crab are caught commercially in the Sea of Japan, Okhotsk Sea, and the eastern Bering Sea.

Shrimp stocks were found in greatest concentrations northwest of the Pribilof Islands, in the Gulf of Anadyr, and off Cape Navarin in the early 1960s, but stock levels remain low after extensive exploitation in the mid-1960s. The United States and Canadian pink shrimp fisheries are mostly within the territorial sea area and are not discussed further.[42] A small shrimp fishery is located off the eastern peninsula of Korea.[43]

Snails are taken by Japan in the eastern Bering Sea along the continental shelf northwest of the Pribilof Islands.[44]

## Cephalopods

There are many species of squid, but the common squid (*Todarodes pacificus*) constitutes 90 percent of the total squid catch by Japan in the Japan Sea, west coast of Hokkaido, and East China Sea.[45] Squid migrate seasonally in response to changing water temperature, currents, and availability of food, and winter along both coasts of southern Japan and on both sides of the Korean peninsula. In spring and summer, squid range as far north as Kamchatka.[46] Squid, predominantly *Loligo opalescens*, are also found in the temperate waters along North America but are only lightly exploited by fisheries at the present time. Other species have a more northwest distribution. Squid feed on small crustaceans, fish and mollusks.[47]

## Marine Mammals

Over fifty species of marine mammals are found in the North Pacific. The polar bear (*Ursus maritimus*) is largely an ice-living mammal, while seals and walruses spend time in rookeries for mating and pupping. The whales, dolphins, and other marine mammals are exclusively water-dwelling animals. One species of marine mammals, the Stellar's sea cow (*Hydroanalus gigas*) is known to have been exploited to extinction prior to 1800, and the Japanese fur seal (*Zalophus californianus japonicus*) is thought to be extinct despite possible sighting off the coast of the Republic of Korea.[48] Not all species are considered to be of commercial importance; only the northern fur seal (*Callorhinus ursinus*), sperm whale

(*Physeter macrocephalus*), minke whale (*Balaenoptera acutorostrata davidsoni*), sei whale (*B. borealis*), and fin whale (*B. physalus physalus*) are currently exploited. The blue whale (*B. musculus musculus*), humpback whale (*Magaptera novaeangliae*), bowhead whale (*Balaena mysticetus*), grey whale (*Eschrichtius robustus*), and black right whale (*Balaena glacialis*) are reserved from harvest by the International Whaling Commission, but subsistence harvest of bowhead whales is maintained by Alaskan Eskimos.

Five separate populations of northern fur seals are recognized in the North Pacific. They are identified by their breeding grounds on the Pribilof Islands, Komandorskiye Islands, Robben Island, Kuril Islands, and San Miguel Island. Seals are present at these locations only during summer and fall months. During the winter, they are pelagic, and some migrate as far south as northern Mexico on the North American side, and to central Japan on the west. Fur seals feed mainly on fish and take various species depending on availability. In the northern part of the range fur seals are known to take mostly herring, capelin, pollock, sand lance, deep sea smelt, and squid.[49]

The distribution of whales in the North Pacific is largely within several hundred miles of the coastlines of the continents, although some have been noted over much wider areas during seasonal migrations. The sperm whale is found in the North Pacific from southern Japan to as far north as Cape Anadyr on the Asian side, and from the Aleutian Island chain all along the coast of North America. It is not found in the northern part of the eastern Bering Sea. The minke whale has a distribution similar to the sperm whale, but it is found throughout the Bering Sea. The sei whale appears to occupy an area somewhat more offshore than the sperm and minke, and is not found in the Bering Sea.[50] The baleen whales of the North Pacific feed on small plankton, while the toothed whales, like the sperm whale, eat squid, octopus, and various species of demersal fish.[51]

## Seabirds

Large numbers of seabirds exist in the North Pacific area. Among the most numerous families are the *Alcidae*, such as murres and auklets, the *Laridae*, or gulls and terns, and the *Procellariidae*, such as fulmars and shearwaters. Most species are found in the coastal areas during warmer months and migrate offshore or to more southerly latitudes in colder months. Many species breed in the North Pacific but some breed in the southern hemisphere and visit only during the summer. The food required and methods of capturing it differ greatly from species to species even within families. One example of this variation is seen in the *Alcidae*, where one group of species feeds exclusively on planktonic crustaceans, another almost exclusively on fish, and a third group on both.[52] Relatively little commercial use is made of seabirds at the present time.

## Seaweeds

Seaweeds are found throughout the coastal areas of the North Pacific region. Commercial exploitation of both natural and artificially established seaweed beds is carried out in many areas in the Northwest Pacific and in southern California. The cold waters off Kamchatka and Alaska limit the production of seaweed in the north, and the warmer waters of the South China Sea limit the production in the south. The principal species include various kelps (*Laminaria spp.* and *Undaria pinnatifida*) and lavers (*Porphyra*).[53]

## THE DEVELOPMENT OF FISHERIES

Unfortunately, much of the information on fisheries in the Northwest Pacific is not available. It is hoped that in future studies, data from the Soviet Union, Democratic Peoples Republic of Korea, and People's Republic of China can be provided. Two main periods can be distinguished in the development of fisheries in the North Pacific, which roughly correspond to the time before and after World War II. The prewar period can be characterized by a trend from artisanal fisheries to organized commercial exploitation, including some distant-water operations, especially by Japan; the postwar period is characterized by what Borgström called a "revolution" in the expansion of distant-water fisheries, technological improvements in fishing equipment, and increasing scale of operations.[54]

In the period between the end of the war and the eventual extension of the coastal state 200-mile jurisdictions over fisheries, a virtual explosion took place in fisheries development. The development in the North Pacific is particularly striking as the distant-water fishing fleets of, first, Japan, then the Soviet Union, and finally South Korea and others, entered the largely undeveloped groundfish fisheries off the coasts of North America and the Soviet Union and competed for available stocks—even to the point that certain stocks were depleted.

### Canada

Development of salmon resources has been the mainstay of Canadian Pacific fisheries. Beginning in 1835 with the export of salt-cured salmon to Hawaii, the Canadian fisheries expansion accompanied changes in technology and access to markets. The utilization of refrigerated railroad cars at the end of the nineteenth century permitted frozen salmon to be sold in the midwestern markets of Canada and the United States. Introduction of mechanized heading and cleaning equipment and powered fishing vessels also contributed to the growth of the salmon industry. A year-round fishery developed for halibut; herring fisheries were developed to provide bait and other products. Progress in fishery development on the Pacific coast of Canada was rapid, with the amalgamation of processing plants and business organization facilitated by relatively high prices for salmon and halibut products, which bore the shipping charges to market areas.[55]

Despite the overall trend in development of large-scale fishing in the North Pacific, not all nations participated to the same degree. Canada, for example, retained its traditional emphasis on salmon, halibut and herring. It has maintained a rather stable production of fish but has experienced an actual decline in the catches of some important species. Total salmon catches averaged 82,400 metric tons per year in the period between 1950 and 1954, while between 1970 and 1974 they amounted to only 72,500 MT. Halibut catches also declined from over 20,000 MT in the 1960s to 13,600 MT in 1972. Catch of other species increased enough to keep production, in terms of quantity, relatively constant at just over one million metric tons. Only a small amount of aquaculture is practiced in Canada, although salmon hatcheries are important and much has been done to improve spawning habitat for salmon.

## Japan

Japan has a long history of coastal fisheries. Its first expansion beyond coastal waters was to Sakhalin at the end of the 1700s for salmon fishing. One of the consequences of Commodore Perry's efforts to conclude a treaty with Japan in 1854 was the opening of the Japanese port of Shimonosecki to American whaling vessels for resupply.[56] A similar treaty between Japan and the Czar of Russia (1) provided for mutual extraterritorial rights, (2) defined the boundary in the Kurils, and (3) maintained joint occupation of Sakhalin, all of which related to the significant Japanese salmon operations along the Russian coast. In 1875, Japan gained all the Kuril Island chain in exchange for renouncing rights to Sakhalin in a convention with Russia. During this time, Japanese fisheries for salmon and fur seals in waters off Russia increased considerably. Following the Russo—Japanese War, the Treaty of Portsmouth in 1905 provided a return of Sakhalin to Japan, and Japanese fisheries interests were not long in reestablishing their operations in the Okhotsk and Bering seas. Fisheries were administered under a 1907 agreement between the two countries, but Japan had by far the greatest capacity to exploit and process fish from the area, and by 1917 had quintupled the 1908 catch.[57]

During the period between the Soviet revolution and the beginning of World War II fishery disputes intensified, and by 1930 the naval skirmishes between the two nations, primarily over fisheries, became international news. This was largely a result of Japanese high-seas salmon fishing initiated off the Russian coast in 1926.[58]

During the same period, Japan's expansion into Taiwan, Korea, and Manchuria added considerably to the Japanese catch and more than offset the losses in northern waters. Large-scale fishing was developed in the Yellow Sea and East China Sea. Trawl fisheries for halibut and flounder were started in the eastern Bering Sea in 1930, after successful mothership operations for king crab were started there the same year.[59] Salmon fishing in the eastern Bering Sea was explored in the mid-1930s but was met by vigorous American objections.

Japan rapidly redeveloped, and exceeded, the fishing capacity lost in World War II. Most of the larger vessels in the Japanese fleets were destroyed by U.S. submarines and warships during the war because they were used for military transportation.[60] Japan also lost important fisheries concessions in the Kuril Islands, Sakhalin Island, and Kamchatka area, as well as the production from occupied territories. The smaller vessels in the coastal fleet were not as heavily impacted, but they were not adequate to supply the serious food deficit in Japan after the war. Investment in fisheries was limited to areas inside the MacArthur Line by the Allied Occupation government immediately after the war. This limited Japanese fishing to the western Pacific in waters near Japan. When this policy was liberalized in 1952, the Republic of Korea declared the Peace Line (Rhee Line), which was intended to protect the developing Korean fishery in the East China and Yellow seas. Fishery conflicts developed with the Soviet Union in March 1956 when they closed Peter the Great Bay in the

Sea of Japan and established the Bulganin Line, which enclosed the Okhotsk Sea and Kamchatka areas (maps of these boundary lines are in Appendix A, figs. 1 and 2).

Restrictions on fishing in waters near Japan and their need for animal protein prompted the government of Japan to encourage the development of distant-water trawl fishing in the Yellow Sea and East China Sea, but political difficulties with the Republic of Korea and China prevented full expansion. Subsequent to the signing of the United States–Japan Peace Treaty in 1951, with its provisions requiring that Japan negotiate agreements with coastal states, some of Japan's China Sea fleets were shifted to the Asian and North American coasts of the Bering Sea.[61] This coincided with a decision by their government to reduce overcapacity in coastal fleets and develop a high-seas salmon fishery.[62] Three categories of licenses for distant-water fisheries were issued by the Japanese government: (1) North Sea mothership fleets, consisting of a large processing vessel accompanied by numerous catcher boats and support ships; (2) North Sea trawlers, which are large stern trawlers capable of storing considerable quantities of catch and of staying at sea for long periods; and (3) the Hokutensen fleets of smaller trawlers, whose name means literally "vessels transferred to the north."[63]

These fleets targeted on groundfish in the eastern Bering Sea, starting in 1954 with yellowfin sole and switching to pollock as other stocks declined. In 1953 Japanese mothership vessels resumed the fishery for king crab in the Bering Sea, and a record catch of over 10 million crabs was attained in 1964. Bilateral arrangements were negotiated between Japan and the United States to conserve the stocks of king crab and to reserve a larger share for domestic U.S. harvests. The crab fishery by distant-water nations was then oriented to tanner crab in 1965, and by 1970 a record 17 million crabs were taken. While this level of fishing did not impact heavily on the substantially underexploited tanner crab stocks, it was necessary to ensure that catches did not greatly exceed these levels. Bilateral negotiations led to reductions in the amount of tanner crab available to Japan. Exploitation of pink shrimp stocks on the continental shelf northeast of the Pribilof Islands began in 1961 and produced record catches in 1963, but subsequently the catches declined drastically as a result of possible overfishing and/or changes in environmental conditions in the area.[64]

The specific exclusion of Japan from Soviet and North American coastal salmon fisheries, as a result of war settlements, prompted Japan to reinstate its high seas salmon fisheries in the area beyond Soviet territorial waters and west of the abstention line of the 1952 INPFC agreement with Canada and the United States. While the abstention principle worked reasonably well as a management tool, it is estimated that some 3.5 percent of the high seas catch of salmon by Japan in the Bering Sea and Aleutian area was of North American origin.[65] Impact on the stocks of Soviet origin was considerably greater, and continued negotiations between Japan and the Soviet Union have resulted in increasingly restricted catch quotas. Japan has significant production of marine products from aquaculture of shellfish, seaweeds and fish. Salmon, too, are artificially propagated in northern rivers. This aquaculture production is highly labor, energy, and resource intensive and produces a high-cost product, usually for specialty markets.

### Democratic People's Republic of Korea (DPRK)

Pre-World War II fisheries in Korea were rather limited, as fishing was considered a menial occupation and farmers engaged in it only as a sideline for their other activities. During the Japanese occupation of Korea certain fisheries were modernized, but the resources were not exploited for Korean benefit. The main part of Korean fishery remained traditional and small-scale.[66]

### Republic of Korea (ROK)

The Republic of Korea lost 50 percent of its fishing boats and many skilled marine workers in World War II. Government postwar fishery development plans were never carried out due to the outbreak of the Korean War in 1950. It was not until after the Korean War that serious efforts to modernize the industry could be taken.[67] Most of the ROK distant-water activities took place outside the North Pacific area, but a substantial pollock fishery was developed off the Soviet Union, and some expansion took place in the northern Sea of Japan. In 1966, Busan National Fisheries University made an exploratory survey of fish resources in the eastern Bering Sea.[68] In 1968, an ROK trawl fishery for groundfish began in that area, primarily for pollock. There was some fear that an ROK high-seas salmon fishery might develop in the North Pacific but agreement was reached between the United States and the Republic of Korea that provided for Korean abstention from salmon, halibut, and crab fishing in the North Pacific in exchange for help in developing salmon runs and oyster culture, and permission to fish less important stocks in the Bering Sea.[69] Aquaculture for seaweeds is practiced off the southern coasts of the Republic of Korea and shellfish are produced in many bays along the eastern and western coastlines. Aquaculture has been a significant factor in seafood exports in recent years.

### Union of Soviet Socialist Republics (USSR)

Fisheries in Russia before the revolution were largely in internal seas and freshwater, with limited fishing in coastal areas near western population centers. Lavrischchev attributes this to the lack of requisite technical bases for the exploitation of the open ocean basins.[70] The fleet of Czarist Russia consisted of small sailing vessels, and fish processing was done by hand-craft enterprises. In 1913, salmon comprised 89 percent of the total fish catch in the Far East. Salmon was caught mainly by intercepting them in coastal areas on their return to spawning grounds. No adequate transportation linkages existed that were suitable for conveying fish from Siberia to the western part of the country where markets were available; therefore, considerable amounts were sold for export to Japan.

Relatively little was done to develop fisheries in the region until 1925, when "Dalrybtrest," the Far East Fishery Agency, was founded. Under the Second Five-Year Plan (1933–1937), substantial investments were made in port facilities, cold storage, and processing as part of a larger Soviet strategic effort to develop and populate the Far East and Siberia.[71] Soviet whaling in the North Pacific began in 1932 with the launching of the first flotilla, the *Aleut*, based in the Far East. Despite these efforts, fisheries in the Far East and Siberia contributed a small proportion of the total USSR catch in relation to the inland seas and other marine areas.[72]

The Soviet Union was the second nation to undertake major distant-water fisheries activities in the North Pacific. During the war, fisheries on the coasts of Siberia and the Far East were rapidly developed in order to supply fish products to the soldiers fighting on the European and Asian front lines. Catches rose from 55,700 tons in 1940 to 120,400 tons in 1943. In the Far East, development of new fishing grounds off Kamchatka resulted in a catch of 400,000 metric tons in 1944. This heavy fishing resulted in a subsequent drop in stocks after the war.[73] In 1948, Soviet catches in the North Pacific were only 133,000 metric tons, but they had recovered to 190,000 metric tons by 1953.[74] The decision to develop distant-water fishing capabilities was apparently based upon a variety of factors, including the needs to provide a source of protein for national consumption at a cost lower than that in agriculture, provide employment,[75] replace imports,[76] and generate foreign exchange.[77] The development of fisheries in the North Pacific region by the Soviets was later than that of the Atlantic region, which was probably due to the high cost and technical difficulty of transporting fish from the Far East and Siberia to centers of demand.[78]

The Soviet expansion in the northeastern Pacific was preceded by a comprehensive scientific investigation of fishery resources and the marine environment in 1958. In 1959, Soviet fleets began to fish for groundfish and herring in the eastern Bering Sea. By 1962–63, the effort was extended into the Gulf of Alaska and the Aleutians, and in 1966 a major development of hake stocks off Oregon and Washington was undertaken.[79] These harvests in the northeastern Pacific accounted for an average of 26 percent of the Soviet Pacific Ocean catch and 10 percent of their total national catch.[80] While the Japanese effort was 90 percent concentrated in the eastern Bering Sea, only 40 percent of the Soviet effort was directed to that area, owing to the major fisheries in the Atlantic and elsewhere.

Soviet fishing for king crab in the Bering Sea began in 1959 and resulted in a catch of over 3 million crabs per year from 1961–63. By 1971, however, as a consequence of depletion of king crab stocks by a combination of Soviet, Japanese, and American effort, the Soviet Union agreed in bilateral negotiations with the United States to cease harvesting king crab. The tanner crab fishery, begun in 1965, followed a similar course. Pink shrimp stocks in the Bering Sea, which the Soviets began to fish in 1963, were largely gone by 1965.

The second area of Soviet fisheries expansion in the North Pacific was off the west coast of Japan. Beginning in 1955, Soviet fleets began taking saury with stick-held dip nets in these waters. In 1961, they also began harvesting mackerel in the north and gradually extended this fishery as far south as the Izu Islands by 1968.[81] The actual size of the Soviet fleet in waters off Japan is unknown, but it has been estimated to range from several score to 100 large trawlers, purse seiners, motherships and transport boats. The Soviet Foreign Ministry reported a catch of 200,000 metric tons (MT) in 1973 in Japanese waters, but Japan estimates the catch was on the order of 200,000–300,000 MT. The Soviet claims catches as high as 500,000 MT.[82] In recent years, Soviet fleets have harvested the relatively lightly utilized sardine stocks off northern Japan. The Soviet Union has so far not developed much mariculture in the Northwest Pacific, but it does have a considerable program on salmon propagation.

## United States (U.S.)

The early fisheries in the United States, like Canada, targeted on salmon and halibut, and the factors affecting the fishing of these species were much the same both sides of the border. In contrast, there was a substantial U.S. industry developed on the exploitation of marine mammals, primarily whales and fur seals. In addition, fleets from California participated in the development of the cod fishery off Kamchatka and in the Okhotsk Sea during the period 1863–1909.[83] Some fishing for halibut also occurred in that area in the 1890s. Other fisheries, like those for salt herring, sardine, and rockfish were developed; and dogfish were exploited for some time as a source of Vitamin A.[84]

Development of the hydroelectric capacity of the Columbia River and other major salmon spawning streams interfered with salmon runs in the 1930s; other land use and forestry practices also had an impact. The combined effect of such activities, the overfishing of salmon stocks, and the overcapacity of the fishing fleets to harvest prompted the United States to expand efforts to enhance escapement and to artificially propagate salmon smolt.[85]

United States' Pacific fisheries were little affected by World War II. The main species fished continued to be salmon and halibut. In 1947, United States crab vessels began operating in the Gulf of Alaska and, to a small extent, in the eastern Bering Sea. Expanding domestic markets encouraged large-scale development of Bering Sea stocks of crabs in the early 1970s.[86] Commercial tanner crab fisheries began in 1961 and increased rapidly thereafter to the point where almost 36,000 MT worth over $16 million were caught in 1975.[87] Development of shrimp peeling technology for small shrimp in 1949 set the stage for a major expansion in Alaskan shrimp fisheries in the late 1950s.[88]

The United States has not participated in the great expansion of international distant-water fisheries in the North Pacific, or in the competition for groundfish stocks. U.S. efforts have been aimed primarily at protecting stocks fished by domestic fleets, and encouraging the conservation of fish stocks developed by other nations on the high seas near the United States coastlines in areas like the Bering Sea. Overall, the catches of groundfish in the North Pacific have remained relatively constant at 70,000 MT, although the proportion of individual species has changed somewhat. Total salmon catches declined from over 200,000 MT in 1960 to approximately 100,000 MT in 1973. Large incidental catches of crab and halibut in the foreign trawl fisheries in the northeastern Pacific have reduced the productivity of those resources for American fishing interests.

The United States, like Canada, Japan, and the USSR, is engaged in large-scale programs for salmon propagation. Research efforts on mariculture are largely related to salmon, although considerable effort has been given to shellfish.

## Other Nations

Little is known of fisheries in the People's Republic of China (PRC) and their development during the pre-World War II period. For the most part, fisheries were small-scale, and marine catches accounted for two-thirds to three-quarters of the total catch.[89] Under Japanese occupation some districts increased levels of production. The coastal area of China is considered to be one of the most productive marine areas in the world, although much of this area lies south of the 30° N latitude boundary of the region used here.

The PRC and the Democratic People's Republic of Korea (DPRK) do not report much on fishing activities in the North Pacific area. It is known that China has greatly expanded its freshwater fish culture because it is considerably less costly than investment in fishing vessels as long as undeveloped freshwater areas still exist.[90] According to some estimates, the marine production of China amounts to less than one-third of the total production,[91] whereas it previously accounted for two-thirds of the production. North Korea is known to have developed a small distant-water fleet that operates in the waters off the Soviet Union.[92] Taiwan began fishing for sablefish and pollock off Alaska in 1970; Poland, East Germany, and Bulgaria have also initiated fisheries there. China has extensive seaweed mariculture.[93]

## Trends in Development of Fisheries

By 1977 the combined catch of all nations fishing in the North Pacific had reached over 20,000,000 MT of fish and shellfish. Approximately 10 percent (1.8 million MT) was derived from the Northeast Pacific, and 90 percent (18.6 million MT) from the Northwest Pacific. The seven nations located on the perimeter of the North Pacific together accounted for nearly 50 percent of the total world catch of fish from all areas; of this amount, over one-half came from the North Pacific. (See table 2.2.) Note that the trend in total catch from the Northeast Pacific shows a slight decline in recent years, and the trend in the Northwest Pacific shows a substantial increase over the period 1970−1977. Considering only marine harvests, the North Pacific accounts for over 30 percent of the world total.

Table 2.3 shows the percentage of world total catches taken by nations bordering the North Pacific in 1975 and reveals the percentage of that amount harvested in the North Pacific. Japan and the Soviet Union accounted for approximately 15 percent and 13 percent respectively of the world catch. Over 90 percent of the Japanese catch and 33 percent of the Soviet catch came from the North Pacific. All of the Chinese and North Korean catch comes from the North Pacific. The United States and Canada obtain only 12.5 percent and 13 percent of their respective catches from the North Pacific, although the value per unit quantity of the species caught there is relatively high. ROK catches are nearly 90 percent from the North Pacific.

Examination of recent trends in the national harvests of fish in the northeastern and northwestern Pacific (table 2.4) reveals some important facts. Canada and the United States do not catch any fish in the Northwest Pacific. China and the Democratic People's Republic of Korea do not harvest fish in the Northeast Pacific. Of the three nations—USSR, Japan, and ROK—that harvest fish in both areas (1) the Soviet catch in the northeastern Pacific has decreased on a percentage basis and its catch in the northwestern Pacific has increased, (2) the Japanese share of the catch in both areas has remained essentially the same, and (3) the ROK harvest has shown a small increase in the share of catch in the Northeast Pacific and a slight decline in the Northwest. On the basis of quantity, the total catches by all nations in

## TABLE 2.2

### NORTH PACIFIC FISH HARVESTS COMPARED TO WORLD HARVESTS (1970–1977)

#### (IN METRIC TONS)

| | World | NE Pacific | NE Pacific as % of world harvest | | NW Pacific | NW Pacific as % of world harvest | | North Pacific | North Pacific as % of world harvest |
|---|---|---|---|---|---|---|---|---|---|
| | | | *Marine* | *Total* | | *Marine* | *Total* | | |
| 1970 | 70,696,400 | 2,652,400 | 4.3 | 3.8 | 12,977,400 | 21.1 | 18.4 | 15,629,800 | 22.2 |
| 1971 | 71,288,700 | 2,307,500 | 3.8 | 3.2 | 14,585,300 | 23.7 | 20.0 | 16,892,800 | 23.2 |
| 1972 | 66,924,400 | 2,774,800 | 4.9 | 4.1 | 14,932,600 | 26.3 | 22.3 | 17,707,400 | 26.4 |
| 1973 | 67,677,900 | 1,901,800 | 3.3 | 2.8 | 17,027,900 | 29.7 | 25.1 | 18,929,700 | 27.9 |
| 1974 | 71,340,000 | 2,332,840 | 3.8 | 3.3 | 17,279,010 | 28.3 | 24.2 | 19,611,850 | 27.5 |
| 1975 | 71,003,700 | 2,240,399 | 3.7 | 3.2 | 17,714,072 | 29.4 | 24.9 | 19,954,471 | 28.1 |
| 1976 | 74,717,200 | 2,408,606 | 3.8 | 3.2 | 18,122,216 | 28.3 | 24.3 | 20,530,822 | 27.5 |
| 1977 | 73,501,000 | 1,765,170 | 2.8 | 2.4 | 18,607,692 | 29.7 | 25.3 | 20,372,862 | 27.7 |

Source: Food and Agriculture Organization of the United Nations, *Yearbook of Fisheries Statistics*, vols. 39, 40, and 42, tables A-1, C-61, and C-67 (Rome: 1974, 1975, and 1977).

Note: Comparable data are not available for the North Pacific for the 1960–1970 period (percentage calculations by the author).

TABLE 2.3

PERCENTAGE OF WORLD FISH HARVESTS TAKEN BY
NORTH PACIFIC NATIONS (1960—1977)

|  | 1960 | 1965 | 1970 | 1975 | 1976 | 1977 |
|---|---|---|---|---|---|---|
| Canada | 2.3 | 2.4 | 2.0 | 1.4 | 1.5 | 1.7 |
| Korea (DPRK) | – | – | 1.4 | 2.1 | 2.1 | 2.2 |
| Japan | 15.5 | 12.9 | 13.2 | 14.8 | 14.3 | 14.6 |
| People's Republic of China (PRC) | 14.5 | – | 8.8 | 9.7 | 9.2 | 9.4 |
| Korea (ROK) | 1.1 | 1.2 | 1.1 | 3.0 | 3.2 | 3.3 |
| USSR | 7.6 | 9.5 | 10.3 | 14.0 | 13.6 | 12.7 |
| USA | 7.0 | 5.1 | 4.1 | 4.1 | 4.3 | 4.2 |

Source:  Calculated from data in Food and Agriculture Organization of the United Nations, *Yearbook of Fisheries Statistics*, vols. 39, 40, and 42 (Rome: 1974, 1975, and 1976).
(Percentage calculations by the author.)

both areas of the North Pacific have increased markedly, although the rate of increase slowed in the middle 1970s.

Table 2.5 presents the catch by nations in the North Pacific. Japan (50.1%) takes by far the largest percentage of fish from the North Pacific, although this figure has declined in recent years as Soviet catches (17.1%) and ROK catches (10%) have increased. The amounts taken by the other nations have declined slightly on a percentage basis so that by 1975 their catches were as follows: China (12%), DPRK (4.1%),Canada (0.7%), and USA (1.8%).

It appears that an increase of from 25—50 percent in the fish catch in the North Pacific is unlikely in the next 10—15 years, even though there are several unexploited species like saury and squid in the northeastern Pacific. In addition, only relatively small increments of total catch can be expected from management programs to rebuild depleted stocks of salmon, halibut, Pacific ocean perch, yellowfin sole and others, although improved salmon and halibut fisheries would yield considerable revenue.[94] Development of technologies to exploit underutilized species and the creation of markets for the products constitute important barriers to the expansion of these fisheries under conditions of rapidly increasing energy and labor costs. Aquaculture is also unlikely to supply large amounts of food protein from marine organisms, but it is likely to supply an increasing demand for specialty items that command high prices. It should be noted that without management of fish stocks, instead of little or no gain in production, a loss would be anticipated.

In the brief span of 30 years, North Pacific fisheries have increased in quantity from less than 8 million metric tons to nearly 20 million metric tons (including freshwater catches). Both the Northwest and Northeast Pacific catches have been greatly expanded during this period. While the catch in the northeastern area is only about one-seventh the catch in the northwestern area, the catch of groundfish and crabs in the eastern Bering Sea, Aleutian Islands, and Gulf of Alaska have shown a greater rate of growth than fisheries in the Northwest Pacific. Previously, there was virtually no harvest of groundfish species in these areas, and in recent years the harvests have exceeded two million metric tons of fish. Still the

## TABLE 2.4

### North Pacific Fish Harvests as a Proportion of Total National Harvests (1960–1977)

(In Metric Tons)

| Nation | Year | Total world harvest | Marine harvest | NE Pacific harvest | NE Pacific harvest as a % of total | NW Pacific harvest | NW Pacific harvest as a % of total | Total N. Pacific harvest | N. Pacific harvest as a % of national harvest |
|---|---|---|---|---|---|---|---|---|---|
| Canada | 1960 | 934,500 | – | – | – | – | 0 | – | – |
| | 1965 | 1,262,300 | – | – | – | – | 0 | – | – |
| | 1970 | 1,388,800 | 1,345,200 | 116,700 | 8.4 | – | 0 | 116,700 | 8.4 |
| | 1975 | 1,020,893 | 978,414 | 132,986 | 13.0 | – | 0 | 132,986 | 13.0 |
| | 1976 | 1,132,258 | 1,092,591 | 180,902 | 16.0 | – | 0 | 180,902 | 16.0 |
| | 1977 | 1,280,401 | 1,235,565 | 204,821 | 16.0 | – | 0 | 204,821 | 16.0 |
| DPRK (Korea) | 1960 | – | – | – | – | – | – | – | – |
| | 1965 | – | – | – | – | – | – | – | – |
| | 1970 | 1,000,000[a] | – | – | 100 | 1,000,000[a] | 100 | 1,000,000[a] | 100 |
| | 1975 | 1,500,000[a] | – | – | 100 | 1,500,000[a] | 100 | 1,500,000[a] | 100 |
| | 1976 | 1,600,000[a] | – | – | 100 | 1,600,000[a] | 100 | 1,600,000[a] | 100 |
| | 1977 | 1,600,000[a] | – | – | 100 | 1,600,000[a] | 100 | 1,600,000[a] | 100 |
| Japan | 1960 | 6,192,700 | – | – | – | – | – | – | – |
| | 1965 | 6,907,700 | – | – | – | – | – | – | – |
| | 1970 | 9,366,500 | 9,198,700 | 1,390,800 | 14.8 | 7,178,400 | 76.6 | 8,565,200 | 91.4 |
| | 1975 | 10,524,204 | 10,324,871 | 1,113,803 | 10.6 | 8,526,648 | 81.0 | 9,640,451 | 91.6 |
| | 1976 | 10,662,188 | 10,461,501 | 1,105,067 | 10.4 | 8,583,264 | 80.5 | 9,688,331 | 90.9 |
| | 1977 | 10,733,316 | 10,525,498 | 808,715 | 7.5 | 8,847,620 | 82.4 | 9,656,335 | 89.9 |
| Peoples Republic of China | 1960 | 5,800,000 | – | – | – | – | – | – | – |
| | 1965 | – | – | – | – | – | – | – | – |
| | 1970 | 6,255,000[a] | 2,102,000[a] | – | 0 | 2,102,000[a] | 33.6 | 2,102,000[a] | 33.6 |
| | 1975 | 6,880,000[a] | 2,312,000[a] | – | 0 | 2,312,000[a] | 33.6 | 2,312,000[a] | 33.6 |
| | 1976 | 6,880,000[a] | 2,312,000[a] | – | 0 | 2,312,000[a] | 33.6 | 2,312,000[a] | 33.6 |
| | 1977 | 6,880,000[a] | 2,312,000[a] | – | 0 | 2,312,000[a] | 33.6 | 2,312,000[a] | 33.6 |

## TABLE 2.4 (Continued)

### NORTH PACIFIC FISH HARVESTS AS A PROPORTION OF TOTAL NATIONAL HARVESTS (1960–1977)

#### (IN METRIC TONS)

| Nation | Year | Total world harvest | Marine harvest | NE Pacific harvest | NE Pacific harvest as a % of total | NW Pacific harvest | NW Pacific harvest as a % of total | Total N. Pacific harvest | N. Pacific harvest as a % of national harvest |
|---|---|---|---|---|---|---|---|---|---|
| ROK (Korea) | 1960 | 455,200 | – | – | – | – | – | – | – |
| | 1965 | 640,400 | – | – | – | – | – | – | – |
| | 1970 | 842,700 | 842,100 | – | 0 | 818,000[a] | 97.1 | 818,000 | 97.1 |
| | 1975 | 2,133,667 | 2,124,858 | 58,738 | 2.8 | 1,914,869 | 89.7 | 1,973,607 | 92.5 |
| | 1976 | 2,405,266 | 2,390,280 | 30,714 | 1.3 | 2,034,689 | 84.6 | 2,065,403 | 85.9 |
| | 1977 | 2,419,019 | 2,393,133 | 24,509 | 1.0 | 2,039,348 | 88.4 | 2,063,857 | 89.4 |
| USSR | 1960 | 3,051,000 | – | – | – | – | – | – | – |
| | 1965 | 5,099,900 | – | – | – | – | – | – | – |
| | 1970 | 7,253,100 | 6,399,700 | 747,600[a] | 10.3 | 1,447,600 | 20.0 | 2,195,200 | 30.3 |
| | 1975 | 9,935,606 | 8,991,636 | 572,597 | 5.8 | 2,719,035 | 27.4 | 3,291,632 | 33.2 |
| | 1976 | 10,133,670 | 9,363,360 | 496,704 | 4.9 | 2,751,709 | 27.2 | 3,248,413 | 32.1 |
| | 1977 | 9,352,204 | 8,581,342 | 185,120 | 2.0 | 2,942,795 | 31.5 | 3,127,915 | 33.5 |
| USA | 1960 | 2,814,700 | – | – | – | – | – | – | – |
| | 1965 | 2,724,300 | – | – | – | – | – | – | – |
| | 1970 | 2,891,600 | 2,810,900 | 297,300 | 13.7 | – | 0 | 397,300 | 13.7 |
| | 1975 | 2,898,373 | 2,826,754 | 346,785 | 12.0 | – | 0 | 346,785 | 12.0 |
| | 1976 | 3,175,558 | 3,099,262 | 435,257 | 13.7 | – | 0 | 435,257 | 13.7 |
| | 1977 | 3,101,544 | 3,029,713 | 477,862 | 15.4 | – | 0 | 477,862 | 15.4 |

Source: Food and Agriculture Organization of the United Nations, *Yearbook of Fisheries Statistics*, vols. 39, 40, and 42 (Rome: 1974, 1975, and 1977). (Percentage calculations by the author.)

[a]Estimates by Food and Agriculture Organization of the United Nations.

TABLE 2.5

PERCENTAGE SHARE OF TOTAL NORTH PACIFIC FISH HARVEST (1970—1977)

|  | Canada | DPRK | Japan | PRC | ROK | USSR | USA | Total[a] |
|---|---|---|---|---|---|---|---|---|
| Northwest Pacific |  |  |  |  |  |  |  |  |
| 1970 | — | 8 | 55 | 16 | 6 | 11 | — | 96 |
| 1975 | — | 8 | 48 | 13 | 10 | 15 | — | 94 |
| 1976 | — | 9 | 47 | 13 | 11 | — | — | 96 |
| 1977 | — | 8 | 48 | 12 | 11 | 16 | — | 95 |
| Northeast Pacific |  |  |  |  |  |  |  |  |
| 1970 | 4 | — | 52 | — | — | 28 | 11 | 95 |
| 1975 | 6 | — | 50 | — | 3 | 26 | 15 | 100 |
| 1976 | 8 | — | 46 | — | 1 | 21 | 18 | 94 |
| 1977 | 12 | — | 46 | — | 1 | 10 | 27 | 96 |
| North Pacific |  |  |  |  |  |  |  |  |
| 1970 | 1.0 | 6 | 55 | 13 | 5 | 14 | 2 | 96 |
| 1975 | 1.0 | 8 | 48 | 12 | 9 | 17 | 2 | 97 |
| 1976 | 1.0 | 8 | 47 | 11 | 10 | 16 | 2 | 95 |
| 1977 | 1.0 | 8 | 47 | 11 | 10 | 15 | 2 | 94 |

Source: Calculated from data in Food and Agriculture Organization of the United Nations, *Yearbook of Fisheries Statistics*, vol. 40, 1975, and vol. 42, 1977 (Rome: FAO), tables A-1, C-61, and C-67.

[a] Annual totals for each region do not equal 100% because of catches by other nations in the region and rounding error.

total harvest from this area is less than the total increase in Northwest Pacific catches between 1970 and 1977. Most of the increase can be attributed to the Japanese development of fish processing technologies for utilizing Alaska pollock, and to the increased use of this species in the form of frozen blocks of fillets by the Soviet Union and ROK.

## SOCIOECONOMIC DESCRIPTORS

In this section, a few of the more important economic and social aspects of the fisheries are discussed as a tentative means of comparing the size and nature of fishery-related activities between North Pacific nations. The descriptors chosen for discussion are employment in the fishing industry, size of the fishing fleet, international trade in fishery products, and domestic consumption of fishery products. The intent of the discussion is to identify the trends in some of the major variables in the fishery industries of the various nations.

Substantial effort has been made to obtain comparable data from each national source. Where fishing takes place in more than one ocean region, as is the case for Canada, the USSR and the U.S., an attempt is made to determine the proportion of employment, fleet, international trade, and consumption attribution to North Pacific fisheries, using the percentage of the weight of the catch from the Pacific relative to the total catch. At the high level of aggregation of data used in this study, the descriptions are rather general. This is intended as a first cut, with the expectation that future studies will further refine the figures. Focus is on the period between 1960 and 1977, particularly the more recent years.

No inferences can be legitimately made on the basis of these descriptors as to how important fisheries are for any given nation. Considerably more research and refinement is necessary to make such analysis possible. Given the paucity of data, it is unlikely that such efforts would meet with success without serious cooperative efforts by all nations involved to develop, standardize, and report these data.

## Employment

National employment statistics are assumed to give a reasonably satisfactory basis for identifying the magnitude of and trends in fishery employment. Fishery employment statistics leave much to be desired in terms of defining who is counted as being employed in fishing. This generally includes both marine and freshwater fisheries and full and part-time or seasonally-employed persons, although the question of whether or not persons employed in processing are included is often left unanswered. The approach used here is to accept the largest number accorded to fisheries employment published by the relevant national agencies.

Of the nations where official statistics are available (summarized in table 2.6), Japan leads in total employment with 480,000 (1975). The Republic of Korea is second with 322,000 (1975), United States third with 136,000 (1973), and Canada fourth with 51,000 (1974). On the basis of published statistics, the amount of U.S. fisheries employment attributable to the North Pacific is about 34 percent, and for Canada 17 percent. At least 90 percent of fisheries employment in Japan and South Korea is located in the North Pacific, based on catch weight data. The Soviet Union is estimated to employ 750,000 persons in fishing, processing, and administration,[95] of which 160,000 are estimated to be employed in the Far East and Siberian fisheries.[96] There is an additional number (20,000) of seasonal cannery workers imported to the Far East from other areas. In 1959, Chinese employment in fisheries was estimated at 1,500,000 persons, although only about one-third are employed in marine areas.[97] No North Korean data or estimates are available.[98]

Employment in fisheries, when compared with the economically active population, shows considerable differences among nations. These are probably of greater importance as a measure of economic and social significance than the sheer number of persons employed, although the linkages have not been adequately researched. About 3.5 percent of South Korean workers were employed in fisheries. Comparable figures for the other nations are: Japan, 1 percent; Canada, 0.8 percent; USSR, 0.4 percent; and the United States, 0.2 percent. Average employment in fisheries is more important in British Columbia than in the rest of Canada because in British Columbia 1.5 percent of the working population is employed in fisheries. Fisheries employment for the state of Alaska, and perhaps for Washington and Oregon, exceeds the national average in the United States, yet the percentage of total employment remains small.

The trend in fishery employment by nation generally shows a fairly rapid decline in number of persons employed as coastal fishing fleets are converted to capital-intensive rather than labor-intensive operations. Job opportunities in other sectors of the economy siphon off workers and marginal and part-time fishermen find it increasingly difficult to maintain their activity. In Japan, employment in fisheries fell from over 626,000 persons to

478,000 between 1962 and 1975, and the rate of decline over the most recent 5-year period was 12 percent. South Korean fisheries employment registered a decrease of almost 50 percent between 1966 and 1975. Canadian employment in fisheries decreased by 26 percent between 1965 and 1972, and the decline in British Columbia was a drop of 24 percent during the period. Total fisheries employment increased by 5 percent in the United States between 1960 and 1973, although there is an overall decrease when compared to 1950. On the west coast of the United States, the number of people employed in fisheries has increased by 33 percent since 1960, despite virtually no change in output. Note that these changes in fisheries are relative only to fisheries employment—not to total employment.

## Size of Fleet

One indirect measure of investment in fisheries is the size of the fishing fleet, although investment in fishing fleets must be adequately complemented by docking, processing, distribution, and personnel training to be effective. Emphasis is placed on vessels over 100 gross registered tons (GRT), since most vessels engaged in international fisheries are large vessels. All nations in the North Pacific have considerable fleets of smaller vessels operating in coastal waters. Some of these, like Canadian and American salmon trollers, are involved in international fisheries. Table 2.7a, Fishing Vessels, and table 2.7b, Factory Vessels, show the number and size of vessels in the fishing fleets of North Pacific nations. The number and size of the fleets are an inadequate data base on which to develop an analysis. More data are required on age and structure of the various categories of vessels, and their equipment and deployment. Still, some useful comparisons can be made about the relative size of national fleets in the North Pacific.

Available data in 1978 show that the Soviet Union leads the nations of the North Pacific and the world in total tonnage of fishing vessels over 100 GRT, with nearly 3.6 million GRT. This constitutes over 40 percent of the world total tonnage in that category in 1976. Japan, with 926,000 GRT, is second with 11.5 percent of the world total. The Republic of Korea, United States, and Canada trail with 427,000 GRT (4.9%), 252,000 GRT (2.9%), and 149,000 GRT (1.7%) respectively. Approximately one-third of the Soviet Union tonnage is used in the North Pacific according to the proportion of the weight of catch derived from that area. This total Soviet North Pacific fleet figure corresponds fairly closely to the Japanese North Pacific fleet on a proportional basis, but it is twice as large as that for the Republic of Korea fleet and much greater than the fleets of either Canada or the U.S. DPRK (3,000 GRT) and China (4,000 GRT) report very small fleets.

All nations have increased the size of their fleets since 1969. The world average increase in GRT, based on the index year 1969 = 100, is 173 for the over-100 GRT category. Canada (120), Japan (129), and USSR (139) were below the world figure, while the United States (229) was above it. The Republic of Korea (612) greatly exceeded the world average rate of increase; it is easier to double the size of the Korean fleets than to increase the total size of the larger Japanese and Soviet fleets. This is not to suggest, however, that a significant increase in the Korean fleet has not been made. No index data are available for DPRK or China.

In terms of factory vessels and carriers, the contrast is even more striking. The United

TABLE 2.6

TRENDS IN FISHERIES EMPLOYMENT IN THE NORTH PACIFIC (1950–1976)

| | I. National fisheries employment | | | II. Employment in North Pacific fisheries | | | |
|---|---|---|---|---|---|---|---|
| | Total | Change by 5-Year period | % Change by 5-Year period | N. Pacific | Change by 5-Year period | % Change by 5-Year period | N. Pacific % national fish. empl. |
| **Canada[a]** | | | | *Br. Columbia* | | | |
| 1955 | 78,511 | | | 12,836 | | | 16.3 |
| 1960 | 78,171 | − 340 | − 0.5 | 15,159 | +2,323 | +18.1 | 19.4 |
| 1965 | 78,157 | − 20 | 0 | 13,000 | −2,159 | −18.7 | 16.6 |
| 1970 | 63,145 | −15,150 | −19.2 | 11,647 | −1,353 | −10.4 | 21.0 |
| 1972 | 57,384 | − 5,761 | − 9.2 | 9,902 | −1,745 | −15.0 | 17.3 |
| 1974 | 50,877 | − 6,507 | −11.3 | 11,906 | +2,004 | +20.2 | 23.0 |
| 1976 | 63,385 | +12,508 | +24.6 | 13,764 | +1,858 | +15.6 | 21.7 |
| **DPRK (Korea)** | (not available) | | | Total fisheries employment in the North Pacific on the basis of origin of catch by weight is 100%. | | | |
| **Japan[b]** | | | | | | | |
| 1962 | 626,000 | | | Total fisheries employment in the North Pacific on the basis of origin of catch by weight is approximately 90%. | | | |
| 1968 | 594,000 | −32,000 | − 5.0 | | | | |
| 1970 | 549,000 | −45,000 | − 7.6 | | | | |
| 1975 | 478,000 | −71,000 | −12.9 | | | | |
| 1976 | 469,700 | − 8,300 | − 1.7 | | | | |
| **Peoples Rep. China[c]** | | | | | | | |
| 1959 | 1,500,000 | (probably increasing) | | Approximately 500,000, or 33%, are employed in North Pacific area by weight of catch. The remaining 67% are employed in inland fisheries. | | | |

Total fisheries employment in the North Pacific on the basis of origin of catch by weight is approximately 90%.

| | | | |
|---|---:|---:|---:|
| **ROK**[d] | | | |
| (Korea) | | | |
| 1962 | 462,525 | | |
| 1965 | 546,394 | + 83,869 | +18.1 |
| 1970 | 367,645 | − 178,749 | −32.7 |
| 1975 | 322,911 | − 44,734 | −12.2 |
| 1976 | 327,489 | + 4,578 | + 1.4 |
| | | | |
| **USSR** | | | |
| 1968 | 321,500[e] | (incl. processing & administration) | |
| 1975 | 750,000[g] | | |

160,000 in Far East and Siberia[f]

| | | | | Pacific States | | | |
|---|---:|---:|---:|---:|---:|---:|---:|
| **U.S.**[h] | | | | | | | |
| 1950 | 161,463 | | | 31,691 | | | 19.6 |
| 1955 | 130,431 | − 30,032 | −19.2 | 31,439 | − 252 | − 0.7 | 24.1 |
| 1965 | 128,576 | − 1,855 | − 1.4 | 34,778 | +3,339 | +10.6 | 27.1 |
| 1970 | 140,538 | + 11,962 | + 9.3 | 42,142 | +7,364 | +21.2 | 30.0 |
| 1973 | 135,745 | − 4,793 | − 3.5 | 46,381 | +4,239 | +10.0 | 34.2 |
| 1975 | 166,000 | + 30,255 | +18.2 | 44,840 | −1,541 | − 3.3 | 24.3 |

Sources:

[a] Fisheries and Environment Service, *Annual Statistical Review of Canadian Fisheries*, vols. 6 and 10 (Ottawa: 1973 and 1979, respectively); 1974 data from Organization for Economic Cooperation and Development, *Report on Fisheries of Member Countries 1977* (Paris: OECD, 1977).

[b] Statistics and Information Department. *Annual Statistical Yearbook on Fisheries and Agriculture* (Tokyo: Ministry of Agriculture, Forestry and Fisheries, various years) (in Japanese).

[c] Clinton Atkinson, "Northeast Asian Fisheries" delivered at Institute for Marine Studies, University of Washington, Seattle, Washington, November 16, 1976.

[d] Office of Fisheries, Republic of Korea, *Yearbook of Fisheries Statistics 1977* (Seoul: 1978).

[e] N. P. Sysoev. *Economics of the Soviet Fishing Industry* (Jerusalem, Israel: Program for Scientific Translations, 1974).

[f] Paul Dibb, *Siberia and the Pacific: A Study of Economic Development and Trade Prospects* (New York: Praeger Special Studies Program, 1974).

[g] U. S. Senate Committee on Commerce, *Soviet Oceans Development* (Washington, D.C.: U.S. Government Printing Office, October 1976).

[h] National Marine Fisheries Service, *U.S. Fisheries Statistics* (Washington, D.C.: U.S. Government Printing Office, various years).

## TABLE 2.7a

### FISHING VESSELS OF NORTH PACIFIC NATIONS IN RELATION TO TOTAL WORLD FISHING FLEET (1969, 1976, 1978)

| Country | | 100–499 GRT | | | 500–999 GRT | | | 1000 GRT & above | | | Total | | | % Total world fleet over 100 GRT | | | Increase in GRT Index (1969=100) |
|---|---|---|---|---|---|---|---|---|---|---|---|---|---|---|---|---|---|
| | | 1969 | 1976 | 1978 | 1969 | 1976 | 1978 | 1969 | 1976 | 1978 | 1969 | 1976 | 1978 | 1969 | 1976 | 1978 | 1978 |
| Canada | # | 388 | 393 | 389 | 65 | 90 | 92 | 5 | 5 | 6 | 458 | 488 | 487 | 3.7 | 2.6 | 2.5 | 120 |
| | GRT | 75,648 | 9,966 | 78,951 | 41,437 | 59,136 | 61,180 | 7,049 | 7,211 | 8,728 | 124,134 | 146,313 | 148,859 | 2.4 | 1.7 | 1.7 | |
| | # | – | – | 1 | – | – | – | – | – | 1 | – | – | 2 | – | – | 0.01 | – |
| | GRT | – | – | 267 | – | – | – | – | – | 2,600 | – | – | 2,867 | – | – | 0.03 | |
| Japan | # | 1,900 | 2,845 | 2,618 | 67 | 65 | 46 | 100 | 103 | 93 | 2,067 | 3,013 | 2,757 | 16.9 | 15.9 | 14.4 | 129 |
| | GRT | 467,108 | 715,542 | 665,573 | 46,188 | 45,337 | 33,585 | 215,731 | 246,244 | 227,045 | 719,089 | 1,007,123 | 926,203 | 14.1 | 12.2 | 10.5 | |
| Peoples Republic of China | # | – | – | 8 | – | – | 1 | – | – | – | – | – | 9 | – | P | 0.05 | – |
| | GRT | – | – | 2,923 | – | – | 827 | – | – | – | – | – | 3,750 | – | – | 0.04 | |
| | # | 135 | 528 | 624 | 16 | 32 | 29 | 2 | 23 | 26 | 153 | 583 | 679 | 1.25 | 3.1 | 3.5 | 680 |
| | GRT | 23,095 | 136,943 | 158,419 | 10,931 | 24,455 | 22,759 | 3,036 | 65,463 | 70,912 | 37,062 | 226,861 | 252,090 | 0.73 | 2.7 | 2.9 | |
| USSR | # | 1,872 | 2,133 | 1,940 | 335 | 869 | 939 | 397 | 831 | 942 | 2,604 | 3,833 | 3,821 | 21.3 | 20.3 | 19.9 | 139 |
| | GRT | 415,416 | 451,615 | 401,256 | 299,960 | 553,228 | 600,651 | 1,138,551 | 2,185,887 | 2,562,801 | 1,783,992 | 3,190,730 | 3,564,708 | 35.1 | 38.7 | 40.5 | |
| USA | # | 818 | 1,715 | 1,807 | 52 | 122 | 122 | 3 | 39 | 45 | 879 | 1,876 | 1,974 | 7.2 | 9.9 | 10.3 | 229 |
| | GRT | 148,342 | 270,191 | 280,075 | 33,917 | 93,129 | 91,090 | 4,277 | 51,254 | 56,733 | 186,536 | 414,574 | 427,898 | 3.7 | 5.0 | 4.9 | |
| World | # | 10,079 | 15,389 | 15,447 | 1,266 | 1,980 | 2,031 | 876 | 1,554 | 1,720 | 12,227 | 18,923 | 19,198 | 100 | 100 | 100 | 173 |
| | GRT | 2,166,550 | 3,292,060 | 3,295,394 | 872,173 | 1,374,932 | 1,384,448 | 2,014,405 | 3,601,093 | 4,117,458 | 5,082,098 | 8,241,085 | 8,797,000 | 100 | 100 | 100 | |

Source: *Lloyd's Register of Shipping*, Statistical Tables 1969, 1976, 1978.

Note: 2,000 GRT and above (GRT = Gross Registered Tons)

| | | 1969 | 1976 | 1978 |
|---|---|---|---|---|
| Japan | # | 44 | 56 | 52 |
| | GRT | 128,760 | 180,536 | 169,423 |
| Korea (DPRK) | # | – | – | 1 |
| | GRT | – | – | 2,600 |
| Korea (ROK) | # | – | – | 13 |
| | GRT | – | – | 52,233 |
| USSR | # | 382 | 692 | 801 |
| | GRT | 1,118,857 | 1,962,947 | 2,333,182 |
| USA | # | – | – | 1 |
| | GRT | – | – | 2,500 |

# TABLE 2.7b

## FISH FACTORY VESSELS AND CARRIERS OF NORTH PACIFIC NATIONS IN RELATION TO TOTAL WORLD FISHING FLEET (1969, 1976, 1978)

| | | 100–1999 GRT | | | 2000–3999 GRT | | | 4000 GRT & above | | | Total | | | % Total world fleet over 100 GRT | | |
|---|---|---|---|---|---|---|---|---|---|---|---|---|---|---|---|---|
| | | 1969 | 1976 | 1978 | 1969 | 1976 | 1978 | 1969 | 1976 | 1978 | 1969 | 1976 | 1978 | 1969 | 1976 | 1978 |
| Canada | # | 2 | 2 | 1 | – | – | – | – | – | – | 2 | 2 | 1 | neg. | neg. | 0.12 |
| | GRT | 2,028 | 357 | 102 | – | – | – | – | – | – | 2,028 | 357 | 102 | | | 0.003 |
| DPRK (Korea) | # | – | – | 3 | – | – | – | – | – | 3 | – | – | 6 | – | – | 0.78 |
| | GRT | – | – | 8,500 | – | – | – | – | – | 27,690 | – | – | 36,190 | – | – | 1.06 |
| Japan | # | 39 | 44 | 58 | 3 | 5 | 6 | 16 | 14 | 12 | 58 | 63 | 76 | 14.0 | 5.1 | 4.9 |
| | GRT | 21,606 | 25,390 | 21,640 | 10,425 | 15,312 | 19,042 | 137,343 | 143,003 | 125,079 | 169,374 | 185,705 | 165,761 | 8.4 | 8.7 | 9.9 |
| Peoples Republic of China | # | – | – | 11 | – | – | – | – | – | 1 | – | – | 12 | – | – | 1.55 |
| | GRT | – | – | 10,025 | – | – | – | – | – | 5,043 | – | – | 15,068 | – | – | 0.44 |
| ROK (Korea) | # | – | – | 8 | 1 | 3 | – | 3 | 3 | 5 | 4 | 6 | 12 | 1.0 | 0.8 | 1.6 |
| | GRT | – | – | 8,585 | 3,500 | 8,500 | – | 21,618 | 27,690 | 42,434 | 31,118 | 36,190 | 51,019 | 1.5 | 1.0 | 1.5 |
| USSR | # | 102 | 164 | 236 | 56 | 119 | 101 | 146 | 264 | 241 | 304 | 574 | 578 | 73.4 | 78.8 | 75.0 |
| | GRT | 56,170 | 99,808 | 135,766 | 178,469 | 392,715 | 329,537 | 1,386,582 | 2,539,245 | 2,376,705 | 1,621,221 | 3,031,768 | 2,842,008 | 80.6 | 84.0 | 83.6 |
| USA | # | 8 | – | 7 | – | 1 | – | 1 | 1 | 1 | 1 | 10 | 8 | neg. | 1.4 | 1.03 |
| | GRT | 1,361 | – | 1,169 | – | 3,805 | – | 4,011 | 4,011 | 4,011 | 4,011 | 9,177 | 5,180 | 0.3 | 0.3 | 0.15 |
| World | # | 168 | 276 | 362 | 66 | 138 | 120 | 180 | 314 | 289 | 414 | 728 | 771 | 100 | 100 | 100 |
| | GRT | 95,939 | 169,202 | 203,918 | 209,125 | 449,088 | 385,835 | 1,705,109 | 2,989,175 | 2,811,734 | 2,012,172 | 3,607,465 | 3,401,487 | 100 | 100 | 100 |

Source: *Lloyd's Register of Shipping*, Statistical Tables 1969, 1976, 1978

Note: 10,000 GRT and above (GRT = Gross Registered Tons)

| | | 1969 | 1976 | 1978 |
|---|---|---|---|---|
| Japan | # | 4 | 5 | 3 |
| | GRT | 54,805 | 72,492 | 48,405 |
| Korea (DPRK) | # | – | – | 2 |
| | GRT | – | – | 20,472 |
| Korea (ROK) | # | – | – | 1 |
| | GRT | – | – | 23,800 |
| USSR | # | 66 | 129 | 123 |
| | GRT | 929,495 | 1,738,958 | 1,652,625 |
| World | # | 79 | 146 | 138 |
| | GRT | 1,099,979 | 1,974,537 | 1,865,941 |

States, Canada, DPRK, and China, with primarily coastal fishing fleets in the North Pacific, have almost no vessels in this category. Even Japan and the Republic of Korea, with large distant-water fleets, account for only 6 percent of the vessels in this category. The Soviet Union dominates with 84 percent.

The disparity between the GRT size of the Soviet fishing fleet and its share of the world fish catch raises questions about the efficiency of the Soviet fishing activity. These are explored in a recent publication by the U.S. Senate Committee on Commerce, but without a great deal of further refinement of data and analysis it is not possible to account for the discrepancy.[99]

## International Trade

The increase in international trade in fish products has been one of the greatest changes in the fisheries development in the North Pacific. Not only have national capacities to harvest fish from off the coastlines of other nations increased, but considerable quantities—both in terms of weight and value of fish products—are exchanged to meet demand in domestic markets. The recent history of trade development is most revealing.

The relative importance of trade in fishery products to the economies of five North Pacific nations can be seen in table 2.8. Exports of fish products from all countries listed at least doubled between 1971 and 1976. South Korean exports rose by an astounding factor of 12 during that period. Imports of fish products into the United States more than doubled, and imports by Canada and Japan tripled and quadrupled respectively. Japan switched from a net exporter to a net importer in 1971, and joins the United States in the latter category. The Soviet Union, South Korea and Canada continued to export in increasingly larger quantities as of 1976.

Fisheries exports in terms of value constituted a small proportion of total exports of Canada (1.5%), Japan (1.5%), USSR (0.7%), and the United States (0.3%) in 1971. On the other hand, ROK exports of fish were 8.5 percent of total exports, although the proportion for that country is declining after reaching a maximum of over 20 percent in the early 1960s. Data from DPRK and China are not available, although China is known to export some fish and shellfish.

In terms of value, fresh and frozen fish products constitute the largest proportion of the fish products traded. Most of this value comes from trade in products made from tuna, which are not treated in this study because most tuna is caught outside the study area. The next most important trade item is salmon. Significant trade in dried seaweed takes place between South Korea and Japan, and trade in sea urchin ovaries and roe of herring, pollock, and salmon is increasing between Canada and the United States with Japan.

Canada exports fish primarily to the United States, Japan, and the United Kingdom; and imports from the United States and Japan. In 1976, Japan exported the largest amounts of fish products to the United States, Netherlands, Philippines, and Taiwan; and imported largely from South Korea, Spain, Taiwan, and the Republic of China. Under a policy aimed at generating foreign exchange, South Korea exported mostly to Japan, the United States, and Spain; and imported relatively small amounts of fish. The Soviet Union exported fish to

TABLE 2.8

TRADE IN FISHERY PRODUCTS BY NORTH PACIFIC NATIONS (1970–1976)

($10^6$/$ US)

| Country | Year | Total exports | Fishery | | | Fishery exports as % of total exports |
|---------|------|---------------|---------|---------|-------------|-------------|
| | | | Exports | Imports | Net balance | |
| Canada | 1971 | $ 18,271 | $282 | $ 59 | $ +223 | 1.5 |
| | 1975 | 36,679 | 461 | 135 | +326 | 1.2 |
| | 1976 | 38,128 | 601 | 183 | +417 | 1.6 |
| Japan | 1971 | 24,040 | 367 | 405 | − 38 | 1.5 |
| | 1975 | 57,609 | 576 | 1,296 | − 720 | 1.0 |
| | 1976 | 67,225 | 743 | 1,895 | −1,152 | 1.1 |
| ROK (Korea) | 1971 | 1,352 | 115 | − | (+ 115)$^a$ | 8.5 |
| | 1975 | 5,427 | 429 | − | (+ 429)$^a$ | 7.9 |
| | 1976 | 8,115 | 567 | − | (+ 567)$^a$ | 7.0 |
| USSR | 1970 | 12,800 | 90 | 17 | + 74 | 0.7 |
| | 1973 | 29,038 | 302 | 16 | + 286 | 1.0 |
| USA | 1971 | 44,137 | 136 | 913 | − 778 | 0.3 |
| | 1975 | 106,977 | 305 | 1,637 | − 720 | 0.3 |
| | 1976 | 113,323 | 382 | 2,277 | −1,895 | 0.3 |

Sources: Data for 1971 (except Republic of Korea) from Food and Agriculture Organization of the United Nations, *The Relative Importance of Trade in Fishery Products*, FIE/C/314 (Rome: FAO, 1973), revised from table 11, pp. 7–9.

Data for 1975–1976 Canada, Japan, United States from Organization for Economic Cooperation and Development, *Report on Fisheries of Member Countries 1977* (Paris: OECD, 1977), pp. 72, 73, 158, 159, 249, 250.

Data for the Republic of Korea from Office of Fisheries, Republic of Korea, *Yearbook of Fisheries Statistics 1977* (Seoul: 1978), p. 235.

Data for 1973 USSR from Food and Agriculture Organization of the United Nations, *Yearbook of Fisheries Statistics; Fishery Commodities* (Rome: FAO, 1974).

Total export data for 1976 Canada, Japan, and the United States from World Bank, *World Development Report, 1978* (Washington, D.C.: August 1978). Values for 1970 and 1973 USSR calculated from 1976 figures, using average growth rates for the period 1970–1976.

Note: Comparable data are not available for Deomcratic Peoples Republic of Korea and Peoples Republic of China. Totals reported are for all fish products traded by each nation since it was not possible to determine the amount of trade derived from harvests in the North Pacific.

$^a$ROK net trade balance data is approximated by total fishery exports, since imports are small.

a variety of countries, but its most important trade in species caught in the Pacific appears to be salmon sold to Japan and western Europe. The United States exported principally to Canada, Japan, and western Europe; and imported from Canada, Japan, and western Europe.

Fish product prices in Japan rose faster than the total consumer price index between 1964 and 1974. During that period, fish prices nearly tripled (from 60 to 175, 1970 = 100), while consumer prices doubled (from 75 to 155, 1970 = 100).[100] The price index of receipts by fishermen in Canada trebled between 1956 and 1973 (from 91 to 288, 1960– 62 = 100), and retail prices of fishery products are assumed to reflect that trend.[101] The average price of all species of fish marketed in Korea stood at 63 won/kg in 1967 and rose to

110 won/kg in 1972, then dropped to 64 won/kg in 1973. By 1976, the average market price for all species was 131 won/kg, a doubling in price over a period of ten years.[102] In the United States, fish product prices have risen considerably since World War II, and recent trends suggest that, within certain limits, prices will continue to rise because of increased demand. For example, despite an 11 percent increase in the quantity of fish landed and increased imports, the average ex-vessel price for 1976 was 23 percent above the 1975 level.[103]

These data on international trade in fish products should be treated carefully, since there are many different ways for reporting imports and exports and it has not been possible to standardize the reporting in this study. It has also not been feasible to separate out the trade in fishery products that originate in the North Pacific, or to segregate trade that occurs solely between nations in the North Pacific. Data for this section are not available from the Republic of China, North Korea, or the Soviet Union.

## Consumption

Japan leads the nations fishing in the North Pacific in the consumption of fish, shellfish, and seaweeds with an annual per capita consumption of over 68 kg. (See table 2.9.) In decreasing order of the amount of consumption of fish products, the Soviet Union is second with 16.5 kg, United States third with 5.9 kg, and Canada fourth with 5.5 kg. No national domestic statistic for South Korean consumption has been found, although one estimate of 22.4 kg is available, on the basis of total catch divided by population. The Chinese people reportedly consumed 3.6 kg in 1964–1966, while North Koreans consumed slightly more—7.6 kg in 1969.

Fish protein as a percentage of total protein supply (table 2.10) for the North Pacific countries in the period 1964–1966 ranged from 3–4 percent for Canada, United States, USSR, China, and North Korea, and 7 percent for South Korea, to 20 percent for Japan. Fish as a percentage of animal protein (including fish, dairy products and meat) ranged from as low as approximately 5 percent for Canada and the United States to as much as about 60 percent for Japan and Korea.

The factors that explain these consumption patterns are a complex blend of religious and traditional preferences, availability of substitutes, domestic agricultural considerations, and international trade policies. The overall trend in the region appears to be toward increased total consumption of fish, although the proportion of fish in the total diet may decrease.

Japan's enormous consumption of fish is in part due to the difficulty of producing protein substitutes at an acceptable price, given the limited amount of arable land that can be devoted to agriculture, and the large population. Religious preference—the Buddhist aversion to eating meat—has also been partially explanatory in this regard, although this appears less important to younger persons and people with higher incomes.[104] Government policies to assist domestic agriculture, particularly the restrictions on beef and poultry imports force the price of these commodities upwards and make fish products relatively cheaper. While total per capita consumption of fish is increasing as total protein intake rises, the proportion of total animal protein supplied by fish has dropped from over 75 percent in

TABLE 2.9

CONSUMPTION OF FISH PRODUCTS BY NATION (1960–1976)

(KG/PER CAPITA/YEAR)

| | Fresh/Frozen | Paste | Processed | Canned | Total |
|---|---|---|---|---|---|
| *Canada*[a] | | | | | |
| 1960 | 3.5 | | 0.8 | 1.5 | 5.6 |
| 1965 | 3.4 | | 0.6 | 1.8 | 5.8 |
| 1970 | 3.2 | | 0.4 | 1.7 | 5.3 |
| 1975 | – | | – | – | 5.8 |
| *DPRK (Korea)*[b] | | | | | |
| 1969 | | | | | 16.9 |
| *Japan*[c] | | | | | |
| 1960 | 20.0 | 11.3 | 13.6 | 2.1 | 47.1 |
| 1965 | 20.1 | 16.6 | 13.5 | 1.1 | 51.4 |
| 1970 | 21.7 | 24.7 | 14.1 | 0.8 | 61.3 |
| 1975 | | | | | 67.4 |
| 1976 | | | | | 67.3 |
| *PRC (China)*[b] | | | | | |
| 1964–66 | | | | | 7.6 |
| *ROK (Korea)*[d] | | | | | |
| 1972 | | | | | 22.4 |
| *USSR*[e] | | | | | |
| 1960 | | | | | 9.9E |
| 1965 | | | | | 12.6E |
| 1970 | | | | | 15.4E |
| 1975 | | | | | 17.0E |
| *USA*[f] | | | | | |
| 1961 | | | | | 4.9 |
| 1965 | | | | | 5.0 |
| 1970 | 3.1 | | 0.2 | 2.0 | 5.3 |
| 1976 | | | | | 5.9 |

Sources:

[a]Fisheries and Marine Service, Environment Canada, *Annual Statistical Review of Canadian Fisheries 1973* (Ottawa: 1976), p. 25. Data for 1975 are from Fisheries and Marine Service, Environment Canada, *Annual Statistical Review of Canadian Fisheries*, vol. 9 (Ottawa: 1977), p. 40.

[b]Clinton Atkinson, "Northeast Asian Fisheries," lecture delivered at the Institute for Marine Studies, University of Washington, Seattle, Washington, November 16, 1976.

[c]Ministry of Agriculture, Forestry and Fisheries, *Food Supply Table* (Tokyo: 1976).

[d]Food and Agriculture Organization, United Nations, *The Relative Importance of Trade in Fishery Products*, FIE/C/314m (Rome: FAO, 1973).

[e]M. A. Kravanja, "The Soviet Fishing Industry: A Review," in Committee on Commerce, U.S. Senate, *Soviet Oceans Development* (Washington, D.C.: U.S. Government Printing Office, 1976).

[f]National Marine Fisheries Service, National Oceanic and Atmospheric Administration, *Fisheries of the United States* (Washington, D.C.: U.S. Government Printing Office, various years).

the 1950s to less than 50 percent at the present time.[105] Since the early 1960s the Japanese diet has shifted toward a more Western style, and by 1972 the per capita level of protein intake was almost the same as that in Europe.[106]

The two-fold increase in per capita fish consumption in the Soviet Union is the result of a concerted effort to increase the protein supply through government investment in fishing.

TABLE 2.10

IMPORTANCE OF FISH IN FOOD SUPPLY, NORTH PACIFIC NATIONS

|  | Fish as % of protein supply 1964–66 | | Per capita consumption 1970 (Kg/yr) | |
|  | Total protein | Animal protein | Fish | Meat |
|---|---|---|---|---|
| Canada | 3.8 | 5.7 | 16.9 | 93.3 |
| DPRK (Korea) | 4.8 | 57.1 | 16.9 | 8.3 |
| Japan | 20.5 | 57.8 | 60.7 | 15.7 |
| Peoples Republic of China | 4.2 | 27.0 | 7.6 | 17.3 |
| ROK (Korea) | 7.0 | 64.4 | 22.4 | 8.2 |
| USSR | 3.3 | 8.4 | 24.9 | 47.4 |
| USA | 3.4 | 4.8 | 15.0 | 119.3 |

Source: Revised from Food and Agriculture Organization of the United Nations, *The Relative Importance of Trade in Fishery Products*, FIE/C/314 (Rome: FAO, 1973).

Note: This table is apparently calculated by dividing total nominal fish catch by total population and does not correct for waste and industrial uses. The figures do not correspond to published national sources for fish consumption but they may reflect the relative contributions to food supply from various protein sources.

Development of fish protein sources was thought to be considerably less expensive,[107] and politically more viable, than to increase productivity in Soviet agriculture.[108] Still, fish supplies only 8.4 percent of total animal protein in the Soviet Union.

Consumption of fish in the United States has been increasing slowly since the early 1960s, and it now accounts for 4.8 percent of protein intake. The rise may be a widespread acceptance of direct frozen fish and prepared fish foods for home and institutional consumption and a possible switch to diets containing less fat and meat by some sizeable groups in the society. Since recreational fish catches of both marine and freshwater origin are not recorded in the consumption statistics, the values for the United States are probably understated. According to some estimates, the marine recreational catch is almost equal to the commercial catch of edible fish and most of the recreational catch is directly consumed by the angler.[109]

Canadian fish consumption has declined slightly since 1955, possibly as a result of increased affluence, the rise of fish prices, and the relative availability of other animal protein. Fish accounts for a somewhat larger proportion of the animal protein in Canada (5.8%) than in the United States.

Fresh and frozen fish constitute the major part of the fish consumed in all countries. Only a narrow selection of fish species are regularly consumed in the United States and Canada, compared with the broad spectrum of fish food products in Japan and the Republic of Korea. Consumption of products produced from surimi have more than doubled between 1960 and 1974 in Japan. This corresponds to innovations in fish food processing of large quantities of Alaska pollock, the prime source of raw material for fish paste.

## SUMMARY

The distribution of fish throughout the North Pacific is primarily coastal. It is associated with the continental shelf and upper continental slope and influenced by many interacting environmental conditions. The pre-World War II development of coastal and offshore fisheries intensified greatly after the War, particularly in the northeastern Pacific. Tremendous investment was made in developing ocean-going fishing vessels for operations in distant waters and the coastal fleets converted from labor-intensive to capital-intensive techniques utilizing sophisticated gear and fish finding methods. Employment in fisheries has declined considerably in most areas in the postwar period. International trade in fish and fish products has shown a dramatic increase in the 1970s, and consumption has increased despite generally rising prices.

As a consequence of these developments, the need to perform scientific research to provide a more stable basis for future development of fish stocks, and management of presently exploited stocks, has increased. The need for comprehensive international arrangements to facilitate such research has also become more obvious.

# 3

# Traditional Regime for Fisheries Management

One of the inevitable consequences of attempting to manage fisheries as a common property resource is that authority and effective control over the stocks are fragmented, sometimes severely. The process of international management then becomes, in large part, a matter of continuously negotiating ad hoc arrangements, bilaterally or multilaterally, to solve particular problems. The pattern of such negotiations usually involves an introduction of constraints upon particular distant-water fishing parties expressed in terms of an extension of the coastal states' authority over fishing beyond the territorial sea. Seen from a global perspective, therefore, the management of world fisheries under the traditional (i.e., preextended jurisdiction), open-access regime is characterized by a patchwork quilt of arrangements relating to specific stocks and/or areas. These arrangements include long-term, multilateral agreements, long-term bilateral agreements, and short-term bilateral agreements. (See Appendix B for a list of agreements for the North Pacific.)

The North Pacific Ocean is no exception to this rule and the work by Kasahara and Burke describes the shortcomings of the traditional regime with telling clarity.[1] The purpose of this chapter is to provide a synoptic view of the structure of the traditional regime based on the existing literature. It is a necessary baseline for a discussion of the conflicts that have arisen over time, and for an analysis of recent major extensions in coastal state jurisdiction over living resources.

## CLAIMS TO EXCLUSIVE ACCESS

Claims to exclusive access for fishing in the North Pacific have traditionally been close to what was perceived to be international law.[2] The most comprehensive authority was, of course, claimed for internal waters and the territorial sea. However, there have been long-standing differences over the outer limits of the territorial sea that were aggravated by the events occurring in the First and Second United Nations Conferences on the Law of the Sea (UNCLOS I and II) in 1958 and 1960. In connection with these difficulties, problems related to claims for extended fisheries conservation zones grew more acute. There has been one conflict on the question of historic bays, and several others relating to living resources on the continental shelf.

Of the seven countries bordering the rim of the North Pacific Ocean in 1955, four claimed a three-mile territorial sea (Canada, China, Japan, and U.S.); two claimed twelve miles (North Korea, USSR); and one claimed between 20−200 miles without prejudice to freedom of navigation (South Korea).[3] Since 1955, the trend has been toward extending coastal state authority, either in the territorial sea or for fisheries conservation zones. For instance, in the territorial sea, the People's Republic of China claimed twelve miles in 1958 and Canada did likewise in 1970.[4]

The movement toward extended fisheries conservation zones by countries bordering the North Pacific has been even more pronounced, but until 1976, and with the exception of the Republic of Korea, these have been limited to twelve miles. For the USSR, North Korea, and China, fishing was subsumed under the territorial sea provisions. Canada, however, first passed the Territorial Sea and Fishing Zone Act on July 16, 1964, retaining a territorial sea of three miles but extending its jurisdiction over fishing to twelve miles. This was later included in the new territorial sea legislation of 1970.

The United States retained a territorial sea of three miles but under the terms of Public Law 89-658 of October 14, 1966 extended its exclusive jurisdiction over fisheries to twelve miles. Of the seven states of the North Pacific, Japan has been the most conservative with respect to extending jurisdiction over fisheries. The Japan−Republic of Korea Fisheries Agreement of June 22, 1965, reciprocally recognized the right of each party to set up an exclusive fishing zone of twelve miles relative to each other. Until 1977, Japan had refrained from any generally applicable extension of its exclusive fisheries jurisdiction. The problem over historic bays arose briefly in 1957, when the USSR closed Peter the Great Bay on the basis that this was "historic waters" and access for fishing was prohibited.[5] In spite of objections by other states, that action remained in force.

The Convention of 1958 gave the coastal state sovereign rights over the continental shelf and its resources beyond the territorial sea to a depth of 200 meters or beyond that "to where the depth of the superjacent waters admits to the exploitation of natural resources."[6] Furthermore, Article 2 (4) defined natural resources as consisting of "mineral and other non-living resources of the sea bed and subsoil together with living organisms belonging to sedentary species, that is to say, organisms which, at the harvestable stage, either are immobile on or under the sea bed or are unable to move except in constant physical contact with the sea bed or the subsoil."

The problem this generated over living resources in the North Pacific related to several species of crab exploited by Japan near the coasts of the USSR and the U.S. The U.S. and the USSR were parties to the Continental Shelf Convention but Japan was not and could not be bound by those provisions without its consent. South Korea was also not a party to the Convention but claimed sovereignty over the shelf and the superjacent waters out to 200 miles. The solution to this problem took the usual form of special bilateral agreements, which imposed certain constraints on Japanese fishing but avoided addressing the question of principle.

One of the bilateral agreements was the Japan—U.S. King Crab Agreement signed on November 25, 1964, and extended to 1966, 1968, and 1970. Under its provisions, Japanese effort and catch were significantly reduced, although both governments reserved their positions on the question of the status of king crab as creatures of the shelf or as living resources of the high seas. The U.S.—USSR King Crab Agreement of February 5, 1965, and extended to 1967, 1969 and 1971, recognizes that king crab are creatures of the shelf and reduced the catch limits for Soviet nationals and fishing vessels in specified areas of the Bering Sea. The Soviets were claiming the same rights vis-à-vis the Japanese in the West.

The situation existing between the USSR and Japan on crab, however, was more complicated. The Annex to the Convention concerning Fisheries on the High Seas of the Northwest Pacific Ocean, signed at Moscow on May 14, 1956, and entered into force on December 12, 1956, dealt with crab but the provisions were deleted in 1970.[7] They prohibited the taking of female and immature crab in the Convention area, permitted the retention of the incidental catch of female and immature crab if not in large quantity, and imposed a series of gear restrictions.

The U.S. Agreements with Japan and the USSR regulating king crab fishing in the eastern Bering Sea in 1969 resulted in an agreement between the USSR and Japan regulating each other's crab fishing on the U.S. continental shelf in the eastern Bering Sea. This agreement was initiated by the U.S. and it "allocates tangle net crab grounds in the Bering Sea and reserves an area for pot fishing."[8] Because both Japanese and Soviet fleets were involved in fishing the same area, the allocation is in the form of strips ten and twelve nautical miles wide alternately assigned to Japan and the USSR.[9]

The last agreement relating to crab fishing between the USSR and Japan dealt with the Northwest Pacific via an Exchange of Letters Concerning Crab Fisheries, signed in 1969 or 1970. The occasion was the declaration of sovereign rights over the natural resources of the continental shelf by the USSR.[10] The resolution here is similar to the U.S.—Japan King Crab Agreement in which Japanese fishing for king, tanner, abura, ibara, hair and hanasaki crab in the western Bering Sea, off Kamchatka and off Sakhalin, was subject to catch quotas, size limits, closed areas, and other restrictions, with the basic question of principle remaining untouched.[11]

## INTERNATIONAL ARRANGEMENTS

The North Pacific Ocean produces more fish per year than any other region of similar size in the world ocean. The area between 20° N and the northern tip of the Bering Strait alone produced about 20 million metric tons in 1973 and 1974, most of that (over sixteen million tons) was produced from the Northwest Pacific. Historically, only a small fraction of this resource has been subject to the exclusive jurisdiction of the coastal state. A few species have been subject to varying degrees of international management, but most of the 20 million MT were subject to no management at all.

In the following section we give a synoptic view of multilateral long-term, bilateral long-term, and bilateral short-term international arrangements. The multilateral and bilateral long-term agreements are compared in terms of the following dimensions: participants, objectives, scope (species, geography and time), organizational competence to prescribe, and decision-making procedures, actions and effects. The bilateral short-term agreements are compared in terms of the specific substantive problems they are meant to resolve, namely, gear conflicts, access to areas subject to national jurisdiction, allocation of stocks, research activities and dissemination of data and information, and visits aboard fishing vessels.[12]

## MULTILATERAL LONG-TERM AGREEMENTS

There have been only three examples of multilateral long-term agreements in the traditional regime for the management of fisheries that are specific to the North Pacific.[13] They are the North Pacific Fur Seal Commission (NPFSC), the International North Pacific Fisheries Commission (INPFC), and the Commission for Fisheries Research in the Western Pacific (CFRWP).

### Participants

The current NPFSC was created in 1957 between Canada, Japan, the USSR, and the U.S. A precursor to this arrangement, however, dates back to 1911. The INPFC was created in 1952 by Canada, Japan and the U.S. The CFRWP was established in 1956 by the People's Republic of China, Korea, Vietnam and the USSR. Mongolia became a member in 1958. Other states of the Western Pacific Basin are also entitled to adhere.[14]

### Objectives

Two of the three multilateral arrangements, the NPFSC and the INPFC, deal directly and indirectly with both conservation and allocation. The third, CFRWP, deals only with the encouragement of research and information exchange in fisheries, oceanology and limnology.[15] The objectives of the Fur Seal Convention[16] are: "to take effective measures toward achieving the maximum sustainable productivity of the fur seal resources of the North Pacific Ocean,"[17] to provide for international cooperation and coordination in carrying out the necessary scientific research,[18] to prohibit pelagic sealing in the entire area north of 30° north latitude,[19] to establish the North Pacific Fur Seal Commission,[20] "to prohibit the importation and delivery into and the traffic within its territories of skins of fur seals taken in expressly authorized circumstances,"[21] and to share the catch according to a prearranged formula between the four countries (Canada, Japan, USSR, USA).[22]

The objectives of the INPFC arrangement[23] are: "to ensure the maximum sustained productivity of the fishery resources of the North Pacific Ocean,"[24] to establish an international commission to promote and coordinate necessary scientific studies[25] with respect to stocks of fish identified in the Annex, to determine annually whether any species qualifies for abstention as described in Article IV,[26] to consider later additions to the stocks described in the Annex,[27] and to study and recommend joint conservation measures for any stock of fish substantially exploited by two or more contracting parties and not yet covered by a conservation agreement between them.[28] The objectives of the CFRWP were to coordinate the planning of joint research activities and to facilitate the exchange of information by organizing conferences and publishing proceedings.

## Scope: Species, Geography, Time

The number of species involved in these arrangements was very small. For instance, the Fur Seal Convention referred primarily to fur seals, though the Commission was authorized to investigate ecosystem relationships, especially those involving predator-prey links. While the INPFC arrangement theoretically could be applied to all high-seas fisheries that contracting parties considered subject to the abstention principle, the species identified in the Annex to the Convention were halibut (*Hippoglossus stenolepis*), herring (*Clupea pallasii*), and five species of salmon (*Oncorhynchus keta, kisutch, nerka, gorbuscha*, and *tschawytscha*). There were no formal species limitations imposed on the CFRWP.

The geographic area usually encompassed by these arrangements was very wide indeed. The NPFSC applied to the entire North Pacific, including the Bering Sea, Okhotsk Sea and Sea of Japan. The CFRWP area included the Sea of Japan, the Yellow Sea, the East China Sea, and the South China Sea.

The INPFC arrangement is more complicated. Article I of the Convention stipulates that: "[T]he area to which this Convention applies . . . shall be all waters, other than territorial waters, of the North Pacific Ocean which, for the purposes hereof, shall include the adjacent seas." In the Annex, however, there are narrower specifications to the Northeast Pacific and eastern Bering Sea for halibut, herring and salmon. Given their migratory pattern and the degree of intermingling of stocks of salmon of North American and Asian origin in the central North Pacific, the salmon arrangements were especially difficult and later proved to be very controversial.

The westernmost boundary of the salmon arrangements was the line of meridian 175° west longitude. Though this later became rigid for reasons briefly described in chapter 1, a Protocol to the Convention stipulates that it was meant to be flexible:

> The Governments of the United States of America, Canada and Japan agree that the line of meridian 175° West Longitude and the line following the meridian passing through the western extremity of Atka Island, which have been adopted for determining the areas in which the exploitation of salmon is abstained or the conservation measures for salmon continue to be enforced in accordance with the provisions of the Annex to this Convention, shall be considered as provisional lines which shall continue in effect subject to confirmation or readjustment in accordance with the procedure mentioned below.
>
> The Commission to be established under the Convention shall, as expeditiously as practicable, investigate the waters of the Convention area to determine if there are areas in which salmon originating in the rivers of Canada and of the United States of America intermingle with salmon originating in the rivers of Asia. If such areas are found, the Commission shall conduct suitable studies to determine a line or lines which best divide salmon of Asiatic origin and salmon of Canadian and United States of America origin, from which certain Contracting Parties have agreed to abstain in accordance with the provisions of Article V, Section 2, and whether it can be shown beyond a reasonable doubt that this line or lines more equitably divide such salmon than the provisional lines specified in sections 1 (c) and 2 of the Annex. In accordance with these

determinations, the Commission shall recommend that such provisional lines be confirmed or that they be changed in accordance with these results, giving due consideration to adjustments required to simplify administration.[29]

With respect to time, all arrangements are open-ended. The CFRWP, however, now appears to be defunct. Annual sessions were held up to 1964 and China formally withdrew in 1967.[30] The seat of the Commission was in Peking. While no notifications of intent to withdraw have been filed with the NPFSC, the United States filed such a notification with the INPFC in 1977 as a signal that the arrangements had to be renegotiated to conform with recent legislation significantly extending coastal state jurisdiction over fisheries.

## Organizational Competence to Prescribe and Decision-Making Procedures

As is usually the case with international fisheries management organizations, the Commissions' competence to prescribe for conservation, allocation, enforcement, and accommodation of fishing practices is quite narrowly circumscribed.

In the case of the Fur Seal Commission, by Article V of the Treaty, this body is authorized to:

(a)  formulate and coordinate research programs;
(b)  recommend these coordinated research programs to the respective Parties for implementation;
(c)  study the data obtained from the implementation of such coordinated research programs;
(d)  recommend appropriate measures to the Parties on the basis of the findings obtained;
(e)  recommend to the Parties . . . the methods of sealing best suited to achieve the objectives of this Convention.

Clearly, the Commission is only an advisory body. The allocation of catch among the contracting parties is specified in the Treaty itself. (Annually, the rookery states [USSR and USA] must deliver 30 percent of the catch to Canada and Japan.) Decision making within the Commission is on the basis of unanimity and each of the four parties has one vote. Authorized officials of the contracting parties may board any vessels suspected of offending against the prohibition on pelagic sealing. If evidence of such offense is observable, the vessel may be seized and persons arrested. Once this action is taken, however, the vessels and persons must be turned over to officials of the flag state, which has jurisdiction for the institution of proceedings and the application of penalties.

The INPFC is similarly constrained. The Commission essentially promotes and coordinates national research efforts specified in the Convention. Article III stipulates that the Commission shall determine annually whether stocks of fish specified in the Annex qualify for abstention; investigate claims that other stocks qualify for abstention and should be added to the Annex, decide and recommend joint conservation measures, request parties to report the conservation measures adopted, compile and study records, and, with the permission of the parties concerned, appraise the effectiveness of the conservation methods adopted. Decisions on whether any stock qualifies for abstention are to be made on the basis of unanimity. Procedures for enforcement are similar to those of the NPFSC arrangement and, indeed, to most other treaties relating to fisheries.[31]

The competence of the Western Pacific Commission was even more circumscribed than the NPFSC and the INPFC. That body was restricted to recommending joint research programs to be conducted by national agencies, organizing annual scientific meetings and disseminating the results thereof. It was not empowered to make recommendations for conservation or allocation of stocks of fish.

*Actions*

The NPFSC arrangement in 1957 sought to prohibit pelagic sealing on a commercial basis and, to this end, wrote into the Convention an allocation that gave 70 percent of the annual catch to the rookery states (USSR, USA) and 30 percent to the two states formerly involved in pelagic sealing (Canada, Japan). The Convention did permit, however, continued pelagic sealing by the four parties for research purposes. The limit currently in effect was achieved in 1963 and is stated in the Protocol amending the Interim Convention as being no more than 2,500 seals in the eastern Pacific and 2,200 seals in the western Pacific.[32]

The Protocol also sought a more equitable division of the direct and indirect costs of research in the western Pacific. To this end, Canada and Japan agreed to forego for three years, beginning the seventh year after entry into force of the Convention, the delivery of sealskins by the USSR as required by the convention (i.e., 30% of the catch) and accept instead 1,500 sealskins each for this period.

The 1911 treaty had reversed the decline of fur seals primarily by prohibiting harvest at sea. Although commercial harvesting at sea is prohibited, one of the stated duties of the Commission is to study whether or not pelagic sealing in conjunction with land sealing could be permitted in certain circumstances without adversely affecting achievement of the objectives of the Convention. The Commission has come to no conclusion about permitting pelagic sealing in conjunction with land sealing and the prohibition against sealing at sea remains in effect.[33]

The 1957 Interim Convention was extended in 1963 with minor changes in the research program to be carried out by the party governments. In 1969, an exchange of notes continued the terms of the Convention for six years. In 1976, a protocol extended the Interim Convention four years and made several small changes in the scientific research program to be carried out by the governments and in the duties of the North Pacific Fur Seal Commission.

When the first four-nation fur seal treaty (United States, Great Britain on behalf of Canada, Russia and Japan) became effective in 1911, the northern fur seal herds had been decimated, and the Pribilof Islands herd reduced from over 2 million animals to about 300,000.[34] From 1911 to the mid-1950s, no fur seals were harvested commercially at sea except for some taken by Japan during World War II. During this same period, no females were intentionally harvested on land, except that some may have been taken during World War II on the western Pacific rookeries. Harvested males were predominantly in the 3- and 4-year-old age groups. Between 1941, when Japan abrogated the 1911 treaty, and 1957, Pribilof Islands fur seals were managed through an agreement with Canada.

The only measures of population size available through the entire period of recovery of the Pribilof Islands fur seal herd, starting in 1911 and extending to the present time, are (1) annual counts of territorial males with females and of adult males without females, and (2) numbers of animals harvested. By the early 1940s the number of territorial males had reached a peak and the harvest was no longer increasing. In the 1950s biologists responsible for management of the Pribilof Islands fur seals decided that a greater yield could be obtained by a reduction in herd size, primarily by a controlled killing of females. This opinion was reinforced by discussions that took place during the period of negotiations leading to the signing of the 1947 Interim Convention on Conservation of North Pacific Fur Seals. The consensus during these negotiations was that the harvest could be increased by decreasing the size of the herd. As a result, in 1956 the United States made a determined effort to reduce the size of the Pribilof Islands herd primarily by harvesting females and also by relaxing somewhat the restrictions on the harvesting of males. This program of reducing the population size continued through 1963. At that time, it was decided that the number of pups being born was at the desired level to give the maximum harvest, and from 1964 through 1968 the objective was to stabilize the herd size. This effort to achieve stability was not entirely successful, and in 1968 the pup estimate was below that calculated for maximum yield. As a result, no commercial harvest of females took place in 1969, and none since that year.

Following the cessation of the harvest of female fur seals, some increase has occurred in the number of pups born. The average number of pups born in 1969 and 1970 on St. Paul Island, where about 80 percent of the Pribilof Islands herd are found, was 232,000; in 1975, the latest census year for all the St. Paul Island rookeries, about 278,000 pups were born.[35]

In recent years, the harvest on St. Paul Island has remained remarkably stable. From each of the 1971–1974 year classes, the harvest was between 25,000 and 27,000 males.[36] For the ten-year period prior to 1956, when the herd reduction program was initiated, the average annual harvest of males on St. Paul Island was about 52,000.[37] Some of the reduced take has resulted from size limits and a shorter season, but most of the reduction is caused by a decrease in the number of harvestable males.

The Pribilof Islands herd reduction program did not achieve the expected results. In an effort to obtain a better understanding of factors regulating herd size, the Commission decided in 1973 that St. George Island should be used primarily for research purposes, at least for several years. During the research period, no commercial harvest took place on St. George Island. Before that time the Island provided an average of about 20 percent of the total Pribilof Islands fur seal harvest, although this percentage had decreased somewhat by 1973. One of the expected results after commercial harvesting stopped on St. George Island was that over a period of years the number of animals on the island would gradually reach a peak. An objective of the study during this period of herd growth was to attempt to measure biological factors that limit population size.

In 1973, the first year there was no commercial harvest on St. George Island, the number of pups born was about 60,000.[38] In 1978 the number of pups born was about 47,000,[39] a surprising decline in a population that was expected to increase as a result of the harvest ban starting in 1973. Further substantiation of a decrease in pups born on St. George

Island came from one of the major rookeries that had been established as an area of intensive research effort. For the period from 1975 through 1978, the average number of adult females in this study site gradually decreased from 673 to 328 (unpublished data NMML).

The evidence from both islands indicates that productivity of the fur seal herd did not increase as expected after the herd reduction program began in 1956. The decrease in the number of fur seals on St. Paul Island did not result in a greater harvest, and the cessation of all commercial harvesting on St. George Island did not result in an increase in the number of pups. The reasons are not clear. The causes could include (1) an increase in the amount of contaminants in the Pacific Ocean; (2) an increase in entanglement of fur seals in netting discarded from foreign fishing operations; (3) a disruption in the structure of the herd caused by the harvest; (4) a decrease in the food supply of fur seals caused by intensive foreign commercial fisheries that began in the late 1950s; and (5) insufficient information about the population dynamics of the herd. Natural long-range changes in the environment may also have had an adverse effect on herd productivity.

The management policy for St. Paul Island fur seals at the present time is to allow pup production to increase to the maximum number. This is being accomplished by a ban on the harvest of females and by a size limit on harvestable males to insure that there is an adequate escapement of males into the breeding population. If factors limiting pup production on St. Paul Island are similar to those on St. George Island, the number of pups that can be produced may be near, or at, a maximum. Pup estimates that were made on the St. Paul rookeries in 1979 and 1980 will yield evidence on this question when they become available.

In recent years, multispecies management of living resources of the oceans has been emphasized. The terms of the 1957 Fur Seal Convention were remarkably progressive in obtaining an understanding of the interrelationships of various species in the marine environment. The Convention gave scientists of the member nations a mandate to study the relationship of fur seals to other fish and shellfish resources. U.S. scientists have, as a result, obtained information on the food of fur seals. These studies indicate that the Pribilof Island fur seals consume about a million metric tons of food in one year.[40] Much of this comes from the eastern Bering Sea and Aleutian area, which is also one of the richest regions of human food fish production in the world. In 1977, the allowable commercial harvest in the eastern Bering Sea and Aleutian Islands region was about 1.3 million MT of groundfish, of which 950,000 MT were pollock. Fur seals consumed about 600,000 MT of food in the same area.[41] The six species of pinnipeds in this region consume about 2.2 million MT of fish, which is considerably more than the harvest by the commercial fishery.

Although we have emphasized the fur seals on the U.S. Pribilof Islands, about 25 percent of the northern fur seals are found on Soviet islands. At the time the Fur Seal Treaty of 1911 went into effect, the western Pacific herds had been decimated even more severely than the Pribilof Island herds. Fur seals are now harvested in the western Pacific on the Commander Islands and Robben Island, and there is a smaller, unharvested, herd on the Kuril Islands. These islands are all under the control of the Soviet Union. By far the largest number of western Pacific fur seals breed on the Commander Islands. A Soviet scientist, P. G. Nikulin,[42] estimated that the Commander Islands population was over 1 million before its depletion, and F. G. Chelnokov believes that there were 25 rookeries on these islands in the last century and the population may have numbered from 1.5 to 2.0 million.[43]

In spite of harvest restrictions similar to those for the Pribilof Islands, only four of the original 25 rookeries on the Commander Islands are now occupied. About 265,000 animals are on the Commander Islands, 165,000 on Robben Island, and 33,000 on the Kuril Islands.[44] Before the Commander Islands fur seal population can approach its original size, rookeries that were completely decimated must be reoccupied. Fur seals are so site-specific, however, that extinct rookeries have not yet been recolonized, and it is possible that the active Commander Islands rookeries must reach maximum density before reoccupation of extinct rookeries takes place. The single rookery on Robben Island is close to the size that will yield maximum production, and the Kuril Islands population is slowly recovering from severe depletion.

The INPFC has been subject to much more controversy than the NPFSC. Most of the controversy relates to salmon stocks, though there has been one major episode involving halibut as well. The intent of the U.S. and Canada in negotiating the INPFC arrangement was to seek protection for the species listed in the Annex to the Convention vis-à-vis Japanese fishing operations. The principal catalyst for this was Japanese high-seas fishing of Bristol Bay sockeye salmon stocks.

At the time the Convention was negotiated in 1952, there had not been a major scientific research effort to determine the extent of westward migration of salmon of North American origin. The line of meridian 175° was chosen as a convenient *provisional* line because it was thought that this boundary gave sufficient protection to the stocks in question. As a result of large-scale increases in research efforts under the INPFC arrangement, later evidence was produced showing that substantial amounts of Bristol Bay sockeye migrate west of 175° W, and that substantial amounts of salmon of Asian origin migrate east of 175° W.[45]

While the line was meant to be provisional and changed as results of research indicated, the new line had to be based on evidence that the allocation thereby effected was "beyond a reasonable doubt" more equitable than the provisional line. Moreover, such a judgment had to be unanimously agreed to by the parties. This proved to be impossible, and was rendered even more difficult when the Japanese—USSR arrangement of 1956 made the meridian of 175° W its easternmost boundary. The Japanese were thereby caught in a potentially severe squeeze by the U.S. and Canada in the east and the USSR in the west.

The level of controversy was so high that during the first five years of its life (1953–1958) the Commission was not allowed to make any judgments on the status of the stocks specified in the Annex to the Convention relative to their qualification for abstention (Article III). Between 1959 and 1962, however, it was possible for the Commission to agree that herring stocks off the U.S. coast and off northern British Columbia no longer qualified for abstention.[46]

In 1962 the Commission was also able to agree that the halibut in the eastern Bering Sea in the area between the Pribilof Islands and the Aleutian Chain no longer qualified for abstention. There were two major reasons for this decision. First, the U.S. could not prove full utilization of the resource by its nationals. Second, and perhaps more important, the

U.S. wanted to demonstrate that the Convention worked, and thereby to facilitate its retention vis-à-vis salmon when the arrangement had to be renegotiated in 1963. As a result, a quota of 11 million pounds of halibut was given to the Japanese in the area in question. By 1963 a major conservation problem was in store for the halibut resource since about 30 million pounds (15,140 metric tons) were taken out of the Bering Sea, east and west of 175° W.[47] In 1964, however, the catch dropped to about 10 million pounds (4,969 MT).

As indicated previously, while the major task of the treaty establishing the INPFC was to provide protection for salmon, halibut, and herring east of 175° W via the abstention principle, the major task of the Commission was to promote and coordinate studies of conservation measures that would maintain the stocks at the level of maximum sustained productivity, that is, maximum sustained yield (MSY). Furthermore, the Commission was not given an independent research staff; its role was purely administrative. National research agencies were to be responsible for all operations. This is more than a pro forma provision, as Kasahara and Burke point out:

> The North Pacific Commission does establish its own research program, at least in broad outline, but the actual research is carried out by agencies of the three member governments. The Commission's Standing Committee on Biology and Research does attempt to coordinate the tentative research plans of each national section and the Executive Director also serves a coordinating function as plans mature and are revised and modified. However, passages in the annual reports seem to reflect a desire to make it completely clear that each national agency retains full and final control over the scope of its research efforts.

> . . . [T]he Committee on Biology and Research (CBR) devotes a predominant share of its labors to the question of the intermingling of American and Asian Salmon. The information relevant to the distribution and origin of salmon comes to the Committee from the individual national members and the Committee, or its subcommittees on salmon, are supposed to advise the Commission on its meaning and effect. What is instructive about this is that the CBR subcommittees are directed to reach agreement on how the data should be interpreted, but are also expected to report differing views if agreement cannot be reached. It is highly likely that this procedure emphasizing decentralized research, coupled with the need for agreed interpretations of it, accounts for the comment by knowledgeable observers that research results have come to be viewed merely as bases for negotiation.[48]

Turning to the western Pacific, there is very little information available on the work of the CFRWP. Park reports that the Commission organized a series of joint research activities, including fishing resources surveys in the Yellow and East China seas, and a joint China−USSR investigation of tides around Hainan Island.[49] Meetings of the Commission, at which scientific papers were presented, were held annually until 1964.

## Effects

It is clear that the fur seal arrangements have solved the problem of pelagic sealing by limiting actual harvesting to the rookeries in the U.S. and USSR, and by sharing the annual catch with Canada and Japan as a means of forestalling their reentry into the fishery. There are no provisions relative to new entrants in this arrangement, but in this case there need not be for long-term stability to be achieved.

The absence of a provision for new entrants, however, threatened the stability of the INPFC when the Republic of Korea fishing vessels began high-seas fishing for salmon. This problem was overtaken by extensions of jurisdiction after 1976. On balance, the INPFC has been a success. It served to contain conflict over Japanese high-seas salmon fishing, provided a mechanism for arriving at satisfactory allocations, facilitated a certain softening of the Japanese position on management of high-seas salmon fishing after the agreement was made with the USSR in 1956 for the Northwest Pacific, and stimulated an enormous increase in high quality, detailed research on North Pacific salmon resources.

There is not enough information available to allow an assessment of the long-term effects, if any, of the CFRWP.

## BILATERAL LONG-TERM AGREEMENTS

### Participants

In contrast to only three multilateral agreements, there are six sets of long-term bilateral agreements, demonstrating that the participants prefer specific ad hoc arrangements framed to deal with particular problems. In the Northeast Pacific, there are the International Pacific Halibut Commission (IPHC) and the International Pacific Salmon Fisheries Commission (IPSFC), both between the U.S. and Canada. In the Northwest Pacific, there are four sets of agreements, governmental and nongovernmental: between Japan and the USSR; Republic of Korea and China; and China and the Democratic People's Republic of Korea.

The Halibut Commission was created by the Convention for the Preservation of the Halibut Fishery of the Northern Pacific Ocean and Bering Sea of 1925, which was amended in 1937 and revised in 1953. The Salmon Commission was created in 1930 by the Convention for the Protection, Preservation and Extension of the Sockeye Salmon Fisheries in the Fraser River System, and was amended in 1956. In the Northwest Pacific, there have been several nongovernmental agreements between the Fishery Association of China and the Japan—China Fishery Association of Japan. The first was signed in 1955, extended in 1956 and 1957, and expired in 1958. The second was signed in 1963 and expired in 1965. The third was signed in 1965, extended in 1967, 1968, 1969, 1970, 1973, and 1974, and expired in 1975. The fourth was signed in 1970 and was specifically limited to the regulation of seining operations; it was extended in 1974 and expired in 1975. These were all replaced by an intergovernmental Agreement Concerning Fishing Operations in the Yellow Sea and the East China Sea signed on August 15, 1975. This agreement followed a Joint Declaration issued in September 1972 after the resumption of formal relations between China and Japan.[50]

Other agreements in the Northwest were: the agreement between Japan and the USSR, the Convention Concerning Fisheries on the High Seas of the Northwest Pacific Ocean, signed in 1956 and amended in 1970; the agreement between Japan and the Republic of Korea, Agreement on Fisheries, signed in 1965 (under the traditional regime, there were no formal agreements, governmental or nongovernmental, between Japan and the Democratic People's Republic of Korea); and, an agreement between China and North Korea, signed on August 25, 1959.

## Objectives

The ad hoc nature of the six sets of arrangements in the bilateral category produces a wide variety of objectives, some of them insufficient even for the limited tasks identified. The Halibut Commission, for instance, is empowered to issue regulations that are "designed to develop the stocks of halibut in the Convention waters to those levels which will permit the maximum sustained yield and to maintain the stocks at those levels . . . ."[51] Not a single provision of the Treaty relates to the economic dimension of management, with the consequence that the Commission is not empowered to introduce limited entry schemes.[52] In contrast, the objectives of the Salmon Commission are formulated in a somewhat broader fashion: (a) to protect, preserve, and extend the sockeye salmon fishery of the Fraser River;[53] (b) to protect, preserve, and extend the pink salmon runs of the Fraser River;[54] and (c) to apportion the catches equally on an annual basis between fishermen of the U.S. and Canada.[55] These objectives as stated in the Treaty are very general in nature. The first operational objective of the IPSFC was to solve the problem of the significant decline in the Fraser River sockeye runs. Over time, the Commission has also become particularly interested in warning about the effects of conflicts in use.

In the Northwest Pacific, the objectives of the successive agreements between Japan and China relate primarily to the maintenance of order in the conduct of Japanese fishing operations in the Yellow and East China seas. Between 1950 and 1955, as many as 158 Japanese fishing vessels were seized by Chinese authorities in retaliation for the Japanese pro-Nationalist Chinese official position.[56] The Japanese fishing industry was therefore very interested in establishing arrangements that would provide safety of operation. Since there were no formal relations between the two countries, the industry, with support from the government (which was late in coming), created a special mechanism called the Japan—China Fishing Entrepreneurs' Association. This was later expanded into a broader Japan—China Fishery Association of Japan, which opened negotiations with the Fishery Association of China in January 1955.[57]

The initial agreement set a pattern for creating specified fishing zones in the Convention area and regulating the Japanese fishing effort in terms of size of fleet and length of season. In addition, the Japanese were excluded from three military zones and an East China Motor Trawl Prohibition Zone set up by the Chinese. The current intergovernmental agreement signed in 1975 states the objectives as being the preservation and effective utilization of fisheries resources in the Yellow and East China seas and the maintenance of order in conducting fishing operations.[58] The Seine Fishing Agreement of 1970 was intended to limit the Japanese fishing effort for mackerel by cutting their take to 50 percent of the pre-1970 level, which was about 400,000 MT.

The Japan—USSR Convention concerning the High Seas Fisheries of the Northwest Pacific Ocean of 1956 states the usual objectives of coordinating measures to maintain the maximum sustained yield of the stocks, and to promote and coordinate scientific research on the stock.[59] The Convention also regulated Japanese high-seas fishing for salmon of Soviet origin, and imposed certain limits on Japanese operations as far east as the meridian 175° W. Limits were also placed on Japanese crab and herring fishing operations in the Northwest Pacific.

The Japan—Republic of Korea agreement of 1965 put to rest a long-standing conflict between the two countries, the last episode of which was generated by the establishment of the Rhee Line in 1954. The primary objectives of this agreement were the reciprocal recognition of a right to establish a twelve-mile exclusive fishing zone, the establishment of a joint regulation zone and a joint resources survey zone outside the twelve mile limit, and the provisions for equal sharing of the catch taken in the joint regulation zone.[60]

The objectives of the China—North Korea agreement are reported as being "the full and rational exploitation of marine resources in the Yellow Sea by both parties in a joint endeavor to develop fisheries and relevant projects."[61] However, the text of this agreement is not generally available, nor is information about the actions of the parties pursuant to this treaty.

## Scope: Species, Geography, Time

Except for the Japan—USSR arrangement, all of these agreements tend to be narrower in scope than the multilateral agreements. For instance, in the Northeast Pacific, only three species are included: halibut, sockeye salmon, and pink salmon. In the Northwest Pacific, the Japan—USSR agreement deals with salmon, two species of king crab (deleted in 1970), and herring. In both the Japan—ROK and Japan—China agreements, all species are included within a narrowly defined geographic area, and the same may be true of the China—North Korea agreement.

The Halibut Convention and the Japan—USSR agreement apply to a larger geographic area than any of the others. The area covered for halibut includes the entire Northeast Pacific and the eastern Bering Sea; for the Japan—USSR arrangement, the area includes the western Bering Sea, Northwest Pacific, Okhotsk Sea, and Japan Sea. The Salmon Convention, however, is limited to a very narrow coastal strip beyond the Fraser River—to a point defined by a line drawn from Bonilla Point, Vancouver Island (Canada) to the lighthouse on Tatoosh Island (U.S.).[62] The Japan—China arrangement is limited to the East China and Yellow seas, the Japan—ROK agreement is limited to the southern portion of the Japan Sea, the Korea Strait and the eastern Yellow Sea. And the China—North Korea agreement is even more restricted since it applies only to the Yellow Sea.

Except for the Japan—China nongovernmental agreements, all agreements were treated from the beginning as long-term arrangements. The Halibut Convention stipulated that it would remain in force for five years and thereafter "until two years from the date on which either Contracting Party shall have given notice to the other of its desire to terminate it."[63] The Salmon Convention was even more open-ended; it was to be in force for over sixteen years, with a requirement of one year's notice of intent to terminate.[64] Similarly, the Japan—USSR agreement stipulates a period of ten years in force with a one-year notice required for termination.[65] The Japan—ROK agreement stipulates a period of five years in force with one-year notice required for terminations.[66] No information is available on the China—North Korea arrangement.

The most complicated arrangements with respect to time are shown by the four Japan—China nongovernmental agreements. Each was made initially for one or two years but extended for a total of seventeen years. The special agreement on seining operations lasted five years. The current intergovernmental agreement, signed in 1975, was initially in force for a period of three years with only a three-month advance notification required for termination.

## Organizational Competence to Prescribe, and Decision-Making Procedures

As described previously, the Halibut Convention has a single objective: to develop and maintain the stocks at the MSY level. The mechanism established to pursue this objective was the IPHC, consisting of three Commissioners appointed by each contracting party. Interestingly enough, decisions are not based on unanimity but on a majority that includes at least two Commissioners from each side.[67] The terms of reference of the Commission fall overwhelmingly into the category of research for conservation. "This Commission shall make such investigations as are necessary into the life history of the halibut in the Convention waters and shall publish a report of its activities and investigations from time to time."[68]

The Convention is entirely silent on how those investigations are to be carried out. The only relevant sentence is: "Joint expenses incurred by the Commission shall be paid by the two Contracting Parties in equal moieties."[69] Nevertheless, one of the first acts of the IPHC was to hire a Director of Investigations and staff. At the time, a major research effort on Pacific halibut did not exist. Some research was being done in the United States but little or none was being carried out in Canada. A coalition of two prominent and influential figures, W. F. Thompson and W. Freeman, the publisher of the *Pacific Fisherman* in Seattle who had close contacts with the Canadians involved, successfully organized the movement to create an independent scientific staff.[70] This same coalition was successful in the case of the Salmon Commission.

The IPHC and the IPSFC were the earliest regional fishery and management commissions to be created. There was therefore more flexibility in the situation, which allowed some experimentation. Given the accumulation of experience and vastly expanded research capabilities on both sides at the present time, participants agree that it would have been virtually impossible to create an independent research staff for the IPHC in the late 1970s.

The Convention is fairly explicit on the kinds of conservation regulations that the Commission is empowered to issue: they include dividing the Convention waters into areas, establishing open and closed seasons in each area, limiting the size of fish and the total catch by season in each area, regulating the incidental catch, fixing the size and character of gear, regulating the operation of vessels through licenses, collecting statistics, and prohibiting fishing of immature halibut.[71]

The Convention is silent on the direct allocation of the catch, although, quite clearly, the Commission indirectly affects allocation by virtue of setting total catch limits by area, regulating catch-per-unit-effort (CPUE), and enforcement provisions. The data on total catch distribution between the U.S. and Canada from 1926 to 1975 show that between 1926–1935 Canadians took only 17.1 percent of the catch, while Americans took 82.9 percent.[72] Between 1946–1955, the distribution was 37.3 percent and 62.8 percent, respectively. Between 1966–1975, the distribution was 51.3 percent and 48.7 percent, respectively.

The procedures that apply to enforcement of IPHC regulations state that duly authorized officers of either contracting party may seize any U.S. or Canadian boat for cause, but only the flag state may prosecute and impose penalties.[73] However, Skud points out that there are gaps as well as conflicts in the Enabling Acts of the U.S. and Canada on these issues.[74] The same penalties for violations are not prescribed; the U.S. Act does not delegate enforcement authority to state officers, and this is critical in waters off Alaska.

The Convention is also silent on the competence to prescribe for accommodation of fishing practices. The impact of domestic (U.S. and Canada) and foreign (Japan and USSR) trawling fleets on the halibut resource over time has been major and adverse, and the Commission is not empowered to negotiate with anyone on this issue. Admittedly, when the Commission was given management authority in 1932, the job it faced was fairly straight-forward. It had responsibility for a single species, single gear (setline) fishery, and it was possible to regulate fishing intensity directly and effectively. Twenty years later, however, the situation changed drastically with the negotiation of the INPFC arrangement. It was necessary to prove that halibut stocks were being fully utilized vis-à-vis Japan, which was not a party to the controls written into the Halibut Convention. This was especially difficult because proving that the stock qualified for abstention meant that the Commission had to prove that increased fishing effort did not produce increased yields. This led to continuous increases in fishing effort until 1956, when the commission decided the MSY level had been reached.

At the same time the Commission was allowing an increase in domestic fishing effort, a major trawl fishery began to be developed in the Northeast Pacific and eastern Bering Sea by the USSR and Japan. The Japanese incidental catch of halibut in the eastern Bering Sea, for example, increased from 168 metric tons (MT) in 1958 to 9,212 MT in 1971.[75] The Soviet incidental catch for the same area went from zero in 1958 to 2,307 MT in 1971. In the Northeast Pacific, the Japanese catch increased from 390 MT in 1964 to 1,816 MT in 1973, with a dip to 995 MT in 1971. The Soviet incidental catch for the same area fluctuated considerably, from 1,290 MT in 1962 to 8,435 MT in 1965, 2,070 MT in 1971 and 3,495 MT in 1973. It is important to realize that most of the halibut caught incidentally were younger and smaller than those caught in the setline fishery, and that the eastern Bering Sea stocks migrate to the Northeast Pacific. The loss in recruitment to the Northeast Pacific stocks was therefore amplified by the loss to the eastern Bering Sea stocks.

Skud has demonstrated that the decline in CPUE within the domestic fishery began when the yield loss from foreign trawling was relatively low.[76] He attributes this to increased pressure put on the stocks by the domestic fishery to test estimates of maximum sustainable yield in order to prove abstention. However, it is clear that the yield loss was compounded by later increases in incidental catch by foreign trawling.[77] It is also possible that reduced recruitment is explained in part by adverse environmental conditions or reduced spawning stocks, as well as by trawling.[78]

After the stocks began to decline, the Commission tried to reduce catch limits, but legally they could impose restrictions only on the setline fishery and not on the Japanese—Soviet trawl fisheries. This was the cause of a burgeoning conflict between Japan and the U.S. In the context of the INPFC arrangements, the U.S. sought to limit Japanese fishing on the major grounds of the setline fishery from December to May. Efforts to stimulate the development of U.S. and Canadian trawl fisheries in the Northeast Pacific and eastern Bering Sea now compound this problem for the IPHC.

The Salmon Convention also neglected to spell out the ways in which the Commission would carry out its investigative and allocative functions, but the same coalition of Thompson and Freeman saw to it that the Commission acquired a Director and staff. The structure of the Salmon Commission is the same as the Halibut Commission. Each party appoints three commissioners and decisions are based on a majority of at least two from each side.

The Commission is empowered to "make a thorough investigation into the natural history of the Fraser River sockeye salmon, into hatchery methods, spawning ground conditions, and other related matters.[79] In 1956, pink salmon was added to the IPSFC's responsibilities. The objective of restoring the runs led to granting significant competence to prescribe for conservation. Permissible actions included making improvements in spawning grounds, constructing and maintaining hatcheries, leasing ponds and other facilities; making recommendations to the two governments concerning obstructions to the ascent of returning salmon, limiting or prohibiting the taking of salmon in waters of the Convention area, allowing exceptions on licensing conditions by the state of Washington and the Dominion of Canada for waters on their side of the boundary,[80] and prescribing mesh size regulations to allow the proper escapement.[81]

Since the allocation provisions are written into the Treaty, it is the job of the Commission to divide the runs equally between U.S. and Canadian nationals. This is technically a very complicated task that involves regulating open and closed seasons and deciding on the amount of escapement necessary, rather than setting catch quotas.

Quite clearly, the Salmon Commission has been delegated far more authority than any other regional fisheries commission. Some authority was reduced in 1956 as a result of a provision written in the Protocol that expanded Article VI of the Convention. In addition to the decision-making requirements that have been mentioned, the Protocol added the following paragraph:

> All regulations made by the Commission shall be subject to approval of the two Governments with the exception of orders for the adjustment of closing or opening of fishing periods and areas in any fishing season and of emergency orders required to carry out the provisions of the Convention.[82]

With respect to enforcement, Kasahara and Burke point out:

> The functions of the Commission in enforcement of its orders and regulations differ from others only because so much proscribed activity can transpire within each Party's territory, with the predictable result that responsibility for enforcement is placed in the hands of the territorial administration. In high seas regions, the Convention provisions are like those noted regarding halibut and fur seals, i.e., each state may arrest any vessel but judicial proceedings take place in the state in which the vessel belongs.[83]

In the Northwest Pacific, three of the four long-term bilateral agreements make provision for some institutionalized body, like a Commission or a Committee. The Japan—

USSR Treaty, for instance, established the Japan—Soviet Northwest Pacific Fisheries Commission.[84] This Commission is composed of two national sections each consisting of three members appointed by the contracting parties. Decisions are made on the basis of unanimity. Like the Halibut Commission, the tasks of the Japan—Soviet Commission relate primarily to conservation and research for conservation purposes, though it indirectly affects allocation via the possibility of setting total catch limits for five species of salmon, two of king crab (until 1970), and herring.

Article IV of the Treaty specifies that the Commission may: (1) consider the appropriateness of coordinated measures being enforced by the parties and, if necessary, revise the Annex on the basis of scientific findings; (2) where indicated in the Annex, fix the total annual catch of a stock; (3) specify the kind and scope of statistics and reports required; (4) prepare and adjust coordinated research programs and recommend them to the two governments; (5) submit annual reports; and (6) make recommendations to the two governments regarding conservation and increase of fishery resources in the Convention area.

The Commission has nothing to do with enforcement; this matter is entirely reserved to the governments, and the normal rules apply as specified in Article VII.

The Japan—ROK Treaty also established a Japan—ROK Joint Fisheries Commission to make recommendations on the creation of the joint resources survey zone, and to issue conservation regulations for the joint regulations zone. The powers of this Commission have been summarized by Oda:

> Within the joint regulation zone, which is demarcated by the lines as indicated in the attached map . . . , the provisional regulation measures described in the annex are to be implemented with respect to dragnet, seine, and mackerel-angling fishing by vessels of over 60 tons, until such time as conservation measures necessary to maintain maximum sustained productivity of fishery resources are implemented on the basis of sufficient surveys (Article 3). Enforcement and jurisdiction in this joint regulation zone, including the halting and boarding of vessels, are exercised only by the party whose flag the vessel flies. Each party is obliged to give the exercise pertinent guidance and supervision of its own nationals and vessels in order to ensure that they faithfully observe the provisional regulation measures, and to carry out domestic measures, including appropriate penalties against violation thereof (Article 4). It is noted with interest that both parties, in the agreed minutes between the two countries, agree to respect the other's domestic fishing ban areas, i.e., that either government will take necessary measures to prevent fishing vessels of its country from engaging in fishing operations in the fishing ban areas of the other.
>
> Conservation measures in the joint regulation zone as prescribed in the annex are based principally on orthodox conservation measures applicable to both parties, such as size of fishing vessels, mesh size, and power of fish-luring lights. It is beyond the scope of this paper to consider the appropriateness of these measures in light of fishery science. It should be noted with interest that, in addition to these measures, conservation measures designed to enable Japan and the Republic of Korea to catch equal amounts of fish are provided for in terms of the maximum number of fishing vessels or fishing units in operation. In fact, in the agreed minutes between the two countries, the standard amount of the total annual fish catch by dragnet, seine, and mackerel-angling by fishing vessels of not less than 60 tons is made equal at 150,000 tons with an allowance of 10 percent upwards or downwards. Thus, the Japan-Republic of Korea agreement on fisheries is notable because it incorporates orthodox fishery regulations and the idea of equal sharing of sea resources as well.

The Japan-Republic of Korea Joint Fisheries Commission, composed of two national sections, was established to effectuate the purposes of this agreement (Article 6). All resolutions, recommendations, and other decisions of the Commission are made only by agreement between the national sections. The Commission is empowered (Article 7) to make recommendations to the parties with respect to: (1) scientific surveys conducted for the study of fishery resources in waters of common interest, and regulation measures taken within the joint regulation zone on the basis of such survey and study; (2) the extent of the joint resources survey zones; (3) measures for the revision of the provisional regulations made on the basis of results of deliberation on matters concerning them; (4) measures to be taken on the basis of deliberation on necessary matters concerning the safety and order of operation among the fishing vessels of the parties and methods of handling accidents on the sea between the fishing vessels of the parties; (5) the enactment of schedules of equivalent penalties for violations of the agreement; (6) measures concerning various technical questions arising from the implementation of the agreement.

Any dispute over interpretation and implementation of the agreement is to be settled first through diplomatic channels. When this fails, an *ad hoc* arbitration board is supposed to settle the matter. This board is composed of three arbitrators, one to be appointed by each party and the third to be agreed upon by the two arbitrators. Both governments have agreed to abide by any award made by the arbitration board (Article 9). This arbitration clause is unique; only the European Convention on Fisheries of 1964 has a similar provision. This is an indication of the difficult and complicated fisheries problems faced by Japan and the Republic of Korea, as well as the distrust that each party holds against the other.[85]

The nongovernmental agreements between Japan and China made no provision for the establishment of a joint commission. However, the intergovernmental agreement signed in 1975 establishes a Japan–China Fishery Joint Committee.[86] The Committee is composed of six members, three appointed by each side. Decisions are to be on the basis of unanimity. The tasks of the Committee are: (1) to conduct studies on the extent to which the Treaty is being enforced by both sides; (2) to recommend revision of the Annex as necessary; (3) to exchange fisheries data and conduct studies on conditions affecting fisheries resources; and (4) to conduct studies " . . . as occasion demands as to preservation of fishery resources in the agreed-upon waters and other related problems . . ." and make recommendations to the two governments.[87] These terms of reference are the most restrictive of all the joint bodies in the North Pacific.

## Actions

A detailed accounting of the regulations enacted by the Halibut Commission for the domestic fishery is available.[88] The Commission issues a wide range of regulations including those on area definition, closed seasons, catch limits by area, closed areas, size limits, gear restrictions, licensing, and the like. There have been several major problem areas that need attention, which are described by Skud.[89]

In addition to the restricted focus on MSY, which does not allow the Commission to deal with the problem of entry limitation, the 1953 Convention contains no proviso that allows in-season emergency actions. All IPHC actions must be approved by the governments of the U.S. and Canada; this means that real-time response to emergency situations is impossible. Consequently, "the fishing season has been curtailed as an extra precautionary measure to limit fishing effort."[90]

The biggest operational problem of the IPHC has been the foreign trawl fisheries, though there may be a major problem with the development of domestic trawling as well. Skud points out that "Canadian and U.S. federal agencies have been promoting the development of domestic trawl fisheries, but neither these bodies nor the state agencies have initiated measures to manage their trawl fisheries to reduce the incidental catch of halibut."[91]

As already mentioned, the IPHC was not empowered to deal with the parties of foreign trawling directly (i.e., Japan and the USSR). After catches began to decline, and a steady decline in CPUE for the domestic fishery was evident, the Commission sought to reduce catch limits and institute closed seasons and other measures against the Japanese and Soviet trawl fisheries. These are succinctly described by Hoag:

> Realizing the importance of the trawl fisheries and recognizing that trawling will continue even if national fishing zones are extended, IPHC proposed a scheme that would reduce the incidental catch of halibut but allow the continuation of a profitable trawl fishery. . . . In 1973, IPHC recommended that foreign trawling be prohibited in particular areas of the Bering Sea during the winter months when the incidence of halibut was high but trawl effort was low. Other areas would remain open to trawling year-round and the closed areas would be open to fishing the remainder of the year, thereby allowing time and area to conduct a productive trawl fishery. At the annual meeting of INPFC (November 1973, Tokyo), the governments of Canada and the U.S. supported the proposal, but it was not accepted by Japan. In subsequent negotiations, Japan agreed to prohibit trawling in parts of the southeastern Bering Sea from December to March 1974. Analysis of additional data, however, showed that the incidence of halibut also was high during the spring and that additional closures were needed. In response to a second proposal by IPHC in 1974, trilateral negotiations continued, and Japan agreed to extend the duration and area of the Bering Sea closures for 1975. Further, closures were adopted in the northeast Pacific as a result of bilateral negotiations between Japan and the U.S. Closures also were discussed with the USSR on several occasions and similar agreements finally were reached for 1976–1977 during U.S.–USSR bilateral negotiations.[92]

It was estimated that the Bering Sea closures for Japan and the USSR, reinforced by reductions in the Japanese total groundfish catch between 1972–1974, should reduce the incidental catch of halibut by about 60 percent of the highest year (1971).[93] In the Northeast Pacific, however, because halibut are more widely distributed, closed areas are not as effective as they are in the Bering Sea.

The major external factor affecting the work of the Salmon Commission has been the type and intensity of industrial and other development in or near the Fraser River. Internally, however, the Commission was faced initially with three constraints in the performance of its tasks:

(1)  That the International Pacific Salmon Fisheries Commission shall have no power to authorize any type of fishing gear contrary to the laws of the State of Washington or the Dominion of Canada.

(2)  That the Commission shall not promulgate or enforce regulations until the scientific investigations provided for in the convention have been made, covering two cycles of sockeye salmon runs, or eight years.

(3)  That the Commission shall set up an Advisory Committee composed of five persons from each country who shall be presentatives of the various branches of the industry (purse seine, gillnet, troll, sport fishing, and one other), which Advisory Committee shall be invited to all nonexecutive meetings of the Commission and shall be given full opportunity to examine and to be heard on all proposed orders, regulations or recommendations.[94]

The primary function of the Commission at first was to launch a major research effort designed to support restoration of the runs. In this connection, the Commission discovered that the blockage of migration was at Hell's Gate Canyon in the Fraser River. This large-scale blockage was successfully circumvented at a cost of $2 million, and supported, inter alia, the construction of fifteen fishways.[95] It is fair to say that the Commission was spectacularly successful in restoring the runs and subsequently developing research. In fact, Crutchfield and Pontecorvo argue that "we look in vain for any other comparable success in physical rehabilitation of a salmon resource on the Pacific Coast, or for any other investment of $2 million in fishery enhancement with an equivalent return."[96]

The major difficulty in the Commission's research is the great variance around mean values of expected runs.[97] In addition to this basic problem are other difficulties, like the complexity of the regulatory alternatives and the short period of time available to harvest the resource.[98] On an annual basis, the Commission makes estimates of runs, escapement, and total catches as a basis for initial regulations, which are then submitted for review to the various constituencies.

> As the fishery develops each season, information received daily from the industry and sampling data gathered during days when the commercial fishery is closed enable the Commission staff to formulate an increasingly clear picture of the size, timing and racial composition of the run. The major regulatory tool employed intra-seasonally is the time closure. Each week the Commission announces open periods by regulatory areas for each of the three major types of gear. This pattern of closure—generally, four to five days per week—may be modified on a short-run basis for two reasons: to adjust for unexpected changes in the size or timing of runs, and to equalize catches by Canadian and American vessels.[99]

This work is made much more difficult and complicated by high variability in the movement of fish through the river system, in the flow rate of the Fraser River at particular junctures, and in the migratory routes used by the fish. These difficulties are keenly felt by the Commission in making decisions on the amount of escapement to allow in order to facilitate an equal division of the catch between Canadian and U.S. fishermen. The division is also affected by the placement of dams in the river system (as proposed by the U.S.), and on the foregoing of schemes for energy production (as proposed by Canada).[100]

Turning to the Northwest Pacific, we find that there is a dearth of information relating to the actual work of the Commission or Joint Committees once they have been established. We cannot say what major decisions and actions have been taken or what difficulties have proved to be the most persistent. For instance, with respect to the Japan–USSR Convention of 1956, Kasahara and Burke declare: "[f]or various reasons, this Commission is even less of an independent body than others in the North Pacific—indeed, it is difficult at times to believe that there *is* such a body in existence."[101]

The primary purpose of this mechanism, it appears, is to limit the Japanese catch of salmon of Soviet origin. This inference is made because the definition of the Convention area excludes the territorial sea and internal waters of the Soviet Union, where most salmon are taken by Soviet fishermen.[102] It is even more interesting that the Convention leaves the door open for extension to any and all fishery issues between the two parties in the Northwest Pacific.[103] However, where the Commission cannot make compromises on levels of Japanese fishing, even for salmon, the negotiations are removed to a much higher ministerial level for decision.[104] As in the Northeast Pacific, the parties also have recourse to specific ad hoc bilateral agreements as well. Therefore, it appears that the potential of this Commission to be comprehensive in scope has never been realized.

Some information on actual annual decisions of the Commission relating to salmon and king crab is available from Oda. Apparently, the Commission imposed increasing limitations on Japanese high-seas fishing for salmon between 1957, when the Japanese catch was 120,000 MT, and 1961, when the Japanese catch was down to 65,000 MT.[105] During that time, Japanese fishing for salmon was not regulated everywhere in the Convention area, so in the unregulated areas Japanese fishing continued as before. This situation changed in 1962 when areas initially regulated were grouped into Regulation Area A, and areas hitherto unregulated were grouped into Regulation Area B. The Japanese catch in Area A further declined from 55,000 MT in 1962 to 52,500 MT in 1967. In Area B an initial catch limit of 60,000 MT in 1962 declined to 55,500 MT in 1967. Apparently, these reductions have been quite contentious, and have consumed most of the Commission's time.[106]

Professor Shoichi Tanaka also testifies to the contentiousness of these negotiations, and suggests that one of the major reasons lies in the extent of divergence on stock assessments between the scientists of the two countries.[107] As he records the extent of divergence within the Scientific and Technical Committee of the Commission from 1967–1976, the views on sockeye were widely divergent for every session except the fourteenth in 1970; the situation was only marginally better for chum salmon where the parties were in agreement twice (1967 and 1972); for pink salmon the views were widely divergent for six out of ten sessions, agreement was reached only once (1975), and partial agreement three times (1972–1974). Conversely, the situation for coho and chinook salmon was quite good. Chinook had a perfect agreement score, and the views were divergent only once on coho in 1968.[108]

The Commission's work on herring involved setting size limits from 1956–1971, and enacting closed areas and effort limitations in the Okhotsk Sea in 1970 as a result of major expansions in Japanese fishing.[109] As a result of the Soviet implementation of a 200-mile zone in 1977, Japanese herring fishing in the Okhotsk Sea is now totally prohibited.

Between 1956 and 1970, the Commission allocated the catch of king crab in the Convention area between Japan and the USSR on the basis of several formulas. Between 1958 and 1965, the ratio used was 3:2 in favor of the USSR. In 1965, this was changed to 7:4, and in 1967 to 2:1, to apply in 1969.[110] However, in 1970 king crab were taken out of the Convention Annex and became the subject of a separate bilateral agreement.

Even less information on the work of the Japan–ROK Joint Fisheries Commission is available. Park mentions that the interfishing problem within the joint control zone has been solved. There have been no further unauthorized seizures of fishing vessels and neither party moved to abrogate the treaty after its five-year mandatory period.[111] But we have no information at all on the Commission's annual regulatory decisions, the surveys it has sponsored, and the effects of its management measures on the stocks.

A somewhat different view of the Treaty's effectiveness has been described by Tanaka. He argues that even after the Treaty was signed, ROK authorities continued to control Japanese fishing rather "rigidly" and to seize Japanese boats.[112] These incidents have decreased with time but there have been conflicts in fishing operations of both fleets in the joint regulation area and in the East China and Yellow seas. As a result, a nongovernmental agreement was concluded between the fishing industries of the two countries but the conflicts did not cease.

As previously mentioned, similar fishing problems between Japan and China in the East China and Yellow seas were regulated by a series of nongovernmental agreements. These agreements placed restrictions or prohibitions on Japanese operations in stipulated areas; they did not require joint action and therefore a commission was not created. The major tasks were to control Japanese fishing operations (by the Japan—China Fishery Association of Japan), to comply with the area and effort regulations of the agreement, and to maintain surveillance and enforcement by both parties. The intergovernmental agreement of 1975 created a Japan—China Fishery Joint Committee but very little information is available on its work since 1975.

Tanaka reports that the Japanese members of the Committee proposed that a joint resources survey be conducted, but the Chinese refused on the grounds that such collaboration would contravene their three principles of self-reliance, independence, and achievement of a planned economy.[113] But the Japanese catch in the Convention area is not at all trivial. The trawl fishery produces more than 200,000 MT per year, and the purse seine fishery, targeting primarily on mackerel and jack mackerel, produces more than 300,000 MT per year.[114]

## Effects

The long-run effects of the Halibut and Salmon Commissions have been substantial, though both mechanisms must now be adapted to changed circumstances and are in the process of being renegotiated. The Halibut Commission has produced the most complete record of fisheries statistics of any fisheries commission in the world. The total domestic catch has declined substantially since 1963 as a result of the complex factors previously described. While total production has declined, the effects of management for the domestic industry have been salutary, but there is an increasing need to deal with the problem of limiting entry. The Salmon Commission has perhaps been the most successful of all. It is, undoubtedly, the only example of a fisheries commission with a comprehensive delegation of authority to manage a resource.

Compared to these two bodies, the bilateral commissions of the Northwest Pacific appear to be very weak. The Japan—USSR Commission is similar in operations to the INPFC and has been one of the means, prior to extended jurisdiction, for the USSR to limit (sometimes drastically) Japanese catch of salmon, herring, and king crab. The joint commission, however, appears to have no life apart from member governments. This is even more true of the Japan–ROK Commission and the Japan–China Joint Committee. Both of the latter arrangements, however, appear to have considerable utility for attenuating a specific source of conflict between the parties.

## BILATERAL SHORT-TERM AGREEMENTS[115]

Practically all the long-term arrangements were expected by the contracting parties to endure for a considerable time period, and most of them have respectable longevity. Some contain specific provisions that do not permit new developments to be taken into account by the parties, particularly extensions of territorial sea or fishing limits. In other respects, too, these broad arrangements are so structured that they cannot reliably accommodate new situations, or resolve the problems that arise from them. These considerations lend emphasis to the generally pragmatic approach that has prevailed in the North Pacific; and they partially explain why short-term, specialized, and sharply focused bilateral agreements are used to confront newly created problems.

The use of temporary agreements on limited, if important, subjects is now common on both sides of the Pacific.

### Northeast Pacific Bilaterals

Prior to extensions in national jurisdiction in 1976 there were nine ad hoc bilateral agreements in force in the eastern North Pacific north of Mexico. The U.S. was a formal party to six of them, the other parties being the USSR (3), Japan (2), and Canada (1). The USSR and Canada have concluded two agreements between themselves and Japan and the Soviets have one. This latter accord is especially interesting because it allocated crab fishing areas in the Bering Sea on the U.S. continental shelf. The U.S. in other agreements with the Soviet Union and Japan had agreed on crab catch quotas for both states. The Soviet–Japan agreement was a mechanism for allocating areas to the two states within which they were able to catch some of the quota permitted them in the separate agreements with the U.S.

Of the remaining eight agreements, only the U.S.–Canadian accord can be considered to involve reciprocal fishing relations. This is because the U.S. and Canadian fleets have historically fished in each other's waters, but do not journey to the western Pacific to fish off other coasts. All of the other agreements deal solely with a foreign fishery operating off the coast of the U.S. or Canada; two concern Soviet fishing off Canada, and five Soviet and Japanese fishing off the United States. In summary, prior to 1976 the eastern Pacific bilaterals were mainly concerned with one overall objective: the accommodation of the interests of the coastal state with those of distant-water fishing states. Even the U.S.–Canadian bilateral can be regarded in this light in some degree, although in this instance there is a symmetry of interest because both sides are coastal and distant-water vis-à-vis the other.

The several agreements concern various elements of five major problems in which the coastal and distant-water distinction plays a significant role. These problems are: (1) gear conflicts, (2) access to areas subject to national jurisdiction, (3) allocation of stocks, (4) research activities and dissemination of data and information, and (5) visits aboard fishing vessels.

## Gear Conflicts

The problem of accommodating the simultaneous use of incompatible types of fishing gear is sufficiently pervasive and complex that seven of the nine subject agreements contain provisions on the matter, and two are devoted almost wholly to it. The scale of attention given to gear conflicts reflects the intense feelings generated by the problem, with a consequent high potential for violent, if isolated, confrontations among fishermen and vessels. The deprivations of property and income inflicted by the loss of fixed gear or damage to mobile gear are not trivial, and may have near catastrophic effect on the fishermen's livelihood.

The major method adopted for resolving the problem of using incompatible gear in the same area is to prohibit the use of mobile gear during specific periods that are important for fishing by set gear. For example, the U.S.–USSR agreement of February 12, 1971 (continuing and modifying one originally concluded December 14, 1964) established six areas off Kodiak Island, Alaska. It identified the areas by coordinates, and provided that fishing operations using mobile gear would not be conducted during particular intervals of time, ranging from five to eight months. A slightly different provision applied to the area dealt with in another U.S.–USSR agreement of the same date concerning the Pacific Ocean off the continental United States. In Paragraph 7 of this agreement, the parties agreed to refrain from using mobile gear between 200 and 1000 meters during a few days' interval and in a following period of seven days to "take additional precautions to avoid gear conflicts."

The Canada–USSR agreement of January 22, 1971, on provisional rules of navigation and fisheries, was aimed at both avoiding gear conflict and accommodating each other's presence in the same grounds using incompatible gear or practices. The rules contain detailed provisions for (1) identifying and marking fishing vessels; (2) marking nets, longline and other fishing gear; (3) additional visual and sound signals to be used by fishing vessels; (4) signals for trawling and drift netting; (5) light signals for purse seining; (6) conducting fishing operations in relation to other vessels and gear; and (7) observations as to compliance with these rules.

Special emphasis was placed in the U.S.–USSR agreements on notifying trawling operators of the location of fixed gear, including its use outside areas from which mobile gear was periodically excluded, and on enjoining the use of adequate marking devices for fixed gear. Paragraph 5 of the Kodiak Gear Conflict agreement created a special communications arrangement for informing the Soviet trawling fleet of locations of fixed gear outside the prohibited areas off Kodiak. Other provisions of these agreements urged special efforts on all concerned to protect fixed gear, to employ suitable markers, to exchange information about markers and their manner of use, and to conduct research on more effective and practical marking methods.

The Canadian–USSR agreement on provisional rules on navigation and fisheries safety also contained provisions for communications about fixed gear. Article 5.7 states that the authorized officers of each party "shall maintain continual contact and notify each other of the places of concentrations of their fishing fleets, and of immovable fishing gear. . . ."

One matter not explicitly handled in the U.S. – USSR agreements was the consequences of damage to fixed gear, either as a result of noncompliance with the agreement or otherwise. The Kodiak Gear Conflict agreement provided that "Each Party will immediately inform the other of damage to its fishing gear caused by the vessels or gear of the other Party in the northeastern Pacific Ocean, through the arrangements provided for in Paragraph 5 or through diplomatic channels." However, there is no mention of what is to follow, if anything, from transmission of such information. Nor does the agreement say how the party is to establish evidence that damage occurred to fixed gear at a particular place and time.

The U.S. – Japanese agreements were even more obscure on what happens if damage occurs. The U.S. – Japan Agreement Concerning Certain Fisheries Off the U.S. Coast, dated December 11, 1970, provided that "to prevent conflict of fishing gear, Japanese nationals and vessels will refrain from certain types of fishing in various areas of Alaska and Washington at various times." The Agreed Minutes attached to the notes exchanged by the parties state merely: "It is recognized to be appropriate that, with respect to cases of gear conflicts which may arise between the fisheries of the two countries, prompt consultation is to be held between the Parties concerned as necessary in each case." The remedies available are not elaborated.

The Canada – USSR agreement on provisional rules has considerably more detail on reporting procedures regarding incidents in the fisheries or violations of the rules. In addition to an account of the factual events involved, the reports that inform of an incident are to include an estimate of the damage resulting, the opinion of the authorized officer regarding the reasons for the incident, and proposals for settling the incident.

## Access to Areas of National Jurisdiction

The major reason for bilateral fishery agreements in the eastern North Pacific is to be found in the expansion of fisheries limits beyond the territorial sea. However, these agreements do not pertain to an accommodation between distant-water and coastal interests only within the claimed exclusive fishing areas. The agreements between the U.S. and Japan and the U.S. and USSR, and to a lesser extent the Canada – USSR accord, are concerned with these areas, but also with adjustments in mutual relations concerning fisheries beyond national jurisdiction. The creation of exclusive fishing zones provided the occasion, at least in this area of the North Pacific, for a trade-off between the coastal states and the two main distant-water states. The form this trade-off took was to grant coastal state permission for Japanese and Soviet fishing and fishery operations within the exclusive fishing zones (or part of the territorial sea for Canada) in specific locations; in return Japan and the USSR would refrain from or modify their fishing activities in areas of the high seas beyond national jurisdiction.

The objective of this bargaining was to secure continued efficient fishing operations for Japan and the Soviet Union within the areas claimed for coastal jurisdiction that were of particular interest to them. In return, the coastal states secured protection of coastal fisheries or species of special interest to coastal fishermen by securing an agreement by Japan and USSR to refrain from all or some fishing in particular areas outside the claimed zones at specified times.

Usually the trade-off in these agreements was explicit. In the U.S.—USSR accord, however, the benefit to the U.S. was obscured by exceptions that, in fact, favored U.S. fishermen. Thus, the U.S.—USSR agreement of February 12, 1971 provided that "both Governments will take appropriate measures to ensure that their nationals and vessels refrain (1) from conducting bottom trawl fishing in specified areas at specified depths at named times and (2) from conducting a specialized fishery for rockfish in the waters off the coast of the United States of America south of 48° 10′ North Latitude.'' Since a later sentence in the paragraph states that "the provisions of this paragraph shall not apply to vessels under 110 feet in length,'' and U.S. fishing vessels were less than 110 feet in length, the effect was to except U.S. fishing from the previously mentioned obligations.

The U.S.—Canadian agreement differed somewhat from the other bilaterals because it dealt with the situation of two states that wanted to continue fishing in waters of the other's exclusive fishing area. As might be expected from their long history of cooperation in fishery matters, the agreement established a right of access for each party to the exclusive fishing areas of the other. However, not all fisheries in Canada or the U.S. are open to entry by outsiders. The arrangement completely prohibits fishing for any species of clam, scallop, crab, shrimp, lobster, or herring. In addition, fisheries already fully utilized are not to be exploited further. For fisheries not already fully utilized, the conditions of exploitation are to be agreed to in advance of opening the fishery.

In addition to provision for access to exclusive fishing areas, both the U.S.—Soviet and Canada—Soviet bilaterals provided for port access by certain vessels. In the former agreement, each government agreed to facilitate appropriate port entry for research vessels of the other that were engaged in joint research, within the scope of each party's domestic laws and regulations. A more significant concession was made by the U.S. in agreeing to take special measures to facilitate the entry (into Seattle and Portland) of no more than four Soviet fishing vessels or fishery support vessels each month. The logistic problems of distant-water fleet operations make this provision of some importance to the USSR. The Canada—USSR agreement permitted port calls only by Soviet supply vessels "for the purpose of obtaining water, provisions, and other supplies in accordance with the customs and immigration laws of Canada.'' Loading activities within the claimed zones were also accommodated in certain instances.

## Allocation of Stocks

All of the bilaterals to which the U.S. was party, except for the Kodiak Gear Conflict agreement with the Soviets, dealt in one way or another with allocation of stocks. The U.S.—Canadian agreement clearly allocated by effect when the parties agreed that their nationals could not engage at all in certain fisheries in the waters of the other. Further, the decision that fully utilized fisheries were to be left alone by new foreign entrants was an allocation that assured the coastal state a 100 percent share of this fishery.

The U.S. crab agreements with both Japan and the USSR dealt most explicitly with allocation. In the former instance, the agreement recorded an accommodation between states with wholly opposing views over rights to the resource. Japan believed that king and tanner crabs were high-seas resources and "that nationals and vessels of Japan are entitled to continue fishing for king crabs and tanner crabs in the eastern Bering Sea." For its part, the U.S. believed these crab were resources of its continental shelf "over which the coastal state . . . has exclusive jurisdiction, control, and rights of exploitation." Japan, nonetheless, agreed in the latest bilateral (December 11, 1970) to limit its annual commercial catch of king crab for 1971 and 1972 to 37,500 cases (one case being equivalent to 48 half-pound cans), and of tanner crab for the same years to 14,600,000 crabs with an allowance of 10 percent. The limit for the king crab catch was a drastic reduction of previous allowable catches—from 85,000 cases in 1969–1970 and 185,000 cases in 1965–1966. The provision for tanner crab was new to the 1970 agreement; this species is not dealt with in earlier bilaterals.

Implementation of the two crab agreements between the U.S. and Japan and the U.S. and the Soviet Union had given rise to a third agreement between Japan and the USSR. This agreement, which originally was suggested by the U.S., who served as a broker in its conclusion, allocated tangle net crab grounds in the Bering Sea and reserved an area for pot fishing. The allocated areas took the form of strips alternately assigned to Japan and the USSR, the strips rotating annually between them.

The two other bilaterals with Japan and the Soviet Union also provided for certain allocations. In the U.S.–Japan agreement of December 11, 1970, on Certain Fisheries Off the United States Coast, Japan was allowed to continue certain fishing within the U.S. exclusive fishing zone, but agreed that its fishing effort would not exceed the level of 1966. For the privilege of continued fishing, Japan undertook to refrain from certain types of fishing outside the specified areas and periods. In addition, Japan agreed that in the mid-Atlantic area covered by agreements between the U.S., USSR, and Poland, its vessels and nationals "would not harvest those particular species covered by the agreements to such an extent as to impair the objectives of the said agreements."

The U.S.–USSR agreement of February 12, 1971, applicable to the northeastern part of the Pacific Ocean off the United States coast, had several provisions potentially effecting allocation. The USSR was permitted to fish within specified areas of the U.S. exclusive fishing zone but agreed, as did Japan, to limit fishery effort to 1966 levels. The USSR agreed also that "statistics on fishing effort and catches by species in these areas will be provided on a regular basis." In other provisions of the accord, the USSR agreed to refrain from fishing on the high seas with the intended effect of benefiting the U.S. fisheries for certain species in these regions. As noted earlier, vessels under 110 feet in length were excepted from the exclusionary effect of Paragraph 5, meaning that U.S. vessels were given preferential access to the specific area and fishery mentioned in this paragraph.

In short, the U.S. bilaterals with Japan and the USSR aimed at allocating living resources by prohibiting fishing in certain places, allowing it in others, and putting express limits on fishing effort in some of the places where fishing is allowed.

## Research Operations and Dissemination of Information

The three bilaterals between the U.S. and the USSR were notable for their emphasis upon scientific research involving fisheries in the eastern North Pacific. The most important concerned the northeastern part of the Pacific Ocean off the U.S. Pacific Coast. This agreement originally came into effect February 13, 1967, and in Paragraph 9 provided:

> Both Governments consider it desirable to expand fishery research in the northeastern part of the Pacific Ocean on species of common interest, both on a national basis and in the form of joint investigations. The competent agencies of the two Governments will arrange for the exchange of scientific data and results of research on the fisheries, for meetings of scientists and, when appropriate, for participation by scientists of each Government in investigations carried out on board research vessels of the other Government. Each Government will, within the scope of its domestic laws and regulations, facilitate entry into appropriate ports for research vessels of the other Government engaged in such joint research.

Pursuant to this arrangement, the two states have held annual meetings of scientists, alternating between Moscow and Seattle, to exchange views on the fisheries in the area. In addition, Soviet research vessels have been permitted access to the U.S. exclusive fishing zone. These research arrangements sometimes pose difficulties in implementation. On one occasion when the U.S. had misgivings about Soviet performance, coupled with locally intense dissatisfaction over the appearance of Soviet research vessels in the fishing zone, Soviet access under the agreement was suspended.

The 1971 agreement, which replaced the 1967 agreement as amended and extended, repeats the substance of Paragraph 9 (elevated to Paragraph 1), and adds details. It states:

> The competent agencies of both Governments shall ensure the following, at least on an annual basis:
> (a) An exchange of scientific and statistical data, published works and the results of fishery research;
> (b) Meetings of scientists and, in appropriate cases, the participation of the scientists of each Government in fishery research conducted on the research vessels of the other Government.

The U.S.—Canada bilateral of April 24, 1970, has a somewhat similar provision on scientific cooperation. The parties agree to continue and expand cooperation in both national and joint research programs on species of common interest off their coasts. Appropriate agencies arrange for exchanges and periodic joint reviews of scientific information.

The Canada—Soviet agreement on cooperation in fisheries also places considerable weight on cooperation in research through participation in research on board each other's vessels, cooperative investigations based on coordinated planning, the exchange of scientific and fisheries data, and meetings of scientists.

The U.S. crab agreements with Japan and the USSR bear resemblance to each other in their provisions regarding research. In the latter bilateral, the parties accepted the specific obligation to study the king and tanner crab and to exchange (annually by November 30) the data resulting from their study, including estimates of maximum sustainable yield. Scientific personnel engaged in studying these resources were exchanged. The Japanese—U.S. agreement was substantially the same, except that the parties referred the study to the INPFC, which transmitted research data and findings to both parties.

Even the Kodiak Gear Conflict accord with the USSR contains provisions on research. The U.S. agreed to carry out further research to develop a more effective and practical method for marking the location of fixed gear, and Soviet technicians were supposed to cooperate.

## Visits Aboard Fishing Vessels

In light of the obligations assumed by the parties to the various bilaterals, it is not surprising that there was some concern over surveillance of operations to see that they conformed to the agreements. Various methods were adopted. In one U.S.—USSR bilateral it was agreed to arrange for visits by representatives of fishermen's organizations of the two states to the other's fishing vessels operating in the northeastern part of the Pacific Ocean. At least two such visits should occur during each fishing season. Although these visits were not on an intergovernmental level, and did not therefore amount to an official appraisal of the activities observed, they were important for maintaining confidence in the usefulness of the bilateral agreements.

The U.S.—USSR crab agreement differs in that it explicitly addresses the enforcement question. Paragraph 3 states, in part:

> Either Government shall, if requested by the other Government, provide opportunity for observation of the conduct of enforcement of the provisions of this Agreement and for that purpose shall permit duly authorized officers of the other Government to board its vessels engaged in the king and tanner crab fisheries in the eastern Bering Sea. These officers will make a report on the results of their observations; the report will be forwarded to the flag government for appropriate action if such should be necessary.

The crab agreement between the U.S. and Japan was less detailed, merely providing that each government, on request of the other, will provide opportunity for observation of the conduct of enforcement.

The Japan—USSR agreement of 1969 on crab fishing grew out of the activities of the Japan—USSR Northwest Pacific Fisheries Commission. Partially in response to the Commission's activities, the two governments had taken various measures from 1958 to 1968 to restrict fishing and to avoid conflicts, including allocation of fishing grounds between the fleets of the two nations. In 1969, after the USSR proclaimed sovereign rights over the natural resources of the continental shelf, the two states began negotiations that culminated in a separate agreement on crab fishing. As in the case of the Japan—U.S. crab agreement, the disputed legal position was left unresolved; the parties agreed to limit the number of vessels and to establish catch quotas for particular species in named areas. Fishing grounds for the various crab fisheries were specified and closed seasons, size limits, and other restrictions provided.

## CONCLUSIONS

Three characteristics of the traditional regime for fisheries management in the North Pacific stand out after this survey. The first is the ad hoc, disjointed, highly specific approach. The second is the great variety of details flowing from official concern with specific problems and circumstances. While a surprisingly large number of bilateral and multilateral commissions were operative, most of them were weak, being severely constrained by lack of resources and by formal constraints written into their charters. Only two maintained independent scientific staffs. The dominance of national governmental control was pervasive.

The third characteristic of the traditional regime is that most of these weak commissions had responsibility for vast areas of the oceans, but their responsibility was limited to very few species so that the gaps in coverage are striking. The gaps have been summarized by Kasahara:

> While the present international fishery management regime consists of a complex network of ad hoc arrangements, some of the largest high seas fisheries in the area which have real or potential international implications are not covered by any of the existing agreements. Most of the trawl fisheries conducted by the USSR, Japan, and South Korea in the Bering Sea, the northeastern Pacific, and off Kamchatka and the North Kurils, are not subject to any international regulations. The present total catch of these fisheries alone is estimated at 3 million metric tons a year. Other large fisheries that are internationally unregulated include herring fisheries conducted by the USSR and Japan in the central and eastern Bering Sea; saury fisheries in the western Pacific by Japan, the USSR, and Korea; mackerel fisheries off Northern Japan by Japan and the USSR; and squid fisheries by Japan and South Korea. Furthermore, much of trawl and purse seine fishing in the East China Sea and the Yellow Sea is not internationally regulated except for the activities in the regulatory areas of the Japan−South Korea agreement and the Japan−China agreement. There is no comprehensive China Sea fishery agreement participated in by all parties fishing there. The only international regulations concerning tuna fisheries are those for yellowfin tuna in the eastern tropical Pacific.
>
> Thus, in spite of the various specific agreements for fisheries in the North Pacific, well over 90% of the total catch comes from fisheries currently not subject to international regulation. This by itself may not be considered a serious defect, as most of these fisheries have not yet become difficult international issues. A real problem is the lack of mechanisms for monitoring the status of these fisheries and resources on which they are based, to predict international management problems likely to arise, and to accommodate consultations to resolve them in a timely fashion.[116]

Given these inadequacies, it is not surprising that the governments of the North Pacific region were engaged in continuous negotiations over fisheries problems. The arrangements could not, and did not, provide a framework for an efficient resolution of fisheries conflicts. Problems proliferated, and dissatisfactions in the Northeast Pacific became linked to the global emergence of a move toward comprehensive extensions of coastal state jurisdiction over living and nonliving resources.

# 4

# Conflicts Over Living Resources Under Traditional Fisheries Regime and Trends Toward Extended Coastal State Jurisdiction

This chapter focuses on the conflicts from which the legal regime emerged prior to extended jurisdiction and examines the trends nationally and internationally that led to claims by coastal states to extend their jurisdiction. It provides a background for understanding current and future conflicts in the North Pacific under extended jurisdiction.*

The concept of conflict at an international level leads to terminological difficulties since the types of interaction are so varied. Conflict conjures up visions of violent confrontation at sea and acerbic diplomatic negotiations at one end of the spectrum; at the other end it can describe a subtle biological argument among fisheries scientists over the distribution of fish stocks, stock size, and impact of fishing operations. The use of the term *conflict* in this chapter is broad and encompasses any situation in which the positions taken by various nations are significantly different and in opposition to each other.

Since this analysis deals with the positions taken by individual states, the term *claim* is used to describe what is discerned as their position, either as stated or as inferred from their actions. These claims are not always clearly stated, nor are they necessarily consistent for all issues and areas. Many of the claims are hidden under the cloak of negotiations held behind closed doors and are fully known only to the participants. Still other claims are cosmetic and mask overriding political conflict under the guise of fishing conflicts. To the extent that it is possible to identify the claims, this is done.

Conflicting claims of North Pacific states can be categorized as claims to prescribe for management with respect to conservation, allocation of stocks, accommodation of fishing practices, and enforcement of regulations. These categories overlap somewhat, since one regulation to conserve stocks may result in de facto allocation of stocks and/or delimitation of boundaries by excluding some participants, or it may result in restrictions on the use of certain gear in defined areas.

*Since this chapter covers only the period prior to extended coastal state jurisdiction, or approximately 1977, discussions of the conflicts are not current, but are updated in chapters 5, 6, and 7.

The above categories can be further divided, where appropriate, to discuss conflicts related to fish species or groups of species, such as halibut, salmon, crab, marine mammals, and seaweeds. Where fisheries conflicts do not relate directly to certain species, as in boundary and fishing zone delimitation questions, they are considered under categories defined by pairs of conflicting nations. Discussion of the conflicting claims for management over time leads to an analysis of the way in which these and other factors can be seen to constitute trends toward extended coastal state jurisdiction.

The basic conflict over fisheries in the North Pacific stems from the claims by coastal states to reserve fishery resources off their coasts for domestic exploitation where existing fishing capacity is sufficient to harvest the resources, and the competing claim of distant-water fishing nations for open access to these waters for fishing by all nations, particularly themselves. Therefore, the claims are discussed with respect to their relative "inclusivity" and "exclusivity" of access to resources.[1] Inclusivity refers to the degree to which all prospective nations are able to participate in the harvest of living resources in a particular area, and exclusivity refers to the degree to which participation in this harvest is limited or restricted to one or several states.

Examination of all the fisheries conflicts in the North Pacific is not feasible. Most attention is given to conflicts that have been in evidence after 1950. In this analysis there is probably a bias toward more extensive treatment of conflicts relating to the Northeast Pacific, since information on that area is more readily available. The claims by the Soviet Union, for example, are inferred from actions or are accepted as expressed in the literature written about the Soviet Union, rather than coming from original sources and consultations with Soviet analysts.

## GENERAL CONSIDERATION OF FISHERY CONFLICTS

While conflicts over management of living resources in the North Pacific tend to attract much attention in the news media, the conflicts themselves are usually minor parts of the overall foreign policy conflicts among the affected parties. The distant-water fisheries component of a nation's fishing industry often has been accorded a prominent role in fishery policies because of its international political importance as well as its economic contribution. This is not to contend that international fisheries conflicts are not important or do not merit serious consideration, but that they must be seen in the proper perspective. Within a nation like Japan, the world's foremost fishing nation, fisheries represent a relatively small but important contribution to national employment and income. The post-World War II difficulties between Japan and the Republic of Korea (ROK), for example, are more a legacy of enmity inherited from long-standing disputes between the two countries than conflicts over fisheries. Fisheries have been treated as a pawn in Japan's overall power politics with the People's Republic of China (PRC) and the Soviet Union (USSR). Still, when compared with the North Atlantic, with its many fishing nations and long history of international fisheries, the North Pacific has relatively few participants and conflicts. This, however, has not lessened the severity of conflicts or made them easier to resolve.

It is useful at the outset to characterize the positions of the main fishing nations in the North Pacific. These generalizations are more fully developed with respect to specific conflicts later in the chapter. Since the basic conflict in the North Pacific is between coastal fishing nations and distant-water fishing nations, the interests of North Pacific nations with respect to each is decribed separately.

## Coastal Fishing

All North Pacific nations maintain large coastal fisheries but only Canada, Democratic People's Republic of Korea (DPRK), China, and the United States are principally coastal fishing nations, based on catches adjacent to their own coasts versus fishing in foreign waters.

Canada and the United States engage in some distant-water fishing for tuna in the Pacific, but this generally takes place in more southern waters than those considered here. In addition, Canada and the United States have maintained traditional reciprocal fishing arrangements in boundary waters for many years. While these reciprocal fisheries constitute international fisheries, the cooperation that has characterized the arrangements has been remarkably good over a long period of time. There have been some conflicts, especially since the extension of jurisdiction to 200 miles.

For the most part, the species caught are a relatively few high-valued species like salmon, halibut, herring and, more recently, crab. Other species like walleye pollock, hake, and squid have been largely ignored. The basic position of Canada and the United States regarding foreign fishing is to reserve important stocks for domestic fishermen and to accept foreign fishing for species of little or no present domestic commercial interest. With respect to both foreign and domestic fishing, there is a strong conservation policy. Conservation, in this case, is defined as a commitment to scientific management of stocks of fish to permit their orderly development, and to avoid depletion. This conservation policy has been relatively successful for domestic fisheries and has been applied with moderate success to foreign fleets.

Japan has considerable fisheries in its coastal areas. After some problems of depletion during and after World War II, these coastal fisheries have been maintained at a relatively constant high level. Japan has maintained a strong position in support of a limited 3-mile territorial sea and fisheries zone,[2] and until quite recently had very little concern with foreign fishing in its coastal waters.[3] The Soviet Union has expanded its range of operations into northern Japanese waters in recent years to catch sardines and other species that Japan did not fully utilize. The Republic of Korea, with an increase in size and quality of fleets, has expanded her fishing capacity into the northern Sea of Japan, where Japan previously had undisputed dominance but no claim for jurisdiction.

The ostensible goal of fisheries in Japan is to maximize the amount of fish caught for consumption. Fishery science is used to assess the location and size of stocks as an aid in fisheries development. Results of scientific research do not produce the same sort of conservation measures and regulations that are adopted by government agencies in Canada and the United States. Instead, fishermen in the coastal and offshore areas of Japan are expected to act in their own self-interest to protect the stocks of fish over the long run, and to adjust levels of catch appropriately.[4] It is not possible to discuss all the differences between the approaches used in the United States and Canada and in Japan, but these two approaches (i.e., regulation by government agency and self-regulation by fishery cooperatives) color the thinking of persons involved with coastal fisheries management from each country.

The Soviet Union has developed an extensive fishery in its coastal waters in the Northwest Pacific in the Bering Sea, northern Sea of Japan and Okhotsk Sea. Still, many of the resources cannot be harvested solely by Soviet fleets, and distant-water fishing nations like Japan, Republic of Korea, and Democratic People's Republic of Korea, have engaged in fishing for underutilized species off the Soviet coasts. The Soviet Union has sought to reserve certain species like crab, herring, and salmon for its domestic fishing fleets, as a conservation measure, and for economic and food reasons. The Soviet approach to fisheries management to a certain extent resembles a combination of the Canadian–United States and Japanese policies, although it has developed indigenously to meet certain needs. There is a strong bias toward using science in the exploration for, and development of, fishing grounds, yet there is apparently a strong central control over the operations of the fishing fleets so certain species are not overharvested. As in the other North Pacific fishing nations, fisheries science is only one aspect that determines the fishing policy of the Soviet Union. Unfortunately, relatively little published information is available on the operations of the Soviet fisheries and the basic determinants of policy.[5] The PRC and DPRK also have extensive coastal fisheries but little is known of their development and management.

## Distant-Water Fishing

Canada and the United States have virtually no distant-water fishing activities that impinge on other nations that fish in the North Pacific. Most of the distant-water fishing by these nations is in the tropical tuna fishery of the central and southern areas of the Pacific Ocean. The Canadian effort is on a much smaller scale than the U.S. effort. The People's Republic of China appears to have no distant-water fishing capabilities at the present time. The DPRK pursues some distant-water fishing for pollock off the coasts of the Soviet Union but not much information is available on that operation.

Japan, Republic of Korea, and the Soviet Union have extensive distant-water fishing operations in the North Pacific. Japan and the Republic of Korea have most of their distant-water fisheries in the North Pacific, whereas less than one-third of the Soviet distant-water activities are there owing to its substantial fishery in the Atlantic and other areas.

Distant-water fishing nations attempt to ensure maximum access to the fisheries of coastal nations. Both the Soviet Union and Republic of Korea have long recognized the claim of coastal nations to 12-mile coastal fishing zones. Japan, prior to the mid-1970s, was reluctant to recognize such zones and maintained that a nation may only reserve a 3-mile territorial sea. The Soviet Union, Canada, and the United States have accepted coastal state control over the management of the living resources of the continental shelf, but Japan has not done so except in the most indirect fashion. For each of these nations, the relationship between the protection of their coastal fisheries against foreign fleets, and the access of their distant-water fleets to the coastal waters of other nations has been a difficult balancing act. Efforts to protect a domestic stock like salmon, for example, could establish a precedent that would prejudice a national claim to harvest other resources, like tuna, off the coasts of other nations.

Three major lines of argument appear to be used by distant-water fishing nations with respect to fishing in the high seas beyond the territorial waters claimed by coastal states. These can be briefly summarized as follows: (1) outside territorial waters, all living resources are available to those who can capture them; (2) if stocks outside territorial waters are to be managed for purposes of conservation, and limits placed on catches, the policy should be made by international agreements under which all states compete on an equal basis for the total allowable catch, or for shares based on traditional catches; and (3) where the living resources off a coastal state are not fully utilized by that state, they should be made available to anyone who can utilize them.

Continued harvesting success in distant-water areas is dependent upon the conservation of fish stocks, but the competition between fleets of distant-water fishing nations can, and has, resulted in overfishing. Thus, the behavior of distant-water fishing fleets under competitive conditions is not so much an anticonservation policy as a policy that maximizes the share of catch taken by each nation under uncontrolled conditions. The end result, however, is that conservation goals are not achieved.

Japan enforced voluntary restrictions on licensing its fishing fleets in the Bering Sea and Gulf of Alaska,[6] and the Soviet Union presumably was in a position to control the activities of its fleets in the same areas. Unfortunately, without an overall coordinating mechanism to adjust the exploitation of each nation to the available stocks, the fishery resources in these areas were vulnerable to overfishing.

There are also cases where the behavior of distant-water nations is not motivated so much by competition as it is by a disregard for the principles of conservation. The end result is an overharvesting of certain fish resources as part of an economically motivated strategy of pulse fishing; stocks of one area are purposefully depleted and then the fleets move on to other areas or species. This practice sometimes can be justified on an economic basis, but it generally contradicts the philosophy of resource conservation.[7]

In addition to the distant-water fleets of the North Pacific nations mentioned above, many other nations began distant-water fishing activities in the North Pacific in the 1970s. Taiwan, Bulgaria, German Democratic Republic, and Poland made their appearance during this time. This posed an additional threat to fish stocks in the area due to added harvesting pressure without any means of coordinating limits on fishing effort. In general, the catches of these nations were small relative to the catches of the coastal and distant-water fishing nations, and contributed marginally to the depletion of fish stocks.

As could be easily predicted, the positions of the coastal nations and distant-water fishing nations were in conflict. The goal of conserving fish stocks declared by the coastal states was viewed by distant-water fishing nations as a thinly veiled guise to reserve certain species for the domestic fisheries of the coastal state. Similarly, the distant-water fishing state claim to international management under equal access considerations was seen by coastal states as a ploy to assure distant-water fleets a larger share of a particular fishery.[8] This coastal state–distant-water state dichotomy is simplistic and is shown to be more complicated in the course of this analysis. Still, it is a highly useful way to characterize the bases of the conflicts that occurred in the North Pacific.

The basic trend in distant-water fisheries conflicts, as elaborated below, has been toward greater exclusivity in management claimed by coastal states. This is seen in the claims to extended territorial waters and contiguous fisheries zones that were made in the 1960s in the Northeast Pacific. Creeping jurisdiction threatened the claims of distant-water fishing nations to greater inclusivity in management arrangements. In addition, even under joint exploitation and management agreements, there was a trend toward increasing the share allocated to the coastal state, and a trend toward restricting fishery practices that impacted most heavily on distant-water fishing nations. These changes prior to the extension of national jurisdiction to 200 miles did not lead, however, to a change in the claims by all nations fishing in the North Pacific for flag state enforcement of fisheries regulations.

## CLAIMS TO PRESCRIBE FOR MANAGEMENT

### Claims to Prescribe for Conservation

#### Sealing

The first major international conflict over conservation of living resources in the North Pacific involved pelagic sealing. Both Russia and the United States (after its purchase of Alaska in 1867), instituted regulations to protect the northern fur seals while they were on land through leases, licensing, and concession arrangements to sealers. These regulations applied to the Pribilof Islands and Commander Islands. The Robben Island stocks, under Japanese ownership, were regulated as outlined in "Regulations for the Control of Fisheries in Hokkaido," which defined the scope of control to territorial waters and prohibited foreign vessels from catching or hunting sea fishes and animals by any means within the range of a cannon shot (3 miles).[9]

These regulatory schemes resulted in a profitable harvest of fur seals for Russia and the United States. In the late 1860s, however, Canadian vessels began to harvest fur seals from the Pribilof Islands on the high seas; by the mid-1880s these harvests were having a substantial impact on the fur seal stocks.[10] The President of the United States, Grover Cleveland, signed an act in 1889 that warned persons entering the Bering Sea that they would be arrested if they engaged in pelagic sealing. The British response to this warning, on behalf of Canada, was rapid. Britain asserted the right of Canadian vessels to harvest fur seals on the high seas. The British proposed a prohibition on both land and pelagic harvest of seals that was unacceptable to the United States,[11] and President Harrison ordered United States' revenue cutters to arrest Canadian sealers in 1890. This action almost led to a naval confrontation, and Britain prepared to send four warships to the Bering Sea. Reports of the grossly depleted status of fur seal stocks prompted a proposal from the United States in 1891 for a moratorium on fur seal harvests. This led to a *modus vivendi* between Great Britain and the United States in that year whereby Britain agreed to a prohibition of pelagic killing of fur seals with a limited land-based harvest on the condition that the conflict would be submitted to arbitration.

The conflict was submitted to a tribunal in Paris in 1893. The American position was that the decline in the fur seal stock was strictly because of indiscriminate pelagic sealing, which took a disproportionate number of females and nursing young. The British contended that the proportion of females in the catch was small and that excessive land-based killing was at fault.[12] The United States argued that its ownership extended to the full migratory range of the fur seal since the seals regularly returned to the same islands and could thus be considered as domestic animals.[13] The Paris Tribunal ruled that the United States could not prescribe conservation regulations for areas of the high seas but was limited to its own three-mile territorial sea. In order to solve the problem, the Tribunal proposed a zone of 60 miles around the Pribilof Islands where pelagic sealing would be banned for Canadian and United States citizens.

Since fur seals migrate far beyond these limits, pelagic sealing could continue. Furthermore, neither Japan nor Russia was bound by the decision of the Tribunal. Russia, however, tried in 1893 to prohibit fur sealing within 10 miles of its coast and for 30 miles around the Commander Islands. Great Britain denied Russian jurisdiction over its sealers within this zone, but consented to the regulations in an agreement signed that year, to protect the seal populations. The United States also protested Russian claims but settled the conflict in 1894 by signing an agreement similar to that between Great Britain and Russia.[14] (See list of Agreements in Appendix B.)

Japan began pelagic sealing in the Pribilof area in 1896 and stocks began to decline at an even more precipitous rate. In 1911 the United States invited Great Britain, Japan, and Russia to negotiate an agreement to prohibit pelagic sealing. By that time, Russia had also become alarmed at the reduction in its fur seal herds due to pelagic sealing. Russia had apparently excluded Japan from shore-based harvest of fur seals in the Northwest Pacific in the 1907 Russo–Japanese Fishery Convention, but did not claim, as the United States did, to regulate the high-seas pelagic fur seal hunt outside its territorial waters for purposes of conservation.[15] Under the 1911 Fur Seal Covention,[16] the coastal states were granted sole management authority over the land harvest of fur seals and the pelagic sealing nations were granted an annual payment of 15 percent each of the coastal state harvests. Japan agreed to provide 10 percent each to Canada, Russia and the United States of the harvests from Robben Island.

In 1940, Japan abrogated the fur seal agreement because it maintained that the population of fur seals had increased to such a degree that the Japanese domestic fishing industry had been damaged.[17] Canada and the United States instituted a provisional agreement in 1942 that continued the ban on pelagic sealing.[18] During World War II, Japan lost its seal rookery on Robben Island to the Soviet Union, and during the Allied occupation Japan voluntarily prohibited pelagic fur sealing.

An agreement was again negotiated between Canada, Japan, USSR, and the United States in 1956 on fur sealing, which closely followed the provisions of the 1911 agreement.[19] It is important to note that this agreement does not constitute a recognition of coastal state jurisdiction over fur seals. Article I (3) of the 1956 convention states clearly that "nothing in the convention shall be deemed to affect in any way the position of the parties in regard to the limits of territorial waters or to the jurisdiction over fisheries." The Japan—U.S. agreement on the contiguous fisheries zone in 1967[20] requires that Japan refrain from trawling, crab fishing, and longline fishing in the vicinity of St. Paul Island to protect fur seal harvests.[21]

### Salmon

The salmon fishery conflicts date from the turn of the century. They are most easily analyzed by separating the conflicts in the Northwest and Northeast Pacific, and by discussing the development of the conflicts in both areas during the pre-World War II and post-World War II periods.

Agreements related to Japanese access to fisheries, in particular for salmon, in Russian waters exist from as early as 1855, but the main agreement is the Russo—Japanese Fishery Convention of 1907, which followed the peace settlement between those nations in 1905 (Treaty of Portsmouth and the Russo—Japanese Peace Treaty). This agreement established an inclusive regime for fisheries in Russian waters that recognized the land-based operations by Japan on the Pacific coast of Russia. The revolution in Russia resulted in a period of instability in the salmon fishery arrangements from 1917 until 1925, when a formal agreement that basically reinstated the provisions of the 1907 agreements could be signed. During this period Japanese fishing boats were sometimes accompanied by Japanese warships in what was termed a "self-help" fishery.[22]

In addition to the overall fisheries agreement negotiated in 1907, Russia claimed a 12-mile territorial zone in its 1911 law for the control of maritime fisheries. Japan protested this position as being inconsistent with the Russo—Japanese fishing treaty, and maintained that a 3-mile territorial sea was the limit according to international law. The Soviet claim was a serious impediment to Japanese fisheries, particularly for crab fisheries, which operated close to the Soviet coast. Protests by Great Britain and Norway over the Soviet 12-mile zone softened the position and by 1926 word was received in Japan that fisheries would be permitted within 3–12 miles of the Soviet coast.[23]

Immediately after conclusion of the 1925 agreement with Japan, the Soviet Union initiated negotiations to revise the agreement to be more in accord with its policy of developing a socialist society. This meant a limitation of the Japanese fishery. Some of the conflicts were over the methods of exercising fishery rights and problems of the laborers in the operation of fish processing facilities.[24] Borgström reports that considerable numbers of Japanese workers were seasonally employed in USSR shore-based fish processing centers, and that the annual migration of many, and full-time residence of other, Japanese citizens was viewed as a problem by the Soviet Union, which wanted to develop the Far East region with its own citizens.[25]

These negotiations led to the signing of a fishery convention in 1928, but many disputes continued to arise over Japanese claims for the stabilization of its existing fishing areas, abolition of the auction system of fishing grounds, and a fixed conversion rate for the ruble.

The Soviet Union claimed priority for its government-operated fishing area.[26] Fisheries relationships, primarily over salmon, deteriorated until the outbreak of World War II.

The deterioration in the relationship between Japan and the Soviet Union can be seen in the gradual reduction in salmon fishing lots allocated to Japan, and in increasingly stringent restrictions placed on the location of the lots, the fishing practices, and gear used by Japan. To offset this decreasing share of the lots, Japan instituted offshore fishing for salmon and salmon processing on board factory vessels in the late 1920s.[27]

The increasingly hostile climate for salmon and other fisheries in the Northwest Pacific, along with the development of at-sea fish processing capacity, caused some Japanese salmon fishing and processing vessels to enter the Bristol Bay fishery in 1936 on a three-year experimental basis, licensed by the Japanese government.[28] This action caused great distress among American fishing interests and pressure was brought to bear on the government to intervene. Legislation claiming ownership of the salmon resources was introduced in Congress, and boycotts of Japanese goods were threatened. The United States Department of State intervened, and by March 1938 had obtained the assurance of the government of Japan that, without prejudice to the question of rights under international law, Japan would refrain from operating salmon mothership fleets in the Northeast Pacific. At this time, the United States did not claim a property right in salmon fisheries but called attention to the sacrifice of its citizens in developing and protecting the salmon resources of its rivers.

The informal settlements of the salmon fishing conflict did not constitute a long-term solution to the problem and the macropolitical climate surrounding the issue no doubt had considerable bearing on the settlement.

> When the agreement was negotiated, the United States was in a favorable position diplomatically as regards Japan, as the latter country was deeply involved with the war in China in which the neutrality of the United States was of cardinal importance. It was obviously in Japan's interests to avoid making an issue over fishing rights which would have imposed further strain on diplomatic relations already tense.[29]

The post-World War II development of conflicts over salmon fisheries is more complicated than the pre-World War II developments. The conflicts center around (1) the abstention principle contained in the 1952 Convention on High Seas Fisheries between Canada, Japan, and the United States;[30] (2) the provisions of the 1956 agreement on High Seas Fisheries in the Northwest Pacific between Japan and the Soviet Union;[31] (3) conflicts over interception of salmon stocks in the waters of Canada, United States, Japan, and the Soviet Union; and (4) the conflicts between the Republic of Korea and other North Pacific nations over salmon fisheries. While the ostensible purpose of the international agreements mentioned above was to conserve the stocks of salmon, it cannot be denied that a major effect of the agreements was to reserve salmon stocks for the coastal fisheries of the United States, Canada, and the Soviet Union where domestic salmon fishing capacity already exceeded the available stocks. Japan's principal dissatisfaction with the agreements was that they restricted the location of salmon fishing activities, limiting the share of the stocks that the Japanese fleet could otherwise harvest on the high seas.

Following the Japanese surrender, Allied occupation forces took over the administration of Japanese affairs. One of the early measures was to restrict Japanese fisheries to limited areas surrounding Japan and to high-seas areas directly to the west of Japan. This area, commonly referred to as the MacArthur Line,* despite its more rectangular configuration, was established to contain the Japanese fishing fleet and prevent incidents between Japan and other nations over fisheries. Because of the expansion of the Japanese salmon fleet into the Bering Sea in the 1930s, the United States was particularly concerned that a similar development should not occur after the war. Therefore, it sought to restrict the range of operation of Japanese fleets. This concern was evidenced by the exchange of notes between Prime Minister Yoshida and Secretary of State Dulles in 1951, which extracted a promise from Japan to prohibit fishing by its nationals where unilateral or international regimes were in existence and where Japan·had not fished prior to 1940.[32]

Pursuant to the provisions of the Peace Treaty in 1952, Japan entered into negotiations with the United States and Canada for fisheries off the coast of North America, and salmon in particular. Canada and the United States wanted to protect salmon stocks fished by their own citizens from Japanese fishing, and thereby promote management and conservation of stocks by reducing competition. The objections of the two nations to Japanese high-seas fishing for salmon, on conservation grounds, were that immature salmon were caught in the high-seas fisheries, that the high-seas fishery made scientific management of individual stocks more difficult, and that large numbers of salmon were injured and dropped out of high-seas gill nets. Japan contended that the natural mortality rate of the fish stocks by the time they were caught in coastal fisheries was higher than the increment of growth of immature fish and injuries due to use of gill nets.[33] Japan also contended that the abstention principle had no status as a permanent measure for regulation of fisheries, but that it could be used in a temporary or transitional sense. Furthermore, the abstention principle stood in direct opposition to fisheries as being one of the freedoms of the high seas.[34] Perhaps the greatest obstacle to Japanese acceptance of the abstention principle was that it could set an undesirable precedent for other Japanese fishery negotiations.[35]

The appeal to the abstention principle by Canada and the United States did not establish ownership over a resource, but did result in a claim for management authority outside of territorial waters and thereby increased the exclusivity of the fishery. Under the Convention, as described in chapter 3, Japan was excluded from salmon fishing east of a line that was set provisionally at 175° west longitude. At the time of the signing of the Convention, this line was thought to be the farthest westward migration of North American stocks of salmon. Later research demonstrated that this was inaccurate, and that considerable numbers of Asian and North American salmon cross back and forth across the line.[36] This fact precipitated attempts by the United States, starting as early as 1957, to obtain an agreement to shift the abstention line farther west, to as far as 170° east longitude.[37] The United States' proposals were regularly rejected by Japanese negotiators on the grounds that there was not clear scientific evidence that guaranteed that any line other than the 175° west longitude

*See map in *Atlas of Marine Use in the North Pacific Region*, p. 6.

abstention line would result in better conservation of salmon stocks or in a more equitable "sacrifice" for conservation purposes.

Canada was also affected by the abstention principle: Canadians had agreed to abstain from fishing for salmon in the Bering Sea, in return for which Canada retained its traditional salmon fisheries off southeast Alaska. On the U.S. side, this concession was clearly motivated by the desire to protect U.S. salmon fishing.

The post-World War II salmon fishery conflicts in the Northwest Pacific between Japan and the Soviet Union stemmed largely from the change from a basically inclusive fishery arrangement prior to the war to a more exclusive arrangement favoring the Soviet Union following it. Japan was restrained from fishing in Soviet waters by the MacArthur Line until 1952. Even after that date, since no peace settlement had been negotiated between the two countries, Japan avoided fishing in the waters near Kamchatka and the northern Kurils.[38] After the war, the Soviet Union openly asserted its claims to a 12-mile territorial sea. Japan, without the powerful navy that had provided some bargaining leverage and protection for fisheries prior to the war, was forced to acquiesce.[39] This was important because Japan and the Soviet Union were technically at war until 1956. Still, the Japanese high-seas salmon fisheries took 64 million salmon in the mothership fishery and 47,000 MT of salmon in the land-based fishery in 1955.[40]

The Soviet Union was alarmed at the amount of Japanese catch, particularly since it consisted, to a large extent, of fish that spawned in Soviet waters. Fisheries negotiations, however, could not commence until some agreement could be obtained on the overall settlement of diplomatic relations between the countries, and the negotiations for normalization of diplomatic relations between Japan and the Soviet Union were protracted because of the difficult problem of the reversion of the southern Kurils to Japan. In March 1956 the Soviet Union declared the Bulganin Line,* possibly as a negotiating tactic to force a decision by Japan on the northern islands questions.[41] The Bulganin Line provided for exclusive Soviet control over fisheries within an area that is bounded on the west by the Soviet Union and on the east by a line running southward from Cape Olyutorsky to approximately 48° north latitude. Foreign and Soviet fishing within the zone was allowed only from May 15 to September 15, and a total quota of 50,000 MT was set. Foreign fishing (meaning Japanese fishing) was allowed only with special permission from the Ministry of Fisheries of the USSR.

In addition to the proclamation of the Bulganin Line, the Soviets drastically stepped up the harassment of Japanese fishing vessels off its coast in 1955 and 1956 as can be seen in table 4.1. The seizure of such a large number of Japanese fishing vessels and crew members was an important reason why Japan agreed to a more rapid normalization of relations with the Soviet Union than it might otherwise have preferred, and for the decision to shelve consideration of the northern islands as part of the settlement. This opened the way for signing the Japan—USSR Convention on High Seas Fisheries in the Northwest Pacific Ocean in May of 1956. The Bulganin Line, therefore, was never applied to Japanese

*See Appendix A, figure 1, for a map of this line.

TABLE 4.1

JAPANESE FISHING VESSELS SEIZED AND RELEASED BY THE USSR
1946–1976

| Year | Seized Vessels | Seized Crew | Vessels Sank | Crew Drowned | Returned Vessels | Returned Crew | Retained Vessels | Retained Crew |
|---|---|---|---|---|---|---|---|---|
| 1946 | 7 | 52 | | | 6 | 43 | 1 | 9 |
| 1947 | 1 | 3 | | | 2 | 12 | | |
| 1948 | 19 | 159 | | 2 | 14 | 85 | 5 | 72 |
| 1949 | 28 | 492 | | 2 | 28 | 522 | 5 | 40 |
| 1950 | 45 | 276 | 1 | | 32 | 280 | 17 | 36 |
| 1951 | 47 | 368 | 2 | 1 | 25 | 328 | 37 | 75 |
| 1952[a] | 3 | 26 | | | | 47 | 40 | 54 |
| 1952[b] | 44 | 364 | 1 | 5 | 35 | 305 | 48 | 108 |
| 1953 | 44 | 340 | | | 53 | 416 | 39 | 32 |
| 1954 | 65 | 537 | 2 | | 62 | 533 | 40 | 36 |
| 1955 | 125 | 1,104 | | 1 | 127 | 1,112 | 38 | 27 |
| 1956 | 131 | 1,207 | 3 | 1 | 81 | 1,187 | 85 | 46 |
| 1957 | 99 | 944 | 2 | | 69 | 949 | 113 | 41 |
| 1958 | 80 | 557 | 2 | | 51 | 568 | 140 | 30 |
| 1959 | 91 | 774 | 1 | | 43 | 773 | 187 | 31 |
| 1960 | 58 | 476 | | 1 | 14 | 467 | 231 | 39 |
| 1961 | 89 | 579 | 2 | | 41 | 568 | 277 | 50 |
| 1962 | 72 | 506 | 1 | | 26 | 422 | 322 | 134 |
| 1963 | 31 | 326 | 1 | | 16 | 448 | 336 | 12 |
| 1964 | 35 | 268 | | | 10 | 229 | 361 | 51 |
| 1965 | 40 | 450 | | | 19 | 480 | 382 | 21 |
| 1966 | 34 | 294 | 1 | 6 | 18 | 281 | 397 | 28 |
| 1967 | 47 | 315 | | | 11 | 303 | 433 | 40 |
| 1968 | 40 | 346 | | 1 | 15 | 324 | 458 | 61 |
| 1969 | 39 | 363 | 2 | 12 | 12 | 379 | 483 | 33 |
| 1970 | 22 | 190 | 1 | | 13 | 204 | 491 | 19 |
| 1971 | 27 | 272 | | | 21 | 277 | 497 | 14 |
| 1972 | 36 | 234 | 1 | | 17 | 227 | 515 | 21 |
| 1973 | 25 | 186 | | | 15 | 187 | 525 | 20 |
| 1974 | 33 | 246 | | | 16 | 248 | 542 | 18 |
| 1975 | 43 | 291 | 2 | 4 | 21 | 273 | 562 | 32 |
| 1976[c] | 14 | 78 | | | 16 | 95 | 560 | 15 |

Source: Japan Maritime Safety Agency, quoted by William H. MacKenzie, "Japan–USSR Negotiations on Safe Fishing and Reversion of Disputed Islands in the North Pacific: 1945–1977," *Marine Affairs Journal*, no. 5 (January 1978).

[a] Through April 27, 1952 (e.g., before the San Francisco Peace Treaty entered into force).

[b] From April 28, 1952 to the end of 1952.

[c] Through June 30, 1976.

fisheries or to fisheries of other nations. It appears that the Bulganin Line still exists as a Soviet claim vis-à-vis foreign fishing fleets, but it does not apply to nations with bilateral fishing agreements with the Soviet Union.

The conclusion of the fisheries agreement between Japan and the Soviet Union was not a solution to all the claims between the two countries. As summarized by Zengo Ohira, the basic positions of the two countries were as follows: The Soviet Union claimed (1) that it had made efforts to conserve and increase the stocks of fish for many years; (2) that the fishing industry, and salmon in particular, was an essential industry for the Soviet Far East; and (3) that scientific evidence showed a reduction in salmon stocks as a result of Japanese intensified fishing. Japan contended (1) that ocean resources should be managed by international agreement, (2) that regulations for conservation should be based on scientific investigations, and (3) that the measures should not discriminate against other parties. Japan also argued that the Soviet Union had not presented scientific evidence that proved that Japanese high-seas fishing had reduced the salmon stocks.[42]

The 1956 agreement provided for prohibiting the use of movable salmon fishing gear within 40 miles of the coast of either party. In successive years, between 1958 and 1962, these prohibited areas were enlarged over the protests of Japan.[43] In 1957 Peter the Great Bay was closed to Japanese fishing,[44] and the entire Okhotsk Sea was closed to Japanese salmon fishing.[45]

The original Northwest Pacific Fisheries Convention agreement applied to waters north of 45° north latitude. Japanese land-based salmon fleets had been operating in the area south of that line and catching considerable quantities of Soviet spawned salmon. This prompted the Soviet Union to insist that the Convention area be expanded to include the operations of the land-based salmon fleets. Quotas were adopted for Japanese fishing in the areas that were less than previous total catches from both areas.[46] It should be noted that the Japanese — Soviet Commission set quotas only for Japanese high-seas fishing, since the coastal Soviet catches were regulated by domestic regulations and the Soviet Union has no high-seas salmon fishery.

The relationship between Canada and the United States in managing salmon resources has been exemplary. Under the terms of the International Pacific Salmon Fisheries Convention as amended, the two countries have shared equally in the conservation, rehabilitation, regulation, and harvest of sockeye salmon from the Fraser River since 1930, and of pink salmon from the Fraser since 1956.[47] Through several informal arrangements, the U.S. and Canada have cooperated in conducting research and coordinating regulations related to salmon fisheries. A 1970 agreement (as modified in 1973) between the two countries provided for reciprocal fishing privileges of each country's salmon troll fisheries off the coast of the state of Washington and the west coast of Vancouver Island.[48] To a certain extent, this cooperation has been encouraged by the need to present a unified stance in opposition to the common threat of foreign harvest of North American salmon stocks.[49] However, the cooperation has been perceived as a common benefit to both countries.[50]

The migratory nature of the salmon and the geographic propinquity of the two countries enables the fisheries of both countries to intercept salmon bound for the other country. The intercepting fisheries can threaten adequate escapement and, therefore, the conservation of the salmon runs. The U.S. and Canada have convened negotiations since 1971 to resolve the salmon interception problems.

Over 200 separate salmon interception fisheries of mutual concern to Canada and the United States have been identified. For purposes of illustration, these interceptions can be broken down into five categories.

1. Interception of northern British Columbia salmon by the United States, notably the purse seine fishery at Noyes Island[51] and the gill net fishery at Cape Fox-Tree Point in which sockeye and pink salmon runs of the Nass and Skeena rivers are caught.
2. Interception of Alaskan salmon by Canada in the gill net fishery for chum salmon in Portland Canal, in the gill net and purse seine fishery for pink salmon in Dixon Entrance, Hecate Strait, and Chatham Sound, and in the troll fishery on the Fairweather grounds.
3. Interception of salmon bound for Canadian portions of the Stikine, Taku, Alsek, Yukon, and Columbia rivers by the United States.
4. Interception of salmon bound for southern British Columbia by the United States, the most important of which are the pink and sockeye of the Fraser River taken by net fisheries in northern Puget Sound.
5. Interception by Canada of salmon that originate in Washington and Oregon in the troll fishery for chinook and coho salmon off West Vancouver Island and the Washington coast.

Both Canada and the United States support the river-of-origin principle, which provides that each nation should have the opportunity to harvest salmon native to its own rivers. The Canadian position has been that in applying the river-of-origin principle the nations should attempt to reduce existing interceptions of salmon bound for the other country. The United States has argued that historic fisheries must be given adequate consideration, and that reduction in interceptions should not result in hardship to the participants in the fishery. Both countries agree that if reduction of interceptions cannot be achieved, the interceptions should be balanced in value. The strong interest shown by Canada and the United States in resolving the salmon interception conflicts is due to the desire by both countries to increase salmon stocks substantially through rehabilitation and enhancement programs. Both countries are reluctant to make these investments until they can be assured that the benefits will accrue to their own fisheries. However, the size and the complexity of the salmon interception problems have delayed their resolution.

The final topic related to international conflicts over salmon resources in the North Pacific was the potential entry of the Republic of Korea (ROK) into the high-seas salmon fishery in the late 1960s. Through foreign aid and domestic investment, the ROK was engaged in a massive effort to develop its fishing fleets—coastal as well as distant-water. One fishery that was considered for entry was the high-seas salmon fishery. In the Northeast Pacific, Canada and the United States strongly opposed Korean entry. Presumably, Japan also opposed Korean entry in that area, since it would upset the existing arrangements. The close ties, economic and political, between Korea and the United States made it undesirable for Korea to jeopardize the more important long-term relationships for the marginal benefits to be gained from salmon fishing, and Korea acquiesced to the United States opposition. In crucial bilateral negotiations with Korea, an agreement was reached in 1972 whereby the United States would provide technical advice on shellfish sanitation and salmon propagation to Korea.[52] In the same agreement, Korea agreed to refrain from fishing for salmon and halibut in the northeastern Pacific east of the 175° west longitude abstention line.

In the Northwest Pacific, the entry of the Republic of Korea into the high-seas salmon fishery was definitely opposed by Japan, since the Soviet Union let it be known through informal channels that any salmon caught by Korea would be deducted from the Japanese quotas.[53] Johnson suggested that Japan withheld as much as $90 million from an assistance fund for Korea because it disapproved of loans for constructing fishing vessels that might be used in high-seas salmon fisheries. It is also reported that Japan denied passports to technicians under contract to advise Korea, and that there was a possibility that Korean fishing vessels would be excluded from making port calls in Japan.[54] Kasahara offers two additional reasons why the Republic of Korea did not develop high-seas salmon fisheries in the Northwest Pacific. First, they lacked diplomatic relations with the Soviet Union and seizures of Korean vessels would surely result in difficult negotiations to return the vessels and crew members. Second, the government of Japan and the Japanese industry might place major restrictions on the import of seafood products from Korea in retaliation.[55]

## Halibut

After the original difficulties over joint management of halibut were resolved by the establishment of the International Pacific Halibut Commission (IPHC),[56] the Canadian—American relationship over management of halibut stocks was remarkably free of conflict until the extension of fishery zones in the mid-1970s. Two conflicts have arisen over foreign entry into the North American halibut fishery and a third conflict has developed over the impacts of foreign trawl fisheries on halibut stocks. Halibut are less abundant in the Northwest Pacific and therefore do not constitute a target fishery in that area.

The first conflict occurred in the winter of 1936−37 and involved the possible entry of the *Thorland*, a British refrigerator ship manned by Norwegians, into the halibut fishery in the North Pacific. The North Atlantic halibut fisheries were declining because of overharvesting, and the North Pacific stocks, which were being rebuilt by the careful management of the International Pacific Halibut Commission, were eyed as potential stocks for harvest by European nations that were not bound by the halibut convention in the North Pacific. Canadian protests sent to Great Britain probably influenced the decision not to send the vessel to the Pacific, although events surrounding World War II also contributed to a declining European interest in the halibut stocks of the North Pacific. Both Canada and the United States precluded future European involvement in Pacific halibut fisheries with their respective legislation implementing the 1937 revisions of the North Pacific Halibut Convention. This legislation provided that the governments of the two countries could prevent the use of territorial waters and ports by nonsignatory parties to the Convention if they were engaged in fishing for halibut.[57]

The second conflict was part of a larger discussion related to the concept of the "abstention line" east of which Japan was not to fish for salmon, halibut, and herring under the International Convention for High Seas Fisheries in the North Pacific Ocean signed by Canada, Japan, and the United States in 1952. The main purpose of the Convention was to conserve fish stocks and, in effect, to reserve for North American fishing interests all stocks that could be demonstrated to be fully utilized by Canada and the United States. Japan resented this provision because it provided unequal access to an international fishery on the high seas. Japan would have preferred joint management of stocks under conditions of equal access.[58]

Halibut, under the aegis of the IPHC, was showing signs of a successful recovery to full population in the Bering Sea area by the early 1960s. Japan pressed for an examination of halibut stocks under the provisions of the International North Pacific Fisheries Commission (INPFC) to see if halibut qualified as a fully utilized species under the abstention principle. INPFC ruled that proof of full utilization was lacking and that Japan could fish for halibut in the Bering Sea. The INPFC set a catch limit for that area which was much in excess of previous levels.[59]

It has been suggested that an important reason why the U.S. agreed to remove halibut from the abstention was to preserve the credibility of the full utilization provisions in the INPFC agreement relative to salmon.[60] If Japan were not convinced that INPFC decisions for abstention from halibut fishing were based on scientific grounds, the renegotiation and renewal of the INPFC agreement on salmon in 1963 might be jeopardized.

The large catches of halibut in the Bering Sea in 1963 and later had a negative impact on the stocks of halibut in the area. Due to the interrelationships between migratory halibut stocks, the impact of overfishing in the Bering Sea may also have influenced Gulf of Alaska stocks. Only through severe restrictions on the halibut fishery, recommended by IPHC and concurred in by INPFC, has there been some positive response in halibut stocks. Additional protection was provided by bilateral agreements between the United States and Poland, and the U.S. and Republic of Korea (Poland and ROK had traded access to ports, fishing zones, and loading areas) for agreement to abstain from halibut fishing.

The situation for halibut was complicated by major increases in foreign trawling effort in the northeastern Pacific area in the 1960s, and the concommitant rise in incidental trawl catch of halibut. In 1971, an estimated incidental catch of 13,589 metric tons of halibut was taken in the Northwest Pacific trawl fishery.[61] In the same year, the total catch of the longline fishery for halibut from all areas was 35,855 MT.[62] The IPHC had regulatory authority over only Canadian and American halibut fisheries, and could seek to bring pressure to bear on Japan only through the INPFC. Appealing to the INPFC did not yield significant results because INPFC decisions are on the basis of unanimity and the position of Japan was opposite to that of Canada and the United States.[63] In addition, the INPFC convention did not provide a formal regulatory authority over groundfish stocks. IPHC also sought to reduce incidental catches by trawlers of the Republic of Korea and USSR through bilateral negotiations.

The United States bilateral negotiations were more successful. In these negotiations, the United States offered distant-water trawling nations access to ports, loading zones in the territorial sea, and access to fishing within the 9-mile contiguous fishery zone in exchange for an agreement that they would not trawl fish in certain areas during specified seasons when halibut are more vulnerable to being caught in trawls. With this type of arrangement, the United States traded a more inclusive regime in some of the areas under its otherwise exclusive jurisdiction for a more exclusive regime in otherwise international waters. This arrangement was more a *modus vivendi* than a declaration of a claim to regulate for conservation, but the effect was basically the same in terms of greater coastal state control over foreign fisheries.

Although the arrangements recommended by the IPHC could not be fully carried out through INPFC arrangements or the bilateral negotiations, they reduced the incidental catch of halibut, and by the mid-1970s halibut stocks showed signs of increasing.[64]

## Crab

Both the United States and the Soviet Union made claims to regulate crab fisheries by foreign nations outside their territorial waters for the purpose of conservation. These claims basically sought to change the status of king and tanner crabs from resources of the high seas to resources of the continental shelf managed exclusively by the coastal state. Some measures had been considered for the crab fisheries prior to 1960 to avoid the typical overfishing cycle in North Pacific fisheries, but at that time there was not an internationally acceptable method for regulation of crab stocks.

The 1958 Geneva Conference on the Law of the Sea produced a convention that dealt with the living resources and other resources of the continental shelf.[65] The Convention on the Continental Shelf provided that the coastal state could exercise jurisdiction over living resources of the continental shelf, and defined them as "living organisms belonging to sedentary species, that is to say, organisms which, at the harvestable stage, either are immobile on or under the seabed or are unable to move except in constant physical contact with the seabed or the subsoil."[66] This agreement did not receive enough ratifications to bring it into force until 1964.

In 1964, after having ratified the Convention on the Continental Shelf, and after the requisite number of other nations had ratified the agreement, the United States could argue that the Continental Shelf Convention had the force of international law among signatory nations. Legislation was passed in the U.S. in May 1964 that, in part, made it illegal for a foreign vessel to take any resource of the continental shelf of the United States without prior agreement.[67] The United States made a claim against the Soviet Union and Japan for crab fisheries in the eastern Bering Sea, Gulf of Alaska, and the Aleutian Islands area when crab catches reached extremely high levels in the early 1960s, and catch per unit effort began to decline drastically. Furthermore, the domestic industry in the United States was rapidly increasing and there was a desire to reserve crab stocks for national benefit.

Since the Soviet Union had already ratified the Convention on the Continental Shelf there was no protest forthcoming on its behalf. Japan had not ratified the Convention and was not bound by the agreement. Furthermore, Japan did not recognize the U.S. contention that crabs were living resources of the continental shelf since, at times, crabs were able to move with a swiminglike motion that propelled them off the shelf.[68] The United States went to great lengths to show that crabs were creatures of the continental shelf by filming their movements.[69]

The conflicting claims were compromised in consultations between the two governments. The United States recognized the historical crab fisheries of Japan on the continental shelf, and Japan recognized the right of the United States to manage the crab for the purposes of conservation. Agreement was reached in 1964 on a *modus operandi* that would allow Japanese crab fisheries to continue without prejudice to the legal positions held by either nation.[70] Japan's adherence to the agreements leads to the conclusion that there was de facto recognition of coastal state exclusive jurisdiction over living resources of the continental shelf, although Japan did not formally accept such a policy.[71]

The Japanese–Soviet conflict over crab resources on the continental shelf evolved along different lines. The Soviet Union claimed the right to regulate king crab fisheries in the Northwest Pacific in the 1956 agreement with Japan. Although Japan did not raise the question of regulating the resources of the continental shelf at this time, it insisted that nothing in the agreement be considered to affect its position with respect to the limits of the territorial sea or jurisdiction over fisheries. During the negotiations on the 1958 Geneva Convention on the Continental Shelf, the Soviet Union sought to have crustaceans, including crabs, declared resources of the continental shelf, but the move was defeated.[72] In 1969, Japan and the Soviet Union negotiated a new treaty concerning several species of crab on the USSR continental shelf. The Soviet Union objected to continued regulation of king crabs under the 1956 agreement with Japan because crabs, they argued, were creatures of the continental shelf and not the high seas. Japan insisted that a statement of nonprejudice to territorial claims and fisheries jurisdictional claims be inserted. Under the terms of the agreement, king crab fishing by Japanese motherships in Soviet waters was banned in 1974, and the next year all Japanese fishing for king crab was prohibited.[73] This move was only partially compensated by increased quotas for other crab species in Soviet waters.

In terms of the claims to management of crab fisheries, the Soviet Union and the United States instituted regulations that prohibited the harvest of females and immature males, and controlled the location of crab fishing gear. United States regulations limited the size of mesh used in tangle nets and set quotas for the allowable catch on its continental shelf by Japan and the Soviet Union. The Soviet Union also used quotas to regulate Japanese operations on its continental shelf. These practices were increasingly restrictive for all species of crab and gradually led to the establishment of exclusive king crab fisheries for coastal states in the North Pacific.

## Whaling

Whaling in the North Pacific has increasingly become an area of conflict between the policies of the United States and those of Japan and the Soviet Union. These nations and Canada are all members of the International Whaling Commission (IWC). In the 1967 Japan–United States Contiguous Fishing Zone Agreement, Japan was permitted to whale within the American contiguous zone except in the area between 163° W and 150° W longitude. Under marine mammal and endangered species legislation passed in the early 1970s, the United States prohibited the taking of whales by its citizens other than a relatively small but controversial take of bowhead whales by native Alaskan peoples.[74] Whaling by other nations in the contiguous zone of the United States was stopped. In addition, it was forbidden to import whale products of any kind into the United States. When the import controls were implemented, they impacted heavily on the major producers, Japan and the Soviet Union, since the United States used approximately 30 percent of all whale products in 1970, at the time the action was taken.[75]

Another important aspect of the United States' position is the push by American delegations to IWC meetings for greater protection of whales than Japan and the Soviet Union consider necessary. The United States has been a strong supporter of scientific management of whale stocks and has resisted attempts of other nations to set international quotas for whales in the North Pacific and other areas at higher levels than those recommended by the IWC's Scientific Committee. In 1972, the United States proposed a one-year moratorium on whaling to the Commission, but it was not accepted by enough other members. The continued harvest of the bowhead whale by United States citizens, despite its protection by IWC regulations, has been criticized in IWC meetings.[76] With respect to whaling, no nation made a unilateral claim for exclusive jurisdiction (except for the limited action by the United States noted above) for purposes of conservation prior to extended jurisdiction, but conflict exists over the measures to be taken to protect whale stocks on the high seas under inclusive management.

### Herring

Herring in the North Pacific is specifically referenced in both the 1952 Canada—Japan—United States INPFC agreement and the 1956 Japanese—Soviet fishing agreement. In each, herring is one of the species mentioned for which coastal states have made a claim to reserve fully utilized stocks for their own citizens. The basic rationale for these national claims has been described in the preceding discussions on salmon and halibut and need not be repeated here. One aspect of the conflict that deserves further emphasis is Japan's claim that the United States and Canada, in applying the abstention principle only to Japanese fisheries, were unfairly discriminating against Japan since other nations, like the Soviet Union, were not excluded from the herring fishery in the northeastern Pacific.

In response to this claim, herring was removed from abstention under the INPFC Convention for Alaskan waters in 1959. Subsequently, herring stocks off the coast of the United States south of the Strait of Juan de Fuca (1961) and on the west coast of the Canadian Queen Charlotte Islands (1962) were also removed from abstention.[77] The herring stocks in Canadian waters south of 51°56' north latitude, however, remained reserved under the abstention principle.[78] In addition, the reciprocal fishing agreements between Canada and the United States provided that there would be no fishing for any species of herring by citizens of one nation off the coast of the other.

Japan considered that the Soviet claim to management of herring for conservation purposes impinged on the freedom of high-seas fisheries. The 1956 Japan—Soviet Convention established a minimum size for herring but allowed a small incidental catch of immature fish at the discretion of the Commission. The Commission established to implement the Convention set a 10 percent limit on incidental catches in 1957 and raised the minimum size limit of herring in 1958.[79] Declines in the stocks of herring prompted the establishment of closed areas in the coastal waters of the Korfo−Karagin area, Gizhiga Bay, and Peuz-hinskaya Bay in 1969.* Commercial catches were prohibited after 1970 to permit the stocks to recover.[80]

## Other Fisheries

Following the conclusion of World War II, Japan lost all the fisheries in waters near nations it formerly occupied and was restricted to fishing within the confines of the area established by the MacArthur Line. After the signing of the peace treaty between the Allied Powers and Japan in 1952, the Allied Occupation of Japan ended and the MacArthur Line was lifted. Before the line was abolished, the ROK, which had pursued an ambitious program to restore its coastal fisheries, declared its sovereignty over adjacent waters in a Presidential Proclamation in 1952. The declaration was prompted by the fear that Japan's superior fishing techniques and equipment would exhaust Korea's fishery resources.[81] In the declaration, which established a fishing area reserved for Korean fisheries extending as much as 200 miles into the seas surrounding that country, Korea claimed the right to regulate fisheries and other resources on the high seas adjacent to its territorial waters in order to reserve the fish resources for its own citizens.[82] The line of demarcation was called the Peace Line (also the Rhee Line after Syngman Rhee, president of the Republic of Korea at that time).**

Japan rejected the Korean claim as a direct contradiction of the international law of the high seas.** The 1952 Peace Treaty with the Allied Powers provided that Japan was obligated to negotiate fisheries arrangements with all parties involved with its international fisheries. Korea, while not a signatory party to that agreement, benefited by it and main-tained the Rhee Line until an agreement for fishing was negotiated with Japan. Fishery talks were proposed by Korea as early as 1951, but Japan declined to negotiate at that time, pleading lack of preparation.[84] Korea was suspicious of the Japanese reluctance to negotiate with them when Japan had already concluded agreements with Canada and the United States.[85] Negotiations dragged off and on for over fourteen years until agreement was finally reached in 1965.[86] During the course of the negotiations between Japan and Korea, the emphasis "gradually turned from disagreement as to whether the actions taken by the Republic of Korea were violations of international law to the setting up of equitable fishery regulations to be agreed upon by themselves."[87] Several problems contributed to the delay in arriving at agreement.[88] First and foremost was the considerable hostility and distrust remaining between the two countries after 40 years of colonial rule by Japan, and centuries of prior conflict. Second, the Korean War and military precautions complicated the differ-ences in position; during that period, the Clark Line was established 12 miles offshore from Korea and was patrolled by the naval forces of the United Nations. The Clark Line was intended to regulate all small boat traffic in coastal Korean waters including Japanese fishing vessels.[89] Third, the Korean government zealously enforced the provisions of the Peace

*See *Atlas of Marine Use in the North Pacific Region* for map of these areas, p. 25.
**See Appendix A, figure 2, for a map of this line.

Line, with the result that during the negotiations 326 fishing vessels were seized by Korea and nearly 4,000 crew members were detained. Of these vessels, 185 were sunk or not returned to Japan, and some $20-25 million of damage was done to the Japanese fishing industry.[90] Even when it was agreed to halt seizures of vessels during the negotiations in 1959, the conflict continued as seen in table 4.2. It is important to note that in 1952, when the Peace Line was established, over 2,400 Japanese fishing vessels with a total crew size of 3,500 were estimated to be fishing within the Clark Line area, and their annual catch was worth approximately $20 million.[91]

The 1965 settlement brought an end to the open fisheries conflict between Japan and the Republic of Korea. One significant aspect of the agreement was Japan's acceptance of a 12-mile exclusive fisheries management zone for the Republic of Korea and for its own coastal fisheries. This marked the first formal concession Japan made to its staunch policy of a three-mile territorial limit as the maximum admissible claim under international law. Japan made it clear that the acceptance did not amount to a change in policy, rather it constituted an exception made under special circumstances.

The rapid expansion of the Korean fishing fleet brought some vessels into the northern Sea of Japan in 1966, but no real problems were experienced in this traditional preserve of

TABLE 4.2

JAPANESE FISHING VESSELS SEIZED BY KOREA, 1946–1962

| | Seized | | Returned | | Not yet returned | |
|---|---|---|---|---|---|---|
| | Vessels | Persons | Vessels | Persons | Vessels | Persons |
| 1947 | 7 | 81 | 6 | 81 | 1 | 0 |
| 1948 | 15 | 202 | 10 | 202 | 5 | 0 |
| 1949 | 14 | 154 | 14 | 151 | 0 | 0 |
| 1950 | 13 | 165 | 13 | 165 | 0 | 0 |
| 1951 | 45 | 518 | 42 | 518 | 3 | 0 |
| 1952 | 10 | 132 | 5 | 131 | 5 | 0 |
| 1953 | 47 | 585 | 2 | 584 | 45 | 0 |
| 1954 | 34 | 454 | 6 | 453 | 28 | 0 |
| 1955 | 30 | 498 | 1 | 496 | 29 | 0 |
| 1956 | 19 | 235 | 3 | 235 | 15 | 0 |
| 1957 | 12 | 121 | 2 | 121 | 10 | 0 |
| 1958 | 9 | 93 | 0 | 93 | 9 | 0 |
| 1959 | 10 | 100 | 2 | 100 | 8 | 0 |
| 1960 | 6 | 52 | 0 | 52 | 5 | 0 |
| 1961 | 15 | 152 | 11 | 152 | 4 | 0 |
| 1962 | 15 | 116 | 4 | 116 | 11 | 0 |
| 1963 | — | — | — | — | — | — |
| 1964 | 9 | 99 | 7 | 99 | 2 | 0 |
| | 310 | 3,757 | 128 | 3,749 | 180 | — |

Sources: Seizures 1947–1962 from Shigeru Oda and Hisashi Owada, "Annual Review of Japanese Practice in International Law 1961–1962," *Japanese Annual of International Law* (1964), 8:99–131.

Seizures 1964 from Shigeru Oda and Hisashi Owada, "Annual Review of Japanese Practice in International Law III 1964," *Japanese Annual of International Law* (1966), 10:67.

Note: These totals do not necessarily reflect the final settlement with respect to vessels and persons seized, since data are incomplete.

Japanese fishing interests until later. By 1975, the scale of Korean operations had increased to the point where Japan requested, and Korea agreed, that Korean vessels would refrain from fishing within 12 miles of the Japanese coast in that area, which was not covered in the earlier agreement.[92] A final area of conflict between Japan and the Republic of Korea was in the fisheries in the South and East China seas where operations of the fleets of both nations resulted in troubled relationships. This was addressed in a private-level fisheries agreement, but the problems did not completely cease.[93]

The fishery conflict between Japan and the People's Republic of China (PRC) began in 1950, when the latter seized Japanese vessels fishing beyond the confines of the MacArthur Line and in waters claimed by PRC in the East and South China seas. At the time the PRC was established it took a hostile stance toward Japan, as can be seen in the PRC–Soviet Amity, Alliance and Mutual Aid Treaty (1950), in which Japan was regarded as a common enemy. The fact that the PRC sent volunteers to North Korea and that Japan was a staging ground for United Nations troops during the Korean War exacerbated the already strong anti-Japanese feelings.[94] As seen in table 4.3, PRC engaged in a serious effort to harass Japanese fishing activities until shortly before a nongovernmental fishing agreement was signed in 1955.

After World War II Japan was eager to expand its fishing activities into areas fished prior to the war, and the China seas were the most accessible. In 1950, PRC had established but not officially announced a number of military, fishing, and other zones off its coastline. Japanese fishing vessels, assuming that PRC claimed only a three-mile territorial sea, were

TABLE 4.3

JAPANESE FISHING VESSELS AND CREW SEIZED BY
THE PEOPLE'S REPUBLIC OF CHINA, 1950–1962

|  | Seized | | Returned | | Not yet returned | |
|---|---|---|---|---|---|---|
|  | Vessels | Persons | Vessels | Persons | Vessels | Persons |
| 1950 | 5 | 54 | 0 | 54 | 5 | 0 |
| 1951 | 55 | 671 | 1 | 660 | 54 | 0 |
| 1952 | 46 | 544 | 14 | 543 | 32 | 0 |
| 1953 | 24 | 311 | 11 | 309 | 13 | 0 |
| 1954 | 28 | 329 | 28 | 326 | 0 | 0 |
| 1955 | 1 | 10 | 1 | 10 | 0 | 0 |
| 1956 | 2 | 24 | 2 | 24 | 0 | 0 |
| 1957 | 0 | 0 | 0 | 0 | 0 | 0 |
| 1958 | 20 | 245 | 16 | 245 | 4 | 0 |
| 1959 | 2 | 24 | 2 | 24 | 0 | 0 |
| 1960 | 1 | 12 | 0 | 11 | 1 | 0 |
| 1961 | 2 | 25 | 2 | 25 | 0 | 0 |
| 1962 | 0 | 0 | 0 | 0 | 0 | 0 |
| Total | 186 | 2,249 | 77 | 2,231 | 109 | 0 |

Source: Shigeru Oda and Hisashi Owada. "Annual Review of Japanese Practice in International Law," *Japanese Annual of International Law* (1964), 8:128.

Note: Totals are given as of the end of 1962.

often seized. Because the governments of Japan and the PRC did not have diplomatic relations, it was difficult to ascertain the precise reasons for the seizures, or to arrange for release of the prisoners and vessels. Returning fishermen indicated that trespassing on PRC fishing grounds, espionage, violation of territorial waters, and obstruction of coastal fisheries were the main charges.[95]

The conclusion of an informal fisheries agreement in 1955 resulted in fairly peaceful fishing operations in the China seas. Only a few vessels were seized, even though the PRC cited 273 instances where Japanese fishermen violated the boundaries and/or internal laws and regulations, and Japanese patrol boats in the area detected 470 violations.[96] The agreement provided for a zone of up to 60 miles off the PRC coast that was reserved for domestic fisheries. The original agreement in 1955 provided for a military zone south of 29° north latitude where no foreign trawling could take place. In 1957 the military zone was shifted southwards to 27° north latitude. The Japanese government protested that the PRC claim contradicted international law, but acquiesced to this arrangement provided that it was applied to all nations.[97]

In 1958, following an incident involving destruction of a PRC flag hoisted in Nagasaki, there was a sudden worsening of relations between the two countries and PRC resumed seizing vessels and refused to renew the informal agreement on fisheries. The areas claimed under PRC jurisdiction were far greater than Japan acknowledged as acceptable claims under international law, but without formal diplomatic relations relatively little could be done to argue the case.[98] As the fishing controversy developed in the 1960s it became apparent that the fishery problems were far more a consequence of the overall relationship between the countries than the result of the fishery conflicts themselves.[99]

Numerous other fishery conflicts existed in the North Pacific that involved conservation of living resources, but relatively little is known in detail about them because they were often of a sensitive political nature. Practically no information is available on the relationship between the Democratic People's Republic of Korea (DPRK) and PRC. PRC and DPRK have negotiated an agreement for fishing in the East China Sea but little is known about what it entails. Park suggests that this agreement has led to successful cooperation.[100] Similarly, DPRK and the Soviet Union had an agreement on fisheries in the southern Okhotsk Sea prior to extended coastal state jurisdiction. DPRK apparently declared a "sensitive area" as much as 100 miles wide in the Sea of Japan and some Japanese fishing vessels were seized there.[101] The Soviet position with respect to the DPRK sensitive areas is not known, however. In 1975 a DPRK patrol boat attacked a Japanese fishing vessel in the Yellow Sea. And the ROK and DPRK are in conflict in the demilitarized zones separating the two countries, where seizures of fishing vessels are frequent.

The position of the Republic of Korea with respect to PRC and the Soviet Union is quite delicate, since it does not have diplomatic relations with either country. Korea caught pollock within 200 miles of the Soviet Union prior to the extension of jurisdiction, but apparently avoided coming close enough to the coastlines to bother the Soviets. It appears that ROK has taken a similar cautious policy with respect to PRC. The Soviet Union and the PRC are engaged in an ideological dispute that has stifled discussions of fishing matters.

## Claims to Prescribe for Allocation

Along with the claims to regulate fisheries for purposes of conservation, major conflicts over the determination of allocations have also existed. Arrangements for allocation of fish stocks have been a part of nearly every fishing agreement signed in the North Pacific, either explicitly or implicitly. In the North Pacific, allocations have been set for salmon, halibut, herring, crab, walleye pollock, and other groundfish under various agreements made prior to extended jurisdiction. Some of the different forms allocation has taken are seen, for example, in (1) the requirements to set a catch quota under the Japan–Soviet 1956 agreement;[102] (2) direct controls on fishing effort in the Japan–Republic of Korea agreement in 1965;[103] (3) allocation of fishing grounds as in the Japan–Soviet crab fishing agreement of 1969;[104] (4) the abstention principle under the tripartite international North Pacific Fisheries Convention in 1952;[105] and (5) various combinations of these methods. Allocation arrangements are definitely made easier to negotiate in the North Pacific due to the ability of the governments of Japan, People's Republic of China, Republic of Korea, and the USSR to control directly the level of entry into a certain fishery, and to monitor the catch. For Canada and the United States, allocation is complicated by the fact that the fishing industry tends to view limitations on entry as a violation of rights.

The basic conflict over allocation is quite simple. Each party to an agreement governing a given fishery desires to harvest as much fish of a certain species or group of species as possible, and any limits on, or reductions in, the permissible catch level are strenuously resisted. In general, scientific evidence that fish catches must be limited to conserve stocks must be shown to obtain agreement, although the onus of proof often falls on the state that desires to limit total catch.[106]

Since the allocation agreements are often the products of protracted formal and informal negotiations in which scientific, political, economic, and other factors can be of great importance, it is difficult to know what has motivated certain allocation decisions or to discern which principles have been applied.[107] Historical catches have been used in the determination of allocations in the North Atlantic but this principle is of relatively less importance in the North Pacific, where only a few nations have had significant involvement in particular fisheries. The types of conflicts over allocations that have occurred between coastal states and distant-water fishing nations in the North Pacific have concerned claims over (1) application of allocation arrangements to previously unallocated stocks at the request of the coastal state, (2) reduction of quotas for purposes of conservation, (3) reduction of foreign quotas to assure coastal state fishing interests a larger share, and (4) exclusion of foreign fishing entirely. These conflicts are discussed with respect to fisheries for certain species and species groups.

### Salmon

Between Japan and the Soviet Union, allocation of leases for coastal salmon fishing lots was made in addition to other restrictions reserving coastal and river fisheries for the Soviet Union. Between 1924 and 1935, the total number of lots allocated to Japan increased from 229 to 378, but the percent of total lots decreased from 88 percent to 50 percent in the respective years.[108] In 1939, some 40 fishing grounds were closed for strategic reasons by the Soviet Union, although intensive negotiation efforts by Japan ameliorated somewhat the negative impacts of this action. The limitations on coastal catch were also somewhat offset by Japanese use of salmon motherships on the high seas.

Following the conclusion of the Japan–Soviet fisheries agreement in 1956, salmon quotas have been fixed on an annual basis.[109] The quotas apply only to Japanese high-seas fisheries. In 1962, the Soviets insisted on extending the salmon quotas to the areas south of 45° north latitude, since Japanese catches in that area had expanded rapidly after the quota was applied to the Northwest Pacific north of that line.

Japan protested the original reduction in its salmon catch from the 1955 catch of 170,000 MT to 65,000 MT under the quota set by the Soviet Union for 1956.[110] In 1957, the first allocation established by the joint Japan–Soviet Fisheries Commission was set at 125,000 MT. With minor exceptions, due to the nature of the biennial fluctuations in runs of pink salmon, the Japanese quota has been gradually reduced each succeeding year. This is partly a consequence of reduction of the total harvest in order to protect the stocks, and partly of the Soviet position that the catch by Japan and the Soviet Union should be equalized.[111]

The negotiation of the salmon quotas and other arrangements has consistently been a long process that reflects the difficulties in obtaining agreements between Japan and the Soviet Union. Between 1957 and 1961 the negotiations took 52, 100, 122, 107, and 105 days in the respective years.[112] Sometimes the talks involved intervention of high-level foreign ministry officials from Japan in order to obtain eventual settlement. Oda suggests that the difficulties experienced in the negotiation had relatively little to do with differences in scientific views with respect to salmon conservation,[113] and Tanaka substantiates this for more recent years.[114]

Salmon quotas may have been used by the Soviet Union to bring pressure on Japan to conclude a peace treaty, and for the normalization of diplomatic relations. It has been suggested that salmon negotiations between Japan and the Soviets have been used as a pawn in the conflict between the Soviet Union and the PRC, although without inside knowledge it is not possible to know what effects these relationships have actually had on allocations. Japan argues that the Soviets, who engage only in coastal salmon fishing, have "subordinated an overall policy of high-seas fisheries for salmon to conservation policies unilaterally pursued by the Soviet Union within her territory," and this results in a more exclusive regime.[115]

In the Northeast Pacific, salmon allocation under the INPFC abstention principle was applied to Japan east of the 175° west longitude line, to Canada in the Bering Sea, and extended in separate agreements to the Republic of Korea and Poland. The prohibition on salmon fishing in the convention area was a de facto claim by the United States and, in part, Canada, to allocate all stocks of salmon to domestic fisheries because it was possible to show that the stocks were fully utilized.

Canada and the United States have strongly desired to relocate the abstention line farther westward to protect the known areas where salmon of North American origin are found on the high seas. Japan resisted this claim because conclusive proof was lacking about the distribution of salmon stocks in this area, and because considerable stocks of salmon of Asian origin migrate across the existing abstention line and are therefore made less accessible to high-seas fisheries by Japan. Japan proposed in the early 1960s that western Aleutian salmon stocks should not be subject to the abstention line, since they were not utilized by the United States or Canada. This conflict has simmered slowly since the INPFC agreement.

Canada and the United States have long agreed to a 50-50 allocation of Fraser River pink and sockeye salmon runs, but in recent years Canada has become increasingly adamant about renegotiating the Fraser River agreement. Canada claims that the sacrifices of not using the Fraser River for hydroelectric power generation and other purposes has been borne solely by Canada.[116] In addition, Canada has argued that the investment made by the United States in rebuilding the Fraser River runs has long since been amortized and should not be considered in the negotiations.[117] Still, Canada recognizes the need to maintain some sort of agreement with the United States because Fraser River salmon stocks migrate through the internal and territorial waters of the United States. The United States claims that the Fraser River runs constitute a historic fishery between the two countries, that joint management is necessary, and that the United States has contributed financially and scientifically to the successful rebuilding of the fishery and should, therefore, be entitled to continue to fish. Actual implementation of the allocation arrangements has been fairly well coordinated and functions fairly well, although there were conflicts over the interception of stocks covered by the convention but intercepted outside the convention area.

## Crab

Allocation of king crab and later tanner crab and other crab species has occurred in the North Pacific.[118] The trend in both the northeastern and northwestern areas has been toward reserving an increasing share for the coastal state and decreasing the allocations to foreign fishing nations. The Japanese west Kamchatka king crab fisheries were allocated 320,000 cases of canned crab in 1958, the first year allocations were applied to crab in the Northwest Pacific; this amounted to 40 percent of the total allocations. By 1969 the allocation had been decreased to 216,000 cases and only 33 percent of the catch. In 1975, Japan was excluded from king crab fisheries in the west Kamchatka region. The decreasing quotas on king crab prompted Japan to shift its crabbing operations to tanner and other crab species in the Okhotsk Sea and western Bering Sea, but the quotas for these areas have also been reduced. Similarly, allocations to Japanese and Soviet crab fisheries in the Northeast Pacific have been reduced as American crab vessels have expanded their fisheries into areas formerly fished by Japan and the Soviet Union.[119] By the early 1970s the quotas on king crab were so low that the Soviet Union no longer fished for king crab and Japan sustained only a token effort. Tanner crab stocks have followed a similar pattern, although there were substantial Japanese crab fishing efforts as late as 1976 since domestic capacity had not fully developed to harvest, process, and market that species. Reciprocal arrangements do not exist between Canada and the United States for crab fisheries.

## Halibut

Halibut was removed from its protected status in the Bering Sea in 1962 by the INPFC, and a quota of 5,000 metric tons was set for Japanese fishing. This proved to be more than that stock could support, and the quota for halibut in that area was drastically reduced. Halibut allocations were not made by the IPHC between Canada and the United States prior to extended jurisdiction, since the halibut fishery took place on a reciprocal basis. In recent years, halibut catches have been about equal.

## Herring

By 1959 herring no longer qualified for protection under the abstention principle of the INPFC, and the prohibition of Japanese fishing was removed except in certain Canadian waters. In 1971 the United States expressed concern over the reduced stocks of the eastern Bering Sea herring and negotiated a quota of 37,600 MT for Japan's fishing fleets. This quota was lowered in 1975 to 18,000 MT.[120] Soviet herring catches were also limited for the first time in that year with a quota of 30,000 MT. Since the Canadian herring fishery is an important fishery in British Columbia, Canada has successfully sought to retain protection for stocks near its coast. Under the INPFC abstention principle, stocks south of 51° 56' north latitude and north of the Straits of Juan de Fuca are reserved for Canada.[121] Canada and the United States do not have reciprocal fisheries for herring.

Herring in the Northwest Pacific are allocated under a complex system of area and time closures combined with quotas. In general, the extremely poor condition of stocks in most areas has led to very strict limits and closures in the northern areas since 1970.[122]

## Other Fisheries

Catches of pollock and other groundfish in the Northeast Pacific were made subject to allocation under bilateral agreements in the early and mid-1970s, when it became apparent that stocks were being depleted by unregulated fishing.

The pollock catch quota for Japan in the eastern Bering Sea was reduced from 1.5 million MT in 1973 to 1.1 million MT in the period from 1975 to 1977.[123] The Soviet Union was assigned a quota for pollock of 210,000 MT in 1975. The Soviet Union's annual catch of hake off the Washington, Oregon, and California coasts was limited to 150,000 MT during the period from 1971 to 1975. Pacific ocean perch were regulated by quotas in the Aleutian region and along the northwest coast of the United States. It appears that Japan and the Soviet Union accepted the quotas established by the United States in bilateral consultations and agreed that they were necessary to promote conservation of fish stocks, even though each preferred larger quotas.[124] Catches by the German Democratic Republic, Poland, Republic of Korea, and Taiwan were not regulated by quotas prior to extended jurisdiction.

Marine mammals in the North Pacific provide an interesting example of allocation arrangements that fix the share of the total catch allocated to each signatory nation but limit harvesting to the coastal states. Under the 1957 Fur Seal Convention,[125] fur seals harvested by the Soviet Union and the United States are allocated 70 percent to the harvesting nations and 15 percent each to Canada and Japan, with minor modifications for seals taken for scientific research.

Total catch quotas for whales in the North Pacific have been set under the aegis of the International Whaling Commission since 1966.[126] The total catch quotas, however, were originally set above the existing harvest levels, which were already too high to protect the stocks and therefore did little to conserve them.[127] In addition, the early IWC quotas were set for the region but not on an individual species basis. The United States has taken a strong stance in favor of reducing whale quotas in the North Pacific since 1970. Japan and the Soviet Union continue to support higher quotas, and considerable debate occurs over the interpretation of data and calculation of stock sizes for the species to be harvested. The actual allocation of the total catch quota to individual nations is not done by IWC. Japan and the Soviet Union, the major whaling nations in the North Pacific, appear to use percentage of historical catches as the allocation rule for dividing the IWC North Pacific whale quota between themselves.[128]

Allocation of stocks under the Japan—Republic of Korea agreement of 1965 provides only for overall limits on catch to be obtained by the two nations in their fisheries in the joint fisheries zone. This limit is 150,000 MT for each nation. The Japan—People's Republic of China agreement of 1975 does not allocate the stocks by quota. Little is known about the allocation arrangements in the other agreements for fisheries in the Northwest Pacific. Presumably the catch by the Democratic People's Republic of Korea is regulated by a quota set in negotiations with the Soviet Union. The Democratic People's Republic of Korea—People's Republic of China agreement provides for cooperation but presumably not allocation.[129]

It appears that distant-water fishing nations have been persuaded to accept quotas on crab, herring, and halibut in the Northeast Pacific in consultation with the coastal states on the basis that reduction of fishing effort is necessary to protect the stocks under principles of scientific management. Probably the willingness of the United States to permit access to ports for reprovisioning, and its contiguous zone for loading and fishing, was an incentive of some importance to Japanese and Soviets in their acceptance of the quotas in the Northeast Pacific.

## Claims to Accommodate Fishing Practices

Along with the claims to prescribe regulations for conservation and allocation, coastal states have also made claims to accommodate fishing practices. These claims involve two classes of interaction: gear conflicts and incidental catches. Gear conflicts can be defined as physical damage inflicted by the use of one type of gear on other types of gear, or as an unacceptable rate of damage to the targeted fishery stock due to nonselectivity of the gear employed. In contrast, incidental catch can be defined as the inadvertent capture of species of fish, not the object of the fishery being pursued, that leads to a negative impact on the stocks of nontargeted species. Causes of gear conflicts are varied. The most serious conflicts in the North Pacific have been caused by the use of mobile fishing gear (like trawls) in areas where fixed gear (like crab pots and setlines) are being employed. The major incidental catch problems have occurred in the northeastern Pacific and involve halibut and Pacific ocean perch.

## Gear Conflicts

Discussion of gear conflicts in the Northeast Pacific is limited to two types of interaction: (1) those related to trawl fishing and pot fishing for crabs and sablefish (blackcod), and (2) those related to dragnet or trawl fishing for groundfish and shrimp. As a measure of the scale of conflict, the U.S. Coast Guard reported that during a five-year period in the early 1970s, 250 claims of gear damage amounting to $600,000 were made by the American fishing industry.[130]

As early as 1964 and 1965, Japanese and Soviet trawlers operating in the southeastern Bering Sea and the western part of the Gulf of Alaska near Kodiak Island interfered with and caused direct damage to crab fishing carried out by Americans in the same areas.[131] This led to the United States establishing extensive areas reserved for crab pot fishing, and eliminated trawl fishing in these areas through bilateral agreements with Japan and the Soviet Union. These areas have been adjusted and expanded in subsequent negotiations and have resulted in a substantial reduction in gear conflicts. Serious conflicts also arose between Japan and the Soviet Union over crab operations in the eastern Bering Sea. In 1967, at the instigation of the United States, Japan and the Soviet Union reached agreement on dividing the crabbing grounds into eight strips 10–12 miles wide to be shared equally by the two countries on a rotating basis. The cooperation of foreign fishing nations in reducing gear conflicts of this type, even though they occurred on the high seas, was obtained by the United States in exchange for permission to fish within the contiguous zones of the United States for species not utilized by domestic fisheries, for loading zones in territorial waters, and for entry into ports for reprovisioning and other purposes.

Several other gear conflicts are worthy of mention, although they did not reach the severity of the crab-groundfish problem. Conflicts between fixed and mobile gear occurred in the halibut longline fishery, but the conflict over gear interactions was not as significant as the incidental catch problem associated with the Soviet and Japanese trawl fisheries and halibut. The settlement of the incidental catch problem (discussed below) also ameliorated the gear conflict. Conflicts between Canadian salmon troll fisheries and Soviet trawlers on the fishing grounds southwest of Vancouver Island led to bilateral negotiations between the two countries in which the Soviet Union agreed to restrict its operations beyond the twelve-mile contiguous fisheries zone of Canada for authorization to use West Coast Canadian ports for transshipment.[132]

The mere physical presence of large Japanese and Soviet trawlers was a formidable sight to Canadian and American domestic fishermen. Even if they produced no direct damage, the psychological effect of foreign fishing fleets in the same areas fished traditionally by coastal fishermen was enough to raise appeals for government protection.[133]

Besides the gear conflicts mentioned above, discarding gear in areas where it interfered with subsequent fishing activity became an increasing problem. Other boats fishing in the area suffered damage to their gear and lost time disentangling their gear from the discarded gear, and marine mammals and seabirds were trapped in the meshes of the cast-off nets and drowned. Provisions requiring that worn or damaged gear not be discarded on the fishing grounds have been included in recent bilateral agreements.[134]

The frequency and severity of damage claims arising out of gear conflicts involving the Soviet Union and the United States, and the virtual impossibility of seeking judicial settlement in American and Soviet courts, made it desirable for the two nations to agree on a claims settlement procedure in a bilateral agreement in 1972.[135] Poland and the United States have a similar agreement for the Northeast Atlantic, which would presumably also apply to the North Pacific although no claims have been made for that area. Under the U.S.–USSR Fisheries Claims Board, 72 cases had been handled by 1976, of which 28 involved incidents in the Northeast Pacific. Of these claims, 11 were accepted and total damages of nearly $63,000 were paid by the Soviet Union to American claimants.[136] Of the remaining 17 claims, 5 were refused on the basis that they occurred prior to the period the Board was permitted to consider claims; 7 were dropped because the Board could not rule in favor of the claimant; 3 were deficient as submitted; and 2 were withdrawn by request of the claimants. The U.S.–USSR Fisheries Claims Board facilitated the settlement of claims put forth by nationals of one country against nationals of another but, more importantly, it established a set of rules that each party recommended to their nationals to reduce the number of conflicts.

In the Northwest Pacific, the major gear conflict appears to be that between Japan and the Soviet Union in the northern Sea of Japan, off Hokkaido, and along the Pacific coast of Japan. The Soviet Union expanded fishing operations in these areas in the late 1960s in pursuit of sardines and mackerel that migrated along the coast. Soviet vessels were reported to have entered Japanese territorial waters, and substantial damage was done to the Japanese coastal and offshore fishing activities. Table 4.4 shows the increasing damage claims against the Soviet Union reported to the Japanese government by persons fishing in the areas. This led to negotiations between the two governments in 1974, and an agreement was

TABLE 4.4

JAPANESE DAMAGE CLAIMS AGAINST THE SOVIET UNION, 1971–1976

| Year | Within 12 mi | | Outside 12 mi | | Total | Damage value (mill. yen) |
|------|------------------|------------------|------------------|------------------|-------|--------------|
|      | No. of incidents | Percentage in area | No. of incidents | Percentage in area | | |
| 1971 | 16 | 40 | 24 | 60 | 40 | |
| 1972 | 0 | | 15 | 100 | 15 | |
| 1973 | 11 | 9 | 112 | 91 | 123 | 64 |
| 1974 | 675 | 65 | 367 | 35 | 1042 | 340 |
| 1975 | 97 | 30 | 230 | 70 | 327 | 89 |
| 1976 (4–12) | 184 | 61 | 117 | 39 | 301 | 58 |
| Total | 983 | (53) | 865 | (47) | 1848 (100) | |

Source: Fishery Agency of Japan, 1977.

signed in 1975 that related to boat markings, lights and signals on fishing boats, and other controls. These measures resulted in a reduction in claims for damages by roughly two-thirds with respect to the number of incidents and the amount of damages claimed.[137] Despite the submission of the claims to the Soviet Union under the claims settlement provisions of the agreement, no compensation had been paid to Japanese fishermen by the Soviet Union as of late 1977. The Japanese government, however, provided compensation amounting to over $3 million to the affected fishing interests.[138]

Conflicts between the Soviet Union and Japan on crab fishing operations off the west coast of Kamchatka brought about the creation of national operation zones in that area. The zones were exchanged on an annual basis.

Japan and the Republic of Korea have persistent gear conflicts in the East China Sea outside of the joint regulation area established by agreement, and expanded Korean fisheries in the northern Sea of Japan have caused some damages in that area.[139] The latter dispute has been ameliorated by negotiations between the two governments under which Korea agreed to restrict its fishing to areas 12 miles outside the Japanese coast.

Both the Japan—Republic of Korea and Japan—People's Republic of China agreements established areas that were restricted to use of specific gear during certain time periods. Furthermore, the Japan—Korean agreement also placed limits on the amount of gear that could be used within the given areas. All of these provisions resulted in a reduction of gear conflicts in the area, regardless of whether or not that was the prime reason for agreement.

## Incidental Catch

Incidental catches have presented significant conflicts between nations fishing in the Northeast Pacific but have apparently not posed major problems in the Northwest Pacific. This can perhaps be explained in part by the nature of the fisheries operations and management philosophies, and in part by the special conditions existing in the Northeast Pacific. The Northwest Pacific nations tend to view trawl fishery harvests more in terms of the total catch than of the species composition, although the latter is not entirely neglected. Thus, species like halibut caught in trawls receive no particular treatment. In the Northeast Pacific, halibut, Pacific ocean perch, and salmon comprise the bulk of catches by North Americans, and other groundfish species have been traditionally neglected. Canada and the United States have developed fishery management policies oriented to the protection of certain species; these policies conflict with the efficient operations of foreign trawl fisheries. The fact that halibut and Pacific ocean perch are found in greater commercial aggregations in the Northeast Pacific than in the Northwest Pacific has also contributed to the development of different national approaches to fisheries management.

Halibut have been managed under a bilateral agreement between Canada and the United States since 1923. Until the mid-1960s halibut catches had been rising in response to the successful management of the International Pacific Halibut Commission (IPHC). The development of large-scale, multispecies foreign trawl fisheries commenced in the Northeast Pacific in the 1960s, and halibut were caught along with other species of groundfish. It is estimated that over 13,500 MT of halibut were caught by foreign trawlers in the Northeast Pacific in 1971.[140] This constituted an incidental catch roughly equal to one-third of the strictly regulated commercial setline halibut fishery, and 95 percent of the halibut catch in the Bering Sea.[141] The trawl-caught halibut tended to be younger than setline-caught halibut, and this produced a negative impact on both yield and recruitment of the stock. This situation resulted in a precipitous decline in the stocks of halibut available for Canadian and American halibut fleets, and brought domestic pressure to bear on the governments to reduce the incidental catch rates by foreign trawlers.

In 1970 and 1971, Japan and the Soviet Union agreed to certain restrictions on trawling in areas where halibut were found, but the restrictions were inadequate to bring about full recovery of the stocks. The IPHC proposed that certain areas of the Bering Sea and Northeast Pacific be closed to foreign trawling during periods when the catch of halibut in trawls was high. This proposal was accepted in bilateral negotiations between the United States and Japan in 1975, and the United States and the Soviet Union in 1976. In surveys conducted in 1975 the abundance of juvenile halibut had already increased in the Bering Sea.[142] It is expected that the closure will increase the catch of commercial halibut setline fisheries in the future.

The incidental catch of crab in the trawl fishery of the eastern Bering Sea was also a problem. The INPFC Subcommittee on King and Tanner Crab estimated that foreign trawl fishing in that area captured over 100 million tanner crabs per year, and that about 60−70 percent of the catch was killed before it could be returned to the water.[143] Since the estimates for the total tanner crab stock size range from 2.4 to 3.5 billion crabs, more information is needed to assess the impact of this catch on the stocks. The incidental catch of tanner crabs on a numerical basis was six to eight times the level of the commercial catch.[144]

The situation for incidental catches of salmon was less clear, but was an important political issue. American and Canadian commercial salmon fishermen claimed to have observed foreign fleets setting nets to capture salmon and taking salmon incidentally in their groundfish trawls in the Northeast Pacific.[145] Because it was not possible for enforcement officials to investigate the reports as the foreign vessels were operating outside North American jurisdiction, it was difficult to determine the validity of the charges made.[146] Whether or not catches of salmon were intentional or inadvertent had little to do with the demands to remove foreign fishing fleets from the coastal areas. The mere presence of foreign fleets was an irritant to many coastal fishermen.

Another example of incidental catch problems occurred in the Soviet Union's Pacific hake fishery off the coasts of Washington and Oregon. When the catch of Pacific ocean perch declined in the Gulf of Alaska in 1964−65, the Soviet Union shifted its fleet to fishing for perch off the northwestern coast of the United States. This led to a rapid decline in the perch stocks in that area and the Soviets began targeting on Pacific hake.[147] In addition to hake, the Soviets caught Pacific ocean perch in their trawls. This led to continued pressure on depleted stocks of perch and the end of a domestic fishery for that species. The depletion of a stock of importance to domestic fishermen through incidental catches exacerbated demands for government intervention, which led to the establishment of restricted trawling in areas off the Washington and Oregon coasts in 1970 and 1971.

Considerable interest was generated over the problem of seabird and Dall porpoise mortalities in the high-seas salmon gill net fishing of Japan prior to extended jurisdiction. It was estimated that each year between 214,000–715,000 seabirds and some 14,000 Dall porpoise were being caught incidentally in this fishery.[148] Precisely what impact this has on seabird or porpoise populations is unknown, but the U.S. considers the large numbers of incidentally caught species undesirable because of its interest in protecting marine animals, and because it violated international agreements protecting migratory birds.

The desire to protect the operations of coastal fishing fleets, and the species caught by them, from the damage inflicted by distant-water fishing fleets brought about a considerable amount of diplomatic maneuvering on the part of coastal states in the Northeast Pacific. Attempts were made to reduce gear conflicts and to provide a means of obtaining compensation for the damages when they occurred. Similarly, the interests of the coastal state in protecting certain species and the interests of foreign trawling nations in efficient operations produced conflict over the incidental harvest of crab, halibut, hake, and salmon. This conflict resulted in restricted seasons, areas, and quotas. Distant-water fishing nations have been reluctant to accept regulation of gear conflicts and incidental catches on the high seas, but have responded to the need to regulate stocks for conservation. They have been willing to cooperate with coastal states in exchange for port privileges, loading privileges in protected territorial seas, and limited access to contiguous fishing zones for fishing.

## Claims to Enforce Prescriptions

After claims have been made to regulate fisheries for purposes of conservation, and prescriptions have been made for allocation and accommodation of fishing practices, it is necessary to enforce these controls if they are not voluntarily accepted. The basic regime for fisheries enforcement in the North Pacific did not differ substantially from other world fishing regions, although the capacity to implement the regulations was probably greater. The coastal state had sovereign enforcement authority within territorial waters, and by the mid-1970s coastal state enforcement was generally recognized for contiguous fishing zones of 12 miles. On the high seas, each nation retained enforcement authority (flag state authority) over its own fishing vessels.

Enforcement authority over foreign fishing vessels operating in the territorial sea, contiguous fisheries zone, and on the high seas can be modified by international agreement to make it relatively more exclusive or inclusive. In the fisheries agreements between nations fishing in the North Pacific, most of the enforcement functions were reserved for the flag state, as can be seen in table 4.5.

Due to the extensive areas of the North Pacific and the long coastlines of many bordering nations, it was virtually impossible to monitor all fishing activities for violations, even when monitoring efforts were strategically directed in certain important fisheries. Much of the success of enforcement activities in the area therefore relied upon voluntary compliance by other fishing nations and the deterrent effect of penalties for violations, loss of fishing time when vessels were seized, and so on.

While the overall problem of enforcement conflicts had been reduced to a fairly low level by the mid-1970s, past conflicts were major, and sometimes violent. The most severe

## TABLE 4.5

### Enforcement Provisions of Selected Fisheries Conventions in the North Pacific

| | General enforcement scheme | Implementation and enforcement | Stop and board | Inspection or search | Arrests | Seizure | Conduct of prosecutions | Penalties | Other |
|---|---|---|---|---|---|---|---|---|---|
| Fraser River Salmon Convention | 2 | 10 | | | 40 | 50 | 60 | 70 | |
| Convention for the Regulation of Whaling | 1 | 10 | | 32 | 40 | 50 | 60 | | |
| International Convention for the High Seas Fisheries of the North Pacific Ocean | 2 | 11 | 21 | 33 | 41 | 51 | 60 | 70 71 | 80 81 |
| Convention for the Halibut Fishery of the North Pacific | 2 | 10 | | | 40 | 50 | 60 | 70 | |
| Convention on the High Seas Fisheries of the Northwest Pacific Ocean | 2 | 10 | 22 | 31 | 43 | 53 | 60 | 70 | 80 |
| Interim Convention on the Conservation of North Pacific Fur Seals | 2 | 10 | 22 | 31 | 42 | 52 | 60 | 70 72 | 81 83 |
| Agreement Between Japan and Korea on Fisheries | 1 | 10 | 20 | 30 | | | | 71 | 82 |
| U.S.–Japan Fisheries Off the Coast of the U.S. and Salmon Fisheries | 1 | 12 | | | | | | | |
| U.S.–Japan King and Tanner Crab Fisheries in the Eastern Bering Sea | 1 | 12 | | | | | | | 85 84 |
| U.S.–USSR King and Tanner Crab Agreement | 1 | 12 | 23 | 34 | | | | | 85 |
| U.S.–USSR Fisheries Problems in the Northeast Pacific Ocean | 1 | 12 | | | | | | | |
| U.S.–USSR Fishing Operations in the Northeastern Pacific Ocean | 3 | | | | | | | | |

Source: After William T. Burke, Richard Legatski, and William W. Woodhead, *National and International Law Enforcement in the Ocean* (Seattle: Washington Sea Grant Publication in Cooperation with the Institute for Marine Studies, University of Washington Press, 1975), pp. 184–192.

Key:

*General Enforcement Scheme*
1. Enforcement by flag state.
2. Joint enforcement of some functions; flag state enforcement of some functions.
3. No specific enforcement provisions.

*General Implementation and Enforcement Provisions*
10. General requirement to adopt laws, regulations or measures to give effect to the provisions of the agreement with specific reference to penalties.
11. Requirement that the party or parties concerned adopt laws, regulations, or measures to enforce the agreement in conservation areas. The abstaining party or parties may observe conduct of enforcement in conservation areas. Otherwise, the same as 10.
12. Requirement that contracting parties take measures to insure their nationals and vessels conduct fishing with due regard for the conservation of the stocks of fish, and other provisions of the agreement.

*Stop and Board*
20. Stopping (and presumably boarding) by flag state only.
21. Boarding by authorized officials of any party.
22. Same as 21, but with a reasonable ground requirement.
23. Boarding by duly authorized officials of one contracting party of other's vessels permited upon request.

*Inspect or Search*
30. Inspection by flag state only.
31. Search by authorized official of any party provided that there are reasonable grounds.
32. Observation by international and/or national observers on vessels and at land stations.
33. Search of fishing vessel's equipment, books, documents, or other articles, and questioning of persons on board by authorized official of any party.

*Arrest*
40. Arrest by authorized official of any party.
41. Same as 40, but with reasonable grounds requirement.
42. Arrest by authorized official of any party after search and with reasonable grounds.

*Seizure*
50. Seizure by authorized official of any party.
51. Same as 50, but with reasonable grounds requirement.
52. Seizure by authorized official of any party after search and with reasonable grounds.
53. Seizure by authorized official of any party if it becomes clear as the result of a search that a violation hs been committed.

*Conduct of Prosecutions*
60. Flag state prosecution or disposition of offenses.

*Penalties*
70. Penalties imposed by flag state.
71. Commission may recommend equivalent penalties.
72. Provides for forfeiture of fishing gear and illegally taken catch.

*Other*
80. Reporting of national implementation required.
81. Reporting of enforcement activity required.
82. Requires adoption of measures to prohibit landing and selling of illegal lobster.
83. Dispute settlement system provided.
84. Requires reporting of inspection results to the flag state.
85. Requires each contracting party to permit other contracting party to observe the conduct of enforcement of the provisions of the agreement.

conflicts were in the northwestern Pacific between Japan and, respectively, People's Republic of China (PRC), Republic of Korea (ROK), and the Soviet Union. The conflicts basically stemmed from Japan's refusal to recognize the military and fishing zones of PRC, the Peace Line established by ROK, and the Soviet Union's claim to the northern islands— the Habomai group, Shikotan, Kunashiri, and Etorofu.

Japan exerted considerable control over its fishing industry through its license policy for distant-water fishing activities and by sending patrol boats along with the fleets in most major fishing areas.[149] The fact that so many Japanese vessels and crew members were seized in PRC, ROK, and Soviet areas indicates that Japan considered the claims by the coastal nation to be contrary to international law, and therefore deliberately asserted its rights to fish on the high seas, or in the case of the northern islands, in what it claimed as Japanese waters. Japan preferred to protest the seizures through diplomatic channels rather than to acquiesce to the unilateral claims. If Japan had ceased fishing in the disputed areas, it was concerned that it might be considered a de facto recognition of the coastal state action. In each case, the coastal state placed pressure on Japan to sign an agreement to reduce the conflict; the coastal states increased their harassment of Japanese vessels through enforcement of unilateral claims.[150]

The relationship between Japan and the PRC under the nongovernmental enforcement of the agreement tended to fluctuate independently of the level of violation of the agreement, which indicated that fisheries were not the only issue at stake.[151] In general, the signing of bilateral agreements between Japan and the other nations resulted in a decrease in the recorded violations, although the dispute with the Soviet Union has still not been resolved, and Soviet enforcement of its claims results in continued protest by Japan.

Other conflicts over enforcement have existed between Japan, Democratic People's Republic of Korea, and the Republic of Korea. These have been violent at times and have had a generally deterrent effect on violations of the imprecisely defined fisheries and military zones claimed in the area. Considerable care is taken by the Republic of Korea to avoid violations of Soviet and People's Republic of China fishing zones and other areas, since it does not have diplomatic relations with them. Japan also objected to the enforcement of the Clark Line against Japanese fishing vessels by the United Nations naval ships. The Republic of Korea, on the other hand, was upset when the measure was suspended in 1953.[152] Japan and the Republic of Korea disputed the ownership of Takeshima-Dokto Island; Japanese fishing fleets for squid and other species in the Sea of Japan were advised by a temporary administrative order to avoid conflict with the Republic of Korea by remaining 12 miles outside the island.[153]

Under the Northwest Pacific Ocean Fisheries Convention of 1956, Japan and the Soviet Union agreed to enforcement by officials of either contracting party if there was reasonable cause to believe that a fishing vessel was violating the terms of the agreement. At the time of signature, this applied only to areas north of 45° north latitude. In 1962, when the provisions of the salmon agreement were extended south of that line, the Soviet Union sought to extend its enforcement jurisdiction. This was resisted strenuously by Japan, since the area was wholly on the high seas and Japanese fishing vessels were the only ones engaged in fishing for salmon there. The conflict was settled by allowing Japan to voluntarily enforce the regulations in 1963 but, thereafter, Japanese patrol vessels were required to carry a Soviet official observer on board.[154]

Japan has felt powerless to resist the incursion of the Soviet fishing fleet in Japanese waters. Since Japan claimed only a three-mile territorial sea and not an extended fisheries zone, the Soviet fleets could fish close inshore. This disturbed coastal fishing communities and damaged many coastal fisheries, but Japan had no grounds for seizure of the Soviet ships. Even where there were violations of the three-mile territorial sea, Japan was reluctant to seize Soviet ships for fear of Soviet retaliation by harassment of the large Japanese fisheries in Soviet waters.

In the Northeast Pacific, enforcement problems have not reached the scale of conflict they attained in the Northwest Pacific. Between Canada and the United States, under the INPFC, the Halibut Convention, Salmon Fishing Convention and Reciprocal Fishing agreements, the enforcement authority of either nation included inspection and seizure by any member of a vessel of another party to the convention that was in violation of the agreement, and return of the vessel to the state of origin for prosecution.

An early conflict embroiled Great Britain and the United States in controversy over the right of the United States to enforce its presidential declarations in 1889 and 1890, proclaiming the authority to regulate for sealing in the Bering Sea. This raised the threat of naval confrontation until the revenue cutters of the United States were recalled to Seattle, and the British warships in Japan and British Columbia were not dispatched.[155] One instance has been noted where several Japanese sealers were killed by American enforcement agents who were attempting to enforce the ban on pelagic sealing and land-based harvest by foreigners in the Pribilof Islands.[156]

A total of 31 vessels in the Japanese high-seas salmon fisheries fleet were observed in violation of the abstention line during the period from 1961 to 1975. Most of these violations occurred close to the abstention line, although a few vessels were noted as much as several hundred miles inside the areas.[157] No Canadian vessels have been observed in violation of the abstention line. Japan, as the state of origin, was responsible for prosecution of the reported violations of INPFC agreement. Concern has been expressed by North Americans that the punitive measures taken by Japan were inadequate.

Given the extensive enforcement efforts of the U.S. Coast Guard and National Marine Fisheries Service personnel in waters of the United States prior to extended jurisdiction, it is generally concluded that enforcement is effective and that compliance is high. One example that supports this view points to the record of no violations by the Soviet fleet posted in their large hake fishery off the coasts of Washington, Oregon, and California between 1966 and 1976.[158] Most fleets from nations with substantial fisheries in the northeastern Pacific are accompanied by patrol boats that monitor the fleet activity to prevent violations. The Soviet Union even has a fleet commander who directs and monitors the activities of the fleet. These actions reduce the conflicts with Canada and the United States.[159]

## THE TREND IN FISHERIES CONFLICTS

The overall trend in fisheries conflicts in the North Pacific can be characterized along several dimensions. First, the assertion of coastal state control over the right to prescribe regulations for purposes of conservation has resulted in agreements with distant-water fishing nations that basically legitimize claims between the contracting parties. This represents a movement away from the inclusive regime of the high seas to a more exclusive control by the coastal state. Second, the claim by the coastal state to allocate certain important fishery resources has resulted in an increasing share being allocated to the coastal state. Third, the number and severity of gear conflicts and incidental catch conflicts have increased along with the intensity of fishing effort in the North Pacific. Completely satisfactory means were not found to resolve them, although such measures as gear sanctuary areas and closed seasons reduced the conflicts significantly, and claim settlement procedures were adopted to provide compensation for damages. Fourth, some of the more severe enforcement conflicts of post-World War II were resolved through international agreements. Others, like the Japan–Soviet conflict on the northern islands, continue to cause problems for fisheries. In short, the conflicts have shifted from confrontation on the high seas to discussion at the negotiating table. Still the pressure remains from coastal nations to continue to expand control over fish stocks near their coastlines and to increase their share of allocated catch.

## TRENDS TOWARD EXTENDED COASTAL STATE JURISDICTION

Although our focus is on the North Pacific Ocean, we do not suggest that the stimulus for extended coastal state jurisdiction over fisheries originated here as a response to the problems faced by the U.S. and Canada vis-à-vis the distant-water fleets of Japan, the USSR, the ROK, and others. The trend toward extended jurisdiction was in evidence at the first Codification Conference on the Law of the Sea hosted by the League of Nations in 1930; it was accelerated by the unresolved conflicts on the territorial sea at the First and Second United Nations Conferences on the Law of the Sea in 1958 and 1960; and it became the dominant mode of coastal state action during the decade 1968–1978 coincident with activities related to the Third United Nations Conference on the Law of the Sea. *Actions taken by Canada and the United States, substantially affecting the pattern of interaction on fisheries issues in the North Pacific, have therefore to be understood primarily in a global context.*

### Trends in the Law of the Sea and Actions by Canada and the United States

One of the many ironies that plague attempts to codify the Law of the Sea is that each conference that has been called to stabilize the limits of coastal state jurisdiction has accelerated the trend to wider limits. For example, prior to the League Conference in 1930, clearly a predominant number of states adhered to a three-mile territorial sea with no extensions of authority beyond that for fishing. Of twenty-two states that replied to a questionnaire distributed by the Preparatory Committee for the Conference, sixteen were in favor of a three-mile territorial sea, two were in favor of four miles, two were in favor of six miles, one was in favor of eighteen miles, and one advocated whatever limit the coastal state unilaterally preferred.[160]

By the end of the Conference in 1930, nineteen states were in favor of three miles, four were in favor of four miles, ten were in favor of six miles and one was in favor of twelve miles.[161] At that time, Portugal led the fight for extending coastal state jurisdiction over fisheries by first advocating a territorial sea of eighteen miles, then falling back to twelve, and finally offering a compromise of a six-mile territorial sea and a six-mile exclusive fisheries zone.

At the end of the Second UN Conference on the Law of the Sea, a number of states (22) still adhered to a three-mile territorial sea but a clear majority (33) were in favor of limits broader than three miles.[162] The most popular options for extended limits were six miles (ten states) and twelve miles (thirteen states). Perhaps the most dramatic moment of the 1960 Conference occurred when the compromise of a six-mile territorial sea with a six-mile exclusive fishing zone failed of adoption by a single vote.

In 1960 only four states (Chile, Costa Rica, El Salvador, and Peru) advocated a territorial sea of two hundred miles. In 1980, as the Third United Nations Conference on the Law of the Sea (UNCLOS III) was drawing to a close, fifteen states had enacted 200-mile territorial seas and eighty-four had unilaterally extended exclusive jurisdiction over fisheries out to two hundred miles. Moreover, the Draft Convention produced by the Conference gives the coastal state sovereign rights over living and nonliving resources in an economic zone extending two hundred miles from the baseline used to measure the territorial sea, the breadth of which is now declared to be twelve miles. Within this economic zone, the coastal state has the competence to determine the allowable catch and its own capacity to harvest all or any portion of that catch. This competence is nonreviewable.

The course by which two former stalwart defenders of a three-mile territorial sea, Canada and the United States, came unilaterally to adopt legislation extending their exclusive jurisdiction over fisheries to a distance of 200 miles from their coasts was long, tortuous, and different. The Canadian experience has already been analyzed in detail by Barbara Johnson.[163] She shows that Canada began to espouse unilateral action only four years after the failure of the Second UN Conference by passing the Territorial Sea and Fishing Zones Act in 1964. This Act established a contiguous zone for fishing extending nine miles beyond the territorial sea of three miles. An amendment to this Act in 1970 extended the territorial sea to twelve miles.

As preparations for the Third United Nations Conference on the Law of the Sea got underway in 1971, there began to be a convergence in points of view on the Economic Zone—Patrimonial Sea between the Latin American and African Groups. These were quite firmly cemented by 1972, and the position was formally espoused by Canada between 1973 and 1974. These developments occurred simultaneously with U.S. and Canada moves within the International Commission for the Northwest Atlantic Fisheries (ICNAF) to extend coastal state control over fisheries. The position adopted in 1970, however, called for the recognition of preferential rights for the coastal state rather than outright ownership of all living resources within the extended zone.

The longer it took for the Law of the Sea Conference to resolve outstanding differences on other issues, the more intense the demands became for unilateral action on domestic fisheries in Canada and the U.S., and in May 1975 the Fisheries Council of Canada publicly called for such action. This reinforced continuing Canadian moves to exert coastal state control within ICNAF. However, as the Spring 1976 session of UNCLOS III in New York again produced no agreement on a Treaty, it appeared that the Canadian government yielded to internal pressures for unilateral action and announced that a two-hundred-mile exclusive fisheries zone would go into effect on January 1, 1977. This decision, in turn, had major impact on Canadian bilateral negotiations within the ICNAF arrangement. It also raised the issue of bilateral negotiations with the United States.

The United States move toward extended jurisdiction over fisheries involved far more internal dissension than Canada's and, in fact, antedates the First and Second UN Conferences on the Law of the Sea. The first action of the United States in this direction was the "Presidential Proclamation with Respect to Coastal Fisheries in Certain Areas of the High Seas" made on September 28, 1945. It is important to emphasize that this Proclamation did not actually assert extended jurisdiction over high-seas areas, although in conjunction with the Proclamation on the Continental Shelf, it certainly precipitated such claims by West Coast Latin American states.

The Proclamation sought to "establish conservation zones in those areas of the high seas contiguous to the coast of the United States wherein fishing activities have been, or in the future may be, developed and maintained on a substantial scale."[164] It was aimed in fact at the increasing Japanese fishing effort on the sockeye salmon runs out of Bristol Bay, a concern that eventually led to the negotiation of the INPFC arrangements with Japan and Canada.

> The Truman fisheries proclamation was never, however, implemented into law. . . . [T]he proclamation *per se* asserts no claim to exclusive fisheries jurisdiction over high seas fishing areas off the coast of the United States. Instead, it is stated, the purpose of the fisheries proclamation was to establish, as U.S. policy, that where fishing activities were developed or maintained jointly by the United States and other nations, conservation zones would be established—but only pursuant to agreement between the United States and such other nations. The domestic implementation of this proclamation has been mainly through State Department attempts to negotiate international agreements to protect certain species of fish which were threatened by the Japanese, most notably the salmon.[165]

The next attempt to extend U.S. conservation authority came in 1952 with the negotiation of the INPFC arrangements, which have already been described.

As previously mentioned, although some sporadic Japanese fishing for bottomfish occurred in the Bering Sea prior to World War II, major increases in fishing effort of a continuous nature did not occur in the Northeast Pacific until the latter half of the 1950s, and in the Northwest Atlantic until early in the 1960s. In the case of the Northeast Pacific, the two major distant-water participants were the USSR and Japan. In the Northwest Atlantic, these two were also involved, but in addition the fleets of seventeen or eighteen other countries were fishing heavily off the coasts of the U.S. and Canada. Growing foreign fishing effort increased the difficulties of the U.S. and Canadian coastal fishermen who consistently claimed that they were faced with preemption of grounds, startling increases in gear conflicts and gear loss, declining domestic catches of preferred species, and increasing harvest of incidental or directed catches of preferred species by the foreigners. The discontent this generated (as did high-density fishing by Japanese and Soviet fleets in the Northeast Pacific) led to more frequent demands to exclude foreign fisheries by fishermen's organizations in New England, Alaska, and Washington. Coincidentally, the senators and congressmen from these areas were rather powerful figures in the U.S. Congress, so fishermen began to exert a much greater influence on U.S. policy than their numbers and significance in the national economy would normally have allowed them.

The first direct result of this growing influence was the Bartlett Act of 1964, sponsored by Senator E. L. Bartlett of Alaska, which prohibited foreign fishing within the three-mile territorial sea of the United States and on the continental shelf.[166] An amendment to this Act was passed in 1966 extending U.S. exclusive jurisdiction over fisheries nine miles beyond the outer limit of the territorial sea.

The reason that proposals to extend U.S. jurisdiction over fishing beyond twelve miles generated such intense internal conflict is that U.S. interests vis-à-vis the oceans are more varied than Canada's, several interests being mutually exclusive, or at least severely incompatible. This is demonstrated quite clearly in the U.S. approaches to the Law of the Sea negotiations, particularly between 1971 and 1974. These interests are analyzed by Miles:

> For example, from the very beginning it was clear that the U.S. conceptualized the major problems of UNCLOS III as involving a trade-off between resources and navigation. The U.S. proposed as a package a solution including a 12-mile territorial sea, a guarantee of unimpeded passage through straits used for international jurisdiction and preferential rights for the coastal state over demersal species beyond 12 miles based on a formula involving the harvesting capacity of the coastal state. Later, separate treatment was claimed for anadromous and highly migratory ocean species (mainly tuna).
>
> This policy is a striking example of the way in which states attempt to reconcile their own conflicting internal interests while negotiating with the outside world. The initial perception of the trade-off between resources and navigation clearly signalled U.S. preoccupation with security interests as its highest priority. However, the willingness to trade on the governmental position regarding fisheries was constrained by nervousness within the Department of Defense (DOD) about 'creeping jurisdiction' and by the need to reconcile the conflicting interests of the U.S. fishing industry divided among coastal fishermen (mainly demersal species), salmon fisheries, and long-distance fisheries for tuna and shrimp. The DOD concern was met by restricting extended coastal state jurisdiction to fisheries and by vesting control over allowable catch in international organizations which all signatory coastal states would be obliged to join. Conflicting fisheries' interests were initially reconciled by separating out coastal species, over which the U.S. would exercise extended jurisdiction, from anadromous and highly migratory species.
>
> There was an appealing elegance to this formulation but it was only an initial submission in a very long series of negotiations. The implication, therefore, was always that as the U.S. moved towards the opposing coalition, as it would have to in order to get a treaty, it was more likely to

compromise on the living resources than on either the military interests or the nonliving resources. In fact, at the beginning, the U.S. package included a significant concession on mineral resources in the continental shelf, but this was vigorously and continuously opposed by U.S. oil companies. It was therefore not likely that further concessions would easily be forthcoming. In any event, most coastal states seemed to be moving towards control of the entire continental margin. The compromises would, as a result, have to be at the expense of the fishing industry, the shipping industry, including oil companies as owners of tanker fleets, and the oceanographers. The latter two were embroiled as the proponents of the economic zone began to do just what DOD feared, i.e., facilitate the creeping of coastal state jurisdiction.[167]

At the same time that pressures for a 200-mile economic zone were rapidly gaining ground in UNCLOS III, the U.S. and Canada were cautiously extending coastal state jurisdiction in the International Commission for the Northwest Atlantic Fisheries (ICNAF). By 1972 the preferential rights system initiated in 1970 was fully in place. "Twenty-three agreements were negotiated by ICNAF in 1972, fourteen of which provided for national quotas in the area. Negotiated on the basis of the '40-40-10-10' formula, these agreements allocated an extra 10 percent for coastal states, thereby recognizing for the first time the preferential rights of the coastal states to Convention area fisheries."[168] These were followed in 1973 by an innovation in the approach to enforcement, whereby agents of the coastal states were permitted to board and inspect foreign fishing vessels in the areas affected. In 1973 also, the U.S. promoted another innovative approach in ICNAF, this time dealing with the regulation of fishing effort in the Convention area.[169]

The turning point for the U.S. position came in the Caracas session at UNCLOS III in 1974, where the U.S. delegation acknowledged that they would accept exclusive state jurisdiction over fisheries to two hundred miles in return for specified guarantees relating to navigation through international straits and the economic zone. Having accepted such a condition in UNCLOS III, the U.S. government began to lose the battle with internal supporters of unilateral action inside and outside of the U.S. Congress. For instance, in June of 1973, Senator Warren Magnuson of Washington introduced Bill S.1988 calling for the unilateral establishment of a 200-mile exclusive fisheries zone by the United States on an interim basis. The bill was successfully opposed by the Administration on the grounds that it would have jeopardized the Law of the Sea negotiations. Even though the bill passed the Senate in 1974, it died in the House from deliberate inaction.

As in the case of Canada, however, the longer the Law of the Sea Conference took to arrive at agreement, the greater internal pressures became for unilateral action since all existing fisheries conflicts continued unabated. In 1975, therefore, two new bills were introduced in the Congress: HR 200 was introduced in the House on January 14, 1975 by Congressman Gerald Studds of Massachusetts on behalf of himself and a large number of cosponsors. Later, on March 5, 1975, S. 961 was introduced in the Senate by Senator Magnuson. Eventually, a revised, combined version of both bills became the Fisheries Conservation and Management Act of the United States (Public Law 94−265) on April 13, 1976. This Act established a two hundred mile exclusive fisheries zone effective March 1, 1977. Its particulars differed most importantly from the Revised Single Negotiating Text,

Part II, in three respects, relating to anadromous species, highly migratory species, and enforcement.[170] The Administration had lost not only this battle with the Congress but also a subsequent one relating to U.S. participation in ICNAF. Not only was the Department of State required to give notice of intent to withdraw from the Convention in 1976, but the Congress insisted on withdrawal in 1977. Canada, however, chose to remain a member and to transform ICNAF into a mechanism for sharing the surplus with foreign fishing countries.

## Responses of the USSR, Japan, the Democratic People's Republic of Korea, and the People's Republic of China

While the phenomenon of extended fisheries jurisdiction has global significance for Soviet and Japanese fleets, table 4.6 shows that the Northeast Pacific and the Northwest Atlantic were critical for the USSR, while the Northeast Pacific was more important for Japan.

Extensions of coastal state jurisdiction off North America affected 18 percent of the USSR total catch in 1975. But, more importantly, extensions by coastal states in the Northeast Atlantic, while affecting only about 240,000 MT of Soviet catch, posed a problem of protecting Soviet stocks against fishermen of northeastern Atlantic states, in whose waters Soviet fishermen would no longer be allowed to fish. However, once extension of jurisdiction was considered by the USSR, there was no reason to limit the extension to the North Atlantic, given the global phenomenon and the size of Soviet resources in the Northwest Pacific.

This juxtaposition of events is the origin of the chain reaction that rapidly swept across North Pacific fisheries in 1976–1977. For the Japanese, the problem posed was most severe. Data presented in table 2.3 (chapter 2) show that the North Pacific accounted for more than 90 percent of the total Japanese catch between 1971 and 1975. In 1975, about 65 percent of the Japanese total catch was taken within 200 miles of Japan; of the remainder, by

TABLE 4.6

SOVIET AND JAPANESE CATCHES IN THE NORTHWEST ATLANTIC AND NORTHEAST PACIFIC, 1974–1976

(IN METRIC TONS)

| Country | Northwest Atlantic | | | Northeast Pacific | | |
|---|---|---|---|---|---|---|
| | 1974 | 1975 | 1976 | 1974 | 1975 | 1976 |
| USSR | 1,161,000 | 1,167,000 | 853,000 | 697,700[a] | 611,700[b] | 582,600[c] |
| Japan | 29,000 | 25,000 | 26,000 | 1,097,300[a] | 1,113,800[c] | 1,140,200[d] |

Sources: For the Northwest Atlantic: *ICNAF Statistical Bulletin*, vol. 26, 1977. For the Northeast Pacific:

[a]*FAO Yearbook of Fisheries Statistics*, no. 40 (1975) (Rome: 1976).

[b]NOAA, NMFS. *Marine Fisheries Review*, 39, 8 (August 1977).

[c]U.S. Dept. of State, Telegram to U.S. Embassies in Tokyo, Moscow, Warsaw, Seoul, Taipei, and Mexico. (Unclassified) November 31, 1977.

[d]Wlodzimierz Kaczynski, chap. 7, this volume.

far the lion's share (about 75 percent) was taken within the 200-mile zones of the USSR and the U.S.[171]

The ROK's problem was similar to Japan's. Table 2.3 (chapter 2) shows that the North Pacific accounted for between 90–94 percent of the total catch between 1971 and 1975. Most of this was in the form of Alaska pollock (*Theragra chalcograma*) taken within the Soviet 200-mile zone. While extension of jurisdiction by the U.S. was a serious problem since about one-third of the Korean catch would thereby be affected, extensions by the USSR would amount to a disaster; the ROK did not maintain diplomatic relations with the USSR and would therefore have to withdraw all its vessels.

During bilateral fisheries negotiations in November, 1976, the USSR accepted extension of U.S. jurisdiction over fisheries and indicated that their vessels would comply with U.S. law from March 1, 1977.[172] The implication was clear that the Soviets were contemplating extending their own jurisdiction, which in fact was done on December 10, 1976.[173] Faced with this act, and with continued near-shore fishing by Soviet fleets off its coasts, the government of Japan reluctantly extended its own jurisdiction to 200 miles on May 2, 1977. This action took effect on July 1.

Following the Japanese action, the North Koreans announced extension of their jurisdiction on June 21, 1977 to take effect on August 1.[174] However, on August 1 the North Koreans announced that, coincident with the new economic zone, a "military border" would be established extending ". . . as far as 50 miles from the baseline of the territorial sea limit on the Japan Sea side and coincid[ing] with the 200-mile economic zone on the Yellow Sea side . . . ."[175] The North Korean government later specifically banned all Japanese fishing within its economic zone, and the absence of diplomatic relations between the two countries reportedly hampered Japanese attempts to negotiate.

The amount of catch affected by this closure, as shown in table 4.7 was estimated to be 80,700 MT within both the economic zone and the military zone, where 2,580 Japanese vessels had been operating. Given the scale of operations, and therefore the potentially significant employment effects of closure for the Japanese, negotiations were conducted on a nongovernmental basis between the Korea Federation of Eastern Sea Fisheries Cooperative Associations and the Japan–Korea Fisheries Council of Japan. The Provisional Agreed Minutes Concerning Cooperation in Fisheries, signed on September 6, 1977 in Pyongyang, applied during the period October 1, 1977 to June 1978. The DPRK undertook to guarantee fishing by "petty fishermen" of Japan with limits placed on vessels larger than 200 tons.[176]

Neither the PRC nor the ROK show immediate inclination of extending their jurisdiction to 200 miles. Recall that for the ROK, the Rhee Line was superseded by the agreement with Japan in 1965. Since that time, apparently, the limits of the territorial sea have been three miles. However, reports in mid-December 1977 indicated that the National Assembly had approved a bill to establish a twelve-mile territorial sea.[177] There have been no reports of South Korean consideration of establishing an economic zone. There have been some indications from the Chinese Communist Party Vice-Chairman, Teng Hsiao-ping, that ". . . China was studying the timing of the establishment of its 200-mile fishing zone."[178]

TABLE 4.7

NORTH KOREAN EXTENDED JURISDICTION AND JAPANESE FISHERIES, 1976
(ESTIMATED IN METRIC TONS)

| | | Yellow Sea | Japan Sea | | |
|---|---|---|---|---|---|
| Type of fisheries | No. of vessels | Within 50-mile military zone | Within 50-mile military zone (A) | Within 200-mile economic zone outside A | Total |
| Otter trawlers (Flounders) | 200 | 11,000 | 0 | 0 | 11,000 |
| Squid | 2,000 | 3,000 | 6,200 | 62,000 | 65,000 |
| Puffer fish | 60 | 500 | 0 | 0 | 500 |
| Pink salmon | 300 | 0 | 120 | 1,080 | 1,200 |
| Deep sea red crab | 20 | 0 | 0 | 3,000 | 3,000 |
| Total | 2,580 | 14,500 | 6,320 | 66,080 | 80,700 |

Source: Regional Fisheries Attaché, American Embassy, Tokyo.

Note: Impact is within the 50-mile Military Zones of the Yellow Sea and the Japan Sea, totalling 20,820 MT (14,500 MT + 6,320 MT), valued at $27 million (Yen 8,000 million), or 25% of the total value of $135 million (Yen 40,000 million) for the 80,700 MT catch.

In chapter 5 we give a comparative analysis of coastal state Acts extending exclusive jurisdiction over fisheries in the North Pacific and consider the implications of such Acts for the patterns of fishing and the problems generated.

# 5

# Extended Jurisdiction: A Comparative Analysis of the Acts and Management Regimes

This chapter identifies and discusses significant similarities and differences between coastal state extensions of jurisdiction in the North Pacific and national measures for this purpose and the Draft Convention on the Law of the Sea of UNCLOS III. Differences between the legislative Acts of the coastal states raise questions of reciprocity and retaliation that may be available, whereas similarities relate to the possible creation of "international law" through uniform national legislation. The Draft Convention presumably reflects an international consensus on the issues; therefore, a primary concern here is to note points of deviation from this consensus by the Acts of national legislation, as well as noting what effect such differences might have on the implementation of national measures. Further questions might be raised as to whether or not a regional international law or some other approach might be more appropriate in instances where deviations are uniform among the Acts of national legislation.

This examination is concerned specifically with the North Pacific Ocean and several of the countries adjacent to it: Canada, China, Japan, North Korea, South Korea, the Soviet Union and the United States. The principal pieces of national legislation examined include:

Canada: The Fisheries Act (1970)[1] and the Fishing Zones of Canada (Zones 4 and 5) Order (1976)[2]. (These two pieces of legislation comprise what is commonly referred to as the "Fisheries Act").

Japan: Law on Provisional Measures Relating to the Fishing Zones[3] (the Japanese Fishing Zone Law).

USSR: Edict on Provisional Measures for the Preservation of Living Resources and the Regulation of Fishing in Marine Areas[4] (the Soviet Edict)

U.S.: Fishery Conservation and Management Act of 1976[5] (FCMA)

The text of the North Korean extension of national jurisdiction is not generally available; the interpretations given reflect Japanese newspaper reports. The People's Republic of China has not extended its jurisdiction but has issued statements relating to its position on the two-hundred-mile zone. South Korea has not claimed a two-hundred-mile zone.

The focus of this chapter is on living resources and activities related to their management. It begins with the general scope of coastal state authority over fisheries, focusing on the objectives and the geographic, functional, and species coverage of the legislation. Following this, the areas of prescriptive jurisdiction are set out in more detail, including allocation principles and the degree of coastal state authority over anadromous stocks. Next, enforcement jurisdiction of coastal states and national enforcement provisions are discussed, and respective management systems are outlined. Finally, an attempt is made to predict the future jurisdictional aspects of the zones.

## GENERAL SCOPE OF AUTHORITY

### General Objective

In the broadest sense the overall objective implicit in all legislation is to maximize the benefits accruing to the respective countries. This is to be done while satisfying the objectives explicitly stated in the various Acts. All legislation stresses such goals as the need to ''conserve and protect or manage'' the living or fishery resources, as well as the need to promote and maintain ''optimum utilization of the resource.''

A prerequisite for attainment of any of these objectives is the establishment of an effective management regime. Prior to unilateral extension of coastal state jurisdiction, many fishery resources in the North Pacific did not fall under any regulatory arrangements. New institutional mechanisms were required to promote development of a regime that would ensure the conservation and optimum utilization of living resources. Changing jurisdictional concepts resulted in unilateral actions to extend coastal state authority. Whether or not the national acts extending jurisdiction do indeed set up effective management systems is discussed in more detail later in this chapter.

### Geographic Coverage

Although the Draft Convention provides that the coastal state may establish a territorial sea not to exceed twelve miles,[6] the United States continues to adhere to a three-mile territorial sea. The other countries in the North Pacific all claim a twelve-mile territorial sea.

Canada widened its territorial sea to twelve miles by amending the Territorial Sea and Fishing Zone Act in 1970.[7] In 1958, China declared a twelve-mile territorial sea and has since closed the Gulf of Po Hai and the northern Yellow Sea for reasons of national defense. On May 2, 1977, the Japanese Diet issued the Law on the Territorial Sea[8] which extends Japan's territorial sea to twelve miles, maintaining the three-mile limit in four designated areas: Soya Strait, Osumi Strait, and the eastern and western channels of the Tsugaru Strait.

In December 1977, the National Assembly of the Republic of Korea passed legislation proclaiming a twelve-mile territorial sea. The Strait of Korea is not subject to the twelve-mile territorial sea extension, as it is considered to be an ''international waterway'' in nature. The twelve-mile limit became effective in April of 1978.

Changing jurisdictional concepts have resulted in the extension of zones of functional jurisdiction. The Draft Convention provides for the establishment of an exclusive economic zone that extends beyond the territorial sea of the coastal nation to two hundred miles from the baseline of the territorial sea.[9] The unilateral coastal state actions taken in the North Pacific uniformly extend jurisdiction to two hundred miles from the territorial sea baseline. However, these zones are functionally much more limited than the exclusive economic zone envisioned by the Draft Convention.

The actual extensions of national jurisdiction in the North Pacific occurred within a relatively short period of time, although the issue had been the subject of lengthy debate in Canada and the U.S. Discussion of unilateral extension to a two hundred mile jurisdiction began as early as 1969 in Canada, with mounting concern about pollution in the Arctic regions. Serious consideration was given to extending fishery jurisdiction in mid-1975, and bilateral negotiations were begun shortly thereafter. The U.S. had been debating the issue of extending fishery jurisdiction since the summer of 1973, when Senator Magnuson introduced the first bill to establish an exclusive 200-mile zone.[10] The official decisions to go to unilateral action to extend fishery jurisdiction were made in the Spring of 1976 by both Canada and the U.S. The Canadian "fishing zones" became effective on January 1, 1977, as stipulated by the Fishing Zones of Canada Order (Zones 4 and 5).[11] The enabling legislation for U.S. extension of its authority, the Fishery Conservation and Management Act of 1976, called for the fishery conservation zone to become effective on March 1, 1977.[12]

Following the Canadian and U.S. announcements, the Soviet Union issued the Edict on Provisional Measures for the Preservation of Living Resources and the Regulation of Fishing in Marine Areas, extending the Soviet zone in December 1976.[13] Japan continued to protest these extensions, maintaining that they were inconsistent with conventional international law. Finally, on May 2, 1977, the Japanese Diet issued two significant laws pertaining to its seaward jurisdiction, the Law on the Territorial Sea[14] and the Law on the Provisional Measures Relating to the Fishing Zones,[15] which extends Japanese jurisdiction over fishery resources. However, in an attempt to avoid exacerbating delimitation problems, Japan did not establish boundary limits at two hundred miles throughout its archipelagic range.

On July 1, 1977, North Korea issued a declaration stating its intention to establish an exclusive economic zone of two hundred miles, as well as a military boundary of fifty miles, both effective as of August 1, 1977. The military boundary, as enforced, has many of the attributes of a territorial sea, while the area extending from the seaward limit of the fifty-mile military boundary to the outer limit of the two hundred mile exclusive economic zone has been designated as the "provisional fishing zone" of North Korea.[16]

While Chinese statements indicate that every country may claim an exclusive economic or fishery zone up to two-hundred miles, it has not done so. Communiques released in the fall of 1977 indicated that the Chinese had considered establishing a two-hundred-mile exclusive fishing zone and reserved the right to do so at any time.[17]

Problems of delimitation of either territorial sea or extended zone boundaries have arisen in almost every instance. The measurement of the baselines can be a contentious issue. For example, the U.S. measures its territorial sea from the low-water line along the coast and does not employ straight baseline regimes along rugged or island-fringed coasts. Canada's territorial sea, on the other hand, is measured in part from the low-water line, and in part from straight baselines joining the outermost points along irregular coasts. It is difficult to separate delimitation problems generated by the desire to control fishery resources from those created by continental shelf deposits and/or strict territorial disputes. Most of the disputed areas encompass significant fishery resources. Although efforts are made to keep fishery issues separate from strict boundary issues, such conflicts may have significant impacts on the control of fishery resources. The substance of these conflicts is discussed in chapter 6, and are mentioned here because they are germane to the delimitation principles included in the Draft Convention.

In the northeastern Pacific, boundary disputes between Canada and the U.S. have arisen over the Straits of Juan de Fuca, between Washington State and the Province of British Columbia. Such disputes are the subject of ongoing negotiations between Canada and the U.S.

The delimitation issue in the northwestern Pacific is far more complex, involving up to six countries.[18] Disputes are focused in three areas: the area between the Sea of Japan and the Okhotsk Sea, the Sea of Japan, and the East China Sea.

Japanese-Soviet disputes focus on four islands situated between the Sea of Japan and the Okhotsk Sea: Kunashiri, Etorofu, Habomai, and Shiketan. Both nations claim these islands as part of their territory, although the Soviets occupy them at the present time. A similar Japanese-Soviet dispute involves Takeshima Island in the Sea of Japan. The status of Takeshima Island is further confused by the fact that the island, known as Tok-to in Korean, could be included in the South Korean territorial sea, if the sea was extended to twelve miles.[19]

In the East China Sea, Japan, China, and Taiwan are all involved in a dispute over Senkaku Island. Also, in January of 1974, Japan and South Korea concluded the ''Japanese-South Korean Agreement on Joint Development of the Continental Shelf,'' which marks an area of the continental shelf in the East China Sea as a zone to be developed and exploited jointly by the two nations. However, China claims inviolable sovereignty over the East China Sea continental shelf and issued a statement in June 1977 protesting the agreement.[20]

None of the above conflicts has been resolved, nor does it appear likely that they will be in the near future. A major impediment is the lack of a universally accepted method for dealing with such problems. The most prevalent system is through bilateral negotiation between states adjacent or opposite to each other. But there are the inevitable differences of opinion as to which delimitation principle to follow.

Earlier formulations of the Draft Convention had set out a general rule stating that the median, or equidistance, line principle was to be used ''taking into account all relevant circumstances.''[21] Indeed, this principle may be the only method that can be readily applied in the case of the two hundred mile zone. For the most part, Japan and North and South Korea appear to be utilizing this method;[22] however, where competing claims exist, the

Chinese want to apply strict "geologic/geographic criteria."[23] Application of such criteria could have a significant impact on the boundary between Japan and China. Thus far, the Soviet Union appears to be following the median line principle. In September 1977 the USSR claimed the median line as the Soviet territorial sea limit in waters between Soviet-occupied Kunashira Island and Shiretoho in eastern Hokkaido (the Nemuro Strait), where the twelve-mile territorial seas of Japan and the Soviet Union overlap. This claim was issued in the form of a warning to Japanese fishing vessels inspected by a Soviet patrol boat.[24] It is impossible to discern whether or not this claim represents consistent, official Soviet policy.

## FUNCTIONAL COVERAGE AND DEGREE OF EXCLUSIVITY

The functional jurisdiction claimed by countries in the legislation examined here differs little between zones. The Draft Convention offers perhaps the broadest authority over the greatest number of users. The coastal state may claim:

(a)  sovereign rights for the purpose of exploring and exploiting, conserving and managing the natural resources, whether living or non-living, of the seabed and subsoil and superadjacent waters, and with regard to other activities for the economic exploitation and exploration of the zone.[25]

Coastal states may also exercise jurisdiction over such uses as the establishment of artificial islands and structures, marine science research, and the preservation of the marine environment.[26] The freedom of navigation, overflight, and the laying of submarine cables and pipelines are purportedly not subject to coastal state control within the exclusive economic zone.[27] Articles 61−73 of the Draft Convention focus exclusively on the regime governing living resources within the exclusive economic zone (see Appendix D for complete text). Coastal state authority extends to the living resources themselves, as well as to all activities related to the exploration and exploitation of such resources. This authority is both prescriptive and enforceable in nature and appears on the surface to be relatively unrestricted in its scope and application. Yet, it is subject to some modifications.

The Draft Convention places certain obligations on coastal nations with respect to their contingent rights of use. For instance, the coastal state must ensure "proper conservation" of the resources, taking account of the "best scientific evidence available"[28] when doing so. The coastal state must also promote the "optimum utilization" of the resource and is obligated to allow foreign access to the surplus of the allowable catch.[29]

As set forth in the Fishing Zones of Canada (Zones 4 and 5) Order, Canada extended "the areas under the fisheries jurisdiction of Canada . . . by prescribing additional fishing zones of Canada pursuant to the Territorial Sea and Fishing Zones Act."[30] The legislation indicates that Canada has the responsibility to conserve and protect the living resources within the designated areas off its Atlantic and Pacific coasts. The extension of jurisdiction does not pertain to activities other than those connected with the resources themselves, the harvesting of the resources, and fisheries research.[31] Although the Fisheries Act extends

Canadian zones of competence, other legislation governs the zones as well. For example, the Coastal Fisheries Protection Act restricts foreign fishing vessels from entering Canadian fishing zones unless duly authorized.[32] Amendments to the Canadian Fisheries Act that went into effect on September 1, 1977, generally provide for broader regulation and greater protection of the aquatic environment, and institute more severe penalties for poaching.

Law No. 31 establishes the fishing zone within which Japan has jurisdiction over "fisheries and similar activities."[33] This includes the competence to regulate the exploitation of the fishery resources, giving Japanese fishermen exclusive rights to the resources within the zone. Foreign fishing is prohibited, except as prescribed by the Ministry of Agriculture and Forestry Ordinance.[34] The Fisheries Law also extends Japanese authority over fishery research or any research that requires the "taking and catching of marine animals or plants within the fishing zone." Approval of the Minister of Agriculture and Forestry is required before such research commences.[35]

The North Korean fifty-mile military border that was implemented with its exclusive economic zone (EEZ) appears to have characteristics similar to a territorial sea.[36] North Korea claims that all "foreigners . . . shall be prohibited from conducting any action" within the military border (this includes the surface, water column and air space). Civilian ships, *excluding fishing boats*, and civilian aircraft may transit the military zone with the permission of North Korean authorities.[37]

Specific references in the North Korean proclamation concerning foreign fishing operations in the two-hundred-mile zone have not been made generally available. However, an agreement has been concluded between Japanese and North Korean private concerns. The agreement allows for the provisional continuation of Japanese fishing activities in the EEZ. The North Koreans have issued statements indicating that South Korean fishermen may operate in the zone, although it is not known to what extent they may do so.[38]

The Soviet Edict extends Soviet control to two hundred miles for "the preservation of living resources and the regulation of fishing."[39] Sovereign rights are exercised only over fishery and other living resources and activities related to the exploration, exploitation, and preservation of such resources.[40] Soviet fishermen have exclusive rights to the resources, although foreign fishing may be conducted pursuant to Articles (3) and (4) for the surplus.

The Edict is rather ambiguous in its use of "exploration research." Article (3) expressly prohibits "exploratory and other operations connected with commercial fishing," except when bilateral agreements have been reached. This prohibition is reiterated in the Japanese—Soviet Provisional Fisheries Agreement.[41] One might interpret Article (3) as restricting only fishery research that is related to commercial exploitation. This is evidenced by the banning of a Japanese research vessel doing exploratory work on cuttlefish in the Soviet zone.[42] There is, however, a fine line between so-called "pure" and "commercial" research and it is doubtful whether the Soviets will bother to make the distinction. Furthermore, the exclusion of fishery research vessels may precede the prohibition of research in other marine areas as well.

Under the Fishery Conservation and Management Act (FCMA), the U.S. claims "exclusive fishery management authority" within the fishery zone for the purpose of conserving and managing "the fishery resources off the coasts of the U.S."[43] U.S. jurisdiction is extended only to activities related to living resources (i.e., it does not purport to affect any other activities within the zone). However, the U.S. claim has been extended to navigation in the zone through pollution control regulations as set out in the 1978 amendments to the Federal Water Pollution Control Act.[44] U.S. fishermen have preferential rights to access to and use of the fishery resources within the zone, anadromous species throughout their migratory range, and the living resources of the continental shelf.[45]

## Species Coverage

The Draft Convention articles on living resources within the EEZ cover all living resources that move in or through the zone at some time during their life cycle, excluding sedentary species, as defined in paragraph 4 of Article 77.[46] The coastal state has regulatory authority over and rights of access to all stocks, including transboundary stocks and highly migratory species.[47] The latter two species come under the Draft Convention but may not be covered in as comprehensive a way as other species. Both Articles (63) and (64) call for cooperation among the relevant countries to ensure conservation and optimum utilization of such stocks; this may be done directly or through appropriate regional or international organization. The Draft Convention also covers anadromous and catadromous species.[48] Article 65 reiterates the right of a coastal state or international organization to exercise authority over the exploitation of marine mammals within their respective purviews.

The Canadian Fisheries Act of 1970,[49] which is applicable to the fishing zones, defines "fish" to include "shellfish, crustaceans and marine animals."[50] This Act includes reference to anadromous species,[51] certain catadromous species,[52] marine mammals,[53] sedentary seals,[54] lobsters,[55] and marine plants.[56] It is assumed that such species are subject to the fisheries jurisdiction that extends to 200 miles.

The Japanese Law lists "marine animals and plants" within the fishing zone as subject to Japanese jurisdiction. These terms are not defined in the Law. However, Article 6 expressly excludes highly migratory species, which are to be prescribed by Cabinet Order, from Japanese authority, whereas Article 12 states that Japan has jurisdiction over anadromous species.[57]

The Soviet Edict states that the sovereign rights of the USSR extend to the fish and other living resources, as well as to the "migratory species of fish" within the limits of the Soviet zone.[58] Although not clearly defined in the Edict text, living resources and fish are defined in the Japanese–Soviet Provisional Fisheries Agreement. Living resources include the fisheries in the area adjacent to the coasts of the Soviet Union in the northwestern Pacific, all species of anadromous fish, and Soviet continental shelf species. Fish include finfish, mollusks, crustacean and all other marine animals and plants.[59]

The FCMA is quite specific in stating which species fall under U.S. purview. The text sets out that U.S. management authority covers "finfish, mollusks, crustacean, and all other forms of marine animal and plant life."[60] It also includes anadromous species, even beyond the fishery zone,[61] and the continental shelf fishery resources,[62] expressly excluding marine mammals, birds, and highly migratory species (which are defined to include only tuna).[63]

## PRESCRIPTIVE JURISDICTION

### Activities Within National Jurisdiction

Under the Draft Convention and the coastal state Acts presented here, the coastal state has prescriptive jurisdiction over activities and operations that pertain to living resources. The primary focus is on the exploitation of the fishery resources (i.e., fishing). The Draft Convention does not define exactly what activities constitute fishing. Rather, it gives the coastal state the exclusive authority to regulate exploitation of the living resources. The emerging principles of expanded coastal state authority over living resources within the exclusive economic zone (EEZ) leads one to expect that the exploitation referred to in the text incorporates all facets of exploitation—exploratory research,[64] harvesting, processing (if done within the EEZ), and transporting.

This broad scope of authority, extending over the range of all fishing-related activities appears in the national zones as well. If not incorporated in the legislation explicitly, the authority is exercised by the nations by regulation of activities within the zone. The Canadian Fisheries Act provides the responsible Canadian entity with the authority to manage and control the catching, loading, handling, transporting, possessing and disposing of fish within its fishing zones.[65] This definition of fishing has been expanded to include an attempt to catch fish as well as the actual capture.[66]

The Japanese Fishing Zone Law states that Japan has "jurisdiction over the catching and taking or culturing of marine animals and plants."[67] The Law does not define these terms further. The Soviet Edict is somewhat more explicit, extending Soviet control to the "commercial catching of fish and other living resources," as well as to "other operations connected with such commercial fishing."[68] This implies that control extends to all harvesting, processing, and transporting operations associated with fishing.

Similar language is found in the Japanese—Soviet Provisional Fisheries Agreement, although the definition of fishing in the Agreement is not as direct as in the Soviet Edict.

> Article 3. "Fishing" means from (A) to (D), listed below:
> (A) The catching of fish.
> (B) Attempts to catch fish.
> (C) Other activities, which can reasonably be expected to result in the catching of fish.
> (D) Operations on the sea to assist directly or to prepare for the activities listed from (A) to (C).

Whereas, in the Soviet Edict, Article 3 states: "The commercial catching of fish and other living resources, as well as exploratory and other operations connected with such commercial fishing." This supports the assumption that Soviet control extends to *all* fishing-related activities, as noted above. The definition of fishing in the Provisional Agreement does not clarify the Japanese intent, as "fishing vessels" are defined by the Provisional Agreement to be:

> ships and vessels which are being used, or are equipped to be used, for (A) and (B) listed below:
> (A) Fishing.

(B) Operations related to fishing (including such operations as preparations for fishing, supplying of ships, storing, transporting, processing, and the loading and unloading of fish).[69]

It is difficult to predict what the Japanese policy on the regulation of processing vessels will be exactly. Yet, as Japan subscribes to the Provisional Agreement, it is likely that Japan is willing to use the broadest definition of "catching and taking" of living resources, thus including "all operations related to fishing."

Section 3 of the FCMA provides definitions for "fishing" and "fishing vessels."

(10) The term "fishing" means—
    (A) the catching, taking, or harvesting of fish;
    (B) the attempted catching, taking, or harvesting of fish;
    (C) any other activity which can reasonably be expected to result in the catching, taking or harvesting of fish; or
    (D) any operations at sea in support of, or in preparation for, any activity described in sub-paragraphs (A) through (C).
Such term does not include any scientific research activity which is conducted by a scientific research vessel.[70]

This definition does not specifically include processing operations, although the definition of fishing vessels does encompass processing activities.[71] In amendments to the FCMA passed in 1978, the U.S. was granted the capability to establish criteria for permitting foreign processing vessels to come within the United States fishery conservation zone and purchase fish from the United States.[72] The 1978 amendments were passed to clarify the intent of Congress to encourage development of the entire United States fishing industry, harvesting and processing alike. Further, the amendments give preference to U.S. fish processors of fish harvested by U.S. fishermen: only fish in excess of the amount that can be utilized by U.S. processors are available to foreign processors. The determination of the amount of fish available to foreign processors is included in the various fishery management plans, and is calculated from the estimate of domestic processing capacity. The determination of domestic processing capacity and the extent of the preference to be given to domestic processors is the focus of considerable debate. The initial interim regulations for guidelines for development of fishery management plans to include processing capacity were published in the *Federal Register* on October 20, 1978; these were subsequently modified and published again on February 7, 1979.[73] Final regulations have yet to be established, as several major elements remain unresolved (for example, the amounts and kinds of data required to determine domestic processing capacity, and the question of price and its relation to processing capacity).[74]

## Allocation Principles

The Draft Convention is quite explicit in requiring the coastal state to pursue fishery management schemes that will ensure "optimum utilization of the living resources in the exclusive economic zone," while continuing to take proper conservation measures at all times.[75] This obligation does not prejudice the coastal state's right to the use of the resources but rather provides that foreign nations be granted access to harvest that amount of the total allowable catch (TAC) that cannot be harvested by the coastal state.

Article 61 (1) allows the coastal state to determine the allowable catch for fisheries within its zone, subject to the constraint that such determinations must be based on the "best scientific evidence available." Article 62 (2) goes on to allow the coastal state to determine its capacity to harvest stocks within its zone. Despite the above constraint, the coastal state is vested with virtually full control over the living resources in the zone. Yet, Article 62 (2) could be read as providing a restrictive effect on coastal state discretion. This article may in fact lend support to the argument that the coastal state cannot automatically reduce the total allowable catch so that it equals the domestic harvesting capacity.

While the coastal state may not arbitrarily set the TAC, it is questionable whether "best scientific evidence available"[76] is a sufficient constraint. A critical question is left unresolved: since it is inconceivable that all the relevant data will be available, who decides what constitutes the "best scientific information?" Essentially, this decision is left to the coastal state. Other factors, such as the maintenance of "friendly relations among nations," may serve as constraints on arbitrary determinations of allowable catch. Yet, given the diversity of scientific methods, and, thus, the variability in results, this is bound to be an area of contention between the coastal states and foreign fishing countries.

Should the coastal state's determination of either the TAC or the surplus available to foreign fishermen be questioned, there is no effective provision for challenge in the Draft Convention. Whether or not the settlement of disputes provisions found in Part XV are applicable to fisheries issues remain an open question.[77] Article 297(3)(a) of Part XV states quite clearly that, with regard to the living resources of the sea, the discretionary competence of the coastal state is nonreviewable.[78] However, the provisions of this article do not preclude judicial review at the national level. In the United States, for example, judicial review is permitted under the FCMA.[79]

Canada is committed to granting foreign fishermen access to its fishery resources, although it does not subscribe explicitly to the principle of "optimum utilization." Canada reserves the right to determine, internally, the TAC for stocks within its zone,[80] and to assess the harvesting capacity of Canadian fishing industries. The TAC for each fishery and the harvesting capacity is reportedly based on a variable range of data and parameters.[81] Foreign fishing nations are given allocations based on the determination of the surplus. The Canadian allocative process has been more flexible than the system prescribed by the Draft Convention; foreign fishing nations are guaranteed considerably more voice in this process as the bilateral fishery agreements stipulate that "appropriate consultations" with the foreign fishing nation are required prior to the allocation of the surplus.[82]

Japan does not expressly commit itself to the concept of "optimum utilization"; however, the Japanese Fishing Zone Law does grant limited foreign access to resources that are beyond the capacity of domestic fishermen to harvest. The "limit of catch" shall be decided on the rather vague basis of "fishery resource trends supported by scientific evidence."[83]

The Soviet Edict notes the need to seek "optimum utilization" of living resources within its marine areas. Without jeopardizing its exclusive rights to the resources, the Edict promises to allow foreign access; such access is to be granted on the basis of bilateral agreements or "other arrangements."[84] The requirement of concluding a bilateral agreement prior to gaining access to the Soviet zone appears to be mandatory. This is substantiated in practice; for example, an agreement was concluded with Japan before Japanese fishermen could commence fishing in the Soviet zone. As in other Acts, the foreign allocation is the surplus portion of the "total annual permissible catch." On the basis of "scientific data," the Soviet Union determines the total permissible catch and the domestic harvesting capacity.[85] Yet the "permissible catch" can be, and in practice is, arbitrarily lowered to prevent foreign fishing.[86] No formal review provision is provided, and it is questionable whether the negotiation process can provide the necessary check on the use of unsubstantiated or altered data. This is particularly noteworthy in light of the relatively poor negotiating position of Japan vis-à-vis the Soviet Union.

To be within the letter of the FCMA, the U.S. must permit foreign access to any portion of the "optimum yield" that domestic fishermen do not harvest, if such allocation is consistent with the provisions of the Act.[87] It is clearly within the purview of the U.S. to determine the "optimum yield" for each fishery under its jurisdiction, as well as to assess the domestic harvesting capacity. As in the Draft Convention, the intent of the legislation would be circumvented if the optimum yield and the domestic harvesting capacity were determined to be equal for the sole purpose of "keeping the foreign fishermen out." All conservation and management measures must be determined on the basis of the "best scientific information available," although this raises the same ambiguities and questions as found in the Draft Convention provisions.

Criteria for allocation among foreign countries of the surpluses are set out in Article 62 (3) of the Draft Convention. The allocation process must include consideration of such relevant factors as: the rights of landlocked and geographically disadvantaged countries; the paramount interests of the developing countries in the region; the rights of traditional fishing interests; and cooperation in scientific research efforts. Further provisions for the landlocked and geographically disadvantaged countries are found in Articles 69 and 70, respectively. The net gain for these countries is virtually nothing—what paragraph (1) of each article gives them, paragraphs (2) and (3) take away. For example, Article 69 (1) gives the landlocked countries the right to participate in the exploitation of living resources within the EEZ of adjoining states, and stipulates that such exploitation shall be negotiated through bilateral or other arrangements. Paragraph (2) goes on to subject paragraph (1) to Articles 61 and 62, which give the coastal state ultimate authority, thereby negating any bargaining power the landlocked country might have gained initially.[88]

Canada, in negotiating bilateral fishery agreements prior to the implementation of its fishing zones, appears to have relied heavily upon traditional fishing rights.[89] Express criteria is not given in any of the Canadian legislation pertaining to foreign fishing. "Positive sanctions" are incorporated into the allocation process. This allows a nation's willingness to assist in conservation and research efforts to be considered during the allocative decision process.

Allocation of the surpluses among foreign fishermen in the Japanese zone is based on reciprocity alone.[90] Japan has concluded bilateral fishery agreements with the Soviet Union and South Korea, and a private agreement with North Korea; these agreements allow Japanese fishermen to fish in their zones, and they are granted limited access to the Japanese zone.

It is difficult to tell from the rather cryptic communiques available exactly what criteria the North Koreans use when granting foreign fishermen access to their zone. Thus far, they have granted access only to countries that historically fished the area.

Criteria for determining the allocation of the surplus are not set out in the Soviet text. There is no apparent recognition of historic fishing rights or of cooperation in conservation and research efforts. Japanese−Soviet negotiations on fishery agreements for 1977 and 1978 gives reciprocity considerable weight by both countries. Both countries grant access to their own zones in order to gain access to the other's. Another example is found in South Korea. Although it appeared initially that the South Koreans would be completely excluded from the Soviet zone, in September 1977 they agreed to import pollock from the Soviet Union via Japan in order to obtain fishing rights near the Kamchatka Peninsula.[91]

The allocation among foreign nations of the total allowable level of foreign fishing (TALFF) is based upon specific criteria set out in Section 201 in the FCMA.[92] The Secretary of State, in cooperation with the Secretary of Commerce, determines the allocation, considering:

(A) whether, and to what extent, the fishing vessels of such nations have traditionally engaged in fishing such fishery;

(B) whether such nations have cooperated with the United States in, and made substantial contributions to, fishery research and the identification of fishery resources;

(C) whether such nations have cooperated with the United States in enforcement and with respect to the conservation and management of fishery resources; and

(D) such other matters as the Secretary of State, in cooperation with the Secretary, deems appropriate.[93]

Lack of reciprocal extension of fishing privileges by another nation is grounds for exclusion from the allocation process.[94]

In an effort to stop whaling operations occurring outside the purview of the International Convention for the Regulation of Whaling, an amendment to the allocation process, as set out in the FCMA, was passed in 1979.[95] The amendment states that the Secretary of Commerce shall certify a foreign nation whose nationals "directly or indirectly, are conducting fishing operations or engaging in trade or taking, which diminishes the effectiveness of the International Convention for the Regulation of Whaling."[96] The law then requires the Secretary of State to reduce a certified nation's allocation by not less than 50 percent after a remedial period of 365 days, if the country has not taken the actions necessary to remove the certification. The amendment was aimed at Japan, a leading supporter of pirate whaling operations.[97] This amendment represents a clear deviation from prevailing allocative criteria; it uses access to fishery resources as a lever to attain nonfishery-related objectives. Whether this precedent is followed by other countries for other purposes remains to be seen.

Under the Draft Convention, the coastal states' prescriptive jurisdiction extends to regulations governing the "licensing of fishermen, fishing vessels, and equipment." This may also include the levying of compensatory fees.[98]

Canadian law requires that foreign fishing vessels wishing to engage in any fishing activities[99] obtain a license, which is issued by the Fisheries and Marine Service.[100] Fees were not imposed on foreign fishermen in 1977, which was considered a transition year. A fee schedule was instituted in 1978, requiring foreign fishing vessels and their support vessels to pay $1.00 per gross registered ton, and the fishing vessels to pay an additional fee for each day of fishing.[101]

In the Japanese zone, once the foreign allocation has been determined, vessels seeking access must apply to the Minister of Agriculture and Forestry for the required permission and permits before fishing operations commence.[102] Fishing or permit fees are imposed, pursuant to Article 8 (1) of the Fishing Zone Law, although Article 8 (2) allows suspension of fees in certain unspecified circumstances. The fee charge is not specified.

It is interesting to note that, while details of the North Korean exclusive economic zone are unavailable, the provisional agreement concluded privately between Japanese and North Korean fisheries associations stipulates that fishing fees will not be levied in this instance. Further, it does not appear from the translation of the text of the agreement that licenses or permits will be issued by the North Korean government, but rather that the Japanese will be responsible for determining which vessels shall fish in the North Korean zone.[103]

A permit is required for foreign fishing vessels of countries that enter into the required bilateral agreements with the Soviet Union.[104] Such permits are issued in accordance with national catch quotas.[105] Fees are not explicitly required in the Soviet text and the information available does not indicate whether or not fees have been imposed.

Vessels of nations that have concluded a Governing International Fishery Agreement with the U.S. must apply for the permits required under Section 204 of the FCMA; such permits must be issued before the vessel engages in fishing activities.[106] Certain permit fees are required, the cost of which is to reflect the aggregate cost of administering the zone (i.e., costs incurred for conservation, management, research, administration, and enforcement). A 1978 amendment to the Fishermen's Protective Act places a surcharge on foreign fishing fees (not to exceed 20 percent) to provide compensation to U.S. fishermen for certain damages or losses occurring in the U.S. fishery conservation zone, regardless of the cause. The FCMA allows the imposition of fees on domestic fishermen as well.[107] The law states that these fees are not to exceed administrative costs; yet this may not be as inclusive as it appears, as some permits may be subject to broader-based charges.[108]

## Anadromous Stocks

Two discrepancies are apparent between the various articles governing anadromous stocks. The inconsistencies occur in the definition of "state of origin" and the extent of jurisdictional claims.

In the Draft Convention, anadromous species are covered by Article 66. Paragraph (1) states that the state of origin shall have the "primary responsibility" for anadromous stocks.[109] The state of origin is defined as states in whose rivers anadromous stocks "originate." Originate, however, is not specifically defined. It could be interpreted as referring to stocks that actually spawn in a nation's rivers or to stocks that merely pass through the rivers while migrating to the sea.

The Canadian definition appears to be equally ambiguous. As evidenced in Canadian bilateral fishery agreements, Canada defines "state of origin" as "states in whose fresh waters anadromous stocks originate."[110] The Soviet Edict does not refer to anadromous stocks specifically—referring only to "migratory species of fish."[111] The bilateral agreements to which the Soviet Union is a party do not provide general guidelines for determining which species constitute "migratory species." Rather, the agreements address specific fisheries, such as the northwestern Pacific salmon and salmon trout fisheries.

The Japanese and U.S. definitions are quite similar. Japan claims jurisdiction over the anadromous species that spawn in the fresh waters of Japan.[112] The FCMA is slightly more specific, designating those species of fish "which spawn in fresh or estuarine waters of the U.S. and which migrate to ocean waters" as falling under U.S. jurisdiction.[113] By so defining anadromous species, some stocks that might be considered to originate in the U.S., following the Draft Convention provisions, are excluded from U.S. jurisdiction. An example of this are stocks that spawn in Canadian waters but enter the sea through U.S. waters.

The second inconsistency is the extent of coastal state jurisdiction over the anadromous stocks. The Draft Convention provides that the state of origin shall have full authority over the regulation of anadromous stocks and the fishing of these stocks within its exclusive economic zone,[114] and that the other countries, through whose zones the fish may pass, shall voluntarily cooperate in the conservation and management of the anadromous stocks.

Fisheries for anadromous stocks are to be conducted only in waters landward of the outer limits of the zone, except where "economic dislocation" would result from the prohibition of such fisheries outside the 200-mile limit. This allows for the continuation of high-seas salmon fisheries, notably the Japanese operations in the North Pacific. This article was negotiated privately between the U.S. and Japan from 1972 to 1974 in an attempt to provide the incentive necessary to keep the Japanese from uncontrolled fishing of salmon on the high seas. As worded, only existing fisheries of this nature are eligible for the exemption, thus assuring the Japanese that others, such as the South Koreans, cannot enter the fishery. This article was renegotiated during the March–May 1978 session of UNCLOS III in response to Soviet concern for their anadromous stocks outside the zone. The following was appended to Article 66 (3) (a).[115]

> With respect to such fishing beyond the outer limits of the exclusive economic zone, states concerned shall maintain consultations with a view to achieving agreement on terms and conditions of such fishing giving due regard to the conservation requirements and needs of the state of origin in respect of these stocks.

This new version of Article 66 does not appear to mean very much; it merely obligates the state of origin to consult on such matters, it does not carry the obligation to agree.

Canada, as expressed in its bilateral agreements, would confine exploitation of anadromous stocks to the areas under national fisheries jurisdiction. Multilateral arrangements would then be negotiated in instances where the stocks passed through the waters of nonstates of origin.[116]

The Japanese law appears to extend jurisdiction beyond its fishing zone, although it is obviously not in its interest to do so. The translated article is unclear but could be interpreted to read that Japan intends to manage its anadromous stocks beyond 200 miles, yet shall do so through international cooperation.[117]

The Soviet and U.S. acts explicitly extend their respective jurisdictions beyond the 200-mile limit. Generally, state of origin jurisdiction over anadromous stocks extends throughout the stock's migratory range, except where such stocks are in the territorial waters or the recognized economic or fishery zones of another country.[118]

It does not seem that these inconsistencies will generate significant conflicts, especially in light of the fact that all aspects of anadromous fisheries in the North Pacific will probably be negotiated separately. As Japan conducts the primary high-seas salmon fishery at the present time, the agreements will focus on Japanese operations. Should provisions similar to the Draft Convention be accepted, there will essentially be no state of origin enforcement beyond the 200-mile limit without the consent of the Japanese.

## Highly Migratory Species

Article 64 of the Draft Convention deals with highly migratory species. A listing of the species falling into this category is provided in Appendix G. Species included are tuna and tunalike species, and all cetaceans.

Article 3 serves to fractionate the authority over these resources between the coastal state and international organizations. The coastal states have the competence to regulate such species within their respective economic zones. Paragraph (1) of the Article extends the coastal state's competence to regulate highly migratory species passing through their zones outside the EEZ, whether or not the country participates in the fishery. Then Article 64 obligates the coastal state to cooperate in the management of the resources beyond the 200-mile limit; this may be done directly or under the auspices of relevant international organizations. It should be noted that this Article does not obligate the coastal states to follow management or conservation measures recommended by such organizations or groups.

The Canadian Fisheries Act does not appear to address the problem of jurisdiction over highly migratory species specifically. However, Canada follows the jurisdictional principles set out in the Draft Convention and claims exclusive jurisdiction over highly migratory species.

Foreign fishermen are expressly not excluded from harvesting highly migratory species in the Japanese fishing zone,[119] nor are they required to obtain approval from the Ministry of Agriculture and Forestry for such fishing activities.[120] Stocks constituting highly migratory species are to be prescribed by Cabinet Order and are not defined in the Law. The Japanese have extensive distant-water tuna fleets; one assumes the government is hesitant to set a precedent that could be turned against Japanese fishermen. Thus, highly migratory species are expressly excluded from Japanese jurisdictional claims.

The United States also specifically excludes highly migratory species from its jurisdiction.[121] But highly migratory species are defined to include only tuna in an attempt to reconcile the interests of the billfish fishermen, and the interests of the U.S. distant-water tuna fleets. The recreational billfish fishermen wanted assured protection for the billfish stocks, and the tuna industry was concerned that U.S. claims to jurisdiction over tuna would set a precedent other countries, primarily Latin American, could use to justify their jurisdictional claims over tuna resources within 200-mile limits.

No guidance is given in the Soviet Edict as to which stocks the Soviets propose to include under "migratory species of fish."[122]

All species of cetaceans (whales, dolphins, and porpoises) are listed as highly migratory species in the Draft Convention, Annex I, and thus fall under Article 64. The inclusion of cetaceans in Article 64 is of serious concern to prowhale conservation groups. It was their hope that all reference to cetaceans could be deleted from Article 64. Attempts to delete cetaceans from the highly migratory species list have not been successful and efforts later shifted to focus on changes in the Article that would strengthen the protective measures for whales; the existing language generally weakens the international system with respect to protection of whales, dolphins, and porpoises.

Article 64 imposes a duty on nations that fish for such species to cooperate so as to ensure conservation of the species. Conservation, as used in the Draft Convention, is defined in terms of "optimum utilization"[123] and "maximum sustainable yield";[124] conservation does not appear to incorporate notions of preservation and nonconsumptive uses, principles that many believe must be considered in the management of cetaceans. Particularly upsetting to those individuals is the use of MSY in this context, as even the International Whaling Commission has rejected MSY as being inappropriate for the basis of marine mammal management.

## ENFORCEMENT JURISDICTION

### Invocation

The Draft Convention gives the coastal state enforcement jurisdiction, allowing it to take such measures as may be necessary to ensure compliance with its management regime. Toward this end, the coastal state may board, inspect, arrest, and institute judicial proceedings against vessels and crew suspected of operating in violation of the coastal state's laws and regulations. In instances of arrest and detention, vessels and crew are to be released immediately "upon the posting of a reasonable bond or other security."[125] The coastal state may place observers aboard foreign fishing vessels for the purposes of enforcement monitoring, data collection, or training.[126]

Canadian fisheries officers are empowered by the Foreign Fishing Regulations to board, search, and inspect log books, gear, and catch.[127] The 1977 amendments to the Fisheries Act designated fishery officers as peace officers with powers to serve summonses and warrants. The amendments also call for the forfeiture of illegal catch and of vessels engaged in illegal fishing.[128] Foreign fishermen are subject to the enforcement provisions included in the 1970 Fisheries Act[129] and the Coastal Fisheries Protection Act.[130] Both of these Acts outline similar enforcement procedures.

Procedures to enforce regulations applicable to the fishing zones of Japan or the Soviet Union are not set out in the respective national legislation. Article 6 of the Soviet Edict provides that "measures of observance" may be taken.[131] The Japanese—Soviet Provisional Fisheries Agreement stipulates that a "public official" of the Soviet Union may board and inspect Japanese fishing vessels within the agreed areas. These vessels, as guaranteed by the Japanese government, must reimburse the Soviet Union for any expenses incurred by such officials.[132] Thus far, this procedure has been the practice in the northwestern Pacific. Japanese vessels suspected of being in violation of Soviet regulations or territory are boarded, inspected, and either detained until sufficient bond has been posted or the fine paid, or released as soon as payment of the fine has been guaranteed.

The FCMA invests U.S. enforcement officers with the power to board, search, and inspect any fishing vessels suspected of violating any provision of the FCMA, with or without a warrant. Gear, equipment, and catch are also subject to such inspection and possible seizure.[133] An arrangement for observers, similar to that provided in the Japanese—Soviet Provisional Fisheries Agreement, has been established by the U.S. Foreign fishing vessels are required to make available, at no cost to the U.S., accommodation for an observer. Observers will be assigned to individual vessels for periods of time at the discretion of the U.S.; they are to perform various tasks as directed by the appropriate regional council. For example, in the North Pacific, observers are to "measure daily catch rates, estimate species, size, and age composition; collect other biological data as appropriate; determine location and duration of hauls; and observe gear dimensions and performances."[134] Thus far, observers in the North Pacific have not been given enforcement duties or powers.[135]

## Application

The arrest or detention of vessel and crew is available to the coastal state in all of the legislation examined here, including the Draft Convention. This does not necessarily include imprisonment. It is incumbent upon the coastal state to promptly notify the flag state should such actions be taken.

The Draft Convention leaves it to the discretion of the coastal state to prescribe a set of penalties. It stipulates that such penalties may not include imprisonment or corporal punishment, unless the flag state so agrees.[136] Neither the Japanese Law nor the Soviet Edict provides explicitly for imprisonment of foreign fishermen. Thus far, all detained violating vessels have been released by both nations upon payment of fines or assurance of such payment. The Japanese Law provides that fishing permits may be suspended or cancelled in the event of violation of fishing regulations or restrictions prescribed by the Minister of Agriculture and Forestry.[137] Further negative sanctions include the imposition of fines of varying severity, not to exceed $200,000; these are applied by administrative procedures.[138] The forfeiture of vessels, gear, and catch or products may also be invoked, or the monetary value of the vessel may be substituted.[139] Penalties available under the Soviet Edict include:

"minimal" fines applied through an administrative process; fines imposed by judicial review; arrest and detention of vessels and crew; and seizure and confiscation of vessel, equipment, gear, and catch.[140]

By Section 61 of the Fisheries Act of Canada, violators of the Act may be liable for certain penalties, including the imposition of fines, imprisonment, or both.[141] The maximum fine available is $25,000 and jail sentences can go up to two years. The 1977 amendments provide an innovation in the use of fines, these being imposed on domestic as well as foreign fishermen. The amendment allows for "ticketing" and obviates court appearances for minor offenses (e.g., fine of $100 or less).[142] Permit and license modification, suspension, and cancellation existed prior to extended jurisdiction and have been used extensively by the Canadians as an effective enforcement measure. This practice is being continued.[143]

Despite preextension concern about Canada's capacity to patrol its zone adequately,[144] to date, Canada's enforcement record has been quite good. A large part of the success of the enforcement measures and general management of the zone hinges on the computerized data base system known as FLASH (Foreign Fishing Vessels Licensing and Surveillance Hierarchical Information System). The computer system keeps track of foreign vessels operating within the zone and can provide details on fleet activities, percentage of quota caught, what each vessel can fish for, where, when, and with what gear.

The U.S. legislation provides for the assessment of a civil penalty that shall not exceed $25,000 for each violation, yet this may be applied every day the violation continues.[145] Criminal penalties may also be imposed under the FCMA and may include either a fine of not more than $100,000, or imprisonment for a maximum of ten years.[146] The question remains open whether or not the U.S. will incarcerate the captain and/or crew of violating vessels. This sanction has already been softened somewhat in the GIFA with Japan. In the Agreed Minutes, which do not have the same status as the Agreement itself, Section 3 states that the U.S. government agrees to recommend to courts that penalties not include imprisonment or any other form of corporal punishment.[147]

Forfeiture and sale of the vessel, gear, or catch is provided for in Section 310 of the FCMA. It has been the practice of the U.S. government to allow cash settlements to be accepted as payment in lieu of forfeiture of the vessel. Further sanctions may be invoked against a vessel's permit: a foreign fishing permit may be modified, suspended or revoked.

All the national legislation is directed primarily at foreign fishermen, although portions of the Canadian and U.S. acts are applicable to domestic fishermen as well. In terms of enforcement procedures, Canada does not appear to make a significant distinction between the two groups, levying similar penalties against both. Soviet and Japanese domestic fishermen are governed by regulations other than those set out in the legislation extending jurisdiction. As such regulations are not readily accessible, in English, a comparison of domestic and foreign enforcement procedures is not possible.

The FCMA appears to discriminate against foreign fishermen since they are subject to criminal penalties, while the U.S. fishermen generally are not. It is difficult to decipher the intent of the FCMA on this point. Section 309 states that a person is guilty of a criminal offense if he commits any act prohibited by portions of Section 307 (1) and (2). Section 307 (1) (D), (E), (F) and (H) deal with the enforcement of the provisions of the Act. Basically, anyone hindering, impeding, or interfering with such enforcement or assaulting authorized enforcement officers are subject to criminal penalties. It is not entirely clear that there are not instances in which domestic fishermen might commit such actions and would thus be subject to the criminal penalties. Section 307 (2) is aimed expressly at foreign fishermen, requiring them to have a permit authorizing them to fish or again be subject to criminal sanctions.

## MANAGEMENT REGIMES

This section focuses on the management schemes instituted under the national legislation extending jurisdiction to 200 miles. Basically, it sets out the definition of "conservation and management" under the various acts. The management entities are identified and a sketch of the management procedures is provided where available. The comparability of the management systems on a detailed basis is limited; thus, each segment of the individual management regimes is not compared separately; rather, the entire system is presented by country.

### Draft Convention

The Draft Convention provisions give rather general guidance for management. As set out in Articles 61 and 62,[148] the coastal states' management regimes must protect the living resources within its jurisdiction from overexploitation, while promoting the optimum utilization of the resources. Conservation is then defined as maintaining or restoring exploited resources at population levels that can produce maximum sustainable yield (MSY). The MSY is to be qualified by relevant environmental and economic factors. The notion of ecosystem management is clear in paragraph (3) of Article 61, by requiring the consideration of the interdependence of stocks. This is reiterated in paragraph (4), which stresses that all of the effects of harvesting a particular stock must be taken into account. The Draft Convention does not address the institutional mechanisms required to implement the above provisions.

### Canada

Canada's management regime parallels the relevant provisions of the Draft Convention: it is committed to optimum utilization of the living resources and to managing the marine ecosystem as a single entity. Canadian policy, however, deviates from all the other legislation as it states that the concepts of MSY and "full utilization" are "inapplicable to the management of resources on an ecosystem basis."[149] MSY does not adequately account for species interaction, incidental catches, or other stochastic events. Nor do such principles provide a rationale for limiting entry into the fishery. Canada believes that exclusion of these factors does not allow optimal utilization of their living resources; therefore, Canadian management is based on a "best use" of the resource principle. This principle entails the determination of an effort-to-catch ratio based on the "optimization of benefits to society."[150]

The federal institutional management structure includes the Ministry of State for Fisheries, the Fisheries and Marine Service, and five regional Fisheries Management divisions of the Fisheries and Marine Service. Fundamental decisions concerning resource management are purportedly reached jointly by industry and government. This process involves all levels of government—federal, provincial, and local—and may be done either through informal discussions between managers and representatives of the fishermen or through regional or national meetings.[151] Foreign fishing nations are afforded the opportunity to consult with the Canadian management officials before the allowable catch and foreign allocations are set. It is incumbent upon the Canadian government to hold such consultations, as set out in the bilateral fishery agreements. Assessment of the Canadian domestic harvesting capacity is done internally; the consultations with foreign nations being held simultaneously with this assessment. This allows a somewhat greater degree of flexibility in determining the foreign allocations.[152]

Operationally, a fishery management program is developed separately for each stock or group of stocks that constitute an established fishery. Program development has been described as unsystematic, and of varying degrees of reliability. Stock assessment differs for the Atlantic and Pacific coasts. For Pacific stocks, scientific data are available from provincial sources and some socioeconomic data have been maintained. The Pacific fisheries are divided into two groups: salmon and herring fisheries and bottomfish fisheries. The allowable yield for salmon and herring is determined by "management teams of biologists and economists" working in British Columbia. The government sets the quotas and gear restrictions for Canadian and foreign bottomfish fisheries.[153]

The domestic management system is dedicated to the expansion of commercial fisheries production. Fisheries development is linked to the restructuring of the industry.[154] The reduction of fishing intensity and relief for congested fleet segments are primary management strategies. A system of entry control is applied to all commercial fisheries, moderated only by government commitment to minimizing the disruptive impacts of such changes.[155] An experimental license limitation program for the British Columbia salmon fishery has been in existence since 1969.[156] Similar regulations have been passed to restrict entry into the British Columbia herring fishery. How effective these programs have been is the subject of considerable debate.[157]

## Japan

The Japanese law extending jurisdiction does not discuss a specific management regime for the fishing zones of Japan. It is difficult to discern exactly what is meant by "conservation and management" in the Japanese law. One notes that as access to the fishery resources of other nations is curtailed, Japanese coastal fisheries receive higher priority. To this end, the Japanese management regime for coastal fisheries is set up to "meet the requirements of the spirit of the UNCLOS provisions." This could be interpreted to mean that the conservation of living resources is ensured based on ecosystem management, since it is officially held that fisheries "should be managed so as not to endanger the living resources and the ecosystem of the seas."[158]

The basis for fishery resource management should reflect "well-planned demand and supply policy," as well as utilization and marketing improvement policies. In light of this, the maximum sustainable economic yield (MSEY) for each fishery is sought. One notes in government and industry statements that the primary emphasis of the management regime continues to be development and increased productivity for both existing and new species. The notion of protection of the resources may be stated in these policies, yet it appears that productivity and sustained supply continue to be the major concern of the Japanese management scheme.

Management powers are vested in the Ministry of Agriculture and Forestry. This includes the power to prescribe regulations relating to all aspects of fishing within the fisheries zone.

## Soviet Union

Conservation is defined somewhat more broadly by the Soviets. Although committed to the "rational exploitation of resources," conservation measures are primarily methods of ensuring stocks of production input.[159] In most instances, the Soviets seek "maximum utilization" of the resources, regardless of the biological consequences. Natural resources play a vital role in Soviet development and the primary concern has been to seek ways to harness natural resources to suit the needs of technologies designed to maximize economic production. Commitments to the quality of the natural environment, to conservation in the sense of protection, and to the application of regulations in these areas are mainly auditory. There appears to be a general indifference to environmental degradation in the Soviet Union.

While developing a large-scale research effort to evaluate the fishing potential of new areas and species, there is essentially no established Soviet management regime. All management is done by the State, given State ownership of the fishing industry, and all directives are issued from the higher levels.[160] There appears to be no coordination between various natural resource agencies, and it is quite unlikely that any semblance of "ecosystem management" exists. The basis for management is the expectation of catching yield forecasts, this being related to the gross fish catch that is to be taken during a given time period, normally corresponding to the 5-Year Plans. For the most part, biological factors are the only other considerations taken into account besides production-supply considerations.

The concept of "optimum utilization" is found in Soviet policies;[161] however, this does not appear to incorporate economic or social factors.[162] As elsewhere, the responsibility for maintaining or increasing production from resources and the responsibility for protecting them are lodged in the same agency. Given the apathetic attitude toward conservation, plus severe production quotas, it is not difficult to imagine that production will receive priority.

Eastern Bloc countries in general, and the Soviet Union specifically, have shown little or no initiative in the past to protect the stocks harvested by their distant-water fleets.[163]

Based on the assumption that "fish not caught up to their biological yield are wasted," the Soviets have harvested stocks at or above their MSY levels. With the advent of the extended zones, Soviet scientists are purportedly advocating strict regulation of catch and even Soviet fishermen have come to realize the deficiencies of the still pervasive principle of "catch at any price."[164] There has been no substantial evidence to support these claims.

Bemoaning the declines in abundance of sundry stocks, the Soviet solution is to ease up on the traditional, presently overexploited fisheries and target on the untapped resources to make up the difference in catch. Notable examples of this are krill and other potential substitutes on lower trophic levels. The emphasis continues to be one of technological progress rather than a combination of technology and protection. There appears to be little evidence that the Soviets are taking steps to protect their own stocks. This is difficult to document as few publications concerning such matters are available. On 25 February 1977, the USSR Council of Ministers issued the *Regulation on the Protection of Fish and Other Living Resources in the USSR's Coastal Waters*. This might provide an indication of Soviet coastal conservation measures, but it is not generally available as yet. Therefore, one must look to the Soviet Edict in this area.

Article 4 provides that the total annual catch shall be determined on the "basis of the respective scientific data." What constitutes relevant scientific data varies in interpretation. In the past, the Soviets have launched large-scale fisheries research programs, an example of this being the Soviet Fisheries Investigations in the Northeast Pacific. The research done during these investigations appears to have emphasized the collection of geomorphological and hydrological data, interspersed with biological information on individual species. Once compiled, the results were used to evaluate potential fishing areas to assure the "efficient and intensive exploitation of the ocean's riches."[165] In essence, the research sought to identify areas with commercially exploitable concentrations of fishery resources. Recent statements indicate that this perspective has changed little. One report indicated that Soviet research continues to focus on the collection of hydrographic conditions and the basic patterns of distribution and size of biological resources in developing a scientific basis for large-scale fisheries.[166]

Domestic fishermen have virtually no access to the management system, at least not in the same sense as found in U.S., Canadian, or Japanese fishing interests. The Soviet Minister of Fisheries, in the Ministry of Agriculture and Forestry, institutes management measures at his discretion, constrained only by the prescribed production forecasts. It is quite inconceivable that policies of the Soviet Ministry of Agriculture and Forestry could be reviewed in the judicial sense or that litigation contesting the levels of allowable catch or other determinations could be initiated.[167]

## United States

The Fishery Conservation and Management Act of 1976 (FCMA) outlines a very detailed, complex management system. Although adhering to the conservation and management principles set out in the Draft Convention, the FCMA provides a more explicit procedure for achieving specific management objectives.

In the FCMA:

> The term "conservation and management" refers to all of the rules, regulations, conditions, methods, and other measures (A) which are required to rebuild, restore, or maintain, and which are useful in rebuilding, restoring, or maintaining, any fishery resource and the marine environment; and (B) which are designed to assure that -
>
> (i) a supply of food and other products may be taken, and that recreational benefits may be obtained, on a continuing basis;
>
> (ii) irreversible or long-term adverse effects on fishery resources and the marine environment are avoided; and
>
> (iii) there will be a multiplicity of options available with respect to future uses of these resources.[168]

This definition is not significantly different from that given in the Draft Convention except in its detailed nature. It stresses proper utilization of the resources, seeking at all times to avoid overexploitation. Subparagraph (ii) begins to address the question of a broader based management system that incorporates the marine environment as well. The definition may present problems for institutions responsible for implementing the procedures; demonstrating compliance with this may be difficult, given the technical difficulties of identifying causative factors in the ecosystem changes (i.e., identifying natural effects as opposed to the effects of human activities).[169]

The FCMA also mandates the attainment of optimum yield (OY) from each fishery. Optimum yield is defined in the following rather broad manner:

> The term "optimum," with respect to the yield from a fishery, means the amount of fish −
>
> (A) which will provide the greatest overall benefit to the Nation, with particular reference to food production and recreational opportunities; and (B) which is prescribed as such on the basis of the maximum sustainable yield from such fishery, as modified by any relevant economic, social, or ecological factor.[170]

There are numerous problems with this concept, as previously defined. For example, no criteria are given that indicate how the "greatest overall benefit to the Nation" is to be determined—a host of values could be subsumed under this rubric. Of significance to the management schemes is the requirement to use a modified MSY when determining the OY for each fishery. The inclusion of social and economic factors requires the incorporation of a broader data base and, if possible, a "multidisciplinary interpretation of that data."[171] Often such data are inadequate or completely lacking, and methods of integrating discipline-specific data in a "multidisciplinary" scheme are still relatively untested.

Section 301 of the FCMA sets out the standards for fishery conservation and management. They reiterate the requirement of achieving the optimum yield and of basing conservation and management measures on the best scientific information available. The standards also address the management of interrelated stocks, as well as the need to consider the relationship between the resources and natural variations in the environment.[172]

Jurisdiction over the fishery resources with the U.S. 200-mile zone is split: the individual coastal states have jurisdiction to three miles, as qualified by Section 306 of the FCMA;[173] the rest of the zone falls under federal purview. To facilitate a more directed management, the FCMA provides for the establishment of Regional Fishery Management Councils. The Councils are responsible for instituting appropriate conservation and management programs in the form of fishery management plans. Scientific and Statistical Committees and other advisory panels are to be established to provide technical assistance to the Councils while developing these plans.[174] These groups are expected to have an active and direct role in the development of the fishery management plans.

The FCMA is also quite explicit in setting out the contents of the fishery management plans. They are to contain the conservation and management measures, including documentation of how these were derived, a detailed description of the fishery, appropriate MSY and OY determinations, again adequately documented, and the harvesting capacity of U.S. fishermen and the resulting amounts to be made available for foreign fishing.[175]

Management measures are subject to extensive review. The Councils must review and revise the fishery management plans on a continuing basis,[176] and the Secretary of Commerce also has review powers.[177] The plans are subject to public scrutiny and the public input required by the FCMA is substantial. Public hearings must be conducted by the Regional Councils[178] at appropriate times and in appropriate locations.

Time constraints under the FCMA are severe. To conform with the required procedure, a minimum of 75 to 135 days must elapse.[179] However, the North Pacific Fishery Management Council reports that the preparation schedule for fishery management plans takes over 300 days, not including the time it takes to prepare the first draft for presentation to the Council.[180] Procedural and substantive questions may be raised as the plans fail to meet specified deadlines or as the plans receive less, rather hurried consideration in the initial development process in an attempt to make the deadlines. This problem may ease as the procedures and techniques of plan development are refined.

The inflexibility of the FCMA process limits the responsiveness of the management system to natural dynamics of the resources and the environment. Emergency regulations may be established in instances where immediate action is crucial to the protection of the stocks; however, these measures may be, and are, contested—to the detriment of the resources. This leads one to question the appropriateness of such explicit procedures in natural resource management. While we are not aware of an instance in which significant harm to the resource has resulted because of procedural delays, the possibility is not unlikely. A management system that is beset by procedural requirements must frequently resort to emergency measures, giving the system an ad hoc nature not unlike the management systems prevalent prior to FCMA.[181]

## THE FUTURE MANAGEMENT REGIME

This section examines the conclusions that can be drawn from the preceding comparisons on a more theoretical level. It is divided into two parts: the first sets forth general conclusions and predicted future bounds of zonal jurisdiction and the second concerns the possible creation of "regional law."

## Predictions

It is clear that the "fishery zones" in the North Pacific will continue to expand in scope. Generally, nations do not respond functionally. In the case of the 200-mile zones nations have made claims to regulate specific uses within a specific area, rather than claiming authority to prescribe solely for the use of the area. The result is that once the area is claimed, it is quite simple to expand the functional coverage until the zone is the "functional equivalent of a territorial sea."

In fact this has been and continues to be borne out, both globally and regionally. The 1977 amendments to the Canadian Fisheries Act, which are aimed quite explicitly at environmental degradation, illustrate the point. The amendments are considered by the government to be "habitat amendments," prohibiting the destruction of fish habitats and providing a mechanism for reviewing, restricting or prohibiting proposed undertakings.[182] Canada has long sought to incorporate such pollution controls within its national purview, and obviously intends to further pursue such policies.

The northeastern Pacific appears to be in a much more stable situation than the northwestern Pacific. The participants in the Northeast Pacific are relatively few and the rules of the game are well-delineated. Potential conflicts exist in several areas; however, they are quite evident and can be avoided or countered before retaliatory measures are invoked. For example, numerous problems have arisen between the U.S. and Japan concerning Japanese allocations in the Northeast Pacific. Still, these are negotiable and it is hoped that neither side will present a position so unreasonable as to endanger negotiations. To the extent that the FCMA is procedurally inflexible, if inequities are perceived by the foreign fishing state, conflicts may be intensified[183] and the acceptability of the FCMA eroded.

A second area that has significant potential for conflict is the increased competition between Canadian and American fishermen for resources off their adjacent coasts. Now that the foreigners have been removed or sufficiently restricted in their access to these areas, the competition between the fishermen will intensify. In essence, they can no longer blame the foreign fishermen and will have to deal with a problem that may have existed all along, camouflaged by foreign fishing. This will be particularly true for transboundary stocks.

The northwestern Pacific is quite another matter. The situation appears quite unstable and the potential for retaliatory action is high. Various reasons for this could be posed. First, there is an unmanageable number of participants, several of whom are unknown variables with respect to their ocean policies. This creates a large uncertainty factor.

Second, there is the intractable problem of delimitation in the Northwest Pacific. No resolution of the conglomerate of issues involved here can be expected in the near future. The nature of the conflict is such that separation of the functional areas in these disputes is impossible. Therefore, claims to living resources are entwined with similar claims to oil and gas deposits or strict territorial issues. Tensions are more likely to worsen in this area before they improve.

Another weak point is the annual Japanese–Soviet fisheries negotiations. These will become increasingly difficult and it is impossible to predict how long the notion of "mutual benefits" and the need to consider reciprocity will hold this tenuous relationship together.

## Creation of Regional Law

The everyday interactions of states generate an interdependency among them that is both real and perceived. The degree to which nations or groups of nations are, or perceive themselves to be, dependent influences each state's expectations of the benefits or costs to be derived from reciprocal or retaliatory action. The extent to which the individual state views reciprocity as a means by which to accrue benefits determines its reliance on, and its adherence to, such an alternative.

Adherence to reciprocity strengthens the relationship of dependence and creates a pattern of action among the states in which the action of one is predicated upon the action of another. McDougal and Feliciano refer to this as the "interdetermination of decisions."[184] This relates to a state's expectations of benefits and costs to be derived from a reciprocal course of action. As long as this spherical decision-making process is perceived as beneficial by all those involved, retaliation is not sought. Adherence to reciprocal alternatives rather than retaliatory ones tends to ameliorate external conflicts and, thus far, has been borne out in the North Pacific Ocean.

The perceived need for, and the reliance upon, reciprocity is strong, as is evidenced in the policies and legislation of the North Pacific countries. The need for reciprocity is not uniform among these nations, given the distribution of resources. The Japanese and the Soviets are in a substantially different position from Canada and the U.S. in this respect. Yet the wording of the Canadian bilateral fisheries agreements and the FCMA indicate that the willingness to extend similar rights of access carries the same force as actually doing so. In the North Pacific it would be extremely difficult to separate the generally held claims from those established through a process of reciprocity.

To what extent, then, does reciprocity contribute to the creation of international law? Does it have a role in this area and if so, what is its role? Certainly, the practice of incorporating reciprocal agreements into formal documents has a contributing effect. If two nations agree on a course of action or a rule to be mutually applied, and over time others acquiesce to the action or rule, the rule may develop into customary international law. In essence, reciprocal measures often represent the initial formalization of supranational norms. This is not to discount tacit reciprocal practices, as these, too, may be acceptable interactions between states, and over time may come to constitute international law.

The link between reciprocity and the creation of international law may be tenuous, yet in the North Pacific a case for this might be made. It rests, however, in the rather strong assumption that many of the similarities in national legislation are attributable to the desire to institutionalize or formalize reciprocal measures. At the very least, many of the similarities are the result of the pattern of interactions referred to above. This interdetermination of decisions is inherent in the interactions concerning living resources and historical patterns of use. The uniformity of the national legislation suggests the potential for agreement among these nations on the recognition of certain rules as norms for some form of supranational law.

The North Pacific countries examined here constitute a region, both geographically and functionally, in terms of the process of ocean use relating to living resources. In this instance then, it seems quite reasonable to propose that the similarities may represent the creation of a regional law, rather than a globally accepted international law.

In a broad sense, a form of regionalism can be seen as evolving with respect to the management of living resources. For the short term, the regional law might not be formalized. Nor must the concept of North Pacific "living aquatic resources" regionalism be institutionalized—it can exist as "implicit regionalism" and still maintain the same functions. Formalization of regional law is no more a requirement for regionalism than is the "express establishment of regional arrangements."[185] The lack of either or both of these need not diminish the force of the regional law.

The source of international law is a seemingly endless debate. Presently, it is generally accepted that the Draft Convention is very close to being customary international law. Therefore, those portions of the national legislation that are consistent with the Draft Convention can be considered to reflect international law. Those provisions that diverge from the Draft Convention, yet are consistent among the North Pacific legislative acts, can be thought to represent regional law. Those claims that are in conflict with both international and regional law will continue to be resolved separately by multilateral or bilateral arrangements.

It is open to question whether or not the Draft Convention, if adopted, would entirely preempt the regional law or the individual legislation. In the case of the former, the inconsistencies are minimal. Should the regional law diverge from the Draft Convention, the international provisions could be circumvented by general regional agreement, either formal or tacit, or by bilateral or multilateral arrangements among specific members of the regional group. As long as the inconsistent provisions are not applied to countries outside the region without their consent, such provision would not necessarily be in violation of the prevailing international law. In all instances, an adopted Draft Convention would place certain limitations on the scope and objectives of any regional law.[186]

Should inconsistencies occur between the coastal state legislation and the Draft Convention, the question of preemption is not clear. The lack of acceptability of national claims that are largely inconsistent with the Draft Convention could create serious enforcement problems for the coastal state. In most instances, the coastal state will probably seek to remedy any differences between its law and the adopted Law of the Sea (LOS) treaty.

The methods for coming into compliance with the Draft Convention vary. The Canadian Fisheries Act is generally subject to future amendments, thus the amendment process would be used to accommodate an international treaty. Article 16 of the Japanese Fishing Zone Law provides that in the event an international treaty addressing fishing zones comes into existence, the provisions of that treaty shall apply. This appears to provide for automatic preemption.

The Soviet Edict provides that the "work of UNCLOS III" will be taken into account in subsequent legislation, and stresses that the regimes set out in the Edict are provisional in nature. One, therefore, assumes that a UNCLOS treaty would be readily incorporated in Soviet legislation. There is no automatic termination of the FCMA upon the effective date of a LOS treaty. Section 401 provides that the FCMA may be brought into conformity with a comprehensive treaty by amendment to the regulations promulgated under the FCMA.

## CONCLUSION

The similarities between national legislation are extant and the inconsistencies relatively few. The actual claims made by the respective countries appear to be generally unchallenged and may, in fact, be unchallengeable if they are seen as establishing a body of regional law. Conflicts will arise not in reference to the claims themselves, but rather in response to the implementation procedures and application processes. The global trend toward expanding functional authority within the zones will most likely persist in the North Pacific until all valuable ocean uses come under coastal state control.

# 6

# Assessment of the Implications of Extended Coastal State Jurisdiction

What does extended coastal state jurisdiction over fisheries imply for the North Pacific and how can these implications be assessed? Extended coastal state jurisdiction over fisheries was proposed as a means of solving some continuing, severe problems for coastal states without large distant-water fleets. The objectives of the FCMA, for example, reflect a major concern with these problems: to ensure conservation of the stocks by extending exclusive coastal state authority and control over all fish except highly migratory species within 200 miles of the U.S. coast, and beyond 200 miles in the case of anadromous and continental shelf fishery resources; to encourage negotiation, implementation, and enforcement of international fishery agreements related to highly migratory species; to promote domestic commercial and recreational fishing; to provide for the preparation and implementation of Fishery Management Plans based upon determination of optimum yields; to establish Regional Fishery Management Councils; and to encourage development of fisheries currently underutilized or not utilized by U.S. fishermen, including bottomfish off Alaska.

The effects of extending U.S. jurisdiction over fisheries must therefore be assessed in terms of these objectives, in particular the extension of management authority and control in terms of conservation, the effects such extension will have on the pattern of allocations of various stocks, and the invention (and effects) of policies designed to encourage development of U.S. harvesting and processing capacity. In our relationship with Canada, the objectives are not spelled out directly and total production on the Pacific Coast is very small.

This chapter focuses on foreign fleets and the kinds of adaptations attempted. Extended jurisdiction has solved some problems, particularly those relating to conservation, but it has created some new problems, both for the foreign fleets and the coastal states.

In the Northwest Pacific, the situation is much more complicated than in the Northeast. In the Northeast, coastal state objectives are predominantly related to conservation, imposing controls over foreigners and developing domestic capacity. In the Northwest where large distant-water fleets are owned by coastal states and their nationals the problems are mainly a reaction to a global phenomenon. The situation became severe when the USSR used her extended jurisdiction to completely exclude the South Korean fleet from Soviet waters in the Pacific, drastically reduce the Japanese catch in Soviet waters, and (as part of the price for Japanese access to the Soviet zone) significantly increase its own catch in Japanese waters.

In addition, external political conflicts significantly affect the course of bargaining over fisheries in the Northwest Pacific.[1] Extensions of coastal state jurisdiction over fisheries allowed the Soviet Union to increase diplomatic pressure on Japan by linking settlement in fisheries issues to Japanese acquiescence on the Northern Territories question. Japan has agreements with China, North Korea, and South Korea. However, the North Korean problem is made more difficult because the North Koreans claim a 50-mile security zone; but accommodation between North Korea and Japan allows the former to put pressure on South Korea. Exclusions from the Northwest Pacific lead South Korea to increased attempts to expand in the Northeast Pacific, especially via joint ventures, primarily at the expense of Japan and the USSR.

These are the major implications of extended coastal state jurisdiction over fisheries in the North Pacific, and the following assessment focuses on what we consider to be four major categories of the issues raised: (a) claims to prescribe for management, (b) claims to delimit boundaries, (c) claims for access to markets, and (d) the long-term implications of fisheries management under extended jurisdiction. Given the configuration of the specific problems analyzed, the assessment of claims to prescribe for management is subdivided geographically between the Northeast and Northwest Pacific, and functionally between questions of conservation, allocation, enforcement, and accommodation of fishing practices.

The analysis included here focuses on the initial period of transition between 1976 and 1979. Since 1978, the situation in the Northwest Pacific has stabilized, albeit temporarily, since that equilibrium of roughly equal catches by the Japanese and Soviets in each other's zones is based on fundamentally unstable biological conditions. The Japanese seek primarily demersal species in the Soviet zone and yields can be managed on a long-term basis. The Soviets, however, seek primarily coastal pelagic stocks in the Japanese zone and these are subject to violent fluctuations over shorter periods of time. It is not clear at this point what will happen in the event that the Soviet catch declines precipitously while the Japanese catch remains stable.

In the Northeast Pacific, the situation is highly dynamic. The major developments have occurred with respect to anadromous species and two species of tanner crab (*Chionoecetes bairdi* and *C. opilio*) for which U.S. fishermen now take the entire optimum yield, and Japanese high-seas fishing for salmon of North American origin has been severely curtailed. On the other hand, the extension of U.S. authority over all demersal species in the eastern Bering Sea and Gulf of Alaska has not yet been accompanied by major expansions of U.S. catches because the economics are still adverse. Most development so far has been restricted to a narrow range of joint ventures in which U.S. fishermen catch fish for foreign processors and deliver to them at sea.

Although an unconventional and promising approach to the management of groundfish fisheries in the Bering Sea and Aleutian Island area is proposed in the 1981 Amendment

Package to the Fishery Management Plan (FMP), the Plan itself is not in force as of November 1981, so not much change has been introduced to the existing regulations governing the conduct of fishing operations. Substantial changes will be introduced, however, once the Plan and its various amendments enter into force.

## CLAIMS TO PRESCRIBE FOR MANAGEMENT: THE NORTHEAST PACIFIC

### United States

The Northeast Pacific fish stocks are divided into seven categories for the purpose of examining the specific claims to prescribe for management. The categories are Bering Sea and Aleutian Islands groundfish, Gulf of Alaska groundfish,[2] halibut, tanner crab, high-seas salmon, U.S.–Canada salmon, and Pacific groundfish. The management regime established by Canada for its Pacific coast is treated separately.

Management measures established for the various categories can be general or specific in nature. Such measures may prescribe for conservation purposes or for accommodation of fishing practices, although these are not always readily separable. Regulations aimed at preventing or reducing incidental catches are considered to be conservation measures (particularly in the case of groundfish versus halibut, given the depleted state of the halibut resource).

Total catch levels and allocations are determined by the following process: The maximum sustainable yield (MSY)[3] of a given species is determined; MSY should reflect the sustainable yield of the stock within a prescribed management area, and the best scientific information available should be used in the determination. The MSY is then used as the basis for determining the allowable biological catch (ABC), and eventually the optimum yield (OY)[4] for the stock. ABC is a deviation, either plus or minus, from MSY for primarily biological reasons, whereas optimum yield deviates from ABC for economic, social, or ecological reasons. Optimum yield may be higher or lower than ABC. Determination of the total allowable level of foreign fishing (TALFF)[5] is made by subtracting the expected domestic annual harvest from the optimum yield.[6] The TALFF is then allocated among foreign fishing nations desirous of harvesting a particular species, if they are party to a Governing International Fisheries Agreement (GIFA).[7] The allocation carries the stipulation that vessels of the foreign nation adhere to such management measures as may be prescribed and pay the requisite fees.

Management measures and allocations are discussed by the categories set out above. Enforcement provisions are more general in their application and invocation and are examined in a separate section.

### Bering Sea and Aleutian Island Groundfish

*Management Measures*—The data in table 6.1 represent the conservation and allocation determinations for 1977, 1978, and 1979 for species included in the Bering Sea and Aleutian Islands groundfish category: Alaska pollock, yellowfin sole, other flounders,

## TABLE 6.1

### BERING SEA AND ALEUTIAN ISLANDS GROUNDFISH STOCK ASSESSMENTS AND ALLOCATIONS

| | | Pollock | Yellowfin sole | Other flounders | Pacific ocean perch | | Sablefish | | Pacific cod | Herring | Atka mackerel | Squid |
|---|---|---|---|---|---|---|---|---|---|---|---|---|
| | | | | | EBS | AI | EBS | AI | | | | |
| Optimum Yield[a] | 1977[b] | 850,000 | 106,000 | 105,000 | 6,500 | 15,000 | 5,000 | 2,500 | 58,000 | 18,670 | | 10,000 |
| | 1978[c] | 950,000 | 126,000 | 159,000 | 6,500 | 15,000 | 3,000 | 1,500 | 70,500 | 18,670 | 24,800 | 10,800 |
| | 1979[c] | 950,000 | 106,000 | 139,000 | 6,500 | 15,000 | 3,000 | 1,500 | 58,000 | 18,670 | 24,800 | 10,000 |
| U.S. Capacity | 1977 | | | | | | | | | | | |
| | 1978 | 0 | 0 | 0 | 0 | 0 | 0 | 0 | 0 | 10,000 | 0 | 0 |
| | 1979 | 0 | 0 | 0 | 0 | 0 | 0 | 0 | 0 | 10,000 | 0 | 0 |
| Reserve | 1977 | | | | | | | | | | | |
| | 1978 | 0 | 0 | 0 | 0 | 0 | 100 | 0 | 500 | 0 | 0 | 0 |
| | 1979 | 0 | 0 | 0 | 0 | 0 | 600 | 0 | 1,500 | 0 | 0 | 0 |
| TALFF | 1977 | 950,000 | 106,000 | 105,000 | 6,500 | 15,000 | 5,000 | 2,400 | 58,000 | 200,000 | 22,000 | 10,000 |
| | 1978 | 950,000 | 126,000 | 159,000 | 6,500 | 15,000 | 2,900 | 1,500 | 70,000 | 8,670 | 24,800 | 10,800 |
| | 1979 | 950,000 | 106,000 | 139,000 | 6,500 | 15,000 | 2,400 | 1,500 | 56,500 | 8,670 | 24,800 | 10,000 |
| Japan | 1977 | 792,300 | 62,100 | 61,500 | 2,800 | 6,500 | 3,600 | 2,000 | 38,100 | | | 10,000 |
| | 1978 | 792,300 | 68,700 | 100,790 | 3,100 | 6,200 | 2,340 | 1,170 | 49,680 | 2,580 | 2,000 | 10,350 |
| | 1979 | 774,630 | 61,910 | 81,842 | 3,090 | 6,190 | 1,480 | 920 | 35,690 | 2,413 | 2,000 | 5,900 |
| Republic of Korea | 1977 | 40,000 | 0 | 0 | 0 | 0 | 400 | 200 | 0 | | | 0 |
| | 1978 | 60,000 | 200 | 710 | 300 | 700 | 210 | 125 | 2,520 | 20 | 100 | 270 |
| | 1979 | 85,000 | 2,600 | 2,600 | 300 | 700 | 370 | 230 | 1,600 | 450 | 1,750 | 1,750 |
| Taiwan | 1977 | 5,000 | 0 | 0 | 0 | 0 | 200 | 0 | 0 | | | 0 |
| | 1978 | 5,000 | 150 | 150 | 25 | 50 | 75 | 40 | 150 | 10 | 100 | 60 |
| | 1979 | 5,000 | 150 | 150 | 25 | 50 | 30 | 20 | 100 | 25 | 100 | 100 |
| USSR | 1977 | 112,700 | 40,800 | 40,000 | 3,500 | 8,100 | 600 | 200 | 17,200 | | | 0 |
| | 1978 | 92,700 | 56,950 | 57,350 | 3,075 | 8,050 | 275 | 165 | 17,650 | 6,060 | 22,600 | 120 |
| | 1979 | 60,370 | 40,590 | 53,658 | 3,010 | 7,885 | 370 | 230 | 16,110 | 5,657 | 20,450 | 1,750 |
| Poland | 1979 | 25,000 | 750 | 750 | 75 | 175 | 150 | 100 | 500 | 125 | 500 | 500 |

Sources:

[a] Optimum yield figures reflect total allowable catch.

[b] 1977 data taken from Bering Sea and Aleutian Islands Groundfish Draft Fishery Management Plan, July 1978.

[c] 1978 and 1979 data taken from *Fisheries of the United States, 1978*, Current Fishery Statistics No. 7800, National Marine Fisheries Service, NOAA, Department of Commerce, April 1979.

Pacific cod, Pacific ocean perch, sablefish, Atka mackerel, and squid. The permit require-ments of the FCMA remain in force at all times, and all foreign fishing vessels as defined in the Act must have a valid permit on board. Restrictions for Bering Sea and Aleutian Islands groundfish fisheries consist primarily of area closures.

In general, a management unit (or subunit where specific quotas apply) is closed to all fishermen of a nation for the remainder of the year after that nation's allocation of any species or species group, as listed in table 6.1, is reached. This measure is designed to "discourage foreign fleets from covertly targeting on depleted species" and to prevent damaging by-catches after the allowed catch has been taken.[8] This provision, in the Bering Sea and Aleutian Islands area as well as other regions, has been the source of considerable contention. The foreign fishermen maintain that the provision is extremely difficult to live with, especially when incidentally caught species receive small quotas. If the foreign nation accurately reports its catch of all species subject to quotas (which it is required to do whether or not the fish are retained),[9] its target fisheries will be terminated before its quota is achieved. This argument is countered by the U.S. officials, who maintain that the provision and its potential consequences provide the incentive necessary to spur development of fish gear that reduces incidental catch and waste. It has also been argued that this provision may encourage false reporting of incidental catches in an attempt to skirt the provision.[10]

The trawl fisheries are subject to more specific restrictions. For example, there is to be no trawling year-round in the "Bristol Bay Pot Sanctuary." This provision is designed to prevent incidental catch of juvenile halibut, which are known to concentrate in this area, as well as to accommodate fishing practices (i.e., to prevent conflicts between foreign trawling gear and U.S. king and tanner crab pots). Furthermore, there is to be no trawling from December 1 to May 31 in the "winter halibut savings area" to protect winter concentrations of juvenile halibut and spawning concentrations of pollock and flounder. While there is no limitation on foreign longline vessel days in the Bering Sea,[11] longlining landward of the 500 m isobath in the winter halibut savings area is limited to June 1 to November 30.[12]

There were no gear restrictions in force for the Bering Sea groundfish up to 1979. Gear limitations listed for 1977 in the Preliminary Management Plan were expressly deleted from the subsequent supplements to the Plan. To accommodate the fishing practices of U.S. fixed gear operations and small, inshore fishery vessels, as well as to prevent catch of localized inshore species important to U.S. fishermen and natives, there is no foreign fishing within 12 miles of the baseline used to measure the territorial sea (with some exceptions in the western Aleutian Islands). To measure adequate supplies of spawners and roe-bearing herring for domestic inshore areas, there is no fishing for herring by foreign fishermen east of 168° W longitude.[13]

*Allocation*—In the Bering Sea and Aleutian Islands regions, the extension of manage-ment authority and control was primarily for conservation purposes; the development of U.S. harvesting capacity, however much desired, is not the primary consideration in this instance. In terms of the allocations to the individual foreign countries, reciprocal fishing interests and traditional fisheries are the primary criteria. The total allowable level of foreign fishing has continued to approach the optimum yield, except in the case of herring, which has a considerable domestic take. Some of the fluctuations in allocations appear to reflect changes in the optimum yield determinations. This is true of flounders, sablefish in both the Bering Sea and Aleutian Islands, and Pacific cod.

The pattern of allocation among foreign fishing nations in the area has changed somewhat. A major reallocation of Alaska pollock occurred from 1977 to 1979, with Japan losing some of their allocation and the Soviet Union experiencing a significant loss. In the case of Atka mackerel, the increased allocation to the Republic of Korea appears to have come directly from the Soviet Union's allocation. Japan has suffered a significant reduction in its squid allocation, the difference being made up by the Republic of Korea and Taiwan. The U.S., therefore, has apparently been willing to compensate the ROK in the eastern Bering Sea, at the expense of Japan and the USSR, for losses suffered in the Northwest Pacific.

## Gulf of Alaska Groundfish

The principal commercial groundfish species represented in the Gulf of Alaska fishery are: Alaska pollock, Pacific cod, sablefish, Pacific ocean perch, flounders, other rockfishes, Atka mackerel, squid, and other species.

*Management Measures*—The regulatory provisions in effect in the Gulf of Alaska were designed to protect and rebuild the halibut resource of the area and, subject to that constraint, encourage "as rapid a growth as possible of the U.S. groundfish industry."[14] Although halibut is regulated separately, the potentially severe effects of trawl fisheries, and perhaps

TABLE 6.2

EX-VESSEL VALUES AS BASIS FOR FEE SCHEDULES, BERING SEA AND ALEUTIAN ISLANDS

| | Average ex-vessel value (per metric ton) | | | |
|---|---|---|---|---|
| | 1977[a] | 1978[a] | 1979[b] | |
| Pacific cod | 251 | 282 | 359 | |
| Other flounders | 318 | 387 | 407 | |
| Herring | 161 | 344 | (100) | roeless |
| | | | (991) | with roe |
| Atka mackerel | 130 | 138 | 223 | |
| Other groundfish | 45 | 48 | 49 | |
| Sablefish | 372 | 399 | (1477) | longline-caught |
| | | | (551) | trawl-caught |
| Squid | 82 | 55 | 458 | |
| Pollock | 98 | 84 | 176 | |
| Pacific ocean perch | | 280 | 356 | |

[a]*Federal Register*, 42,195 (October 7, 1977), 54588–54590. Ex-vessel values are used in calculation of poundage fees.

[b]*Fisheries of the United States*, Current Fishery Statistics No. 7800, National Marine Fisheries Service/NOAA (April 1979), p. xviii.

of the sablefish setline fishery, on halibut requires consideration of conservation measures designed to minimize such effects.

*Conservation*—To reduce uneven exploitation on concentrated stocks, the TALFF for all species has been apportioned to individual statistical areas. To minimize the incidental catch of nontarget species and prevent overexploitation of small stocks, once a nation's allocation of *any* species or species group in an individual statistical area has been exceeded, that nation's fishermen may not fish in that area for the remainder of the year.[15]

Several time-area closures were established to protect the halibut resources, primarily by reducing the incidental catch. Areas closed to foreign trawling are 140° W – 147° W from January 1 to February 15 and November 1 to December 31 (this is to prevent possible high incidental catches of crabs, as well as to accommodate domestic fixed crab gear); and the restriction of gear in the sablefish longline fishing to longliners (hook and line) or pot gear.[16]

*Accommodation of Fishing Practices*—Many of the management measures in the Gulf of Alaska were established to allow initial and continued development of domestic fisheries. Foreign fishermen may not retain any of the following species or species groups when caught incidentally to the target species: (1) salmonids, (2) Pacific halibut, (3) shrimp, (4) herring, (5) "creatures of the continental shelf," and (6) scallops. Year-round closures are in effect in the following areas for foreign fishermen: (1) landward of 12 miles as measured from the territorial sea baseline (to prevent conflicts with established, inshore domestic fisheries), (2) within three U.S. fishing sanctuaries (to provide for expansion of domestic setline sablefish fisheries), (3) the Davidson Bank (to provide for development of domestic groundfish fisheries), and (4) east of 140° W is closed to setline fishing (to prevent conflicts with the development of the U.S. sablefish fishing). To prevent interference with the opening of the halibut season, foreign trawling is not allowed in the three "Kodiak halibut areas" five days before to five days after the opening of the domestic halibut setline fishery.

*Allocation*—The total TALFF for Gulf of Alaska groundfish has decreased substantially from approximately 260,000 metric tons (MT) in 1977 to approximately 190,000 MT in 1979. The individual species stock assessments and national allocations are shown in table 6.3. Unlike the Bering Sea and Aleutian Islands regions, the Gulf of Alaska allocations to foreign nations reflect an increased U.S. interest in, and capacity to harvest, several of the groundfish species. Sablefish is illustrative of significantly reduced levels of foreign fishing.

Japan has suffered the greatest loss in sablefish. Reductions in Japan's allocation were not reallocated to other foreign nations, rather the optimum yield (OY) determination was reduced. Sablefish has been one of the most contentious issues in the Gulf of Alaska. This is the most important American groundfish species apart from halibut, and the one of keenest competition between Japanese and American fishermen. In question here is the Japanese allocation, the OY upon which it was based, and the closed areas. An example of this problem is set out below. Similar contentions arose in other fisheries, such as Alaska pollock.

Initially, the Japanese requested that the 1978 quota be maintained at the 1977 level— 19,500 MT, yet the final draft FMP lowered the Japanese allocation to 4,400 MT with a 3,000 MT reserve, based on the OY and domestic capacity determinations. The 1978 OY

# TABLE 6.3

## GULF OF ALASKA GROUNDFISH STOCK ASSESSMENTS AND ALLOCATIONS

| | | Pollock | Pacific cod | Sablefish | Pacific ocean perch | Other rockfish | Flounders | Atka mackerel | Squid | Others | (Totals) |
|---|---|---|---|---|---|---|---|---|---|---|---|
| Optimum Yield | 1977[a] | 126,000[d] | 6,300[d] | 22,000[d] | 30,000[d] | — | 37,500[d] | 22,000[d] | —[d] | 16,200[d] | 258,200 |
| | 1978[b] | 168,800 | 40,600 | 15,000 | 25,000 | 7,600 | 33,500 | 24,800 | 2,000 | 16,200 | 282,600 |
| | 1979[c] | 168,800 | 34,800 | 13,000 | 25,000 | 7,600 | 33,500 | 24,800 | 2,000 | 16,200 | 187,479 |
| U.S. Capacity | 1977 | 1,000 | 5,000 | 4,500 | 3,000 | — | 7,000 | 0 | 0 | 1,300 | |
| | 1978 | 17,700 | 15,500 | 4,000 | 1,100 | 2,000 | 9,200 | 0 | 0 | 0 | |
| | 1979 | 6,100 | 4,000 | 4,000 | 400 | 700 | 1,300 | 0 | 0 | 300 | |
| Reserve | 1977 | — | — | — | — | — | — | — | — | — | |
| | 1978 | 0 | 0 | 800 | 0 | 0 | 0 | 0 | 100 | 500 | |
| | 1979 | 66,900 | 4,996 | 3,250 | 3,950 | 1,750 | 4,850 | 2,750 | 500 | 2,350 | |
| TALFF | 1977 | 125,000 | 1,300 | 17,550[e] | 47,000 | — | 30,500 | 22,000 | — | 14,900 | |
| | 1978 | 151,100 | 25,100 | 10,200 | 23,900 | 5,600 | 24,300 | 24,800 | 1,900 | 15,700 | |
| | 1979 | 87,700 | 14,304 | 5,750 | 19,950 | 1,425 | 21,450 | 22,050 | 1,500 | 13,350 | |
| Japan | 1977 | 44,100 | (1,445)[e] | 13,900 | 19,800 | 2,700 | 18,700 | 0 | — | 5,800 | |
| | 1978 | 40,740 | 14,722 | 8,750 | 6,448 | 1,510 | 21,370 | 2,000 | 1,155 | 5,090 | |
| | 1979 | 18,474 | 6,200 | 4,950 | 5,232 | 1,113 | 19,218 | 1,758 | 180 | 3,672 | |
| Mexico | 1977 | 0 | 0 | — | 0 | 0 | 0 | 0 | — | 0 | |
| | 1978 | 6,000 | 2,400 | 100 | 1,000 | 224 | 100 | 100 | 450 | 500 | |
| | 1979 | 20,000 | 4,400 | 100 | 2,089 | 273 | 100 | 100 | 800 | 1,430 | |
| Poland | 1977 | 6,000 | 0 | 0 | 0 | 0 | 0 | 1,000 | — | 200 | |
| | 1978 | 15,840 | 798 | 50 | 2,428 | 636 | 100 | 1,030 | 50 | 1,455 | |
| | 1979 | 6,729 | 300 | 50 | 1,125 | 154 | 140 | 874 | 160 | 839 | |
| Republic of Korea | 1977 | 35,800 | — | 1,600 | 500 | 100 | 0 | 0 | | 0 | |
| | 1978 | 31,810 | 1,662 | 1,000 | 5,001 | 1,185 | 200 | 100 | 145 | 2,595 | |
| | 1979 | 13,828 | 500 | 550 | 3,800 | 738 | 150 | 130 | 170 | 2,452 | |
| USSR | 1977 | 63,100 | (1,010) | 0 | 8,700 | 1,200 | 1,800 | 21,000 | — | 12,400 | |
| | 1978 | 56,710 | 5,518 | 100 | 9,023 | 2,045 | 2,030 | 21,570 | 100 | 6,060 | |
| | 1979 | 28,669 | 2,904 | 100 | 7,704 | 1,572 | 1,842 | 19,188 | 190 | 4,957 | |

Sources:

[a] 1977 Preliminary Management Plan for Gulf of Alaska Groundfish September 1976.

[b] 1978 data taken from *Fisheries of the United States, 1978*, National Marine Fisheries Service, NOAA, (April 1979), p. xxiv.

[c] 1979 Personal communication, Dr. Fred Olson, National Marine Fisheries Service, Washington, D.C. Data include reallocations made through May 1979.

[d] Optimum yield in 1977 is represented by Total Allowable Catch.

[e] Represents an incidental catch of 2% of the trawl catch.

had been set at 10,000 MT (12,000 MT lower than 1977) to allow rapid rebuilding of the stocks, and to account for reported declines in Japanese CPUE in the Aleutian Islands region. Comments received from the Japanese insisted that the OY could be raised by at least 1,100 MT, as justified by Japanese CPUE statistics for the Bering Sea, Aleutian Islands, and Gulf of Alaska, which indicated an increase of 10% between 1975 and 1976.[17] The original OY figure simply could not be justified biologically, and the sablefish OY was eventually raised to 15,000 MT.

In August 1978, the Japanese submitted further requests concerning the sablefish resources of the Gulf of Alaska. They urged that in order to avoid unnecessary hardship on Japanese longliners, the reserve allocations be released, and any unutilized domestic annual harvest (DAH) be reallocated for stocks east of 140° W longitude.[18] They also requested that Japanese longliners be allowed to fish in this area during the U.S. longline vessel ''off season'' and that a 20 percent (100 m) allowance be given in areas of depth contour restrictions.

Of further concern to the Japanese was the closing of four areas in the Gulf of Alaska to foreign fishermen. The Japanese claim that the sablefish resources of the Bering Sea, Aleutian Islands, and Gulf of Alaska intermingle to such an extent that there was no biological basis for the closed areas.[19] Furthermore, the closure of these areas was not necessary to prevent conflict between U.S. domestic fishermen and Japanese fishermen; other U.S. regulations prohibit foreign longlining shoreward of the 500 meter depth contours, where most of the domestic fishermen operate. The closed areas in Southeast and Yakutat also impair the effectiveness of longlining operations: the Japanese established that such closures would eliminate 40−50 percent of the total longlining in the open areas. A compromise was reached on this point. The North Pacific Council allowed Japanese fishing west of 141° W in the Cape of St. Elias area.

In addition to reductions in foreign allocations, there have also been changes in the patterns of allocation among foreign fishing nations. Generally, the traditional fishing nations have experienced reductions in their allocation to accommodate the Mexican fishery.[20] Notable among such reallocations are the reductions in Japan's Alaska pollock and squid fisheries, while Mexico received significant increases in their allocations for both species.

*Quotas by Subarea*—Five subareas were established in the Gulf of Alaska region: Shumagin, Chirikof, Kodiak, Yakutat, and Southeast. Allocations in this region are made by subarea. The Japanese objected strenuously to the allocation of quotas for various species by subarea. They maintained that this procedure was not necessary for the conservation of the stocks and, given the migratory nature of the stocks, the distribution of the fish might not balance with the assigned quotas. This could seriously impair the efficiency of fishing operations and could possibly damage the resource if the area abundance did not coincide with the area quota. The United States maintained that these area allocations were designed to permit each nation to take its allocation with a minimum amount of interference from other nations in each area, and to permit the by-catch in each area to be as large as possible. Allocations by fishing area were also made in 1979, keeping in mind the possible reallocation of additional resources (reserves).[21]

TABLE 6.4

EX-VESSEL VALUES AS BASIS FOR FEE SCHEDULE, GULF OF ALASKA

| | 1977[a] | 1978[b] | 1979[c] | |
|---|---|---|---|---|
| Pacific cod | $251 | $282 | $ 359 | |
| Pacific flounders | 318 | 387 | 407 | |
| Other rockfishes | 350 | 298 | 356 | |
| Atka mackerel | 130 | 138 | 223 | |
| Other groundfish | 44 | 48 | 49 | |
| Alaska pollock | 98 | 84 | 176 | |
| Pacific ocean perch | | 280 | 356 | |
| Sablefish | 372 | 399 | (1,477) | longline-caught |
| | | | ( 551) | trawl-caught |
| Squid | 82 | 55 | 458 | |

Sources:

[a]*U.S. Federal Register*, 42,27 (February 9, 1977), 8176, 8177

[b]*Marine Fisheries Review*, 40,1: 29.

[c]*Fisheries of the United States*, 1978, Current Fishery Statistics No. 7800, p. xviii, National Marine Fisheries Service/NOAA (April 1979).

## *Halibut*

There are essentially two components to the halibut question: incidental catch by foreign fishermen, and Canadian—U.S. management of the halibut resources. The first comes under the purview of either Canada or the U.S. separately, and has been dealt with peripherally in preceding sections. The issues involved in the joint management of halibut are more complex. A potential problem lies in the incidental catch of halibut by domestic trawlers; this is becoming increasingly significant as the U.S. groundfish fishery expands.

*Canadian—U.S. Management of Halibut*—Even with the extension of jurisdiction, the International Pacific Halibut Commission (IPHC) temporarily retained jurisdiction over the U.S. and Canadian setline halibut fishery. The fishery was regulated pursuant to the regulations adopted in accordance with the Pacific Halibut Fishery Convention between Canada and the United States, which entered into force October 28, 1953 and allowed reciprocal fishing in the Canadian and U.S. zones. The treaty was scheduled to expire April 1, 1979, or to be renegotiated as required by the FCMA. Under the FCMA, the Secretary of State, in cooperation with the Secretary of Commerce, must renegotiate any treaty pertaining to fishing within the U.S. 200-mile conservation zone that is inconsistent with the purposes, policies, or provisions of the FCMA. The 1953 Halibut Convention was determined to be inconsistent with the FCMA in several aspects and therefore required renegotiation.

Reciprocal access was the focal issue in the negotiations concerning the Halibut Convention. Yet the animosity between the two countries over fisheries and related issues had intensified. Since 1926, Canada had taken an estimated 36 percent of the halibut catch, the U.S. 64 percent. The amount nationals of each nation have taken off the other's coast has been declining steadily, particularly since 1971. Previous research has shown that there is definitely transboundary movement of halibut stock components. While both countries clearly have the option of eliminating the other's fishery in its zone, they cannot control interceptions in the other's waters. Further, U.S. fishery management councils must take the intermingling of stock components into account when prescribing management measures for halibut.[22] Thus, it was essential that some form of communication with Canada be maintained regarding management of halibut resources.

Nonetheless, on April 1, 1979, the U.S. gave notice of its intention to terminate the Convention in two years. In August 1977, the two governments had appointed special negotiators to address boundary and related resource issues of joint concern, including the future of the Convention. By February 1979, tentative agreement had been reached with Canada on new fisheries arrangements off the west coasts of both countries, including essential elements of a revised halibut convention. The new agreement, consisting of a Protocol (with Annex) amending the Convention for the Preservation of the Halibut Fishery of the Northern Pacific Ocean and Bering Sea, and a Note (with Annex) dealing with West Coast halibut and groundfish arrangements, entered into force March 29, 1979, when an exchange of Notes between the two governments was completed.

The International Pacific Halibut Commission was continued under Article III of the Protocol; it retains its research functions, making such investigations as are necessary into the life history of the Pacific halibut. The Commission may, with the approval of the parties, regulate the halibut fishing operations of fishermen of both countries, as set out in Article III, Section 3, of the Protocol. Regulatory measures include fishing seasons, catch limits, and gear size and restrictions, and are set by areas and subareas to obtain the appropriate distribution of fishing effort. These regulatory areas were established to allow for fluctuations in abundance of individual stock components. Specific seasons and catch limits are assigned by regulatory area in accordance with the assessment of stock abundance and to protect juvenile halibut and concentrations of halibut on the spawning grounds.

Under Article II, each party has the right to enforce the Convention and any regulations adopted under it against its own nationals and fishing vessels in all Convention waters, and against nationals or fishing vessels of either party, or third parties, in that portion of the Convention area in which it exercises exclusive fisheries jurisdiction.

Accompanying the Protocol amending the Halibut Convention was an agreement relating to West Coast groundfish. The new agreement consists of two parts—a Note and an Annex. The Note makes clear that the nationals and vessels of the United States may fish for groundfish in the maritime area off the west coast of Canada, in which Canada exercises exclusive fisheries jurisdiction. The Annex spells out in detail the procedures and restrictions governing the fishing operations in that maritime area.

Although several minor interpretive problems arose in the initial implementation, this agreement has been much less problematic than the U.S.–Canada East Coast fisheries agreements. A problem exists, however, with the take of albacore off British Columbia by U.S. fishermen. Canada seized several U.S. fishing vessels during the Fall 1979 season on the charge of illegal fishing in the Canadian zone. The U.S. replied that it did not recognize

Canadian jurisdiction over highly migratory species. In the negotiations the Canadians attempted to link the questions of development of a herring fishery by the state of Washington, and the Canadian share in the 1978—1979 halibut harvest, to the settlement of the albacore issue.[23] However, this attempt was unsuccessful.

The issue was settled by a Treaty on Pacific Coast Albacore Tuna Vessels and Port Privileges, which was signed in Washington, D.C. on May 26, 1981 and entered into force on July 29, 1981. This Treaty is "[w]ithout prejudice to the respective juridical positions of both Parties regarding highly migratory species of tuna. . . ." It therefore regulates not the catch of albacore but the vessels of either nationality by imposing a requirement for notification prior to entry into the fishery, and by stipulating ports in either country that vessels may enter, land and transship their catches upon payment of nondiscriminatory tuna landing fees. Catches may also be sold for export in bond or, upon payment of the applicable customs duties, sold locally.

## Incidental Catch

Foreign fishermen are strictly prohibited from targeting on halibut, yet significant amounts of halibut are caught incidentally by other groundfish fisheries. Prior to the extension of jurisdiction, this incidental catch was controlled by bilateral agreements between the U.S. or Canada and the foreign trawling nations. With the advent of extended jurisdiction, the foreign groundfish fisheries came under the purview of the coastal states and regulation of incidental catch was incorporated into the management measures governing the groundfish fisheries. In the Northeast Pacific, regulations of this kind relate primarily to the Bering Sea, Aleutian Islands, and Gulf of Alaska groundfish fisheries, as sketched below. In the Bering Sea and Aleutian Islands region, the following areas are closed to foreign fishing during the specified period to protect juvenile halibut that concentrate in the areas:

(a) Bristol Bay Pot Sanctuary closed to foreign trawling year-round
(b) Winter Halibut Savings Area from December 1 to May 31
   (i) closed to foreign trawling
   (ii) closed to longlining landward of the 500 m isobath

In the Gulf of Alaska, areas closed to foreign trawling to protect concentrations of spawning halibut are:

(a) 140° W — 147° W from January 1 to February 15 and November 1 to December 31
(b) 147° W — 157° W from February 16 to May 31
(c) East to 157° W and landward of the 500 m isobath is closed year-round to the setline fishery (to protect juvenile halibut as well as the spawners)

A further restriction was instituted in the Gulf of Alaska to reduce the incidental catch of halibut: from January 1 to May 31 and from December 1 to 31, only pelagic trawls can be employed in areas where foreign trawling is permitted during these time periods. Although dissatisfaction was expressed over the area-time closures for trawling, the restrictions placed on longlining and demersal trawls were the most contentious issues. The Japanese lodged protests against these limitations, citing numerous reasons. Requesting that the restrictions be applicable only to trawling, the Japanese urged that the 500 m depth limitation on longlining be rescinded since Pacific cod, the target species in this instance, was intended to ameliorate the effects of a smaller sablefish allocation.[24] The argument against imposing the pelagic trawl restriction was based on the contentions that (1) the conservation of halibut could be accomplished with the establishment of closed areas, closed seasons, and restriction by depth of water (i.e., the use of gear limitations is redundant); (2) such restriction hampers the efficient use of existing equipment; and (3) it prevents effective harvest of other species.[25]

The Japanese further noted that the ratio of incidentally caught halibut in the summer versus the winter was statistically produced and may not be that relevant under actual conditions.[26] It should be noted that current observer reports and research indicate that the incidental catch rate is estimated to be .267 individuals per metric ton for the entire region. This is much lower than previously, the decline being attributed to the closure of critical areas to trawling and, in some instances, longlining.[27] Observer reports from the Gulf of Alaska, monitoring the Japanese longline cod fishery west of 157° W, indicate approximately 2.5 halibut per metric ton in waters less than 500 meters.[28]

## Tanner Crab

The tanner crab fishery focuses on two species: *Chionoecetes bairdi* and *Chionoecetes opilio*, with the commercially more desirable *C. bairdi* constituting 90−95 percent of the catch. Presently, tanner crab is harvested primarily by domestic commercial fishermen and Japanese nationals fishing in the eastern Bering Sea. The management measures set out for this fishery have generated considerable debate, the area closures being the most contested.

*Conservation*—Regulatory measures designed to ensure conservation of the stocks are relatively straightforward and apply to domestic and foreign fishermen alike. The stocks are regulated by geographical areas to allow for selective application of conservation measures based on stock differences such as variations in time of molting, breeding, and softshell conditions.[29] To assure continued reproductive levels, the taking of female crabs is prohibited, as is the retention of male crabs having less than a 5.5 inch (140 mm) carapace width, except in Prince William Sound, where the size limit is 5.3 inches. Gear restrictions have been imposed to protect nonlegal crabs. Legal gear for tanner crab includes pots, ring nets, or scuba; foreign fishermen are limited to the use of pots. Seasonal closures are in effect, as required by the tanner crab life cycle. Closed seasons seek to encompass molting, peak breeding of oldshell females, and egg hatch periods.[30] For foreign fishermen, the season opens at 0001 hours on March 1, with no specific termination date or time.[31]

*Accommodation of Fishing Practices*—Area restrictions on the Japanese fishermen in the Bering Sea were instituted to minimize conflict between domestic and foreign harvesting (in terms of gear interference), competition for concentrations of crab, and incidental catches of *C. bairdi*. The objectives found in the Fishery Management Plan (FMP) state clearly that these measures are designed to accommodate the expanding U.S. tanner crab fishery. Gradually the Japanese crabbing operations have been pushed northward. In 1975 the Japanese fishery operating east of 164° W longitude and south of 55°30' N was eliminated. The 1977 Preliminary Management Plan (PMP) set the southern boundary at 56° N latitude in the Bering Sea and throughout the Northeast Pacific;[32] and the 1978 FMP further expanded the restricted area, prohibiting Japanese operations south of the 58° N latitude. This area limit coupled with the 1978 allocations generated a furor among the Japanese and U.S. government officials.[33] A substantive objection relating to the physical characteristics of the area north of 58° N was raised by the Japanese. They claimed that ice would hamper the harvest during the initial days. During the FMP deliberations Japanese pictures were submitted showing the ice covering that lasted for 50 days during the first fishing months of the season.[34] However, at the March meeting of the North Pacific Council, satellite photographs, taken by the National Oceanic and Atmospheric Administration (NOAA) Satellite Service, were presented. While they quite clearly showed ice formations existing during the initial stages of the tanner crab season, there was no indication that the ice was interfering with the fishery operations.[35]

*Allocation*—The allowable level of foreign fishing on tanner crab has not decreased since the implementation of the U.S. fishery conservation zone. However, the Japanese have not been able to harvest *C. bairdi*; the prohibition on the foreign taking of *C. bairdi* was rescinded in the amended Preliminary Management Plan published in mid-March 1978.[36] These regulations were modified to prohibit Japanese tanner crab operations south of 58° N. Given the natural cessation of occurrence of *C. bairdi* north of 58° N, it is difficult to estimate what amount of *C. bairdi* would be taken. In spite of predictions to the contrary, the 1978 regulations and allocations did not significantly diminish their take of tanner crab.[37] In 1979, the regulations were further amended to allow the Japanese to harvest 2,500 metric tons of *C. opilio* between 54° N and 58° N latitude, west of 173° E. (See table 6.5.) Retention of *C. bairdi* is still prohibited.[38]

*Fee Schedule*—The average ex-vessel value used in calculating the poundage fees applicable to tanner crab remained the same in 1978 as in 1977: $441 per metric ton. In 1979

## TABLE 6.5

### TANNER CRAB
### STOCK ASSESSMENT AND ALLOCATION
### (METRIC TONS)

| Date | OY | Reserve | Initial DAH | Initial TALFF |
|---|---|---|---|---|
| May 1977 | 12,497 | | 0 | 12,497 |
| 1978 | 16,360–17,268 | | 1,360–2,268 | 15,000 |
| (N. of 58° N, revised) | | | | |
| | 18,000–20,000 | | | |
| 1979 | 68,556 | 0 | 53,556 | 15,000 |

the ex-vessel value rose to $661. A permit fee of $1.00 per gross registered ton per year for fishing vessels, and 50¢ per gross registered ton per year for processing vessels (with an upper limit of $2,500), were also assessed.[39]

## High-Seas Salmon Fisheries of Japan

Both national and international legislation support claims of the "states of origin" to manage anadromous stocks within and beyond their fishery zones. The provisions relating to this are discussed in detail in the previous chapter. The U.S. acknowledges the right of the Japanese to continue their high-seas salmon fishery, but claims the right to manage anadromous stocks of North American origin on the high seas. Prior to the extension of fishery jurisdiction, this was done through the INPFC; the FCMA, however, requires that previously concluded international fishery agreements be renegotiated and brought into accordance with the provisions of the Act.[40] To this end, in February 1977, the U.S. gave notice of its intention to withdraw from the INPFC in one year unless the treaty was renegotiated to be consistent with the FCMA. These negotiations began in October 1977 and ended in April 1978, when a new agreement was reached; the new treaty has since been ratified by the U.S. Congress.

*Management Measures*—Although it is claimed that, fundamentally, the abstention provisions of the North Pacific Fisheries Treaty were set to assure the conservation of salmon of North American origin, the resources are in fact being conserved to maintain U.S. and Canadian salmon fisheries. In essence, the management measures are set to accommodate fishing interests, although periodic requests for abstention from fishing specific species are submitted for conservation purposes. For example, during 1977 Japan continued its operations west of 175° W, taking salmon primarily of Asian origin, although North American salmon were particularly vulnerable to the mothership salmon fishery. United States scientists noted that the Bristol Bay sockeye salmon run was at or near the low point in its cycle and the western Alaskan chinooks continued to exhibit poor abundance. For these reasons, the National Marine Fisheries Service in the January 1977 Final Environmental Impact Statement—Preliminary Management Plan for High-Seas Salmon Fisheries of Japan recommended that "species restrictions be imposed on Japan's high seas salmon fishing in 1977 to keep interceptions of North American salmon at as low a level as possible." Such restrictions could only come about through a negotiated agreement between the U.S. and Japan, which did not materialize in time for the 1977 season.

Under the new treaty, the management regime operates on an area-time closure system. Japanese salmon fishery operations (this includes both the Japanese mothership operations and the land-based driftnet fishery) in the waters of the Convention area are regulated as follows:

    1. Fishery operations will be allowed:
       (a) North of 56° N (lat.), east of 175° E (long.) and outside the U.S. fishery conservation zone beginning on June 26 (Japan Standard Time) (1500 June 25 GMT) of each year, the Japanese mothership fishery shall conduct no more than 22 mothership fleet days in the

area between 175° E. (long.) and 180° (long.) and no more than 31 mothership fleet days in the area between 180° (long.) and 175° W (long.).

(b) North of 46° N (lat.), between 175° E. (long.) and 170° E. (long.), outside the U.S. fishing conservation zone, salmon fishery operations shall not begin before June 1 (Japan Standard Time) (1500 May 31 GMT) of each year.

(c) West of 175° E (long.), within the U.S. fishery conservation zone, salmon fishery operations shall not begin before June 10 (Japan Standard Time) (1500 June 9 GMT) of each year.

(d) Such operations will not be allowed:
East of 170° E (long.) the southern limit of the Japanese mothership fishery and the northern limit of the Japanese land-based fishery shall remain at 46° N (lat.) West of 170°E (long.) the southern limit of the Japanese mothership fishery shall not extend south of the 46° N (lat.), and the northern limit of the Japanese land-based fishery shall not extend north of 48° N (lat.).

2. There shall be no salmon fishery east of 175° E (long.), except for areas specified above, unless such operations are agreed to for a temporary period by Canada, Japan, and the U.S.[41]

The treaty defines a mothership fleet day as "one mothership with no more than forty-one catcher boats present during a portion of any one calendar day." While there are no specific gear or fishing procedure limitations, any modifications that might affect current fishing efficiency are subject to examination by the Treaty parties. Such modifications may result in a change in the number of authorized fleet days.[42]

Requirements for reporting of biostatistical information continue to be prescribed by the INPFC; it is anticipated they will remain as they were previously, with emphasis given to improving the data received from the Japanese land-based driftnet fishery.

Fishing vessels engaged in Japanese salmon fishery operating within the fishery conservation zone are required to have on board a valid registration permit issued by the U.S. government. Such vessels are also required to accommodate "scientific observers," bearing all expenses incurred by such accommodation.[43]

A Certificate of Inclusion relating to the incidental taking of marine mammals is normally required; this requirement was suspended for the period ending June 9, 1981.[44] During this time, the U.S. and Japan conducted joint research to study the effect of the Japanese salmon fishery on marine mammal populations. Specifically, a Japanese–U.S. research program was established to study the role of the Dall porpoise in the North Pacific gillnet fishery. The Japanese collected and furnished all available relevant data associated with the incidental take, and the U.S. agreed to supply equipment and training for the data collection and to analyze life-history data. The eventual goal was to develop gear for porpoise mortality reduction.[45]

On the basis of the research results produced in 1978, 1979, and 1980[46] and on the basis of a ruling by Administrative Law Judge Frank W. Vanderheyden in Seattle, Washington on March 5 and 6, 1981, the Acting Administrator of NOAA issued a decision limiting the Japanese high-seas salmon fishery in the North Pacific to an incidental take of 5,500 Dall porpoise, 450 northern fur seals, and 25 northern sea lions. The permit was effective on June 10, 1981 for three years.[47] National Marine Fisheries Service was required to continue to monitor the fishery to ensure that quotas were not exceeded.

*Allocations*—The following summary of information was compiled by the National Marine Fisheries Service on salmon in relation to the high-seas salmon fisheries of Japan. The numbers given below reflect estimates of the average annual catches of salmon of both North American and Asian origin by the Japanese mothership fishery for five areas, as illustrated in figure 6.1. These areas represent the time-area closures set out in the new INPFC treaty, as described in the preceding portion of this section dealing with management measures. The time-area closures, based primarily upon the distribution and migration of mature and immature sockeye salmon, have implications for the total Japanese salmon catch.

Under the 1978 INPFC arrangements, Area B is open to Japanese salmon fishing from June 1 of each year. Maturing sockeye salmon of North American origin are still in this region at that time; therefore, this time restriction is not expected to alter significantly the Japanese catch. Immature North American sockeye do not generally enter the area until after June 20 and are not subject to great fishing pressure.

Area C is open to salmon fishing operations after June 10 of each year. By that time,

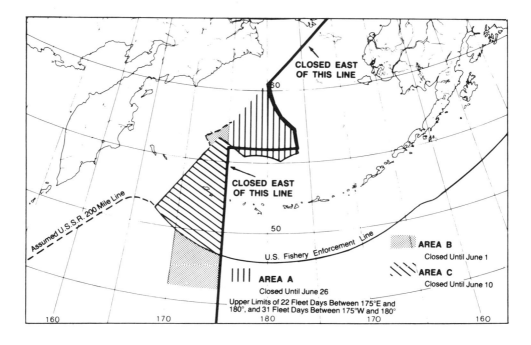

Fig. 6.1 *Time-Area Closures for Japanese High-Seas Salmon Mothership Fishery 1978.* Source: Drawn on the basis of Annex 1, "International Convention for the High Seas Fisheries of the North Pacific Ocean 1952 (as amended 1978)." Available in International North Pacific Fisheries Commission, *Handbook,* INPFC Doc. 2271 (Vancouver: INPFC, March 1980). (See *Atlas of Marine Use in the North Pacific Region,* accompanying this volume, p. 6, for a more detailed map.)

virtually no mature sockeye salmon of North American origin are in the area. Immature sockeyes enter the area after June 20 and are subject to somewhat greater fishing pressure than those in Area B.

The delayed opening of the salmon fishing season in Area A, to the 26th of June each year, will result in the loss of all the mature sockeye salmon. Immature sockeyes occur in this area after June 30; however, the Japanese operations may target on other species, thereby reducing the catch of immatures. Area D is now completely closed to Japanese high-seas salmon fishing.

Under the old INPFC, Japan's average annual take of North American salmon (between 1964 and 1973) was 2,545,000 fish. By individual species this breaks down as follows: Sockeye, 2,137,000; Pink, 17,000; Chum, 175,000; Coho, 24,000; and Chinook, 192,000. It was expected that the 1978 Protocol would reduce interceptions between 75 and 85 percent, the expected Japanese take ranging from no more than 670,000 salmon of North American origin to as little as 400,000 fish, assuming the closure of the Soviet zone and assuming a level of fishing effort equal to that fished during 1964—1973. At the 400,000 fish level, this would be broken down as follows: Sockeye, 240,000; Pink, 0; Chum, 86,000; Coho, 0; and Chinook 74,000.

## U.S.—Canada Salmon

Management of U.S.—Canada salmon resources functions quite differently from the other U.S.—foreign fishing nation management regimes. The U.S. does not have a "true" GIFA with Canada; fisheries are conducted under bilateral arrangements. Reciprocal fishing off the coasts of the two countries has been maintained by bilateral agreements since the extension of fisheries jurisdiction from 3 to 12 miles in the 1960s. With the extension of jurisdiction to 200 miles, the countries agreed to maintain the traditional pattern of reciprocal fishing. This had to be done through negotiation; separate negotiations were undertaken in 1976 to resolve bilateral fishery issues.

In 1977, boundary and fishery negotiations were combined. However, as the negotiations on the boundary disputes stalled, it was agreed that an interim agreement for fisheries was necessary to maintain the reciprocal fishing patterns for 1977. On February 24, 1977, a Reciprocal Fisheries Agreement was concluded after considerable negotiation; it entered into force on July 26, 1977.

The appointment of special negotiators in August of 1977 marked the beginning of a concerted effort by the governments of both nations to reach agreement on maritime boundaries and fishery and hydrocarbon resources. The negotiators met several times during the next few months, producing in October, 1977, a joint report of the principles recommended by them for "a comprehensive maritime boundaries and resource settlement."[48]

Throughout this process, there were separate negotiations to establish a regime for the management of Pacific Coast salmon; again, a principal feature of the regime was to be continued reciprocal fishing. The overall Reciprocal Fisheries Agreement expired on December 31, 1977, yet reciprocal fishing was continued in "good faith." Early in 1978, it was apparent that it would not be possible to reach a comprehensive settlement in 1978 and further interim measures would be required. Such measures were agreed to by Canada and the U.S. on April 11, 1978 in the form of an Annex,[49] extending, as amended, the Reciprocal Fisheries Agreement of 1977.

Other disputes arose between Canada and the U.S. on these issues. One concerned the level of effort that had existed previously (the Canadians claimed quite a few more boat-days than the U.S. had calculated), and another focused on catches (Canada alleged the U.S. had exceeded its catch limits along the East Coast). An important issue for the Canadians was the continuation of the Canadian salmon troll fishery after September 15 on Swiftsure Bank to the 50-meter contour. The Pacific Management Council's salmon management plan proposed the closing of the salmon troll fishery in U.S. waters on September 15—this would apply to Canadian trollers as well as U.S., even though the area in question was part of the maritime boundary issue. The U.S. indicated a willingness to make an adjustment of the Juan de Fuca maritime boundary along the 50-fathom contour on Swiftsure Bank, pending satisfactory resolution of other maritime issues. However, unless the overall long-term agreement could be reached, it would be difficult for the U.S. to apply provisionally the adjusted boundary to allow Canadian trolling after September 15. The Canadian response was quite clearly that the continued acceptance of an interim fisheries agreement for 1978 hinged on the satisfactory resolution of this issue. Should a situation develop where Canadian salmon trollers were unable to complete their season in this area, the reciprocal fisheries "relationship" would be "adversely affected"—implying that retaliatory action would be in order.[50]

Prior to the beginning of Canadian fishing operations in the U.S. zone, scheduled to begin May 1, 1978, an injunction was sought on behalf of the Washington trollers to halt such fishing. The injunction was granted on the grounds that legislation was required to bring the 1978 agreement with Canada into force since the agreement contained provisions affecting Canadian fishermen that were not in accordance with the FCMA. In this instance, the executive branch of the government could not allow foreign fishing under the FCMA, but could allow it by a properly concluded and authorized international agreement. Without such an agreement, the executive branch had to comply with the FCMA. This injunction did not directly halt Canadian fishing in the U.S. zone.

On June 1, 1978, Canada terminated its provisional acceptance of the agreement. Canada required U.S. fishing vessels to cease fishing operations in Canadian waters on two days' notice; the U.S. responded in kind, evicting Canadian fishermen from U.S. waters. This situation prevailed for approximately three weeks until U.S. legislation was signed, giving the President authorization to lift the ban on Canadian fishing off U.S. coasts for the rest of the year if reciprocal access was reinstated. Reciprocal access was not reinstated for the 1979 fishing season.

During the last quarter of 1978, the separate negotiations on Pacific salmon continued to focus on the persistent problems of salmon fisheries management. Major discussion topics included the implementation of a mechanism to limit interceptions, the possible impacts of intercepting fisheries on domestic enhancement programs, and the institutional arrangements applicable to the Fraser River fisheries and fisheries of transboundary rivers. General agreement was reached on the following points at the last round of talks held in early February, 1979.[51] A Discussion Draft Agreement was developed that would create a new Pacific Salmon Commission, subject certain fisheries to interception limitations, and provide for research and management cooperation.

A Pacific Salmon Commission would be created and would have at least three panels: (1) a Northern Panel to deal with salmon originating in rivers whose mouths are situated north of a point to be defined; (2) a Southern Panel to deal with salmon originating in rivers whose mouths are situated south of that point, other than those stocks for which a Fraser River Panel would be responsible; and (3) a Fraser River Panel to deal with salmon originating in the Fraser River and its tributaries. There was also a possibility that a fourth panel could be developed, one that would deal with salmon originating in transboundary rivers, i.e., those rivers that arise in Canada and flow to the sea through the United States.

In the Spring of 1979, two events occurred that were to have major effects on the development of the negotiations. First, the U.S. negotiator, Donald L. McKernan, died and was replaced by Dr. Dayton L. Alverson. Second, internal difficulties within both delegations over the direction of the negotiations increased to the point where domestic approval seemed in question. The respective negotiators, Dr. Alverson for the U.S. and Dr. Michael P. Shepard for Canada, therefore, decided on a major midcourse shift in strategy.[52]

The "objective" situation remained supportive of an agreement. Both countries had extensive and imaginative plans for salmon enhancement and had had enough success to have a clear idea of its potential. On the other hand, most stocks were subject to interception by fishermen of both nationalities, which retarded investment in salmon enhancement. Both parties also faced very difficult domestic problems that were unlikely to be solved without simultaneous or prior settlement of the international problem.

The strategy for negotiations, therefore, shifted to a search for joint gain in which the parties sought to (1) stabilize interceptions in the short term, (2) cooperate to maximize the production of salmon on a case by case basis, and (3) arrange for the equitable sharing of results. With respect to sharing, the emphasis was on the following principles: (1) each country should benefit from its own enhancement; (2) the parties should work gradually to derive a formula that would give each country a share equal to its total national production, though this required the development of species equivalents.

Having adopted a strategy that sought to maximize joint gain, the parties found they could make rapid progress, and the direction the solutions were taking was very different from that developed under the prior mode, which emphasized distributive bargaining. The goal shifted from the detailed design of a commission to the framing of principles that would guide management and procedures for collaboration, cooperation on enhancement, and making deals with respect to interception. In the latter case, the U.S. had a need to receive adequate benefits from its previous investments in the IPSFC, whereas Canada sought compensation for deferring industrial development of certain transboundary rivers.

By October 1980, the parties were in sight of a solution, though, at the time of writing (December 1981), this had not yet been achieved. The course of action agreed upon called for the conclusion of

. . . a general framework Convention which would include a series of binding principles and a series of specific provisions related to an initial salmon interception limitation scheme, management of stocks bound for transboundary and Fraser rivers, and technical resolution procedures. A Commission (with appropriate subsidiary panels) would be formed immediately on ratification to implement the Convention during the first year in which the Convention comes into force.

Once the Convention is in place, it would be necessary for the Parties to negotiate further detailed implementation provisions regarding specific fisheries and approaches to management, development, research and monitoring.[53]

## Pacific Groundfish

The Pacific groundfish management regime covers Pacific hake (Pacific whiting), Pacific ocean perch, other rockfishes, flounders, sablefish, jack mackerel, and others for the California, Oregon, and Washington region. Halibut is excluded, being regulated by the International Pacific Halibut Commission (IPHC). Although the regulatory measures imposed on foreign fishermen have "merit on a biological basis,"[54] their primary function is to reduce spatial conflict between domestic and foreign fishermen, and to assure adequate resources for domestic fisheries.

*Management Measures*—Foreign fishing for hake is conducted by pelagic trawl only, the minimum mesh size being 100 mm stretched measure. Generally, foreign fishing in the California–Washington region is permitted only from 0800 GMT June 1 to 0800 GMT November 1 each year (there appears to be some discrepancy here, as part of the Fishery Management Plan (FMP) indicates there is an area in the California–Washington region that is open to foreign trawling year-round).

Specific time-area closures are as follows for foreign fishermen:

1. 47°30′ N to U.S.–Canada boundary is closed year-round (to accommodate domestic fishing operations).
2. U.S.–Mexico boundary to 39° N—closed year-round (again to prevent conflict with domestic fisheries and to prevent exploitation of juvenile Pacific hake).
3. "Columbia River Pot and Recreational Fishery Sanctuary" and "Klamath River Pot Sanctuary"—closed year-round.
4. 39° N to 47°30′, landward to 125°40′ W—closed from November 1 to May 31 (to prevent harvest of juvenile Pacific hake).[55]

*Allocations*—Allocations to foreign nations in this region for the allowed target species have decreased dramatically due to the increased ability of U.S. fishermen to harvest Pacific groundfish. Some of the individual national reductions, notably in the Soviet allocation, is a reallocation to accommodate the Mexican fishery.

*Statistical Reporting*—Statistical reporting requirements are incorporated in the foreign fishing regulations issued each year. The requirements are similar for all fisheries, although some are necessarily tailored for specific species and management areas. Generally, the requirements entail keeping daily fishing logs to be used as the basis for reports required for each species. Logs contain such information as vessel name and number, date, time of set and haul of each tow, starting and ending position of each tow (latitude and

TABLE 6.6

PACIFIC GROUNDFISH

STOCK ASSESSMENTS AND ALLOCATIONS

| | Year | Pacific hake | Pacific ocean perch | Other rockfish | Flounders | Sablefish | Jack mackerel | Others |
|---|---|---|---|---|---|---|---|---|
| Optimum Yield | 1977 | 130,000 | 1,000 | 18,000 | 31,000 | 7,000 | 55,000 | 4,200 |
| | 1978 | 130,000 | 1,000 | 18,000 | 31,000 | 7,000 | 55,000 | 4,200 |
| | 1979 | 198,900 | 1,000 | 18,000 | 31,000 | 7,000 | 55,000 | 4,200 |
| U.S. Capacity | 1977 | 6,800 | | 17,400 | 30,875 | 6,750 | 51,000 | 3,600 |
| | 1978 | 10,000 | | 18,040 | 30,880 | 6,879 | 51,000 | 3,600 |
| | 1979 | 50,000 | 907 | 17,809 | 30,581 | 6,851 | 50,533 | 3,455 |
| Reserve | 1977 | | | | | | | |
| | 1978 | | | | | | | |
| | 1979 | 39,780 | 25 | 318 | 40 | 40 | 1,193 | 199 |
| TALFF | 1977 | 123,200 | | | | | | |
| | 1978 | 120,000 | | | | | | |
| | 1979 | 109,120 | 0.062%[a] | 0.8%[a] | 0.1%[a] | 0.5%[a] | 3.0%[a] | 0.5%[a] |
| Mexico | 1977 | 0 | 0 | 0 | 0 | 0 | 0 | 0 |
| | 1978 | 1,800 | | 15 | 2 | 2 | 100 | 9 |
| | 1979[b] | 6,000 | 4 | 48 | 6 | 6 | 180 | 30 |
| Poland | 1977 | 18,000 | | 234[d] | 18[d] | 37[d] | 2,000 | 88[d] |
| | 1978 | 28,930 | | 231 | 29 | 29 | 1,950 | 145 |
| | 1979[c] | 11,868 | 8 | 95 | 12 | 12 | 356 | 59 |
| USSR | 1977 | 105,200 | | 1,366[d] | 107[d] | 213[d] | 2,000 | 572[d] |
| | 1978 | 89,270 | | 714 | 89 | 90 | 1,950 | 446 |
| | 1979[c] | 67,252 | 42 | 538 | 67 | 67 | 2,018 | 336 |
| Unallocated | 1977 | | | | | | | |
| | 1978 | | | | | | | |
| | 1979[b] | 24,000 | 14 | 192 | 24 | 24 | 720 | 131 |

[a] Incidental catch not to exceed the established percentage of the Pacific hake TALFF.

[b] As of May 1979.

[c] As of June 1979.

[d] Authorized as an incidental catch in 1977.

longitude), bottom depth (averaged over length of tow), depth of gear during tow, and estimates of landed catch, including discards.

Weekly reports must be submitted, on a vessel-by-vessel basis, giving the catch of the species allocated to the nation, number of days actually fished during the seven-day period, fishing areas, and area code numbers. Monthly statistical reports contain effort data such as vessel-days on the grounds by vessel class and gear type, or in numbers of pots hauled (for tanner crab) and catch in metric tons of target species, and unavoidable catches of other species.

Annual reports are submitted by each country whose fishing vessels operate in the area. They include effort data by ½° latitude by 1° longitude statistical area, by the specific species groupings. Fleet disposition reports are also required of all foreign vessels entering the fishery: the date of entry into the fishery conservation zone, time of entry, position at which fishing activities begin, and the species and amounts of fish on board. Similar reports are required upon completion of fishing activities.

Further requirements are included, one being that accommodations for observers must be provided by the foreign fishing vessel upon request by the United States. Failure to adhere to these requirements can result in the modification, suspension, or revocation of a vessel's permit.

## Enforcement

Under the FCMA, the Department of Commerce (in this instance primarily NOAA/ NMFS) and the U.S. Coast Guard are charged with enforcing the provisions of the Act, although the Coast Guard has the major share of the responsibility.[56] They may utilize such things as the services, personnel, and facilities of any other state or federal entity to do so.

The extent of federal enforcement jurisdiction varies. Although the state retains jurisdiction within its boundaries, and thus the authority to enforce state regulations, the Act allows for federal preemption of state authority outside internal waters if the state violates or inhibits implementation of the Act.[57] There are two instances in which enforcement authority is claimed beyond the 200-mile zone for continental shelf species and anadromous stocks. There are likely to be few quarrels with the extension of control over continental shelf species beyond the zone, as such coverage is consonant with the 1958 Convention on the Continental Shelf.[58]

A potentially contentious issue did exist regarding anadromous stocks. The FCMA allows the enforcement of prescriptions for anadromous stocks throughout their migratory range (i.e., beyond the U.S. fishery conservation zone).[59] In an effort to avoid conflict, this claim is modified somewhat by the Governing International Fisheries Agreement (GIFA) with Japan, Japan being the only principal high-seas salmon fishing nation. Paragraph 2 of the Agreed Minutes requires the U.S. to notify and consult with Japan before any enforcement action is taken "with respect to anadromous beyond the fishery conservation zone." The 1978 INPFC negotiations reaffirmed Japan's agreement to allow U.S. enforcement of high-seas salmon regulations.

The major portion of the U.S. enforcement effort is directed at foreign fisheries; the enforcement philosophy has been to gain compliance by foreign fishing fleets (as opposed to attempting to eliminate all violations), and to impress upon domestic fishermen that regulations pertaining to them *will* be enforced.

Both direct and indirect sanctions are available under the FCMA. Direct sanctions include civil forfeitures;[60] formal enforcement provisions such as arrest, boarding, search, seizure, and arrest (this may involve either civil or criminal penalties);[61] and issuance of citations.[62] Indirect sanctions may include decreased allocations or measures taken against the vessel's fishing permit.[63] For the most part, these sanctions are generally accepted as being within a nation's authority. Yet the potential for discriminatory enforcement exists in three instances: invoking the forfeiture sanction against only foreign vessels, assessing civil penalties primarily against domestic fishermen, and applying criminal sanctions as specified in Section 309.[64] The most difficult issue here is the imposition of criminal sanctions, which include the imposition of fines, imprisonment, or both.[65] As set out in Section 309, criminal sanctions do not apply to every violation listed in Section 307;[66] the exclusions have the effect of insulating domestic fishermen from these sanctions. Furthermore, imprisonment or corporal punishment of any kind is expressly prohibited by the Draft Convention,[67] placing the national law in conflict with current international consensus. It should be noted that the present policy has resulted in a heavy use of citations and a minimal use of criminal sanctions.[68] The imprisonment sanction is further modified in the Agreed Minutes to the GIFA with Japan and the GIFA with the Republic of China. In both instances, it is stated that "appropriate U.S. representatives will recommend that penalties for violation of fishing regulations not include imprisonment or other forms of corporal punishment."[69]

Enforcement patrols are using an "active fishing area" method of surveillance via air and sea patrols. Such patrolling is seldom devoted to the enforcement of a single management plan, but rather monitors compliance with FCMA statutory requirements and management regulations set out in the individual plans for a region.

United States enforcement officers are vested with the power to board, search, and inspect any fishing vessel suspected of violating any provision of the FCMA, with or without a warrant. Gear, equipment, and catch are also subject to such inspection and possible seizure.[70] Enforcement officers have a policy of foregoing "casual interchange" with the crew of foreign fishing vessels to impress upon them the serious nature of a boarding.[71] Many enforcement officers have undergone intensive language training, even though each foreign fishing vessel must have at least one English-speaking person aboard to facilitate enforcement procedures. The Japanese have distributed "English handbooks" to all fishing vessels as a short-term measure.[72]

An arrangement for observers is also available under the FCMA: foreign fishing vessels are required to make available, at no cost to the U.S., accommodation for an observer.[73] For the most part, observers are not given enforcement duties or powers, yet they can be considered part of the overall enforcement scheme because their reports may serve as the basis for subsequent surveillance activities. In the North Pacific region, the primary function of an observer is to collect biostatistical data for management purposes.

## Summary

The categories used in this section were made because each region and/or grouping of species presents a unique set of responses to extended jurisdiction. These responses reflect the short-term implications of extended jurisdiction. In general, however, the U.S. has successfully asserted exclusive management authority and effective control over all living resources found within 200 miles of its coasts, and beyond in the case of anadromous and continental shelf resources. In this context, a very real effort is being made to ensure conservation of the stocks. Scientific research has been expanded considerably and the quality of the available data base is being markedly raised. The enforcement effort is also comprehensive and effective.

The Bering Sea and Aleutian Islands fisheries remain predominantly foreign, and thus the short-term implications of extended jurisdiction involve changes in the patterns of allocation among the foreign fishing nations involved. It would be rather bold to attempt to predict when U.S. harvesters may begin to take over these fisheries; much will depend on the success of fisheries development efforts in the Gulf of Alaska.

The Gulf of Alaska is illustrative of the transition from predominantly foreign fisheries to United States-dominated fisheries in the short-term. Private initiatives and clear policy directives from the U.S. government[74] indicate that development of the U.S. fishing industry is the single most important short-term objective for the Gulf of Alaska region.

With regard to species, the area off the Washington, Oregon, and California coasts exhibits yet another response to extended jurisdiction that is similar to both the Bering Sea, Aleutian Islands, and the Gulf of Alaska areas. Off the U.S. Pacific Coast only two of the groundfish species are available for foreign harvest—Pacific hake and jack mackerel. Quotas for other species are made only to account for their incidental catch in the hake fishery. Domestic ventures have shown considerable interest in the hake fishery, and it is reasonable to expect that foreign fishermen in this area face continued reductions as the U.S. fishery develops.

In all three of these areas there have been changes in the patterns of allocations among the foreign fishing nations. Initially, the allocations were based primarily on traditional fishing. Allocations of resources available for foreign fishing off the U.S. Pacific Coast for 1978 were made on the basis of: (1) reciprocal fishing interests (e.g., Mexico), (2) an increased pollock allocation to the Republic of Korea as a result of their de facto elimination from their traditional pollock fishery off the Soviet coast, and (3) prorated adjustments in 1977 allocations.[75] These allocation factors were applied in 1979 as well, with increased emphasis being placed on reciprocal fishing interests.[76] It is reasonable to expect that reciprocal fishing interests will remain the primary consideration for allocation, especially as the U.S. domestic fishing industry develops and interest in U.S.–overseas fishing ventures increases. Accommodation of foreign nations that face severe reductions in other zones will not remain a strong criterion in the allocation process. As the U.S. industry expands, the need for foreign markets will increase; countries facing elimination of their distant-water fisheries could serve as ready markets for U.S. domestically caught fish.

Although foreign fishing has remained relatively constant, the Japanese face considerable pressure from the developing U.S. tanner crab industry. Stock assessments conducted during 1979 indicate that the available resource is not as large as previously thought. Furthermore, the U.S. catch has been larger than anticipated, indicating that U.S. capacity is increasing and, in 1979, there was every indication that the Japanese should expect no allocation, or a very small allocation, in 1980. In fact, the Japanese allocation in 1979 was 14,000 MT. However, this declined to 7,500 MT in 1980 and none in 1981.

The long history of cooperation in managing the transboundary halibut resource appears to be overcoming the increased tensions between the U.S. and Canada on fisheries issues. There have been some minor problems with the implementation of the new Halibut Convention but these have been resolved without significant difficulty. While reciprocal fishing is in the process of being phased out, there is no reason to believe that cooperative research and management will not continue as outlined in the Protocol Amending the Halibut Convention. However, some uncertainty affects the long-term future of the Halibut Convention since, as with the U.S.–Canadian salmon relations, the cooperative management of halibut is quite dependent on relations between the two countries.

## Canada

Earlier in this chapter we said that Canadian objectives have not been spelled out as directly as have the U.S. objectives under the FCMA. However, in reality, Canadian objectives in extending control over fisheries appear to have been quite similar to the American objectives, as Snow points out:

> Canada has adopted the objective of optimum utilization but has avoided the problems associated with a legal definition that promise to plague the American managers in the future. This has been possible because 'optimum utilization' has carefully been kept out of Canadian legislation and regulations. To understand the Canadian approach, it is necessary to piece together treaties, Law of the Sea position papers, policy statements, and public statements by senior officials.
>
> Regulations made under the authority of S.34 of the Fisheries Act can prescribe the total allowable catch for a fishery and allocate among nations. All that finds its way into regulation form are the foreign nation quota allocations.[77]

Consequently, the foreign quota allocations that are shown in Table 6.7 are not only small but relate only to a few species and are declining rapidly. The quotas in 1978 and 1979 cover only sablefish and hake, except in the case of U.S. vessels for 1979, where a variety of species of groundfish are included. Only Japan, Poland, and the USSR are involved, in addition to the U.S. Whereas Japan was taking 11,000 MT in 1977, their quota was cut to 5,500 MT in 1979. The Polish quota was 12,500 MT in 1977, and reduced to 5,000 MT in 1979. The Soviet quota likewise declined from 7,500 MT in 1977 to 1,000 MT in 1979.

Regulations pertaining to the foreign fisheries in the Canadian zone of the Pacific Coast are stated in the Foreign Vessel Fishing Regulations, of the Fisheries Act (SOR/77-50) of December 29, 1976. Limits are placed on incidental catches of hake, rockfish, and sablefish (#25), and the season is closed for all species from November 30 to December 31 every year (#26). Gear restrictions are in force for sablefish and hake and, previously in the case of Japan, for rockfish (Schedule VII).

TABLE 6.7

FOREIGN ALLOCATIONS IN THE CANADIAN PACIFIC
EXTENDED FISHERIES ZONE, 1977–1979

(METRIC TONS)

| Country | Species | 1977 Allocations | 1978 Allocations | 1979 Allocations |
|---------|---------|------------------|------------------|------------------|
| Japan | Sablefish | 3,000 | 2,200 | 1,000 |
|  | Hake | 5,000 | 5,000 | 4,500 |
|  | Rockfish | 3,000 | 0 | 0 |
| Poland | Hake | 7,500 | 6,500 | 5,000 |
|  | Dogfish | 5,000 | 0 |  |
| USSR | Hake | 7,500 | 6,500 | 1,000 |
| USA | – | – | – | 3,250 |
| TOTAL |  | 31,000 | 20,200 | 14,750 |

Source: Offshore Commercial Fisheries Division, Fisheries and Environment Canada, Fisheries and Marine (Vancouver, British Columbia: July 16, 1979), personal communication.

## CLAIMS TO PRESCRIBE FOR MANAGEMENT: THE NORTHWEST PACIFIC

Let us recall briefly the chain of events relating to the extension of national jurisdiction during the period 1976–1977. For the North Pacific Ocean, the first extensions occurred in the Northeast with the U.S. and Canada. These were followed by the USSR, North Korea, and (purely as a protective measure against the USSR) Japan. China has not extended its marine jurisdiction to 200 miles, nor has the Republic of Korea. However, on May 1, 1978, South Korea implemented new territorial sea limits to twelve miles.[78]

Major perturbations in the traditional regime were generated as a result in USSR–Japan, North Korea–Japan, and South Korea–USSR relationships. The situation relative to China–Japan, China–North Korea, and Japan–South Korea remains as described in chapter 3 for conservation, allocation, enforcement, and accommodation of fishing practices. The Japan–South Korea relationship on fisheries, however, continues to be affected by the historic conflict over Takesima Island. For instance, in early May 1978, Korean patrol boats ordered Japanese fishing vessels operating off Takesima Island to move beyond the recently implemented twelve-mile territorial sea.[79] The Japanese National Offshore Cuttlefish Fishery Association claimed that about 100 vessels had to curtail operations, and they began to put pressure on the Japanese government to take protective action. The Japanese Cabinet, in response, rejected the South Korean claim and committed patrol boats and helicopters to "protect" Japanese fishing vessels, but they were authorized to patrol only up to twelve miles off Takesima Island.[80]

The Republic of Korea (ROK) continues to be faced with a catastrophic situation relative to the USSR zone, and continues to try to get increased allocations for pollock in the Northeast Pacific from the U.S. at the expense of the Japanese. Given the fact that the ROK and the USSR maintain no formal diplomatic relations, the ROK is at a severe disadvantage in the Northwest Pacific in attempts to secure some redress. However, it appears that the absence of diplomatic relations does not necessarily preclude the creation of a *modus vivendi*. It all depends on the USSR.

There were reports in early 1978 of an informal arrangement between the USSR and the ROK via Japan, whereby the ROK imported a certain amount of fresh fish (pollock) from the USSR, paying in hard currency, and in return was to be given a small allocation in the Soviet zone. It is difficult to get detailed information on this arrangement but Korean sources claim that the "deal has not really been consummated." Apparently, the ROK bought fish from Soviet vessels via Japan but found the fish almost unusable for the fresh fish market because it had not been sorted and was of poor quality. In return, the Soviets have not provided any direct allocations for the ROK, and later reportedly refused to meet and talk.

The absence of formal diplomatic relations is also affecting Japanese–North Korean arrangements, but to a much lesser degree. The North Korean zone came into effect in August 1977, and at that time all Japanese fishing operations within the zone were formally proscribed.[81] However, as early as May 1977, Japanese and North Korean parliamentarians had agreed to set up a committee of experts to prepare for private-level agreements on trade and fishery matters.[82] The fisheries agreement was signed on September 6, 1977 (its terms are described in chapter 4).[83] Subsequent to this, somewhat minor problems arose in connection with the negotiation of a more comprehensive agreement scheduled for conclusion by the end of June 1978.

Part of the problem was generated by North Korea's simultaneous enactment of a "military warning zone" that extends out to sea fifty miles beyond the baselines used to measure the territorial sea. All Japanese fishing operations are prohibited in this zone, and enforced by North Korean patrol boats.[84] Access to this zone for the Japanese is clearly hampered by the absence of formal diplomatic relations between the two governments. The leniency with which offending Japanese fishermen have been treated, accompanied by statements of friendliness on the part of the North Korean government, suggest that the latter intends to use this issue as a means of facilitating formal recognition by Japan, to the displeasure of South Korea. This interpretation is reinforced by the favorable reception President Kim Il Sung gave to the Japanese Socialist Party delegation sent to Pyongyang to negotiate an extension of the current agreement in May 1978.[85] The extension was agreed to but no termination date was publicly stated, so it is unclear how long the agreement will be in force.[86]

The major problem of Northwest Pacific fisheries (at least in terms of scale) since the implementation of extended coastal state marine jurisdiction involves the reciprocal access of Japan and the USSR to each other's zones. In this connection, the legitimacy of claims to prescribe for allocations were contentious only in respect to the Northern Territories issue. The real controversy surrounded the conditions of access, including the amount of the allocation to be awarded each party. These issues deserve detailed treatment. The analysis is divided between groundfish, coastal pelagic, and crab resources on the one hand (all of which fall completely within the zones), and anadromous (salmon and salmon trout) resources on the other, which necessitates the regulation of high-seas fishing beyond 200 miles as an added complication.

Table 6.8 shows the total Japanese catch for 1975 in the Soviet zone, and the estimated annual catches of the USSR and others in the Japanese zone.

As the negotiating situation developed, the Japanese sought to stay as close to a million ton allocation in the Soviet zone as possible. The Soviets sought not only a significant cut in Japanese catches, in order to recoup Soviet losses resulting from extensions of jurisdiction elsewhere, but also to continue to fish in the Japanese zone and, more particularly, to fish for sardines *within the Japanese twelve-mile territorial sea*. The latter would have been by itself an extraordinarily difficult demand for the Japanese government to accept. But the difficulties were significantly compounded when the Soviets linked establishment of the zone to Japanese recognition of their ownership of four Northern Territories—Habomai, Shikotan, Kunasiri, and Etorofu Islands—which had been in dispute since the end of World War II. An additional quirk generated further complications. Earlier, a Soviet pilot had defected to Japan in a new MIG-25 and, under pressure from the U.S., the Japanese government immediately turned over both the MIG and the pilot to the Americans. This angered the Soviets greatly and their delegation informed the Japanese fisheries delegation in Moscow that this issue was the source of considerable difficulties.

To maintain entry to this valuable traditional fishery in the Soviet zone, Japan was

### TABLE 6.8

JAPANESE TOTAL CATCH FOR 1975 IN SOVIET ZONE AND ESTIMATED
ANNUAL CATCHES FOR FOREIGN FISHERMEN IN THE JAPANESE ZONE
(IN THOUSAND MT)

| 1975 Japanese catch (April–Dec) in Soviet zone[a] | | Estimated annual catches, foreign fishermen in Japanese zone[b] | |
|---|---|---|---|
| Alaska pollock | 459 | USSR | 300–400[c] |
| True cod | 26 | ROK | 5–10 |
| Squid | 127 | PDRK | unknown |
| Saury | 122 | PRC | nil |
| Sand lance | 50 | Taiwan | 1 |
| Stone crab | 12 | | |
| Snail | 3 | | |
| Flounder | 57 | | |
| Others | 58 | | |
| Total | 914 | | 306    411 |

Sources:

[a]Quoted in U.S. Dept. of Commerce. *Survey of Foreign Fisheries, Oceanographic, and Atmosphere Literature* (Washington, D.C.: #C-20, 1977, p. 9. Taken from *Asahi Shimbun*, #32847 (May 26, 1977), p. 1.

[b]Ibid., p. 6.

[c]The Soviets claim their catch in the Japanese zone has been greater than 500,000 tons.

compelled to negotiate a temporary agreement to permit its fishermen to continue to fish there after the zone went into effect on April 1, 1977. As negotiations were in progress at that time, permits to Japanese fishermen were delayed another month. Only after a marathon negotiating process, lasting eighty-five days, and after repeated breakdowns that compelled the Japanese Minister of Agriculture and Forestry to go to Moscow three times, was agreement formally reached on May 27, 1977.[87]

The negotiations over the important catch quotas were completed rather quickly despite the drastic cuts experienced by the Japanese. The agreement was only for the period from April to December and permitted a catch of 455,000 tons as shown in table 6.9. This amounted to something like a 46 percent cut compared to 1975.[88] By contrast, American and Canadian cuts in North American waters were only about a third as great. Fishing for salmon, trout, and herring was completely forbidden in the Russian zone. Even with such drastic cutbacks on Japanese fishing in the Russian zone, the permitted Japanese catch was still quite large—possibly larger than the Russians were taking in their own zone at that time.[89]

Primarily as a result of Japanese perceptions that the Soviets were secretly trying to

TABLE 6.9

INITIAL JAPANESE PROPOSALS AND FINAL ALLOCATIONS FOR
FISHING IN THE SOVIET ZONE, APRIL–DECEMBER 1977

(IN THOUSAND MT)

| Species | Proposed for April–December 1977 | Agreed for June–December 1977 |
|---|---|---|
| Alaska pollock | 49 | 100 |
| True cod | 25.3 | 19 |
| Squid | 120 | 132 |
| Saury | 50 | 63.4 |
| Anchovy | 30 | NA |
| Tuna | 5 | NA |
| Sand lance | 78.3 | 79.3 |
| Tanner crab | 2 | 2.3 |
| Stone crab | 1 | 5.3 |
| Horsehair crab | 0.8 | 0.82 |
| Snail | 3.5 | 3.5 |
| Flounder | 9 | 9 |
| Wachna cod | 7.4 | 10.4 |
| Young yellowfin tuna | 21 | NA |
| Ocean perch | 7 | 6.9 |
| Atka mackerel | 5 | 1 |
| Shrimp | NA | 1.2 |
| Octopus | NA | 1.9 |
| Other species | 40.7 | 19.8 |
| Total | 455 | 455.8 |
| Total catch taken in March, 1977 | | 245.0 |
| Combined total | | 700.8 |

Source: Consulate of Japan, Anchorage, Alaska, letter to James H. Branson, Executive Director, North Pacific Fishery Management Council, June 20, 1977, ref. JC77-119, p. 9.

secure Japanese recognition of Soviet occupation of the four Northern Territories, the Japanese government preferred to break off negotiations, even at the severe costs this entailed for the Japanese salmon fishery. It was reported that agreement on a set of principles had been arrived at in the session of February 28—March 1, but difficulties in drafting the joint communique stalled announcement of this agreement.

The three principles reportedly were: (1) the parties agreed to discuss introduction of a temporary measure to permit continued fishing during the 1977 season; (2) the Soviets agreed to guarantee the safety of Japanese fishing vessels operating in the "Northern Seas" during the discussion of the temporary measure; (3) a long-term bilateral fisheries agreement would be negotiated to replace the 1956 Treaty.[90] In reporting these negotiations to the House of Councillors, the Japanese Minister of Foreign Affairs said that the temporary measure would be implemented by an administrative agreement between the two governments; that it would not replace the existing bilateral treaty; and that, in the negotiations for the new long-term bilateral agreement, Japan would have to acknowledge the Soviet 200-mile zone.[91] These principles were affirmed in an exchange of notes issued on March 3.

The second round of negotiations began in Moscow on March 15. The Japanese revealed that the Soviets had offered an allocation of 600,000 MT exclusive of salmon and herring, in return for which the Soviets demanded an equal amount of saury and sardine to be taken from within the Japanese zone.[92] Presumably, this would have included the Soviet demand to fish within the Japanese territorial sea, since a significant portion of the Soviet saury and sardine catch was taken there.

We have no detailed information on additional proposals and counterproposals for the remainder of the second round, or the third round in Moscow in May. On the basis, however, of controlled government leaks to various Japanese newspapers, it appeared that Soviet claims to exercise extended fisheries jurisdiction around the four Northern Territories remained the major stumbling block. In May, the Japanese Minister of Agriculture and Forestry, Mr. Zenko Suzuki, indicated that Japan had made some concessions to the USSR on this issue.[93] Apparently, Japan was seeking some way to settle the fisheries conflict without conceding Soviet ownership of the four islands. The Soviets, in turn, appeared to have accepted the final Japanese proposals of mid-May because agreement was announced on May 18.[94] The operative principle on the major stumbling block was that the demarcation of the Soviet 200-mile zone would not affect Japan's territorial claims to the four islands. It appeared also that in return for this, the USSR still wanted Japanese acquiescence to continued Soviet fishing within the new Japanese territorial sea.

Pending resolution of the jurisdictional issue, the salmon talks had been suspended since March. The Japanese high-seas salmon fisheries of the Northwest Pacific (i.e., in the areas falling under the jurisdiction of the Joint Japanese—Soviet Commission) had consistently declined in production from a high of 120,400 MT in 1963 to 91,000 MT in 1975.[95] In 1976, the Joint Commission had cut the Japanese quota again to 80,000 MT after the Japanese had proposed a quota of about 95,000 MT.[96] The Soviets, on the other hand, had proposed a quota of about 62,000 MT.[97] Both parties settled at 80,000 MT, but the Japanese actually took about 82,000 MT.[98] As a result of extensions of Soviet jurisdiction in 1977, the quota agreed on was 62,000 MT, which the Soviets had proposed the previous year. This figure was incorporated into the Japanese—Soviet Provisional Fisheries Agreement signed in Moscow on May 24.

On the two crucial jurisdictional issues, the text of the agreement states the compromises in the following way: (1) the Preamble declares that the two governments recognize the "sovereign rights of the Soviet Union toward living resources for the surveys, development, and conservation thereof" as prescribed in the decree issued by the Presidium of the Supreme Soviet on December 10, 1976; and (2) Article 2 declares:

> The right of the Japanese people and fishing vessels to conduct fishing . . . , will be given, based on the principle of mutual interests, in the form of granting the rights to the Soviet people and fishing vessels to continue their traditional fishing operations in the offshore waters of Japan.[99]

The arrangements on enforcement, similar to those described in Chapter 3, are continued in the Provisional Agreement. Very difficult new rules were imposed on the Japanese relative to the conduct of fishing practices. The areas in which allocations were to be distributed were widely separated. The Japanese claimed that this would have significantly adverse impacts on the CPUEs and, in some cases, might even make it difficult for vessels to take their quotas.

On his return from Moscow, one of the leaders of the Japanese delegation, Mr. Akira Matsura, then Director of the Office of Ocean Fisheries, Japan Fisheries Agency, gave a press conference in which he indicated that bartering arrangements would play a prominent role in the negotiations for a long-term agreement, to be held during 1978.[100] Similar arrangements were proposed earlier by the USSR as a means of gaining access to Japanese technology.

In February of 1977, President Nakabe of Taiyo Fisheries Company returned to Tokyo from Moscow and revealed that as part of the negotiations between Taiyo and the USSR on exportation by Taiyo of plants and machinery, the USSR proposed barter arrangements in lieu of cash payments.[101] These proposals were unacceptable to Taiyo. In exchange for a canning plant, a 1,500 ton freezer unit with building and fish processing machinery, the Soviets offered Taiyo the following allocations: 30,000 MT of onago, 3,000—5,000 MT of pelagic armorhead, 600 MT of whale meat, and 25,000—26,000 MT of Alaska pollock to be delivered over three years.[102]

Apparently, Taiyo turned down these arrangements only under pressure from the Japan Fisheries Agency because such a large allocation of pollock to a single company would have had an adverse effect on the Japanese government's bargaining posture in the scheduled negotiations with the Soviets. The disadvantage thereby incurred would have been felt primarily by the "smaller domestic fishing companies and fishing families."

The Soviet—Japan Interim Fisheries Agreement to enable Soviet fishermen to enter the new Japanese 200-mile fishery zone was signed on August 4, 1977, in Tokyo.[103] The interim agreement covered the period from July to December, 1977, and went into effect on the date of signing by the fishery ministers of both countries. It reduced the Soviet catch by about 31 percent over the same period of the year before—somewhat less than the reductions for the Japanese in the Russian zone. This was intended approximately to reciprocate, but also to encourage the Russians to be more generous in the long-term treaty to be negotiated during 1978 for subsequent years.

Soviet fishermen are wholly excluded from the new territorial sea, where they caught most of the highly prized sardines. However, to make this assertion of Japanese sovereignty more palatable to the Soviets, the Japanese offered to barter sardines *caught by Japanese fishermen* for pollock *caught by Soviet fishermen*. But implementation of this arrangement was difficult because of the danger of making transfers at sea and overhandling, which damages the fish when brought into Japanese ports for transfer to Soviet ships.

The general implementation of the Japanese 200-mile fisheries zone has certain peculiarities that should be kept in mind. The Japanese relationship with the USSR differs from its relationships with China and South Korea on fisheries matters. West of 135° east longitude, the 200-mile zone has not been put into effect in order to avoid applying zone restrictions to South Korean or Chinese fishermen. Under the existing fishery agreements with both China and the Republic of Korea, Japanese fishermen have satisfactory entry to offshore waters of those countries. The Japanese government did not want to disturb current arrangements by enforcing the new zonal regulations, at least not until South Korea and China had enforced their own extended zones or terminated the current fishery treaties. [104] Only the new 12-mile territorial sea applies west of 135°.

Since the agreement with South Korea already provides for a 12-mile exclusive fishery zone (Article 2), the new 12-mile territorial zone did not add restrictions on existing arrangements under the Japan—Korean Fishery Agreement. [105] In addition, the territorial sea in five important straits is kept at three miles. [106] This avoids conflict with Japan's position at the Law of the Sea Conference in support of a new regime for the world's international straits. The use of the straits by American nuclear submarines is also preserved; entry of U.S. submarines into territorial waters is forbidden by current Japanese government policy. The straits in question are Soya, Tsugaru, East Tsushima, West Tsushima, and Osumi.

Tables 6.10 and 6.11 compare the effects of enclosures in the North Pacific as a whole on the operations of the Japanese fleet.

## The Japan—USSR Negotiations on the Long-Term Bilateral Fishery Agreement, 1978

Issues related to salmon were separated from other long-term bilateral fishing issues, and negotiations proceeded rapidly on the others. The first round was held in Moscow in late November and early December, 1977. As an opening offer, the Soviets proposed to hold the Japanese to the March—December, 1977, quota of 700,000 MT. The Japanese objected that this did not take into account the large catches of January and February, 1977. In return, the Japanese proposed to allocate 378,000 MT to the Soviets from the Japanese zone. The Soviets then objected on the ground that Soviet fishermen should receive the same allocation as the Japanese in the Soviet zone. [107] By December 16, however, the parties managed to

TABLE 6.10

CURTAILMENT OF JAPANESE FISHING VESSELS
IN THE NORTH PACIFIC, 1977

| Type of vessels | Number 1976 | Number to be curtailed 1977 | Number of surviving vessels 1977 |
|---|---|---|---|
| Salmon | 2,327 | 555 | 1,772 |
| Crab | 124 | 57 | 67 |
| Herring | 205 | 205 | 0 |
| Medium trawlers | 154 | 57 | 97[a] |
| Offshore trawlers | 253 | 50 | 203 |
| Snail | 37 | 7 | 30 |
| Mothership trawl fleets | 20 | 20 | 0 |
| Other | 123 | 103 | 20 |
| Total | 3,243 | 1,054 | 2,189 |

Source: Japan Fisheries Agency, Japan Trawlers Association, various fisheries newspapers. Prepared by the Regional Fisheries Attaché, American Embassy, Tokyo.

Note: Curtailment is primarily in the USSR Exclusive Fisheries Zone.

[a]Of the 97 medium trawlers (Hokkutensen), 22 are fishing within the Soviet zone, 62 are within the U.S. zone, 5 are used for krill fishing in the Antarctic, 5 fish off Mauritania, and the remaining 3 are used as stock research vessels in adjacent waters of Japan.

TABLE 6.11

CURTAILMENT OF JAPANESE FISHING VESSELS
IN THE UNITED STATES' 200-MILE EXCLUSIVE FISHERIES ZONE

| Type of vessels | Number 1976 | Number to be curtailed 1977 | Number of surviving vessels 1977 |
|---|---|---|---|
| Motherships | 6 | 0 | 6 |
| Catcherboats | 108 | 20 | 88 |
| SURIMI FLEETS | 114 | 20 | 94 |
| Surimi trawlers | 17 | 4 | 13 |
| Frozen fish trawlers | 41 | 0 | 41 |
| LARGE NORTH PACIFIC TRAWLERS | 58 | 4 | 54 |
| NORTHWEST ATLANTIC TRAWLERS | 17 | 2 | 15 |
| NORTH PACIFIC LONGLINE/GILLNET | 22 | 0 | 22 |
| SNAIL BOATS | 19 | 1 | 18 |
| Motherships | 2 | 0 | 2 |
| Catcherboats | 12 | 0 | 12 |
| BRISTOL BAY CRAB FLEETS | 14 | 0 | 14 |
| TOTAL | 244 | 27 | 217 |

settle on 850,000 and 650,000 MT, respectively. The details are provided in Tables 6.12 and 6.13.

For Japan, the 1978 allocation is only 15 percent less than the 1975 catch of 996,000 MT. For the first time, data on the Soviet catch in the Japanese zone are available, and the 1978 quota is only 15,000 MT less than the 1976 catch. Both sides, it seemed, were relatively generous with each other. Though information on the details of the negotiations is scarce, there were no reports in the Japanese press of Soviet demands to continue fishing within twelve miles of the Japanese coast. Nothing more was heard, it seems, of the proposal

TABLE 6.12

JAPANESE QUOTA FOR 1978 IN THE SOVIET 200-MILE FISHERIES ZONE

| Species | Quota (metric tons) |
|---|---|
| Pollock | 345,000 |
| Squid | 146,400 |
| Sand lance | 65,200 |
| Flounders | 30,300 |
| Ocean perch | 22,000 |
| Cod | 44,700 |
| Wachna cod | 15,500 |
| Atka mackerel | 11,000 |
| Shrimp | 500 |
| Saury | 68,600 |
| Octopus | 3,500 |
| Other fish | 80,800 |
| Red tanner crab | 2,300 |
| Crabs | 4,100 |
| Snail | 2,500 |
| Tuna and skipjack | 6,400 |
| Sharks (excl. dogfish) | 1,200 |
| Total | 850,000 |

Source: Regional Fisheries Attaché, U.S. Embassy, Tokyo.

TABLE 6.13

SOVIET QUOTA FOR 1978 IN THE JAPANESE 200-MILE FISHERIES ZONE,
COMPARED WITH THE SOVIET 1976 CATCH IN THE SAME AREA
(IN METRIC TONS)

| Species | 1978 Quota | 1976 Catch |
|---|---|---|
| Sardine & mackerel | 318,000 | 287,000 |
| Pollock | 80,000 | 174,000 |
| Itohikidara (Remonema) | 138,000 | 138,000 |
| Saury | 20,000 | NA |
| Sand lance | 30,000 | 30,000 |
| Other | 64,000 | 36,000 |
| Total | 650,000 | 665,000 |

to barter sardines for pollock. The biggest cuts that the Japanese had to sustain were on pollock, crab, and shrimp.[108]

There was one new development in early 1978 that deserves mention. Two Japanese fishing companies, Marubeni Corp. and Hoko Fishing Co., negotiated a joint venture with the Soviet Fisheries Ministry on the basis of which they were allowed to take 3,000 MT of tanner crab off Kamchatka in return for supplying equipment and fishing know-how to the Soviets.[109] In addition, the two companies agreed to turn over 25 percent of the catch to the Soviets. But this joint venture was disallowed by the Japan Fisheries Agency for both internal and external reasons.

The Agency claimed that: (1) there was no guarantee of continued Japanese crab fishing after the expiration of the one-year contract; (2) there was a danger of increasing monopoly of Japanese fishing in Soviet waters by only a few Japanese firms under this type of arrangement; (3) the Soviets might be induced to switch to joint ventures as the sole means for allowing access to Japanese fishermen; and (4) joint venture agreements with the Soviets should be signed either by the government or by the industry as a whole and not by individual companies.[110] This policy on joint ventures was modified in early 1979, however, as a result of an arrangement worked out between the Japan Fisheries Association and the Hokkutensen Trawler Federation. Joint fishing operations are now permitted as a means of easing the problems faced by the offshore fleet. These operations also assure large companies continuing supplies of fish. However, the season lasts only from January to March and the primary target is pollock roe.[111]

The negotiations over salmon were a little more difficult and complicated because at the same time the Japanese were renegotiating the INPFC arrangements for the Northeast Pacific with the U.S. and Canada and were facing continued Soviet efforts to reopen the Article on anadromous species (Art. 66) in the Informal Composite Negotiating Text (ICNT), precursor to the Draft Convention. Japan at first proposed to continue negotiations with the Soviets on fishing operations and the high-seas salmon quota in early February, but these negotiations were delayed until March and April.

The Japanese were hoping to hold the 1978 quota at the same level as the 1977 quota (62,000 MT). However, the Soviets proposed: a quota of 35,500 MT, a fishing season lasting from May 1 through July 1, and a closure of the grounds north of 44° N and west of 175° E. The Japanese were stunned and proposed to barter technical cooperation in salmon propagation for a Soviet agreement to remain at the 1977 quota. The Soviets refused.[112]

The Japanese claimed that the Soviet proposal would result in the death of the Japanese industry, since the proposed quota was almost half the previous year's. The Soviets proposed that salmon of Soviet origin caught in the Japanese 200-mile zone be included in the Japanese quota and, in addition, the Soviets would close the most productive fishing grounds to Japanese salmon fishing. Given the fact that the proposed fishing season was forty days less than the previous year's and the major fishing ground for the land-based drag-net fleet was to be closed, there was some question whether it would even be possible to achieve a quota of 35,500 MT.[113]

As the negotiations continued in April, the Soviets raised their offer to 41,000 MT, and later to 42,500 MT. The Japanese agreed to the latter figure, though negotiations had not concluded on the question of closure.[114] The new quota represents a reduction of 31.4 percent from the 1977 quota. In terms of fishing operations, each Japanese vessel is given a catch quota. This does not represent a change for the operation of mothership fleets, but is a substantial change for the small and medium-sized drift gill-net vessels.[115]

The fishing season was extended from May 1 to August 10, except in the case of pink salmon, on which agreement remained tied to the question of closure. The Soviets had retreated somewhat from their initial position but the Japanese were seeking more concessions on this issue. However, the Soviets showed absolutely no interest in trading more salmon for either Japanese construction of twelve salmon hatcheries or two integrated research centers, or for Japanese willingness to pay a "fisheries cooperation fee."[116]

The reduction in the Japanese quota was calculated to result in the curtailment of additional vessels (two motherships, seventy-three catcher boats, and eighty-nine medium drift gill-net vessels)[117] from the Japanese fleet.

These agreements, on April 29, constituted the new Japan—Soviet Fisheries Cooperation Agreement, which was scheduled to replace the 1956 Treaty. With respect to the outstanding issues, the USSR moved towards acceptance of a fisheries cooperation fee. However, the Japanese had initially proposed a rate of 3.5 percent of the value of the quota. This had subsequently been increased to 5.6 percent. The Soviets, on the other hand, were insisting on 10 percent with the intention of using the revenues gained to excavate riverbeds to facilitate natural spawning of salmon.[118]

The other outstanding issue concerned the resumption of Japanese kelp harvesting around Kaigara Jima Island off Hokkaido. Since this issue was linked to the sensitive jurisdictional issue connected with the Northern Territories question, a solution was found in a private-level agreement between the Japan Fisheries Association and the Soviet Ministry of Fisheries. The major stumbling block here appeared to be the license fee. The Association claimed it was willing to pay ¥ 60 million but the Soviets were demanding ¥ 100 million.[119]

The conditions of fishing would allow 329 boats to operate during a season lasting from June 10 to September 30. The ¥ 100 million figure was derived by applying a rate of 15 percent of the value of the catch. This represented a sixfold increase from the rate for 1976 which was ¥ 52,000 per boat or a total of ¥ 17 million.[120]

With some changes in the conditions, the Japanese Fisheries Agency seemed more willing to consider joint venture arrangements with the Soviets than previously. The Soviets asked again for six joint ventures. The Agency was willing to authorize five involving the taking of shrimp, tanner crab, blue king crab, and horsehair crab. However, the Agency was willing to allow only firms that had fished in the Soviet zone in the past to participate in joint ventures.[121] Trading houses were specifically excluded.

Information on actual enforcement activities is very scarce but one story in the *Yomiuri Shimbun* for June 2, 1978, indicated that since June, 1977, the Soviets had enforced against eighty-eight cases of Japanese violations: sixty-five in 1977 (June to December), and twenty-three in 1978 (January to May). In the first formal judgment delivered, with the heaviest penalty imposed, the Soviets seized a 350-ton Japanese vessel, the *Nitto-maru*, on May 25, confiscated it and imposed fines of U.S. $100,000 plus U.S. $1,350,000 for damages to Soviet continental shelf resources.

## CLAIMS FOR ACCESS TO MARKETS: THE NORTHEAST AND NORTHWEST PACIFIC

The major issues in claims for access to markets are twofold. The first involves the question of import restrictions on certain products imposed by the Japanese, and the second relates to the conditions under which joint ventures in fisheries are permitted between Japanese, Korean, and Soviet firms, on the one hand, and U.S. firms or fishermen on the other. In certain respects, the two issues are linked and both raise collaterally questions of allocation as well.

### The Problem of Import Restrictions

Difficulties that have emerged between the U.S. and Japan on the question of import restrictions go far beyond the fisheries sector. The issue perhaps has its origins in the large Japanese trade surpluses of recent years compared to the growing U.S. balance of payments problems. These, in turn, are linked to concerns expressed by other advanced industrial countries in the Organization for Economic Cooperation and Development (OECD) that the Japanese rely too heavily on a vast array of barriers, the purpose of which is to retard the free entry of foreign goods into the Japanese market. These charges are heatedly denied by the Japanese,[122] but the conflict definitely exists in the fisheries sector where there are widespread restrictions on imports.

Tables 6.14 and 6.15 show the value of Japanese fisheries imports and exports relative to total imports and exports.

TABLE 6.14

VALUE OF JAPANESE FISHERIES IMPORTS VERSUS
VALUE OF TOTAL IMPORTS, 1967–1976
(IN U.S. $1,000)

| Year | Fisheries imports (A) | Total imports (B) | (A)/(B) % | Exchange rate to U.S. $1.00 |
|------|----------------------|-------------------|-----------|------------------------------|
| 1967 | $ 191,573 | 11,663,087 | 1.64 | 360 yen |
| 1968 | 200,374 | 12,987,243 | 1.54 | 360 yen |
| 1969 | 260,676 | 15,023,536 | 1.74 | 360 yen |
| 1970 | 318,412 | 18,881,168 | 1.69 | 360 yen |
| 1971 | 436,887 | 19,686,485 | 2.22 | 351 yen |
| 1972 | 617,980 | 23,470,711 | 2.63 | 308 yen |
| 1973 | 1,099,173 | 38,111,101 | 2.88 | 273 yen |
| 1974 | 1,106,985 | 61,905,418 | 1.79 | 292 yen |
| 1975 | 1,298,078 | 57,811,539 | 2.25 | 297 yen |
| 1976 | 1,897,808 | 64,744,675 | 2.93 | 297 yen |

Source: Fisheries Trade Statistics, Japan Fisheries Agency, 1967–1976. Compiled by Office of the Regional Fisheries Attaché, U.S. Embassy, Tokyo.

TABLE 6.15

VALUE OF JAPANESE FISHERIES EXPORTS VERSUS
VALUE OF TOTAL EXPORTS, 1967−1976
(IN U.S. $1,000)

| Year | Fisheries exports (A) | Total exports (B) | (A)/(B) % | Exchange rate to U.S. $1.00 |
|------|-----------------------|-------------------|-----------|-----------------------------|
| 1967 | $326,143 | $10,441,572 | 3.1 | 360 yen |
| 1968 | 350,603 | 12,971,662 | 2.7 | 360 yen |
| 1969 | 346,893 | 15,990,014 | 2.2 | 360 yen |
| 1970 | 390,882 | 19,317,637 | 2.0 | 360 yen |
| 1971 | 417,839 | 23,911,020 | 1.7 | 351 yen |
| 1972 | 526,554 | 28,591,143 | 1.8 | 308 yen |
| 1973 | 635,508 | 36,745,153 | 1.7 | 273 yen |
| 1974 | 691,659 | 55,506,436 | 1.2 | 292 yen |
| 1975 | 568,000 | 55,708,126 | 1.0 | 297 yen |
| 1976 | 743,546 | 67,119,927 | 1.1 | 297 yen |

Source: Fisheries Trade Statistics, Japan Fisheries Agency, 1967−1976. Compiled by Office of the Regional Fisheries Attaché, U.S. Embassy, Tokyo.

Over the last decade, the value of Japanese fisheries imports relative to total imports increased from 1.64 to 2.93 percent. Conversely, the value of fisheries exports to total exports declined from 3.1 to 1.1 percent. This means that the net balance of fisheries exports to imports went from +U.S. $134,570,000 to −U.S. $1,154,262,000. The ratio of the value of fisheries imports to exports increased from .59 in 1967 to 2.55 in 1976. The break occurred in 1971 and rapidly increased from 1971 to 1976. This trend is attributed to the combined effect of extended jurisdiction and significant increases in the value of the yen.[123]

With respect to the trends relative to Japan's major trading partners on fisheries products, tables 6.16 and 6.17 show the value and quantity of Japanese fisheries imports and exports for 1967−1976 with the top ten countries in each case. The rank order for imports is (1) Republic of Korea (ROK), (2) Taiwan, (3) Indonesia, (4) India, (5) Thailand, (6) U.S., (7) Spain, (8) Canada, (9) China, and (10) Australia. The rank order for exports is (1) U.S., (2) U.K., (3) Netherlands, (4) Taiwan, (5) Federal Republic of Germany, (6) Canada, (7) Australia, (8) Philippines, (9) Hong Kong, and (10) Switzerland.

On the dimension of fisheries imports, South Korea has been so far the most significant trading partner for Japan, accounting for 16.6 to 20.5 percent of total value over the decade. However, data for 1977 and 1978 show South Korea's share declining to 19.61 and 14.67 percent respectively.[124] The second in rank up to 1976, Taiwan, is only about half as important as the ROK. The U.S. share of the Japanese market between 1967 and 1976 was quite small, fluctuating from 7.66 percent in 1967 to 5.0 percent in 1976. However, major changes in the U.S. rank occurred in 1977 and 1978. The U.S. overtook both Taiwan and South Korea in 1978, garnering 16.3 percent of the Japanese imports, up from 9.6 percent in 1977.[125] The value of Japanese imports from the U.S. in 1978 was $532 million. Looking at Japanese exports, however, yields a strikingly different picture. The U.S. has been by far

## TABLE 6.16

### JAPANESE FISHERIES IMPORTS FROM TOP TEN COUNTRIES, 1967–1976

#### (IN ORDER OF VALUE IN 1976)

| Country | 1967 Quantity (MT) | 1967 Value ($ Million) | 1968 Quantity (MT) | 1968 Value ($ Million) | 1969 Quantity (MT) | 1969 Value ($ Million) | 1970 Quantity (MT) | 1970 Value ($ Million) | 1971 Quantity (MT) | 1971 Value ($ Million) |
|---|---|---|---|---|---|---|---|---|---|---|
| South Korea | 32,010 | 32 (16.67%) | 26,302 | 32 (16%) | 30,159 | 34 (13.03%) | 40,781 | 39 (12.26%) | 58,262 | 49 (11.21%) |
| Taiwan | 4,098 | 4 | 13,704 | 7 | 10,729 | 12 (4.6%) | 27,106 | 25 ( 7.86%) | 29,335 | 38 ( 8.70%) |
| Indonesia | 1,420 | 1 | 666 | 2 | 4,109 | 7 | 5,336 | 11 | 10,186 | 24 ( 5.49%) |
| India | 2,357 | 5 | 3,275 | 7 | 4,931 | 12 ( 4.6%) | 6,480 | 15 ( 4.72%) | 9,873 | 25 ( 5.72%) |
| Thailand | 5,302 | 11 | 4,627 | 12 ( 6%) | 6,819 | 16 ( 6.13%) | 7,445 | 16 ( 5.03%) | 13,913 | 23 ( 5.26%) |
| United States | 14,963 | 15 ( 7.66%) | 10,220 | 17 ( 8.64%) | 22,949 | 26 ( 9.78%) | 14,148 | 24 ( 7.59%) | 14,018 | 29 ( 6.68%) |
| Spain | 23,160 | 5 | 12,763 | 3 | 11,017 | 3 | 21,844 | 7 | 49,470 | 27 ( 6.18%) |
| Canada | 2,358 | 3 | 2,618 | 4 | 2,016 | 3 | 4,120 | 5 | 8,763 | 10 |
| China | 35,399 | 20 (10.42%) | 27,811 | 16 ( 8%) | 20,904 | 19 ( 7.28%) | 21,035 | 30 ( 9.43%) | 25,192 | 31 ( 7.09%) |
| Australia | 1,983 | 6 | 1,919 | 7 | 4,531 | 15 ( 5.75%) | 4,877 | 16 ( 5.03%) | 5,510 | 21 ( 4.81%) |
| Other | 207,900 | 80 | 260,238 | 9³ | 235,464 | 114 | 221,387 | 130 | 173,550 | 160 |
| TOTAL | 330,950 | 192 | 370,143 | 200 | 362,628 | 261 | 374,569 | 318 | 398,072 | 437 |

## TABLE 6.16 (Continued)

### JAPANESE FISHERIES IMPORTS FROM TOP TEN COUNTRIES, 1967–1976

#### (IN ORDER OF VALUE IN 1976)

| Country | 1972 Quantity (MT) | 1972 Value ($ Million) | 1973 Quantity (MT) | 1973 Value ($ Million) | 1974 Quantity (MT) | 1974 Value ($ Million) | 1975 Quantity (MT) | 1975 Value ($ Million) | 1976 Quantity (MT) | 1976 Value ($ Million) |
|---|---|---|---|---|---|---|---|---|---|---|
| South Korea | 96,691 | 80 (12.94%) | 129,518 | 173 (15.74%) | 151,494 | 215 (19.42%) | 199,606 | 288 (22.19%) | 260,362 | 390 (20.5%) |
| Taiwan | 31,070 | 56 ( 9.06%) | 40,548 | 93 ( 8.46%) | 34,944 | 98 ( 8.85%) | 52,600 | 149 (11.48%) | 51,925 | 184 ( 9.6%) |
| Indonesia | 15,930 | 49 ( 7.93%) | 21,975 | 81 ( 7.37%) | 21,800 | 84 ( 7.59%) | 25,274 | 99 ( 7.63%) | 28,927 | 163 ( 8.5%) |
| India | 12,958 | 40 ( 6.47%) | 24,033 | 65 ( 5.91%) | 20,498 | 60 ( 5.42%) | 30,780 | 94 ( 7.24%) | 28,742 | 138 ( 7.2%) |
| Thailand | 17,003 | 33 ( 5.34%) | 24,684 | 52 ( 4.73%) | 15,697 | 44 | 22,706 | 70 ( 5.39%) | 24,625 | 97 ( 5.1%) |
| United States | 9,470 | 25 ( 3.98%) | 28,519 | 89 ( 8.08%) | 14,388 | 56 ( 5.05%) | 19,365 | 73 ( 5.65%) | 21,077 | 96 ( 5.0%) |
| Spain | 52,880 | 28 ( 4.53%) | 42,473 | 35 | 54,378 | 61 ( 5.51%) | 55,738 | 66 | 69,468 | 94 ( 4.9%) |
| Canada | 10,328 | 24 ( 3.88%) | 18,533 | 64 ( 5.82%) | 10,786 | 49 | 16,331 | 45 | 20,271 | 93 ( 4.8%) |
| China | 31,517 | 50 ( 8.09%) | 31,200 | 76 ( 6.92%) | 37,349 | 99 ( 8.94%) | 34,910 | 76 ( 5.86%) | 31,661 | 83 ( 4.3%) |
| Australia | 6,039 | 28 ( 4.53%) | 7,182 | 40 | 7,204 | 38 | 6,215 | 38 | 8,653 | 71 ( 3.7%) |
| Other | 196,763 | 205 | 289,770 | 331 | 235,603 | 303 | 246,890 | 300 | 268,806 | 489 (25.7%) |
| TOTAL | 480,649 | 618 | 658,425 | 1,099 | 604,141 | 1,107 | 710,415 | 1,298 | 814,517 | 1,898 (100.0) |

Source: Fisheries Trade Statistics, Japan Fisheries Agency, 1967–1976.
Compiled by the Office of the Regional Fisheries Attaché, U.S. Embassy, Tokyo.

## TABLE 6.17

### Japanese Fisheries Exports to Top Ten Countries, 1967–1976

(In order of value in 1976)

| Country | 1967 Quantity (MT) | 1967 Value ($ Million) | 1968 Quantity (MT) | 1968 Value ($ Million) | 1969 Quantity (MT) | 1969 Value ($ Million) | 1970 Quantity (MT) | 1970 Value ($ Million) | 1971 Quantity (MT) | 1971 Value ($ Million) |
|---|---|---|---|---|---|---|---|---|---|---|
| United States | 108,700 | 92 (28.2%) | 117,057 | 103 (30.0%) | 109,368 | 104 (29.9%) | 145,499 | 117 (29.8%) | 125,122 | 114 (27.3%) |
| United Kingdom | 34,886 | 49 (15.03%) | 50,262 | 59 (16.81%) | 32,431 | 37 (10.66%) | 35,752 | 47 (12.02%) | 32,247 | 45 (10.77%) |
| Netherlands | 47,573 | 12 | 11,253 | 7 | 23,372 | 9 | 39,458 | 14 | 57,620 | 20 ( 4.78%) |
| Taiwan | – | – | – | – | 14,338 | 3 | 20,366 | 5 | 22,870 | 6 |
| West Germany | 16,011 | 20 ( 6.13%) | 16,099 | 21 ( 5.98%) | 16,908 | 23 ( 6.63%) | 22,380 | 25 ( 6.39%) | 14,769 | 20 ( 4.78%) |
| Canada | 7,045 | 7 | 5,680 | 6 | 7,567 | 8 | 9,778 | 11 | 25,322 | 14 |
| Australia | 8,939 | 9 | 7,401 | 9 | 9,479 | 11 | 9,559 | 10 | 13,390 | 14 |
| Philippines | 56,347 | 20 ( 6.13%) | 59,752 | 20 ( 5.70%) | 52,718 | 16 | 52,304 | 16 | 55,773 | 19 ( 4.55%) |
| Hong Kong | 2,179 | 7 | 2,136 | 8 | 2,890 | 11 | 3,106 | 11 | 2,525 | 9 |
| Switzerland | 1,666 | 13 | 2,200 | 11 | 2,469 | 12 | 3,001 | 10 | 2,703 | 10 |
| TOTAL incl. others | | 326 | | 351 | 489,322 | 347 | 578,876 | 391 | 635,245 | 418 |

## TABLE 6.17 (Continued)

### JAPANESE FISHERIES EXPORTS TO TOP TEN COUNTRIES, 1967–1976

(IN ORDER OF VALUE IN 1976)

| Country | 1972 Quantity (MT) | 1972 Value ($ Million) | 1973 Quantity (MT) | 1973 Value ($ Million) | 1974 Quantity (MT) | 1974 Value ($ Million) | 1975 Quantity (MT) | 1975 Value ($ Million) | 1976 Quantity (MT) | 1976 Value ($ Million) |
|---|---|---|---|---|---|---|---|---|---|---|
| United States | 216,153 | 194 (36.8%) | 243,667 | 226 (35.5%) | 191,060 | 214 (30.9%) | 85,776 | 128 (22.5%) | 109,414 | 192 (25.8%) |
| United Kingdom | 25,338 | 41 ( 7.78%) | 18,283 | 39 ( 6.13%) | 14,819 | 38 ( 5.49%) | 18,213 | 42 ( 7.39%) | 19,635 | 50 ( 6.72%) |
| Netherlands | 46,105 | 16 | 30,653 | 15 | 97,274 | 49 ( 7.08%) | 81,276 | 33 ( 5.18%) | 82,490 | 40 ( 5.38%) |
| Taiwan | 25,059 | 10 | 17,386 | 22 | 39,674 | 20 | 57,206 | 28 | 50,634 | 40 ( 5.38%) |
| West Germany | 32,210 | 25 ( 4.74%) | 10,668 | 32 ( 5.03%) | 7,625 | 28 | 9,965 | 33 ( 5.81%) | 6,622 | 31 |
| Canada | 14,073 | 19 | 14,645 | 27 | 11,925 | 24 | 11,356 | 23 | 11,529 | 30 |
| Australia | 13,116 | 15 | 14,699 | 20 | 22,106 | 29 | 14,665 | 18 | 15,884 | 29 |
| Philippines | 46,050 | 17 | 38,492 | 19 | 44,137 | 28 | 50,172 | 26 | 37,443 | 28 |
| Hong Kong | 7,006 | 13 | 1,744 | 17 | 2,003 | 15 | 2,807 | 18 | 1,821 | 25 |
| Switzerland | 14,485 | 15 | 4,068 | 23 | 2,375 | 16 | 3,227 | 16 | 3,030 | 21 |
| TOTAL incl. others | 667,066 | 527 | 687,372 | 636 | 718,726 | 692 | 603,334 | 568 | 650,350 | 774 |

Source: Fisheries Trade Statistics, Japan Fisheries Agency, 1967–1976.
Compiled by the Office of the Regional Fisheries Attaché, U.S. Embassy, Tokyo.

the largest market for the Japanese fishery products, accounting for 28.2 percent in 1967, 36.8 percent in 1972, 22.5 percent in 1975, and 25.8 percent in 1976. This trend dipped to 21.4 percent in 1977[126] but climbed back up to 27.2% in 1978.[127]

The question of import restrictions on fisheries products in Japan emerged as a difficult issue during 1977, both as a result of the unfavorable trade balances of the previous decade and the implementation of extended jurisdiction in the U.S. Specifically, the issue turns on Japanese prohibitions on the import of surimi (made from pollock) and the implications of this for the Northeast Pacific. Since pollock constitute the largest single allocation for Japan in the Northeast, U.S. fishermen and processors would like to expand their export trade with Japan in this direction. The stumbling block is the Japanese import prohibition on surimi. In Japan this is part of the significant domestic political constraints on Japanese responses to U.S. trade policy. The most politically potent problem is the extreme protectionism of the agricultural sector in Japan, of which import prohibitions on surimi are simply a reflection.

To a certain extent, this policy is similar to the official policy of the governments of China, North and South Korea, and Taiwan. The primary objective of exports of fisheries products for these countries is the accumulation of foreign exchange. Consequently, they maintain a variety of tight controls on imports of fisheries products via the necessity of seeking approval of a government purchasing agency for each transaction, or through quotas or high tariffs.[128]

During 1977 in the North Pacific Fishery Management Council, several Council members seemed to want to link the issue of increasing the Japanese allocations on tanner crab (*C. opilio*) in the eastern Bering Sea to the issue of import restrictions on surimi in Japan. This move did not go very far at the time but it later blossomed into a salient problem for the Japanese.

On February 14, 1978, Governor Jay S. Hammond of Alaska wrote to Ambassador John Negroponte, Deputy Assistant Secretary for Oceans and Fisheries Affairs in the Department of State. Governor Hammond strongly protested the import restrictions maintained by both Japan and South Korea on a species for which they had received significant allocations from the U.S. zone. He stated specifically:

> In reviewing the FCMA, I cannot discern a convincing justification for the willingness of the State Department to allocate U.S. fisheries resources to nations which refuse to import U.S. fisheries products of the same type. After foreign nationals catch and process U.S. fish taken from the FCZ, they use the products (1) to satisfy their domestic needs and (2) to control other markets, including the United States market. Thus, while being excluded from foreign marketing opportunities by import restrictions, U.S. producers are concurrently stifled at home by the dominance of foreign fisheries products, many of which originated in waters subject to U.S. jurisdiction. Therefore, notwithstanding enactment of the FCMA, foreign interests have essentially locked up these resources, preventing any development or expansion of the U.S. fishing industry.

Later that same month, the North Pacific Council met in Anchorage and unanimously adopted a Resolution expressing the same points made by Governor Hammond. This

Resolution was also communicated to Ambassador Negroponte by Chairman Harold E. Lokken, who argued:

> The Council passed this Resolution, not only in support of the position taken by the Honorable Jay Hammond, Governor of the State of Alaska, in his letter to you of February 14, but also in the firm conviction that import restrictions by countries such as Japan and the Republic of Korea on species for which those same countries receive large allocations in the FCZ off Alaska unfairly restrict the development of the U.S. fishing industry. Not only do such quotas or, as in the case of the Republic of South Korea, outright embargos, deny access to important markets to U.S. fishermen, but they tend to give those countries unfair access to the U.S. marketplace. U.S. fishermen must have the opportunity to compete fairly on the world marketplace, but large allocations of species such as Alaska pollock to Japan, which restrict or prohibit the import of those same fish from the United States, give them an unfair competitive edge in both their own market and on the world market.[129]

In an attempt to seek more direct action on this issue, members of the North Pacific Council succeeded in getting Senators Warren Magnuson and Henry Jackson of Washington and Senator Ted Stevens of Alaska to cosponsor a Bill (S.3050) dealing with the regulation of foreign fish processing vessels in the U.S. zone. Most of this Bill addresses the question of joint ventures primarily. However, one part of the Bill (Section 4 [B]) deals with the problem of import restrictions:

> In deciding whether to approve such an application [of a foreign processing vessel], the Secretary may consider whether the applicant nation imposes any tariff or non-tariff conditions on the importation of fish or fish products which are greater than those imposed by the United States.[130]

These initiatives did not meet with favor in the Administration. There were two responses. Ambassador Robert S. Strauss, then Special Representative for Trade Negotiations, responded to the Resolution passed by the North Pacific Council in the following way:

> We support fully the Council's desire to expand U.S. fish product exports. However, we have taken a slightly different approach to achieving access to the fish markets of other nations than that recommended by the Council.
> We are now engaged with nearly 100 other nations in an effort to expand world trade through a reduction in trade barriers worldwide. This is the seventh series of such multilateral trade negotiations which have occurred since World War II.
> In this current round, which is known as the Tokyo Round, we have made requests of nations for a reduction in tariff and non-tariff barriers to the expansion of U.S. fish product exports. These requests were specially designed to take advantage of the export potential in under-utilized species.[131]

The second Administration response came in the form of a letter from Douglas J. Bennet, Jr., Assistant Secretary for Congressional Relations, Department of State, to James T. McIntyre, Jr., Director of the Office of Management and Budget, commenting on S.3050.[132] Secretary Bennet made the following points:

The Department is opposed to the proposed legislation, which is not consistent with U.S. Government policy regarding controls on exports. We believe that S.3050 contains several provisions which would be detrimental to the international trade policy objectives of the United States and which could set a precedent for foreign export restrictions on raw material and supplies needed by American firms. . . .

Another element of the proposed legislation which could seriously undermine the international trade objectives of the United States is the provision that the Secretary of Commerce may consider, before granting fishing permits, whether the foreign nations applying for such permits have trade barriers against the importation of U.S. fish or fish products. Such criteria would set a precedent which other countries could cite as justification for placing restrictions on U.S. access to materials in an effort to gain concessions on U.S. tariffs or other import restrictions. For example, foreign countries could deny U.S. vessels the right to fish in their 200-mile zones unless the U.S. lowered its barriers against importation of processed tuna. The United States has consistently held that the sale of raw material and resources in international markets should be free from restrictions based on trade or political considerations. We are currently negotiating with Japan on access to its market for our processed fish. Japan now has barriers to such imports. We believe that we can obtain concessions without instituting a new restrictive policy that would jeopardize our access to the raw materials of other countries.

These events at least succeeded in triggering interesting responses in Japan and the ROK. For the Koreans, the problem was not at all difficult. The basis for import restrictions on surimi was to conserve the government's supply of foreign currency reserves. Faced with a drastic curtailment of supply of pollock, it made sense to remove impediments to possible access to new supplies either by direct allocations or via joint ventures. The ROK therefore eliminated its restrictions on the importation of surimi.[133]

The Japanese situation is more complicated in two respects. First, Japan finds itself caught by declining pollock allocations in both the Soviet and U.S. zones. In the U.S. zone, there are *two* potential competitors (i.e., U.S. fishermen and the ROK). The Japan Fisheries Agency fears that if they reject the demand to remove import restrictions on surimi, their pollock allocations will be cut drastically in retaliation. However, if they agree to remove such restrictions, they run the risk of severe short-run cuts in their allocation as a means of giving U.S. fishermen the opportunity to catch and sell pollock to Japan.[134] If this occurs, there might be similar moves on the Soviet side.[135]

But there is a further and more difficult complication arising from internal political divisions in the Japanese fisheries industry. As the *Yomiuri Shimbun* argues: "the Japanese import restriction is a necessary measure in order to avoid economic dislocation of the Japanese fishing industry and is not designed to apply to the United States alone."[136] Quite large constituencies of the Minister of Agriculture, Forestry, and Fisheries are situated in Hokkaido and northern Honshu. The constituents are primarily from fishing families and small to middle-sized cooperatives and firms. They are the ones most likely to suffer directly and in the short run from lifting the ban on the importation of surimi. However, the large fish processing and trading companies are agitating in favor of lifting the ban as a means of relieving increasing restrictions on the supply of surimi, and are continuing to seek special arrangements with the USSR and the U.S.[137] The Fisheries Agency has so far resisted these attempts, even though the major companies and trading firms have now begun to lobby the Ministry of International Trade and Industry as well.[138]

## The Problem of Joint Ventures

Joint ventures in fisheries take a wide variety of forms.[139] More than 200 existing examples seem to fall into two distinct categories: equity and contractual. Many joint ventures proposed for the North Pacific since 1976 are of the contractual type and involve either U.S. fishermen catching fish for foreign processing vessels in the U.S. zone, or Japanese fishing companies exchanging technology for increased allocations of particular species in the Soviet zone. However, there appears to be growing Japanese equity participation in Alaskan and British Columbian processing firms as a further means of ensuring trading companies a stable access to low-cost raw material.[140] In the case of the USSR, ROK, and Poland, the objectives pursued are fairly straightforward, the prime objective being guaranteed access to stable and sufficient supplies. The Canadian case is also a simple one, since it is feasible for the federal government to avoid paying developmental costs by arranging with foreign fishermen to keep a portion of the resource themselves for a fee, and to sell a portion directly on the Canadian market.

The situation for Japan and the United States is more complicated because objectives are heavily skewed by difficult internal political considerations. For Japan the problem is the necessity of protecting fishing families and small to medium-sized fishing operations. In addition, there is the question of attempting to forestall the adoption of joint ventures as the only means of getting access to the Soviet zone. In the U.S., the problem is twofold. First, the barrier of the Jones Act prohibits the direct landing of unprocessed fish caught by foreign fishermen in the U.S. zone. Second, goals expressed in the FCMA are conflicting and ambiguous. The development of fisheries for "the greatest overall benefit of the nation" is not necessarily always compatible with regional development of either harvesting or processing capacities. Moreover, proposals that call for development of U.S. harvesting capacities are objected to by U.S. processors on the ground that this would foreclose their own development.

Let us for a moment leave aside the internal political problems of the U.S. and Japan and consider the objectives that might be sought by the large distant-water fishing states and the coastal states in the Northeast Pacific. Japan and the USSR are the primary distant-water states, though Japan is involved in most of the joint venture arrangements in fisheries around the world and therefore has the widest experience as shown in table 6.18.

Japan also has the largest number of equity joint ventures with both Alaskan and British Columbian firms as shown in tables 6.19 and 6.20.

The objectives of the large Japanese fishing and trading companies reflect concern for domestic consumption, rates of return on investment, stable access to supplies of low cost raw material, and control of a market that consists of Japan, South Korea, Canada, the U.S., and Western Europe. They therefore operate on a scale that is qualitatively different from any other participant. As Kaczynski points out in chapter 7 of this book, the dynamics

TABLE 6.18

JAPANESE JOINT VENTURES IN FISHERIES

| Type of fishery | Latin America | Asia & Oceania | Africa | North America | Europe Mid-East | TOTAL |
|---|---|---|---|---|---|---|
| *Fishing* | | | | | | |
| Trawl fishery | 4 | 3 | 7 | — | 1 | 15 |
| Shrimp trawl fishery | 4 | 20 | 7 | — | — | 31 |
| Skipjack angling | — | 7 | 2 | — | — | 9 |
| Tuna longlining | 1 | 2 | 1 | — | 1 | 5 |
| Other (1) | 6 | 3 | 2 | 5 | — | 16 |
| *Mariculture* | | | | | | |
| Eel | 1 | 16 | — | — | — | 17 |
| Pearl | — | 4 | — | — | — | 4 |
| Other (2) | — | 8 | — | 2 | — | 10 |
| *Processing* | | | | | | |
| Frozen seafood | 5 | 10 | 5 | 4 | 1 | 25 |
| Canned seafood | 2 | 2 | 1 | 13 | — | 18 |
| Other (3) | 4 | 20 | 2 | 16 | 1 | 43 |
| TOTAL | 27 | 95 | 27 | 40 | 4 | 193 |

Source: U.S. Department of Commerce. *Survey of Foreign Fisheries, Oceanographic and Atmospheric Literature*, No. C-20, 1977, p. 6. Taken from *Suisan Shuho*, No. 799 (25 April 1977), p. 4.

driving the operations of the Socialist Bloc of distant-water fishing states are quite different. These countries reflect a concern for internal food shortages and the problem of domestic versus foreign currency outlays. The purchase of fish from a coastal state, like the U.S. or Canada, would necessarily involve hard currency expenditures; but unprocessed fish costs less than processed fish and they can afford to pay more for unprocessed fish than either U.S. or Canadian processors.

We have already described the arrangements that have been permitted in the Northwest Pacific. In the Northeast Pacific, four proposals have been made for the U.S.: two involve the ROK, one involves the USSR, and one involves Poland.

## The Korea Marine Industry Development Corporation Proposal

The Korea Marine Industry Development Corporation (KMIDC) proposed a contract with U.S. fishermen for the delivery to Korean processing vessels in the U.S. zone of pollock caught by U.S. vessels in the Gulf of Alaska. Originally, the amount proposed for 1977 was 130,000 MT. This figure was substantially scaled down to between 30,000–40,000 MT. The Koreans proposed to pay 5¢ per pound with an additional ½¢ per pound at the end of the season. After the fifth year of operation, vessels remaining continuously on contract would derive an additional ½¢ per pound. The proposal called for the Koreans to provide three vessels—two processors and a transport vessel—and for U.S. fishermen to provide five catcher boats via R. A. Davenny and Associates.[141]

# TABLE 6.19

## Japanese Investment in Alaskan Fisheries

| Japanese investors | U.S. subsidiaries | Date of investment | Equity (capital stock) Percent | $1,000 (U.S.) |
|---|---|---|---|---|
| Taiyo | Pacific Alaska Fisheries | 12/65 | 49 | 50 |
| | B & B Fisheries | −/67 | 70 | 305 |
| | Western Alaska Enterp. | 11/67 | 100 | 550 |
| | B & B Fisheries | −/74 | 30 | 131 |
| | NEP TOTAL | | | 1,036 |
| Nichiro Mitsubishi | Orca Pacific | 6/66 | 50 | 1,000 |
| | Hilton Seafood | 7/73 | 50 | 81 |
| | Sand Point Packing | − | 50 | |
| Nichiro | Nichiro Pacific | 8/67 | 100 | 300 |
| | Adak Aleutian Proc. | 6/73 | 30 | 33 |
| | NEP TOTAL | | | 333 |
| Marubeni | North Pacific Proc. | 6/72 | 50 | 250 |
| | Marubeni Alaska Seaf. | 6/72 | 100 | 600 |
| | Bering Sea Fisheries | 6/72 | 25 | 135 |
| | Juneau Cold Storage | 4/73 | 25 | 25 |
| | King Crab | 4/73 | 49.9 | 1,500 |
| | Kodiak Fishing | 4/73 | 25 | 130 |
| | Ward Cove Pack. | 11/73 | | |
| | Juneau Fishing | 11/73 | | |
| | Alaska Ice & Storage | | 100 | |
| | Alaska Pacific Seaf. | | 100 | 100 |
| | Columbia-Ward Fish. | | 25 | |
| | Cordova Bay Fisheries | | 50 | |
| | New Eng.-Marub. Export | | | |
| | New Eng.-Marub. Seaf. | | | |
| | Point Chehalis Packers | | | |
| | St. Elias Ocean Products | | | |
| | Togiak Fisheries | | 49.9 | 256 |
| Nippon Suisan Mitsui | Morpac | 6/73 | 37.6 | 405 |
| | Morpac | −/76 | 60 | 646 |
| | NEP TOTAL | | | 1,051 |
| Nippon-Suisan | Universal Seafood | 6/74 | 49.9 | |
| | Intersea Fisheries | 3/75 | 40 | |
| | Dutch Harbor Seafood | | 25 | |
| | Nippon Suisan (USA) | | 100 | 300 |
| Kyokuyo | Kyokuyo (USA) | −/73 | 100 | 300 |
| | Whitney Fidalgo | 10/73 | 97.9 | 11,000 |
| | Mokuhana Fisheries (M/V) | | | |
| | Nefco-Fidalgo Packing | | 50 | |
| C.Itoh Hokuyo | New Northern Proc. | 3/74 | 50 | 500 |
| C.Itoh | Roy Furfjord | | | |
| Iwakiri Fisheries | Alaska Marine Prod. | −/74 | | |
| Ak. Pulp | Harbor Seafoods | | 100 | |
| Alaska Shokai | JAD Alaska Shoji | | | |
| Kyodo Kumiai | JCT Alaska | 6/73 | 100 | 10 |
| Kenai Fisheries | R. Lee Seafoods | | 20 | |
| Kamai Fisheries | William Sound Fisheries | | | |

Source: Taken from Per O. Heggelund, ''Japanese Investments in Alaskan Fishing Industry'' in *Alaska Seas and Coasts*, 5,4 (October 1977), 9.

TABLE 6.20

## Foreign Investment in the B.C. Fish Processing Industry

| Foreign investors | Canadian companies | Equity (capital stock) (%) | Debentures ($1000) | Date |
|---|---|---|---|---|
| **UNITED STATES** | | | | |
| New England Fish | The Canadian Fishing Company | 100.0 | – | – |
| Consolidated Foods Corporation | Con. Foods Corp of Canada | 97.6 | | |
| Con. Foods Corp of Canada | Booth Fisheries Can. | 100.0 | | |
| % Foreign Invest. (% FI) | Booth Fisheries Can. | 97.6 | – | – |
| Washington Fish and Oyster | Dennis Shellfish | 100.0 | – | – |
| Americo | Reliance Fish | 39.0 | – | – |
| Swiftsure Fisheries (Seattle) | East Pacific Enterprises | – | 75 | Jan. 1977 |
| Joe Kristek (US) | Transcoastal Enterprises | 33.0 | | |
| Floria Musladin (US) | Transcoastal Enterprises | 33.0 | | |
| % FI | Transcoastal Enterprises | 66.0 | – | – |
| **JAPANESE** | | | | |
| Nichimo Trading | S.S.I. Sea Products | 30.0 | 150<br>300 | Feb. 1975<br>June 1976 |
| Nigata Trans. and Constr. | Tohto Ocean Commerce | 35.0 | – | – |
| Nikko Shoji | Aero Trading | 100.0 | – | – |
| Sumitomo Shojikaisha | Western Canada Seafood | 100.0 | – | – |
| Nippon Suisan Kaisher | Pacific Rim Mariculture | 19.0 | 250 | Mar. 1978 |
| Nozaki Trading | Quality Fish | – | 500 | Jan. 1978 |
| Nozaki Trading[a] | Delta Food Processors | – | 1,000 | Jan. 1976 |
| Bank of Tokyo | Tohcan | 48.0 | | |
| % FI | Tohcan | 50.2 | | |
| Tohcan | Westerham Capital | 50.0 | 500[b] | Aug. 1977 |
| % FI | Westerham Capital | 25.1 | | |
| Westerham Capital | Norpac Fisheries | 50.0 | 1,150[b] | Feb. 1974 |
| Toshoko | Wescan Fisheries | 30.0 | | |
| Kyoei Shokai | Wescan Fisheries | 30.0 | | |
| Toshoko (Am) | Wescan Fisheries | 15.0 | | |
| Fukuyama/Sugiyama | Wescan Fisheries | 25.0 | | |
| % FI | Wescan Fisheries | 75.0 | | |
| Wescan Fisheries | Norpac Fisheries | 50.0 | | |
| % FI | Norpac Fisheries | 50.0 | – | – |
| Norpac Fisheries | Carlyle Fisheries | 100.0 | | |
| % FI | Carlyle Fisheries | 50.0 | – | – |
| Norpac Fisheries | Carlyle Packing | 100.0 | | |
| % FI | Carlyle Packing | 50.0 | – | – |
| Norpac Fisheries | National Fisheries | 11.1 | | |
| Carlyle Packing | National Fisheries | 80.9 | | |
| % FI | National Fisheries | 50.0 | – | – |

TABLE 6.20 (Continued)

FOREIGN INVESTMENT IN THE B.C. FISH PROCESSING INDUSTRY

| Foreign investors | Canadian companies | Equity (capital stock) (%) | Debentures ($1000) | Date |
|---|---|---|---|---|
| *JAPANESE Cont'd.* | | | | |
| Fukuyama/Sugiyama | Norpac Fisheries | – | 300 | Aug. 1974 |
| | | | 100 | July 1969 |
| Fukuyama/Sugiyama | Lions Gate Fisheries Ltd. | 16.7 | | |
| % FI | Lions Gate Fisheries Ltd. | 0.8 | – | – |
| % FI | S. Fukiyama[c] | 4.9 | – | – |
| Kibun Co. (B.C.) | North Sea Products | – | 400 | Apr. 1975 |
| | | | 400 | Mar. 1977 |
| Marubeni | Cassiar Packing | 49.8 | | |
| % FI | Cassiar Packing | 49.8 | – | – |
| Marubeni | Tonquin Enterprises | 20.0 | | |
| Cassiar Packing | Tonquin Enterprises | 45.0 | | |
| % FI | Tonquin Enterprises | 44.5 | 1,140[d] | |
| Tonquin Enterprises | Tofino Packing | 100.0 | | |
| % FI | Tofino Packing | 44.5 | 1,140[d] | |
| Tonquin Enterprises | Port Alberni Fish | 100.0 | | |
| % FI | Port Alberni Fish | 44.5 | – | – |
| Marubeni | Tonquin Enterprises | – | 2,420[e] | Aug. 1976 |
| Marubeni | Tofini Packing | – | 2,420[e] | Aug. 1976 |
| Marubeni | Port Alberni Fish | – | 2,420[e] | Aug. 1976 |
| Marubeni | Oakland Fisheries | – | 3,500 | Aug. 1977 |
| Marubeni | Central Native | | | |
| Marubeni | Fishermen's Co-op | – | 500 | Jan. 1978 |
| Marubeni | Fishermen's Co-op | – | 1,500 | Sept. 1976 |
| Marubeni | Fishermen's Co-op | – | 4,500 | Jul. 1975 |
| Millbanke Ind.[f] | Fishermen's Co-op | – | 500 | Jul. 1975 |
| Tonquin Enterprises | S.&K. Processors | – | 104 | July 1974 |
| Mitsubishi Canada | Oakland Industries | – | 800 | Feb. 1974 |
| | | | 750 | Sept. 1976 |
| Hoko Fishing[g] | Oakland Fisheries | 36.0 | – | – |
| Toshoku Canada | Tradewind Seafoods | – | 225 | Mar. 1978 |
| Total Debentures | | | 19,664[h] | |
| Total Japanese Debentures | | | 19,589[h] | |

Sources: This table and notes were taken from: Trevor B. Proverbs, *Foreign Investment in British Columbia Fish Processing Industry* (Vancouver, B.C.: Canadian Dept. of Fisheries and the Environment, Fisheries and Marine Service Industry Report No. 105, July 1978), pp. 13–16; 1978 Search of Registered Offices; Statistics Canada. Inter-Corporate Ownership, 1975. (Ottawa; Queen's Printer, 1978); Will McKay, *An Investigation of Foreign Influence in the B.C. Fishing Industry* (Vancouver: Environment Canada, 1975); Russ Freethy, *Jurisdiction, Legislation and Provincial Policy for the B.C. Commercial Fishing Industry* (Victoria: Marine Resources Branch, 1976).

[a]An agreement was made between Nozaki Trading and Delta Food Processors that Delta would issue a $1,000,000 debenture if certain conditions arose, but this situation did not occur.

## TABLE 6.20 (Continued)

### Foreign Investment in the B.C. Fish Processing Industry

[b]Norpac Fisheries issued $500,000 and $1,150,000 debentures to Tohcan and Westerham Capital, respectively.

[c]It was not indicated in *Inter-Corporate Ownership 1975* who the foreign interests were.

[d]McKay reported that Tonquin Enterprises and Tofino Packing had a $1,140,000 debenture outstanding with Marubeni. $140,000 was on term loan with $1,000,000 available on an operating loan basis. The exact date when this debenture was issued is not known.

[e]Marubeni Corporation purchased this debenture from Tonquin Enterprises, Tofino Packing (1965), and Port Alberni Fish.

[f]Millbanke Industries was purchased by the Central Native Fishermen's Co-op in July 1975. Marubeni had controlled 50 percent of Millbanke's shares.

[g]As of April 30, 1978, Oakland Fisheries had redeemed the shares held by Hoko Fishing. Oakland could accept financing from Marubeni within two months.

[h]Includes debentures issued to foreign companies and Canadian companies with some degree of foreign investment. Total does not include two debentures issued to S. Fukuyama and I. Sugiyama by Norpac Fisheries, as the percentage of foreign ownership in S. Fukuyama is only 5 percent and the origin of these shareholders has not been determined. The total also does not include a debenture that was agreed upon by Nozaki Trading and Delta Food Processors. (See *a*.)

## *The USSR Ministry of Fisheries (Sovrybflot)—Bellingham Cold Storage Proposal*

Sovrybflot and Bellingham Cold Storage formed an equity joint venture in 1976, called Marine Resources, in which each partner holds an equal amount of capital stock. The purpose of the joint venture is to fish for species that are not utilized by U.S. fishermen, mainly hake and pollock. The fish are caught by U.S. fishermen and processed by two vessels provided by Sovrybflot in the U.S. zone. The product is sold on the international market. During 1978, the trial operation was expected to produce between 10,000–20,000 MT. Marine Resources proposes to pay 6¢ per pound for hake and pollock. Eventually, the two processing vessels will be able to accommodate fifteen U.S. trawlers. The trial operation during 1978 was scheduled to utilize only three.[142]

## *The Poland—Mrs. Paul's Kitchens Proposal*

Mrs. Paul's Kitchens proposed a contract joint venture with Poland in which Polish trawlers would harvest and process 60,000 MT of pollock in the Gulf of Alaska and the entire product was to be reprocessed and sold in the U.S.[143]

## *The ROK—Ketchikan Proposal*

Ketchikan Pisces proposed to join with two South Korean companies to form an entity called Alexander Fisheries. The proposal would allow two Korean freezer vessels in the U.S. zone to purchase excess salmon from U.S. fishermen during the summer of 1978. In addition, Alexander Fisheries would be allowed to harvest 4,000 MT of sablefish to be processed in Ketchikan.[144]

## Policy Issues

These proposals raised several major questions of policy. The KMIDC proposal split the Alaskan fisheries community. Those in favor of allowing the joint venture were the Governor of Alaska and the small fishermen, particularly of southeastern Alaska, where the operation was to be located. Those against included the processors, the king crab association based on Kodiak (called the United Fishermen's Marketing Association), and the Alaska Fishermen's Union.

The arguments for were basically that such joint ventures were permissible when they targeted on species not utilized by U.S. fishermen, and where domestic processing and marketing capabilities did not exist. Under these circumstances, joint ventures would allow fishermen to increase their income and develop the capability for midwater trawling.[145] The processors argued that such joint ventures would prevent the development of U.S. processing and marketing capabilities, and would be contrary to the intent of the FCMA. The ventures would make it very difficult for the U.S. industry to raise the necessary capital to compete because the foreign processor had much lower labor costs and did not have to comply with a variety of U.S. regulations established by agencies like the Environmental Protection Agency and the Food and Drug Administration.[146]

The Kodiak Fishermen's Wives Organization argued that the joint ventures should be prohibited because foreign processors could take advantage of loopholes in the U.S. vessel ownership and manning laws.[147] The argument focused on the effects such joint ventures would have on opportunities for the section of the fleet that was most suitable for targeting on unutilized species. They feared that foreign vessels and crews could, in a variety of ways, be registered as U.S. entities and thereby short-circuit the development of the U.S. fleet.

Virtually the same arguments were made against the Marine Resources joint venture relative to the production of hake resources under the jurisdiction of the Pacific Fishery Management Council.[148]

It appeared at this time that the U.S. government had no policy on the question of joint ventures, and that cautious beginnings resulted from the controversial actions of the two Councils. The North Pacific Council specifically disapproved the KMIDC proposal for 1977 and deferred a decision on the Marine Resources proposal, thereby killing it for 1977. However, at its May 1977 meeting, the Chairman of the North Pacific Council requested the NOAA office of the General Counsel to provide an analysis of the legal questions raised by the KMIDC proposal. A response was provided on May 23.[149]

The legal questions identified were as follows: (1) Must a foreign-flag processing vessel have a permit in order to process fish within the 200-mile zone? (2) Do fish caught by U.S. vessels in the FCZ (fisheries conservation zone) and sold to foreign-flag processing vessels in the FCZ count against that country's allocation? (3) If a permit is approved, what control does the U.S. have over the amount of fish processed by such foreign processing vessels? (4) Does Sec. 611.10 (b) of the Foreign Fishing Regulations issued by the National Marine Fisheries Service prevent the issuance of permits to the six KMIDC vessels? (5) Can the Secretary amend preliminary management plans and the interim regulations implementing them?

The responses to the questions posed were as follows: (1) foreign-flag processing vessels must have a permit in order to process fish in the U.S. zone; (2) fish caught by U.S. vessels in the U.S. zone and sold to foreign-flag processing vessels in the U.S. zone would *not* count against that country's allocation; (3) control over the amount of fish processed by foreign-flag vessels would be exercised via the permit which could specify conditions and restrictions applicable to operations; (4) Sec. 611.10 (b) of the Foreign Fishing Regulations did not by itself prevent issuance of permits to the KMIDC vessels; (5) the Secretary had the power to amend the Preliminary Management Plans and their implementing interim regulations.

Two additional opinions delivered by the Alaska Regional Counsel in June 1977 and March 1978 served to clarify the remaining grey areas. During the May 1977 meeting of the North Pacific Council, the following question was raised: Once permits are issued, does the Secretary have the power to restrict processing and transporting by such vessels later in the season, as an emergency measure, in order to prevent the total U.S. and foreign catch from exceeding the total allowable catch as specified in the Preliminary Management Plan? In response to this question, the suggestion was made in the meeting that the Secretary did have this power under Section 305 (d) of the FCMA which allows promulgation of emergency regulations to amend existing regulations that implement the Fishery Management Plans.

The Office of the NOAA General Counsel, however, thought that a serious question existed whether Section 305 (d) "could be relied upon as a method for regulating a fishery when a PMP [Preliminary Management Plan] is in place."[150] As a more effective measure, the Regional Counsel recommended that "permits issued to KMIDC vessels could simply include a restriction which allows them to receive and process fish from U.S. vessels until the optimum yield in the fishery is attained by the combined U.S. and foreign harvest."[151]

The second opinion came in response to a query by the General Manager of the United Fishermen's Marketing Association, Thomas Casey. Mr. Casey asked whether a foreign processing vessel could process fish while it was located in the territorial sea of the U.S. The response was that the FCMA [Section 307 (2) (A)] prohibits foreign vessels from engaging in fishing within state boundaries. Section 3 (10) of the Act defines all support activities as fishing but only if they are conducted "at sea."

> We presently interpret the term "at sea" to encompass all oceanic waters extending outward from the baseline of the territorial sea *except* for ports and harbors. Therefore, the FCMA does not cover support activities (such as processing) conducted by foreign vessels in the internal waters of a state or at ports. In addition, for some areas of western Alaska where permanent port facilities are not reasonably available, we are considering the appropriateness of designating particular locations as "constructive ports" which would be beyond the scope of the FCMA.
>
> It should also be noted that while the FCMA does not apply to the activities you describe when they occur in internal waters or at a port, State laws as well as other Federal laws (i.e., Customs laws, EPA, etc.) may apply.[152]

This question had actually been raised in 1977 concerning the operation of some Korean vessels in port at Bristol Bay engaged in processing herring caught by U.S. fishermen. The

Coast Guard had queried the Customs Service on the issue. The response was that a foreign-flag processing vessel could receive, process, and store fish within the U.S. territorial sea but would be prohibited from transporting fish or fish products between points within the territorial sea or to a U.S. port.[153]

With respect to the questions raised concerning foreign ownership of fishing vessels and U.S. fishing and fish-processing companies, the Alaska Regional Counsel, NOAA, summarized for the North Pacific Council Federal Maritime Statutes Affecting Joint Ventures in Fisheries.[154]

> In general terms, for an existing fishing vessel to enjoy treatment as a U.S. vessel, it must (1) have been built in the United States, and (2) if owned by an individual or a partnership, all owners must be U.S. citizens, or, if owned by a corporation, that corporation must be incorporated under the laws of the United States or any State thereof, the president or other chief executive officer and the chairman of the board of directors must be citizens of the United States, and no more of its directors than a minority of the number necessary to constitute a quorum can be non-citizens.
>
> If the amount of foreign ownership of a corporation is more than a controlling interest (usually 50 percent), the acquisition of existing fishing vessels by the corporation would require approval of the Maritime Administration under the Shipping Act of 1916. Under present regulations, however, if acquisition is of a new fishing vessel (not previously documented), no Maritime Administration approval is required, even if foreigners own 100 percent of a domestic corporation making such an acquisition.

On February 8, 1978, the National Marine Fisheries Service (NMFS) proposed an interim policy governing the purchase of fish from U.S. fishermen by foreign processing vessels in the U.S. zone.[155] This interim policy was to be applicable only to permit applications submitted under the Preliminary Management Plans in effect on January 1, 1978. As described by NMFS, the major objectives of the interim policy were twofold: (a) to prevent the emergence of conservation problems caused by unexpected increases in U.S. fishing efforts that result in optimum yield levels being exceeded; and (b) "to preserve foreign market opportunities for U.S. fishermen when such sales or deliveries would not unduly affect the development of other segments of the U.S. fishing industry."

Permit applications for such joint ventures, therefore, were to be approved only when (1) the optimum yield for the fishery would not be exceeded; (2) the capability and intent of the U.S. fishing industry to harvest fish to be sold or delivered would exceed the capability and intent of the U.S. industry to process such fish; and (3) the relevant foreign vessel had the capability and intent to process such fish.

This interim policy was more congenial to the North Pacific Council than to the Departments of the Treasury and State. The Treasury had three major objections to it: (1) the Department of Commerce had no authority under the FCMA to regulate or enhance the capacity utilization of the U.S. fish processing industry; (2) the regulation proposed would ensure 100 percent utilization of domestic capacity before permits were issued to foreign vessels without any prior consideration of demand conditions or rates of efficiency; (3) the

Department of Commerce had offered no economic analysis of the impacts of the proposed policy on fishermen, fish processors, and consumers.[156]

The Department of State objected to the fact that the proposed interim policy sought to impose export controls on food, and thereby had the effect of seriously jeopardizing broader U.S. interests vis-à-vis international trade. Moreover, in specifying the two objectives that the interim policy sought to achieve, no standards were provided by which the Secretary's satisfaction was to be determined, and no consideration was paid to problems of national security, short supply, and foreign policy, without which export controls cannot be imposed.[157]

The North Pacific Council in its meeting of February 23–24, 1978, wished to see the interim policy expanded and applied to Fishery Management Plans as well as to Preliminary Management Plans. The Council reiterated the point that one of the main justifications for developing such a policy was the development of the domestic fish processing sector.[158] The Council also requested that allocations for resources to be caught by U.S. fishermen and sold to foreign processors in the U.S. zone should come from the foreign countries' allocation and not that reserved for U.S. fishermen.

In response to the strong objections raised by Treasury and State, NOAA announced major substantive changes in the proposed interim policy on April 26, 1978. Joint ventures would now be approved once they met the requirements of the Act and other applicable law.[159] Henceforth, the special interests of U.S. domestic processors would not be a necessarily limiting condition on the approval of such permit applications. The KMIDC–Davenney Associates and the Sovrybflot–Marine Resources joint ventures would therefore be permissible. However, the Poland–Mrs. Paul's Kitchens joint venture could not be included in the former category, which called for all harvesting to be done within the U.S. zone by Polish vessels. Polish vessels would be allowed to take only the quota allocated to Poland.

Let us return to S.3050 and its companion, H.R. 12630, introduced into the U.S. House on May 9, 1978, by Rep. Donald Young of Alaska.[160] This legislation has three objectives. We have already dealt with the third, which allows the Secretary of Commerce to consider whether any nation applying for a permit to engage in a joint venture imposes artificial trade barriers against the importation of U.S. fish. However, the first two objectives (1) permit joint ventures only if U.S. processors do not have adequate capability to process the fish caught by U.S. fishermen; and (2) impose license fee requirements in the FCMA on processing vessels as well.

The Department of State again took the opportunity to oppose S.3050 as being inconsistent with U.S. policy on export controls.[161] The restrictions on the sale of fish by U.S. fishermen to foreign processors, the Department of State contended, "could prevent American fishermen from obtaining the prevailing market price for their fish by creating a buyer's market for U.S. processors. . . . These provisions also put restrictions on U.S. exports, not because of a serious domestic shortage of the raw material . . . but simply as a means to provide processors abnormally low-priced fish for processing."

The North Pacific Council, however, at its meeting on May 26, 1978, favored S.3050, specifying the following amendments to PL 94-265 (the FCMA):

1. To require that the interests of the seafood processing industry be weighed equally with those of other segments of the fishing industry.
2. To direct the Secretary of Commerce to evaluate the effect of any proposed action under the FCMA on the seafood processor and the development of the entire United States fishing industry.
3. To specify that foreign processing vessels be authorized to purchase fish caught by vessels of the United States in the U.S. fishery conservation zone only if:
   a. The domestic seafood processing industry lacks the capability to process the fish;
   b. The conservation and management provisions of the 200-mile Act are satisfied; and
   c. The Secretary evaluates the many considerations relevant to whether the authorization would in the long-term benefit the domestic fishing industry and the United States economy.
4. To grant the Regional Councils greater input into the decision-making process prior to the granting of permits for foreign processing vessels.

While the future of S.3050 and HR 12630 seemed to be uncertain in the Spring of 1978, given the concerted opposition of the Departments of State and the Treasury, the legislation passed both Houses of Congress and was signed into law (PL 95-354), as an amendment to the FCMA, on August 28, 1978. The new policy governing joint ventures in which U.S. fishermen may sell to foreign processors definitely gives preference to U.S. processors. Such applications may be approved only if it is determined by the Secretary that U.S. processors either do not have the capacity to process the amount of fish requested, or will not utilize their capacity on those species; only the difference between domestic harvesting and processing capacity is available for joint ventures.

During the January, 1979, meeting of the North Pacific Council, several questions arose concerning the effects of PL 95-354 on existing Fishery Management Plans of the Council, particularly the Gulf of Alaska Trawl and the Tanner Crab plans. The office of the NOAA Regional Counsel of Alaska sought to clarify these issues in a Memorandum to the Council on February 20, 1979.[162]

The amendment, which went into effect on August 28, 1978, amended the FCMA to clarify Congressional intent that the entire U.S. fishing industry, including processors, should benefit from the FCMA's assertion of extended jurisdiction. The FCMA, as now amended, appears to provide three options for utilization of fishery resources in the FCZ. Ranked in order of preference, these options are: first, harvesting and processing by the U.S. fishing industry; second, harvesting by U.S. vessels but processing by foreign vessels; and last, harvesting and processing by foreign fishing industries. When deciding to which of these categories fishery resources will be allocated, the Council must provide a sufficient amount of fish to satisfy the highest, unfilled level of preference.[163]

Both the Gulf of Alaska Trawl and the Tanner Crab plans conformed to the new amendment.

A detailed evaluation of the entire approach to the joint ventures problem in fisheries as adopted by the U.S. and Canada is provided in the second volume of this series. However, joint ventures in the U.S. appear to be on a much firmer footing than they were before the processor amendment was passed because most joint ventures proposed involve species that the U.S. processors cannot yet come even close to handling the full optimum yield. But the effect of this approach has been to intensify the competition between joint ventures and straight allocations for foreign fishing. This implies an increasing conflict between new-comers like South Korea and Poland on the one hand, and the traditional Japanese fishermen on the other.

The argument that joint ventures would hinder development of American processing capacity deserves careful scrutiny (and this is provided in the forthcoming volume) because the foreign allocations for principal species are very large and there are excellent prospects for long-run increases in the real prices of fillets and blocks. To the extent that the *real* costs of joint ventures are actually below those of shore-based processors, there is no reason why development of American processing capacity should be interpreted as forcing fishermen to take a lower price in order to subsidize a real source of economic inefficiency (i.e., higher costs and lower quality incurred in transferring hake and pollock into a shore-based plant).[164]

## CLAIMS TO DELIMIT ECONOMIC ZONES AND OTHER BOUNDARIES: THE NORTHWEST PACIFIC*

Japan's Law No. 31 on Provisional Measures Relating to the Fishing Zone refers only to the taking of marine animals and plants in the zone beyond the 12-mile territorial sea, and extends to 200 nautical miles in case there is no overlapping with opposite or adjacent states. (Articles 2 and 3). As already noted above, the fishing zone is not applied for the time being west of 135° east longitude to prevent application to foreign fishermen to the northwest and southwest of Japan. This applies particularly to South Korea and China, with which Japan has satisfactory fishing treaties; nor have those two countries attempted to implement an extended fishing zone, although they are actively considering its merits and demerits. Only a twelve-mile territorial sea applies in this region of the southern portion of the Sea of Japan, the Yellow Sea, and the East China Sea. Generally, foreign fishing is prohibited within the territorial sea areas.

The problem of overlapping claims has thus not become serious with respect to Japan, South Korea, and China, though some precise delimitation on the continental shelf has taken place between Japan and Korea with application to mineral exploration and exploitation. A precise delimitation of the continental shelf has been agreed to by Japan and Korea between 32°57' and 36°10' north latitude. The Agreement Between Japan and the Republic of Korea

*This section was written by Professor Frank Langdon, Dept. of Political Science, University of British Columbia.

Concerning the Establishment of the Boundary in the Northern Part of the Continental Shelf Adjacent to the Two Countries specifically states in Article III that it does not apply to the superjacent waters.[165] It seems likely that the boundary of Japan's extended fishery zone would follow this line, and would become authoritative for any economic activities claimed to come under the jurisdiction of the two countries. It also seems likely that the claim to delimitation for the purposes of mineral exploitation would apply to international fishing operations in the superjacent waters. The current agreement, ratified in the summer of 1978, applies only to the two countries negotiating it and not to all foreign states.

To the east of Japanese and Soviet territory toward the central Pacific, where there is no opposite state for great distances, the claiming of fisheries jurisdiction for 200 miles simply involves measuring from the low watermark or a base line connection point in their territories. Such a zone can be claimed from the principal inhabited islands. It is in the shelf areas where neighboring states are closely opposite or adjacent, as in the case of Japan and the Soviet Union, Japan and Korea, and Japan and China, that difficult problems arise. Overlapping claims have been made even when no legal steps have been taken to implement them.

The use of a median line to determine an acceptable boundary has been emphasized by Japan, which hopes thereby to maximize its share of intervening continental shelf areas. This line is drawn at a point equidistant between two different territories. The delimitation line agreed to between Japan and Korea relies upon such a method.[166] In the more contentious shelf area in the East China Sea, there will have to be a three-way division between Japan, China, and the Republic of Korea in an area where substantial amounts of oil may be discovered.

China and Korea have relied upon the natural prolongation principle or extension of the land as the primary basis for claiming most of the shelf area for themselves.[167] The discussions at the United Nations Conference on Law of the Sea III and the opinion of the International Court of Justice in the North Sea Continental Shelf cases tend to favor the natural prolongation principle. Both Korea and China would probably prefer a boundary drawn at the deepest point in the trough between the Japanese islands and the mainland which would insure their access to most of the oil. In Japan, some would be prepared to argue that the Asian continental margin extends to the deep trenches on the ocean side of the Japanese islands. In that case, all of the enclosed seas would be part of the shelf and division by median lines would be appropriate.

In the aftermath of the North Sea cases, the coastal states ignored the slight depression in the bottom of the North Sea in dividing up the sea areas among them. Japan and the Republic of Korea reached a solution of their shelf dispute in the southern portion of their shelf that is cooperative, despite the failure to resolve the question of ownership or delimitation.

## Petroleum in the East China and Yellow Seas

Predictions of valuable oil deposits under the East China Sea were made by a geophysical survey sponsored by the United Nations Economic Commission for Asia and the Far East in 1968.[168] No exploration has been carried out in the ensuing decade except for some close inshore drilling by China in the Gulf of Po Hai. The Republic of Korea, Japan, and the Republic of China were all quick to grant concessions to their own and major oil companies but no drilling of any importance has gone ahead in view of the overlapping claims and the fear of antagonizing the Chinese People's Republic.

The friendly relations established by the United States and Japan with the Peking government led to discouragement of American-based oil exploration on the shelf off South Korea and close to Taiwan in areas where concessions did not overlap. The Korean legislation of January 1970 established a mining area on the shelf close to Japan which almost completely overlapped the area claimed by Japan using the median line principle.[169] The Korean government claimed the shelf up to the Japanese Goto Retto offshore from western Kyushu, where a marine trough from 200–1000 meters in depth runs south along the Ryukyu Islands. They claimed the shelf to the bottom of the trough as the natural prolongation of the land of the Korean Peninsula.

In Seoul, at the Sixth Regular Japan–Korea Cabinet Ministers' Meeting in September 1972, the Koreans proposed that both countries put aside the question of ownership of the shelf and develop the oil resource jointly.[170] Negotiations subsequent to that proposal produced an Agreement Between Japan and the Republic of Korea Concerning Joint Development of the Southern Part of the Continental Shelf Adjacent to the Two Countries, which was signed in December, 1974.[171] It was only in the spring of 1977 that the Japanese Diet ratified the treaty because of strong opposition by the antigovernment parties and some sections of the governing Liberal Democratic Party. Because the legislation to modify the Japanese mining law, which only authorizes exclusively Japanese development, had not been passed, the actual beginning of exploration had to wait upon this final Diet action. This was completed in Spring 1978. The Korean ratification process had been long completed and the Korean government pressed the Japanese government to act, failing which, the ROK proposed to go ahead unilaterally with the exploration of the shelf area.

This agreement to proceed with exploration and development on a basis of sharing proceeds equally, without coming to agreement on the vexing delimitation question, suggests one way to solve such disputes. As installations are very vulnerable to any use of force, it is probably essential to insure that the principal parties are in agreement, or that peaceful activity can proceed. Interference by a third party is not to be ruled out, however. The joint development plan has been subjected to continual protest and disapproval by China, which claims its rights in the shelf are infringed by any Japanese or Korean action. Japan gave prior notice of the joint plans when Foreign Minister Ohira was in Peking in 1973, before the initial negotiations with Korea had been completed. Japan has repeatedly offered to discuss the shelf question with China but has been rebuffed on the ground that any solution to the delimitation question in the Yellow and East China seas must be done on a multilateral basis with all the parties involved. South Korea's recent attempts to talk with Chinese authorities have been rebuffed because China refuses to recognize that South Korea is a legitimate government and recognizes only the North Korean government as the legitimate government of all of Korea. Japan, in turn, has repeatedly stated its view to China that no rights of China are infringed by the Japan-Korean agreement, since that part of the shelf would not be awarded to China under a median line solution to the problem.

The Southern Shelf agreement is intended to deal only with petroleum, but it does touch on fishing and navigation. Exploration and exploitation of resources are subject to action suits for damages in case they affect other legitimate activities in the shelf area. The two governments have agreed that adequate provision will be made to prevent pollution or damage to fishing in the area. This has been done to appease fishermen who will be inconvenienced or even adversely affected.

Unlike the shelf dispute over delimitation and ownership, which primarily affects oil and gas resources, the handling of fishery matters has proved more amicable and limited in scope. Japan has effective fishery treaties with both South Korea and China as previously noted, which permits the joint use of the waters in question for fishing purposes. But the question of bottom-dwelling resources resembles disputes over land territory to a certain extent. For the time being, Japan has exempted its 200-mile fisheries zone claim from application to its two western neighbors, pending their own action in a similar direction.

The new 200-mile zone of the Korean People's Republic, which has combined security considerations with fishery regulation, has introduced a disturbing and extreme element. By claiming a right to interfere with or sanction innocent passage or peaceful transit in much of the fishing zone, it goes beyond even the usual treatment of territorial waters. The apparent disarray within the North Korean government, the paucity of information on applicable regulations, and the frequent shift of policy on the new zone resemble similar confusion in the trade and diplomatic relations of the country. The steps taken by the North are also provocative toward the South, which may be pushed into action on its own fishing zone, although thus far it has moved with considerable circumspection.

The overall pattern of the impact on fisheries of other problems, such as petroleum, is to complicate the fisheries issues; but the need to find some viable solution to permit fishing to continue and to prevent the escalation of conflict seems to be determining. Should oil or gas be discovered in large amounts, the urgent need for those resources, as well as the possibility of obtaining them at more reasonable cost, will probably put that issue well above fishing as a national priority of nearly all the countries concerned. In that case, fishermen may have to curtail their activities or accept the interference where they are carrying on joint use of the resources in the same area.

## Territorial Conflicts Over Takeshima and Senkaku Islands

The tiny uninhabited Senkaku or Tiao Yu islands are claimed by Japan, China, and Taiwan. Fishing is carried on in the vicinity by fishermen of all three countries. The islands are also close to the area where rich oil-bearing strata have been predicted. Japan considers that these islands belong with the nearby Ryukyu Islands which have been part of Japan for a century, although they were under American jurisdiction from 1945 to 1972. They are located on part of the shallow shelf area that stretches from China but is cut off by deeper water from the rest of the Ryukyu Islands. Japan's new 12-mile territorial waters should probably apply to them and, in the event of claiming a 200-mile fishing zone in this area, Japan might wish to include them in an extended economic zone.

Since Japan established friendly relations with Peking in 1972 both governments have put aside this quarrel without resolving it, though it occasionally flares up. Neither has attempted oil exploration near the islands. Should exploration be conducted and promising oil deposits located, the dispute over ownership could become acute. If the joint development scheduled for the area near to Kyushu proceeds, and if promising deposits were found there, there would be some incentive to initiate activity further south near to the Senkaku Islands. Even if China offered no more than verbal protests to the Kyushu development, it might attempt more forceful resistance to the Senkaku activity, depending upon the situation at that time. However, because of the ease with which oil installations or exploration can be interfered with, it would probably not proceed if active resistance were likely.

Both China and Japan have strong motives to avoid any worsening of their relations, not only because Japan wishes to enable her fishermen to fish in the waters close to China, but also because it has a strong motive to gain access to oil in its own vicinity and under its own control. It seems unlikely that Japan would permit this to become a serious issue while the actual presence of oil is still somewhat speculative. As the islands themselves are probably of no particular value, if Japan and China were to agree to some sort of joint development of the sea bottom in the vicinity, the question of ownership might be put aside, as in the case of the development close to Kyushu. The local fishery would have to sustain whatever interference or limitation was necessary, in view of the enormous potential value of the oil.

## CLAIMS TO DELIMIT BOUNDARIES: THE NORTHEAST PACIFIC

Compared to the Northwest Pacific, the delimitation problems found in the Northeast Pacific are minor, but are particularly significant for fisheries. The U.S.–Soviet boundary in the Northeast Pacific is relatively stable, whereas the U.S.–Canadian boundary issues have been a politically volatile dispute.

The U.S.–Soviet boundary was set in 1867 in the Convention Ceding Alaska,[172] concluded between the U.S. and the Russian Emperor. The western limit is described in Article I, following a prescribed demarcation starting in the Bering Straits continuing "nearly southwest" through the Bering Sea to include the whole of the Aleutian Islands. With the advent of the 200-mile zone, almost the entire Bering Sea is included in either the U.S. or the Soviet zone, excluding one triangular area, falling approximately between 59° N to 55°30′N and 175° W to 175° E. This boundary has not been the focus of significant debate.

The U.S.–Canadian boundary issues are much more complex, involving the Pacific, Atlantic, and Arctic coasts. The delimitation issues are inextricably bound to resource settlement issues (fisheries and hydrocarbons) on the Pacific and Atlantic coasts. In August 1977, special negotiators were appointed to conduct negotiations on maritime boundaries and related resource issues. The long-term agreement is to include a comprehensive settlement encompassing boundary demarcation and resource arrangements. The focus of the first stage was on resource settlements, leaving the boundary delimitation to be dealt with during the second phase. Yet these issues have become so intertwined that separation has become virtually impossible.

On the Pacific Coast, the specific disputes involve the Straits of Juan de Fuca (between Washington State and the Province of British Columbia) and Dixon Entrance (between Alaska and British Columbia). In the Straits of Juan de Fuca, the established boundary goes west through the middle of the Strait to a point between Tatoosh Point, Washington, and Bonilla Point, B.C. In question here is the continuation of this line. If it continues to follow the midpoint of the Strait, the line would be closer to the U.S. than the U.S.-proposed equidistant boundary, which would be located further west. Of specific interest to the Canadians is the possible adjustment of the boundary along the 50-fathom contour on Swiftsure Bank because of its importance to the Canadian salmon troll fishery.

At the Dixon Entrance, the dispute focuses on the wording of a 1903 document concerning the existence or nonexistence of a territorial sea in the southern portion of Dall Island. The U.S. has proposed the use of the equidistance principle; this would establish a U.S. territorial sea and fishery conservation zone in the Dixon Entrance, which is now controlled exclusively by Canada.[173] Significant fishery resources will be affected by settlement of these issues, among them several stocks of salmon and halibut.

## THE LONG-TERM IMPLICATIONS OF FISHERIES MANAGEMENT UNDER EXTENDED JURISDICTION

In the North Pacific as a whole, the intensity of conflict over claims to conserve and allocate fisheries resources has declined since the extended jurisdiction for all species except salmon. But conflict over the regulation of fishing practices has increased. The issue, therefore, has shifted from what is to be taken or not taken and why, to how it is to be taken. The how can, in fact, be a surrogate for the what, since the array of regulations can adversely affect CPUEs of a distant-water fleet, and the filling of its quota. In addition to claims related to the conduct of fleet operations, conflict over access to markets has also increased significantly.

With respect to the Northeast Pacific, both coastal states have actually implemented exclusive management authority and effective control over fishing within 200 miles of their coasts. This has resulted in major gains in conservation where foreign fishermen previously accounted for a predominant share of the catch on an open-access basis. In the U.S. zone in particular, extended jurisdiction has led to a significant increase in the amount and quality of information available from foreign fishermen as a result of the observer program, and to expanded cooperative scientific research.

The situation in the eastern Bering Sea presents certain interesting differences from the situation in the Gulf of Alaska. For the foreseeable future, the major competition in the eastern Bering Sea trawl fisheries will be between the distant-water fleets, in particular Japan, USSR, ROK, and perhaps new entrants like Poland. Side payments, like cooperation on research projects, are likely to play an increasing role in this competition. While the expansion of coastal state effort into the Bering Sea trawl fisheries is a long-term develop-ment, constraints are likely to be put on the foreign Bering Sea herring fishery as a result of its probable impacts on the abundance and size of herring available for subsistence fishing by the Eskimo communities of the Arctic, Yukon, and Kuskokwim area of Alaska. Rapid growth in the activities of the domestic offshore purse seine fleet and the inshore roe fishery represent additional constraints for the foreigners.

The situation in the Gulf of Alaska will produce a faster rate of foreign phase-out than in the eastern Bering Sea. This is occurring already on sablefish and is emerging on pollock as a result of joint ventures. The major ingredients in this development will be access to markets for American fishermen and the price paid for the fish. Canadian fishermen are unlikely to mount a major effort for groundfish of low market value in the Gulf of Alaska.

With respect to tanner crab resources of the southeastern Bering Sea, the U.S. already has the capability to produce the entire ABC of *C. bairdi*. Physical capacity will not be a problem for production of *C. opilio*, either. Once again, the major variable here is the development of the market for *C. opilio* in Japan and Western Europe, and the special role of Japanese processors based in the United States.

The long-run objectives of the North Pacific Council give very high priority to achiev-ing foreign phase-out on most species of fish caught by foreigners. The Japanese seek to extend this time horizon as long as possible, given the significance of the pollock fishery for Japan. They worry about the "arbitrariness" of optimum yield determinations, as illustrated in the 1978 FMPs for sablefish (Gulf of Alaska Trawl Fisheries) and tanner crab, yet are unwilling to seek redress in U.S. courts on decisions they regard as being arbitrary. The Soviets seek to maintain access to hake, Atka mackerel, and (increasingly) pollock re-sources by joint ventures as well as direct allocations. The ROK and Poland seek increased allocations of groundfish at the expense of the Japanese and Soviets.

An additional effect of extended jurisdiction in the Northeast Pacific, especially in the larger U.S. zone, is that firm annual quotas for each participating foreign nation, combined with relatively low fees, provide a real incentive for each nation to minimize the cost of taking its allotted share. This has become evident in the reduced number of vessels participating in the fisheries in the Gulf of Alaska and off the coasts of Washington and Oregon, where the reduction in vessels has been substantially greater than the actual reduction in quotas.[174] In some respects, therefore, extended jurisdiction has provided foreign fishing nations the opportunity of reducing economic inefficiency in fishing opera-tions generated by the open-access situation. At the same time, smaller quotas and increased regulation have increased potential competition between gear types (e.g., trawlers versus longlines) within particular fleets, especially the Japanese fleet.

In the Northwest Pacific, the situation on fisheries seems to be stable between Japan and China, and Japan and North Korea. In both situations, however, external political con-siderations are the primary determinants. While the Japan—ROK situation is internally stable, the ROK has still not solved its catastrophic shut-out by the USSR. The Japan—USSR relationship on fisheries will continue to dominate fisheries politics in the Northwest Pacific. While Japan has succeeded in deflecting Soviet attempts to link Japanese adaptation to the Soviet 200-mile zone with Japanese recognition of Soviet ownership of the Northern Territories, the Japanese have had to sustain severe dislocations for salmon and herring fleets operating out of Hokkaido and northern Honshu.

In terms of adjustments on the diversity and size of its catch, the worst seems to have passed for Japan. In 1974, 39.4 percent of the Japanese catch was taken from the 200-mile zones of foreign countries, most of this from the North Pacific.[175] In 1975, the figure was 35.5 percent and in 1976 this declined to 35 percent. Japan's total catch in 1976 declined only 0.9 percent, and most of this is accounted for by smaller allocations of pollock in the U.S. and Soviet zones of the North Pacific and significant declines in the mackerel catch in Chinese and South Korean waters.[176]

Since 1976, the emphasis in Japan has shifted to increasing productivity of fisheries within Japan's 200-mile zone and increasing the catch in the high-seas area beyond the Japanese zone. This strategy has so far been quite successful. In 1977, the Japanese catch in waters falling under the jurisdiction of other countries declined to 28 percent, and the trend is still downwards.[177]

Since by far the largest portion of Japanese offshore and distant-water catches consists of pollock, declining allocations in the North Pacific will produce significantly higher costs of operations unless significant numbers of vessels are withdrawn. Joint ventures and barter arrangements are possible alternative mechanisms for assuring access to raw material, but present the Japanese Fisheries Agency with serious internal problems. Increased costs for pollock also raise the question of product substitution and may facilitate reversion to resources from the East China Sea for surimi and/or to Antarctic krill. The major problem of adjustment to extended jurisdiction for Japan is not national in nature but internal, as between the coastal and offshore fisheries and between the fishing families and small to medium-sized firms and the large fishing and trading companies.

A special word should be said about salmon. There are three aspects to this problem: severely restricted Japanese fishing for salmon in the Soviet zone, Japanese high-seas fishing for salmon of North American and Asian origin, and the problem of salmon interceptions between U.S. and Canadian fishermen, which has already been discussed earlier in this chapter. Different approaches to resolution of the management problem have been adopted in each case. With respect to Japanese fishing for salmon in the Soviet zone, the parties have agreed on both quota allocations and time and area restrictions. Major reductions in catch were imposed on the Japanese fishery in 1977, 1978, and 1979 with seriously adverse consequences for the size and composition of the fleets.[178]

The approach adopted in the renegotiation of the INPFC was quite unusual and seems to have been very effective. In the new arrangements no specific quotas were set. Instead, the primary management tools were area and time closures; these imply quotas but, from the coastal states' perspective, relate more to what can be protected under time and area closures, given the mix of mature and immature salmon estimated to be distributed in particular locations at particular times of the year. It is therefore left to the Japanese to decide how many vessels they wish to retire. The new arrangements have resolved the big problem of Japanese high-seas fishing for Bristol Bay sockeye, and appear to be stable for the long run. Questions may be raised about two issues: (1) the impact of Japanese fishing in the "free" area (the so-called "donut" area) in the middle of the Bering Sea on chinook stocks from the Yukon and Kuskokwim regions; and (2) the extent of Japanese fishing, if any, on the northern chum runs.

It is necessary to raise the question whether the stability of the new INPFC arrangement is likely to be adversely affected by the declining Japanese allocations for pollock in the eastern Bering Sea. Obviously, this depends on decisions to be made by the North Pacific Council and the U.S. Secretaries of Commerce and State, but the new arrangements need not be affected. For instance, it is possible to conceive of holding Japanese Bering Sea pollock allocations at a fairly stable level in return for a phased reduction of Japanese import restrictions on surimi. By implication, this means that part of the price the Japanese (and others) must pay will be a faster foreign phase-out on the pollock fishery in the Gulf of Alaska. This possibility raises interesting implications as well for the potential competition between distant-water fishing states.

An additional problem of the future for the North Pacific as a whole concerns the North Pacific Fur Seal Commission, whose Convention must be renegotiated in 1980. These negotiations may be affected by certain portions of the FCMA and the Marine Mammal Protection Act of 1972. The objectives of the Fishery Conservation and Management Act and the Convention on Conservation of North Pacific Fur Seals are written in such general terms that the primary objectives of each can be accommodated. The mechanism for such accommodation has, however, not been established, nor is the relationship understood between the abundance of fur seals (and other marine mammals) and the abundance of fish. Considerable attention is being given to research involving the interactions of marine mammals with commercial and sport fisheries. As new knowledge becomes available, research results can be expected to be included in management plans of the North Pacific and Pacific Fishery Management Councils.

In the late 1960s and early 1970s in the United States, public interest in conservation of marine mammals resulted in the Federal Marine Mammal Protection Act of 1972. Prior to 1972, the principal United States federal marine mammal legislative Acts related to United States involvement with the International Whaling Commission and the North Pacific Fur Seal Commission. The Marine Mammal Protection Act outlines United States policy toward marine mammals under jurisdiction of the United States. The Act states that the primary objective of marine mammal management should be to maintain the health and stability of the marine ecosystem and, consistent with this primary objective, to obtain an optimum sustainable population, keeping in mind the optimum carrying capacity of the habitat. The Fisheries Conservation and Management Act of 1976 extended the jurisdiction of the Marine Mammal Protection Act to 200 miles offshore. In general, fur seals are exempted from the provisions of the Marine Mammal Protection Act, but the Act contains several requirements related to fur seals.

One requirement is that the Convention and the Act should be made consistent with each other insofar as possible. During meetings in 1976 concerning extension of the Convention, the United States proposed to reword parts of the Fur Seal Convention by introducing concepts and terms taken from the Marine Mammal Protection Act. Most of the changes proposed by the United States were not accepted. The concept of "optimum sustainable population" taken from the Marine Mammal Protection Act and recommended by the U.S. for inclusion in the Convention was of particular concern to other member nations. This term had not been used in the scientific literature and its meaning is still being debated, especially in the United States. Therefore, it is not surprising that the term was not acceptable for inclusion in the language of the treaty. After about three weeks of discussions, delegates reached an agreement on a new Interim Convention little different from the previous Convention but extending it for a period of four rather than six years.

The present Convention expires in 1980 and agreement about renewal of the Convention must be reached by October 1979. In the United States, some opinion existed that a four-nation Convention is no longer needed because of the protection afforded Pribilof Islands fur seals within the United States 200-mile zone. As a result there was some uncertainty about the future of the Convention[179] but this dissipated and the Convention was extended in 1980.

We have suggested that claims to accommodate fishing practices and claims over access to markets have increased in significance as a result of extended jurisdiction. We think that conflict over the regulation of fishing practices will be endemic. As the quality of information increases, the coastal states are likely to seek greater specificity of regulations (as well as more regulation in quantity) as a means of exerting greater control over foreign fisheries. Consequently, the enforcement task will be expanded. On the other hand, foreign fishermen are likely to continue to insist on flexibility of fishing operations in order to maintain profitability of the fleets. As explained in chapter 7, however, this will be more of a problem for the Japanese than for the USSR or Poland. Foreign fishermen will also seek to maintain continuity in regulations from year to year and to avoid drastic changes. The coastal state may not share this desire for stability and may seek regulations that provide its stocks the greatest protection.[180]

While claims for access to markets are now significant, it is unlikely that they will be as endemic as claims to accommodate fishing practices. Claims for access to markets appear to be primarily a characteristic of the transition period. As we have argued earlier, a solution to the import restriction problem is easily available. Since the Japanese fear that removing the prohibition on imports of surimi would result in declining allocations of pollock for them in the Northeast Pacific, and since expansion of U.S. fishing operations for pollock in the eastern Bering Sea is possible only in the long term, an efficient solution would be to offer the Japanese stable allocations in the Bering Sea in return for importation of U.S.-caught pollock and surimi from the Gulf of Alaska.

Joint ventures are also likely to expand in the Gulf of Alaska as a means of stimulating development of U.S. harvesting capacity and of ensuring foreigners access to raw material, but these will be constrained by the requirements of the new policy giving preference to U.S. processors.

A final word should be said about the price effects of extended jurisdiction. One of the global effects of extended jurisdiction is that fish prices for preferred species are increasingly being tied to the Japanese market, which is very high indeed. As access to raw material becomes problematic, Japanese fishing and trading companies compete fiercely with each other and the rest of the world. This competition drives prices up even further. In 1977, for instance, the domestic price for fish in Japan increased as much as 20 percent as a result of the combined effects of competition among Japanese firms, hoarding, and an increase in the value of the yen. [181] This development will probably fuel the expansion of U.S. catching and processing capacity for preferred species of groundfish from the Gulf of Alaska in the short run.

# 7

# Alternatives for Distant-Water Fishing States, Primarily in the Northeast Pacific

The events of recent years have made it plain that Northeast Pacific distant-water fisheries have entered into a phase of serious changes in their activities and perspectives for future development. With the extension of national jurisdiction, practically all fishing grounds adjacent to the coastal states were closed to unrestricted foreign operations. The only exceptions were fisheries based on bilateral agreements with coastal states and on surplus quota systems. These alternatives do not satisfy the needs for distant-water fishing nations that have developed a large fishing potential to satisfy the growing demand for fish in their consumption markets. Some of the most important trends are described in the first part of this chapter. In the 1960s, the principal factors in the development of unrestricted distant-water fisheries were investments and growing employment. After extension of national jurisdiction the access to the resource and management of the long-range fleet operations are the decisive factors in their future expansion.

Existing and projected policies of some of the most important users of Northeast Pacific fishery resources are better understood through an analysis of internal and external economic factors that affect activities managed by selected foreign nations. Next to Japan, Eastern Bloc countries belong to the most developed distant-water fishing countries in this region, as measured by technology range, engaged capital investment, and manpower. The purpose of this chapter is to look at one relatively neglected aspect in the expansion of distant-water fisheries; namely, the importance of overseas resources in maintaining their internal food market equilibrium. Thus, the limitations imposed on access to coastal state fishery resources could have immediate adverse impacts on animal protein supplies in distant-water fishing states. This is particularly the case in East European countries, which are facing permanent agricultural production difficulties and very few short-term alternatives for their distant-water fisheries in the world ocean.

Long-range fleets that are displaced from their traditional areas of operation expect to move a large proportion of their fishing capacity into the open ocean (i.e., beyond 200 miles) and over the Antarctic shelves, but this could lead to an enormous increase in operational costs and further declines in the economic efficiency of distant-water fishing. Alternative economic effects of the Northeast Pacific distant-water fisheries are discussed from the points of view of the coastal states and foreign fishing nations.

For the coastal state, the first alternative is to obtain maximum direct benefits of the marine living resources harvested and processed by its domestic fishing industry. The second alternative is to utilize these resources in cooperation with the distant-water fleets. In joint venture operations foreign vessels process fish caught by local fishermen. Joint utilization of selected species, mainly of lower value in the coastal nation's consumer markets, could be seen as a way to develop resources that temporarily cannot be utilized by the coastal fishermen, mainly for economic reasons. The third alternative is to obtain indirect benefits of the coastal fishery resources by allocating them to foreign fleets for license and poundage fees. The net economic revenue of such a management arrangement is obtained after all costs related to the 200-mile economic zone administration and enforcement activities are deducted.

For distant-water fishing nations, the first task is to maintain their former shares in utilization of presently enclosed fishery resources, and minimize access restrictions imposed by the coastal states. Intergovernmental fishery agreements in which the foreign country's traditional fishing rights would be recognized or reciprocity privileges included, seem to be the most important way of achieving these goals. Although cooperative arrangements with coastal fishermen do not allow foreign operators to fully utilize the enormous harvesting-processing potential of their long-range fleets, they consider joint ventures in fisheries a means of producing additional volumes of fishfood products for their domestic consumer markets. These joint ventures are considered not as a means of producing additional income opportunities but primarily as a tool for partially neutralizing access restrictions imposed on foreign fleets by the coastal nations. The benefits and constraints of these alternatives are discussed in the final part of this chapter.

## NORTHEAST PACIFIC DISTANT-WATER FISHERIES IN INTERNATIONAL PERSPECTIVE

### Expansion Prior to Extended Jurisdiction

There are three main reasons to include an international distant-water activities perspective in the North Pacific fisheries analysis: (a) the high mobility of the long-range fleets enabling them to quickly shift their fishing effort from one fishing area to another; (b) the role of the North Pacific fisheries in the volume of total world catch and the value of harvested and processed species; (c) the strong economic and political interests of the most important North Pacific nations (U.S., USSR, Japan, Canada) in marine living resources also located in other marine regions.

Distant-water fisheries expanded principally after the 1960s when some developed fishing nations decided to extend the area of their fleet operation as their coastal resources became insufficient.

Table 7.1 presents the contribution, in the most productive fishing areas, of local and

TABLE 7.1

Catches as Percentage of National Total Taken by Local and Distant-water Fleets
(In Thousand Tons)

| Fishing areas | Years | 1965 Tons | 1965 % | 1967 Tons | 1967 % | 1969 Tons | 1969 % | 1971 Tons | 1971 % | 1972 Tons | 1972 % | 1973 Tons | 1973 % | 1974 Tons | 1974 % | 1975 Tons | 1975 % |
|---|---|---|---|---|---|---|---|---|---|---|---|---|---|---|---|---|---|
| Atlantic Northwest | Local | 1785 | 47 | 2080 | 52 | 2110 | 48 | 2119 | 49 | 2041 | 47 | 2039 | 45 | 1926 | 47 | 1846 | 48 |
| | DW | 1975 | 53 | 1950 | 48 | 2250 | 52 | 2246 | 51 | 2289 | 53 | 2452 | 56 | 2130 | 53 | 1973 | 52 |
| Atlantic Northeast | Local | 8224 | 85 | 9063 | 87 | 9251 | 92 | 9216 | 88 | 9275 | 86 | 9860 | 87 | 10336.8 | 87 | 10592 | 87 |
| | DW | 1396 | 15 | 1281 | 13 | 769 | 8 | 1253 | 12 | 1415 | 14 | 1425 | 13 | 1480 | 13 | 1549 | 13 |
| Atlantic East Central | Local | 603 | 50 | 748 | 49 | 782 | 38 | 1096 | 39 | 1238 | 40 | 1327 | 38 | 1589 | 42 | 1454 | 41 |
| | DW | 597 | 50 | 782 | 51 | 1288 | 62 | 1745 | 61 | 1907 | 60 | 2148 | 62 | 2184 | 58 | 2071 | 59 |
| Atlantic Southeast | Local | 1580 | 72 | 1978 | 75 | 2289 | 74 | 1541 | 62 | 1789 | 60 | 1882 | 60 | 1955 | 67 | 1583 | 61 |
| | DW | 600 | 28 | 662 | 25 | 801 | 26 | 939 | 38 | 1214 | 40 | 1273 | 40 | 975 | 33 | 1004 | 39 |
| Pacific Northeast | Local | 640 | 57 | 476 | 46 | 391 | 38 | 464 | 20 | 521 | 19 | 531 | 28 | 486 | 21 | 780 | 22 |
| | DW | 476 | 43 | 569 | 54 | 643 | 62 | 1844 | 80 | 2255 | 81 | 1352 | 72 | 1831 | 79 | 1761 | 78 |

Source: 1965–1969, J. A. Gulland, "Distant-water Fisheries and Their Relation to Development and Management," Technical Conference on Fishery Management and Development (Vancouver: 1973).

1971–1975, Yearbook of Fisheries Statistics, 1975 (Rome: FAO, 1976).

distant-water fisheries during the decade from 1965 to 1975. It shows that in virtually all parts of the world ocean, distant-water fisheries accounted for a significant part of the catch. In some areas, particularly in the Atlantic and North Pacific oceans, foreign nations harvested a larger volume of the coastal resources than neighboring local nations. The importance of this is greater than it seems because, with a few exceptions,[1] the long-range fleets did not exploit the low market-value species (such as those used in bulk for fish meal) but included many of high value, principally for direct human consumption. For example, the majority of tuna catches were taken by long-range vessels. In the Northwest Atlantic, distant-water fleets were focusing their fishing effort on cod, redfish, flatfishes, herring, and other species of higher demand and price levels.

Unrestricted distant-water fisheries developed very quickly, mainly in marine regions where the density of fish and catch rates were high enough to assure good production yields. This tendency is shown in table 7.2, where catch volumes of the most important distant-water fishing nations were compared in various fishing areas during the decade 1965−1975. The most important fishing grounds where distant-water fleets concentrated their fishing effort include the Northwest Atlantic, Central and Southeast Atlantic, and the North Pacific. In the beginning of the 1970s, distant-water fishing fleets of foreign nations were able to harvest from 4 million to over 4.5 million metric tons of fish off the Pacific and Atlantic coasts of the United States and Canada (table 7.1). During the first years of the 1970s, Japan harvested about 1.5 million metric tons of fish a year in the coastal waters of the Northwest Pacific adjacent to the USSR. This could also be observed in West African fishing grounds where non-African nations recorded a catch volume of 1.2 million metric tons in 1965 and about 3.4 million metric tons in 1973.

After long-range fishing began in a given area it developed at a very high rate until declining stocks, reduced catch rates, or local fishing restrictions made opportunities elsewhere more attractive. This is shown in tables 7.2 and 7.3. Management measures were usually introduced too late, and long-range fisheries developed quickly, resulting in excessive fishing in practically all areas,[2] and a substantial reduction of exploited stocks. According to table 7.3 during the five-year period 1971−1975 the total catch of Northwest Atlantic herring dropped by 40 percent and Northeast Atlantic herring by one-third. At the same time, the total harvest of the South African pilchard (sardine) increased from 393 to 637 thousand tons (i.e., by 162 percent), and the catch of Atlantic capelin grew more than sixfold.

With the reduction of fishing opportunities for traditionally harvested species of higher market value, many distant-water fishing fleets shifted to species of lower market value. When the North Atlantic herring stock could not support the increasing fishing effort of numerous long-range fleets, they began to shift their interest to African sardine, capelin, and other pelagic species to substitute for reduced herring supplies in their local markets. The same thing occurred in cod, redfish, hake, and pollock fisheries. The last few years are characterized by increased interest of distant-water fleets in less developed species that, because of their comparatively lower economic significance, were not formerly harvested or were only partially utilized.

TABLE 7.2

VOLUME OF CATCH BY SELECTED DISTANT-WATER FLEETS, 1965–1975

(IN THOUSAND MT)

| Area and Country | 1965 | 1966 | 1967 | 1968 | 1969 | 1970 | 1971 | 1972 | 1973 | 1974 | 1975 |
|---|---|---|---|---|---|---|---|---|---|---|---|
| *Northwest Atlantic* | | | | | | | | | | | |
| Bulgaria | – | – | – | – | – | 7 | 45 | 41 | 37 | 30 | 28 |
| German Democratic Republic | 93 | 95 | 140 | 182 | 187 | 89 | 142 | 174 | 185 | 131 | 113 |
| Federal Republic of Germany | 181 | 178 | 217 | 281 | 253 | 206 | 134 | 86 | 95 | 83 | 80 |
| Norway | 44 | 43 | 59 | 75 | 54 | 47 | 35 | 43 | 71 | 59 | 53 |
| Poland | 57 | 72 | 120 | 200 | 180 | 216 | 270 | 267 | 255 | 215 | 188 |
| Spain | 234 | 241 | 290 | 341 | 294 | 274 | 269 | 238 | 181 | 188 | 122 |
| USSR | 886 | 841 | 623 | 801 | 987 | 813 | 1042 | 1150 | 1357 | 1157 | 1167 |
| *Atlantic East Central* | | | | | | | | | | | |
| Bulgaria | 3 | 5 | 8 | 12 | 18 | 20 | 15 | 27 | 20 | 26 | 46 |
| Bermuda | – | – | – | – | – | – | 155 | 160 | 161 | – | – |
| France | 31 | 33 | 44 | 58 | 47 | 54 | 48 | 59 | 49 | 54 | 56 |
| Italy | 58 | 65 | 69 | 63 | 62 | 63 | 65 | 64 | 42 | 38 | 30 |
| Japan | 159 | 128 | 169 | 183 | 176 | 143 | 115 | 120 | 113 | 127 | 89 |
| Norway | – | 1 | 1 | 1 | 2 | 92 | 202 | 197 | 131 | 78 | 12 |
| Poland | 24 | 44 | 46 | 34 | 42 | 31 | 33 | 40 | 34 | 37 | 92 |
| Portugal | 46 | 41 | 40 | 37 | 37 | 37 | 47 | 36 | 28 | 30 | 26 |
| Romania | 5 | 7 | 9 | 5 | 11 | 5 | 16 | 33 | 44 | 72 | 78 |
| Republic of South Africa | – | – | – | – | 48 | 350 | – | – | – | – | – |
| South Korea | 1 | 8 | 12 | 14 | 24 | 27 | 40 | 40 | 64 | 75 | 97 |
| Spain | 167 | 182 | 179 | 180 | 178 | 153 | 130 | 244 | 367 | 417 | 417 |
| USSR | 84 | 79 | 153 | 319 | 570 | 613 | 790 | 849 | 942 | 1145 | 1106 |
| *Southeast Atlantic* | | | | | | | | | | | |
| Bulgaria | 10 | 19 | 18 | 33 | 37 | 37 | 32 | 28 | 23 | 20 | 32 |
| Cuba | – | – | – | – | 5 | 21 | 46 | 57 | 57 | 54 | 54 |
| Japan | 112 | 109 | 147 | 99 | 77 | 85 | 113 | 112 | 138 | 129 | 144 |
| Poland | – | – | – | – | – | – | – | 4 | 50 | 62 | 76 |
| Spain | 137 | 189 | 227 | 231 | 217 | 246 | 251 | 209 | 217 | 160 | 196 |
| USSR | 361 | 361 | 251 | 485 | 407 | 423 | 439 | 720 | 649 | 447 | 420 |
| *Northeast Pacific* | | | | | | | | | | | |
| German Democratic Republic | – | – | – | – | – | – | – | – | 5 | 1 | 12 |
| Japan | 342 | – | – | – | – | 1391 | 1188 | 1385 | 964 | 1087 | 1114 |
| Poland | – | – | – | – | – | – | – | – | 2 | 45 | 59 |
| South Korea | – | – | – | – | – | – | – | – | – | – | 3 |
| USSR | 476 | 544 | 570 | 434 | 643 | 748 | 656 | 862 | 380 | 698 | 573 |
| *Southwest Atlantic* | | | | | | | | | | | |
| USSR | – | 73 | 678 | 190 | 93 | 421 | 262 | 46 | 6 | 13 | 9 |

Source: *Yearbook of Fisheries Statistics*, 1969, 1972, 1975 (Rome: FAO).

Although fisheries of coastal nations have also contributed in some areas to overfishing and depletion of their coastal fishery resources (like some West European countries in the North Sea), the general opinion prevails that because distant-water fishing nations had less permanent and direct interests in the fish stocks concerned, they were much slower to admit the need for protection measures. This fact contributed to an increase in conflicts between coastal and distant-water fishing nations, and accelerated the extension of national jurisdiction over most of the attractive marine living resources for long-range fishing operations.

The Soviet Union and Japan are the most developed distant-water fishing countries.

TABLE 7.3

IMPORTANT FISH SPECIES IN LONG-RANGE FISHING OPERATIONS

(IN THOUSAND MT)

| Area and Species | 1971 | 1972 | 1973 | 1974 | 1975 |
|---|---|---|---|---|---|
| NW Atlantic Herring | 740 | 554 | 487 | 433 | 445 |
| NE Atlantic Herring | 1404 | 1362 | 1494 | 1132 | 1078 |
| SE Atlantic Pilchard | 393 | 509 | 473 | 613 | 637 |
| Atlantic Capelin | 58 | 74 | 273 | 291 | 368 |
| NW Atlantic Redfish | 276 | 284 | 313 | 234 | 216 |
| NW Atlantic Cod | 1077 | 1057 | 808 | 793 | 631 |
| NE Atlantic Cod | 1774 | 1685 | 1732 | 2018 | 1791 |
| SE Atlantic Cape Hake | 798 | 1111 | 893 | 727 | 627 |
| NE Pacific Hake | 183 | 120 | 164 | 206 | 208 |
| NE Pacific Alaska Pollock | 944 | 1430 | 690 | 1153 | 1118 |

Source: *Yearbook of Fisheries Statistics*, 1971–1975 (Rome: FAO).

Their long-range fleets in 1976 (without support vessels) took 50 percent of the total world gross tonnage of fishing vessels over 100 GRT. Tables 7.4 and 7.5 include the data taken from *Lloyd's Register of Shipping,* Statistical Tables, 1976, which is used in this evaluation of distant-water fleets. Only a few nations are clearly leading in distant-water fishery activities. As shown in table 7.5, the Soviet Union owns more than half of the world's total tonnage of fishing vessels over 100 gross tons. This fleet is made up of more than 4,300 fishing vessels, factory motherships, and other support vessels, aggregating more than 6.2 million tons. The Soviet fleet continues to increase at a very rapid pace. In the three years from 1974 to 1976 (table 7.6), about 350 vessels were added with an increase in tonnage of over 600,000 gross tons, representing a growth rate of 11 percent. Other East European countries, mainly Poland and East Germany, have also increased their distant-water fishing fleets. Altogether, the Soviet Union and East European fishing fleets make up almost 60 percent of the world's total tonnage in fishing vessels, and 95 percent of the support ships over 100 gross tons in size. Nearly all of this tonnage is in distant-water fleets. The second important group of distant-water fleets is composed of East Asian countries: Japan, South Korea, and Taiwan, although the total tonnage of these fleets is only one quarter of that of the Socialist nations.

The magnitude of these fleets reflects a massive investment, which amounts to several billion dollars, and a tremendous commitment to the exploitation of ocean fishery resources. As we have seen, the global implications of extended coastal state jurisdiction are substantial for these fleets.

In most countries, the rapid build-up of distant-water fishing potential was based (until recently) on the following assumptions: (1) Unlimited potential of world fishery resources; (2) Unrestricted access to the world's richest fishing grounds in the coastal waters of foreign nations; (3) Continuation of the traditional freedom of the seas principle on the world ocean.

Until the early 1970s the concept of ocean fisheries expansion seemed to be quite attractive. The volume of catch increase was closely related to additional fleet capacity and technological progress in the field. These trends are illustrated in figures 7.1 and 7.2 for the

## TABLE 7.4

### Trawlers and Fishing Vessels of Selected Distant-Water Fishing Nations (1976)

| Flag | 100–499 | | 500–999 | | TONNAGE 1,000–1,999 | | 2,000–3,999 | | 4,000 and above | | TOTAL | |
|---|---|---|---|---|---|---|---|---|---|---|---|---|
| | No. | Tons gross | No. | Tons gross | No. | Tons gross | No. | Tons gross | No. | Tons gross | No. | Tons gross |
| United Kingdom | 505 | 115,446 | 82 | 59,234 | 43 | 56,096 | — | — | — | — | 630 | 230,776 |
| Bulgaria | — | — | — | — | — | — | 30 | 77,254 | — | — | 30 | 77,254 |
| Cuba | 127 | 15,497 | 33 | 21,710 | 9 | 11,522 | 19 | 63,263 | — | — | 188 | 111,992 |
| France | 501 | 105,078 | 76 | 48,526 | 25 | 35,830 | 5 | 12,284 | — | — | 607 | 201,718 |
| German Democratic Republic | 79 | 13,629 | 61 | 48,362 | 1 | 1,616 | 13 | 38,988 | — | — | 154 | 102,595 |
| Federal Republic of Germany | 74 | 12,245 | 37 | 32,104 | 14 | 21,201 | 26 | 75,519 | — | — | 151 | 141,069 |
| Greece | 71 | 14,176 | 21 | 13,808 | 10 | 12,210 | 2 | 6,412 | — | — | 104 | 46,606 |
| Italy | 189 | 34,309 | 37 | 25,657 | 20 | 27,856 | — | — | 1 | 4,000 | 247 | 91,822 |
| Japan | 2,845 | 715,542 | 65 | 45,337 | 47 | 65,708 | 46 | 132,126 | 10 | 48,410 | 3,013 | 1,007,123 |
| Korea (South) | 528 | 136,943 | 32 | 24,455 | 11 | 15,331 | 6 | 18,638 | 6 | 31,494 | 583 | 226,861 |
| Norway | 555 | 139,516 | 73 | 52,374 | 5 | 7,054 | — | — | — | — | 633 | 198,944 |
| Poland | 145 | 15,782 | 61 | 43,238 | 29 | 39,029 | 59 | 146,683 | — | — | 294 | 244,732 |
| Portugal | 128 | 31,330 | 17 | 12,006 | 44 | 57,434 | 13 | 29,053 | — | — | 202 | 129,823 |
| Romania | — | — | — | — | — | — | 27 | 73,164 | — | — | 27 | 73,164 |
| Spain | 1,657 | 377,636 | 98 | 69,324 | 78 | 106,441 | 11 | 27,707 | — | — | 1,844 | 581,108 |
| Taiwan | 219 | 56,218 | 7 | 5,280 | 3 | 4,723 | — | — | — | — | 229 | 66,221 |
| U.S.S.R. | 2,133 | 451,615 | 869 | 553,228 | 139 | 222,940 | 687 | 1,932,532 | 5 | 30,415 | 3,833 | 3,190,730 |
| U.S.A. | 1,715 | 270,191 | 122 | 93,129 | 38 | 48,754 | 1 | 2,500 | — | — | 1,876 | 414,574 |
| World Total | 15,389 | 3,292,060 | 1,980 | 1,347,932 | 577 | 822,848 | 954 | 2,659,926 | 23 | 118,319 | 18,923 | 8,241,085 |

Source: *Lloyd's Register of Shipping, Statistical Tables*, 1976.

## TABLE 7.5
### Fish Carriers and Fish Factories in Selected Countries During 1976

| Country | TONNAGE 100–1,999 | | 2,000–3,999 | | 4,000–5,999 | | 6,000–9,999 | | 10,000 and above | | TOTAL | |
|---|---|---|---|---|---|---|---|---|---|---|---|---|
| | No. | Tons gross | No. | Tons gross | No. | Tons gross | No. | Tons gross | No. | Tons gross | No. | Tons gross |
| Bermuda | — | — | — | — | — | — | — | — | 1 | 18,888 | 1 | 18,888 |
| Bulgaria | — | — | 1 | 3,288 | 5 | 28,888 | — | — | — | — | 6 | 32,176 |
| German Democratic Republic | — | — | 3 | 8,046 | 3 | 15,281 | — | — | 2 | 20,386 | 8 | 43,713 |
| Japan | 44 | 25,390 | 5 | 15,312 | 1 | 5,044 | 8 | 65,467 | 5 | 72,492 | 63 | 183,705 |
| Korea (North) | — | — | 3 | 8,500 | — | — | 1 | 7,218 | 2 | 20,472 | 6 | 36,190 |
| Korea (South) | 9 | 9,541 | — | — | 1 | 4,055 | 2 | 14,579 | 1 | 23,800 | 13 | 51,975 |
| Norway | 5 | 1,119 | — | — | — | — | — | — | 1 | 17,583 | 6 | 18,702 |
| Poland | — | — | — | — | 3 | 15,376 | 4 | 31,970 | 2 | 27,747 | 9 | 75,093 |
| Romania | — | — | — | — | 2 | 10,240 | — | — | 2 | 23,798 | 4 | 34,038 |
| Spain | 2 | 2,858 | — | — | — | — | — | — | 1 | 10,413 | 3 | 13,271 |
| U.S.S.R. | 164 | 99,808 | 119 | 392,715 | 98 | 506,215 | 37 | 294,072 | 129 | 1,738,958 | 547 | 3,031,768 |
| World Total | 276 | 169,202 | 138 | 449,088 | 115 | 593,201 | 53 | 421,437 | 146 | 1,974,537 | 728 | 3,607,465 |

Source: *Lloyd's Register of Shipping*, Statistical Tables, 1976.

## TABLE 7.6
### TONNAGE OF FISHING VESSELS AND SUPPORT SHIPS (OVER 100 GRT) OF THE
### MOST IMPORTANT FISHING NATIONS IN 1974 AND 1976
#### (IN THOUSAND GRT)

| Country | 1974 | | | 1976 | | |
|---|---|---|---|---|---|---|
| | Total | Fishing vessels | Support vessels | Total | Fishing vessels | Support vessels |
| U.S.S.R | 5,611 | 2,805 | 2,806 | 6,223 | 3,191 | 3,032 |
| Japan | 1,255 | 1,038 | 217 | 1,191 | 1,007 | 184 |
| Spain | 509 | 496 | 13 | 594 | 581 | 13 |
| USA | 358 | 351 | 7 | 424 | 415 | 9 |
| Poland | 271 | 220 | 51 | 320 | 245 | 75 |
| Korea (South) | 147 | 133 | 14 | 279 | 227 | 52 |
| Norway | 203 | 184 | 19 | 218 | 199 | 19 |
| France | 196 | 190 | 6 | 208 | 202 | 6 |
| East Germany | 147 | 103 | 44 | 147 | 103 | 44 |
| Subtotal | 8,697 | 5,520 | 3,177 | 9,604 | 6,170 | 3,434 |
| World Total | 10,683 | 7,334 | 3,349 | 11,848 | 8,241 | 3,607 |

Source: *Lloyd's Register of Shipping,* Statistical Tables, 1976.

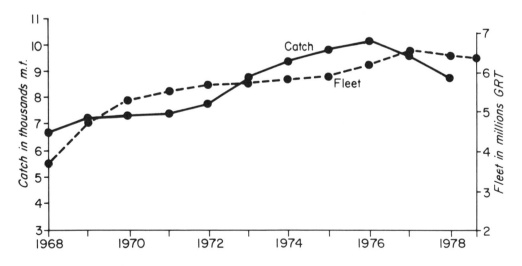

Fig. 7.1. *Volume of Catch and Fleet Capacity in the Soviet Union.* Source: *Lloyd's Register of Shipping,* Statistical Tables (London: Lloyd's Register of Shipping, various years); and United Nations, Food and Agriculture Organization (FAO), *Yearbook of Fisheries Statistics (Rome: FAO, various years).*

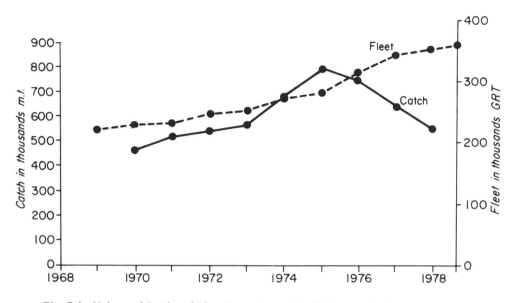

*Fig. 7.2. Volume of Catch and Fleet Capacity in Poland.* Source: *Lloyd's Register of Shipping,* Statistical Tables (London: Lloyd's Register of Shipping, various years); and United Nations, Food and Agriculture Organization (FAO), *Yearbook of Fisheries Statistics* (Rome: FAO, various years).

USSR and Poland. However, due to increased overfishing of the most important commercial fish stocks, and restrictions imposed on fishing grounds by international fishery organizations and coastal nations, these trends could not be maintained.

The latest developments in the legal restrictions of marine fisheries are generating extremely negative effects for the fishing policies of many countries with well-developed fishing potential but inadequate coastal resources. The countries most affected by the 200-mile economic zones are Japan (40 percent of its fish were harvested in foreign waters in 1975), the Soviet Union (about 54 percent), the Federal Republic of Germany (80 percent), German Democratic Republic (70 percent), Romania (63 percent), Spain (54 percent), and Poland (72 percent).

The extension of national jurisdiction around the coastal waters of the U.S., Canada, Iceland, Norway, and the European Economic Community (EEC) countries has had particularly negative effects on the distant-water fishing interests of the Socialist Bloc. Although Australia and New Zealand are rich in coastal fishery resources—and are therefore the potential targets of the Soviet and Eastern European distant-water fishing fleets—they were formerly only partially exploited by the Soviet Union. It is still unknown if Australia and New Zealand will allow foreign fleets to continue fisheries activities in their economic zones. The Republic of South Africa (and Namibia), where large amounts of fish were taken by Socialist and other distant-water fishing fleets, have closed their waters to foreign vessels.

During the last 30 years, Socialist fishing countries have developed massive distant-water fisheries specialized in taking bottomfish species distributed over continental shelves adjacent to foreign coastal states. With growing access limitations and overfishing of commercially important fish stocks in these areas, these distant-water fishing fleets began shifting to other, more abundant fishing grounds. For example, after a few years of exploitation (in the first years of the 1960s) of the North, Norwegian, and Barents seas, the factory trawlers from Russia, Poland and East Germany looked for better yields in the Northwest Atlantic and later in the waters adjacent to the West African coast. In the beginning of the 1970s, Socialist distant-water fleets (Poland and Cuba) started activities in Peruvian waters, while Russian factory trawlers began cooperative exploitation of Chilean hake fishing grounds. At the same time, Polish and German Democratic Republic, and later Bulgarian, fishing vessels entered the Northeast Pacific waters, close to the United States and Canadian coasts. Subantarctic fishery resources have also been quickly developed by these states, and Indian Ocean resources may soon be included in their harvesting activities.

Until 1977, a large percentage of the catch was taken by Socialist fishing fleets 2,000 to 9,000 miles from their base ports at high harvesting costs. Fishery activities became very expensive and consumed large amounts of ever-scarcer energy. The structure of catch suffered an undesirable change from highly valuable species such as cod, halibut, redfish, and herring to the exotic and pelagic species of smaller dimensions, difficult processing, and low market value (sardines, anchovies, capelin, mackerel, and others). Finally, the strategy of constantly shifting the distant-water fleets from one area to another is gradually losing its positive economic effects. There is less room for their activities than before, and the productivity cannot be improved, even by introducing new mangement methods (such as exchange of crews by chartered planes), new types of factory trawlers, or development of new fish products..

## Main Economic Factors—The Case of Socialist Fisheries

The Eastern Bloc nations' share of the Northeast Pacific resource is quite high. In 1976, they harvested about one-third of the total catch volume in this area. According to more recent data, the whole Pacific hake catch (231,000 metric tons in 1976) off the coasts of Washington, Oregon, and California was taken by the Eastern Bloc fleets. The Soviet Union is presently engaged in joint Pacific hake fishing operations with U.S. fishermen, and Poland is negotiating joint ventures for Alaska pollock fisheries. Bulgaria and Poland are buying fresh herring and hake from Canadian fishermen both in Northwest Atlantic and Northeast Pacific coastal waters.

Eastern Bloc fleets not only represent high fishing potential measured by number, tonnage, and technological advancement of harvesting-processing and support ships, but as centrally managed units they can develop operational systems hardly comparable to any western or Asian long-range fishing activities.

One of the most important features of these distant-water fishing fleets is their high mobility, which allows them to shift their effort quickly from one fishing ground to another and to change target species within a much shorter period than it takes for many other fleets. The fact that the Soviet Bloc long-range fishing potential is totally state-owned, and that the

Eastern Bloc governments have a strong influence on the demand patterns in their domestic consumer markets (by offering little choice) makes fishery expansion an integral part of the overall ocean policy of these nations.

Within this framework, Eastern Bloc distant-water fishing fleets are fulfilling two basic goals: (a) to supply raw material and finished fish food products for the local food industry complexes and consumer markets; and (b) to maintain and/or expand Soviet Bloc presence, and the highest possible share of the marine living resources, in the world ocean.

These fleets are interested in harvesting Northeast Pacific fishery resources within existing quota allocation systems as well as through different forms of cooperation with the U.S. and Canadian fishing industries. Some Eastern Bloc consumer markets are familiar with, and largely dependent on, the food fish products based on the species in the Northeast Pacific and Bering Sea (Pacific hake, Alaska pollock, flatfishes, dogfish, Atka mackerel and others).

If coastal state partners decide to enter into cooperative fishery arrangements with Soviet Bloc operators, much better knowledge of Eastern Bloc fishery economies is necessary. Existing and projected ocean policies of the Socialist states could be more accurately forecast through an analysis of internal and external economic factors that affect Eastern Bloc fishing activities managed by these nations.

To illustrate general trends and expected developments in this field, two Socialist distant-water fishing countries were chosen: the Soviet Union and Poland.[3] Both nations are heavily dependent on foreign marine living resources. They each have large distant-water fishing fleets and utilize the same methods of resource exploitation. With Japan, they are the principal foreign users of the Northeast Pacific fishery resources. Finally, the problems, goals, and fishery activities of the USSR and Poland are most representative for all Socialist fishing countries.

The development of food production is actually one of the most important internal socioeconomic problems in all Socialist countries. Agriculture in this area is still unable to supply a sufficient volume of animal protein to the local consumer markets. Despite achievements in this field, serious food supply problems exist in some Socialist countries and will continue into the future.

In the USSR, the consecutive crop failures during 1973, 1974, and 1975 caused a sharp decrease in the number of animals and, consequently, a decline in meat consumption. It is estimated that in 1976 alone per capita consumption of meat in the Soviet Union declined approximately one-quarter.[4] However, the state plans emphasize a continued improvement in the quality of the diet over the 5-year period as a whole. In the 1950–1975 period, in both the USSR and Poland, the rate of growth per capita consumption of fish was higher than for meat and meat products. For example, in Poland meat consumption increased twofold, whereas fish and fish products increased more than fourfold. In the Soviet Union, consumption of fish grew only slightly faster, but it should be stressed that the general level of fish consumption in the USSR was already high, surpassing the consumption levels of many developed nations (table 7.7).

In Poland, the adverse trends of agricultural development are even more pronounced.

TABLE 7.7

PER CAPITA CONSUMPTION OF FISH AND MEAT IN USSR AND POLAND
(IN KG PER YEAR)

| Products/Country | 1950 | 1960 | 1970 | 1975 | 1980 |
|---|---|---|---|---|---|
| *Meat and meat products* | | | | | |
| USSR | 26.0 | 40.0 | 48.0 | 58.0 | 60[a] |
| Poland | 36.7 | 42.5 | 53.4 | 70.0 | 70[a] |
| *Fish and fish products* | | | | | |
| USSR | 7.0 | 9.9 | 15.4 | 16.8 | 18.2[a] |
| Poland | 1.7 | 4.5 | 6.2 | 7.1 | 10.0[a] |

Sources: E. Wisniewski, "Aktualne i przyszlosciowe zadania gospodarki rybnej (The Present and Future Tasks of the Fishing Industry)," *Technika i Gospodarka Morska (Marine Technology and Economy)* no. 3 (309) (Gdansk, March 1977).

Division of International Fisheries Analysis, Office of International Fisheries, NMFS, NOAA (Washington, D.C.: 1976).

[a]Estimation.

Smaller harvests during 1974−1976 and a relatively low production increase of agricultural products created a much lower food supply, which could not meet the existing demand and increased buying power that resulted from higher salaries. In recent years, disposable incomes grew about 10−12 percent per year, while agricultural production grew only 2−4 percent per year. Due to the shortage and price increase of feeds, animal breeding became less economical and more difficult. Consequently, a reduction in the number of cattle and hogs occurred at that time.

In the near future the food situation in Poland is expected to continue to be difficult. The grain harvests are relatively low, fodder reserves are reduced, and imports of these products are very expensive. Any improvement in this situation cannot be forecast for a shorter period than 5−10 years, or even more. Generally, the food problem is actually attaining a crucial role in maintaining the market equilibrium, and is considered by the governments of all Socialist countries as one of the first and most important economic and social tasks.

Fish and fish products are not only considered a necessary diversification of diet in these nations but also an extremely important complement to meat supplies. For example, the Polish fishing industry actually supplies about 5.5 percent of the volume of all protein products; all efforts are made to increase this percentage. Moreover, it contributes to the expansion of exports, and supplies fish meal for national agriculture (in 1975, 46,700 MT). In Poland, capital investment in fisheries is about 23 billion zlotys[5] (approximately $575 million). In the USSR, the total estimated capital investment in only the fishing fleet is about $8.5 billion, and is increasing rapidly each year.[6]

In the Soviet Union, the role of the fishery industry in food supplies is particularly important. Taking into account the protein content of fish and land animals and using Sysoew's methodology of economic evaluation,[7] the total volume of the USSR catch in 1975 released its national agriculture from the necessity of raising about 42 million units of cattle. The actual annual catch of the USSR is the equivalent of about 30 percent of its total cattle stock. The total demand for fish meal in the Soviet Union is about 2.5 million MT. It is expected that the Russian fishing industry will be able to supply at least half this amount. The role of the fishery industry in Eastern Bloc countries is then very important, and the possibilities of its further development from a technological point of view are theoretically unlimited—considering their well-developed shipbuilding industry, particularly in Poland, German Democratic Republic, and the USSR.

According to the official policy of Socialist countries, the fishery industry does not compete with agriculture in supplying protein foods, but rather complements it. Consequently, there is little place for a question of optimal yields of fishery resources, or optimal utilization of all inputs, natural resources, capital, labor, and technological knowledge. The principal task of the fishery industry is to supply as much fish products as it can. A few examples will support this view.

Soviet writers state that to produce 100 kilograms of lightweight beef, it takes a capital investment of 2,000−2,500 rubles. But for a similar amount of fish, only about 1,500−1,700 rubles are necessary.[8] Similarly, less manpower is necessary to produce fish protein products than to produce land animals. However, at least in Poland, the costs of fish protein production are actually as high as the costs for the animal protein delivered by agriculture. For example, the price of 1 kg (2.2 lbs) of fish protein during the period 1970−1975 increased as shown in table 7.8.

TABLE 7.8

PRODUCTION COSTS OF FISH PROTEIN IN POLAND
(IN POLISH ZLOTYS PER KM)

|  | 1970 | 1971 | 1972 | 1973 | 1974 | 1975 |
|---|---|---|---|---|---|---|
| Production costs | 149.5 | 170.7 | 164.0 | 174.1 | 226.4 | 314.3 |
| Percentage of increase 1970 = 100 | 100 | 114 | 110 | 116 | 151 | 210 |

Source: T. Lubowiecki, J. Figiel, Z. Laszczynska, ''Rybolowstwo w Kompleksie Gospodarki Zywnosciowej'' (''Fisheries in the Food Economy Complex''). Sea Fisheries Institute (Gdynia: 1976).

During 1970−1975, fish protein production costs in Poland rose more than 200 percent. This continued during 1976, and it is expected that the real production cost of 1 kg of fish protein is well over 400 zlotys. The production of land animal protein costs are growing more slowly than those of fish, although it is expected that further investments in agriculture will accelerate the costs of production.

The main reasons for the rapid increase of fish protein production costs in Poland and other Eastern Bloc fisheries are the rising costs of construction and operation of the large highly industrialized factory trawlers and support fleets. During the last decade, the costs of harvesting by the Polish distant-water fishing fleet, calculated to a unit of 1 kg of round fish caught, are shown in table 7.9.

TABLE 7.9

HARVESTING COSTS OF THE POLISH DISTANT-WATER FLEET

| Year | Cost in Polish Zlotys (per kg) |
|------|-------------------------------|
| 1965 | 7.93 |
| 1966 | 8.18 |
| 1967 | 9.00 |
| 1968 | 8.17 |
| 1969 | 7.92 |
| 1970 | 8.49 |
| 1971 | 8.80 |
| 1972 | 9.50 |

From 1974 onward, there was a considerable increase in these costs due to such factors as the increase in price of fuel oil and other materials used by fishing vessels, an increase in price of newly built ships in Polish shipyards, a longer distance between fishing grounds and base ports, and an increasing proportion of costly distant-water catches in total fish supplies.

As a result, the harvesting cost per 1 kg of round fish reached in 1974 was about 18 zlotys; the cost of obtaining 1 kg of the final fish food product may then have exceeded 60 zlotys.[9] This cost is higher than the retail price of beef meat sold in the consumer market. The argument for developing industrial fisheries in Eastern Bloc countries, based on the premise that they are less expensive than animal protein production by local agriculture, is at least questionable.

The total deficit of meat supply in the consumer market could be improved in the shortrun only by sharply increasing meat imports. This, however, must be done with hard currencies. The alternative is to look for substitutes and other sources of animal protein. Sea fishery resources are considered an excellent and free-of-hard-currency way to eliminate the existing shortages. Fish are taken from the ocean and processed on board expeditionary fleets built chiefly in Socialist countries; their costs of exploitation are paid with internal "soft" currencies. Consequently, through distant-water sea fishery activities, Eastern Bloc countries are able to harvest any marine living resources with full utilization of internal economic and social factors, eliminating or reducing imports or hard currency outlays.

Another economic factor in USSR distant-water fishing fleet development is that Polish and East German fishing vessels purchased by the Soviet Union contain machinery and equipment imported or built under Western licenses; consequently, the Soviet Union is able to acquire sophisticated marine technology without the expenditure of scarce hard currencies or the necessity of having to sell gold. By exporting a part of the fish production, currencies are generated, which in turn can be devoted to finance emergency fish imports to some Eastern Bloc countries or to pay license fees for fishery activities within the 200-mile economic zones. The fact that industrial fishery activities of Socialist countries are sponsored principally with soft currencies and are totally in the hands of the state-owned companies has a crucial economic effect: susceptibility to current net economic benefits of this industry is practically negligible. It can operate even under adverse economic conditions and negative direct economic effects. The losses are consciously accepted in exchange for benefits derived in other branches of the national economy, like in food balance in the consumer market, employment opportunities, and foreign trade.

According to the forecasts presented by Polish official sources,[10] expected meat shortages in Poland could be eliminated if 320,000–350,000 MT of fish could be supplied to the consumer market in 1978. To this volume, 60,000–90,000 MT of fish products should be added, as they are planned for exportation in the same period. The total expected supply of fish food products by the Polish fishing industry would then reach the level of about 410,000 MT. In 1977, the expected efficiency ratio of the Polish processing industry and distributing network was slightly above 40 percent.[11] This means that in order to produce 410,000 MT of fishery products it would be necessary to catch about 1 million MT of round fish in 1978.

In 1975, the total volume of catch in the USSR was 9,876,000 MT, but consumption was only about 44 percent of the catch (i.e., 4,345,000 MT).

In the Soviet Union, the Academy of Medical Sciences calculated that each Soviet citizen should consume on the average about 18.2 kg (about 40 lb) of fishery products per year to maintain the optimum nutritional balance. Taking into account the present population and existing efficiency ratio of the Soviet fishing industry in deliveries of fish products for human consumption, the required catch level would be about 11 million metric tons per year.

In both countries, official policy is promoting rapid increase of fish consumption. As a consequence, the sea fisheries of Socialist countries are obliged to supply additional volumes of fish, even if traditionally exploited resources are now less accessible and the costs of getting additional catches are growing at accelerated rates.

Another internal factor strongly promoting further development of fishery activities in eastern countries is the employment problem. In the Soviet Union, the number of fishermen in 1975 was estimated at approximately 250,000. Total employment in the fishing industry, including processing workers and service and administrative personnel, is about 750,000.[12] In Poland, the total number of sea fishermen, 80 percent of whom are employed mainly in distant-water fishery activities, is about 16,000,[13] and another 10,000 persons in processing, storage, transportation, and other activities related to the fishing industry. The shipbuilding industry, largely specialized in fishing vessels, employs another 50,000 workers.[14] It should be stressed that the personnel engaged in direct fishery activities and related industries are generally highly trained. It would be extremely difficult to shift those workers to other activities if the fishing industry should considerably reduce its rate of growth.

In countries like the Soviet Union and Poland, the fishing industry became an essential part of the contemporary national economy. In addition to providing a significant contribution to the nation's food supplies, it is also a large user of human and material resources. In Eastern Bloc countries, the main investment effort in fishery development is concentrated in harvesting activities, while land infrastructure (processing, distribution, etc.) is relatively less developed. For example, in the Soviet Union the investment estimates for the current 5-Year Plan were obtained by calculating that about 70 percent of the total fishery investments, estimated at over 4 billion rubles, would be allocated for the modernization and expansion of the fisheries fleet[15] (see table 7.10).

TABLE 7.10

USSR CAPITAL INVESTMENTS IN FISHING FLEET, 1961–1975
(1 RUBLE = $1.32)

| Planning Period | Min. Rubles | Percentages of Increase (1961–1965 = 100) |
|---|---|---|
| 1961–1965 | 1,346.3 | 100 |
| 1966–1970 | 2,484.0 | 185 |
| 1971–1975 | 3,000.0 | 121 |

Source: Milan Kravanja, *Fisheries of the USSR, 1976.* NMFS, Office of International Fisheries (Washington, D. C.: February 1977), p. 425.

During the last few years, increased investments in industrial and, principally, distant-water fishing fleet development did not result in proportional increases in catch. This unfavorable tendency is shown in table 7.11 and figures 7.3 and 7.4. This means that in order to achieve a slight total catch increase it was necessary to pay higher and higher prices. For example, in Poland the distant-water fishing fleet capacity increased only 2.3 percent. The same trend can be observed in the Soviet Union. Increasing inputs are producing decreasing outputs. Undoubtedly, the extension of national jurisdiction over 200 miles will worsen interrelationships and oblige Eastern Bloc fishing nations to reconsider the strategies of their development, both in terms of methods of resource exploitation and intensity of fishing effort.

One of the most significant features, the importance of which became clear only recently, was the fact that the foundations for a modern industrial distant-water fisheries effort were laid on a highly restricted raw material base. The peculiar systems and political context in which East European expansion in massive exploitation of these resources took place made this particular aspect one of crucial importance for the future development of its fisheries.

A second interesting feature of Soviet Bloc industrial fisheries, which also was to have far-reaching repercussions, was the growth of autarchic tendencies. All fishing activities were developed until the mid-70s on a generally noncooperative basis. Coastal resources were harvested by Eastern Bloc distant-water fishing vessels with heavy support of auxiliary fleets without establishing joint ventures or other satisfactory cooperational links with coastal nations. Hence, it was not surprising that in the absence of outside pressures (for example, extension of national jurisdictions on coastal resources) there was little spontaneous movement toward cooperation in joint utilization of these resources with coastal nations.

## Economic Impact of Extended National Jurisdiction

### Utilization of Fishery Resources Within 200-Mile Fisheries Zones

Introduction of 200-mile fisheries zones, particularly by the United States and Canada, but also by the USSR, has direct and far-reaching impacts on the activities of all distant-

TABLE 7.11

RUSSIAN AND POLISH INDUSTRIAL FISHING FLEET CAPACITY

| Country | 1969 | 1970 | 1971 | 1972 | 1973 | 1974 | 1975 | 1976 |
|---|---|---|---|---|---|---|---|---|
| *USSR* | | | | | | | | |
| a. Volume of catch in thousand MT. | 7.082 | 7.828 | 7.785 | 8.209 | 9.005 | 9.600 | 9.876 | 10.074 |
| b. Total capacity of industrial fleet in thousand GRT[a] | 3.405 | 3.997 | 4.902 | 5.100 | 5.383 | 5.610 | 5.931 | 6.223 |
| aa. Percentage of catch increase over prior year period | | 11 | −1 | 5 | 10 | 7 | 3 | 2 |
| bb. Percentage of fishing fleet increase over prior year period | | 17 | 23 | 4 | 6 | 4 | 6 | 5 |
| *POLAND* | | | | | | | | |
| a. Volume of catch in thousand MT. | 408 | 451 | 488 | 527 | 594 | 652 | 679 | 695 |
| b. Total capacity of industrial fleet in thousand GRT[a] | 220,6 | 230,7 | 236,2 | 250,0[b] | 267,8 | 271,3 | 281,9 | 319,8 |
| aa. Percentage of catch increase over prior year period | | 11 | 8.2 | 7.8 | 12.9 | 9.7 | 4.1 | 2.3 |
| bb. Percentage of fishing fleet increase over prior year period | | 5 | 2 | 6 | 7 | 1 | 4 | 13 |

Sources: (USSR) 1976 catch volume, *Pravda* (daily) No. 23 (21358) (January 23, 1977), pp. 1, 2.
1975 catch volume, *Yearbook of Fisheries Statistics*, 1975 (Rome: FAO, 1976).
1969–1974 catch volume, M. Kravanja, *Fisheries of the USSR* (Washington, D.C.: NMFS, 1977).
Fishing fleet capacity, *Lloyd's Register of Shipping*, Statistical Tables 1969–1976.

(Poland) 1976 catch volume, *Morska Gospodarka Rybna* (monthly) (Sea Fisheries Economy) no. 1, Szczecin, Poland, 1977.

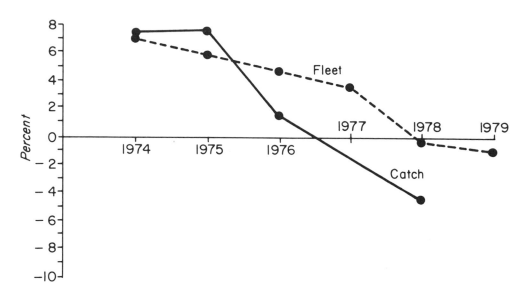

Fig. 7.3. *Fish Catch and Effort Dynamics in Poland.* Source: *Lloyd's Register of Shipping,* Statistical Tables (London: Lloyd's Register of Shipping, various years); and United Nations, Food and Agriculture Organization (FAO), *Yearbook of Fisheries Statistics* (Rome: FAO, various years).

water fishing fleets in the North Pacific Ocean. The most important effect of the new regime is the introduction of catch volume and fishing effort limitations for foreign nations. In harvesting activities, the distant-water fleets are restricted to national quotas, which can be taken within limited time, area, and number of vessels. Quota allocation systems permit the long-range fleets to utilize only part of their up-to-date capacity. Practically all foreign distant-water fishing nations felt the impact of these limitations immediately.

The USSR 1977 catch in the Northeast Pacific was limited to 480,800 metric tons under the terms of the U.S. Fishery Conservation and Management Act. The Soviet allocation figure represents a 17 percent reduction from the 1976 catch level, and a 21 percent reduction from 1975. In terms of quantity, these reductions equal 101,800 metric tons and 130,900 metric tons, respectively.[16]

Implementation of the 200-mile fisheries zone by the Soviet Union and the United States will oblige the Japanese fishing industry to curtail as many as 1,054 fishing vessels, including 555 salmon ships, 205 herring trawlers, 57 medium size trawlers (Hokutensen) and others.[17] Catch quotas for almost all species harvested traditionally in the USSR coastal waters were far below former levels of the Japanese catch, as shown in chapter 6, tables 6.16 and 6.17. The catch quota for Alaska pollock, that regarded as one of the most important species for the Japanese fishing industry, was set at 345,000 metric tons, which, though considerably higher than the initial Soviet proposal of 260,000 metric tons, fell short of one-third of the 1,073,000 tons caught in 1976, and far short of the total expected catches of about 600,000 tons for 1977.[18] We can expect that in the future the Japanese quota allocation on the Soviet coasts will be gradually reduced. The foreign catch quota estab-

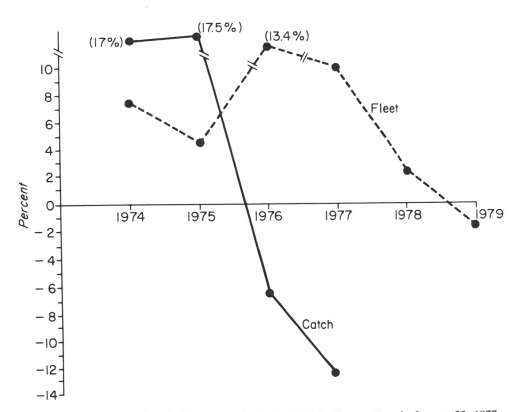

Fig. 7.4. *Fish Catch and Effort Dynamics in the U.S.S.R.* Source: *Pravda*, January 23, 1977, pp. 1 and 2; United Nations, Food and Agriculture Organization (FAO), *Yearbook of Fisheries Statistics* (Rome: FAO, various years); M. Kravanja, *Fisheries of the USSR* (Washington, D.C.: National Marine Fisheries Service, 1977); *Lloyd's Register of Shipping*, Statistical Tables (London: Lloyd's Register of Shipping, various years).

lished by the United States for Poland, both in Atlantic and Pacific coastal waters, can be taken with half the fishing effort used during the freedom of fisheries era.[19] Some distant-water fishing nations lost practically all their fishing privileges for using long-range fleets in fishing grounds that became the extended fisheries zone of coastal states.

The Soviet, Cuban, and Bulgarian distant-water fishing fleets were obliged to withdraw from the Argentinian Patagonian Shelf fishing grounds, which are now included within the economic zone of Argentina. In this fishing area, the Soviet Union increased its catch volume, within one year, from 73,000 tons in 1966 to 678,000 tons in 1967.[20] Introduction of the 200-mile fisheries zones in the North Sea and its adjacent waters eliminated catching opportunities for many European distant-water fishing fleets. Bulgarian, Rumanian, Portuguese, and other vessels are not allowed to catch there at all, while other traditional users like the USSR, East Germany, and Poland suffered drastic reductions of their quotas.

Even in the Baltic Sea, where the most important marine living resources management problems were initially resolved by the Baltic Convention, there is a new trend to share fishery resources according to the theoretically passed national zones. With such a solution, the largest fishery zone will belong to Sweden, while the Soviet Union, Poland, and German Democratic Republic, with the highest Baltic catches, will be the greatest losers.[21]

After implementation of the 200-mile EEZ by the Soviet Union, South Korea lost practically all possibilities of harvesting resources in the Pacific coastal waters of the USSR. Consequently, the pressure on the Northeast Pacific fishery resources by Japan, South Korea, and other countries may increase. It can be expected that, principally for political reasons, Japan will continue its catches within the U.S. and Canadian zones with relatively high quotas in the near future. Probably for the same political reasons Taiwan, and particularly South Korea, will also maintain their former levels of catch within the U.S. 200-mile exclusive fisheries zone, although their quotas for 1977 were lower than catches during 1976. If in the future the U.S. should wish to increase the quota for Japan, South Korea, and Taiwan, and the present total allowable catch (TAC) level for foreign fleets remained unchanged, the possibility for the Eastern Bloc countries to expand fishing activities in the Northeast Pacific could be seriously hampered. For 1977, South Korea, Taiwan, and Poland were allowed to take smaller volumes of fish and, consequently, had to shift a part of their fleets to other fishing grounds or accept less intensive utilization of their catching potential. Since 1977, similar actions by the United States have led to increased rivalry between distant-water states for higher quotas and better conditions of access to the living resources in the U.S. and Canadian fisheries zones.

National quotas allocated for long-range fleets for 1978 widely confirmed these expectations (table 7.12). Japan's quota decreased only 2 percent in 1978, while South Korea received an additional 10,000 MT of Alaska pollock after "additional study of circumstances surrounding de facto Korea exclusion from the Soviet Union."[22] Taiwan received only a slightly increased quota, whereas Mexico was accepted as a newcomer to the U.S. Northeast Pacific fishing grounds with 66,000 MT for 1978.

This volume constitutes 100 percent of what Mexico required from the U.S. for its long-range fleet during 1978.[23] It is a clear recognition of special consideration given to this adjacent coastal state in allocation of U.S. fishery resources. All these additional increments in the share of U.S. surplus resources resulted in a reduction of allocation to the USSR (16 percent) and to Poland (15 percent) in the same year, despite the fact that both countries are contributing substantially to the scientific knowledge of the U.S. coastal resources.[24]

The allocations for 1979 and 1980 also tell an interesting story. Japan retains the largest share of U.S. Northeast Pacific resources (61 percent, 1979; 69 percent, 1980). The USSR, by contrast, declined from 31 percent in 1976 to 25 percent in 1979 and experienced a drastic cut in 1980 (down to 3.8 percent) as a result of the Soviet intervention in Afghanistan. South Korea increased its share to 8 percent in 1979 and 12 percent in 1980, and Poland did likewise, from 1 percent in 1978 to 4 percent in 1979 and 11 percent in 1980. The major beneficiaries of reductions in the Soviet quota have therefore been Japan, South Korea, and Poland. This event has, at least temporarily, eased the problem of competition for access among the remaining distant-water fleets.

With gradually decreasing foreign TACs, allocation problems could be extremely

## TABLE 7.12

### VOLUME OF CATCH AND NATIONAL QUOTAS FOR FOREIGN NORTHEAST PACIFIC FISHERIES

#### (IN THOUSAND MT)

| Country | 1971 | 1972 | 1973 | 1974 | 1975 | 1976 | U.S. quota alloc. 1977 | U.S. quota alloc. 1978 | U.S. quota alloc. 1979[e] | U.S. quota alloc. 1980[e] |
|---|---|---|---|---|---|---|---|---|---|---|
| Japan | 1,188.0[d] | 1,385.3[d] | 964.1[d] | 1,087.3[d] | 1,113.8[c] | 1,140.2 | 1,168.4 | 1,148.6[c] | 1,162,392 | 1,367,240 |
| Soviet Union | 656.0[d] | 869.8[d] | 379.8[d] | 697.7[d] | 611.7[a] | 582.6[a] | 480.8[a] | 402.1[c] | 451,256 | 76,458 |
| South Korea | — | — | — | — | 3.3 | 116.2 | 81.2 | 31.2[c] | 148,635 | 244,768 |
| Poland | — | — | 2.4[d] | 44.7[d] | 58.4[b] | 31.9[b] | 27.2 | 23.2[c] | 79,830 | 224,598 |
| Taiwan | — | — | — | — | — | n.a. | 5.2 | 5.8[c] | 6,243 | 9,020 |
| Bulgaria | — | — | — | — | n.a. | n.a. | — | — | 0 | 0 |
| Federal Republic of Germany | — | — | — | — | — | — | — | — | 0 | 16,484 |
| German Democratic Republic | — | — | 5.3[d] | 1.2[d] | 12.2[d] | n.a. | — | — | 0 | 0 |
| Mexico | — | — | — | — | — | n.a. | — | 66.1 | 29,417 | 25,360 |
| TOTAL | 1,844.0 | 2,255.1 | 1,351.6 | 1,830.9 | 1,799.4 | 1,870.9 | 1,762.8 | 1,737.0 | 1,877,773 | 1,963,928 |

Sources:

[a]*Marine Fisheries Review*, NOAA, NMFS, 39,8 (August 1977).

[b]*Polish Maritime News*, no. 226 (June 1977), p. 18

[c]Telegram from the Department of State to the U.S. Embassies in Tokyo, Moscow, Warsaw, Seoul, Taipei and Mexico, November 30, 1977.

[d]*FAO Yearbook of Fisheries Statistics*, no. 40, 1975 (Rome: 1976).

[e]Northwest and Alaska Fisheries Center, NMFS.

sensitive as the coastal states of the North Pacific Ocean deal with resource users of high catching potential and an increasing demand for fish. They can compete for a higher quota and look for all possible ways to receive better treatment from the coastal nation. Seeking employment opportunities for their long-range vessels, some states may be interested in using them in joint operation with partners that have better access to another nation's surplus quotas. However, it will probably be impossible for overseas countries to effect transfer of their fishing quotas from one nation to another if the latter is not formally permitted to harvest or receive fish in the fishery conservation zone off the Northeast Pacific coasts.[25]

As other fishing grounds adjacent to the USSR coasts, particularly the Northeast Atlantic area, are becoming overexploited, and with extended national jurisdiction gradually restricting Soviet distant-water fishing opportunities, it can be expected that its Far East fishing grounds will become more and more important. Having introduced the 200-mile fisheries zone, the Soviet Union has automatically eliminated South Korean catches in the Okhotsk Sea and Kuril Islands coastal zones, and is gradually decreasing traditional Japanese fisheries in these areas. Northwest Pacific marine living resources of the Soviet Union have become an important asset in its international trade and foreign economic relations.[26] South Korea and Japan can import fresh pollock from the Soviet Union in exchange for fishery facilities or hard currency.[27] Barter deals can be extended on Japanese investments in Siberian natural resources development as well.[28] Limitations imposed by the Soviet Union on Japanese and South Korean fisheries near USSR coasts could open very important export markets for Soviet Far Eastern fish and fish products, which before were harvested directly by these states.[29] However, the Soviet Union and other Eastern Bloc fishing nations advocate the historic rights concept as a basis for their further share in 200-mile economic zone fisheries.[30] In the Northeast Pacific these expectations worked only partially. In allocating quotas for Eastern Bloc fleets, the U.S. excluded Bulgaria and the German Democratic Republic from Northeast Pacific fisheries, although these nations had dramatically increased their Pacific hake harvest in California, Oregon, and Washington coastal waters.

Bilateral agreements with the U.S. and Canadian governments, combined with cooperative links established with these nations' fishing industries, are considered by Eastern Bloc states as an important asset in their efforts to assure a continued presence in the U.S. and Canadian coastal waters. It should be noted that the U.S.–Polish Governing International Fishery Agreement (GIFA) of August 2, 1976 was the first signed with a foreign nation after the U.S. Congress approved the Fishery Conservation and Management Act.

Extension of national jurisdiction over continental shelf fishery resources has created a serious problem for the utilization of the existing distant-water fishing potential of many states. According to the preliminary estimates, the 1977 quota allocated for Poland in the Northeast Pacific could be taken with about 50 percent of its existing long-range fishing fleet. Undoubtedly, in the USSR and other Eastern European countries (German Democratic Republic, Bulgaria, Rumania) excessive capacity will pose a similar problem. It should be stressed that the distant-water fishing fleets of these countries are quite new, their average age being about ten years. In 1976, the total GRT of Eastern Bloc distant-water fleets (including the support vessels) was about 7,017,255 GRT (tables 7.2 and 7.6), and during one year (1975 – 1976) increased by only 362,000 tons (i.e., by 5 percent). The Soviet Bloc fishing fleet accounts for nearly 60 percent of the world fishing tonnage (ships over 100 GRT each). This indicates that a large part of this potential, represented by hundreds of catchers, freezers, factory trawlers and other specialized fishing vessels, could have considerable difficulties in achieving full utilization of their designed capacity when their fishery activities in traditional fishing grounds are suspended or sharply reduced by the coastal nations. Although the Soviet Bloc nations' total share in world fisheries is presently about 16 percent, this does not change the general impact of the 200-mile economic zone; they will suffer the greatest loss.

## High-Seas Living Resources as an Alternative for Long-range Fleets

Catch limitations imposed by coastal nations and resulting restrictions for distant-water fishing fleet operations in the traditionally exploited fishing grounds will reduce the total volume of harvest and employment opportunities for long-range fleets. The United States, Canada, and other nations rich in fishery resources introduced a quota allocation system that permits the distant-water fleets to utilize a part of their current capacity and to take sharply reduced volumes of fish stocks available to foreign countries as a surplus quota. Facing such drastic and perhaps irrevocable changes in world fisheries, distant-water fishing nations are heavily involved in the quickest possible adaptation of their fleets to new tasks and new methods of operation.

Some distant-water countries, particularly Japan, West Europe, the Soviet Union, Poland, and other Eastern Bloc nations, are highly interested in further development of their fishing operations in the high-seas areas that are not included in national jurisdiction zones. This, however, will require adaptation of the existing vessels for open ocean pelagic fisheries as well as super deep-water trawling. According to Soviet scientists, fishing potentialities of the deep seas should be fundamentally reappraised. Numerous species of distant neritic, epipelagic and bathypelagic zones are considered of particular importance. Their present and potential catch levels are presented in table 7.13.

The latest research findings show that depths of over 1,000 meters are considerably more productive than they were believed to be. Soviet research vessels have discovered unknown fish species at depths over 7.5 kilometers (24,600 feet); at this time as few as 7 – 8 deep-dwelling species are the objects of commercial fishing.[31]

Open ocean and super deep-water fisheries will require completely new types of fishing vessels, which will be equipped with stronger propulsion engines and other types of fishing gear. This will imply much higher fuel consumption and, in consequence, higher costs of operation. Adaptation of the existing factory trawlers for such tasks is almost impossible; it would be less expensive to build new vessels. A more realistic alternative seems to be adaptation of some existing fleets for saury fisheries in the South Atlantic and cephalopods of the open ocean. The principal condition for industrial fisheries based on these species is to achieve high-catch yields of the fishing vessel. It is possible that some conventional side trawlers will be adapted for light fishing, which is hopefully the best method for harvesting

TABLE 7.13

PRESENT AND POTENTIAL CATCH OF THE PRINCIPAL
COMMERCIAL SPECIES IN THE WORLD OCEAN

| Regions and species | Catch in million MT | |
|---|---|---|
| | Present | Potential |
| *Pelagic-neritic zones* | | |
| Anchovies | 3.6 | 13.0 |
| Herrings | 2.5 | 5.0 |
| Sardines | 2.8 | 5.0 |
| Mackerels | 5.3 | 6.7 |
| Pollocks | 4.6 | 5.0 |
| Capelins | 2.0 | 3.5 |
| Poutassou | 0.0 | 1.0 |
| Total | 20.8 | 39.2 |
| *Shelf bottom zones* | | |
| Cod | 2.7 | 3.2 |
| Hake | 2.5 | 3.5 |
| Flatfishes | 1.3 | 1.5 |
| Total | 6.5 | 8.2 |
| *Shelf slopes and underwater heights* | | |
| Red snappers, Redfishes | 0.6 | 0.8 |
| Grenadiers, Rattails | 0.05 | 1.5 |
| Other | – | 1.0 |
| Total | 0.6 | 3.3 |
| *Epipelagic zones* | | |
| Large tunas | 1.0 | 1.2 |
| Small tunas | 0.9 | 3.0 |
| Sauries | 0.5 | 1.5 |
| Squids | 0.8 | 5.0 |
| Other | – | 0.5 |
| Total | 3.2 | 11.2 |
| *Antarctic waters* | | |
| Krill | 0.04 | 30.0 |
| Total | 31.1 | 91.9 |

Source: P. A. Mojsiejev, "Biologicheskije resursy mirovogo okeana i perspektivy ich ispolzovanja (Biological resources of the world ocean and perspectives of their utilization)," *Voprosy Ichtiologii* (Problems of Icthyology), 17,5 (106) (Moskva, 1977).

dispersed species in the ocean's upper layers. Another alternative for open ocean activities will be harvesting small organisms that live in light dispersing layers. These organisms could be utilized for reduction and feed production purposes. If the shift into the open ocean species is introduced within a few years, we can expect that part of the existing fishing vessels will be withdrawn from service and placed in local shipyards for long-term modernization work. From a technological point of view, all leading distant-water fishing nations are able to adapt their fleets to new conditions, although the cost of doing so will be extremely high.

Eastern fishing nations, particularly the Soviet Union and lately also Poland, East

Germany, and Bulgaria, are developing efforts to harvest unconventional living resources such as Antarctic krill, cephalopods, and some new fin fishes (numerous pelagic species such as saury and lantern fishes) but, unfortunately, it is still early to get final results; technological and economic obstacles are tremendous and require further efforts and huge costs of scientific investigations.

It should be stressed again that open ocean fisheries will not, at least in the foreseeable future, totally replace the fishing lost in the coastal zones of foreign nations. This applies particularly to the fish species traditionally caught for direct human consumption. Except for subantarctic demersal fish, the majority of presently known open sea species are difficult to catch and expensive when used in processing operations oriented for production of food products for human consumption. Fish meal seems to be the most immediate possibility for open ocean fisheries of small sea organisms. The newest trends in construction of long-range trawlers are confirming this tendency. Fish meal plants on modern factory trawlers will be able to reduce twice or three times as much fish raw material as before (i.e., up to about 100 tons of fish per day).

A rapid engagement in massive exploration of unconventional open sea resources is hampered in many states by the following obstacles: (a) high costs of scientific research, which must be developed over the large ocean areas; (b) lack of information about distribution and volume of the open sea resources (intricate technology of elaboration and generally low processing efficiency of unconventional species measured as a ratio between raw material and processed food product); (c) higher consumption of energy during the super deep-water trawling, light fishing, or electric trawling activities (these techniques are most appropriate in the open ocean harvesting, particularly of some dispersed school fishes). The principal technological shortcoming of the existing distant-water fleets owned by Soviet Bloc countries is the lack of medium- and short-range fishing vessels that could be employed in cooperation with coastal nations, as well as the absence of distant-water ships for open ocean fishing.

Future plans for long-range fisheries development include construction and adaptation activities which can be specified as follows:

1. *Construction of smaller and medium size fishing vessels for international cooperation with coastal nations.* Fishing boats for the exploitation of continental shelf resources within international joint ventures will be characterized by the smaller dimensions, lack of processing plants on board, simple construction, and lower engine power. It is expected that these ships will be handled partially by local crews and operate principally in developing countries with rich coastal fishery resources.

2. *Further development of high-seas fishing fleets able to harvest school fishes, cephalopods, and small sea organisms of fish species of the deepest as well as the upper layers of the water column.* To fulfill this task, reconstruction of numerous fishing vessels is foreseen to adapt them to the operation in new fishing grounds. Also new scientific activities and objectives in ocean exploration are needed, and additional funds allocated in order to: (a) Develop a new fishing gear for mid-water trawling, krill exploitation and, super deep-water fisheries (taking into account low processing yields of open ocean species and

krill as a source of meat for direct human consumption, new harvesting and processing methods and equipment were recently studied during the large subantarctic scientific-commercial expeditions organized by the USSR, Poland, West Germany, and other countries—in Antarctic waters, the final goal is to achieve as high daily catch rates per ship as 150−300 tons of round krill);[32] (b) Increase open-sea catching potential (in 1977, the Soviet Union signed its largest contract with Polish shipyards for construction of a new series of 15 factory trawlers [1,500 DWT each], 4 stern trawlers [750 DWT], and 8 mother-ships [12,000 DWT]). Poland will also build, for the Soviet Union, a series of 5 supertrawlers (3,600 DWT, 390 foot length, 7,200 HP), the largest of their kind in the world. By 1980, these fishing vessels, of modern construction and high versatility and autonomy, will enter into the fisheries. Old contracts also assure new supplies of fishing vessels. For example, the Soviet Union received recently the 27th type B-422 Arctic trawler built for seal hunting and bottom fishing activities. Large series of motherships are also commissioned by earlier orders from the Soviet Union.[33] In 1977 the Polish distant-water fishing potential had to be increased with additional factory trawlers and support vessels; by 1980, about 11 large factory trawlers were constructed and delivered by the home shipbuilding industry. Shipyards of the German Democratic Republic, who specialize in factory trawlers of the "Atlantik" and "Tropik" types produced in large series for the Soviet Union, Romania, and other Eastern countries, have their portfolio full of contracts for many years ahead.

3. *Rapid development of the tuna fisheries.* There are very strong incentives in many distant-water fishing nations to develop tuna fisheries, although they are obliged to look for new fishing grounds and new methods of operations. It is believed in some countries that tuna fisheries can expand beyond present levels of catch. According to Soviet Bloc scientists, tuna resources are still underutilized in all oceans and represent large fishing potential. This particularly applies to smaller tuna species like skipjack (Atlantic Ocean), whose potential catch is estimated about 250,000 tons per year, but its actual harvest is only about 100,000 tons. In the Indian Ocean, the potential skipjack catch is estimated at about 500,000 tons per year, but the present harvest is only 100,000 tons.[34] Eastern European nations are increasing their consumption of tuna, and some of them are importing certain quantities of tuna products. The demand for tuna is expected to increase in this area. While the world price for tuna products is actually very high (about $1,500 per ton), it seems logical for the Eastern Bloc countries to develop their own tuna fleets and deliver these highly valuable species to local markets with reduced (or with no) hard currency outlays; and exports of tuna products will produce additional hard currency incomes. All these factors influenced the decision of the Soviet Union to develop its own tuna fleet. As a result, new tuna vessels ($100 million contract for the Polish shipping industry) will be delivered to the Soviet Union. Under the terms of this contract, Poland will build during 1977−1981: (a) 50 tuna vessels 16 m long; (b) 1 tuna mothership; 32 other vessels, completed by the end of 1980; (c) 10 tuna superseiners (1,800 DWT, 5,000 HP diesel engines, reconnaissance helicopter, and 4 fast launches for rounding up the tuna schools); and (d) 10 tuna super-seiners (3,000 DWT). Tuna fisheries may also be developed by other Eastern Bloc nations, particularly Poland, which is a main producer of tuna vessels in the Soviet Bloc area.

If the Eastern Bloc countries and other nations expand their tuna fisheries, additional pressure will be put on tuna resources, and the economic rent of all present and future users will be decreased. According to many western scientists, tuna fisheries are overcapitalized on a worldwide basis.[35] Unrestricted fleet growth will create serious political problems because of conflicting interests among nations interested in tuna resources.

4. *Expansion of subantarctic fisheries—construction of new and adaptation of existing factory trawlers and support vessels for exploitation of the southern ocean.* Subantarctic ships will be of large dimensions and high engine power to enable them to catch in depths up to 10,000 feet. They and their support ships will operate independently during long periods of time, in all hydrometeorological conditions.

A large majority of the new fishery resources are characterized by a lower percentage of edible parts in relation to the raw material weight. The new distant-water fleets are to be equipped with improved processing equipment to increase average yield of edible fish meat to fish raw material from the existing level of 30−40 percent to 45−55 percent.

These developments indicate that distant-water fishing fleets of the majority of eastern nations will probably not be reduced but increased in the foreseeable future. After certain adaptations or reequipment (chiefly in fishing gear and processing plants), the fleet presently in use will continue its activities where it will be possible to develop them. As previously mentioned, the direct costs and economic efficiency problems will not be considered (mainly in the Soviet Union's case) as a criterion of first importance. Increasing fishing potential for open ocean fisheries and better adjustment of technology, accompanied by more active multilateral and bilateral agreement policies will be the main response of the eastern distant-water fishing nations to extended jurisdiction.

Like the shelf fishing grounds, the open ocean resources may be managed by international organizations in the future. This expectation is based on historical experience in overexploitation of coastal resources and on the results of the uncontrolled harvest of some highly migratory species like tuna, as well as on recent fishing developments on species concentrated in reduced shelf areas around small islands, archipelagoes, formed by underwater mountains, and in the Antarctic coastal waters.[36]

Distant-water fishing countries expect that their early presence in the open ocean fishing grounds (in case such an international management system is imposed) will assure them a more advantageous position in future access to these resources.

## IMPLICATIONS FOR THE NORTHEAST PACIFIC COASTAL NATIONS

### License Fees and Surplus Quota Allocation

As long as the U.S. and Canadian fishing industries are unable to fully utilize their coastal fishery resources, all surplus quotas will be allocated to foreign users. The question arises as to what the economic impact of surplus allocations will be on both foreign and coastal state's interests.

If foreign fleets are allowed to harvest on the basis of quota allocation, they must pay poundage and other fees, which for the coastal state constitute an indirect benefit derived from its resources harvested by other nations. In the Northeast Pacific, the foreign surplus fisheries are the largest in the world. In 1978, the total volume of catch allowed by the U.S. for overseas fleets was as high as 1,737,000 MT (table 7.14). As the optimum yield level of this area is about 1,802,000 MT, foreign nations were allowed to harvest about 95 percent of the existing fishery resources.[37]

According to the ex-vessel prices used for computing poundage fees for 1978,[38] the total value of fishery resources allocated for foreign fleets in the same year was about U.S. $200 million. A new fee schedule requires foreign nations to pay 3.5 percent of the U.S. ex-vessel price of fish. This will make the total value of poundage fees about $7 million. Japan, with its quota in 1978 of 1,149,000 MT, took 66 percent of the total allowable catch for foreign fisheries, and paid nearly $4 million as a poundage fee to the United States. This

TABLE 7.14

VALUE OF CATCH AND POUNDAGE FEES FOR FOREIGN
QUOTA ALLOCATIONS IN THE NORTHEAST PACIFIC

| Country, fishing area and species | Total allowable catch for foreign nation 1978 (metric tons) | U.S. ex-vessel price per MT (U.S. $) | Total ex-vessel value of allocated quota (U.S $) | Poundage fee: 3.5% of ex-vessel price per MT (U.S. $) |
|---|---|---|---|---|
| *USSR* | | | | |
| *Gulf of Alaska* | | | | |
| Pacific Cod | 2,330 | $282 | $ 657,060 | |
| Flounders | 1,500 | 387 | 580,500 | |
| Atka Mackerel | 21,570 | 138 | 2,976,660 | |
| Alaska Pollock | 44,770 | 84 | 3,760,680 | |
| Pacific Ocean Perch | 7,225 | 280 | 2,023,000 | |
| Other Rockfishes | 1,535 | 298 | 457,430 | |
| Sablefish | 100 | 399 | 39,900 | |
| (central & western Gulf) | | | | |
| Squid | 50 | 55 | 2,750 | |
| Other species | 5,000 | 48 | 240,000 | |
| *Bering Sea & Aleutians* | | | | |
| Pacific Cod | 17,500 | 282 | 4,935,000 | |
| Yellowfin Sole | 41,950 | 387 | 16,234,650 | |
| Other Flounders | 55,050 | 387 | 21,304,350 | |
| Atka Mackerel | 22,600 | 138 | 3,118,800 | |
| Herring | 6,060 | 100 | 606,000 | |
| Alaska Pollock | 92,700 | 84 | 7,786,800 | |
| Pacific Ocean Perch (Bering Sea) | 3,075 | 280 | 861,000 | |
| Pacific Ocean Perch (Aleutians) | 8,050 | 280 | 2,254,000 | |
| Sablefish (Bering Sea) | 265 | 399 | 105,735 | |
| Sablefish (Aleutians) | 165 | 399 | 65,835 | |
| Squid | 70 | 55 | 3,850 | |
| Other species (Bering Sea) | 11,145 | 48 | 534,960 | |
| Other species (Aleutians) | 6,365 | 48 | 305,520 | |

TABLE 7.14 (Continued)

VALUE OF CATCH AND POUNDAGE FEES FOR FOREIGN
QUOTA ALLOCATIONS IN THE NORTHEAST PACIFIC

| Country, fishing area and species | Total allowable catch for foreign nation 1978 (metric tons) | U.S. ex-vessel price per MT (U.S. $) | Total ex-vessel value of allocated quota (U.S $) | Poundage fee: 3.5% of ex-vessel price per MT (U.S. $) |
|---|---|---|---|---|
| *USSR (Cont.)* | | | | |
| *Northeast Pacific* | | | | |
| Pacific Hake | 50,300 | 32 | 1,609,600 | |
| Jack Mackerel | 1,950 | 110 | 214,500 | |
| Pacific Ocean Perch & other Rockfishes | 400 | 280 | 112,000 | |
| Flounders | 50 | 387 | 19,350 | |
| Sablefish | 50 | 399 | 19,950 | |
| Other species | 250 | 48 | 12,000 | |
| TOTAL | 402,075 | | 70,841,280 | 2,479,445 |
| *JAPAN* | | | | |
| *Gulf of Alaska* | | | | |
| Pacific Cod | 6,200 | $282 | $ 1,748,400 | |
| Flounders | 15,800 | 387 | 6,114,600 | |
| Atka Mackerel | 2,000 | 138 | 276,000 | |
| Alaska Pollock | 28,800 | 84 | 2,419,200 | |
| Pacific Ocean Perch | 4,650 | 280 | 1,302,000 | |
| Other Rockfishes | 1,000 | 298 | 298,000 | |
| Sablefish (central & western Gulf) | 6,950 | 399 | 2,773,050 | |
| Squid | 30 | 414 | 12,420 | |
| Other species | 4,030 | 48 | 193,440 | |
| *Bering Sea & Aleutians* | | | | |
| Pacific Cod | 38,850 | 282 | 10,955,700 | |
| Yellowfin Sole | 63,900 | 387 | 24,729,300 | |
| Other Flounders | 83,800 | 387 | 32,430,600 | |
| Herring | 2,580 | 100 | 258,000 | |
| Atka Mackerel | 2,000 | 138 | 276,000 | |
| Alaska Pollock | 792,300 | 84 | 66,553,200 | |
| Pacific Ocean Perch (Bering Sea) | 3,100 | 280 | 868,000 | |
| Pacific Ocean Perch (Aleutians) | 6,200 | 280 | 1,736,000 | |
| Sablefish (Bering Sea) | 1,870 | 399 | 746,130 | |
| Sablefish (Aleutians) | 1,170 | 399 | 466,830 | |
| Snails | 3,000 | 600 | 1,800,000 | |
| Squid | 9,870 | 55 | 542,850 | |
| Other species (Bering Sea) | 45,415 | 48 | 2,179,920 | |
| Other species (Aleutians) | 25,900 | 48 | 1,243,200 | |
| TOTAL | 1,148,615 | | 112,355,130 | 3,932,430 |

## TABLE 7.14 (Continued)

### VALUE OF CATCH AND POUNDAGE FEES FOR FOREIGN
### QUOTA ALLOCATIONS IN THE NORTHEAST PACIFIC

| Country, fishing area and species | Total allowable catch for foreign nation 1978 (metric tons) | U.S. ex-vessel price per MT (U.S. $) | Total ex-vessel value of allocated quota (U.S $) | Poundage fee: 3.5% of ex-vessel price per MT (U.S. $) |
|---|---|---|---|---|
| *SOUTH KOREA* | | | | |
| *Gulf of Alaska* | | | | |
| Pacific Cod | 100 | 282 | 28,200 | |
| Flounders | 100 | 387 | 38,700 | |
| Atka Mackerel | 100 | 138 | 13,800 | |
| Alaskan Pollock | 19,870 | 84 | 1,669,080 | |
| Pacific Ocean Perch | 3,203 | 280 | 896,840 | |
| Other Rockfishes | 675 | 298 | 201,150 | |
| Sablefish | | | | |
| (central & western Gulf) | 800 | 399 | 319,200 | |
| Squid | 20 | 55 | 1,100 | |
| Other species | 1,535 | 48 | 73,680 | |
| *Bering Sea & Aleutians* | | | | |
| Pacific Cod | 100 | $282 | $     28,200 | |
| Yellowfin Sole | 100 | 387 | 38,700 | |
| Other Flounders | 100 | 387 | 38,700 | |
| Herring | 20 | 100 | 2,000 | |
| Alaska Pollock | 60,000 | 84 | 5,040,000 | |
| Pacific Ocean Perch (Bering Sea) | 300 | 280 | 84,000 | |
| Pacific Ocean Perch (Aleutians) | 700 | 280 | 196,000 | |
| Sablefish (Bering Sea) | 200 | 399 | 79,800 | |
| Sablefish (Aleutians) | 125 | 399 | 49,875 | |
| Other species (Bering Sea) | 2,800 | 48 | 134,400 | |
| Other species (Aleutians) | 1,600 | 48 | 76,800 | |
| Squid | 50 | 55 | 2,750 | |
| TOTAL | 91,164 | | 9,012,975 | 315,454 |
| *POLAND* | | | | |
| *Gulf of Alaska* | | | | |
| Pacific Cod | 350 | 282 | 98,700 | |
| Flounders | 100 | 387 | 38,700 | |
| Atka Mackerel | 1,030 | 138 | 142,140 | |
| Alaska Pollock | 3,900 | 84 | 327,600 | |
| Pacific Ocean Perch | 630 | 280 | 176,400 | |
| Other Rockfishes | 126 | 298 | 37,548 | |
| Sablefish | | | | |
| (central & western Gulf) | 50 | 399 | 19,950 | |
| Squid | 10 | 55 | 550 | |
| Other species | 395 | 48 | 18,960 | |
| *Northeast Pacific* | | | | |
| Pacific Hake | 8,700 | 32 | 278,400 | |
| Jack Mackerel | 1,950 | 110 | 19,500 | |

## TABLE 7.14 (Continued)

### VALUE OF CATCH AND POUNDAGE FEES FOR FOREIGN QUOTA ALLOCATIONS IN THE NORTHEAST PACIFIC

| Country, fishing area and species | Total allowable catch for foreign nation 1978 (metric tons) | U.S. ex-vessel price per MT (U.S. $) | Total ex-vessel value of allocated quota (U.S $) | Poundage fee: 3.5% of ex-vessel price per MT (U.S. $) |
|---|---|---|---|---|
| POLAND (Cont.) | | | | |
| Northeast Pacific | | | | |
| Pacific Ocean Perch & | | | | |
| other Rockfishes | 80 | 280 | 22,400 | |
| Flounders | 10 | 387 | 3,870 | |
| Sablefish | 10 | 399 | 3,990 | |
| Other species | 51 | 48 | 2,448 | |
| TOTAL | 23,217 | | 1,191,156 | 41,690 |
| MEXICO | | | | |
| Gulf of Alaska | | | | |
| Pacific cod | 4,000 | $282 | $ 1,128,000 | |
| Flounders | 100 | 387 | 38,700 | |
| Atka Mackerel | 100 | 138 | 13,800 | |
| Alaska Pollock | 10,000 | 84 | 840,000 | |
| Pacific Ocean Perch | 1,596 | 280 | 446,880 | |
| Other Rockfishes | 744 | 298 | 39,900 | |
| Sablefish | | | | |
| (central & western Gulf) | 100 | 399 | 39,900 | |
| Squid | 745 | 55 | 40,975 | |
| Other species | 2,000 | 48 | 96,000 | |
| Northeast Pacific | | | | |
| Pacific Hake | 15,000 | 32 | 480,000 | |
| Jack Mackerel | 100 | 110 | 11,000 | |
| Pacific Ocean Perch & | | | | |
| other Rockfishes | 230 | 280 | 64,400 | |
| Flounders | 30 | 387 | 11,610 | |
| Sablefish | 30 | 399 | 11,970 | |
| Reserved quotas for further utilization. | | | | |
| Pacific Cod | 4,000 | 282 | 1,128,000 | |
| Alaska Pollock | 10,000 | 84 | 840,000 | |
| Pacific Ocean Perch | 1,596 | 280 | 446,800 | |
| Hake | 15,000 | 32 | 480,000 | |
| Squid | 745 | 55 | 40,975 | |
| TOTAL | 66,116 | | 6,380,802 | 223,328 |
| TAIWAN | | | | |
| Bering Sea & Aleutians | | | | |
| Pacific Cod | 50 | 282 | 14,100 | |
| Yellow Sole | 50 | 387 | 19,350 | |
| Other Flounders | 50 | 387 | 19,350 | |
| Herring | 10 | 100 | 1,000 | |
| Atka Mackerel | 100 | 138 | 13,800 | |
| Alaska Pollock | 5,000 | 84 | 420,000 | |
| Pacific Ocean Perch (Bering Sea) | 25 | 280 | 7,000 | |

TABLE 7.14 (Continued)

VALUE OF CATCH AND POUNDAGE FEES FOR FOREIGN
QUOTA ALLOCATIONS IN THE NORTHEAST PACIFIC

| Country, fishing area and species | Total allowable catch for foreign nation 1978 (metric tons) | U.S. ex-vessel price per MT (U.S. $) | Total ex-vessel value of allocated quota (U.S $) | Poundage fee: 3.5% of ex-vessel price per MT (U.S. $) |
|---|---|---|---|---|
| *TAIWAN (Cont.)* | | | | |
| Pacific Ocean Perch (Aleutians) | 50 | 280 | 14,000 | |
| Sablefish (Bering Sea) | 65 | 399 | 25,935 | |
| Sablefish (Aleutians) | 40 | 399 | 15,960 | |
| Squid | 10 | 55 | 550 | |
| Other species (Bering Sea) | 240 | 48 | 11,520 | |
| Other species (Aleutians) | 135 | 48 | 6,480 | |
| TOTAL | 5,825 | | 569,045 | 19,917 |
| | Total allowable catch for foreign fisheries | | Total value of U.S. N.E. Pacific resources allocated for foreign nations | Total value of poundage fees |
| GRAND TOTAL | 1,737,012 | | $200,350,388 | $7,012,264 |

Source: Author's calculations based on the National Marine Fisheries Service Fee Schedule for 1978 and quota allocations for foreign fleets.

is 56 percent of the total value of poundage fees paid by all foreign nations in this area.

The Soviet Union receives 23 percent of the total quota allocations, but its contribution in poundage fees is 35 percent, mainly due to the high incidence of flatfish of high ex-vessel value. Together, Japan and the Soviet Union take about 90 percent of the total surplus quota of the United States. Although South Korea's quota increased last year, its share of U.S. surplus is only 5 percent.

The revenues generated by the annual access fee of $1.00 per gross registered ton of each foreign fishing vessel engaged in harvesting within the 200-mile fisheries zone, and $0.50 per GRT charged for any vessel engaged in processing fish but not catching, depends on the total tonnage and number of the foreign vessels employed in surplus fisheries.

In 1977 the total number of foreign fishing vessels engaged in Northeast Pacific fisheries was 696.[39] Assuming an average size of 1,400 gross tons per vessel,[40] the revenue from the access fees would be about $974,400. In sum, the U.S. would thus receive a total revenue from both fees of about $8 million. This revenue is, however, based on the value of fish established arbitrarily by the coastal state. Moreover, some species allocated for foreign fleets are not utilized at all by local fishermen, so the ex-vessel values are based on foreign fish prices.

If the license fees are not used as a management tool to restrict foreign fishing, and are not high enough to prevent foreign long-range fleets from utilizing the allocated surplus solely because of the fee level, then establishing objective criteria to develop the fee schedule is of utmost importance.

It should be noted that the typical and most important component of the distant-water fleet, the factory trawlers, are designed to process the fish at sea and to obtain as high a reduction ratio of raw material to processed products as possible. This leads to better utilization of the production capacity of the factory trawlers, and better coordination between the top season yields of given stocks and the time allotted for fishing activities. Long-range activities would be impossible without the support fleet, which contributes to saving a considerable part of the fishing vessel's harvesting capacity; otherwise harvesting time would be wasted in traveling between the fishing ground and base ports to deliver the fish cargo and receive new supplies. Foreign fleets also employ numerous smaller catching vessels with relatively reduced dimensions and limited processing capacities on board. Their presence on distant fishing grounds is also made possible by the existence of supporting operations; that is, the small catching vessels and freezers deliver fresh or frozen fish to the factory motherships, which process raw material and transfer fish products to the transport ships.

However, support vessels contribute to serious problems of cost increases in distant-water activities. Soviet fisheries offer a typical example of the burden of auxiliary fleets in long-range operations. According to *Lloyd's Register of Shipping,* Statistical Tables, 1976, the support fleet has nearly the same tonnage as fishing vessels over 100 GRT each. This means that each ton of fishing capacity in the Russian fleet maintains an additional ton of support vessel. Other distant-water fishing fleets are less dependent on support vessels, although in Socialist fishing countries each GRT of fishing vessel is economically charged from over 0.3 ton of auxiliary vessel (Poland) to about 0.5 ton in Romania.

A serious burden of auxiliary operations on distant-water fishing activities derives from the high operational costs of the support vessels. For example, the average daily cost of one refrigerated cargo transport vessel is about $4,500, and the freight rate of frozen fish between the U.S. West Coast and Baltic ports is greater than $100, per MT. This has a large impact on the price structure determined on an ex-vessel basis. Figure 7.5 illustrates.

It is difficult to establish uniform ex-vessel prices for a given species when it is harvested by various types of fishing vessels (for example, catchers, freezers, and factory trawlers). If we consider the ex-vessel price for round fish delivered in ice to the fish terminal as a starting point, then the only analogy in distant-water fleet operations can be found when the catching vessel delivers its harvest without previous processing to the support vessel. This delivery of fresh round fish can be carried out through transfer of the cod-end, or cargo operations at sea between the catcher and mothership.

Freezer and factory trawlers are able to freeze round fish on board, as well as carry out

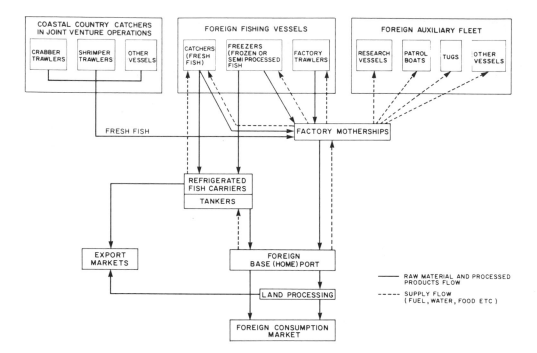

Fig. 7.5. *Distant-Water Fishing Fleet Operation System.* Author's illustration.

numerous processing activities. Factory trawlers process practically their whole catch on board, and are equipped with fish meal plants. Once on board, round fish is selected, put into the trays, frozen, packed and stored in the fish holds. Fish of large dimensions can be frozen and stored individually. Processing can include heading, gutting and even filleting. Usually the vessel is able to process the fish with machines (depending on the kind and size of the fish); however, many times the fish must be processed manually. The crew accepts such work because of the economic incentives offered by the owner; for highly processed products, the crew receives higher wages.

When the fishing trawler delivers its fish cargo to the support vessel, it is usually composed of a large variety of fish products in different stages of processing as shown in table 7.15.

All of the above products are usually delivered to the support vessels. Factory motherships may process the cargo received from the support vessels. Fresh fish can be wholly processed (salting, heading and/or gutting, filleting, and mincing fish meal production), whereas products received from freezer and factory trawlers are stored only. Motherships and transport vessels deliver fish to the home markets, where they are consumed without any further processing, or serve as a raw material for canning, smoking, and making prepared fish food products.

The great complexity of distant-water fishing operations is the origin of numerous difficulties in establishing proper ex-vessel prices. Consequently, the ex-vessel price for fish

TABLE 7.15

FISH PRODUCTS AND PROCESSING ON FACTORY TRAWLERS

| Fish Product | Processing Activities on Board |
| --- | --- |
| Frozen round fish in cartons or bulk | Selection of fish, placement in trays, transportation to the freezers, freezing, packing, transportation to the refrigerated hold, and storage in low temperature. |
| Fish headed, gutted or filleted and frozen in cartons | Primary selection of fish, storage in chilled sea water tanks, final selection, machine or hand heading or gutting, placing in trays, freezing (pre- and postfreezing), packing, transportation operations, storage in refrigerated holds. |
| Fish meal | Selection of trash fish, offal and damaged fishes not suited for human consumption, processing, packing and storage. |

products delivered by freezer and factory trawlers is not compatible with the general understanding of ex-vessel prices in the United States and other coastal states.

Distant-water fishing and auxiliary vessels deliver highly processed or semi-processed fish products; a considerable portion of their costs is for fish processing at sea. It is difficult to identify precisely these costs from other operational expenses, although they can reach one-third or more of all costs at sea if only depreciation of processing equipment, salaries of the crew, energy consumed, handling and storing of fish products, and the like are considered.

The route taken by fish caught by distant-water fishing vessels to the consumer markets is long, not only in geographical terms but principally as a result of multiple handling, processing, and transportation functions added by supporting operations. However, fish food prices in some distant-water fishing nations are kept at artificially low levels. Many governments heavily subsidize distant-water fishing activities since they produce net economic losses. This is a result of low ex-vessel and market prices, which are also established by the governments. For example, in Poland the fishing industry has been requesting higher ex-vessel prices because fishing costs have increased many times, but fish prices have remained the same for at least seven years (1970–1977).

## License Fees Based on Dockside Value in the U.S. Market

For the following analysis, we use Alaska pollock as an example of a species allocated nearly totally to foreign users.

According to the existing information about catch composition for the vessels engaged in Alaska pollock fisheries,[41] the fish cargo brought by the coastal fishing vessel to the harbor is composed of Alaska pollock (65%), cod (15%), flathead sole (5%), rock sole (5%), rex sole (5%), and other flatfish (5%).

The estimated price that the local fishermen could get in the home market would reflect a weighted average of prices applied for all species caught at the same time. In order to establish an average annual ex-vessel price for all the species, it was necessary to determine an actual price level for fish landed currently in the nearest harbors or consumption centers.

Unfortunately, ex-vessel price notations for species of interest are very scarce and incomplete. For Alaska pollock, for example, as well as for many other underutilized species, it is practically impossible to estimate the average annual price f.o.b. Alaskan habors because they are still not landed there for commercial purposes.

In January 1977, the first ex-vessel price notations for Alaska pollock were given for the Seattle fish auction. Of the remainder of the bycatch species, only cod prices are regularly registered in the Seattle fish terminal and, from time to time, in Kodiak, Alaska.

Table 7.16 shows the price notations for 1976 and the beginning of 1977.

Due to the lack of price notations for the flathead sole, we were obliged to include this species in "other flatfish" and, consequently, calculated weighted average price for all sole species. Thus, the final estimation for ex-vessel price, according to expected catch composition, is as follows: Alaska pollock, 8.0 ¢/lb; cod, 13.2 ¢/lb; and flatfish, 14.2 ¢/lb.

Taking into account the expected percentage of individual species to be caught in Alaska pollock fisheries, we can estimate the final ex-vessel price per pound of catch:

| | | |
|---|---|---|
| Alaska pollock | 0.65 lb × 8.0¢ = | 5.20¢ |
| Cod | 0.15 lb × 13.2¢ = | 1.98¢ |
| Flatfishes | 0.20 lb × 14.2¢ = | 2.84¢ |
| Total | 1.0 lb | = 10.02¢ |

We can assume then, that the ex-vessel price that could be considered for Alaska pollock fisheries is about 10¢ per pound, or about $220 per metric ton of round fish f.o.b. Seattle.

This price, however, is highly theoretical; it does not include such important factors as possible price variations related to volume of fish offered by fishermen, storage, processing, and transportation capacities—as well as local market demand for fish products based on Alaska pollock as a substitute for other bottomfish products, particularly cod-derivates.

## Ex-Vessel Price Based on Foreign Notations

Japan, Soviet Union, South Korea, Taiwan, Poland, and Mexico are the foreign users of the Alaska pollock from the eastern Bering Sea and Gulf of Alaska.

To obtain the ex-vessel price of raw Alaska pollock taken in the U.S. fisheries zone by, for example, Japanese distant-water fleets, the price of surimi should be used because most of the catch in U.S. waters is reduced into surimi; only a minor portion is landed as dressed fish. Based on this assumption, the average price of raw Alaska pollock in 1976 (the price of surimi minus the cost of processing, etc.) was 25 yen/kilo.[42] The same methodology of obtaining ex-vessel price is used for other species that could be caught as by-products (i.e., cod and flatfish).[43] According to the Japan Deep Sea Trawlers Association and Japan Medium Trawlers Association, the average 1976 ex-vessel prices for the principal fish species harvested in the Northeast Pacific waters are shown in table 7.17.

Consequently, the ex-vessel price for Alaska pollock fisheries in U.S. coastal waters by Japanese trawlers is about *$114 per metric ton*. This price is based on an assumption that foreign vessels' catch composition will be the same as suggested by the NMFS data

## TABLE 7.16

### Ex-vessel Price Notations in Seattle Fish Terminal for Alaska Pollock and By-catch Species
#### (Round and Iced)

| Species | 1976 (¢/lb) | | | | | | | | | | | | 1977 (¢/lb) | | | Average ex-vessel price for whole period (¢/lb) |
|---|---|---|---|---|---|---|---|---|---|---|---|---|---|---|---|---|
| | J | F | M | A | M | J | J | A | S | O | N | D | J | F | M | |
| Alaska pollock | – | – | – | – | – | – | – | – | – | – | – | – | 8.0 | 8.0 | – | 8.0 |
| Cod | 11.5 | 12.5 | 12.5 | 12.5 | 12.5 | 12.5 | 12.5 | 12.5[a] | 12.5 | 12.5 | 13.8[a] | 13.8 | 15.0 | 15.0 | 15.0 | 13.2 |
| Flathead sole | – | – | – | – | – | – | – | – | – | – | – | – | – | – | – | – |
| Rock sole | – | 19.0 | 19.0 | 19.0 | 19.0 | 19.0 | – | 19.0 | 19.0 | – | – | 20.9 | – | – | – | 19.7 |
| Rex sole | 16.0 | 13.0 | 13.0 | 13.0 | 13.0 | 13.0 | – | 19.0 | 19.0 | – | 13.0 | – | – | 15.0 | – | 14.9 |
| Other flatfish[b] | – | – | – | – | 8.0 | – | 8.0 | 8.0 | – | – | – | – | – | – | – | 8.0 |

Source: *Fishery Market News* (Weekly). (Seattle: NMFS, 1976 and first quarter of 1977).

[a] In Kodiak fish terminal the ex-vessel price for cod in the same month was 20¢/lb.

[b] Based on price given for flounders.

## TABLE 7.17

AVERAGE 1976 EX-VESSEL PRICE OF BOTTOM SPECIES HARVESTED BY JAPAN
(ROUND FISH)

| · Species | Yen/kg | $/kg |
|---|---|---|
| Alaska pollock | 25 | 0.08 |
| Cod | 72 | 0.24 |
| Flatfishes | 40 | 0.13 |
| Weighted average ex-vessel price $/kg based on average catch composition assumed in this chapter. | | 0.114 |

(table 7.16). It is obvious that with a reduction of by-catch in these fisheries the final ex-vessel price for Alaska pollock fisheries would decline to the lower limit of about *$80 per metric ton*. This price is about the same as that paid on the high seas for Alaska pollock purchased from Soviet vessels by Japanese surimi-processing motherships. The round fish price, including some fish with roe, was fixed with the USSR at $81.15 per metric ton for 1977.[44]

Applying lower U.S. dollar and yen exchange rates for 1977 ($1=235 yen), ex-vessel prices in Japan for U.S. Alaska pollock fisheries increased from *$96 to $136 per metric ton* of round fish.

It is much more difficult to establish the ex-vessel price for species harvested in the Northeast Pacific waters by the Soviet Bloc fishing vessels. It is known that the price of fish in its processing and distribution states is maintained at artificially low levels, and fishing operations of distant-water fleets are heavily subsidized. Another problem is the determination of the proper exchange rate for the U.S. dollar and the soft currencies of these states. Ex-vessel prices are fixed by the local authorities in eastern countries and do not necessarily reflect the real market value of fish landed. Table 7.18 illustrates some of these problems.

## TABLE 7.18

AVERAGE EX-VESSEL PRICE FOR ROUND ALASKA POLLOCK AND COD IN THE
USSR AND POLAND (1976)
(PER KG)

| | Pollock | | Cod | |
|---|---|---|---|---|
| Country | Local currency | U.S. $ | Local currency | U.S. $ |
| USSR | 0.25 rubles | 0.19[a] | 0.32 rubles | 0.24 |
| Poland | 2.80 zlotys | 0.07[b] | 2.80 zlotys | 0.07 |

Source: W. Kaczynski. "The Role of Distant-Water and Coastal Fleets in Fisheries of Lower Market Value Species within the 200-mile Economic Zone" (with example of Alaska pollock), Institute for Marine Studies (University of Washington: September 1977).

[a]Ruble-dollar exchange rate applied here is $1.34 per ruble.

[b]Zloty-dollar exchange rate applied is $1 per 42 zlotys (approximate foreign trade exchange rate in 1976).

In the USSR and Poland ex-vessel and retail prices for fish reflect the general tendency in all Soviet Bloc countries to keep the basic food products on a relatively low level. According to many Eastern Bloc economists, food prices should be increased nearly 100 percent[45] to reflect true economic interrelationships between costs of production and market values. It seems reasonable to consider the present price levels for fish in the Socialist countries as informative data only. Taking into account all the above-mentioned precautions, it can be observed in table 7.18 that the ex-vessel price of Alaska pollock calculated in this chapter for the Soviet Union is about $190 per metric ton, whereas the ex-vessel price for cod would be around $240. In Poland, Alaska pollock and cod would cost only $70 per metric ton.

Table 7.19 summarizes the ex-vessel prices for Alaska pollock species of some of the most important users of this resource.

TABLE 7.19

ESTIMATED EX-VESSEL PRICE FOR ALASKA POLLOCK IN
PRINCIPAL HARVESTING COUNTRIES
($ PER MT)

| Country | Price |
|---------|-------|
| United States | $220 |
| Soviet Union | 190 |
| Japan | 96–136 |
| Poland | 70 |

We can expect that Alaska pollock ex-vessel prices in Japan could increase if, after restrictions imposed by the United States and the Soviet Union, Japan is unable to replace this species with another to continue highly demanded surimi production at the current level. Ex-vessel price for Alaska pollock could also increase after implementation of higher license fees for harvesting in the USSR and U.S. economic zone fishing grounds.

## Costs-Benefits Studies as a Basis for Ex-Vessel Price Determination

The costs of fishing effort, together with the benefits realized from these activities by foreign nations, can serve as a basis for establishing proper license fees for given fisheries. Also knowledge of the vessels' age, condition, and construction cost factors are useful for projecting future foreign demand for U.S. fish resources.[46]

Perhaps the most difficult problem in this field is the production costs on board the long-range ships, which usually deliver ready-made fish products for the home or foreign consumer market. The complexity of this problem is illustrated in figure 7.5. It can be seen that the harvesting, handling, processing, freezing, and transportation costs occur mainly on the sea. It is frequently difficult to separate one cost from another. If the vessel is changing fishing grounds or harvesting various species, the costs become more and more complex.

Perhaps the most convenient way to deal with these problems is to establish average daily operational costs separately for harvesting and support ships engaged in the coastal fishing within the quota allocation system. Operational costs of any distant-water fishing vessel are composed of the following items: (1) variable costs of fishing or traveling activities on the sea (fuel oil, food, salaries, packages, fishing gear, etc.); (2) fixed costs of maintaining the vessel in constant technical readiness (repairs, depreciation, insurance, administration, etc.); (3) other direct costs of operation (materials, equipment, etc.); and (4) transportation and support services of auxiliary ships. It is well known that the overwhelming majority of a distant-water fishing vessel's costs depends on the operational time on the sea. Thus, knowing the number of days spent by a given vessel on the sea and its daily costs of operation, it is possible to establish operational costs for given fisheries.

The benefits of the distant-water fishing activities could be calculated by summing the value of fish and fish products based on the existing ex-vessel price for a given species and average percentage of subsidy received by owner from the governmental funds. An actual ex-vessel price increased by state financial support forms a more realistic value of fish cargo delivered by the distant-water fishing fleet to its home distribution network.

## POSSIBLE DIRECT BENEFITS AND CONSTRAINTS OF LOWER MARKET-VALUE SPECIES, USING FOREIGN FLEETS

After implementation of the 200-mile fisheries zone, the United States and Canada became the owners of some of the largest commercial fishery resources in the world. Part of these resources are already intensively exploited by domestic fishermen, in particular all salmon species, shellfish, and some fin fishes such as halibut, haddock, Pacific ocean perch, cod, herring, and others. They are considered to be very valuable, and there is a high demand for them in the local consumer market. It can be expected that the future demand for these fish will be even stronger and, consequently, their price will probably increase.

However, the U.S. and Canadian Northeast Pacific coastal waters are also abundant in species of lower market value, which are only partially utilized or not developed by the domestic fisheries at all. Such species as Alaska pollock, dogfish, hake, Atka mackerel, and others have been harvested for many years exclusively by foreign distant-water fishing fleets. They are able to catch these lower-valued species, preserve or process them on board, and deliver them in large quantities to their home ports. Part of the catch is shipped (in processed state) back to the United States. For example, in 1976 the U.S. imported Alaska pollock fillets frozen in blocks for a value of U.S. $19,804,303.[47]

Extension of national jurisdiction over coastal resources will certainly accelerate the development of underutilized species by local fishermen. It can be expected that in the long run these resources will be harvested principally by the coastal states. This will be done by increasing the existing fishing and processing capacity as well as by improving the economic efficiency with which the resources are utilized.

Full development of underutilized fishing potential in the Northeast Pacific region can be realized through the expansion of large-scale specialized industrial trawl fisheries. This will require the introduction of a new, economically optimal type of fishing vessel, as well as development of a land-based processing industry specializing in these species.

Among the most important species allocated to the distant-water fishing fleets operating in the eastern Bering Sea and Gulf of Alaska are the bottom sea resources, particularly Alaska pollock. The fishing potential of this species is high but only a small part of it is actually taken by the U.S. fishermen (table 7.20).

For 1977, the domestic catch of Alaska pollock was expected to reach only 1,000 metric tons in the Gulf of Alaska, whereas during 1978, it was expected to increase to 17,700 metric tons. In the Bering Sea in 1977, the domestic catch of Alaska pollock was practically nonexistent.

By 1980, the domestic catch of pollock in the Gulf of Alaska was 12,791 MT and, in the Bering Sea, 10,788 MT.[48]

Alaska pollock, unlike many other groundfish species, is a difficult fish to handle. It is subject to rapid deterioration and is difficult to process. These difficulties have been overcome by means of rapid freezing within a few hours after the fish is caught, followed by storage in low temperatures ($-20°C$). However, during long periods of cold storage (about 6 months), this fish deteriorates more rapidly than other species. This particular characteristic of the Alaska pollock is a serious problem from a quality standpoint.

Although highly expensive in operation, the large factory trawlers with processing plants and freezing capacity on board, used by Japan, the Soviet Union, and other distant-water fishing nations, are probably the principal factor in successful development of Alaska pollock resources in U.S. coastal waters. These states were able to successfully develop their processing technologies and find multiple uses for this species in their home consumer markets. In Japan, Alaska pollock is used primarily as a raw material for production of fish jelly, mincemeat, and fresh and cured products; in the Soviet Union, South Korea, and Poland it is used mainly for production of fillets and dressed fish frozen in blocks. Alaska pollock frequently serve as raw material for canned and other prepared fish-food products. A large percentage of the catches are reduced to fish meal. Japanese factory trawlers reduced

TABLE 7.20

ALASKA POLLOCK FISHING POTENTIAL AND ALLOCATIONS FOR
DOMESTIC AND FOREIGN FLEETS
(METRIC TONS)

| Area | 1977 | | | 1978 | | | |
| | Optimum yield (OY) | U.S. capacity | Total quota for foreign fleets | Optimum yield (OY) | U.S. capacity | Total quota for foreign fleets | Reserve (20% of OY) |
| --- | --- | --- | --- | --- | --- | --- | --- |
| Gulf of Alaska | 150,000 | 1,000 | 149,000 | 168,000 | 17,700 | 117,340 | 33,760 |
| Bering Sea and Aleutian Islands | 950,000 | — | 950,000 | 950,000 | — | 950,000 | — |
| Total | 1,100,000 | 1,000 | 1,099,000 | 1,118,000 | 17,700 | 1,067,340 | 33,760 |

Source: *Preliminary Management Plan of the North Pacific Fishery Management Council* (Anchorage, 1977).

nearly 50 percent of their Alaska pollock harvest for fish meal; shore plants only about 6 percent. About 70 percent of the total catch was used for food purposes in 1970. The remainder was processed into fish meal used to feed poultry and fish.[49]

If rationally managed by the coastal state, Alaska pollock distributed in the U.S. 200-mile fisheries zone could support long-lasting fisheries on a large commercial scale. After a certain period, an expected average of one million metric tons would be available annually for fishermen. In managing these resources, the coastal state faces some alternatives related to their allocation and utilization. The most important are:

1. *Continuation of the current system based on quota allocation for foreign countries.* In this case, practically all of the harvestable stock of Alaska pollock would be handed over to foreign nations. As previously mentioned, the economic benefits generated by this management policy depends on the license fees imposed on foreign fishing vessels.

2. *Prompt development of the domestic fishing effort for Alaska pollock with simultaneous expansion of the existing land-based processing capacity.*

It is well known that the U.S. consumer market for Alaska pollock is insufficient. This problem, however, is the result of many factors. The most important problems are the capacity of the existing domestic fishing fleet to catch Alaska pollock, as well as its ability to preserve it on board. According to surveys carried out by NORFISH, at the University of Washington,[50] modern combination crabber-trawlers are the only class of vessel that can feasibly participate in the pollock fishery. These vessels are known to be of sufficient horsepower and size to harvest pollock with otter trawls. In 1979 there were about 225 such vessels in the Alaska region, principally designed for shellfish fisheries. This fleet is not fully utilized, and consequently could catch Alaska pollock after the shellfish season is closed. This effort could bring more than 60,000 metric tons of round Alaska pollock with a net value of more than $10 million.[51]

The above mentioned numbers are obtained as a result of some simplifying assumptions. The most important is that shellfish skippers would enter the Alaska pollock fisheries when their crab and shrimp seasons have been completed. According to the fish-ticket landing data for 1974, when there were substantially fewer vessels in the fleet, there was an excess of fishing capacity in this fleet that, if utilized, could have produced more than one thousand week-unit trips for Alaska pollock. However, according to another author,[52] most of the existing fishing vessels' operating time in the Alaska region is rather fully utilized, and with the yet unharvested potential of other crab species and bottomfish of the Bering Sea, it is obvious that the present fleet must be augmented in numbers to utilize the Alaska pollock fully. Since 1974, the fleet has grown rapidly.

Another factor related to the Alaska pollock fisheries is that the fish deteriorates rapidly and has a very short shelf-life in the hold compared to other species. This considerably hinders exploitation of these resources by present domestic fishing vessels, which generally keep their catches on ice or in refrigerated sea water. Consequently, it will probably be necessary to design a new type of specialized trawler that is capable of keeping the fish in proper freezing temperatures, or to develop some processing activities on board. During the last cooperative research of the Sea Fisheries Institute (Gdynia, Poland) and the National

Marine Fisheries Service (Seattle, Washington) held on board the Polish research vessel *Profesor Siedlecki*, it was confirmed again that for practical purposes the storage life of Alaska pollock is extremely short unless deeply frozen, no matter what kind of preserving media are used (table 7.20). It is practically impossible to store the fresh fish on the deck or in the hold without chilling; the raw material, after six hours of being caught, is not suitable for human consumption.

If existing vessels are to be engaged in Alaska pollock fisheries, the maximum storage time for fish should be shortened in relation to that indicated in table 7.21 by at least twelve working hours. This time is necessary for handling in the harbor, transportation, and freezing or processing the fish in the land-based processing plant.

TABLE 7.21

STORAGE OF ALASKA POLLOCK AND PRESERVING METHOD ON BOARD

| Preserving method | Maximum storage time for human consumption (hours) |
|---|---|
| Stored on the deck in a pen without any chilling media[a] | 6 |
| Stored in refrigerated sea water (RSW) at temperature of 0°C (32°F) | 24 |
| Stored in flake ice (equal proportion of fish to ice) | 48 |
| Stored in slush ice (or slush ice and $CO_2$) | 96 (4 days) |

Source: Preliminary Report, Gulf of Alaska Research Cruise of R/V *Profesor Siedlecki*, First and Second Leg, Fish Processing Technology Laboratory, July 1977.

[a]The question is still open as to whether or not the fish stored for six hours on deck will be suitable for further processing, including subsequent freezing and the changes occurring in this process. This can be decided once all quality estimates are concluded after a six-month period of cold storage of fish.

Consequently, the vessel can keep on board her first haul of fish (a) in RSW, 12 hours; (b) in flake ice, 36 hours; and (c) in slush ice, 84 hours.

If we assume that the average coastal fishing vessel spends about one third of its time at sea for traveling purposes, then the range of operation from the base ports (for example, Dutch Harbor and Kodiak) will be limited to: (a) 4 hours of one-way trip, with 8 hours of harvesting activities; (b) 12 hours of one-way trip, with 24 hours of harvesting activities; and (c) 28 hours of one-way trip, with 56 hours of harvesting activities.

With the average speed of 10 knots, the vessel will be able to operate in fishing grounds a distance up to 40, 120 and 280 miles from her base port (see fig. 7.6). This includes many simplifications, but the general conclusion is perhaps universal for these fisheries, and can be expressed as follows: Unless the fish are deep frozen, all available preservation methods limit the geographical range of the fisheries to one part of the existing Alaska pollock resources, and even then only to partial utilization of their potential.

Foreign experience acquired during the last 15-year period of Alaska pollock harvesting activities indicates that the best way to assure high quality fish raw material for land-based processing plants is by quick freezing the fish immediately after they are hauled on board. Which, then, is the most appropriate fishing vessel for the Alaska pollock domestic

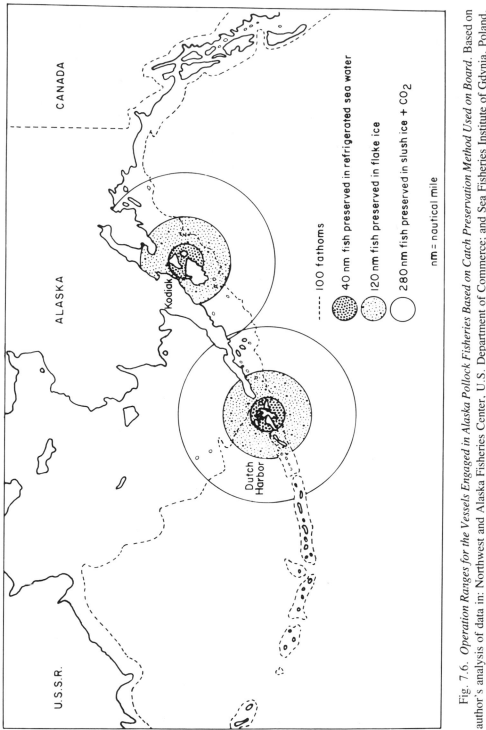

Fig. 7.6. *Operation Ranges for the Vessels Engaged in Alaska Pollock Fisheries Based on Catch Preservation Method Used on Board.* Based on author's analysis of data in: Northwest and Alaska Fisheries Center, U.S. Department of Commerce; and Sea Fisheries Institute of Gdynia, Poland. "Preliminary Report, Gulf of Alaska Research Cruise of R/V *Profesor Siedlecki*, First and Second Leg" (Fish Processing Technology Laboratory of the *Profesor Siedlecki*, July 1977).

fisheries? (a) It will certainly be a medium-sized trawler of rather high sea-worthiness, able to operate in icy conditions to assure the longest harvesting season and access to the northern portion of the northeast Bering Sea. Stern trawlers can carry on harvesting activities in worse hydrometeorological conditions than other types of fishing vessels. (b) The ship should be characterized by a relatively large hold capacity to enable her to carry the greatest volume of catch possible. This is because Alaska pollock will probably maintain its low ex-vessel price. When engaged in harvesting low-value species, profits for the shipowners are feasible only when massive catches are obtained. (c) Freezing facilities of fish or, at least, chilling installations will be required both to maintain the best quality of fish delivered to the processing plant and to increase the range of operation of the vessel. (d) The main propulsion engine should develop the necessary power (probably over 1,000 HP) to assure rather high speed (particularly for the vessels with chilling facilities on board only) and enable it to catch the fish distributed in deeper waters, up to 400−500 meters or even more. (e) All operations on board, particularly handling caught fish and use of nets, should be mechanized or automated to reduce the number of crew as much as possible. (f) If possible, the vessel should be designed for continuous fishing with two interchangeable trawl nets to shorten her time at sea.

Even this short review of the main characteristics of the future U.S. fishing vessel designed for the Alaska pollock fisheries indicates that its price can be rather high. One particularly strong factor is whether the U.S. would be willing to change its laws prohibiting importation of fishing vessels.

It is strongly recommended that Alaska pollock fisheries should be carried out by only a few, but large, specialized fishing companies, which would possibly include harvesting, processing and marketing (exporting) activities. Any dissipation of fishing effort among small individual fishermen to harvest these low-valued species would not be economically acceptable. Only large, financially strong owners would be able to develop the massive production process, and perhaps maintain its satisfactory economic efficiency.

## Processing and Marketing Aspects

The rapid development of Alaska pollock domestic fisheries should be tightly inter-related with simultaneous expansion of a land-based processing industry. Its location in the shortest distance from the most abundant fishing grounds would reduce the time of transportation and preservation of fish on board the fishing vessels. Dutch Harbor seems to be the best existing base port for Alaska pollock fisheries, both in the eastern Bering Sea and the Gulf of Alaska. Generally, the whole processing activities of Alaska pollock species should be centered in the Alaska area. The physical properties of the Alaska pollock flesh, its quick deterioration after being extracted from the sea, and frequent infestation with parasites, require a very careful handling and processing technology. This undoubtedly will contribute to higher costs for the land-based processing plants. The acceptance of Alaska pollock by the U.S. consumer market will be possible if the domestic industry is able to deliver the fish with high grade processing, and with competitive prices in relation to other groundfish products.

In Japan, this question was resolved by the invention of surimi and fish jelly production technologies. There are also many other examples where low-value species have been successfully utilized as a raw material for fish protein concentrate (FPC), fish flakes, fish sausages, and other products. In the United States, the last significant developments were the introduction of fish blocks and portions. According to NMFS researchers, even more product forms based on Alaska pollock as a raw material could be developed in the near future.[53] However, the existing fish processing industry on the Northeast Pacific coast of the U.S. does not have sufficient capacity to absorb massive supplies of Alaska pollock. It is oriented principally to process highly valuable fish and shellfish species like halibut, salmon, crab or shrimp. Lack of interest in development of the processing potential for Alaska pollock is caused by low market prices of fish products based on this species as well as by the strong competition of other fish products derived particularly from cod and other species, and by imported fish products consumed in the U.S. market.

## Joint Development of Lower Market-Value Species

In spite of considerable efforts made by the U.S. to accelerate the exploitation of the lower market-value species, a large part of them will probably not be utilized by the local fishermen for many years. Lack of sufficient and adequate fishing potential as well as nonexistent processing capacity for these species are the important obstacles to rapid development by the domestic fishing industry. However, the most immediate factor influencing the U.S. utilization of lower market-value species is the lack of marketing opportunities. In the present situation, the large scale commercial fisheries based on these resources could perhaps be developed as a source of seafood products sold in foreign markets. The 200-mile fisheries zone creates additional export opportunities for coastal states as a result of harvesting limitations imposed on the distant-water fishing nations and increasing world demand for fish products.

In the short run, U.S. and Canadian exportation of fish-food products based on the low-value species will probably be hampered by price competition of the low-cost fish-producing countries, or by payments difficulties of the potential importing states, particularly Eastern Bloc countries. In addition, distant-water nations that face fishing restrictions of coastal states and hard currency outlays for imported fish products will at first try to find more economically feasible sources of fish supply. They will simply look for new fishing grounds and new species, even if it is more expensive for their domestic economies. It is possible for them to take such measures because of their existing large harvesting potential, which is endangered by partial employment, or even scrapping. Can international cooperation alleviate these problems?

If we confront the most immediate interests of both sides (i.e., coastal states rich in low-value fishery resources, and distant-water fishing countries with large harvesting potential) it is possible to present the following comparative list of factors to stimulate cooperative exploitation of these resources (table 7.22).

With the growing fishing potential for groundfish fisheries of the Northeast Pacific coastal states, the surplus quota for the lower-value species, even after some overfished stocks are rebuilt, will certainly be gradually decreased. For distant-water fleets, one of the

TABLE 7.22

BALANCE SHEET OF COASTAL AND DISTANT-WATER FISHERIES AND
SPECIES OF LOW MARKET VALUE

| Coastal state (with 200-mile fisheries zone) | Distant-water fishing countries |
|---|---|
| Underutilized or partially exploited fishery resources (mainly low-value species) | Absence of or reduced coastal fishery resources. |
| Weak or nonexisting domestic demand for fish products derived from low-value species. | Traditionally high consumption of fish products (Japan, South Korea, etc.) or strong market for fish food as a result of internal agricultural production difficulties (Soviet Bloc countries). |
| Insufficient harvesting and processing potential. | Distant-water fishing fleets with factory trawlers and motherships designed for immediate processing on board. |
| Lack of experience and technology of massive utilization of low-value species for human consumption by local fishing industry. | Wide experience with harvesting know-how and processing technology, preservation and distribution networks. |
| Temporary lack of larger economic benefits for existing fishing industry if engaged in low-value species fisheries. | Massive fisheries, know-how, lower manpower costs (Japan, South Korea, Taiwan) or strong state subsidizing policy (Soviet Bloc countries). |

ways to overcome this tendency is to establish wide cooperative links with the coastal state's fishing industry. Cooperation in scientific research of the coastal fishery resources should be mentioned in particular. Foreign countries expect that cooperation can contribute to the identification of new resources that can produce a surplus potential, to better knowledge of actually exploited stocks, and to a positive attitude of the coastal state in future quota allocations and establishment of commercial cooperation in fisheries.

For example, Eastern Bloc countries that have experienced most recently the highest reductions in their Northeast Pacific fisheries are now seeking commercial cooperation in the form of joint ventures with U.S. and Canadian fishing companies. For the Socialist partners, the best solution will use existing factory trawlers and their crews for fish processing on board the vessels. Part or all of the fish products could be taken back to the Eastern country by auxiliary fleets. This would be in compensation for the foreign partner's costs of operation, the mixed fishing company, and as part of the total profit generated by its activities.

Taking into consideration the existing internal legal arrangements which, in the case of the United States, do not allow the discharge of fish in U.S. ports by foreign fishing vessels, other solutions can be suggested: direct exportation of the fish products from the vessels to foreign markets, or the creation of customs-free zones in U.S. fishing ports where the fish raw material could be processed and then sent abroad.

If a joint venture is not allowed to use the fishing ships of the foreign partner (an alternative undoubtedly least attractive for any foreign fishing country), the foreign partner could purchase the fish raw material from the U.S. fishermen, as has been proposed by the

USSR and South Korea. This form of joint operations is not, however, a joint venture in the strict sense, but rather a contracted sale of fresh fish to the foreign processor. Proposed arrangements by Soviets and South Koreans for Alaska pollock joint fisheries can serve as a confirmation of this principle. Since the catch would be taken by U.S or Canadian fishermen, foreign partners expect that the catch would not be chargeable to their quota allocations but would come out of the share reserved for U.S. or Canadian harvest.

It is obvious that joint fishing ventures are and will continue to be authorized to exploit nonutilized or underutilized species. In Northeast Pacific waters, the principal species could only be Alaska pollock, although Eastern Bloc and Western European countries are far more interested in more valuable fishes like cod, hake, flounders, herring, and rockfish; Japan is interested in Alaska pollock as raw material for surimi.

Joint ventures established by U.S. companies with one country may constitute a serious threat for other foreign interests if they result in reduction of their future quota allocations. For example, the 1977 TAC for Alaska pollock in the Gulf of Alaska was 150,000 MT. Of this, only 1,000 MT was retained for U.S. harvest; 149,000 MT was allocated for foreign nations. The proposed U.S.—South Korean joint venture, which would have harvested 130,000 MT, would have effectively allocated all that amount to South Korea. Thus, if the TAC had remained at the 150,000 MT level in 1978, the amount allocated among other nations would have dropped from 149,000 MT to 20,000 MT.[54] This factor remains important given the criteria for allocations adopted by the U.S. and described in chapter 6.

If we consider U.S. fishing regulations as the only point of reference for the international joint fishing operations in this country, the transfer of product from U.S. fishermen to foreign factory ships seems to be the most feasible solution. Such cooperation could be established on an interim basis, being of short duration with minimal financial engagement of both parties. Equity fishing joint ventures in which only capital from foreign countries (without their fishing vessels in such operations) are also possible, although capital investments in hard currencies would also be made by foreign distant-water states, preferably in coastal countries that offer the best business opportunities. In the United States or Canada, equity joint ventures for underexploited or unexploited species are theoretically possible, but not for highly valuable species like salmon, halibut, and shellfish.

Underdeveloped species are generally of low market price and are difficult to process or preserve. For the time being, they do not assure quick economic return. Alaska pollock can be mentioned as the typical species on which joint ventures could eventually be allowed to concentrate. With hard currency capital engagement, any foreign partner would look for the highest income possible and the lowest costs of exploitation. In fisheries, this goal can be achieved if the joint venture has an opportunity to harvest highly valuable species with boats of low operating costs. Factory trawlers prove to be a high-cost operation.

In the U.S. the ex-vessel price of Alaska pollock is far below the price of cod, but in Eastern Bloc countries these differences are negligible, or do not even exist. There are more examples of this phenomenon involving other species and other countries. Consequently, it is expected that distant-water fishing nations will be very interested in harvesting stocks that are not developed by local fishermen in the U.S.

For both the U.S. and Canada, the joint venture concept deserves careful consideration as a means of quick development of their own harvesting and processing potential. Perhaps the most attractive incentive for U.S. partners is the opportunity to export coastal resources that otherwise would not find their way to the foreign markets. In cooperative fishing activities with distant-water factory trawlers and motherships, coastal fishermen can better utilize their existing fishing fleet and harvest the resources that, being too far from base ports, would not be accessible for them. In the long run, joint ventures may serve as a vehicle to facilitate independent utilization of underutilized resources by the coastal state.

One of the principal conditions of successful international joint ventures operation is the political and social climate existing in the potential host country. Fishery activites, if they are developed by an international company, should be planned for a rather longer period of time, guaranteeing return of invested capital for both sides. The United States and Canada have some interest in joint exploitation of selected coastal resources, but it is based on short-term policies influenced by strong pressures of the local fishing communities. They generally reject broad cooperative links with foreign distant-water fishing nations.

Romeo LeBlanc, Minister of Fisheries of Canada in 1977, announced Canada's basically restrictive policies toward joint ventures in the fishing industry after the 200-mile economic zone. The new policy permits only experimental projects lasting no more than one year, provided that the terms are strict and work to the benefit of Canadian fishermen. LeBlanc expressed concern that even the present small-scale joint ventures (on the Canadian East Coast principally), were causing tension between different elements of the industry and between different regions. He emphasized that in the future, joint ventures in the fishing industry would be tolerated only if they fit into the goals of overall fisheries planning and if they serve primarily as data gathering tools.[55] In the near future, we can thus expect rather reduced possibilities in the U.S. for international cooperation in joint exploitation of the Northeast Pacific coastal resources. For distant-water fishing fleets, the principal alternative in this region is harvesting within a strictly limited entry regime involving license fees and quota allocation at levels that will probably be lowered on a year-to-year basis.

For the U.S. and Canada, it is perhaps true that joint ventures will not be the only and best long-run solution in development of underutilized species within their 200-mile fisheries zone. However, in the short run, joint utilization of these resources with distant-water fishing nations should be considered as a feasible way to gradually change resource exploitation patterns imposed by the 200-mile fisheries zone regime.

## SUMMARY

Long-range fisheries account for a significant part of the catch in virtually all parts of the world ocean. The North, Central, and Southeast Atlantic, and the North Pacific are among their most important areas of operation.

Only a few nations are clearly leading in distant-water fishing activities. The Soviet Union and Japan are the most developed long-range fleet owners. They are also heavily dependent on United States and Canadian coastal fishery resources. Soviet Bloc states taken as a whole possessed, in 1976, almost 60 percent of the world's total tonnage of fishing vessels and 95 percent of the support ships over 100 gross tons in size. The long-range fishing potential of Japan, South Korea, and Taiwan taken all together, is many times lower than that of Soviet Bloc nations. One of the most significant features, the importance of which became clear only recently, is the fact that foundations for modern long-range fisheries were laid on a highly restricted raw material base. Actually, the magnitude of these distant-water fleets reflects a tremendous commitment to the exploitation of ever-scarcer overseas fishing resources.

The principal task of the sea fisheries industry in the Eastern Bloc countries is to complement the animal protein supplies for local consumer markets. Agriculture in these states is still unable to develop sufficiently high production. With increasing demand for meat products, distant-water fisheries are considered an important food-generating activity. Consequently, further development of the fishing industry is strongly promoted by Eastern Bloc governments.

In the Soviet Union, Poland, and other Socialist countries, production costs of fish protein are increasing at accelerating rates. Even small increases of catch have to be paid with higher and higher inputs, both in capital and manpower. Nevertheless, the negative economic results of Eastern Bloc fishing activities, as well as unfavorable changes in patterns of world fishery resources exploitation, do not impede further development of their distant-water fishing fleets. Internal needs, seen from a near-term perspective (meat shortage, employment opportunities, shipbuilding potential utilizations, foreign trade tasks, etc.), are apparently stronger than international obstacles faced by distant-water fleets.

The next decade will thus be characterized by increasing research and fishing efforts in utilization of the open sea living resources as well as continued presence in 200-mile exclusive fisheries zones on the basis of bilateral agreements.

The Northeast Pacific is considered by many fishing nations to be an important and attractive region for their distant-water fishing operations. After implementation of the 200-mile fisheries zone by the Soviet Union, South Korea lost practically all possibilities of harvesting fishery resources in the Pacific coastal waters of the USSR, and will look for new fishing grounds in the Northeast Pacific. The Japanese catch in this area is declining. On the other hand, Mexico was accepted as a newcomer to the U.S. Northeast Pacific fishing grounds. Consequently, the pressure on the Northeast Pacific fishery resources by foreign long-range fleets may increase considerably.

This trend can be extremely unfavorable for Soviet Bloc nations, as the increasing allocations for South Korea, Mexico, or Japan may result in reduction of fish quotas for the Soviet Union and Poland, and may impede future access to these resources for Cuba or East Germany. As a result, a large part of their fishing potential could have considerable difficulties in full utilization of its designed capacity.

High-seas living resources not included in national jurisdiction zones are considered as an important alternative for some distant-water fishing nations, although the costs of their utilization will be extremely high. Tuna fisheries can expand quickly in the Soviet Union and other Socialist nations, and these fisheries have a chance to become the first economically profitable long-range harvesting activity in these states. They will also contribute to an increased pressure on the world tuna resources, and limit the economic rent of all present and future tuna harvesters.

Another alternative for distant-water fishing fleets will be found in Antarctic krill, fish, and squid of the southern ocean. Experimental krill fisheries are developed mainly by the USSR and Japan, while other nations like Poland and West Germany are sending numerous expeditions preceding full-scale utilization of these resources. The krill reserves could provide an outlet for excessive catches of other species, helping at the same time to remove pressure on valuable food fish stocks in other parts of the world. Fin fish, principally bottom species, have already supported large harvesting efforts of the USSR fleets and were probably depleted mainly around subantarctic and Antarctic islands (South Georgia, Kerguelen, etc.).

Operations of distant-water fishing fleets in Antarctic waters will incur high costs and will not be possible without financial support of the governments interested in fishery resources of this area. It is not surprising that State-owned Soviet fisheries are so much more advanced in the rapid transfer of their fleets to the Antarctic fishing grounds.

All these alternatives will not replace full resource utilization within coastal zones. In the Northeast Pacific, foreign distant-water fishing fleets are still allowed to harvest about 95 percent of the disposable fishery resources in this area.

Of the total value of fish taken by foreign fleets, which is about $200 million, the U.S. will recover about $8 million in the form of license and poundage fees. There are many doubts related to the methods and criteria applied in fixing these fees. In the long run, they should be reevaluated and better adjusted to the existing fish prices in the markets of other nations. The value of processed fish product delivered to the home ports by distant-water fishing fleets is hardly comparable to the product of traditional coastal fisheries, which is mainly fresh or iced round fish. If the coastal state were willing to fix its license fee on the foreign ex-vessel price basis, it would be forced to develop extended cost-benefit studies to determine the proper range for fixing the price. Other external factors like world tendencies in ex-vessel prices for similar or substitute species must also be taken into account. Distant-water fleets might relinquish surplus coastal resources if they can find alternative and less expensive fishing opportunities. Local ex-vessel prices of the coastal state could serve as a starting point to establish a final price list for foreign fleets, but this alternative will not necessarily reflect real demand for a given species in distant-water fishing nations.

For the species not harvested at all by the coastal nation, the ex-vessel price as a basis for the license fee is most controversial because it may be established arbitrarily. Internal market prices of the distant-water fishing nation could be taken into consideration, although they frequently do not reflect the real production costs. Many foreign fisheries are heavily subsidized and market prices are artificially low.

It can be expected, however, that in the long run all the coastal surplus resources of the U.S. and Canada will be harvested principally by the coastal fishermen. This will be possible as soon as new fishing and processing potential is built, and economic efficiency of lower market-value species harvesting is improved. The fishing potential of these species, particularly Alaska pollock, is high, although only a small part of it is actually taken by U.S. fishermen.

In spite of many efforts made by the U.S. to accelerate the exploitation of the lower market-value species, a large part of them will probably remain nonutilized by the local fishermen for many years ahead. In the present U.S. market situation, large-scale commercial fisheries, based on the underutilized Northeast Pacific fishery resources, could be developed as a source of seafood products sold in foreign markets. International cooperation in their resource utilization could help resolve some of the existing difficulties the coastal states have in harvesting, processing, and marketing.

With international cooperation U.S. fishermen would be able to begin full-scale harvesting activities much earlier, and perhaps economically more attractively, than with noncooperative fishery activities. If only presently existing U.S. bottom fishing potential in the Gulf of Alaska waters were to be engaged in cooperative Alaska pollock fisheries, and 60,000 tons of fish were to be sold to foreign factory motherships at the price of U.S. $220 per ton, the total value of these deliveries would amount to about U.S. $13 million.

If properly managed by the host country, cooperative fisheries that specialize in some underutilized species can contribute to quicker development of the coastal states' fishing industry based on these species. However, joint ventures are considered by foreign nations to be an attenuation of restrictions imposed within the 200-mile economic zone. Foreign partners offer wide experience in full-scale harvesting activities and export markets for fish products. In joint fishing operations, coastal fishermen could better utilize their existing fishing potential and harvest the resources which, being too far from the base ports, would not be accessible for them.

The responsibility for international cooperation decisions lies with the management agencies of the coastal state. They could accept joint resource utilization if its fits into the goals of overall fisheries policies of the coastal nation. In the case of the U.S. and Canada, joint ventures are not the only long-run solution in the development of underutilized species, although, in the short term, joint utilization of these resources with foreign nations could be economically attractive both for distant-water fleets and coastal fishermen. If, however, the Northeast Pacific coastal states choose a noncooperative utilization of their resources, the principal alternative in this area for distant-water fishing fleets will remain a highly restrictive quota allocation system.

# PART II

# Marine Transportation on the North Pacific

# 8

# International Marine Transportation

This chapter describes the pattern of commercial ocean shipping in foreign trades on the North Pacific. In terms of scale of activity, shipping is one of the most important marine uses. It provides the predominant vehicle for international trade and creates significant global economic benefits. The economic organization of the world's commercial shipping industry is both extensive and complex, and antedates all other attempts at international management of an ocean activity.

Shipborne trade produces certain negative effects, however. Accidents from collisions with other ships or with fixed structures, or from groundings, can result in loss of life and property, oil or chemical spills, and other types of damage to ocean uses, users, and the marine environment. Spillage of waste materials from ships can be an acute problem in congested waters. And commercial shipping operations (coastal, as well as international) can interfere with fishing, recreation, aquaculture, mining, passenger carriage and, due to congestion, commercial shipping itself.

The presentation of commodity trade flow data here serves the dual purpose of facilitating an analysis of international trade relationships and of multiple use conflicts in the North Pacific. Financial aspects are discussed first, and cargo tonnage movements described later in the chapter.

## FINANCIAL ASPECTS OF SHIPPING

Maritime commerce is carried by a fleet of mobile ships ready to respond to commercial opportunities throughout the world. Competition among much of the shipping business, together with fleet mobility, tends to equalize the global price rates at which shipping services are offered. The commercial conditions for petroleum tankers and dry bulk carriers, for example, are largely the same, regardless of the ocean in which they operate. Therefore, in general, it is not reasonable to describe transportation on the North Pacific as unique; it must be described in relation to the global market. However, liner operations, which account for less than one-quarter of the tons of cargo carried annually by shipping, are somewhat different and are described separately.[1]

## The Charter Market for Deep-Sea Trades

Marine transportation can be classified according to two general types of service: charter (bulk) shipping and liner shipping. Charter shipping is nonscheduled, tends to deal in shipload lots, will go anywhere, and sets prices through free competition. Liner trade carries less-than-shipload lots, usually sails on rigid schedules on defined routes, and are ordinarily cartelized.

Charter shipping can be subdivided into the carriage of liquid bulk (crude oil, oil products, chemicals, and other liquid bulk) or dry bulk (grains, metal ores, and coal, for example). The liquid and dry bulk ship charter markets are indistinguishable in the sense that both fit the classic model of free competition. Furthermore, a large fleet of combination dry and liquid bulk carriers can shift between the liquid and dry trades as profit conditions warrant. Thus chartering rates for liquid and dry bulk ship tonnage is unified in price competition, and brokerage houses in New York and London deal in liquid, dry and combination vessels. The preponderance of all chartered vessel tonnage is engaged in the carriage of crude oil, and is the focus of this section. The discussion is specialized but contains valuable information that has gone largely unrecorded in the marine literature.[2]

To explain the functioning and present condition of the world crude oil tanker market, it is best to start with the prices paid for services. These prices are usually quoted according to an index called *Worldscale*. The Worldscale index that describes prevailing transport prices on a given trade route is the ratio of the current market price per long ton of crude oil delivered for a prompt (commencing within a few weeks), single round-trip voyage on that route (called the *spot rate*), to the *flat* or *base rate* price. The flat rate is the price per long ton of oil delivered that would permit a reference tanker vessel operating on the given route to earn only a *fixed hire element* of $1,800 per day, and to recover its fuel costs, port charges, and canal tolls. Table 8.1 lists the reference tanker's characteristics.

### TABLE 8.1

WORLDSCALE REFERENCE CRUDE OIL TANKER CHARACTERISTICS

| Characteristic | Description |
| --- | --- |
| Deadweight tonnage at summer draft | 19,500 long tons (T-2 class Tanker) |
| Summer draft laden in salt water | 30′6″ (9.33 meters) |
| Average service speed | 14 knots (25.9 kilometers per hour) |
| Daily bunker fuel consumption at sea | 28 long tons high viscosity fuel oil |
| Daily bunker fuel consumption in port | 5 long tons high viscosity fuel oil |
| Fixed hire element | $1800/day |
| Where built | Japanese or equivalent cost shipyard |
| Crew nationality | International |

As of 1970, the $1,800 fixed hire element was sufficient to cover the capital (depreciation and amortization), maintenance, insurance, and labor costs (the fixed costs) of the reference vessel. Thus to determine the long-run cost per day of operating a reference tanker on a particular ocean trade route, you would add up the fuel costs, port charges, and canal tolls (i.e., all the variable costs) of operating on that route for one round-trip voyage, divide by the number of days required for a round trip and add them to the fixed hire element. The cost per day converted to a per-ton-of-oil-delivered basis is the *required freight rate* or the rate per ton of oil delivered that the reference ship had to earn to break even when operating on the given route.

As a Worldscale example, suppose that in September, 1978, an oil importer in Japan wanted a tanker to bring in 190,000 long tons of crude oil from the Persian Gulf. This would require a 200,000 deadweight tons (dwt) tanker. By checking with a broker, the importer found that a 300,000 dwt tanker was recently chartered for a similar run at a Worldscale 45. The importer could then feel comfortable if a contract for a 200,000 dwt vessel was made at Worldscale 48, as this was essentially the going rate. Since the flat rate on this trade was $10.14 at that time, Worldscale 48 implied that the importer would pay 48 percent of the flat rate, or $4.87 per long ton of oil delivered. The total transportation cost would be 190,000 times $4.87 or $924,768.

The flat rates are prepared for several thousand petroleum trade routes by the International Tanker Nominal Freight Scale Association of London, England.[3] Sample flat rates for the North Pacific are listed in table 8.2.

The fixed hire element is seldom altered to reflect the effect of inflation on fixed costs, the last adjustment being in 1970. The other elements (fuel costs, etc.) of the flat rate are adjusted for inflation on a semi-annual basis. Thus, the fixed hire element plus fuel and other

TABLE 8.2

WORLDSCALE FLAT RATES FOR THE NORTH PACIFIC BULK PETROLEUM TRADES
(SEPTEMBER 1978)

($ PER LONG TON OF OIL DELIVERED)

| Route[a] | Rate |
|---|---|
| Indonesia to Japan (Dumai) → (Yokohama) | $ 5.26 |
| Indonesia to West Coast USA (Dumai) → (San Francisco) | $10.95 |
| Persian Gulf to Japan (Ras Tanura) → (Yokohama) | $10.14 |
| Persian Gulf to West Coast USA (Ras Tanura) → (San Francisco) | $15.88 |

Source: *Worldscale*, published semi-annually by the International Tanker Nominal Freight Scale Association (see Ref. 3).

[a] Based on full round trip by most economical route

costs is a nominal figure, and is not equal to the required freight rate except at the time the fixed hire element is revised.

The use of the Worldscale index economizes in reporting current global tanker market conditions, since all international tanker trades tend to experience similar trends in Worldscale. Furthermore, one can tell readily from the index whether the market is attractive or unattractive for investors.

The Worldscale index describes the contract price agreed to by buyers and sellers of only a small portion of all the ships operating in the crude oil trades. Roughly one-third of all tankers are owned by the major oil companies (British Petroleum, Exxon, Gulf, Mobil, Royal Dutch Shell, Socal, and Texaco) and are used to carry their own or proprietary cargoes. The rest of the world tanker fleet is chartered from companies with no oil interests (the independents) by the major oil interests for multiple voyages or for extensive time periods. When charter rates for these transactions are recalculated on a per voyage basis, momentary market fluctuations are smoothed out, and the per voyage rate approaches the required freight rate as the length of the charter approaches the vessel's expected lifetime. In view of this, one might ask, Why emphasize the spot rate when describing the market for tanker tonnage when more than 90 percent of all tonnage is not in the *spot market* but is either employed in proprietary carriage or is time-chartered at a different rate?

The spot rate describes the current market price of the *marginal ship* (the ship whose services are employed to bring the supply and demand of shipping capacity into balance at the market price). According to the principle of price equals marginal or opportunity cost in a competitive market, the spot rate describes the opportunity cost for all ships trading regardless of who owns them or how they are actually chartered. Even a ship that is owned by an oil major and is used exclusively to carry proprietary cargoes and is never chartered could be spot-chartered to someone else at any time. Thus, foregoing the opportunity to *let* the ship at the prevailing spot rate is an opportunity cost to owners. The cost equals the spot rate revenue foregone. The same reasoning applies to tonnage on time charter that can always be *relet* in the spot market by those holding the current contract. Thus, the spot rate applicable to the various oil trades describes the opportunity cost of, and therefore the true price of, all tonnage trading whether or not the tonnage has actually been spot-chartered.

Due to the competitiveness of the tanker market, it is rare for the numerical value of the Worldscale index for a particular route to depart significantly from the value for other routes. Small systematic differences between the rates offered on different routes can exist, however, because port depths may restrict the size of vessels, forcing some trades to use smaller vessels than would otherwise be used. Larger vessels are generally more economical per cargo ton to operate than are smaller vessels if a large quantity of oil is to be moved.

Figure 8.1 depicts the Worldscale rates applicable to North Pacific trades. It is evident that Worldscale rates in the trades originating from Indonesia tend to be slightly higher than those from the Persian Gulf. The average-sized tanker fixed for the Indonesia–Japan trade was roughly 50,000 dwt in 1977, whereas it was 100,000 dwt for the Indonesia to U.S. West Coast trade.[4] Smaller tankers are used on the former route because Japan tends to import smaller quantities of Indonesia's heavy, high sulfur crude than of Persian Gulf crude, and

because Japan's imports from Indonesia tend to come from newer producing areas, which
have shallow depth loading berths.[5]

Figure 8.2 shows a longer history of Worldscale rates, indicating that the world tanker
industry is subject to incredible swings in the prices paid for shipping services. The peaks in
rates are referred to as *booms* because owners during those periods may make huge profits by
letting their vessels in the spot markets. In the depressed periods rates barely cover variable

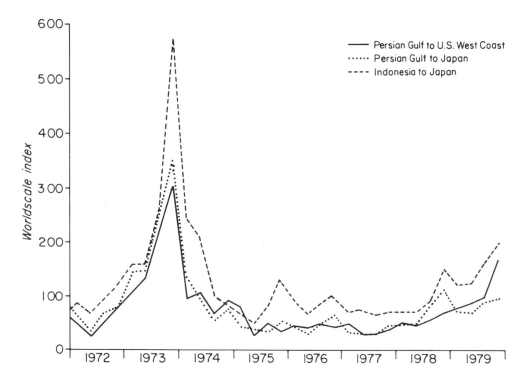

Fig 8.1. *Spot Charter Worldscale Index, North Pacific Ocean Trades* (unweighted quarterly
average). Source: *Chartering Annual* (New York: Maritime Research, Inc., various years). A. Persian
Gulf to U.S. West Coast; B. Persian Gulf to Japan; C. Indonesia to Japan.

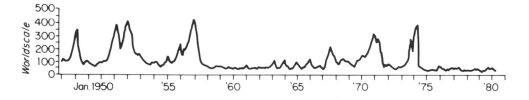

Fig.8.2. *Spot Charter Rate 1947−1980* (Persian Gulf to United Kingdom or Continent). Source:
J. W. Devanney, course notes (Massachusetts Institute of Technology, 1976), and *Seatrade* (various
months).

costs. Rarely is the market at a level where owners are breaking even, although in the long run profits made in the boom periods are sufficient to maintain a continuous market for tanker tonnage.

Because Worldscale was set up shortly after the end of World War II (it was called *Scale* at that time), the reference vessel chosen was the prevalent T-2 tanker. This tanker size is almost completely absent from the deep-sea crude oil trades now, and the world fleet average required freight rate is roughly Worldscale 60, reflecting a 40 percent savings by using larger vessels.

## Recent Events Affecting Freight Rates

Figures 8.3 and 8.4 show the time trend of seaborne exports by weight and value of the world and of the North Pacific rim countries. After the substantial contraction in overall trade that occurred in 1974−1975, visible in the statistics of all the countries investigated, trade began to recover in 1975 and 1976. With the exception of petroleum bulk movements, growth has occurred in almost all commodity categories in recent years. World crude oil shipments suffered a decline in both the tonnage moved by sea and the ton-miles of oceanborne carriage.[6] Furthermore, the growth rate before 1973 in ton-mile demand for crude oil movement was higher (17.6 percent from 1966 to 1972) than for the consumption of oil itself (11.5 percent), making the late 1973 collapse in oil consumption all the more

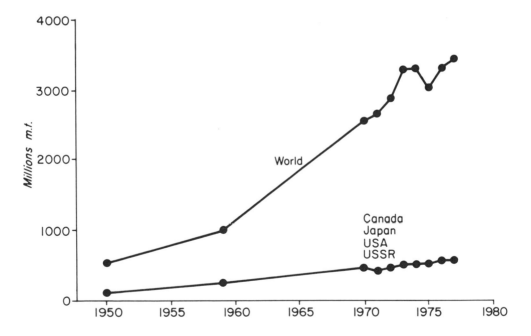

Fig. 8.3. *Total Seaborne World Trade-Exports by Weight.* Source: *United Nations Statistical Yearbook* (New York: United Nations, 1978), table 17. The relatively large proportion of cargo exports from non-North Pacific countries is a consequence of the very large exports of crude petroleum from Middle East countries, which constitute roughly two-thirds by weight of world seaborne cargoes.

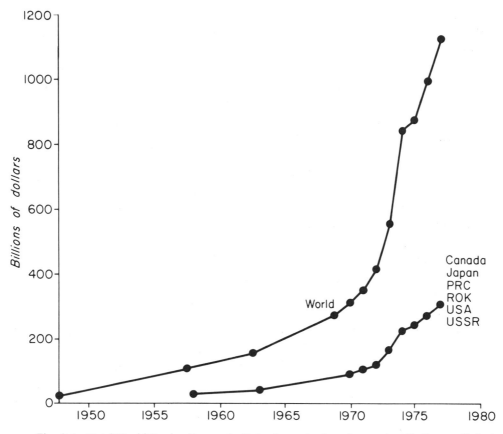

Fig. 8.4. *Total World Trade—Exports by Value* (current prices, free-on-board). Source: *United Nations Statistical Yearbook* (New York: United Nations, 1978), table 149. Includes all modes of transportation, at current prices charged on a free-on-board basis. Excludes trade among the following countries: Democratic People's Republic of Korea, former Democratic Republic of Vietnam, Mongolia, and People's Republic of China.

significant for the world crude oil tank ship fleet.[7] Since the international market for tanker capacity is globally integrated, the 1973 decline in demand for ton-mile carrying capacity resulted in roughly the same proportion of excess tonnage being offered for employment for all trades. That is, if global ship tonnage supply exceeded total global demand by 40 percent after Autumn 1973, which it did, supply would also exceed demand by approximately 40 percent on every individual trade route at that time, including those in the North Pacific.

Had historic growth rates continued, by 1975 the demand for crude oil carriage capacity would have equalled 12,566 million ton-miles instead of an actual 8,882 million.[8] This represents a 29 percent decline from what might have been expected. It was no coincidence that roughly 40 percent of the crude oil tanker fleet was laid up or underemployed in 1975 because many investment and new building decisions prior to that time had been based on extrapolations of the historic growth rate. Significant overcapacity in the crude oil tanker fleet existed through 1979.

A modest market recovery in the deep-sea liquid bulk petroleum trade began in early 1979, when spot rates rose briefly in response to a sudden reduction in the supply of available tonnage. The rising costs of bunker fuel encouraged vessel operators to conserve fuel by slowing their vessels down. This had the effect of contracting the transport capacity of the world tanker fleet and the shrinking supply of capacity resulted in higher bids for vessels and higher Worldscale rates. From the fourth quarter of 1978 to the fourth quarter of 1979, the world supply and demand for deep-sea liquid bulk carriage capacity was in equilibrium at a price roughly equal to that necessary for vessel owners to break even in their trades.

The tanker market experiences one complete cycle of boom and bust roughly every ten years. This cycling is the consequence of the competitive forces of profit-seeking and business acumen (or lack thereof) coupled with the effects of unforeseeable international events. In 1973, the United States, Japan, and Western Europe experienced growth in their economies. The demand for imported oil to fuel this growth resulted in an unprecedented growth in deep-sea petroleum movements. Tanker investment decisions were based on two principal factors: (1) forecasts of future market conditions, and (2) current market conditions. The years 1971 to 1973 were major years for placing tanker orders (tankers which in some cases were later to lie idle for almost 5 years) as a result of the profit levels achieved at that time. In 1973, very large crude carriers (VLCCs, roughly from 200,000 dwt to 400,000 dwt) were getting spot charters at Worldscale 200 for a single voyage, or the equivalent of $7.6 million per voyage from the Middle East to Western Europe, while incurring only $.6 million in variable costs. This yielded a surplus of $7 million to cover the capital investment and labor cost. Since VLCCs then in existence cost on the order of $15 million, two round-trip voyages (requiring about four months) would pay for the ship. New VLCCs costing $32 million at that time could obtain a three-year time charter at the equivalent single-voyage rate of Worldscale 68 that would pay a net of $30 million for two years.[9] Therefore, the tanker owners who were already in the market were making huge profits, and both current owners and new investors were encouraged to place orders for the construction of new tankers on a massive scale. The unforeseen Arab-Israeli war of October 1973 and the ensuing fourfold price increase for imported oil ended the economic growth phase of the Western countries and threw the tanker market into a depression from which it has only recently recovered. Numerous independent tanker owners went bankrupt, including several of long standing in the industry (for example, Hilmar Reksten) and the major oil companies lost heavily on their investments in new tankers.[10]

In July of 1976, total existing tanker tonnage for the first time topped 300 million dwt tons (306,627,000 dwt), having grown 11 percent since 1975. The current distribution of tonnage by flag of registry is shown in table 8.3.

## The United States Domestic Tankship Market

The bulk petroleum trades on the North Pacific Ocean are divided into international and domestic, or coastal, trades. While Worldscale is used to describe all spot activity in

## TABLE 8.3

### Existing Bulk Fleet July 1, 1979
#### (Vessels over 100 gross tons)

| Country of Registry | Crude oil tankers | | Oil/dry bulk combination carriers | | Dry bulk carriers | | Total | |
|---|---|---|---|---|---|---|---|---|
| | Number | 1,000 dwt[a] | Number | 1,000 dwt | Number | 1,000 dwt | Number | 1,000 dwt |
| Liberia | 793 | 104,921 | 145 | 15,908 | 800 | 30,425 | 1,738 | 151,254 |
| Japan | 1,525 | 33,066 | 42 | 5,596 | 370 | 16,012 | 1,937 | 54,675 |
| United Kingdom | 419 | 25,015 | 31 | 3,789 | 186 | 7,666 | 636 | 36,470 |
| Norway | 173 | 24,276 | 35 | 4,099 | 123 | 6,493 | 331 | 34,869 |
| Greece | 432 | 21,341 | 51 | 4,361 | 742 | 21,926 | 1,225 | 47,628 |
| France | 105 | 15,080 | 6 | 1,078 | 42 | 1,603 | 153 | 17,762 |
| USA | 337 | 14,481 | 2 | 143 | 162 | 3,358 | 501 | 17,983 |
| Panama | 331 | 12,314 | 10 | 885 | 343 | 8,572 | 684 | 21,772 |
| Spain | 111 | 9,452 | 5 | 519 | 54 | 1,775 | 170 | 11,747 |
| Italy | 283 | 9,395 | 30 | 3,342 | 113 | 3,957 | 426 | 16,695 |
| USSR | 503 | 7,387 | 8 | 738 | 94 | 2,081 | 605 | 10,207 |
| Singapore | 157 | 5,709 | 4 | 275 | 87 | 2,770 | 248 | 8,754 |
| Fed. Rep. of Germany | 104 | 5,545 | 1 | 73 | 54 | 2,984 | 159 | 8,603 |
| Netherlands | 76 | 4,277 | 0 | 0 | 26 | 1,077 | 102 | 5,355 |
| Sweden | 99 | 4,213 | 4 | 533 | 23 | 927 | 126 | 5,674 |
| Rep. of Korea | 70 | 2,226 | 1 | 46 | 82 | 2,010 | 153 | 4,284 |
| People's Rep. of China[a] | 87 | 1,867 | 1 | 93 | 85 | 2,757 | 173 | 4,717 |
| Canada | 58 | 360 | 0 | 0 | 117 | 2,718 | 175 | 3,079 |
| Dem. People's Rep. of Korea | 4 | 49 | 0 | 0 | 1 | 33 | 5 | 83 |
| Others (138 Countries) | 1,283 | 37,294 | 54 | 4,631 | 704 | 23,268 | 2,041 | 65,194 |
| World Total | 6,950 | 338,777 | 430 | 46,116 | 4,208 | 142,420 | 11,588 | 526,815 |

Source: *Lloyd's Register of Shipping, Statistical Tables 1979* (London: Lloyd's Register of Shipping, 1979).

[a]Deadweight tons

[b]Data incomplete

international trades, the American Tanker Rate Schedule (ATRS or AR) describes charter rates in the U.S. domestic trade. This trade is shielded from the competition of non-U.S.-built and documented tankers by the U.S. cabotage law (Jones Act).[11] The ATRS functions exactly like Worldscale, being a ratio of the prevailing single round-trip voyage price per ton of oil delivered to the flat rate (which is nominally the required freight rate) of a reference tanker. Like Worldscale, it is a fully-deflated index over a period of time, which includes revision of the fixed hire element. Table 8.4 lists the reference tanker's characteristics. Note that the ATRS is based on a larger vessel size, which is more representative of current vessel design practice, than is Worldscale. Table 8.5 lists some sample North Pacific trade flat rates for the ATRS.

## TABLE 8.4

### AMERICAN TANKER RATE SCHEDULE REFERENCE
### CRUDE OIL TANKER CHARACTERISTICS

| Characteristic | Description |
|---|---|
| Deadweight at summer draft | 37,800 long tons |
| Summer draft laden in salt water | 36'8" (11.20 meters) |
| Average service speed | 16 knots |
| Daily bunker consumption at sea | 82 long tons of Bunker C fuel |
| Daily bunker consumption in port | 21 long tons of Bunker C fuel |
| Fixed hire element | $9,000/day (was $2,500 before 1976 revision) |
| Where built | U.S. shipyard |
| Crew nationality | U.S. citizens |

## TABLE 8.5

### AMERICAN TANKER FLAT RATES (SEPTEMBER, 1978)
### ($ PER METRIC TON OF OIL DELIVERED)

| Route[a] | Rate |
|---|---|
| From Valdez, Alaska to: | |
|     Anacortes, WA. | 4.05 |
|     Los Angeles/Long Beach, CA. | 5.85 |
|     Gulf of Panama | 12.31 |
|     New York, N.Y. (via Panama Canal) | 17.64 |
| From Drift River, Cook Inlet, Alaska to: | |
|     Los Angeles, CA. | 5.90 |
|     Anacortes, WA. | 4.16 |
|     New York, N.Y. (via Panama Canal) | 17.75 |

Source: *American Tanker Rate Schedule, Rev. January 1978*, Association of Ship Brokers and Agents, USA, (1978)

[a]Round trip, by most economical route.

Too little spot chartering in the U.S. West Coast petroleum trades occurs to permit construction of a time series of the Pacific trade ATRS index. However, U.S. Gulf of Mexico to north of Cape Hatteras (USNH) has been a major route for many years and the available data on North Pacific fixtures indicates that rates for the USNH route are broadly similar to those applicable to the U.S. Pacific domestic trades. Figure 8.5 plots the trends for USNH trade.

Prior to 1973, U.S. flag tankers operating in domestic trades earned approximately break-even rates. But after 1973 United States domestic tanker rates experienced a boom, thanks in part to the demand for U.S. flag tonnage to move Gulf of Mexico oil to the U.S. East Coast and, since August 1977, to move Alaskan oil to the continental United States.

The domestic U.S. flag tanker market is very profitable and will probably continue to be so for the foreseeable future. The trans-Alaska pipeline output is scheduled to rise slowly from about 1 million barrels per day in 1978 to 2.2 million barrels per day in 1981. Coastwise movement of petroleum products may decline somewhat in the 1980s if national economic activity slows, but the effect on the U.S. flag tanker market will be minimal.

Alternatively, the deep-sea international tanker market has been in a depression since the last boom in 1973, and recent forecasts place the date of the next boom in the mid-1980s.[12] The size of a useful tanker fleet decreases over time as older vessels are scrapped. Also, the demand for imported oil, and thus for ton-miles of shipping capacity,

Fig. 8.5. *Freight Rates in Domestic United States Crude Oil Shipping Trades.* Source: *Chartering Annual* (New York: Maritime Research, Inc., various years). Unweighted quarterly average, U.S. Gulf of Mexico to north of Cape Hatteras for crude oil or "dirty" carriage. Dashed lines are inferred rates when no contracts were reported during the relevant period. Circled points are single contracts for the U.S. Pacific Coast domestic trade.

has declined and will probably show little or no growth; the United States, Europe, and Japan are continuing their efforts to reduce energy consumption.

## Liner Shipments

The market for liner shipping tonnage differs from that of charter shipping; charter shipping fits the classic description of a pure competitive market,[13] but liner shipping is organized into cartels.[14] In the charter market, all actors are price takers (i.e., no firm or decision maker is capable of affecting the prices bid or offered for ship tonnage). In the liner market, ship owners organize into associations called *conferences* and agree among themselves as to the prices the conference will charge for supplying service, and the quantity of ton-mile carriage capacity that each member will place in the conference. An exception is conferences that operate in or out of the United States. United States law requires that conferences be open to all who wish to join, and thus the conferences have little or no control on the ton-mile shipping capacity.[15]

Within each conference, prices for shipping service are set on a commodity-by-commodity basis and since the conferences usually carry a great variety of cargo types, referred to as *general cargo*, the list of prices (or the *tariff* for a conference) may be 300 pages (or more) long.

A conference is usually organized for each one-way trade, so there is a conference that serves U.S. and Canadian West Coast exports to Japan and the Far East (Pacific Westbound Conference), and another conference that serves Japanese and Republic of Korea exports to the West Coast of the United States and Canada (Transpacific Freight Conference of Japan). Although membership is quite variable, usually shipowning firms or *lines* operate as members of both an outbound and inbound conference on the same trade route. The Pacific Westbound Conference contains 22 member lines, a typical number.[16]

Since each conference constitutes a closed market for ship tonnage (except for U.S. trades), the freedom to compete and equalize profit levels among the conferences is somewhat retarded. Therefore, indexed rate trends for a given conference do not describe the condition of the liner markets generally as accurately as is possible for the bulk trades. Rate trends in one North Pacific Ocean open conference have been plotted by the U.S. Justice Department and are thought to be broadly representative of the open conferences (see figure 8.6). The marked upward trend of the plotted index reflects, at least in part, the increase in service quality that has occurred since the late 1960s when the use of containers to carry general cargoes began to be prevalent. The index trend is markedly different from that of the charter trades; liner rates have tended to be constant for long periods accompanied by rate increases, whereas in 1971 and again in 1974 the real price of chartered tonnage fell sharply.

## The Minibridge System

An important trend in West Coast liner shipping began in the 1970s with the increasing use of the *minibridge system*. This entails moving interocean-routed containers via the U.S. transcontinental railroads rather than by an all-water route through the Panama Canal. The

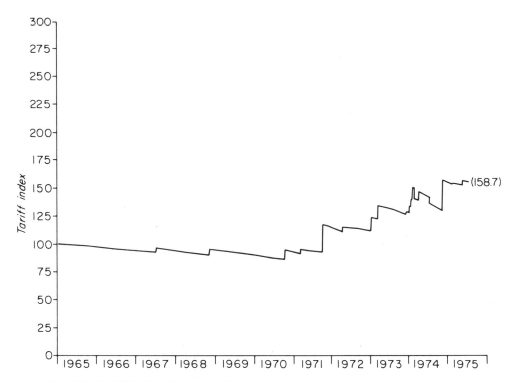

Fig. 8.6. *Tariff Index: Trans-Pacific Freight Conference of Japan—Korea* (general Rate Actions, including Surcharges with Adjustment for Inflation. 1956 = 100). Source: U.S. Department of Justice, *The Regulated Ocean Shipping Industry* (Washington, D.C.: Government Printing Office, January 1977), p. 211.

minibridge is used to transport containers between the U.S. East Coast and Asia or between the U.S. West Coast and Europe. The *landbridge* concept, whereby containers are moved between Europe and Asia across the U.S., has not proved competitive to all-water shipment due to the high costs of two transshipments at the two U.S. coasts.

Two separate increases in the tolls asked at the Panama Canal between 1974 and 1976, amounting to an increase of 45 percent, are reported to have significantly affected the diversion of cargoes to the minibridge.[17]

The freight charge for container shipment on the all-water canal route has been matched by the minibridge promoters for several years, and service overland is as much as four days faster.[18] This may partly explain the drop of over 23 million long tons of cargoes transited through the Canal between 1974 and 1975, which appear to have been diverted to minibridge movements, as noted by John Immer.[19] He observed that between 1970 and 1977 U.S. non-Pacific Coast ports (those on the Gulf of Mexico, Atlantic Coast, and the Great Lakes) experienced a net reduction in liner cargo exports of 4.45 million metric tons, or 22 percent of total liner exports, while U.S. Pacific Coast port liner exports rose 1.96 million metric tons for a 51 percent growth in this cargo category. For imports, non-Pacific Coast U.S. ports suffered a decrease in tonnage of 1.83 million metric tons, or 11.4 percent, while

Pacific port cargo figures grew 2.07 million metric tons, or 57.8 percent. The gains in West Coast liner cargo business is due to their capture of cargoes that once were tributary to non-Pacific Coast ports. These cargoes moved to and from the U.S. North Central states and the Province of Ontario, Canada.

> Perhaps the most important single force causing these changes has been the impact of the railroads. Piggyback [containers carried on a railroad flatcar] is most efficient at great distances, thus its growth minimizes the negative aspects of distance and makes the far-distant port more competitive with the nearer ports. . . . Improvement in container handling and processing through the port is more likely to occur in southern [U.S. Gulf of Mexico] and western ports which will cause the trend toward those ports to continue.[20]

Liner cargoes represent 10 to 30 percent of the cargo tonnage moving through U.S. ports and are thought to be the most valuable and important cargoes for a port because of the large number of jobs and high capital services associated with handling the cargo.

By way of comparison, table 8.6 shows recent trends in the use of the trans-Siberian landbridge, which in recent years has suffered a loss of traffic. The landbridge runs from Vostochny on the Pacific Coast to Leningrad in the Soviet West.

TABLE 8.6

TRANS-SIBERIAN LANDBRIDGE TOTAL TRAFFIC

(20 FT. CONTAINER BOXES)

| 1976 | 1977 | 1978 |
|------|------|------|
| 121,000 | 105,000 | 99,000 |

Source: *Seatrade* (July 1979): p. 119, from Soviet sources. Roughly 70 percent of the movement is westbound.

## PHYSICAL SETTING OF TRADE

The physical setting for international trade on the North Pacific has been well-described by Walter Radius.

> The Pacific Basin covers nearly half the area of the world, Singapore and Panama lie on opposite sides of the globe, separated by 177°41' of longitude. The usual maps of this region are most deceptive, for they picture this half-sphere on a flat surface with the consequent distortion not only of distances but also of the relative positions of the bordering continents. On such maps the western coast of North America faces the eastern coast of Asia. A study of the globe reveals that the shores of these two continents are practically a continuous straight line, and that the shortest distances between the ports of North America and Asia pass close to the Aleutian Islands of Alaska. Therefore, the tendency is for the main flow of transpacific trade to move along the shores of the continents until it veers across the North Pacific Ocean along the Great Circle route.
>
> With almost half the world lying between the two extremities of the Pacific Ocean, Singapore and Panama, tremendous distances must be traversed in order to serve the commerce of this region.[21]

Some representative distances for the North Pacific are as follows: Yokohama to San Francisco (direct), 8,400 km; Yokohama to San Francisco via Hawaii, 10,164 km; Yokohama to Seattle, 7,871 km; Anchorage to Seattle, 2,630 km; Anchorage to Yokohama, 5,682 km; Yokohama to Inchon, 1,982 km; Yokohama to Vladivostok, 1,763 km; and Vladivostok to Namp'o (DPRK), 1,787 km.[22] These are average distances, but actual sailing distance varies with season of the year. Bad winter weather in northern latitudes forces vessels to sail to the south of the great circle route, taking them as much as 905 km south and adding 461 km to the sailing distance on the Yokohama to Seattle route.[23]

In terms of physical routing, there are only two international trade routes across the North Pacific: southern California to Hawaii to Japan, and Seattle–Vancouver, B.C., to Japan. The latter is the most heavily used. Direct routing from other ports on the Pacific rim, either the east or west side, closely parallels these two routes. Thus, almost all trans-Pacific trade, except that routed to pick up or leave cargo and passengers in Hawaii, is routed between the Northwest U.S. Pacific Coast and the northern ports of Japan.

## Patterns of Marine International Trade

Different facets and measurements of seaborne trade on the North Pacific are revealed from records of the types of commodities carried in trade, the tonnage of cargoes moved, the cargo throughput of the ports of loading and discharge, the characteristics of the ports through which the cargoes move, and the time trends describing all of these.

These topics are addressed here in varying degrees of detail. Emphasis is placed on describing cargo movements by type, quantity, and geographic locale of loading and unloading. Inland origins and destinations of trade are traced.

Other significant aspects of seaborne trade are the types, flags of registry, and size of vessels carrying the cargoes. However, published national statistics, the data base used here, do not describe vessel movements. Data on the true origin and destination of cargoes (significant especially for Asian cargoes transshipped through Japan) are also useful for some purposes and are discussed briefly.

Historical and comparative trade data describing cargo tonnage movements are provided to set North Pacific trade in context. Petroleum movements are described in more detail, due to their significance for global economy; petroleum shipments are also a potential source of pollutants in the marine environment, stemming from ship accidents and routine tanker operations.

In order to identify the composition of trade, a judgment had to be made as to the appropriate level of commodity aggregation that would be manageable, yet not lose useful detail. Eight commodity categories[24] were selected:

1. Containerizable General Cargo
2. Marginally and Noncontainerizable General Cargo
3. Petroleum and Petroleum Products
4. Other Liquid Bulk
5. Iron Ore

6. Coal and Coke
7. Grains
8. Other Dry Bulk

These categories were used to separate commodities into groups that tend to move on the same types of ships. A large proportion of the containerizable category now moves on container ships.

Marginally and noncontainerizable general cargo moves on container ships, roll-on and roll-off ships, conventional break-bulk ships, or specialized carriers such as log, pulp, and newsprint carriers. Petroleum bulk and other liquid bulk cargoes are carried on tankers. Dry bulk cargoes, including grains, coal and iron ore, are carried on dry bulk carriers and sometimes on tankers if the latter have been fitted with wide deck hatches and strengthened bulkheads. The latter vessels are called combined carriers (OBOs). Iron ore, grain, and coal have been tabulated separately since Japan and the Republic of Korea import large quantities of these commodities.

Foreign oceanborne trade statistics for Canada (Port of Vancouver only), Japan, and the United States, and total trade for the Republic of Korea (which is mostly oceanborne) were analyzed by grouping commodity types into the above eight categories and distinguishing the commodity flows according to their overseas origins and destinations. The overseas trade regions were grouped into nine categories: (1) United States Pacific Coast (five subregions), (2) Japan, (3) Republic of Korea, (4) People's Republic of China, (5) Democratic People's Republic of Korea, (6) Canadian Pacific Coast, (7) USSR Pacific Coast, (8) Oceania—Southeast Asia (including all countries south and east of Burma, such as Thailand, Taiwan, Singapore, Philippines, Indonesia, Malaysia, Hong Kong, Australia, New Zealand, and other South Pacific Islands), and (9) World Other (including Burma and points west, and countries bordering the Atlantic Ocean and the West Coast of South and Central America). This breakdown groups trades and associated ship movements that tend to follow similar geographic tracks in the North Pacific Ocean.

United States Pacific Coast data were tabulated according to five subregions: Alaska, Puget Sound, Columbia River (including the Oregon and Washington coasts), northern California (San Francisco Bay and points north to the Oregon border), and southern California.[25] Since Japanese, Republic of Korea, and Canadian national trade data sources do not distinguish U.S. Pacific Coast trade from total U.S. trade, Panama Canal data were used to separate trade that passed through the Panama Canal to U.S. and Canadian Atlantic coast ports; they were placed in the World Other category.[26] The year 1976 was selected as the basis for the following discussion. Some data for later years are tabulated when possible.

## North Pacific Trade and Total World Trade

The significance of oceanborne trade on the North Pacific Ocean may be perceived by comparing it with trade elsewhere in the world. Total world exported seaborne cargo tonnage in 1976 was 3,352 million metric tons.[27] Rapid growth in the tons of cargo traded in the 1960s was abruptly halted in 1973 by the fourfold price increase of petroleum, and the subsequent recession in many national economies. The share of seaborne world trade tonnage provided by the U.S., Canada, the USSR, and Japan (trend data on a tonnage basis for the Republic of Korea, the People's Democratic Republic of Korea, and the People's Republic of China are unavailable) was 584 million metric tons, or 18 percent of world seaborne cargo exports by tonnage in 1976.[28] These four countries' seaborne imports totalled 1,162 million metric tons in 1976, or 36 percent of the 3,233 million metric tons of cargo landed in all countries of the world that year.[29]

The value of total world trade exports (figures for oceanborne trade by value are not available) grew rapidly in the 1960s and early 1970s—at an annual average rate of 12.5 percent between 1958 and 1976.[30] High inflation rates after 1969 spurred the growth of trade value to the extent that a decline in the total tons of trade in 1975 (inferred from the 7 percent decline in seaborne tonnage that year) slowed but did not halt or reverse the growth of trade measured by value.

The value of total exports from the People's Republic of China, United States, Soviet Union, Republic of Korea, Canada and Japan was 27.3 percent of the total value of all export trade in 1976 ($271 billion out of a world total of $991 billion).[31] Total world imports by value (differing from world exports by the cost of transport) were $1,021 billion in 1976, and imports for the six North Pacific countries were $363 billion or 36.5 percent of the world total.[32] From the figures for value and tonnage traded for the North Pacific nations, one might conclude that they contribute 25 to 30 percent of world and oceanborne trade. Only a portion of the oceanborne trade of the U.S., Canada, and the Soviet Union moves on the North Pacific Ocean, however, since these countries have ports on other oceans.

Total Soviet Union exports in 1976 were valued at $37.2 billion, while imports were $38.1 billion.[33] Soviet Union seaborne exports were 135 million metric tons, and seaborne imports were 41 million metric tons.[34] No official data are available that distinguish the value or tonnage of Soviet shipborne trade from trade carried by other modes, or that differentiates Soviet Pacific seaborne trade from that moving through Soviet ports on the Mediterranean, Baltic, and Barents seas. However, data are available on the types of cargo carried in overall Soviet foreign trade, and the foreign origins and destinations of the cargo by value.

Due to geographical proximity, it is assumed here that Soviet trade with Oceania—Southeast Asia, Japan, the People's Republic of China, and the Democratic People's Republic of Korea are oceanborne, moving out of Pacific coast Soviet ports, whereas trade to Atlantic Ocean regions, including the U.S., Canadian, Central and South American Atlantic coasts, Indian Ocean regions east of India, and the Pacific coasts of Central and South America are carried overland or via ports in the western Soviet Union.[35] Trade to Pacific U.S. and Canada, and to Cuba—the latter being a major Soviet trade partner—are probably moved through both east and west Soviet ports; trade for these areas requires more detailed analysis to ascertain the portions of trade flowing to and from Soviet Pacific ports.

While it is impossible to ascertain precisely the value of Soviet trade goods moving from Soviet Pacific ports to the Pacific coasts of the United States and Canada and to Cuba, it is possible to estimate the flow with the additional observation that the eastern Soviet regions tend to be sparsely populated but possess rich supplies of natural resources (oil, coal, timber, and metals). Raw material exports would tend to originate there, whereas relatively small quantities of consumer goods moving in Soviet international trade would originate or terminate there. Thus, one might expect 50 percent or more of Soviet exports of raw materials to originate from its Pacific Coast. In addition, one expert estimated in 1970 that Pacific Soviet Union seaborne trade accounts for 13 percent of the total Soviet seaborne trade.[36] This figure is probably closer to 15 percent in 1980 in view of the recent Soviet expansion of the Pacific ports of Nakhodka and Vostochniy.

It is therefore assumed that 15 percent of the total Soviet trade to (and from) the United States, Canada, and Cuba was exported from (imported into) the Soviet Pacific coast, except that this percentage is larger for raw material exports. These assumptions result in the tabulated figures shown in table 5 of the chapter "International Marine Transportation" in the companion to this book, *Atlas of Marine Use in the North Pacific Region*. Soviet Pacific coast exports work out to 6.2 percent by value of total Soviet foreign exports. Imports to the Soviet Pacific Coast are estimated at 15 percent of the total trade by value for 11.2 percent of total turnover, or somewhat less than the anticipated average of 15 percent. The relatively high percent for landings reflects the imports of general cargo in containers and grain, which are shipped by rail via the Soviet transcontinental railroad landbridge to western regions of the country for consumption.[37] If 15 percent of the total Soviet trade by value moves through Pacific ports, and the percentage of seaborne trade by weight is similar, this yields a Pacific Coast export tonnage of 20.1 million metric tons in 1976.

Total oceanborne exports from the Canadian Pacific Coast in 1976 were 33.3 million metric tons, or 27 percent of the 115 million metric tons Canada exported that year.[38] Canadian Pacific Coast imports were 4.3 million metric tons or only 8 percent of Canada's total imports of 56 million metric tons. By value, Canada's Pacific Coast seaborne exports in 1976 were $7.6 billion out of total Canadian exports of $38.1 billion or 20 percent, whereas imports by value were $3.1 billion or 8 percent of total Canadian imports of $37.9 billion.[39]

United States Pacific Coast international oceanborne imports (excluding Hawaii) for 1976 amounted to 64.26 million metric tons, which was 13.5 percent of the total U.S. imports (474.1 million metric tons). Exports in this category equalled 48.76 million metric tons or 20.6 percent of total U.S. exports (235.8 million metric tons). Total oceanborne U.S. Pacific Coast (excluding Hawaii) imports by value for 1976 were $20.13 billion, or 16.6 percent of total U.S. imports ($120.68 billion). Exports in this category equalled $11.19 billion or 9.7 percent of total U.S. exports ($115 billion).[40]

While no time trend of Republic of Korea trade data is available, its total imports in 1976 were 41.1 million metric tons, and its exports (mostly seaborne) were 11.4 million metric tons; its exports totalled $7.7 billion.[41] Equivalent figures for Japan were 577.1 and 71.9 million metric tons and $67.2 billion.[42] The total exports of the People's Republic of China totalled $7.2 billion,[43] and about 80 percent of this is seaborne.[44] Little data are available on the trade of the Democratic People's Republic of Korea. Imports and exports are each estimated at $1 billion (1973); 60 percent of this was with the People's Republic of China and 20−30 percent with the Soviet Union.[45]

The figures for the U.S. and Canadian Pacific seaborne exports by weight, coupled with the assumption that Soviet Pacific exports are on the order of 20 million metric tons, and using a figure of 325 million tons for Japan, which is an average of its import and export tonnage, and 26 million tons for the Republic of Korea, which is also an average for its unbalanced trade, suggest that the North Pacific seaborne exports of the U.S., Soviet Union, Canada, Republic of Korea, and Japan sum to 453 million metric tons, or 13 percent of world seaborne exports in 1976. Since no data on the value of world oceanborne trade are available, we are unable to estimate the relative significance on a value basis of North Pacific oceanborne trade. Overall, it appears that 10 to 15 percent of the global seaborne trade tonnage is moved in the region, and trade by value is probably of equivalent significance. Considering the large expanse of the earth's surface in the North Pacific, the density of ship traffic carrying international trade on average does not appear to be great, but subregions, particularly in areas near the Japanese islands, must be intensively used.

International trade contributes to the economic well-being of countries to different extents. Although no measure of this is fully satisfactory, the most commonly used measure is the ratio of the value of international trade to the gross national product. This ratio for the North Pacific nations is shown in table 8.7 in the fifth column. Note that Japan (.25), Republic of Korea (.64), Democratic People's Republic of Korea (.33), and Canada (.44) depend to a significant degree on international trade. Canada's dependence is largely a reflection of the overland trade it does with the United States along their common border. The Democratic People's Republic of Korea trades extensively with the People's Republic

TABLE 8.7

REGIONAL ECONOMIC INDICATORS: GNP, POPULATION, TRADE VALUE

| Country | Avg. annual real[a] growth rate of GNP per capita (1970–1975 base) | GNP[a] per capita 1976 | Trade value[a] $ Billion | Year | Population[a] mid-1976 (millions) | Estimated total[b] Trade value/(GNP) |
|---|---|---|---|---|---|---|
| Canada | 3.3 | $7,510 | 174 | (1976) | 23.2 | .44 |
| Dem. People's Rep. of Korea | 0.9 | 470 | 7.7 | (1976) | 16.3 | .33[c] |
| Japan | 4.0 | 4,910 | 554 | (1976) | 112.8 | .25 |
| People's Rep. of China | 5.3 | 410 | 343 | (1974) | 835.8 | .04 |
| Rep. of Korea | 8.2 | 670 | 24.1 | (1976) | 36.0 | .64 |
| USSR | 3.1 | 2,760 | 708 | (1974) | 256.7 | .10 |
| USA | 1.6 | 7,890 | 1.697 | (1976) | 215.1 | .14 |

Sources:

[a]World Bank, *World Development Report* (Washington, D.C.: The World Bank, 1978), p. 77.

[b]Except where noted, the value of trade used in this column is the same as that used in the text.

[c]Newspaper Enterprises Association, *World Almanac and Book of Facts 1978* (New York: Newspaper Enterprises Association, 1977).

Note: GNP = gross national product.

of China, and most of this is also probably done over land. Therefore, Japan and the Republic of Korea are seen as the two nations in the region whose economies are most dependent on international oceanborne foreign trade for their economic well-being.

## Trends in Patterns of Commerce

The patterns of ocean commerce generally, and on the North Pacific particularly, have undergone rapid changes in the post-World War II era. In 1943, trade on the North Pacific was summarized as predominantly an exchange of raw materials between two continental areas whose economies were in different stages of development.[46] This kind of trade still goes on but new trade patterns have been added to the old, and old trade patterns have changed. Now Japan, the United States, and Canada are at similar stages of development and exchange large volumes of finished goods. Simultaneously, these countries trade finished goods for raw materials with Southeast Asia, Oceania, and the Asia mainland. Furthermore, in the immediate pre-war period, the United States was a major exporter of bulk goods. "The extent to which the westbound cargoes heavily overbalance the eastbound is the most significant feature of transpacific trade. In 1936, for example, exports from the United States (east and west coasts) to the Far East carried on cargo vessels were almost double the [tonnage of] imports, while tanker exports were twenty-five times tanker imports."[47] As described below, the pattern of North Pacific trade is now both more balanced and much more complex than it was forty years ago.

The most significant trade relationship lying wholly within the North Pacific region is the trade between the Pacific Coast of the United States and Japan. Table 8.8 shows total tonnage and value of cargo exchanged between the U.S. West Coast and Japan 1976 to 1977.

In 1976, the volume of trade moving between the U.S. West Coast and Japan represented 5 percent of Japan's imports that year (577,083 thousand metric tons) and 7 percent of Japan's total exports (71,930 thousand metric tons).[48] Furthermore, it represented 14 percent of Japan's total exports by value ($67,225 million) and 7 percent of Japan's total imports ($64,799 million).[49] Conversely, U.S. Pacific Coast imports from Japan represented 8 percent of total Pacific Coast imports of 1976 (64,266 thousand metric tons) and 57 percent of the exports (48,764 thousand metric tons); the equivalent figures on a value basis are 48 percent (out of $20,133 million) and 40 percent (out of $11,189 million) respectively. Pacific Coast imports from Japan accounted for 8 percent of the value of total U.S. imports in 1976 ($128,872 million) and 4 percent of all U.S. exports ($113,323 million).[50] Thus, for both the U.S. and Japan, their trade link through U.S. Pacific Coast ports accounts for roughly 10 percent of their total foreign trade by value, and accounts for roughly 40 percent of the trade of U.S. Pacific Coast ports. This is a significant component of both countries' total trade, especially considering how narrowly the trade link has been defined here. For example, Japan's trade with the U.S. via U.S. East Coast and Gulf Coast ports is also sizeable, the total being 36,228 million metric tons for just that portion routed via the Panama Canal.[51]

The tonnage and value of trade moving between the Pacific Coast of the U.S. and Japan

TABLE 8.8

U.S. PACIFIC COAST AND ALASKA TRADE WITH JAPAN
(TRUE ORIGIN AND DESTINATION)

| Year | 1000 metric tons | | | Million dollars | | |
|------|---------|---------|--------|---------|---------|---------|
| | Imports | Exports | Total | Imports | Exports | Total |
| 1974[a] | 5,440 | 29,913 | 35,353 | $ 6,401 | $3,891 | $10,292 |
| 1975[a] | 4,116 | 26,161 | 30,277 | 5,425 | 3,605 | 9,030 |
| 1976 | 5,177 | 27,321 | 32,498 | 7,198 | 3,794 | 10,992 |
| 1977 | 6,554 | 26,094 | 32,648 | 9,747 | 3,952 | 13,699 |
| 1978[a] | 8,087 | 30,532 | 38,619 | 13,282 | 5,664 | 18,946 |
| 1979[a] | 8,038 | 38,882 | 46,920 | 14,767 | 8,175 | 22,942 |

Source: U.S. Bureau of the Census, Foreign Trade Data Tapes SM305 and SM705. Data processed by Port of Seattle, March 10, 1979 and July 17, 1980.

[a]Trade figures for Alaska were inadvertently not acquired for this year but were estimated on a constant proportion basis from data available for 1976 and 1977.

were relatively unchanged between 1976 and 1977 (as seen in table 8.8) at a time when the total trade of the two countries was growing (fig. 8.7). This is indicative of the increasing diversification of trade on the North Pacific with nations such as the Republic of Korea (ROK), People's Republic of China (PRC), Singapore, and Hong Kong (for PRC), who are emulating the Japanese model of promoting trade to reap economic gains.

Total Japanese trade in dollar value was $132 billion in 1976[52] as compared to total U.S. West Coast trade totalling $31 billion for that year.[53] Thus, Japan is the single most important trade center in the region. Both Japan and the U.S. have experienced rapid trade growth since the late 1960s, but with a dip in the tonnage values occurring in recent years. Dollar values have grown in spite of the tonnage drop, but inflation effects account for much of this growth.

The foregoing discussion describes the physical movement of cargoes but not the true origin of the cargo (where manufactured), nor true destination (where marketed and consumed). A significant volume of Asian containerizable general cargo exports are temporarily stored in Japan before final shipment to the United States Pacific Coast. In 1976, 1.90 million metric tons (mMT) of containerizable cargo worth $5.1 billion was reported as actually originating in Japan and exported to the U.S. Pacific Coast, as compared to 2.37 mMT worth $6.6 billion that was shipped from Japan to the U.S. Pacific Coast.[54] Most of the 470,000 metric tons of goods that were staged through Japan probably originated in Taiwan, Hong Kong, and the Republic of Korea, these being other ports of call for the liner conference that operates between Asia and the North American Pacific Coast. Similarly, 2.20 mMT of containerizable general cargo worth $2.0 billion was loaded on the U.S. Pacific Coast destined for debarkation in Japan, but only 1.69 mMT worth $1.6 billion was actually consumed there, the remaining .51 mMT presumably was for ultimate consumption elsewhere in Asia.[55] These are the principal trade flows in the North Pacific that evidence significant discrepancies between reported consumption-production and destination-origin figures.

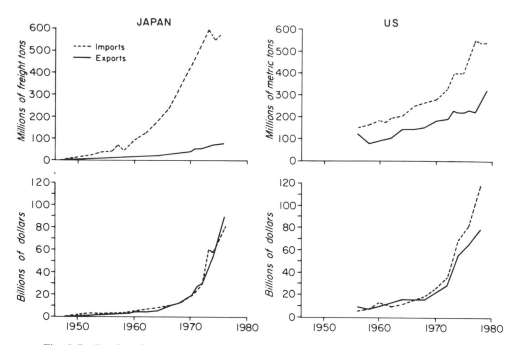

Fig. 8.7. *Total Seaborne Trade of Japan and the United States.* Source: Maritime Administration, U.S. Department of Commerce, *United States Oceanborne Foreign Trade Routes, 1977* (Washington, D.C.: U.S. Government Printing Office, October 1979), Appendix D; U.S. Bureau of the Census, *Highlights of the U.S. Export and Import Trade,* Report FT 990 (Washington, D.C.: U.S. Government Printing Office, December 1978 and December 1979); Geographical Survey Institute, The Ministry of Construction, *The National Atlas of Japan* (Tokyo: The Japan Map Center, 1977), pp. 243 and 247; Prime Minister's Office, Statistics Bureau, *Japan Statistical Yearbook* (Tokyo: Japan Statistical Association, 1980). Japanese data are reported in freight tons. A freight ton equals either 1.113 cubic meters of cargo volume or 1 metric ton, the choice of unit depending on which of the two, when applied to a particular cargo, results in the larger figure for freight tonnage (and thus whichever yields the greatest revenue to the liner conferences who charge for shipment on freight tonnage basis). A Freight Ton is sometimes also called a Revenue Ton.

## Commodity Trades by Country

A wide spectrum of commodities moves in oceanborne trade on the North Pacific. Exported from the North American Pacific Coast are coal, wheat, citrus fruits, molasses, natural gas, forest products, tractors, manufactured goods, and petroleum products; whereas crude oil, fish products, automobiles, coffee, footwear, fertilizers, bananas, salt, rubber, and iron and steel plates and shapes are imported. Japan, the principal trading nation in the North Pacific, imports grains, iron ore, coal and coke, crude petroleum, fertilizers, forest products, wool and soybeans; it exports iron and steel plates and shapes, ships, automobiles, electrical machinery, and a vast array of consumer goods such as cameras, clothing, watches, small appliances, special papers, and furniture. A description of the principal cargo flows from various port regions on the North Pacific rim is given below. Note that this discussion is based on ports of loading and unloading, and not on the basis of true origins and destinations.

The United States Pacific Coast port areas studied were San Diego, Long Beach-Los Angeles, San Francisco-Oakland, Portland, Seattle, and Anchorage. The largest tonnage of total cargo throughput in 1976 was achieved by the geographically proximate ports of Los Angeles and Long Beach, California, handling a sum total of 31.7 million metric tons valued at $13.02 million (53.4 percent of the total business of the eight major Pacific Coast United States ports discussed here). Most of the tonnage moving through these two ports was in the form of petroleum imports, of which 9.09 mMT was from Indonesia, 4.4 mMT from Africa and Venezuela, and 3.87 mMT from the Middle East, out of total Pacific Coast imports of 17.48 mMT.[56]

The next most active port in terms of tons handled was Portland, handling 8.6 mMT valued at $1.73 billion. Portland is primarily a dry bulk port, specializing in exports of grain to Southeast Asia (1.07 mMT), Republic of Korea (ROK) (1.12 mMT), and Japan (1.3 mMT) from total grain exports of 4.34 mMT. In addition, 1.1 mMT of wood chips were exported to Japan.[57]

Of the eight commodity groups, containerizable general cargo tends to be the most valuable per ton for the ports examined, and the most valuable cargo generally. Los Angeles and Long Beach are principally containerizable general cargo ports, handling $8.5 billion worth of this cargo in 1976, or 74 percent of the total cargo for the West Coast ports ($11.55 billion). Most of the Los Angeles-Long Beach's containerizable traffic was imports ($6.29 billion) and of this, most came from Japan ($3.93 billion), Hong Kong ($1.6 billion), and the Republic of China ($.68 billion).[58] Containerizable general cargo accounted for 66 percent of the total value of cargoes imported through Los Angeles and Long Beach in international trade in 1976, but represented only 12 percent of those ports' total tonnage.

Second in the containerizable cargo category was Oakland-San Francisco at $4.24 billion, accounting for 81 percent of the value of their total business. Seattle was third in this category at $3.37 billion, of which $2.8 billion was imports ($1.56 billion from Japan).[59] In addition, Seattle does a substantial containerized cargo trade with Alaska in domestic commerce, which is not documented here.

San Francisco and San Diego, while prominent ports, are small relative to Los Angeles, Long Beach, or Oakland. The former two ports have experienced little growth in the last five years, but Los Angeles has more than doubled the value of its business since 1972. Neither San Francisco nor San Diego have had enough cargo tonnage growth to offset the effects of inflation, and San Diego has actually lost one-half its containerizable general cargo business on a tonnage basis since 1972.

Seattle, while primarily a containerizable general cargo port, exports large volumes of grain to Japan, People's Republic of China, Republic of Korea, Indonesia, the Philippines, and the region lying between the Suez Canal and Vietnam; it imports lumber, gravel, newsprint, cement, and gypsum from Canada and automobiles from Japan.

Despite its remote location, Anchorage did more business in 1976 on a tonnage basis than San Diego, although its business has declined by over one-half since 1975, reflecting the end of the trans-Alaska pipeline construction period.

The Port of Vancouver, B.C. exceeded all other North American Pacific ports in international trade on a tonnage basis (20.7 mMT throughput in 1976 versus 18.6 mMT for runner-up Long Beach and 13.2 mMT for Los Angeles).[60] Trade value data for Vancouver are not available for comparison. While Vancouver trade tonnage has been almost stationary since 1972, both Long Beach and Los Angeles have experienced significant growth. Most of Vancouver's trade is export (87 percent of total trade by weight in 1976), and much of its exports are grain, mainly to Japan (3.13 mMT) and People's Republic of China (800 thousand MT), and coal, again mainly to Japan (3.3 mMT). Vancouver also exports Dry Bulk (other), such as wood chips and cement, and considerable quantities of containerized general cargo to Japan. Like the United States' Pacific Coast ports, Japan is Vancouver's most important trade partner. Vancouver is also an important, if irregular, exporter of petroleum and petroleum products, most of it going to Atlantic region ports, and a steady export averaging .26 mMT tons annually to Japan.[61]

The Soviet Union exports (in total trade) machinery and equipment, petroleum and petroleum products, ferrous metals, chemicals, forest products, cotton fiber, and foodstuffs; it imports machinery and equipment, ferrous metals, chemicals, and consumer goods including food. A brief description of the commodity types carried through Soviet Pacific ports was given in the section on North Pacific Trade and World Trade. The Soviet Pacific port of Nakhodka was the eighth most active Soviet port in 1975, handling 10 mMT that year.[62]

No trade data are available on total, or oceanborne, trade of the Democratic People's Republic of Korea (DPRK), but its seaborne trade is probably quite small; most of its trade moves overland to and from the People's Republic of China. Foreign flag ships are limited to calling at the ports of Namp'o on the west coast and Hamhŭng and Chŏngjin on the east coast.[63]

Republic of Korea's trade is carried on predominantly out of the ports of Pusan, Ulsan, and Inchon. Pusan is the most active by value ($2.69 billion in 1976) with $1.91 billion worth of imports, out of a total national imports valued at $8.77 billion; Pusan's exports totalled $2.79 billion, out of a total national exports of $7.71 billion. Thus, Pusan represented 28 percent of Republic of Korea's foreign trade by value in 1976, while Inchon captured 9.2 percent and Ulsan 12 percent.[64]

Since the Republic of Korea (ROK) does not have an extensive coastline, its trade is described as a unit, and not detailed by port. The Republic of Korea, much like Japan, imports raw materials such as ores, coal, and oil; it exports manufactured and consumer goods. Its major exporting trade is to World Other, passing through the Straits of Malacca and including Southeast Asia from Vietnam eastward. World Other trade represented 4.3 million metric tons (mMT), or 38 percent by weight of Korea's total exports of 11.3 mMT in 1976. The value of exports in the World Other trade was $2.4 billion. The predominant export by weight was Dry Bulk (other) at 2.5 million tons, worth $.11 billion; containerizable general cargo weighed only 1.1 mMT but was worth $1.8 billion.[65] Imports in the World Other trade were worth $2.58 billion, being mostly petroleum (from the Middle East) totalling $1.6 billion, followed by containerizable general cargo totalling $.76 billion. Interestingly, ROK imports no petroleum from Indonesia, even though it is nearer than the Middle East. By value, ROK is heavily deficient in petroleum trade, importing $1.6 billion worth and exporting $.14 billion, much of the latter going to Japan ($69 million) and Hong Kong ($40 million). On a per ton basis, ROK's imports exceed its exports of petroleum 18.4 mMT to 1.2 mMT indicating that it is highly dependent on foreign sources since it has no domestic production.

Overall, ROK exports were less valuable than her imports, producing a balance of payments deficit in the merchandise account of $1.09 billion. It has a comparative disadvantage in the production of energy-related cargoes and noncontainerizable general cargo. These two categories together were in deficit by $2.4 billion. However, this was mostly made up by a merchandise account surplus in containerizable general cargo of $2.1 billion. The overall deficit occurred because trade in dry bulk goods was in deficit by $.73 billion.[66]

Despite the proximity of the People's Republic of China, ROK, for political reasons, did no business with this potential trade partner in 1976, nor with the Soviet Union. Republic of Korea's single most important trade partner is Japan, exporting $1.8 billion worth of goods to Japan in 1976; containerizable general cargo predominated at $1.66 billion. It imported $3.1 billion in merchandise from Japan, mostly containerizable general cargo worth $2.25 billion. By weight, ROK imported 4.7 mMT from Japan and exported 2.6 mMT, mostly containerizable general cargo. Japan accounted for 23 percent of ROK's export value and 35 percent of its import value. On a weighted basis, Japan averaged 30 percent of ROK's trade, compared to an average of 17 percent for the United States.[67]

On a tonnage basis, ROK imports much more than it exports, 41.1 mMT to 11.3 mMT. Almost 45 percent of its imports by weight is petroleum. The next largest category, at 21 percent, is noncontainerizable general cargo, much of it coming from Indonesia and Japan. On the export side, the predominant category is containerizable general cargo, accounting for 39 percent of the export weight, followed by dry bulk (other) at 39 percent.[68]

A balance of tonnage account would show that ROK is in deficit by 2.97 mMT, indicating that much shipping leaves ROK only partly filled or entirely empty.

The People's Republic of China (PRC) exports foodstuffs such as meat, fish, grain, fruits, and vegetables, as well as textiles, yarn, and crude oil; it imports grain, textile fibers, fertilizer, iron and steel manufactures, and heavy machinery.[69] Unlike ROK and Japan, trade is not yet a significant contributor to the Chinese economy but is seen by the Chinese as ''a vital part of the PRC modernization plans.''[70]

The People's Republic of China has recently been opened to increased international trade. The charter of this trade will be strongly influenced by the Chinese development policy of the four modernizations: agriculture, industry, defense, and science and technology. With its shallow ports and limited road, rail, and air transportation facilities and communications infrastructure, it is not likely that China will become a major oceanborne trader for at least 10 years or more. Until its ports can be deepened to the 35- to 45-foot range necessary to accommodate larger modern container, roll-on and roll-off, general purpose break-bulk, and bulk cargo ships, it is likely that China's trade will have to be carried by small, shallow draft cargo vessels, by lightering from larger vessels anchored in deeper waters away from piers and terminals, by use of LASH ships (lighter aboard ship) that carry cargo-filled barges, or by using feeder services to Hong Kong and to Japan. Sixty to seventy percent of China's trade with the United States now moves through U.S. Gulf Coast ports.[71]

China's Gross Domestic Product has grown at seven percent annually, and its foreign trade has grown generally at the same rate; these trends are expected to continue.

Japan is the dominant trader with the People's Republic of China, exchanging whole factories and technology for PRC coal and oil. While the United States did $1.1 billion worth of trade with PRC in 1979, the Japanese signed a trade agreement, effective to 1990, that is valued at $40–60 billion, most of it to be paid for with PRC oil exports (7.6 mMT). In 1976, PRC exports were worth a total of $7.2 billion, of which $1.3 billion went to Japan; the total import figure was $6 billion, of which $1.7 billion came from Japan.[72]

Japan's trade has been described incidentally in the foregoing discussions. In more (but brief) detail, Japan, like the ROK, has a heavily unbalanced trade in terms of cargo tonnage; it imported eight times what it exported in 1976. Imports in the World Other trade accounted for 58 percent, and 339 mMT in 1976, most of this (217 mMT) being crude oil and petroleum products from the Middle East. Japan's principal export trade was also to World Other, shipping 36 mMT or 51 percent of its total exports there in 1976. Japan is truly a global trader, with most of its tonnage going to nations outside the North Pacific region, such as the Atlantic Coast of the United States, Europe, and the Middle East.[73]

## Bulk Petroleum Trades

The available information on U.S. Pacific Coast intraregional oil movement—the only oil movement in the North Pacific Ocean that is not of an international nature—is discussed in this section. For 1977, the only year for which such estimates have been published, the following is known: Cook Inlet, Alaska, production declined from its 1975 maximum of 9.68 million metric tons annually (mMTa) to 6.9 mMTa in 1977. Of this, 4.4 mMTa of crude oil and .99 mMTa of refined products were shipped to unidentified U.S. Pacific Coast refineries. The remaining Cook Inlet production was consumed in Alaska.[74] Cook Inlet natural gas shipments to Japan were .99 mMTa in 1977 (1.06 mMTa in 1976).[75]

Alaska also imported from foreign sources .19 mMTa of crude oil and .49 mMTa of products to meet needs that its own oil production and refining capacity could not fill. U.S. Pacific Coast refineries supplied Alaska with .89 mMTa of petroleum products. By the second half of 1977, roughly 3.48 mMTa of North Slope, Alaska, crude oil was being exported from Alaska, about 2.48 mMTa of which was consumed on the U.S. Pacific Coast and 1 mMTa was transported through the Panama Canal to U.S. Atlantic Coast areas.

Table 14.13 (chapter 14) shows historical and planned crude oil shipments in the PRC-Japan trade. Plans call for increased shipments, growing from 7 mMTa in 1978 to 15 mMTa in 1982, or an increase of 17.8 percent annually.[76] By 1976, oil from the People's Republic of China represented 2.3 percent of total Japanese petroleum imports.

The U.S. received its first shipment of Chinese crude oil, 103,000 metric tons, in early 1979 as part of a contract calling for shipment of 493,000 metric tons over an unreported period.[77]

The Chinese oil exports to Japan and the United States represent an expansion of China's marketing its oil. Chinese exports for earlier years have been reported as shown in table 8.9, although these reports are not consistent with reports for Chinese oil shipments to the DPRK, for example, as given in chapter 14.

Japan imports 99.5 percent of the oil it consumes. In 1978, Japan imported 233 mMT (270 million kiloliters), which was 3 percent less than its imports the previous year.[78] Japan imports most of its oil from the Middle East. Table 8.10 shows Japanese oil import sources. Note that despite great efforts to diversify its petroleum import sources since 1973, Japan has not succeeded in materially reducing its dependence on Middle East oil, and this has kept Japan very sensitive to foreign policy conflicts in that part of the world.

Japan promised at the Tokyo economic summit of 1979 to restrain its growth in oil imports for the next six years to a level of no more than 6.6 percent higher than in 1979. Such restraint is of major importance, because Japan accounts for 18 percent of the world oil

## TABLE 8.9

### CHINESE OIL EXPORTS

### (IN 1,000 METRIC TONS)

|  | 1974 | 1975 |
|---|---|---|
| *Crude Oil* |  |  |
| Japan | 4,000 | 8,100 |
| Philippines | 150 | 650 |
| Romania | – | 500 |
| DPRK | 500 | 900 |
| Subtotal | 4,650 | 10,150 |
| *Products* |  |  |
| Hong Kong | 250 | 630 |
| Thailand | 50 | 80 |
| Cambodia | 500 | 600 |
| Subtotal | 800 | 1,310 |
| Grand Total | 5,450 | 10,460 |

Source: *Platt's Oilgram* as reported in *Japan Petroleum News* (October 7, 1977).

## TABLE 8.10

### JAPANESE PETROLEUM IMPORTS

### (IN 1,000 METRIC TONS)

| Source | Fiscal Year 1972 (to March 31) | | Fiscal Year 1978 | |
|---|---|---|---|---|
| Middle East | 167,753 | 84% | 181,212 | 78% |
| People's Republic of China | 0 | 0 | 7,460 | 3 |
| Others (Indonesia, Malaysia, etc.) | 31,595 | 16 | 43,656 | 19 |
| Total | 199,348 | 100% | 232,328 | 100% |

Source: Henry Hymans, "Oil Imports to Japan Falling," *Seatrade* (July 1979), p 61.

trade. But in order to achieve this goal, it was reported that Japan planned to increase its imports of coal from about 60 mMTa to 100 mMTa in 1985, and to 170 mMTa by 1995, while liquified natural gas (LNG) imports would grow from 8 mMTa in 1977 to 29 mMTa in 1985, and eventually to 50 mMTa.[79] Japanese petroleum imports are the largest single crude oil trade on the North Pacific and employ roughly 14 percent of the world crude oil tanker fleet at any one time.[80]

Recent figures for the oil trades of the Soviet Union are shown in table 8.11. The USSR, like the People's Republic of China, supplies DPRK with crude oil, but the level of this trade is unclear since the United Nations reports total DPRK oil consumption as 1,225 million metric tons for 1975, whereas the combined figure for China and Soviet oil exports to DPRK shown in tables 8.9 and 8.11 is substantially higher.[81] Soviet supplies in the North Pacific come from the pipeline terminus at Vladivostok, and it is assumed here that this is the source for Soviet shipments to Japan, DPRK, and the rest of Southeast Asia. Otherwise, Soviet oil is assumed to move to non-Asian or European destinations from its Western ports and via pipeline. While Soviet oil exports have grown rapidly in the last few years, this growth trend is not likely to continue in light of forecasts of dwindling production in the mid- and late 1980s and beyond.[82] Soviet imports were approximately 7,200 thousand mMT for 1976.

U.S. Pacific Coast international petroleum movements are of lesser magnitude than those already discussed. In 1976, 44.5 mMT of crude oil and oil products were imported from the Middle East and Indonesia, and a small quantity was exported, mainly to the U.S. East Coast.[83] Canadian Pacific Coast petroleum movements were on the order of 300 thousand metric tons imported and 400 thousand metric tons exported.[84] The Canadian

TABLE 8.11

SOVIET OIL TRADES (EXPORTS)

(IN 1,000 METRIC TONS)

| Destination | 1975 | | 1976 | |
|---|---|---|---|---|
| Europe | 113,532 | | 130,711 | |
| Middle East | 208 | | 642 | |
| Asia/Pacific | 4,779 | | 5,121 | |
| Japan | | (1,320) | | (1,773) |
| DPRK | | (1,110) | | (1,061) |
| Other | | (2,349) | | (2,287) |
| Africa | 1,231 | | 1,382 | |
| Western Hemisphere | 10,601 | | 11,198 | |
| U.S.A. | | ( 539) | | (1,059) |
| Canada | | ( 220) | | ( 93) |
| Cuba | | (8,060) | | (8,809) |
| Brazil | | (1,475) | | (1,071) |
| Other | | ( 307) | | ( 166) |
| Total | 130,351 | | 149,054 | |

Source: *The Oil and Gas Journal* (August 15, 1977), which quotes from USSR Ministry of Foreign Trade, 1976, Statistical Summary.

Pacific Coast is supplied by oil pipeline from Edmonton in Alberta Province, and has little need for marine shipment of petroleum cargoes.

## CONCLUSIONS

This survey of the general pattern of trade on the North Pacific Ocean is admittedly brief. Yet it is perhaps the most comprehensive to date. The survey reveals that petroleum and containerized and noncontainerizable general cargoes are the three most important commodity groups moving on the North Pacific; that Japan is the predominant shipping influence; that trade movement is not spread uniformly over the expanse of the ocean, but is concentrated around Japan, extending southward and eastward; and that, with the exception of the Los Angeles–Long Beach shipping area, the intensity of use by international shipping on the eastern side of the North Pacific Ocean is rather low relative to that observed in the western and northwestern North Pacific Ocean.

Industrial development is proceeding in several areas such as Singapore, Republic of Korea, and Taiwan. This is having a visible impact on historic trade linkages because these countries emphasize trade as a means of furthering their economic well-being. The PRC is slowly awakening to the importance of trade, and this will further diversify and complicate the patterns of trade and vessel movements. Petroleum carriers will continue to be employed in the region to supply Japan, and as carriers of the PRC's most politically significant export.

With ocean trade patterns changing and tonnages growing, the possibilities for interference with other ocean uses and users will proliferate, although impediments to trade from this source do not yet appear to be affecting the patterns and levels of trade observed.

# 9

# Existing Regulatory Regime Governing Marine Transportation

This chapter discusses the existing regulatory regime governing vessel navigation and operation on the North Pacific. No multilateral arrangements exist today that explicitly address the North Pacific as a region. The international agreements are primarily global in coverage, but apply to the North Pacific and must therefore be addressed in discussing the management of vessel movements and operations in that area. The discussion is focused primarily upon United States, Canadian, and international arrangements for transportation flow management, although a brief discussion of Japanese regulation of transportation is included.

This discussion addresses the regulation of marine transportation in the North Pacific, but does not address the regulation of the *operation* of the commercial marine transportation industry. It deals with jurisdictional arrangements and regulations intended to assure the safe navigation of ships through the high seas and coastal waters of North Pacific rim nations. Navigation regulations can affect the conduct of business by raising the cost of operation (for example, through requiring the retrofitting of tank vessels with segregated ballast tanks) or by making the risks associated with maintaining service along a particular trade route excessively high. National trade and merchant marine policy may also have important consequences for the nature and distribution of vessel traffic in any area as well, but is not addressed here unless it significantly affects the volume of marine transportation moving in the region.

In discussing national and international regulation of vessel movement and operation, a distinction can be made between measures of the safety and efficiency of vessels in their navigational and operational procedures, and regulations that govern specific vessels and cargoes (i.e., large crude oil and dangerous bulk carriers). In both instances, the objective of regulation is to secure compliance with requirements that facilitate safe navigation without imposing too restrictive requirements upon shipowners and operators. Before discussing specific requirements that affect navigation, the legal context within which maritime commerce occurs is briefly outlined.

# INTERNATIONAL RULES GOVERNING COASTAL STATE JURISDICTION

Efficient and expeditious conduct of maritime commerce requires that vessels navigating outside inland and territorial waters not be subject to conflicting requirements regarding operation and navigation, but should comply with uniform rules and standards. At the same time, these measures must meet the needs of the coastal or port state regarding protection of its territory and citizens. On the international level, negotiations within the Intergovernmental Maritime Consultative Organization (IMCO) have been cumbersome and slow but have resulted in quite a few national conventions, recommendations, and resolutions. These measures have no force of their own and must be ratified and implemented by member nations. Because of the lengthy process of negotiation, and extensive influence that special interests have historically exercised within IMCO, several states have become impatient (including Canada and, recently, France and the U.S.), and have pressed for firmer regulation or unilateral action.[1] These states feel hampered by the nature of the IMCO forum and constituency and by the existing regime of international law governing coastal state jurisdiction over vessel activities in the territorial sea, contiguous zone, and on the high seas.

Coastal state jurisdiction to prescribe regulations applicable to foreign vessels is dependent upon the waters within which the vessel (foreign or domestic) is navigating. In internal waters,[2] a foreign vessel is subject to regulation by the coastal state and has no absolute right of entry into the state's internal waters. The coastal state may prescribe and require compliance with, for example, special navigation regulations as a condition for entry into ports.[3]

In waters seaward of the coastal state's baselines, its jurisdiction diminishes. In the territorial sea, the coastal state still has full sovereignty subject to the right of innocent passage for the international community. Foreign private commercial vessels engaged in innocent passage may be required to comply with reasonable safety and navigation regulations intended to protect the security and well-being of the coastal state.[4] Reasonable measures aimed at reducing ship casualties and pollution incidents appear to fall within such jurisdiction. However, with such a wide disparity in jurisdictional claims by coastal states (territorial seas measure from 3 to 200 nautical miles), the nature and extent of coastal state rights is not settled. Indeed, not only the disparity in area claims, but also the wide disagreement about coastal state powers over navigation and pollution control within the Law of the Sea negotiations has left issues unresolved.

Outside the territorial sea, in the contiguous zone, the coastal state's jurisdiction is limited to the enforcement of fiscal, immigration, customs, and sanitary laws of the coastal state.[5] Certain special agreements under treaties of commerce and navigation with the flag state of vessels calling upon a coastal state's ports may entitle the coastal state to exercise jurisdiction over vessels outside of the territorial sea. Until the past fifteen years the extent of coastal state jurisdiction over vessel activities outside of the territorial sea was negligible.

Vessels on the high seas are subject to the exclusive jurisdiction of the flag state except for one convention that authorizes a coastal state to take certain actions, under conditions of duress, against a foreign oil-carrying vessel that has foundered outside the coastal state's territorial sea and is threatening the state with imminent oil pollution damage.[6] Flag states are required to generate and enforce regulations governing their own vessels when they are on the high seas.[7] Unfortunately, flag states have not always enforced such measures diligently, especially when they are "flag of convenience"[8] states. No effective jurisdiction is possible when these vessels rarely touch base in their "adopted" legal homes. The impatience of many coastal states with lax flag state enforcement of vessel operating standards, and the pollution record of many flag of convenience vessels, has prompted a push for much stricter standards and liability requirements, either within an international forum or by unilateral legislation.

## THE REGULATION OF NAVIGATION

### International

Freedom of navigation entails two principles; one involves the right to enjoy unimpeded progress over the seas, the other requires that navigation be safe with respect to speed, steering, and lights.[9] The first right pertains to the freedom of passage from waters on the high seas through a coastal state's territorial sea. But this can be limited by unilateral jurisdictional claims and by the effects of competing uses of ocean space. The second principle dictates that directions be given to the mariner by the flag state or the appropriate organization.

Until recently the independence of the mariner in determining how his ship is to be navigated has been accepted practice, although subject to some flag state requirements.

> (National legislation) . . . has met, or at the most compromised with, the commercial demands of the shipping industry and it has done so in isolation of the impacts these activities have on interests outside the industry. . . . However, both the independence of the masters and the self regulation by the industry are being increasingly broken down by national and international regulation.[10]

Despite the fact that mariners have, over the centuries, adopted navigating and collision-preventing rules in the absence of any formal authority, this self-regulation by customary adaptation is no longer sufficient. The increasing size and speed of vessels, the increased congestion in traffic (sea) lanes, the decreased maneuverability of ships, and the wider consequences that vessel accidents have upon coastal areas and other uses of the oceanic resources dictate that regulations that go beyond mere safety measures be promulgated outside the industry.[11] These regulations vary due to the type of vessel, type of cargo, nature of geographical area in which the ship operates, and the nature of onboard operations and operating equipment.

The present international rules regarding navigation and collision avoidance can be found in the International Regulations for Preventing Collisions at Sea (1960, with the 1972 amendments) and the convention to which these collision regulations (COLREG) were attached, the International Convention for the Safety of Life at Sea (SOLAS, 1960).

The COLREG, or "rules of the road" Convention,[12] establishes navigational requirements of various kinds intended to give shipmasters a standardized guide to avoid collisions. It prescribes regulations regarding light and sound signals, and establishes international rules dealing with steering and sailing in areas with wide and narrow channels and in both good and poor visibility conditions. The 1960 regulations suffered from a number of weaknesses, however.

1. They failed to address the changed navigating conditions that accompanied faster ships and huge vessels operating in ever more congested sea lanes.
2. They did not adequately address situations where the risk of collision was imminent, but instead dealt only with *avoiding* dangerous crossing situations. No standardized guidance was available to the shipmaster in emergency situations.
3. They did not anticipate the advent of the supership with its chronic maneuverability problems that made it impossible to fulfill all the conditions required in the convention.
4. They did not contain adequate provisions on one of the most vital aspects of navigating a ship, the radar.[13]

These weaknesses and the practical necessity of upgrading the regulations to respond to changing conditions resulted in an IMCO meeting in October 1972, which produced an upgraded set of regulations and amendments that entered into force on July 15, 1977.

The 1972 rules of the road contain many changes dealing with safe speed, operation of vessels in and around traffic separation scheme (TSS) areas, vessels operating in narrow channels, and vessels with restricted maneuverability. The more important regulations include provisions on the use of sophisticated radar,[14] requirements that apply to vessels with deep draught and limited maneuverability (including lighting requirements and the priority given these vessels in navigating),[15] and the requirement that vessels either adhere to IMCO-adopted TSSs[16] or keep clear of these areas.[17]

Prior to the ungraded regulations, IMCO-approved TSSs could be used at the discretion of mariners. This created a potential problem for coastal states that had suggested the adoption of TSSs in international waters off their congested coasts and presented the plans to IMCO for adoption. Optional TSSs provided no real remedy to vessel congestion. Potentially hazardous conditions were cleared up by the adoption of the 1972 rules, which are binding only upon the ships of signatory states. The COLREGs apply to international waters, areas outside coastal states' jurisdiction. Waters inshore of the line of demarcation are subject to coastal state "inland rules of the road."

The 1960 SOLAS Convention addressed various safety-related matters for vessels, including ship certification. Among matters addressed were ship stability requirements, fire protection equipment, lifesaving equipment, radar equipment, safety of navigation and navigation equipment, and the safe storage of goods carried on board.[18] National Coast Guard units, such as the U.S. Coast Guard (USCG), require vessels to display up-to-date SOLAS certificates, and see to it that domestic flag vessels obey reinspection requirements.

## National

Vessel management by coastal states involves more than mere control of vessel movement by the use of traffic separation schemes. It also includes coastal state jurisdictional claims, which by themselves affect navigation through the zones involved. States bordering the North Pacific waters have legislated and promulgated standards applicable to their zones of jurisdiction, whether these zones be clearly acceptable (and standard) regions of jurisdiction (such as territorial seas), or are areas claimed by the coastal state in ways inconsistent with prevailing state practice (such as extensive pollution control claims over vast areas of ocean space). Although legislation and regulation since 1970 has become increasingly concerned with specific kinds of cargoes and vessels, a considerable body of law exists that addresses the safety of navigation in general. A brief discussion of some of this law is given in the following sections.

### United States

Title I of the Ports and Waterways Safety Act (PL 92-340) of 1972 articulates U.S. policy for the regulation of vessels within U.S. ports, granting the Secretary of Transportation and the U.S. Coast Guard rule promulgation and enforcement authority. As a result of this legislation, the Coast Guard for the first time became involved in vessel traffic management.[19] Under the Act, the Secretary of Transportation, in order to guarantee vessel safety and protect the environment, was empowered to (1) establish and operate vessel traffic services at ports and harbors and other congested areas, regulating time of entry, ship speed and size limits, and location of vessel anchorage and moorage; (2) establish traffic separation schemes, with similar regulations; and (3) provide for mandatory pilotage on all navigable U.S. waters that require it.

Pilotage standards are provided for in the Pilotage Act of 1789,[20] which vested authority in the states to regulate pilotage for vessels engaged in international trade. Coastwise and intercoastal trade was and is subject to federal pilotage requirements, including the requirement that such vessels carry on board a licensed federal pilot while in U.S. waters. While confusion may appear possible with different pilotage standards, most state pilots are also federally licensed and the two levels of government cooperate in the performance of this function.

Another important part of vessel management in U.S. waters, vessel traffic systems (VTS), is also run by the USCG, under Title I of the Ports and Waterways Safety Act. Coastal and port areas judged by the USCG to be congested with certain types of large vessels are to establish/incorporate VTSs. Of the five[21] USCG VTSs presently operating, three are on the Pacific coast: the Puget Sound, San Francisco, and Valdez systems.[22]

The U.S. and Canada initiated a joint VTS in the waters of the Strait of Juan de Fuca in August 1974 to coordinate the measures being taken by the Ministry of Transport (MOT) in Canada and the USCG to manage the flow of traffic coming into Puget Sound. The heart of the VTS is a traffic separation scheme in which incoming ships use the south (U.S.) side of the strait, and outgoing ships use the north (Canadian) side of the strait. Vessels report their movements to Coast Guard officers at regular intervals, with traffic centers providing information to mariners to minimize the threat of an accident.[23]

The U.S. and Canada maintain their own vessel traffic schemes for nonborder waters, such as the San Francisco, Vancouver, and Valdez schemes. These schemes differ in requirements and operation but considerably aid the safe navigation of ships.

## Canada

The Ministry of Transport has been granted authority by the Canadian Parliament to make regulations establishing compulsory traffic routes and other controls essential for safe navigation.[24] The Canadian Shipping Act, in addition to prescribing navigational practices and construction requirements for vessels carrying dangerous bulk cargoes, establishes general rules and enforcement measures applicable to mariners.

Canada does not have specific inland rules of the road applicable to British Columbia's coastlines but instead merely applies agreed-upon international rules to vessel navigation. Mandatory pilotage is required in the waters inward from Victoria, though coasting vessels and American-registered ships coming from San Francisco (and north of there) and headed to Alaskan ports are exempted.[25] A voluntary VTS is maintained on portions of the British Columbian coast, where the individuals who are in charge of running the traffic control—called Vessel Traffic Regulators—are also designated as Pollution Prevention Officers by the MOT.[26] They therefore have the authority to issue orders regarding speed, anchorage, pilotage, routes, and may even deny access to vessels they have reason to believe are in violation of Canadian law or are hazardous to the environment.

## Japan

Japanese coastal waters have some of the most intense vessel traffic of any waters in the world. Japan, as the major marine shipping nation in the North Pacific region, must make certain that vessel traffic moving into and out of its many congested ports is not subject to unnecessary navigational hazards. As a result, the Japanese, despite their firm opposition to regulatory measures that restrict vessel movement unnecessarily (because of extensive jurisdictional claims), have implemented international measures (such as the COLREG and SOLAS standards) and have instituted a complex vessel traffic management system.

The International Regulations for the Prevention of Collisions at Sea (1960) have been adopted by the Japanese in their Regulations for Preventing Collisions at Sea (1960). In addition to this, two other laws address the safety of navigation—the Japanese Port Regulations Law and the Maritime Traffic Safety Law. The Port Regulations Law[27] maintains safety and order in all 499 (as of May 1976) ports located in the country. Regulations include navigational provisions, signal requirements, channel safety requirements, anchorage provisions, and steps to be followed at times of accidents. Of the ports governed by this law, 73 (including the Keihan District and the Ports of Nagoya, Kobe and Osaka) are designated as special ports due to their heavy traffic volumes.[28] Vessels navigating in these ports are subject to stricter regulations on anchorage, the handling and storing of dangerous cargoes, and notification of port entry or exit. Harbor masters, who are appointed by the Maritime Safety Agency (MSA), are responsible for the enforcement of regulations on vessel movement and the handling of dangerous cargoes.[29]

The Maritime Traffic Safety Law[30] was enacted to maintain vessel traffic safety in the three most congested navigating areas in Japanese internal waters—the Bay of Tokyo, the Bay of Ise, and the Seto Inland Sea. The law establishes special traffic separation schemes and designates eleven sea routes in these areas. Vessels navigating these routes are required to observe the single lane TSSs, obey certain requirements for vessel speed, and adhere to the regulations governing the number of vessels incoming and outgoing and the behavior of vessels crossing these sea routes.[31] "Huge" vessels (longer than 200 meters) have the right-of-way over smaller steamships and fishing vessels, though these large ships are also subject to requirements. They must announce to MSA traffic operators their intentions to pass through sea lanes, allowing officials and patrol boats to make adequate preparations for their passage. Finally, in the event of an accident, the MSA may prescribe temporary restrictions on navigation freedom in the affected areas.

## REGULATION OF VESSELS CARRYING DANGEROUS CARGOES

### International

A variety of dangerous contaminants find their way into the ocean. Some of them are found naturally in the waters of the ocean, but at very low concentrations; others are the product of man's activity.

International attention has focused on the problem of marine pollution in unprecedented fashion in the past decade. A considerable amount of this attention concerns the contaminants that enter the oceans from shipping operations or accidents, occurrences that cause considerable localized damage to the other uses of coastal oceanic resources (fishing, other shipping, and recreation).

International concern over ship-generated pollution began in the early twentieth century when the international community first perceived the risks associated with oceanic transport of petroleum, which now results in about 17 percent of the total petroleum inflow into the oceans that is attributable to human actions.[32] With increased petroleum commerce after World War II, more and larger vessels traversed the oceans. Several factors have been responsible for the increased jurisdictional claims by coastal states over the navigation of tankers (and other vessels carrying hazardous cargoes) in their coastal waters: (1) the sheer volume of the products moved by ship, a phenomenon caused by the enormous growth in demand for crude oil; (2) the increased concentration of the sources of supply, a development necessitating the use of specific petroleum trade routes; (3) the revolution in the technologies of tanker size, culminating in the rise of the supertanker; (4) the increased multiple uses of the ocean, particularly in the resource and activity-rich coastal areas; and (5) the dissatisfaction of many coastal states with the present national and international regulations governing vessels that carry dangerous cargoes.

International agreements addressing the protection of the marine environment from damages caused by maritime commerce have been drafted and adopted by IMCO. Their standards are a response to several areas of concern associated with oil tanker operations: pollution from deliberate discharge (deballasting, bilge pumping), pollution resulting from accidents and groundings, the rights of coastal states to protect their coastlines against oil pollution, and liability and compensation arrangements in the event of spills. In addition, IMCO has considered the transportation of other toxic substances. International arrangements have also been made by conferences not called by IMCO regarding the regulation of waste dumping activities. The regulatory arrangements addressing these problem areas are discussed in turn.

### Deliberate Oil Discharge

The first international convention regulating the deliberate discharge of petroleum from ships was the International Convention for the Prevention of Pollution of the Sea by Oil (Oil Pollution Convention, 1954).[33] Amendments to the Convention were drafted in 1962 and 1969 and are now in force. The Oil Pollution Convention addresses the intentional discharge of oil from vessels over 500 gross tons.[34] Tankers, as a result of the 1969 amendments on January, 8, 1978, are prohibited from discharging oil into waters within 50 miles of the nearest land, or into other "prohibited areas." Other ships are required to be "as far as practicable" from land during discharges.[35]

Ships greater than 20,000 gross tons are prohibited from discharging oil anywhere at sea unless special circumstances exist.[36] Coastal states have the responsibility to provide facilities for disposal of oil-water mixtures in their ports. Under the 1969 amendments, in waters outside 50 nautical miles, certain limitations apply to the amount of oil to be discharged: the instantaneous rate of discharge shall not be more than 60 litres per mile of an oily mixture not over 100 ppm oily waste in water, with the total quantity released being not more than 1:15,000 of the ship's cargo.[37]

Several aspects associated with enforcement are worth noting. In requiring that tankers carry and maintain a log book of shipboard operations (Article IX of the Convention) it was hoped that coastal, port, or flag states would have means at their disposal to ensure compliance with the Convention requirements by a simple inspection of the log book's contents when the vessel was in port. However, there is no effective way to guarantee that the officers do not doctor the entries. Enforcement of the Convention is left to the flag state,[38] which is called upon to provide for sanctions and penalties severe enough to discourage violations, and penalties equal to those applicable to vessels navigating in waters of its jurisdiction. Little evidence exists to date to indicate that the flag states have taken their responsibilities seriously. Finally, the requirements dealing with operational discharge outside 50 miles are not easily monitored.[39] In sum, the 1954 Convention and Amendments to eliminate certain sources of ship-generated oil pollution have not lived up to the expectations many held for it. In the absence of coastal state authority, clearly not provided for in the Convention, the 1954 Act and the Amendments have had limited effectiveness.

### Accidental Oil Spills

The international community has also addressed pollution of the sea resulting from the collision or grounding of oil tankers in or around the territorial waters[40] of coastal states. Two conventions, drafted in response to the *Torrey Canyon* catastrophe of 1967, attempted to protect the interests of damaged or potentially damaged parties. These are the Convention

Relating to the Intervention on the High Seas in Cases of Oil Pollution Casualties (1969, The Public Law Convention) and the International Convention on Civil Liability for Oil Pollution Damage (1969, the Private Law Convention).

The Public Law Convention[41] grants coastal states the right to intervene on the high seas, beyond the territorial sea, in order to prevent, mitigate, or eliminate the imminent danger of pollution to their coastlines that might follow an accident or marine casualty. The coastal state is required to consult the flag state, seeking its advice on the possible courses of action,[42] unless the danger requires immediate action. Even then, the action taken by the coastal state must be proportional to the threat it faces[43] or it can be required to compensate the vessel owner for the overreaction.[44] The Convention thus attempts to strike a balance between the coastal state's interest in protecting its environment and economic interests of the vessel. At the same time, the flag state and vessel owner's interest is protected from arbitrary action against their vessels.

The Private Law Convention[45] seeks to provide compensation to those who sustain damage from oil spills caused by accidents and casualties, and to determine liability for such payments. It applies to situations arising in the territorial seas of a nation, and actions taken to minimize the consequent damage.

The Convention establishes strict liability for shipowners[46] who may be exempted from liability in the event that the accident resulted from an Act of God, war, or from negligent acts taken by the coastal state.[47] Financial liability is limited to $16.8 million for each incident, unless the shipowner or operator was guilty of willful actions, in which case liability is unlimited.[48] Coastal states may require that private vessels carrying more than 2000 tons of bulk oil cargo must have evidence of insurance or security on board, no matter where the vessel is and irrespective of the flag.[49] Otherwise, the vessel may be excluded. The Convention is now in force, though the U.S. has not yet ratified it.

The Public Law Convention is in force for all Pacific rim nations with the exception of Canada, which claims that it already had the jurisdiction to intervene in such instances via the Arctic Waters Pollution Prevention Act.

## Dumping

The International Convention on the Prevention of Marine Pollution by Dumping of Wastes and Other Matter (December, 29, 1972)[50] regulates the disposal of wastes and other matter into the sea but does not cover wastes from normal ship operations, the placement of matter into the ocean for nondumping purposes,[51] nor wastes from seabed mining. Vessels engaged in dumping are required to secure permits stipulating the type of material to be dumped, the amounts to be dumped, and the time and place of dumping.[52] Certain categories of material may not be dumped, however, due to their toxicity, and other materials may only be dumped in limited quantities[53] and in conformance with issued permits.

Permits are issued and jurisdiction is exercised by state authorities for materials intended for dumping that are loaded in its territory, loaded by a vessel or aircraft registered there or flying its flag, vessels or aircraft loading material that is intended to be dumped in the territorial sea, or fixed or floating platforms under its jurisdiction that are believed to be dumping.[54] Thus, signatory states are required to see to it that the activities are carefully regulated, and they are assigned the necessary power and jurisdiction to do so. They are also to punish offenders, and can determine where vessels or platforms carry out their activities.

Despite the great concern registered by the international community over the threat posed by the entry of radioactive materials into the ocean, relatively few conventions have addressed the problem. This is due, in part, to the fact that there are so few nuclear-powered merchant vessels operating on the sea, and also to the very stringent packaging regulations that apply to radioactive materials carried aboard ships.[55] The dangers associated with nuclear materials emanate from three situations: leakage resulting from a collision; the lethal effects of dumping radioactive wastes; and radioactive wastes released due to normal ship operations.

Collision prevention and careful construction of nuclear-powered vessels were addressed primarily in the SOLAS Convention (1960 and 1974)[56] and in the International Dangerous Goods Code,[57] which addresses nuclear material transport. The SOLAS Convention provided for several things: the careful regulation of labeling, packaging, and classification of dangerous goods, and the imposition of very stringent safety inspection procedures by flag states, who are to approve the construction and installation of vessel reactors and periodically inspect the ships.[58]

Coastal and port states are authorized to grant or deny nuclear-powered commercial vessels access to their ports, depending upon whether the vessels are carrying valid safety inspection certificates, which the flag state issues.[59] Coastal states are also entitled to receive the flag state's evaluation of the vessel before the ship seeks entry there. The standard of evaluation (i.e., that the vessel shall not pose an "unreasonable radiation hazard") is somewhat ambiguous and grants coastal states discretion in their ruling on access.

The SOLAS Convention has several weaknesses. First, warships are exempted from the provisions.[60] These vessels presently constitute the major portion of the nuclear-powered vessel fleet navigating the oceans. Therefore, the Convention addresses only the smallest part of the problem—commercial nuclear-powered or nuclear material-carrying merchant vessels. Second, compliance is not ensured by the reliance upon the "good faith" of nations, and there are no independent sources of monitoring or inspection. Third, the ambiguity about safety standards and radiation hazards constitutes an obstacle to effective enforcement.

The carriage of nuclear materials is addressed in the International Atomic Energy Agency (IAEA) Regulations for Safe Transport of Radioactive Materials.[61] This establishes standards governing the transport and control of radioactive materials and updates the provisions of the 1960 SOLAS Convention.

## National

### Designing, Constructing, and Manning Dangerous Cargo Carriers

The USCG is entrusted with authority to promulgate rules and standards governing the construction of vessels, and to inspect them for compliance with safety standards.[62] The

Coast Guard inspects all U.S. flag vessels, both during their construction and periodically thereafter, to ensure that they pose no hazards to navigation or to the environment. All United States flag ships, including tankers, must carry USCG certificates in order to operate.

Title II of the Ports and Waterways Safety Act (1972, PWSA) expanded the authority of the Coast Guard with respect to regulating tanker operation and construction to protect the waters of the United States and the personnel on board. United States-documented tankers operating anywhere, and foreign tankers navigating within U.S. internal waters, are subject to Coast Guard regulations regarding (1) the design, construction, and maintenance of vessels; (2) the handling of cargo, including petroleum and other dangerous substances, such as chemicals and radioactive materials; (3) lifesaving and environmental protection equipment; (4) the operation and movements of vessels; and (5) the manning of vessels.[63] Public vessels not engaged in commerce, and vessels carrying substances only as fuel or for vessel stores, or which carry oil only in drums and other nonbulk forms, are not subject to some of these regulations.[64]

United States Coast Guard rule-making for vessel design and construction under Title II of the PWSA (the Tanker Act) places limitations on operational discharge and requires that newly constructed tankers of over 70,000 dwt tons be equipped with segregated ballast tanks to separate oil from ballast water[65] in accordance with the Articles of the 1973 IMCO Convention.

The Coast Guard, under 46 U.S.C. 222, sets standards for the licensing of officers and crew on U.S. flag vessels. The rules prescribe the number of crew that must be on board tankers while the vessel is operating. And, under the Tanker Act, foreign flag vessels entering U.S. navigable waters may be boarded to ensure that they meet the manning standards provided for in the SOLAS and the Officer Competency Certificates Convention of 1932.[66] The Competency Convention, as implemented, requires that each officer aboard a vessel hold an appropriate competency certificate based upon experience and an examination. These standards are set exclusively by the flag state.

The documentation process for tankers is also important, inasmuch as it determines which vessels will carry oil to U.S. refineries. United States tankers must be American-owned and either registered or enrolled and licensed in the United States. For U.S. registry, they may be foreign built, but for enrollment they must be both U.S. owned and built.[67] Foreign registered or built tankers may carry oil between U.S. ports and foreign areas, but non-U.S. enrolled foreign built tankers may not (because of the cabotage requirements in the Jones Act) engage in coasting trade. Finally, a U.S. documented vessel must have only U.S. officers and a crew that is 75 percent American. While these measures are intended to subsidize the U.S. shipping and shipbuilding industries, they also have implications for the regulation of navigation by controlling which vessels may serve U.S. ports in certain trades.

## OIL POLLUTION PREVENTION AND CONTAINMENT

The U.S. has implemented the 1954 Oil Pollution Prevention Convention and the 1962 and 1969 amendments by way of the Oil Pollution Act of 1961.[68] The U.S. has ratified the

Public Law Convention but not the Private Law Convention because it feels that the liability coverage is unsatisfactory. The U.S.-accepted conventions aim at the reduction of certain sources of oil pollution.

The Federal Water Quality Improvement Act of 1970[69] regulates the navigation and operation of vessels of any registry in the U.S. contiguous zone. Tankers may be denied access to U.S. ports if they do not carry certificates on board showing proof of financial responsibility. They are also required to carry equipment on board for the clean-up of small spills. This is also required in the Federal Water Pollution Control Act.[70] Proof of financial security and arrangements governing damage reimbursement for spills associated with the transport of Alaskan oil is provided for in the Trans-Alaskan Pipeline Act (TAPS) of 1973.[71] Liability limitations and conditions similar to the Private Law Convention are provided for in the TAPS Legislation.

## ENFORCEMENT

Existing United States law has also entrusted the USCG with general enforcement authority[72] to make inquiries, examinations, inspections, searches and seizures, and arrests in areas of U.S. jurisdiction. In the event of a suspected violation of U.S. laws, USCG officers may board and inspect foreign vessels.

The Magnuson Act[73] provides for the inspection of any vessel at any time it is navigating in U.S. territorial waters. Vessels, under the Tanker Act, must also comply with vessel safety requirements before they are allowed to take any bulk oil on board. Permits are required for these vessels.[74] However, if foreign vessels have certificates on board that are recognized under U.S. law or treaty, then the restrictive regulations for vessel safety do not apply to them.

Denial of entry may occur if vessels do not comply with the standards established in the Tanker Act. Port Captains, as agents of the U.S. government, are charged with protecting U.S. waters and guarantee compliance. In areas deemed hazardous, Title I of the PWSA allows the appropriate officials to restrict vessel traffic, whether within or outside of ports.

Canada has adopted a policy regarding the regulation of tanker traffic and operations that, until recent years, disturbed many of the maritime powers. Canada's concern with protecting its Arctic environment led it to make more extensive jurisdictional claims than most nations up to 1975. This included a redefinition of innocent passage, requiring vessels to comply with certain Canadian standards in order to navigate in Arctic areas. The major thrust of Canadian policy can be found in two pieces of legislation—the Arctic Waters Pollution Prevention Act and Part XX of the Canadian Shipping Act.

The Arctic Waters Act[75] establishes a 100-mile contiguous zone along the Canadian shores north of the 60th parallel within which the Canadians claim authority over vessels for the purpose of protecting the marine and onshore environment. All vessels, irrespective of flag, are required to refrain from the deposition of materials (especially oil) into this area. They are also subject to Canadian standards with respect to vessel operations and construction in order to be guaranteed navigational rights. These include manning, shipboard operating, and navigating requirements, some of which are stricter than international standards.

In order to gain access to these waters, vessels must not only meet the special requirements but must also carry certificates of compliance on board issued by flag states, which may be inspected by Canadian pollution control officers; they must also carry proof of financial responsibility.[76] In the event of a collision or accident within the 100-mile zone, the Canadians maintain the right to take any actions they deem necessary, including the destruction of the vessel, in order to eliminate the hazard.

The Arctic Waters Act was intended to control the actions of vessels that might try to open up the Northwest Passage, but has not been enforced because no oil vessels navigate in this area. The legislation itself is partly responsible for this state of affairs, however, because it discourages major oil corporations from sending vessels through the Canadian Arctic. The main body of functional Canadian legislation is found in the Canadian Shipping Act.[77]

The Shipping Act addresses a variety of matters, including the discharge of pollutants, the use of navigational aids, the methods of retention of oil and water wastes, and the various personnel and manning requirements essential to ensure safe navigation.[78] The discharge of oil from ships of any kind is prohibited in the fishing zones established by Canadian legislation.[79] Like the Arctic Waters Act, the Shipping Act empowers Pollution Control Officers to inspect and seize or arrest a vessel that violates Canadian standards. The vessel may also be fined up to $100,000. Certain equipment must be carried on board tankers, including oil-retention facilities, clean-up equipment, and emergency navigation equipment. These are consistent with IMCO standards.

Surveillance and enforcement is carried out by the Canadian Coast Guard,[80] which is especially interested in seeing this Act complied with to the edge of the 12-mile territorial sea, where the threat of damage is the greatest, and in the delimited fishing zones, which are coterminus in places with the territorial sea. Some ambiguity exists with the extension of the fishing zone to 200 miles. It is not clear whether enforcement of the Shipping Act will extend this far.

## CONCLUSIONS

There is a fairly well-defined set of laws and regulations, both national and international, that applies to the North Pacific and addresses safety of navigation generally, and the navigation and operation of bulk tanker vessels in particular. With respect to the regime for navigation found in the COLREGs and SOLAS, both coastal states and the shipping community have maintained a common interest in the safe conduct of vessels engaged in maritime commerce. These rules and practices have developed over centuries. Only recently has the revolution in maritime commerce and vessel technology indicated that self-regulation by the shipping community is inadequate.

Coastal states find they have particular interests to protect when they promulgate regulations governing access and navigation. The necessity for safe and expeditious commerce in their busy ports, and the multiple uses to which much of this ocean space is put, dictates that the coastal states adopt what may seem to be restrictive standards. As the Washington State tanker law (declared unconstitutional by the Federal courts in 1977 but still in force as a result of a special ruling by the U.S. Secretary of Transportation) indicates, even subnational special interests may drive the process of regulation.

The growing coastal state challenges to the preeminence of flag state jurisdiction reflect the dissatisfaction of many nations with the slow and cumbersome evolution of stricter standards governing international navigation. Canada, France, and now the United States, are in the forefront in advocating greater coastal state jurisdictional powers over vessel operations, particularly tanker operations. As technological changes continue to occur in the shipbuilding industry, the need for an alteration of the specific conditions applicable to navigation in certain areas and the demands by coastal states for control over marine transportation in their coastal areas and economic zones will continue to occur.

The events taking place globally as well as within the North Pacific region demand a reevaluation and alteration of the existing regime governing navigation. As trade in the region grows (generating larger vessels and more ships entering port areas) and as technological changes occur, the nations involved must alter the management arrangements. The norms governing the use of the oceans and the claims made by nations are in a process of change and could lead to dramatic alterations in the historical arrangements governing marine commerce.

# 10

# Emerging Regulatory Trends and Their Implications for Ocean Commerce

Commercial marine transportation in the North Pacific has increased considerably over the past few decades.[1] As a consequence of greater use of, and interest in, marine resources, including shipping, coastal states have attempted to shape the regulatory arrangements governing usage in ways consistent with their interests.[2] An example of this can be found in coastal state jurisdictional claims to regulate access of vessels to coastal waters outside the territorial sea.

In addition to the increasing demand for changes in the regime governing vessel operation and navigation, there are shifts occurring at the national and international level that could affect the conduct of commercial shipping in the North Pacific. These developments, while not directly affecting the spatial patterns of marine transportation in the North Pacific, could affect the intergovernmental climate in the region. They could either encourage or discourage trade and could therefore affect marine transportation in the North Pacific. The objective of this chapter is to discuss the changes that may affect both navigation (and ship operation) and shipping policy.

A few observations must be made. First, the present negotiations in UNCLOS III that affect navigation and pollution will yield some minor changes in the regulation of pollution prevention and navigation. Second, the force motivating increased demands for vessel regulation in UNCLOS III (i.e., changing coastal state perceptions and demands) may in some cases result in unilateral action that goes beyond the measures agreed upon by the international community. Some of these claims to prescribe and enforce new regulations alarm the shipping community and the commercial maritime powers. Third, the states' interest in maximizing the domestic economic, political, and military benefits of trade relationships could affect marine transportation in the North Pacific. New trade agreements, national legislation promoting subsidy and protectionism, and possible new international arrangements regulating the liner conference system (not now in effect) could alter (promote or inhibit) shipping relations between regional partners. This may affect the type and volume of vessels navigating in the North Pacific. None of these observations carry uniquely regional implications, but they do affect the sea trade and navigation of vessels in the North Pacific.[3]

## CHANGING INTERNATIONAL RULES AND THEIR CONSEQUENCES FOR NAVIGATION

The regime that regulates the navigation and access of vessels to waters, both within coastal state jurisdiction and on the high seas, is changing. In IMCO, states continue to discuss and draft regulations for vessel safety and for the prevention of pollution from ships. At the same time that some states are lobbying for more stringent regulations within IMCO, negotiations at UNCLOS III have been aimed at producing a comprehensive text on the law of the sea. Portions of the present negotiating text, the Draft Convention, would, if accepted and ratified, alter the regime for navigation and pollution from ships.[4]

The multilateral instruments discussed below, which include the 1973 MARPOL Convention, the 1978 Protocols emerging from the London Tanker Safety and Pollution Prevention (TSPP) Conference, and the Draft Convention provisions, are not presently in force. Each of them, however, endeavors to alter the present international regime governing ship navigation and pollution prevention. These three, in particular, imply changes with respect both to formal jurisdictional arrangements, and onboard (vessel) construction and operating requirements. Their objective is to eliminate, reduce, or mitigate the impacts of oil pollution resulting from ship operations or casualties.

### The International Convention for the Prevention of Pollution from Ships (MARPOL)

The MARPOL Convention of 1973[5] was intended to replace and update the 1954 International Convention for the Prevention of Pollution of the Sea by Oil standards governing tanker oil discharges, and to apply similar restrictions to bulk carriers transporting other noxious cargoes.[6] It deals primarily with the elimination, or minimization, of operational oil outflows. But it goes much further than the 1954 Convention because it mandates ship operation procedures and construction features designed to reduce oil discharges.

Several items covered in the annexes to the 1973 Convention are worth noting. Annex I, which addresses primarily ships that carry petroleum cargo on board, applies to all tankers over 150 gross tons and to other ships over 400 gross tons, requiring that they carry valid International Oil Pollution Prevention Certificates, which are issued pursuant to vessel inspection and updated at no more than five-year intervals. The flag state assumes responsibility over ships flying its flag. The vessel operational discharge standards provided for in the 1954 Convention, as amended, are made twice as stringent for new tankers (over 150 gross tons) by requiring that the total discharge of oil and oily waste per voyage not exceed 1:30,000 of the vessel's last cargo load. As a way of monitoring the instantaneous rate of waste discharge, all tankers must install an oil discharge monitoring system with an oil content meter that has been approved by the flag state. Port states are required, for their part, to make available at oil loading, repair, and other ports, facilities for the reception of oil residues and mixtures that the vessels retain on board in conformity with the regulations.[7]

The most innovative aspects of the MARPOL Convention are its prescriptions regarding ship operation and construction standards. All new oil tankers greater than 70,000 deadweight tons (dwt) must be equipped with segregated ballast tanks. On these and smaller tankers, retention of oil on board (use of the load-on-top, or LOT, system) is required, as are sludge tank installations and oil-water separators. Appendix 3 of Annex I details the particulars to be followed by ship officers in logging entries in the revised oil record book. The log is an instrument designed to facilitate enforcement.

Annex II calls for similar regulations for owners of vessels that carry noxious chemical bulk cargoes, including prohibiting them from discharging substances within special geographic areas, requirements for port reception facilities, and the format and nature of information to be contained in cargo record books. Annexes III, IV and V deal with the prevention of pollution from ships that carry cargoes in packages or in freight containers, from ship sewage, and from ship garbage, respectively.[8]

Enforcement provisions of the MARPOL Convention incorporate a new concept—port state jurisdiction. Ships that are required to hold valid ship seaworthiness certificates are subject (while in port or at offshore terminals of other states) to inspection by authorized port state officers, who ensure that a valid certificate is carried on board. If such officers expect that the ship's condition doesn't correspond to the particulars in the certificate, further search of the vessel is warranted.[9] If this inspection reveals that a violation has occurred (that the vessel either carries no valid certificate on board, or that the ship's condition does not correspond to the certificate) the port authorities may ensure that the vessel does not sail until it can proceed without posing a threat to the marine environment. Denial of entry to a vessel is also an appropriate sanction against delinquent ships, provided that the party contemplating the action informs the representative of the flag state, or the state under whose authority the vessel is sailing.

Inspection for the purpose of detecting a violation of the *discharge* (of oil, chemicals, sewage, etc.) provisions of the Convention is also allowed. If a violation is detected, the inspecting state reports it to the flag state or the state under whose authority the vessel is sailing, which then takes appropriate action. The flag state may also, in conducting its investigation and evidence-gathering operation, request the port state to pass along further information on the alleged violation. Finally, a port state is authorized to inspect a vessel entering its ports when requested to do so by a state that claims the vessel discharged harmful substances into its waters, provided that proper evidence supports the allegation. Nothing in the MARPOL Convention is to prejudice the process of codification and progressive development of international law occurring at UNCLOS III, nor the present or future claims of states regarding the nature and extent of coastal and flag state jurisdiction. "Jurisdiction" here is interpreted to be consistent with the applicable law of the sea at the time of application of MARPOL. The last provision, as discussed below, could be of great importance when read in conjunction with the Draft Convention by possibly extending some pollution jurisdiction out to the seaward limit of the exclusive economic zone (EEZ).

The 1973 MARPOL Convention, then, takes important steps toward the reduction of operational shipborne pollution and in the application of jurisdiction to ensure compliance with its provisions. However, it is not now in force nor is it likely to be in the near future.[10] Opposition, to two requirements in particular, has become widespread. The first is the requirement that cargo loading (port) states provide the reception facilities necessary for off-loading of oily-water wastes at port areas. Loading states say the expense is unreasonable and consequently are reluctant to ratify the Convention and implement this scheme. The second is the requirement for segregated ballast tanks on board new tankers, and other machinery and LOT procedures aboard existing vessels; the owners of toxic chemical carriers object to the expense involved.

Coastal state pressure for firmer regulation of oil and other bulk carriers has persisted since the MARPOL Conference. The dramatic occurrences of December 1976, when the *Argo Merchant* broke up in waters off Cape Cod, and the (mostly empty) *Sansinena* exploded in Long Beach harbor, and of March 16, 1978 when the *Amoco Cadiz*'s stearing gear failed and the vessel broke up off Brittany (and resulted in the largest oil spill to that time)[11] have increased the resolve of coastal states. The United States has assumed an especially active role, advocating greater coastal state jurisdiction over oil tankers navigating in coastal waters. The U.S. had been leaning in this direction, but the spills of December 1976 catalyzed public opinion. Public pressure was reflected in the decision to hold an International Conference on Tanker Safety and Pollution Prevention (TSPP), which met February 6 – 17, 1978 in London, with representatives from 62 states attending.[12]

## Conference on Tanker Safety and Pollution Prevention

The TSPP, organized under the auspices of IMCO, featured a debate between nations and owners who favored retrofitting segregated ballast tanks (SBT) and those who argued for crude oil washing (COW) as a more cost-effective alternative.[13] A compromise alternative emerged. Two protocols, the Protocol of 1978 Relating to the International Convention for the Safety of Life at Sea, 1974, and the Protocol of 1978 Relating to the International Convention for the Prevention of Pollution from Ships, 1973, were adopted. The former is legally dependent on the SOLAS Convention, meaning that only states signatory to SOLAS are entitled to ratify the protocol. The MARPOL Protocol, on the other hand, may be ratified independently of a commitment to MARPOL 73. In specifically addressing the problem of operational pollution from tankers, both suggest new standards of performance and implicitly address the question of regulation of navigation by coastal states.

The SOLAS Protocol provides that the Cargo Ship Safety Construction Certificate is restricted to five years duration, after which the ship must be reinspected. For tankers older than ten years, there must be an additional intermediate inspection once between the periodic (five-year) inspections.

There are other provisions, too. Steering gear requirements for tankers are toughened, though the ones in the Protocol would not have prevented the *Amoco Cadiz* accident. (The *Amoco Cadiz* foundered one month after the end of the TSPP Conference.) New and existing tankers of 10,000 gross tons and over are required to have back-up steering gear control systems with an alarm system on the bridge indicating if a failure takes place. For existing tankers, this equipment must be installed within two years of the entry into force of the Protocol. The Protocol also calls for dual (independent) radar systems on ships that are over 1,000 gross tons in size, and the fitting of certain tankers with inert gas systems. All COW tankers must have inert gas systems.[14]

The MARPOL Protocol, though containing measures on inspection and certification, primarily deals with equipping existing and new tankers with either COW or SBT to minimize operational discharges. With respect to inspection and certification, the International Oil Pollution Prevention Certificate provided for in the 1954 Convention is valid for only five years, requiring inspection after that time for reissuance.

A detailed description of the MARPOL and SOLAS Protocol provisions are given in chapter 11. They add up to a complex set of size and age formulas, as well as a set of techniques designed to reduce the discharge of oil from tankers. Despite an initial attempt by the U.S. to reduce SBT on all existing tankers, the requirements of compromise resulted in the addition of this set of formulas and technologies.

The TSPP provisions for elimination of operational discharge from tankers, when they enter into force, should at least temporarily end international attempts to prescribe standards for the elimination of oil pollution that results from normal ship operations, though flag states can issue more stringent provisions for their own flag vessels. Compliance with these provisions will be necessary because coastal states that are anxious to see these provisions enter into force will certainly implement them domestically and, where the capacity to do so exists, will police them. While the provisions impose some increased costs on the tanker industry, they should not be prohibitive. Enforcement by concerned states will be made easier by merely certifying, while the vessels are in waters of their jurisdiction, that they are provided with the required equipment. It will be several years before these measures are ratified and fully implemented, although several nations, including the United States, have given notice of their intention to implement them early, before the treaties and protocol enter into force.

### Other Multilateral Instruments of Consequence to Navigation

The IMCO forum has produced several other draft treaties and conventions dealing with vessel safety, the rights of coastal states to intervene on the high seas in order to protect their coasts, liability and compensation provisions to see that damaged parties obtain compensatory relief in the event of major spills, and an insurance requirement for tank vessels before they are granted access to ports and roadsteads.

In the area of liability and compensation, IMCO has drafted, among others, the International Convention on Civil Liability for Oil Pollution Damage (1969, the Private Law Convention) discussed in the previous chapter. Most notable of the other conventions was an attempt by IMCO members in 1971 to increase the amount of financial coverage in the event of ship casualties resulting in oil spills. The International Convention on the Establishment of an International Fund for Compensation for Oil Pollution[15] was signed in 1971 but is not yet in force. This instrument expanded the maximum liability available under the 1969

Convention to roughly $36 million per mishap and suggests that a fund be created by contracting governments to cover the liability risk. The monies for this are to come from a tax on oil imports, assessed at the receiving port, though it is not clear exactly who will be assessed.

Another convention that addresses liability and compensation covers the carriage of nuclear materials, and entered into force on July 15, 1975. This convention, the International Convention Relating to Civil Liability in the Field on Maritime Carriage of Nuclear Materials (1971),[16] establishes liability standards applicable to shipowners, and resolves some of the confusion arising out of prior liability arrangements.

A protocol intended to be attached to the 1969 Public Law Convention was drafted and signed in 1973. The Protocol Relating to Intervention on the High Seas in Cases of Marine Pollution by Substances Other than Oil, which has nearly all of the 15 ratifications necessary, would extend coastal state jurisdiction into the high seas in the event of spills likely to cause serious injury to coastal state waters. Thus, IMCO again attempted to satisfy the demands of uneasy coastal states.

IMCO members have also addressed the need for updating navigation systems and position-fixing equipment, both of which are vital to safe navigation. A conference held in London from April 2 to May 9, 1975 resulted in the (Draft) Convention on the International Maritime Satellite Organization (IMMARSAT).[17] Given the tremendous technological developments in communications technology in the past decade, nations have become interested in obtaining access to high quality navigational information and applying it to commercial vessel navigation. Should IMMARSAT be created, potentially great benefits could accrue to shipping interests.[18] At present, however, there is considerable disagreement about the institutional arrangements for such an organization (i.e., who should control access to it, and who should operate the technology).

## UNCLOS III NEGOTIATIONS AND THE DRAFT CONVENTION ON THE LAW OF THE SEA

The regime governing navigation and pollution as defined by the Draft Convention contains a number of important provisions. These relate to the prescriptive and enforcement powers of coastal states (CS), flag states (FS), and port states (PS).

### Prescription

Coastal states have the authority to legislate behavior regarding certain vessel activities in the internal waters and the territorial seas of the states.[19] In internal waters, a coastal state's authority to prescribe and enforce is extensive and includes the right to set conditions that a vessel must fulfill to gain access to ports. This includes the authority to prescribe operation and construction standards for vessels. These provisions do not differ dramatically from existing international law.

Outside of internal waters, in the territorial sea, the sovereign powers of the coastal state do not entitle it to prescribe operation and construction standards. Subject to the right of innocent passage, the coastal state is entitled to make laws and regulations in conformity with, and giving effect to, the Draft Convention and other international law provisions relating to the safety of navigation and the preservation of the coastal state's environment and living resources. The coastal state may not prescribe design, construction, manning or equipment requirements for foreign vessels, unless these give effect to generally accepted international standards. [20] Coastal states may, "after taking into account" recommendations of intergovernmental organizations (IMCO) and specific conditions, designate sea lanes and vessel traffic separation schemes applicable to ships navigating in the territorial sea.

In the economic zone beyond the territorial sea, however, the coastal state is granted jurisdiction only for the preservation of the marine environment. The regime provided for in the Draft Convention governing the prevention of pollution from ships (Part XII) contains important provisions with respect to both prescription and enforcement.

In the economic zone outside of territorial waters, the power of states to prescribe rules and regulations for the prevention of pollution from vessels is carefully circumscribed. In general, these rules and regulations may be as effective as international standards, but must not have the effect of hampering innocent passage in coastal state waters, [21] including those in the economic zone and the territorial sea. Even if a coastal state wants to establish a special zone, it may not act unilaterally to do so. Instead, it must amass evidence supporting its claim to regulate vessel activities and pass the evidence on to IMCO, which then decides whether to designate such an area. The standards applicable to the special area may not include provisions on the design, manning, construction, or operation of foreign vessels unless the provisions are consistent with international standards. This would prohibit the adoption of standards regulating vessel size and equipment. The recent adoption of new North Sea routes following the *Amoco Cadiz* accident did not include prescriptions on vessel size or equipment.

## Enforcement

The Draft Convention grants jurisdiction to flag states, coastal states, and port states for the prevention of pollution of the marine environment from ship discharges under different conditions.

### Flag States (FS)

Flag states are obligated to apply measures to vessels of their registry to prevent, reduce, or control pollution of the marine environment, no matter where the violation occurs. They must also (1) prevent any vessel not in compliance with the requirements of international rules and standards from sailing; (2) ensure that vessels flying their flag carry on board valid certificates attesting to vessel seaworthiness, as required by international law; (3) conduct an immediate investigation of any vessel violating accepted international rules and regulations, and bring proceedings immediately against the violator vessel, no matter where the violation occurred; (4) upon the written request of any state, investigate an alleged violation by one of its ships to determine if evidence supporting the charge exists and, if so, to initiate proceedings; and (5) apply penalties specified under domestic law adequate to discourage further discharge violations, irrespective of where they occur.

In situations involving pollution outside the territorial sea, where no major pollution damage has occurred in the economic zone, the flag state may preempt coastal state proceedings against the violator vessel, assuming that the coastal state has begun proceedings. The preemption need not be honored, however, if it is not made by the flag state within six months of the initiation of proceedings, or if the flag state has historically disregarded its obligation to enforce international standards.[22] The latter provision departs from the existing scope of flag state jurisdiction.

## Coastal States (CS)

Coastal states are granted enforcement powers under the Draft Convention to apply valid national and international rules governing vessel-source pollution. If a vessel is voluntarily in the port of the coastal state and has violated applicable rules regarding vessel pollution in the territorial sea or economic zone, the CS may institute proceedings against that vessel. If a vessel navigating in the territorial sea has, during its passage there, violated the standards set forth in the Draft Convention or in other valid national and international texts, the CS may undertake physical inspection of the vessel and, if warranted, initiate proceedings against it.

For offenses occurring in the exclusive economic zone by vessels navigating there, the Draft Convention establishes coastal states enforcement jurisdiction. If the coastal state has clear reasons to believe that a violation of accepted rules and standards for vessel discharge has occurred, it may require the vessel to provide information about its registry and its last and next port of call to determine if a violation has occurred. If the CS has reasonable cause to expect that a violation has resulted in ''substantial discharge and in significant pollution of the marine environment,'' it may undertake physical inspection of the vessel to discern if a violation has transpired. Should the coastal state have objective evidence that the vessel has committed a ''flagrant and gross violation'' of accepted national and international standards, and this has resulted in ''major damage or threat of major damage'' to the coastline, related interests, or to the resources of the territorial sea or economic zone, the CS may cause proceedings to be taken against the vessel, even if the violation was within the economic zone but outside its territorial waters.[23] If the violation does not result in major damage, the flag state would, under this wording, still maintain prosecutorial authority. This provision, nonetheless, expands the enforcement jurisdiction of the coastal state beyond the present scope of coastal state authority, which grants authority over vessels not flying its flag only in the territorial sea.

## Port States (PS)

The concept of universal port state jurisdiction, born in the early 1970s, is also contained in the Draft Convention provisions. The PS may, when a vessel is voluntarily in port, undertake an investigation and, if necessary, institute proceedings if the vessel has violated international discharge standards outside of internal waters, the territorial sea, or the economic zone of that state (i.e., anywhere, including the high seas). If, however, the discharge violations have occurred within the economic zone or the territorial sea of another state, the PS may not initiate proceedings against the vessel unless requested to do so by the state damaged or likely to be damaged, or unless the discharge is likely to cause harm to the port state. In conducting an investigation of a discharge violation on a vessel voluntarily in its ports, the PS must comply with requests by other states that have suffered the damage. This includes a duty to provide for the transfer of records and any proceedings initiated by the port state if the other CS suffered damages in its internal waters, territorial sea, or in the EEZ. At that point, all PS proceedings must cease.

States, generally, may also take measures to prevent a vessel from sailing if the vessel does not comply with international seaworthiness standards and therefore poses a threat to the marine environment. The violator vessel may be required to proceed to the nearest appropriate repair port to eliminate the irregularities.

The Draft Convention presents few dramatic changes in the scope of coastal state jurisdiction within the territorial sea or inside internal waters. It expressly prohibits the passage and enforcement of unilateral construction, design, and manning standards. International straits states are not given extensive prescription or enforcement powers within the straits.

In the economic zone, certain fundamental changes are contained in the regime designed by the Draft Convention, though applicable to a very narrow range of events. In the event of flagrant violations resulting in serious pollution of the economic zone, coastal states are authorized to initiate proceedings that may not be preempted. This provision in the text, along with the investigation powers granted to coastal states for minor pollution in the zone, considerably extends coastal state jurisdiction in an area previously regarded as high seas.

The extension of port and coastal state jurisdiction in the economic zone for prevention of marine pollution is consistent with the increasing jurisdictional claims of many coastal states to more extensive ocean space. Therefore, prohibitions against construction and design standards being unilaterally passed by coastal states runs contrary to the desires of several major coastal states, including the United States and Canada. The U.S. has claimed design and construction standards may be enacted by the coastal state to apply to vessels sailing within the TS, though not in the EEZ. Thus, tension continues in the coastal community about prescription and enforcement jurisdiction. The recent *Amoco Cadiz* spill has heightened coastal and port state demands for increased jurisdiction over tankers. Even if the negotiations for a comprehensive UNCLOS III treaty fail, these provisions regarding pollution from ships will probably become customary international law. The provisions of Part XII of the Draft Convention reflect already existing principles of international law as well as rapidly emerging trends.

## CHANGING NATIONAL CLAIMS TO JURISDICTION

Coastal states are not entirely satisfied with the measures taken by the international community to eliminate or reduce pollution from ships. Even where stricter regulations have been drafted, as in the 1973 MARPOL Convention or the 1978 SOLAS and MARPOL Protocols, they have not yet entered into force. Thus, at present a vacuum exists.

The United States, for years an opponent of unilateral coastal state legislation, has recently changed course and drafted legislation granting itself more jurisdiction over bulk carriers, especially tankers. Feeding this growing movement in the U.S. were the catastrophes of December 1976, including the *Argo Merchant* and the loss of life associated with the explosion of the *Sansinena*.[24] Thus, the U.S. has joined Canada as an advocate for greater environmental protection.

## United States

Congress and the administration have drafted some very tough standards that apply to ocean shipping. The Carter administration in 1977 drafted regulations which would, among other things, require that by January 30, 1983, all tankers greater than 20,000 dwt entering U.S. waters be equipped with segregated ballast tanks, sophisticated position-fixing equipment, inert gas systems, and double bottoms (on vessels contracted after January 1, 1978). Vessels presently in existence would be required to retrofit with position-fixing equipment, such as dual radar and Loran-C navigation equipment.[25] The Ford and Carter administrations suggested that IMCO establish radar standards, and that IMCO meet in 1978 to draft new standards of training, watchkeeping, and certification of officers. U.S. pressure for the inclusion of segregated ballast tanks and inert gas systems on vessels of all flags resulted (as noted above) in the early convening of the 1978 London TSPP Conference. The 1978 Tanker and Vessel Safety Act implemented the standards adopted at the TSPP Conference.

Congressional action has been led by Senator Warren Magnuson of the Senate Commerce Committee, who drafted legislation incorporating all of the administration measures into a bill aimed at updating the Ports and Waterways Safety Act.[26] His bill contained provisions for the creation of a 200-mile pollution-control zone. Magnuson also drafted a bill providing for a national liability and compensation act.

Other recent congressional action includes the Clean Water Act Amendments of 1977, sponsored by Senator Edmund Muskie, which amend the Federal Water Pollution Control Act. These amendments are intended to prevent the introduction of any polluting substances into U.S. waters (navigable, internal, territorial), onto U.S. shorelines, or into the coastal waters or other areas that may affect the resources covered by the Fisheries Conservation and Management Act of 1976. This constitutes a claim to regulate for pollution, and hence to regulate navigation within the economic zone of the United States. Congress is authorized, along with appropriate executive agencies, to prescribe vessel waste discharge standards as they relate to various geographic areas, and to provide for the allocation of clean-up costs in pollution accidents. The amendments also authorize enforcement of U.S. standards for vessels over which the U.S. has prior jurisdiction. The language of the Act suggests that this could include a claim to regulate foreign flag "owners, operators, and persons otherwise subject to U.S. jurisdiction" all the way to, and beyond, the fisheries conservation zone. This has caused considerable concern in shipping and international circles here and abroad, though it appears that the Environmental Protection Agency (EPA), one of the major enforcement arms of the legislation, does not intend to enforce U.S. jurisdiction to what the international community still regards to be the high seas.

These measures suggest that the U.S. is serious about regulating vessels that carry dangerous bulk cargoes. Concerned congressional members have even suggested that the U.S. establish a policy that would deny access to vessels with poor safety records. While this will probably not eventuate, the development and utilization of an information system that can ferret out "high risk vessels" would be useful in deterring future violation.

## Canada

While the U.S. has recently shown a high-level interest in firmer coastal state protection rights, Canada has been a lobbyist for such rights for over a decade. This is understandable because Canada believes that major pollution would threaten its fragile and beautiful coastal environment.

There are no major surprises about recent events in Canadian policymaking in the area of environmental protection and vessel regulation. Canadian policy is well known and consistent. The one area of potential interest lies in the implications of the 200-mile resource claims (Fishery Zone) for the regulation of tanker traffic, given the fact that the Canadian Shipping Act is applicable to fishing zones. This could constitute an expansive pollution control zone, but, like the United States, the Canadians do not seem ready to enforce bold claims to jurisdiction. While the presence of oil tankers traveling up and down the British Columbian coast carrying Alaskan oil is not a pleasant thought for most Canadian citizens, vessel transit has not been hindered so far.

## SHIPPING POLICY DEVELOPMENTS OF CONSEQUENCE FOR MARINE TRANSPORTATION

Policy shifts are taking place on the international and national levels that are of considerable importance to the conduct of commercial shipping in the North Pacific region. Although these developments do not impact directly upon the spatial patterns of marine transportation in the North Pacific, they do affect countries involved in shipping. They could also affect the foreign relations climate within which regional trading occurs by facilitating either greater intergovernmental cooperation, or competition and conflict, between the North Pacific rim countries.

The conduct of international shipping in the liner sectors has traditionally occurred in a largely unregulated environment. Shipowners, while abhoring the concept of governmental interference in the conduct of the liner shipping business, have, nevertheless, made a practice of forming steamship conferences along trade routes to pool cargoes, negotiate with shippers and with each other for steamship rates, and to discourage what they claim is disruptive price competition.[27]

While shipper loyalty to the conferences has generally been maintained since the turn of the century by way of both sanctions and incentives, in recent years nations, particularly developing countries (LDCs), have become impatient with conferences. They claim that the conferences exploit their lack of domestic shipping capacity, and are thus prejudicial to their import and export trades.[28] Large numbers of LDCs, along with many other disgruntled shippers around the world, negotiated in the United Nations Conference on Trade and

Development's (UNCTAD) Shipping Committee for a code of conference behavior that they felt would better serve their interests. The result, the Code of Conduct for Liner Conferences,[29] when it is ratified and implemented by the required number of states, will represent a fundamental change in the liner conference system.[30]

Instead of determining the liner carriers along a particular trade route by a process of pooling among conference members, or between them and outside steamship lines through competition, the Code mandates major governmental intervention. The most controversial aspect of the governmental role centers upon the concept of "bilateralism" embodied in the Code. The two governments involved in one international trade route (one importing and one exporting) would utilize national flag shipping line vessels to ship commodities.[31] Each nation's national flag lines would be entitled to carry 40 percent of the available cargo tonnage. The remaining 20% would be reserved to cross-trades. This is radically different from the situation today in which cross-trading is a major source of revenue for several shipping companies. If, however, the trade nations do not have sufficient capacity on hand to carry their apportioned percentage of the cargo, they are entitled to charter additional vessels, thus allowing greater (but temporary) third-party penetration of many two-way trade routes.

Further evidence of the extension of governmental roles in conference affairs is found in the requirement that governments be present at all conciliations involving rate disputes between shippers and shipping companies. Trade relations may be advanced by the adoption of a promotional freight rate. Any decision made by the conference relating to trade between two countries must be made with the agreement of their national shipping lines (i.e., a line that is governmentally controlled) if there is such a line. Also, noncommercial criteria are acceptable to use in determining who will be conference members.

There are a few important implications of the Code. Certain analysts note that the participation formula is inflexible, preventing an easy transfer of liner vessels into and out of markets as conditions demand. This would probably generate overtonnaging and economic inefficiency.[32] Also, the major losers associated with the adoption of the Code would be third flag carriers and, indirectly, the national economies of these carriers, stemming from the bilateralism explicitly adopted in the Code. The extent of their loss is dependent upon several things, however. If nations have considerable shipping capacity and have been served by third flag carriers prior to the Code, these third flag carriers will be pushed out of the trade route. If, however, the trading state has little or no shipping capacity—and no expressed desire to immediately generate national flag tonnage through ship purchasing or shipbuilding—the liner conference carriers that serve the state could continue to serve it after the Code enters into force. To a certain extent, then, some surplus tonnage generated by acceptance of the Code could be shifted to other trade routes serving nations with little or no merchant marine. This could serve as a hedge against massive losses for some liner companies. However, it is likely that if the spirit of the Code is implemented, some liner firms that are heavily committed to third flag trades serving LDCs will be eased out at considerable financial loss.

The impact of the Code upon freight rates is unclear. Abrahamsson contends that freight rates are apt to rise because the bilateral arrangements adopted in the Code would squeeze out a large source of vessel supply that would normally bid the price (freight rate) down. This would lead to, the argument contends, national liners assuming what might approximate monopoly pricing power and result in a reduction in the carriage of lower-valued commodities on conference vessels, due to their (at times) highly elastic demand in export markets.[33]

This outcome—higher freight rates—is not as inevitable as the logic above suggests. Governments would be involved in trade promotion, freight rate determination, and conciliation; they would not be representatives simply of shipowners. They would also have to answer to shippers and shippers' councils, where they exist. Furthermore, in many countries, especially the U.S., governmental agencies are adopting stronger stances against present abuses of conference power, and would not likely become passive bodies simply because the Code entered into force. They represent a broader public interest than that of the shipowning community.

Another check on high freight rates is found in the Annex to Resolution I of the Code. Shippers may not be prevented from choosing between conference and nonconference liners. If freight rates were too high on conference vessels, shippers would be encouraged to contract with nonconference liner vessels. Competition could be preserved then, at least to this extent.

Although the Code of Conduct legitimizes the phenomenon of national merchant marine subsidy and protection, it also puts a brake on the kind of bilateral shipping agreements that have emerged in recent years. Fifty-fifty agreements, so often adopted by the Soviet Union and others in shipping liner cargoes, would be prohibited; thus the code aggravated some merchant marine nations, including the USSR.

It is too early to conclude which of the various interpretations of the Code is correct and what provisions will be implemented. If the Code were implemented, it would affect the traditional conduct of business in the liner sector, but whether it would lead to gross inefficiency and unjust freight rates is an open question. It is uncertain what impact the Code would have upon the trans-North Pacific liner conferences, including primarily Japan, the United States, Canada, and the Soviet Far East Shipping Co. (FESCO) cross-trading ambitions.

Tables 10.1 through 10.3 contain lists of the liner conferences presently serving Japanese, U.S., and Canadian Pacific ports and including trans-Pacific (at times exclusively trans-North Pacific) trade routes. Table 10.4 details FESCO's participation in routes serving U.S. ports. These tables illustrate the present liner conference arrangements on the North Pacific.

The Soviet Union currently engages in 50:50 bilateral arrangements for shipping (or better if it can) by buying goods and shipping them exclusively on Soviet bottoms (imports F.O.B., exports C.I.F.). Japan's merchant marine is beginning to suffer because, to cover costs, it must charge higher freight rates than FESCO, and has lost business to the latter. Japanese shipowners are increasingly using foreign crews and flags to cut costs, thus reducing the percentage of Japanese cargo (imports or exports) carried by Japanese flag vessels. This is why Japan is leaning toward ratification of the UNCTAD Code—to increase

## TABLE 10.1

### Liner Conferences Serving Japanese Ports

Australian and New Zealand/Eastern Shipping Conference
Bay of Bengal/Japan/Bay of Bengal Conference
Far East/Canary Islands, Spanish Sahara, Mauritania Freight Conference
Far East/East Africa Freight Conference
Far East/River Plate/Far East Freight Conference
Indonesia–Japan/Japan–Indonesia Freight Conference
Japan/Ceylon Freight Conference
Japan/Europe Freight Conference
Japan/Gulf of Aden and Red Sea Ports Conference
Japan/Hong Kong and Japan/Straits Freight Agreements
Japan/India–Pakistan–Gulf/Japan Conference
Japan/Indochina Freight Conference
Japan/Korea–Atlantic and Gulf Freight Conference
Japan/Korea–East Canada Freight Conference
Japan/Korea–West Canada Freight Conference
Japan–Latin America Eastbound Freight Conference
Japan–Mexico Freight Conference
Japan/People's Republic of China Freight Agreement
Japan/Philippines Freight Conference
Japan/Puerto Rico and Virgin Islands Freight Conference
Japan/Sabak Freight Conference
Japan/Sarawak Freight Conference
Japan/Saigon Freight Conference
Japan/South Pacific Freight Conference
Japan/Thailand Freight Conference
Japan/West Africa (Angola/Cameroun Range) Freight Conference
Japan/West Africa (Nigeria/Senegal Range) Freight Conference
Japan/West Coast South America Freight Conference
*Trans-Pacific Freight Conference of Japan/Korea
*Australia Northbound Shipping Conference
Brazil/Far East/Brazil Freight Conference
Ceylon/Strait/Hong Kong/Japan Agreement
East Africa/Far East Freight Conference
East Canada/Japan Freight Conference
East Mediterranean and Black Sea/Japan Conference
Ensenada/Japan Freight Conference
*Europe/Japan Freight Conference
Far East Conference
Hawaii/Orient Rate Agreement
Hong Kong/Japan Freight Agreement
Italy/Far East Conference
Malabar/Far East Rate Agreement
*New York Committee of Inward Far East Lines
*Pacific Coast Committee of Inward Trans-Pacific Steamship Lines
*Pacific Westbound Conference
Philippines–Asian Conference
Portugal/Japan Freight Conference
Sabah/Shanghai and Japan Freight Conference
South Africa/Far East Freight Conference
Spain/Far East Freight Conference
Strait/East Asia Rate Agreement
Thailand/Japan Conference
West Africa (Angola/Cameroun Range) Far East Freight Conference
West Africa (Nigeria/Senegal Range) Far East Freight Conference
West Coast of South America/Far East Freight Conference

*Note: Major Liner Conferences

Source: Professor Masao Oda, Tokyo University of Mercantile Marine, Private Communication.

## TABLE 10.2

### TRANS-PACIFIC CONFERENCE AND RATE AGREEMENTS SERVING
### U.S. WEST COAST PORTS AS OF MAY 1975

Trans-Pacific Freight Conference (Hong Kong)
Far East Conference
Pacific Coast/Australasian Traffic Bureau
Pacific Westbound Conference
Trans-Pacific Freight Conference of Japan/Korea
Java/Pacific Rate Agreement
Delhi/Pacific Rate Agreement
Pacific/Indonesian Conference
Hawaii/Orient Rate Agreement
Trans-Pacific American-Flag Berth Operators Agreement
West Coast U.S. and Canada/India, Pakistan, Ceylon & Burma Rate Agreement
India, Pakistan, Ceylon & Burma/West Coast U.S. Rate Agreement
Thailand—Pacific Rate Agreement
New Zealand Rate Agreement
Malaysia/Pacific Rate Agreement
Australia—Pacific Coast Rate Agreement
Trans-Pacific Freight Conference (Hong Kong)/Independent Lines Rate Agreement
Pacific/Straits Conference

Source: Irwin M. Heine, *The United States Merchant Marine: A National Asset* (Washington, D.C.: National Maritime Council), pp. 162, 163.

## TABLE 10.3

### CONFERENCES SERVING WEST COAST CANADIAN PORTS

Delhi/Pacific Rate Agreement—Inbound
India, Pakistan, Ceylon & Burma/West Coast U.S. Rate Agreement—Inbound
Japan/Korea—West Canada Freight Conference—Inbound
Java/Pacific Rate Agreement—Inbound
Malaysia—Pacific Rate Agreement—Inbound
Pacific Coast—Australasian Tariff Bureau—Outbound
Pacific/Indonesian Conference—Outbound
Pacific/Straits Conference—Outbound
Pacific Westbound Conference—Outbound
Philippines—North America Conference—Inbound
West Canada Freight Conference—Inbound

Source: Canadian Transport Commission: Research Branch. *A Study of the Economic Implications of the International Convention on a Code of Conduct for Liner Conferences* (Ottawa: no. ESAB 76-130, 1976), pp. 171—225.

its flag share of its trades and to maintain hard currency reserves.

Canada and the United States, on the other hand, do not carry a large percentage of their trading commodities on their own flag vessels.[34] Canada, presently involved in a debate over the creation of a deep-water fleet, does not have a large merchant marine. The U.S. has employed operating differential subsidies (ODS) to subsidize the operating costs of U.S. flag vessels on designated essential U.S. foreign trade routes. This has helped it assume a moderate role in the carriage of liner cargoes to and from U.S. ports. Roughly 25 percent of its liner cargoes are carried on U.S. flag vessels, which is more than the 5 percent figure that

## TABLE 10.4

### FESCO LINES SERVING U.S. PORTS

FESCO Pacific Lines, FMC-2

    From: Ports in the states of Washington, Oregon, California and Alaska and overland common points

    To:    Kobe, Nagoya, Osaka, Yokohama and Tokyo, Japan and Nakhodka, USSR

FESCO Pacific Lines, FMC-3

    From: Vladivostok, Nakhodka, USSR

    To:    Ports in the states of Washington, Oregon and California and overland common points

FESCO Pacific Lines, FMC-4

    From: Ports in the states of Washington, Oregon and California and overland common points

    To:    Hong Kong

FESCO Pacific Lines, FMC-5

    From: Hong Kong

    To:    Ports in the states of Washington, Oregon and California and overland common points

FESCO Pacific Lines, FMC-6

    From: Ports in the states of Washington, Oregon and California and overland common points

    To:    Manila and various other Philippine ports

FESCO Pacific Lines, FMC-7

    From: Manila and other base ports

    To:    Ports in the states of Washington, Oregon and California and overland common points

FESCO Straits Pacific Line, FMC-8

    From: Ports in the states of Washington, Oregon and California and overland common points

    To:    Port Klang and Penang, Federation of Malaysia and Singapore

FESCO Straits Pacific Line, FMC-9

    From: Port Klang and Penang, Federation of Malaysia, Singapore

    To:    Ports in the states of Washington, Oregon and California and overland common points

FESCO Straits Pacific Line, FMC-10

    From: Ports in the states of Washington, Oregon, California and overland common points

    To:    Bangkok and Kohsichang, Thailand

FESCO Straits Pacific Line, FMC-11

    From: Bangkok and Kohsichang, Thailand

    To:    Ports in the states of Washington, Oregon, and California and overland common points

FESCO Straits Pacific Line, FMC-12

    From: Ports in Washington, Oregon and California and overland common points

    To:    Belawan and other ports in Sumatra, Java and Borneo

FESCO Straits Pacific Line, FMC-13

    From: Sumatra between Langsa and Indragiri (both inclusive)

    To:    Ports in the states of Washington, Oregon and California

FESCO Pacific Lines, FMC-15

    From: Ports in Japan

    To:    Ports in Washington, Oregon and California and overland common points

Source: U.S. Congress, Senate Committee on Commerce and National Ocean Policy Study, *Soviet Oceans Development*, 94th Congress, 2nd Session, October 1976.

Note: Far Eastern Shipping Company also doing business as *FESCO Pacific Lines and FESCO Straits Pacific Line* applies to *all* U.S. foreign trade carriage on U.S. flag ships. The United States has opposed the UNCTAD Code.

FESCO's fleet expansion since 1960 (shown in table 10.5) resulted from a desire for increased Soviet penetration into Soviet foreign, mainly liner, trades. FESCO operates on the North Pacific and its growth in the region and worldwide has been controversial throughout the 1970s.

FESCO's fleet expansion and penetration into Pacific cross-trades began in the late 1960s. Its development was fed by the expansion of settlements in Kamchatka, Sakhalin Island, and in eastern Siberia. These, in turn, were fed by agriculture, timber, and other natural resource development that began then. FESCO fleet expansion has been dramatic, increasing from 877,210 dwt (1945) to greater than 18 million dwt in 1977.[35] The expansion of FESCO's capacity and the cargo it carries has fed the development of the Pacific ports of Nakhodka and Vostochny, which are now not only break-bulk general cargo ports but are also developing considerable container-handling capacity as well. FESCO's vessels and shipbuilding plans include the replacement of container vessels serving West Coast North American and Japanese ports with considerably larger vessels.

Trans-Pacific conference liners are upset about Soviet penetration into conference routes, its offering lower freight rates, and its capturing a growing share of the trade. The Conferences regard this as unfair and as a form of dumping or price gouging, which threatens the continuing profitability of their operations on these routes. FESCO's participation on the U.S. trade route from the Pacific Coast to the Far East (Route #29) has grown rapidly, from 2.97 percent (1971) to 5.9 percent (1976), an increase in tonnage from 159,959 dwt to 485,148 dwt.[36] Total Soviet penetration into all U.S. liner trades is estimated to increase from 2.9 percent (1.43 million dwt 1976) to 6.6 percent (4.48 million dwt 1985).[37] This is particularly upsetting for some U.S. liner operators who feel threatened by the Soviet penetration. In 1971, Soviet participation in U.S. trades was associated primarily with low-valued, break-bulk cargoes of semifinished industrial products and bulk commodities, whereas by 1976, 13 of the top 20 commodities (by value) carried by the Soviets were high-value commodities, and 7 were in the top 10.[38] United States and other

TABLE 10.5

SOVIET MERCHANT FLEET GROWTH

| Year | No. of vessels | Deadweight tons (millions) |
|------|----------------|-----------------------------|
| 1960 | 605 | .9 |
| 1963 | 820 | 5.7 |
| 1966 | 1,070 | 8.9 |
| 1970 | 1,400 | 11.9 |
| 1973 | 1,520 | 13.4 |

Source: U.S. Congress, Senate Committee on Commerce, National Ocean Policy Study. *Soviet Oceans Development*, 94th Congress, 2d Session (October 1976), p. 332.

non-Soviet operators claim that the Soviets are now "creaming off" the best cargo, leaving them to fight over lower-valued commodity cargoes.

While these concerns may be real, the accusations made are debatable. Lurking behind the rhetoric and suspicion is a simple fact: Soviet and other Comecon fleets operate by different rules and practices than Western shipping firms. They have few, if any, operating constraints; no capital costs are charged to FESCO by the Soviet government, and their costs of insurance, bunker fuel, and wages are low. FESCO can, therefore, easily underbid conference liners, though other independent nonconference liners (Zim Line of Israel, for example) do the same. Given these competitive advantages, along with the ambitious developmental goals for Soviet shipping in the Five-Year Plan of 1975–1980,[39] which includes technological modernization, it is not surprising that Western shipowners are upset. And the Soviets have penetrated and operated well, generating the hard currency, employment (social welfare), and economic influence goals they sought. However, the matter of Soviet penetration is quite controversial, and more research is being conducted.

A major question remains: What kind of accommodation can the Soviets and the Western operators come to? Whether the Soviets will live up to the principles embodied in the July 1976 Leningrad accord, promising to enter certain liner conferences in return for a share of the trade is in question. Thus far, the Pacific conferences do not seem pleased with Soviet compliance, and the Soviets have not chartered the agreed-upon percentage of U.S. flag tonnage for carrying their grain purchases. One side claims the other is cheating; the other side claims that Conference vessels are too expensive.

The conferences thus presently operate under conditions of uncertainty. Not all of the illegal behavior undertaken by conferences and their members necessarily relates to Soviet cross-trading vessels. A U.S. Justice Department study concludes that conferences have more than their share of abuses, and condemns the abuses.[40]

It is difficult to predict what will occur in the North Pacific with respect to Soviet shipping and liner conferences. The Soviet presence will certainly continue. The degree of market penetration will depend upon the success or failure of negotiations with the West and could be affected by the entry into force of the UNCTAD Code discussed above. The development of ports and resources in the eastern USSR will continue, however, and the Soviet Union cannot help but be a major actor in both the liner and bulk shipping sectors in the North Pacific.[41] Industrial development in this area, and the existence of the trans-Siberian landbridge, will ensure this.[42]

On both the national and international levels, considerable support is being given to the protection and development of national merchant marines. The UNCTAD Code embodies this and finds support from ambitious shipping nations and from countries (like Japan) who wish to recapture a share of the market. The Soviet penetration into the cross-trades could precipitate more protectionism from the U.S. interests intent on preserving a strong U.S. (liner) flag merchant marine. The situation in the North Pacific is in considerable flux, however. It is too early to ascertain to what degree disruptions, caused at least in part by FESCO, in the liner system will occur and what implications this will have for the region.

## FUTURE DEVELOPMENTS AND THEIR IMPLICATIONS FOR NAVIGATION AND SHIPPING

The United States, Canada, and other North Pacific rim nations have enacted, legislated, and implemented conventions they perceive to be in their national interests. This definition of self-interest is not time-bound; however, as technology and demands change, coastal states will find it necessary to adapt present arrangements to meet new conditions, and at times to adopt completely different ones.

On both sides of the North Pacific, resource development and exploitation is presently occurring. One technology and resource that has not been heavily developed so far, but promises to be very important politically and economically, is oil and natural gas.

In the Northeast Pacific, oil and gas development in the offshore areas has been limited to only one area, until recent years. Offshore oil and gas finds off southern California (in and around the Los Angeles basin) have been moderate, but have been exploited. This has had one practical consequence for shipping—making the creation of well-defined sea lanes mandatory for safe navigation in an area full of potential conflicts between multiple ocean uses. With the increasing price of oil and development of new technology, both catalysts in the push offshore, outer continental shelf oil and gas (OCS O+G) research has begun, with some leasing and development occurring in southern California and in Cook Inlet in Alaska.[43]

The development of offshore oil resources in Alaska will generate even more coastal vessel traffic and necessitate the creation of multipurpose zones. Alaskan waters are rich in living resources that have been tapped by industry and are in the interest of Alaskans to protect. Thus, the possibility of multiple use conflicts is substantial here.

A few other questions surround the shipment of Alaskan oil and gas, and therefore the movement of vessels in the North Pacific. One major question is where will onshore Alaskan oil ultimately be shipped: Puget Sound (for transshipment across the Northern Tier), through the Panama Canal, to Japan in exchange for Gulf oil imported to the East Coast, or some combination of these areas. Environmental impediments have surfaced regarding the Puget Sound oil port, and federal legislation is necessary before oil can be shipped from U.S. oil fields to Japan.

Another question involves the liability and compensation arrangements for the shipment of Alaskan oil. The U.S. Congress, through the Trans-Alaska Pipeline legislation and bills now in committee, has attempted to resolve some of the issues, but is far from satisfying all of the interests.

Another issue remains unresolved. Local areas that are likely to be recipients of Alaskan oil have sought either to make it impossible economically, or to adopt local standards that severely restrict the movement of vessels. The most obvious examples of this are Washington State's attempt to prohibit tankers larger than 125,000 dwt from entering Puget Sound and southern California's protestations about further pollution of the already foul Los Angeles airshed, which has resulted in the demise of the proposed transshipment facility there.

Perhaps in time, with the implementation of safer and more efficient navigation and cargo storage systems, and with the entry into force of the international standards discussed above, many of the fears will abate. This does not address the immediate future, however. Local interests see themselves paying the price for others' benefits, and resent it.

In the Northwest Pacific Ocean, substantial petroleum deposits appear to exist. Oil-bearing sediment is found in the South and East China seas, estimated at 30 billion barrels for the People's Republic of China alone.[44] At present, Japan, the People's Republic of China (PRC), the Republic of Korea, and the Republic of China are at odds regarding delimitation, and development has not been possible thus far. Jurisdictional conflicts over the continental shelf and over some contested islands are enormous.[45] The economic and security implications of oil ownership in this area are significant. While many uncertainties cloud the development of this resource, the multiple use problems already present when development occurs will be aggravated. Traffic congestion in and around these semien-closed waters will likely intensify, making management more difficult.

Natural gas development in the Northwest Pacific Ocean, Siberia, and on Sakhalin is also important.[46] This will feed into the Soviet economy, but, if some of the gas (if it is a large reserve) is to be exported, some of the technological and environmental problems associated with LNG tankers must be solved. While little ecological damage is believed to occur with LNG accidents, the volatility and flammability of the substance is so great that coastal states and ports are reticent about shipping and receiving this cargo.[47] If LNG tankers become a greater part of the trading economy of the North Pacific in the future, the traffic management needs of the region will become more complicated. The same, incidentally, applies to the possible entrance of nuclear-powered vessels into world trade.

Technological developments could have consequences for vessel navigation and safety in the North Pacific. These developments might result in greater coastal state confidence in certain vessel types, therefore reducing some of the demands for unilateral action or international regulations. In addition to the implementation of the inert gas systems and segregated ballast tanks, crude oil washing and clean ballast tank systems on tankers, as required by the two 1978 protocols, operational discharge could be effectively reduced by placing a "little black box" on all larger vessels navigating on the seas. One version of this instrument provides constant read-outs on the discharge of waste oil and water mixtures and, when the reading equals or surpasses that allowed by international law, automatically shuts off further discharge.[48]

The problems of port and waterway congestion in the major regional ports could be reduced somewhat by building superports, provided they are in appropriate areas and are not themselves hazards to navigation. For example, offshore off-loading of petroleum at moorage buoys could increase both efficiency and safety, though questions remain about the best systems of moorage and off-loading. Little evidence exists in the Northeast Pacific to indicate that either of these technological developments is likely to be implemented in the near future.

Improved navigation and vessel safety could result from upgrading vessel radar, bridge-to-bridge communication, vessel traffic systems, and the implementation of a satellite navigation IMMARSAT system. This would allow more accurate short-term planning by vessel traffic managers and allow more sophisticated schemes to be developed for management. With more refined information, Vessel Traffic Services systems in harbors could become more generalized, reducing congestion hazards.

Until recently, most of the attention of the international community has been on the establishment and implementation of more appropriate technologies and equipment aboard vessels. But without a qualified set of officers and crew, even the most sophisticated equipment would be useless. Many of the major accidents resulting in catastrophic pollution have been due, in part, to human error, lack of judgment, or negligence.[49] Increasingly, however, nations are demanding vessels be manned by the most qualified people, rather than simply on the basis of cost containment. This would probably result in certain flag-of-convenience ships, in particular, becoming safer in order to gain access to ports.

## CONCLUSIONS

There is a fairly well-defined set of laws and regulations applicable to the North Pacific, both national and international, that address safety of navigation generally and the navigation and operation of bulk tanker vessels in particular. With respect to the regime for navigation found in the COLREGS and SOLAS, both coastal states and the shipping community have maintained a common interest in the safe conduct of vessels engaged in maritime commerce. These rules and practices have developed over centuries. Only recently has the revolution in maritime commerce and vessel technology indicated that self-regulation by the shipping community is inadequate.

Coastal states, with particular interests to protect, have promulgated regulations governing access and navigation. The necessity for safe and expeditious commerce in their busy ports and the multiple uses to which much of their coastal and offshore ocean space is put dictates that the coastal states adopt, at times, what may seem to be restrictive standards. As the Washington State tanker law (declared unconstitutional by the federal courts in 1977) indicates, even subnational special interests may drive the process of regulation.

The growing coastal state challenges to the preeminence of flag state jurisdiction reflect the dissatisfaction of many nations with the slow and cumbersome evolution of stricter standards governing international navigation. The Canadians, and now the United States, are in the forefront in advocating greater coastal state jurisdictional powers over vessel operations, particularly tanker operations. As technological changes continue to occur in the shipping industry and in commercial trade, the need for an alteration of specific conditions applicable to navigation in certain areas, and the demands by coastal states for control over their coastal areas and economic zones, will continue to occur.

As noted several times, projections of the future trends in trade and shipping commerce are usually wrong, so this endeavor might best be left to astrologers. Unfortunately, it cannot be. The task of assessing the likely regulatory regime for navigation in the North Pacific requires that an assessment of the trends in trade be undertaken. In the North Pacific region, the Japanese economy accounts for much of the vessel movement. Japan and the

United States are the two major maritime traders, as reflected in the vessel route patterns.

While trade patterns say something about the existence or nonexistence of certain trade routes, they say little about the need for vessel regulation that aims to ensure that this process is streamlined and efficient. Analysis of the navigation requirements that vessels must adhere to in order to navigate in coastal areas suggests that coastal and flag states have collaborated with the shipping interests to provide the appropriate navigational aids (charts, buoys, etc.) and technologies that make transport safe. The requirements for safe navigation include the necessity for change in arrangements and information.

The regime for regulation of vessels that carry dangerous substances in bulk is changing today. The provisions of the Draft Convention and the MARPOL and SOLAS Protocols (and Conventions) indicate that the era of unchallenged flag state jurisdiction over vessels is coming to an end. Coastal states have responded to pollution incidents and the presence of large tankers off their waters by demanding that they have jurisdiction to ensure that these ships are safe and seaworthy. Port state jurisdiction has also evolved. Coastal states command greater jurisdiction both with respect to area (note the emergence of the exclusive economic zone in international law) and with respect to functional authority (prescription and enforcement authority over certain aspects of vessel operation). In the North Pacific this coastal state lobbying has been led by the U.S. and Canada. It is conceivable that strong jurisdictional claims could result in some vessels being denied access to various coastal areas in the North Pacific, but this will not likely include the majority of seaworthy vessels involved in international commerce.

The TSPP Conference and the resulting Protocols, along with development of certain technologies, will close most of the regulatory holes in operational oil discharge prevention, answering a large part of the oil pollution problem. Enforcement of these standards is important, however, and the coastal state is in a better position than other enforcement agencies to protect its interests and apprehend offenders.

The future of the liner conference arrangements in the North Pacific is uncertain for two reasons. Should the UNCTAD Code enter into force, it would most certainly affect the makeup of the conferences serving the region, eliminating many of the cross-traders. The Code would alter the very nature of the conference system. The second challenge to the conferences comes from FESCO's penetration into the cross-trades, which destabilized an already unstable situation even more, precipitating a rash of claims and counterclaims. The Soviets have become a major shipping influence in the region, introducing a challenge to the prevailing actors—the conferences. It is too early to determine what will transpire with respect to either of these. It is also premature to determine how this could affect trade arrangements and national merchant marine policies in the nations involved.

The foreseeable future of North Pacific economic development does not portend that major conflicts will eventuate on the Northeast side. With the exception of southern California and possibly the Cook Inlet area of Alaska, traffic and multiple use conditions will not necessitate major adjustments in vessel traffic management in the next ten years or so. On the Northwest side, the picture is quite different, particularly if major oil fields are developed in the South and East China seas. Here, space is already at a premium, and multiple use conflicts are many in coastal areas. With the appearance of oil equipment in the East and South China seas, vessel traffic will need to be carefully managed.

It is hard to conceive of any revolutionary development of technologies that will render the conflicts for ocean space in the Northwest Pacific nonexistent. Perhaps with better navigational equipment and technicians aboard vessels, along with the development of more sophisticated vessel traffic systems onshore, the problems associated with actual vessel movement in crowded areas will be reduced. But it is too early to say when coastal state uneasiness about the revolution in bulk vessel size will subside. With the likelihood of enormous bulk vessels, LNG tankers, and possibly nuclear-powered merchant ships navigating in coastal areas, citizens will be quite uneasy. A way will have to be found to satisfy these reasonable fears without giving in to unreasonable protectionist claims. There is no easy formula for this.

# 11

# New Technologies of Transportation and the Problem of Tanker-Originated Pollution

This chapter discusses the effect of new shipping technologies on the environmental quality of the North Pacific Ocean. The principal technologies of international interest are those designed to reduce tanker-generated oil pollution from accidents or from routine vessel operations that discharge oil into the sea. We therefore consider (1) global tanker-generated oil pollution; (2) tanker-generated oil pollution in the North Pacific Ocean; (3) the environmental and economic consequences of this pollution; (4) the principal vessel-related technologies proposed to ameliorate it; and (5) the international negotiations undertaken to mandate the use of these technologies and their significance for the world, the North Pacific study region, and the United States.

## WORLDWIDE AND REGIONAL MARINE OIL POLLUTION LEVELS

The groundings of the *Torrey Canyon* in 1967 near the United Kingdom, the *Showa Maru* in 1975 in the Malacca Straits, the *Argo Merchant* in 1976 near the northeast coast of the United States, and the *Amoco Cadiz* in 1978 near Brittany, among others, alerted the public to the global and possibly growing nature of accidental oil spills.

In addition to accidents, tankers are a source of marine oil pollution as a consequence of discharges that can occur during a vessel's normal operations. On the return (or ballast leg) of a round-trip voyage, tankers typically sail without cargo. To achieve adequate sea-keeping performance and propeller immersion, standard practice has been to fill 55 to 60 percent of their cargo tank capacity with seawater ballast.[1] Since on most tankers the cargo tanks retain an average of .4 percent of their oil cargo as clingage on tank walls and piping, ballast water and most of the retained oil are mixed.[2] Later, when this ballast water is discharged overboard to make room for new cargo, much of the retained oil goes with it unless the vessel operator takes steps to avoid this, such as practicing load-on-top (LOT), or unless one of several other techniques that avoid the initial mixing of oil and water is used (see the section on Major Technological Alternatives below).

345

Table 11.1, prepared in early 1973, estimates the quantities of hydrocarbons introduced into the world's oceans from tankers and other sources. This table is widely cited but the data used in preparing it were taken before the late 1973 quadrupling of the price of internationally traded oil. This price increase made waste oils more valuable and increased incentives to recycle them via the LOT process. Nevertheless, tankers appear to be a significant source of oil input to the oceans, although by no means the only such source. International efforts have been taken to reduce the estimated 21 percent of total oil input to the oceans coming from tanker accidents and normal operations (1.53 million metric tons annually).

Table 11.2 and figure 11.1 show estimated total world trade in shipborne petroleum, 80 percent of which is crude oil movements. Table 11.3 shows the North Pacific oil trade.

## TABLE 11.1

### Petroleum Hydrocarbons Dumped into the World Ocean

| Source | Percent | Million metric tons annually |
|---|---|---|
| Offshore production | 1.3 | .08 |
| River runoff | 26.2 | 1.6 |
| Transportation/Marine | | |
|     LOT tankers | 5.1 | .31 |
|     Non-LOT tankers | 12.6 | .77 |
|     Tanker drydocking | 4.1 | .25 |
|     Terminal operations | .05 | .003 |
|     Bilges, bunkering | 8.2 | .5 |
|     Tanker accidents | 3.3 | .2 |
|     Nontanker accidents | 1.6 | .1 |
| Coastal refineries | 3.3 | .2 |
| Atmospheric rainout | 9.8 | .6 |
| Coastal municipal wastes | 4.9 | .3 |
| Coastal industrial wastes | 4.9 | .3 |
| Urban runoff | 4.9 | .3 |
| Natural seeps | 9.8 | .6 |
| TOTAL | 100.0 | 6.113 |

Source: National Academy of Sciences, *Petroleum in the Marine Environment* (Washington, D.C.: National Academy of Sciences, 1975), p. 6.

## TABLE 11.2

### World Oceanborne Crude Oil and Products Trade
### (in million metric tons)

| 1965 | 1970 | 1971 | 1972 | 1973 | 1974 | 1975 | 1976 | 1977 | 1978 |
|---|---|---|---|---|---|---|---|---|---|
| 727 | 1,240 | 1,315 | 1,445 | 1,639 | 1,675 | 1,467 | 1,602 | 1,619 | 1,580 |

Sources: Organization for Economic Cooperation and Development, *Maritime Transport: 1977* (Paris: Organization for Economic Cooperation and Development, 1978), p. 131; The British Petroleum Company, *B.P. Statistical Review of the World Oil Industry, 1978* (London: The British Petroleum Company, 1978).

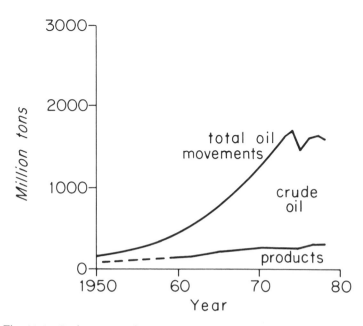

Fig. 11.1. *Seaborne Petroleum Cargo Movements*. Source: G. Victory, "The Load on Top System, Present and Future," *Symposium on Marine Pollution* (London: Royal Institution of Naval Architects, 1973); and United Nations, Organization for Economic Cooperation and Development (OECD), *Marine Transport 1978* (Paris: OECD, 1979).

TABLE 11.3

PRINCIPAL NORTH PACIFIC CRUDE OIL AND PRODUCTS SEABORNE TRADE (IMPORTS)
(IN MILLION METRIC TONS)

| Destination | 1970 | 1971 | 1972 | 1973 | 1974 | 1975 | 1976 | 1977 | 1978 | 1979 |
|---|---|---|---|---|---|---|---|---|---|---|
| Japan | 198 | 215 | 230 | 269 | 266 | 242 | 253 | 260 | 254 | |
| USA (Pacific Coast) | | | | 23.5 | 32.3[a] | 36.3[a] | 48.8 | 56.6 | 28.0[a] | 23.9[a] |
| Republic of Korea | 15.5 | 19.9 | 18.4 | 20.9 | 21.7 | 16.8 | 20.1 | 24.0 | 26.2 | |
| Canada (Pacific Coast) | | | | | 0 | 0 | 6.6 | 7.4 | 7.5 | |

Sources: Edward L. Miles et al., *Atlas of Marine Use in the North Pacific Region* accompanying this volume; Organization for Economic Cooperation and Development, *Quarterly Oil Statistics (Oil Statistics* before 1976) (Paris: Organization for Economic Cooperation and Development, quarterly); *Economic Statistics Yearbook 1979* (Bank of Korea, 1979); Republic of Korea, Bureau of Statistics, *Korea Statistical Yearbook 1975* (Seoul, 1976); United States Maritime Administration, *Essential U.S. Foreign Trade Routes*, 1975; U.S. Census Bureau, Foreign Trade Data Tapes, *SM305* and *SM705* processed by the Port of Seattle, 1979.

Note: These figures exclude liquid natural gas. In addition to the petroleum imports listed above, all four countries export small quantities of petroleum products. Some of these exports are in turn imported by other North Pacific rim nations. In 1976, export tonnages ($10^6$ metric tons) were as follows: Japan .09, mostly to Republic of Korea; Republic of Korea 1.2, one-half to Japan; Pacific Canada .4, one-half to Japan: Pacific USA 4.2, one-half to Japan.

Blanks indicate absence of data.

[a] Data for Alaska were inadvertently not acquired. For 1976 and 1977, the Alaska component were .6 and .8 million metric tons respectively.

Almost all (80 percent) of the North Pacific deep-sea crude oil trade is Japanese imports.

From these figures, we see that North Pacific oil trade constitutes about 19 percent of the total world petroleum trade. Thus, one might expect about 19 percent of the annual oil spill due to tanker casualties, for example, to occur here. Yet, according to the data in table 11.4, the actual incidence has been approximately 1.5 percent of the estimated oil spillage, or much less than expected. Some very large tanker spills have occurred south of the study region, however.[3]

There are three probable reasons for this low oil spillage in the North Pacific. First, most of the oil that is spilled into the world oceans from accidents results from a few very large spills. The *Amoco Cadiz* spilled 200,000 metric tons near Brittany, France; the *Argo Merchant* spilled 27,500 metric tons near Cape Cod, USA; the *Metula* spilled 40,000 metric tons in the Straits of Magellan, South America. No very large spills have been reported in the North Pacific study region in recent years, and thus the oil input in the region should be below its prorated portion of the world annual average. Second, even though 19 percent of the world petroleum moves in this region annually, a far smaller portion on a ton-mile basis is carried here, since the major oil movement in the region—Middle East to Japan—ends with a short 200 nautical miles in the North Pacific Ocean north of 30° north latitude. Third, it is probable that tanker accidents in coastal waters of the North Pacific countries that result in medium and small spills are not well reported, so the data in table 11.4 are almost certainly underestimated, although small spills are not likely to contribute significantly to the total spill figures.

Alternatively, the region's load of discharged oil from tanker washings has been estimated by Wong and his associates to be on the order of 71,500 metric tons annually, or about 1 percent of the estimated total annual oil input to the world's oceans. They estimated that the load of tar carried annually by the Kuroshio Current to the North Pacific is on the order of 25,000 metric tons.[4] Land-based and other nontanker marine sources of petroleum did not appear to be the origin of the tar, leading them to the conclusion that it came from tanker discharges. Wong's estimate of the annual input of petroleum hydrocarbons to the region from tanker washings was based on the facts that crude oil contains 35 percent tar on average and the weathered oil-tar is believed to float in the oceans for approximately 1 year before sinking.[5] The U.S. domestic movements of Alaska oil employ shoreside reception facilities at the cargo loading port for tanker slops, so this trade produces no routine oil discharges.[6]

TABLE 11.4

CRUDE OIL AND PRODUCTS SPILLED IN NORTH PACIFIC TANKER CASUALTIES
(IN METRIC TONS)

| 1966 | 1967 | 1968 | 1969 | 1970 | 1971 | 1972 | 1973 | 1974 | 1975 | 1976 | 1977 | 1978 | 1979 |
|------|------|------|------|------|------|------|------|------|------|------|------|------|------|
| 3,210 | 2,372 | 25 | 774 | 4,902 | 10,335 | 427 | 3,410 | 1,914 | 648 | 9,777 | 3,777 | 52 | 450 |

Source: Edward L. Miles et al., *Atlas of Marine Use in the North Pacific Region* (section on Marine Pollution) accompanying this volume.

Wong found almost no tar in water samples taken from eastern North Pacific waters.

The estimated annual volume of actual oil discharges from routine tank cleaning and deballasting in the study region represents .03 percent of the oil annually carried to Japan, or about 14 percent of the oil that would be discharged from a deballasting vessel that did not practice LOT or another technique for controlling oil discharges.[7] This figure can be compared with data for 1970 reported by Arasaki that roughly 12 percent of all ballast wash waters discharged by tankers that call on Japan and practice LOT occurred north and east of Taiwan Island.[8] The remaining wash waters from LOT operations are discharged in the South China Sea (47 percent) and east of the Malacca Straits (41 percent). These data indicate that the North Pacific study region is relatively unpolluted by oil from tanker washings, and confirm that vessels calling on Japan practice some form of pollution control.

By way of comparison, table 11.5 summarizes all reported oil spills into the North Pacific for the period 1954 to 1979. It shows that 50 percent of all reported oil spilled in the region has come from tanker casualties. This high percentage is well above the figure for the world average of 4.9 percent from tanker casualties reported in table 11.1. The disparity is probably due to underreporting of nontanker casualty spill events in the study region, and because spill sources are not readily observable (for example, oil in river runoff). Table 11.5 also shows that 94 percent of the events and 57 percent of the spill volume of reported tanker casualties in the study region have occurred in the Northwest Pacific. These spills have all occurred within Japan's 200-mile zone. Data were not available for the DPRK, PRC, ROK or USSR.

Table 11.6, in conjunction with figure 11.2, shows that Japanese statistical areas 3, 4, 5, and 10 are reported to have the most oil spillage. This reflects the relatively high level of ocean traffic in these areas since the major Japanese ports of Tokyo and Yokohama are in area 4, Nagoya and Osaka are in area 5, area 10 is the intensely used Seto Inland Sea and area 3 covers the Tsugaru Strait, which connects the Sea of Japan to the Pacific Ocean and is a major throughfare for shipping. In the Northeast Pacific nine tanker casualties resulted in 21,500 tons of oil spillage. Reported casualties in the Northeast Pacific yielded larger outflows per spill than in the Northwest.

To evaluate the consequences of these spills for the North Pacific, and to consider what measures, if any, should be taken, a thorough investigation of the state of international regulation of tanker operations is necessary. Analysis of this problem from a regional perspective is artificial and awkward since most of the mechanisms available for implementing alternatives exist only at the global level. Therefore, our North Pacific region viewpoint is temporarily set aside; we return to discuss implications for the region at the end of the chapter.

## ENVIRONMENTAL CONSEQUENCES

Petroleum hydrocarbon input to the world ocean has concerned national and international lawmakers since World War I.[9] Accidental oil spills and deliberate oil discharges to the oceans as a result of human activity, amounting to 90 percent of the estimated annual

## TABLE 11.5

### Summary of Reported Oil Spills in the North Pacific (1954–1979)
### (spills greater than one metric ton)

| Source | Number of spills | Quantity spilled (metric tons) | % Total number | % Total quantity spilled |
|---|---|---|---|---|
| *North Pacific Total* | | | | |
| Tanker casualties resulting in oil spills | 150 | 50,207 | 45.0 | 50.4 |
| Other vessel-related oil spills | 154 | 12,241 | 46.6 | 12.3 |
| Oil spills from other sources | 28 | 37,129 | 8.4 | 37.3 |
| Total | 332 | 99,577 | 100.0 | 100.0 |
| | | | *%Number spills by source* | *%Quantity spilled by source* |
| *Northwest Pacific Total* | | | | |
| Tanker casualties resulting in oil spills | 141 | 28,675 | 94.0 | 57.1 |
| Other vessel-related oil spills | 110 | 6,857 | 71.0 | 56.0 |
| Oil spills from other sources | 10 | 11,273 | 35.7 | 30.4 |
| Total | 261 | 46,805 | | |
| *Northeast Pacific Total* | | | | |
| Tanker casualties resulting in oil spills | 9 | 21,532 | 60 | 42.9 |
| Other vessel-related oil spills | 44 | 5,384 | 29.0 | 44.0 |
| Oil spills from other sources | 18 | 25,856 | 64.3 | 69.6 |
| Total | 71 | 52,772 | | |

Source: Edward L. Miles et al., *Atlas of Marine Use in the North Pacific Region* (section on Marine Pollution) accompanying this volume.

Note: Included in this table are spills of many types of crude and processed petroleum hydrocarbons. Tanker casualties are reported as a separate category. Illegal discharges and valve malfunctions resulting in spills from tankers are recorded as Other Vessel-Related Oil Spills. Spills from Other Sources include offshore oil production, pipelines, onshore storage, and refining.

Data reported for the Northwest Pacific are almost exclusively for waters in the vicinity of Japan. Four very large tanker spills occurred in Southeast Asian waters below 30° N and are not included in the summary table but are shown in the annex to the list of spills from which this summary is drawn. These four spills are the *Paceocean* (30,000 MT), *British Ambassador* (50,000 MT), *Borag* (32,000 MT), and the *Stoic* (15,000 MT). Three other very large tanker spills occurred elsewhere in the south central and southeast North Pacific Ocean. These were the *R. C. Stoner* (18,000 MT), *Irene's Challenge* (36,000 MT), and the *Hawaiian Patriot* (17,500 MT). Thus, on the order of 80 percent of the spillage of oil from tanker casualties for the entire North Pacific Ocean above the equator actually occurred outside the North Pacific study region and in the band 0° to 30° N latitude. These spills, furthermore, accounted for two-thirds of the oil spilled from all sources, including pipelines, offshore production, and others.

## TABLE 11.6

### OIL SPILLS REPORTED IN WATERS OFF JAPAN (1966–1978)
#### (spills over one metric ton)

| Region | | Number of spills | Quantity |
|---|---|---|---|
| (1) | Tanker casualties resulting in oil spills | 2 | 132 |
| | Other vessel-related oil spills | 5 | 404 |
| | Oil spills from other sources | – | – |
| | Total | 7 | 536 |
| (2) | Tanker casualties resulting in oil spills | 6 | 375 |
| | Other vessel-related oil spills | 3 | 40 |
| | Oil spills from other sources | – | – |
| | Total | 9 | 415 |
| (3) | Tanker casualties resulting in oil spills | 10 | 3,747 |
| | Other vessel-related oil spills | 13 | 497 |
| | Oil spills from other sources | 2 | 2,530 |
| | Total | 25 | 6,774 |
| (4) | Tanker casualties resulting in oil spills | 24 | 3,054 |
| | Other vessel-related oil spills | 20 | 1,095 |
| | Oil spills from other sources | 1 | 9 |
| | Total | 45 | 4,158 |
| (5) | Tanker casualties resulting in oil spills | 15 | 54,773[a] |
| | Other vessel-related oil spills | 9 | 242 |
| | Oil spills from other sources | 1 | 54 |
| | Total | 25 | 55,069 |
| (6) | Tanker casualties resulting in oil spills | 5 | 1,409 |
| | Other vessel-related oil spills | 6 | 357 |
| | Oil spills from other sources | 2 | 172 |
| | Total | 13 | 1,938 |
| (7) | Tanker casualties resulting in oil spills | 14 | 514 |
| | Other vessel-related oil spills | 14 | 1,084 |
| | Oil spills from other sources | 3 | 8,506 |
| | Total | 31 | 10,104 |
| (8) | Tanker casualties resulting in oil spills | 3 | 307 |
| | Other vessel-related oil spills | 5 | 1,176 |
| | Oil spills from other sources | – | – |
| | Total | 8 | 1,483 |
| (9) | Tanker casualties resulting in oil spills | 1 | 6,200 |
| | Other vessel-related oil spills | 4 | 17 |
| | Oil spills from other sources | 1 | 2 |
| | Total | 6 | 6,219 |

TABLE 11.6 (Continued)
OIL SPILLS REPORTED IN WATERS OFF JAPAN (1966-1978)
(spills over one metric ton)

| Region | | Number of spills | Quantity |
|--------|--------------------------------------------|------|-------|
| (10) | Tanker casualties resulting in oil spills | 59 | 6,709 |
| | Other vessel-related oil spills | 25 | 727 |
| | Oil spills from other sources | – | – |
| | Total | 84 | 7,436 |
| (11) | Tanker casualties resulting in oil spills | 2 | 155 |
| | Other vessel-related oil spills | 5 | 218 |
| | Oil spills from other sources | – | – |
| | Total | 7 | 373 |

Source: Edward L. Miles et al., *Atlas of Marine Use in the North Pacific Region* (section on Marine Pollution) accompanying this volume.

[a] Includes 50,000 metric tons of oil spilled by the tanker *British Ambassador* southwest of Chichi-Jima, which is within the Japanese 200-mile zone but not necessarily within the Japan Maritime Disaster Prevention Center's statistical Area 5. Another spill attributed to the Northwest Pacific in table 11.5 but not shown here is from a dry bulk carrier near ROK (1,000 MT).

[b] See figure 11.2.

input (the remainder being from natural oil seeps), may have large-scale and/or long-run deleterious effects on the living resources of the oceans. The distribution in time, space, and degree of oil-related damages to living resources is the subject of extensive research at this time, but only limited generalizations have thus far been drawn by the scientific community. An assessment by the National Academy of Sciences (NAS) summarizes our knowledge.

> The most damaging, indisputable, adverse effects of petroleum are the oiling and tarring of beaches, the endangering of seabird species, and the modification of benthic communities along polluted coastlines where petroleum is heavily incorporated in the sediments. The first two of these effects occur predominantly from discharges and spills of tankers and ship operations. The toxicity and smothering effect of oil caused mortality in all major spills studied, with pelagic diving birds and intertidal and subtidal benthic organisms being most affected. Mortality was greatest where oil spills were confined to inshore areas with abundant biota. The effects were generally quite localized, ranging from a few miles to tens of miles, depending on the quantity of petroleum involved. [10]

According to the NAS report, whether these effects are a prelude to long-lasting and widespread damage to the oceans is unknown.

Scientists have not been able to ascertain the effect of oil spills on fish populations in their natural habitats. Laboratory experiments, in which living organisms are exposed to oil and the results generalized to the ocean environment, have not come readily. Nor has it been possible to account for all physical and chemical parameters that affect living marine species in the case of an actual oil spill. For example, Dr. John Farrington testified that the effect of the *Argo Merchant* spill on the fisheries resources of Georges Bank would probably never be

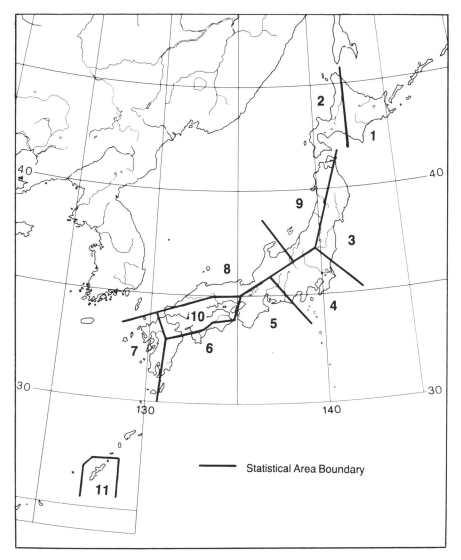

Fig. 11.2. *Japan Maritime Disaster Prevention Center: Statistical Areas.* Source: personal correspondence with Mr. Katsumi Kuzu, director, Japan Maritime Disaster Prevention Center, Tokyo, March 1980.

known because of the unknown effects of other natural stresses on the fish stocks, prior polluting events, and the implementation of the 200-mile exclusive fisheries jurisdiction zone in early 1977, which changed the pattern of fishing effort.[11]

Thus, the known effects of oil discharges and spills from tankers on living resources are bird mortalities and that portion of damage to shallow water benthic organisms that is attributable to nearshore spills (mainly from tanker casualties). Oil discharges from routine tanker operations also are a source of beached and floating tar. These, along with concern for possible unknown threats to living resources and the offensive nature of oil spills near recreational beaches, are the factors that have motivated research into the socioeconomics of marine oil pollution and the search for precautionary and remedial measures by national and international decision makers.

## A SOCIOECONOMIC FRAMEWORK FOR EVALUATING POLICY ALTERNATIVES

Policies proposed and formulated to deal with marine oil pollution can be evaluated for their effects on two types of interests impacting human welfare: (1) the national and international economic consequences of oil pollution, including possibly short-term damage to valuable fisheries, lost recreational opportunities, and reduced shoreline property values; and (2) the ecological or environmental consequences of oil pollution, including damage to nonexploited marine living and nonliving resources (such as seabirds and seascapes), and increased concern for the long-term effects on natural ecosystems.[12]

The decision problem described at its greatest level of generality consists of devising a means of measuring the consequences of policy alternatives in all the relevant policy dimensions, and a means of selecting (via a legitimate political process) a policy that has the community's preferred mix of outcomes. The market mechanism can, in principle, provide an integration of a community's collective valuation of marketable goods and services, the values being expressed as prices; market imperfections can thwart this, however. The environmental consequences of various policies can be measured with more or less accuracy using an appropriate metric, depending on the state of scientific knowledge.[13]

An alternative formulation of the decision problem (but not the one used here) is to assume that the community's assessment of the environmental consequences of the policy alternatives can be measured in monetary units, or money, and are additive to the economic consequences, also measured in money. The decision problem then becomes one of selecting the alternative that results in the minimum total costs.[14]

Market imperfections can be an important cause of excessive oil discharges from accidents. When a tanker casualty occurs and oil pollutes a valuable shoreline, the vessel and cargo owner(s), under historical standards, lose only the value of the vessel and its cargo. However, the economic loss to society also includes cleanup costs and the damage done to shoreline property, living marine resources, and other marine economic uses. These additional losses can be substantial. A metric ton of crude oil was worth about $90 to its owner in 1978, but the cost of only cleaning up an oil spill averaged $655 per ton.[15] A listing of some of the economic costs that a coastal community bears as a result of an oil spill, and an estimate of their magnitude, has been published by Wilcox and Mead.[16]

As a consequence of the failure of the market to account for these extra social costs, the profit-maximizing vessel operator invested only in safety devices, such as good navigation equipment, whose costs were estimated by the operator to be balanced by the value of the cargo and vessel they contributed to saving (or the reduction in insurance premiums resulting from an accident-free record), but not by the value of the cleanup costs avoided, or the recreational and other values the shoreline saved. Consequently, insufficient incentives for safe and clean operation, from a purely socioeconomic perspective, existed under historical (pre-1970s) standards. Furthermore, the impact of an oil spill or discharge on societal interests for environmental amenities was entirely outside the framework of private sector decision making. As a consequence, public action became necessary.[17]

Public action in the tanker pollution context could take any of four forms: (1) regulations requiring use of specific safety and oil discharge prevention devices; (2) regulations requiring the achievement of specific discharge standards, based either on the total amount of oil discharged, or on the concentration of oil in waste water effluents; (3) subsidies to vessel owners to encourage achievement of specific standards; or (4) taxes or fines levied on vessel owners based on the volume of oil outflows or spills or on the cost of cleanup.

Regulatory requirements for use of specific safety and discharge-preventing devices have been frequently used to protect air and freshwater resources. These requirements have the advantage of apparent nondiscrimination and do not impact governmental budgets. However, their use may hinder innovation and prevent the introduction of more efficient equipment. Furthermore, such regulations affect waste outflows only indirectly. A doubling of economic activity and of seaborne oil movements, for example, could double oil effluents to the ocean.

Alternatively, regulations specifying the allowable quantity of vessel effluents (performance standards) but not the technology to use to achieve the limits would not hinder innovation, but would be very difficult to enforce against pollution arising from normal tanker operations occurring at sea where they cannot be independently monitored. Even if enforcement was feasible, effluent quantity limits have the disadvantage of being potentially costly to society because different vessel owners may be subject to greater or lesser costs to achieve the same pollution-avoidance standard. Newer vessels whose pipes, pumps and tanks are in better condition than those of older vessels might be required to spill less oil, while older vessels might be permitted to spill more since the additional cost (marginal cost) borne by the older vessels to engage in nonpolluting operations would be relatively greater than for the newer vessels. Society would be better served in an economic sense by letting operators who find it relatively more costly to reduce oil outflows bear less of the economic burden of oil outflow standards, and other vessels bear more of the burden. For any given level of total tanker fleet oil outflow, the consumption of economic resources would, in principle, be minimized under this arrangement.[18]

To determine the least-cost mixture of standards to be applied to the world fleet of tankers requires detailed information on the relationship of operating costs to oil discharge levels for each vessel in the world fleet. A further layer of complexity can be added if the waste loading varies by region; in this case, the operating area of each individual vessel must be known in order to assign appropriate discharge standards to it, and tankers do not usually have a definite region of operation.

Rather than attempt to collect and analyze the required information, it has been suggested that the regulatory authority employ financial incentives as a means of encouraging each operator to achieve the right standard. Incentives would take the form of fines or taxes against oil discharges, or subsidies to encourage nonpolluting performance. How financial incentives can direct, in a decentralized manner, the achievement of the most efficient level of discharges and abatement costs is described by Freeman et al.[19] The difficulty of enforcing such policies would be significant. Enforcement problems have thus far prevented the adoption of marine pollution charges on a national or international basis.

While both fines and subsidies can lead to an economically efficient allocation of resources, they have quite different effects on social equity. A fine assessed on the quantity of effluents would correct, in principle, for deficiencies of the market system by insuring that vessel owners bear the social costs of avoidable pollution incidents. The vessel owners would have the option of either paying fines or changing their activities, whichever seemed most profitable. If the income from the fine is paid to those whose environment is damaged, this effectively awards the latter the rights to the environmental amenities.

The difficulty of devising practical enforcement mechanisms and the unwillingness or inability of vessel owners to bear responsibility for their activities have not prevented important efforts to assign partial liability to vessel owners for avoidable accidental spills. This is a fine applied to cases where culprits can be identified. Liability conventions and national funds are now in the process of being ratified and implemented, as described in chapters 9 and 10. However, Pearson is of the opinion that pending international liability conventions are not by themselves sufficient solutions to the marine oil pollution problem because they do not fully internalize pollution damage costs to shipowners.[20] Agreements by major oil companies to bear liability, under certain voluntary plans, will be important for several years.

The final points to be made in this section concern the reasonableness of efforts to require different performance, design, and equipment standards for vessels operating in different coastal areas. The U.S. delegation worked strenuously at the IMCO 1973 conference on oil pollution to prevent the adoption of a provision in the ensuing Convention that would have precluded coastal and port states from unilaterally enacting regulations for vessel pollution equipment and design standards more stringent than those established by the Convention.[21] The U.S. position was that such a provision should not be enacted, and each state should be free to impose more stringent standards as it saw fit. Regional differences in the valuation of environmental amenities, such as fisheries and recreational resources, varying perceptions of the as yet unknown hazards posed by oil pollution, and different concerns for the economic costs of pollution prevention, were felt by the United States to imply that tankers should adhere to standards suitable to their region of operation.

The counterargument for including a provision in the Convention that would require that standards be consistent everywhere was that without such consistency each state would be free to set its own standards and a thicket of regulations might grow up. It was argued that this would unreasonably hinder oceanborne trade. While no requirement for global consistency was adopted in 1973, a quid pro quo for not adopting one was extracted from the U.S. delegation; it promised that the U.S. would not stray far from international norms when establishing its domestic regulations.[22]

It is well known that the international tanker trade functions like an idealized, perfectly competitive market. Ease of entry to the trade via investment in new or existing tonnage is a hallmark of the industry. The degree of capital mobility is significant since it has encouraged the development of vessels tailored for individual trades. The Japanese have experimented, for example, with wide beam, shallow draft tanker designs to enable larger tonnage vessels to enter certain shallow ports. Given the mobility of capital movement into and out of the tanker market, and the ability of tanker owners to design their vessels to suit the physical and legal constraints of specific trades if profits can be had thereby, it is highly unlikely that any reasonable range of environmentally motivated standards that affected vessel design and operation and applied only in a limited geographic area would have only a minimal impact on the economics of delivering oil to that geographic area. Reluctant adaptation has occurred, for example, in the case of the U.S. law requiring that U.S. and foreign flag tankers larger than 125,000 dwt be barred from entering Puget Sound for reasons of safety.[23] Thus, neither the desirability nor the feasibility of establishing regulatory standards on a regional basis for tankship operations should be questioned. Other factors such as a desire for international comity may cause governments to resist passing regionally specific standards.[24]

## MAJOR TECHNOLOGICAL ALTERNATIVES

The major design and equipment requirements that have been proposed in national and international forums to reduce the spillage of oil are load-on-top (LOT), fitting existing and new tankers with segregated ballast tanks (SBT), using crude oil washing (COW), fitting double bottoms (DB) to all newly constructed tankers as a means of reducing oil spills from tanker grounding accidents, and inert gas systems (IGS).[25] Furthermore, it has been suggested that the volume of oil spilled in a tanker accident will be reduced if the interior volume of tankers is subdivided into a larger number of smaller cargo tanks. Finally, double bottoms and segregated ballast have been combined to yield a hybrid concept—protective location (PL) of segregated ballast. These proposed requirements are described in the following sections.

### Load-On-Top

Routine tanker operations are a source of oil discharge to the seas. Oil is spilled (1) when water ballast has been placed in cargo tanks and is later discharged at sea prior to cargo loading, carrying with it much of the oil that clings to tank walls after cargo discharge (the oil outflow averages .32 percent of the cargo capacity of the tanks that have been ballasted); (2) when cargo tanks are washed with high pressure jets of seawater to reduce the accumulation of tacky petroleum residues, and the oil-contaminated wash waters are discarded overboard; (3) when cargo tanks are washed with seawater for periodic inspections; (4) when tanks are thoroughly cleaned prior to change of cargo type, which can yield an additional .1 percent of ship cargo capacity in oily sludge and residues; and (5) when the cargo tanks are thoroughly cleaned prior to scheduled dry-docking, which occurs every 12 to 24 months.

As table 11.1 indicates, these activities were thought to contribute 21.8 percent or 1.33

million tons of oil spillage to the seas annually in 1973 from LOT and non-LOT tankers.

When tankers use the technique called load-on-top (LOT), the oily ballast water mixture in the cargo tanks is pumped to a holding or *slop tank* where the oil is allowed to separate from the water by flotation. This step takes place while the vessel is at sea, proceeding from the cargo unloading port back to the cargo loading port. Since crude oil is less dense than water, petroleum fractions that have not dispersed into the water float to the surface of the slop tank. Meanwhile, fresh seawater ballast is added to the "clean" cargo tanks, while nearly oil-free seawater from the bottom of the slop tank is gradually pumped overboard; the oil residue is retained in the slop tank. At the cargo loading port, the seawater ballast from the "clean" tanks can be pumped into the harbor to make room for the oil cargo, which is loaded into the cargo tanks and "on top" of the retained oil in the slop tank. This procedure cannot be used with refined petroleum products because mixing product types in the slop tank would spoil the characteristics of any new cargo loaded.[26] The LOT procedure, when properly performed, reduces the amount of oil discharged routinely to the sea. Our description of LOT is abbreviated and therefore slightly inaccurate.

The use of LOT was encouraged by the 1969 Amendments to the 1954 International Convention for the Prevention of Pollution of the Seas by Oil, which is deposited with IMCO. These amendments came into force in January 1978 but became customary law in 1969 when they were accepted. They are described in chapter 9 and in Pritchard.[27] If LOT was practiced properly by all vessel operators, the input of oil to the oceans from routine tankship operations would be much smaller than it now is. The figures of table 11.1 on oil discharges from routine vessels operations were based on the assumption that 80 percent of the world crude oil tanker fleet practiced LOT with 90 percent efficiency, and that the remainder of the fleet made no effort to retain oil and water mixtures on board. This implies an average effectiveness for the world fleet of 72 percent. When diligently practiced, LOT is capable of reducing oil outflows per voyage to a level of .0067 percent (or 1/15,000th, which complies with provisions of the 1969 Amendments) of vessel cargo capacity, making it 98 percent effective.[28] Were LOT employed this effectively by the entire world tanker fleet, routine tanker operations would discharge .08 million metric tons of oil yearly to the seas.

Actual experience with LOT (under customary law) has been disappointing. M'Gonigle and Zacher report that confidential studies by major oil companies of tanker operations out of the Middle East in 1970 and 1971 revealed that only one-third of the vessels visiting the terminals were using the system properly, another one-third used it with only indifferent success, and the remainder were not using it at all.[29]

IMCO encouragement of the use of LOT has not resulted in the expected level of compliance and oil discharge reduction because neither the enforcement mechanisms nor the anticipated environmental and economic incentives for the ship operators have been adequate. Human errors during ballast water pumping operations, ignorance of the proper techniques, concerns that salt water remaining with the retained slop oils would cause the retained slop oils and cargo mix to be rejected by refinery operators, and short voyages that preclude adequate separation of the oil and water in settling tanks (a voyage of at least 48 hours is necessary) have contributed to the failure of the LOT system to meet expectations.

These problems were sensed when LOT was being evaluated by IMCO. The principal arguments that the 1969 Amendment would encourage LOT use were that LOT was a profitable process for the ship operator since retained oils had some value, and that enforcement of proper operation would be possible by inspecting slop tanks at cargo loading ports to ensure that oil had been retained on board and not discharged on the ballast voyage.[30] However, it was assumed that the authority that would do the inspecting would be oil industry personnel, and enforcement would be undertaken by the nation of registry of the offending vessel (flag state enforcement).[31] In practice, inspections do not appear to have been carried out, and sanctions against offending vessels have not been instituted.[32] Furthermore, financial incentives were inadequate. While crude oil is sold in the Middle East for about $90 per metric ton (1978), oil mixed with seawater requires more sophisticated and expensive separation and refining processes, making it less valuable to refineries. Thus, stipulations were placed on LOT operations specifying the maximum quantities of seawater mixed with oil that refineries would accept.[33]

Financial incentives to retain oil on board depend upon how profits are generated in the oil transport business. Waters et al. pointed out that slops reduce the amount of oil a tanker can load by up to .3 percent of cargo capacity for a 100,000 dwt tanker. If tankers owned by independent operators are paid for their services on the basis of their *bill of lading* weight (amount of oil loaded into the ship as measured at the loading port manifold) the vessel owners have an incentive to arrive at the loading port empty of slops in order to have more space for cargo. Alternatively, these vessels may be paid on the basis of the amount of oil they deliver, but account is taken of the quantities of seawater in the slop tank that is delivered with the oil cargo, so shipowners lose credits for delivering oil mixed with salt water and also lose valuable cargo-carrying capacity by retaining slops from the prior ballast voyage.[34] The incentive in this case is to drain slop tanks of their water content until what remains is primarily oil, pumping quantities of oil and water mixture to sea.

Due to tank clingage, the quantity of oil discharged to the unloading manifold from a tanker that initially loaded oil cargo while empty of slops will be less than the amount of oil loaded aboard by up to .4 percent. The exact amount of clingage and reduced cargo outturn depends on the characteristics of the crude oil carried and the number of cargo tanks that were cleaned on the prior ballast voyage. Alternatively, the amount of oil delivered from a tanker that retained slops and employed LOT will equal the amount loaded aboard, since any reductions in deliveries due to clingage losses in the cargo tanks will be balanced by the amount of oil initially aboard the tanker in the slop tank. Total ship capacity for oil carriage is reduced, however, due to the water in the slop tank, so that efforts to save oil result in slightly higher transportation costs. Integrated oil companies, which have owned about 25 percent of the tonnage of the world crude carrier fleet in recent years, take all these factors into account, balancing the value of the saltwater and oil mixture that is saved with the value of the lost transportation capacity of their fleet of ships. The quadrupling of the posted price of oil in late 1973 should have increased the incentive for the integrated oil companies to conserve oil from the operations of both their own and chartered fleets. In 1975, a survey of vessels calling in the Middle East revealed that ships owned by the major oil companies retained about 50 percent more oil slops on board than did other vessels.[35] This implies a global fleet effectiveness figure of 62 percent. This same source shows that slop retention had increased over the years 1972−1975, implying that global ocean petroleum pollution levels from routine tanker operations have probably not grown significantly since the early 1970s.[36] This improvement in the fleet performance is undoubtedly due to improved financial incentives for practicing LOT. The financial incentive to practice LOT, which did not exist in 1969, came into being in 1973. Thus, the 1969 IMCO amendments alone turned out to have little discernable effect on tanker operations, but rapid increases in the value of oil had an effect on some segments of the world fleet.

## Segregated Ballast Tanks

A second technology for reducing or eliminating the discharge of oil from ships is fitting segregated ballast tanks (SBT) on product, crude, and combination oil and bulk carriers. Since only ballast water and no oil cargo would usually be placed in these tanks, oil and water mixtures would not be created, and deballasting prior to cargo loading would not be a source of oil discharge. In practice, the degree of success of this method of controlling oil discharges depends on: (1) the amount of SBT capacity available relative to the vessel's needs for ballast; (2) the amount of oil slops originating from cargo tank washing undertaken for residue control, for cargo type change, for inspection, and for dry-docking; and (3) the proportion of the world fleet equipped with SBT capability.

General practice has been to ballast a vessel to about 60 percent of its full load displacement for heavy weather sailing, and to 40 to 50 percent for good weather sailing.[37] Thus, between 20 and 40 percent of the vessel's cargo tank volume may be flooded (the higher figure is more common), since conventional tankers normally already have between 10 and 15 percent SBT capacity.[38] Vessels equipped with up to 55 percent SBT capacity should be largely immune from the problem of creating oil and water mixtures in cargo tanks as a consequence of ballasting operations. Smaller volumes of ballast space can be used if it is determined that tank vessels can safely operate at lower drafts.[39] It was proposed in 1977 that all crude oil and oil product carriers then in existence have their pipe and pumping arrangements modified or retrofitted in the near future to create sufficient SBT capacity to obviate the need of using cargo tanks to carry ballast water.

Use of SBT (that is, adding more SBTs to the ship over and above standard practice) as a pollution-preventing measure would not be a complete solution to the problem of oil pollution from tankers for two reasons: not all tanker routine oil discharges come from ballasting operations, and SBTs cannot be cheaply installed on existing ships. Crude oil carriers typically wash a portion of their cargo tanks each voyage with seawater to control the accumulation of tacky residues and sludge, washing all cargo tanks by the completion of every fourth to sixth voyage. The washing process consists of pumping high volumes of seawater through water guns, called washing machines, which are mounted on the vessel's deck and extend down into the cargo tanks. The seawater washes oil and sludge residues to the slop tank.

On a conventional tanker operating at light ballast levels, about 35 percent of total cargo tank capacity is washed each voyage for clean ballasting purposes. An additional 13 percent is washed for residue and sludge control for a total of 48 percent of the total cargo tank capacity. On a SBT tanker, 20 percent of the cargo tanks are washed each voyage for sludge control. Switching from conventional to SBT capacity would reduce oil and water mixture volumes and any pollution resulting from the disposal of these by 58 percent, or a reduction of .63 million metric tons of oil spills annually. However, this figure overstates the overall improvement of SBT pollution-reducing benefits because tankers must occasionally thoroughly wash all cargo tanks with seawater prior to a change in cargo type, or to achieve a gas-free condition for tank inspection. This thorough cleaning is accompanied by demucking operations in which unpumpable residues and sludges, which are typically 50 percent solids and 50 percent hydrocarbons, are hoisted out of the cargo tanks.[40]

These activities would be unaffected by the existence of extra SBT capacity. And tankers that carry petroleum products, or combination oil and dry bulk carriers, may need frequent thorough cleanings prior to cargo change. The exact contribution these activities make to the budget of oil discharges to the sea is unknown but is probably small, being on the order of 20 percent or less. Therefore, it appears that were the world fleet fitted with SBT, 45 to 50 percent of oil discharges from routine tanker operations could be avoided annually, amounting to between .49 and .54 million metric tons if LOT were practiced on the wash waters to the standards assumed by the National Academy of Sciences. Total annual oil outflows to the sea would thus be reduced by 8 to 9 percent.

Retrofitting SBT capacity to the world tankship fleet is not a feasible proposition for international implementation in the near future because it would be both a time-consuming and costly process. Retrofitting SBT on existing ships requires (a) vessel structural changes, including the provision of additional bulkheads and possibly the reinforcement of the bottoms of some tanks; (b) rearrangement of piping and pumps in order to dedicate sets of pipes and pumps to handle either oil cargo or ballast water only; and (c) special coating and corrosion protection in ballast tanks.

The cost of retrofitting between 1,600 and 3,300 crude, product, and combination carriers that are greater than 20,000 dwt in size has been estimated to be between $3.2 and $7.4 billion, assuming 1979 implementation of a retrofit program.[41] The cost per vessel averages $2 million, or about 5 percent of the contract cost of a modern Japanese-built 200,000 dwt tanker. The wide range in the estimated fleet cost stems from uncertainty as to how much of the world tanker fleet would be retrofitted and how much would be scrapped by vessel owners as uneconomical to retrofit. Consumers of oil products would ultimately pay the cost of retrofitting SBTs on the fleet. Due to the perceived high cost, retrofitting SBTs on the fleet has been strongly resisted by tanker owners and by nations that do not want to bear the higher transportation costs for imported oil.

Alternatively, SBT tankers could be used as a long-run method for oil discharge reduction, taking effect as tankers now on the seas are gradually replaced by new SBT tankers. It was estimated in 1973 that fitting segregated ballast tanks to a 250,000 dwt tanker would add 4.5 percent to its construction cost.[42] Leading tanker owners have indicated that they are relatively unconcerned about the costs that would result from national or international mandates to employ SBT on new tankers.[43] Unfortunately, while mandating the use of

SBTs on new tankers would be a feasible method of reducing oil discharges, the effects of such a mandate would not be noticeable for as many as ten or more years.

Clean ballast tanks (CBT) are a variation on SBT in which certain tanks on *existing* vessels are used only to carry water ballast. This differs from SBT in that CBT ships are created by modifying cargo and ballast water piping arrangements without changing tank size from the original design. Usually a CBT tanker has more ballast space and less cargo space than a vessel whose piping and tank arrangement were designed initially for SBT.

## Crude Oil Washing

Another alternative for reducing routine vessel discharges has recently been proposed—crude oil washing (COW), also referred to as waterless washing. In this system, as oil cargo is discharged in port, a portion of the oil is diverted from the discharge piping system and routed to the cargo tank washing machines (see figure 11.3). These machines rotate about the vertical axis and simultaneously the discharge nozzle changes elevation through a preprogrammed arc, blasting the tank walls with a high pressure (160 psi) jet of oil. The jet dissolves tacky residues and lubricates sludge. This permits more complete cargo outturn, reduces the quantity of clingage to less than .1 percent of tank capacity, and reduces sludge quantities normally left in cargo tanks by 65 to 90 percent.[44] Oil in pumps and pipes becomes a larger proportion of potential discharges as tank clingage is reduced. It is assumed that these are thoroughly flushed during a crude wash cycle.[45]

Oil and water mixtures are formed after crude oil washing in the process of filling cargo tanks with water ballast. These mixtures can be handled in the appropriate (LOT) manner if the vessel operator chooses to do so, resulting in oil discharges of less than 1/30,000th of vessel cargo capacity, a level in compliance with new IMCO rules discussed below. Crude oil washing is undertaken in the cargo discharge port, improving the possibilities of enforcing its use since COW operations can be verified by shoreside authorities.

By reducing sludge buildup and increasing the outturn of cargo, an economic incentive to undertake COW is provided shipowners and operators. Operators and owners who are paid on the basis of the amount of oil they deliver can deliver more oil using COW, since less tank clingage and sludge creation occurs so that cargo outturn is increased. Operators paid on a bill of lading weight basis can also earn more due to greater cargo capacity resulting from cargo tanks containing less unpumpable sludge and smaller volumes of slop. Routine water washing of tanks to control sludge buildup is unnecessary when COW is practiced so that only the oil remaining in cargo tanks used for ballast need be mixed with ballast water. Thus, oil residues remaining in about 35 percent of cargo tank capacity are exposed to mixing with seawater ballast, as compared to 48 percent with LOT.

Crude oil washing is not without disadvantages. If there is any water in the oil lines that feed the washing machines during washing operations, and there usually will be small amounts present, static electricity can be created, which can ignite flammable cargo vapors in the cargo tanks. For this reason, it is necessary to install an inert gas system (IGS) on COW-equipped tankers. This is a system that provides cargo tanks containing flammable vapors with low oxygen, high carbon dioxide gas from the main power plant exhaust. The gas is used during cargo discharge and COW operations to displace the air and hydrocarbon

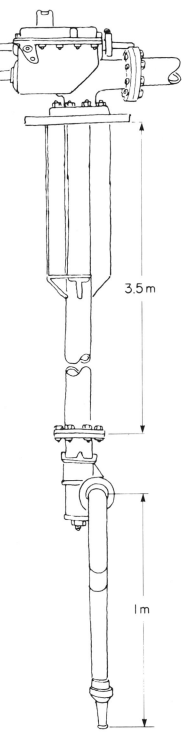

3.5 m

1 m

Fig. 11.3. *Butterworth Systems LAVOMATIC®
Tank Washing Machine*. Source: personal communication, W. O. Gray, Exxon Corporation, New York,
July 1978, and Butterworth Systems, New Jersey, July
1980.

vapor mixture that would otherwise form in the cargo tanks.[46] Installing an IGS, the most costly part of a COW investment, costs roughly $1 million, or 2.5 percent of a typical 200,000 dwt vessel's capital cost.

Since 1969, when three vessels had cargo tank explosions, tanker owners have begun to install IGSs on tank vessels over 100,000 dwt as a safety measure, regardless of whether they used COW. Smaller tankers have not been routinely equipped since the danger of explosions on small vessels is thought to be less.[47]

COW operations produce up to four times the normal quantities of hydrocarbon vapors generated in cargo tanks, amounting to .09 percent of the cargo capacity, due to the increased splashing of oil in the cargo tanks. Tank vapors are a concern to some port communities because they can add to local air pollution.[48]

COW cannot be used on petroleum product tankers because they often carry several different grades of cargo oils that would be contaminated if accidentally mixed in the washing process. Additionally, COW is a process; SBTs are not a process, they are embodied in the vessel's structure. Therefore, concerns have been voiced that enforcement of international standards for COW operations may be more difficult than enforcement of retrofitting SBTs on existing tankers.[49]

In light of the LOT experience, it would seem that enforceability of COW would depend to an important degree on its economic attractiveness to vessel owners and charterers. In this regard, COW offers several advantages over LOT.

Better cargo outturn is achieved, better use is made of cargo capacity, and valuable vessel time is saved prior to dry-docking. An average of six fewer days are reported to be required to bucket and hoist out the unpumpable sludge, which otherwise accumulates during the 12- to 24-month period between scheduled dry-docking. However, COW operations may increase port time at the cargo unloading port while cargo tanks are crude washed. This can result in lost vessel utilization time of up to 10 hours per voyage for a 250,000 dwt vessel if a full wash of all cargo tanks is performed, or a total of 120 hours (5 days) over a 24-month, 12-voyage period between dry-dockings.

An Oil Companies International Marine Forum (OCIMF) study indicates that COW is economic for integrated oil companies, since they take advantage of both the value of the oil saved and the resulting increased transport capacity of their ships.[50] The saving reportedly can amount to $197,000 annually for a 250,000 dwt vessel, implying that proper use of COW would be self-enforcing (see table 11.7). However, vessels operating in trades that make more than six round-trips per year would lose time in port for crude washing operations, and vessels owned by interests who hold no equity in the oil carried, and would not benefit from the value of the oil saved, would have less incentive to invest in a COW capability.

Crude oil washing, however, is like SBT in that part (40 percent) of the total annual cost of employing the system is capital cost. Thus, were national or international law to mandate that COW capability be built into tankers, capital costs would be "sunk" for those vessels complying with the mandate and it would become attractive for even the independent tanker owner to utilize COW effectively. An independent tanker owner's calculation after accounting

TABLE 11.7

CRUDE WASHING ECONOMICS FOR INTEGRATED OIL COMPANY

| Source | Savings/Loss ($1000/year) |
|---|---|
| Oil recovered from sludge | $ 26 |
| Additional capacity gained (sludge) | 31 |
| Clingage recovered | 79 |
| Additional capacity (clingage) | 91 |
| Vessel time saved prior to dry-docking | 81 |
| Reduced cleaning cost at dry-docking | 25 |
| Increased vapor loss | (32) |
| Extended cargo discharge time | (68) |
| Amortization and maintenance | (75) |
| Oil saved due to smaller volumes of slop from tank washing | 20 |
| Inventory gains | 27 |
| Increased energy used in crude washing | ( 8) |
| Net savings | 197 |

Source: Oil Companies International Marine Forum, *Crude Oil Washing*, MEC/MEPC Informal 17 (prepared for the 1978 IMCO Conference on Oil Pollution), 1977.

*Assumptions*

Vessel: Size 250,000 dwt, 6 voyages/year, dry-dock every second year, 70 to 90 washing machines, extended cargo discharge time of 10 hours, full wash of all tanks, six days saved prior to dry-docking. (Note that from one-third to all cargo tanks may be crude-oil washed each voyage, depending on each owner's calculation of the benefits derived from the process.)

Sludge: Buildup first voyage without crude-oil wash—360 long tons; after that, 60 long tons more per voyage.

Clingage: Clingage recovered from COW—1,575 long tons per year.

Costs: Vessel capital cost (Worldscale 60) $27,000/day; freight rate Persian Gulf—Rotterdam $9.62/long ton; cleaning costs saved $50,000, oil value $100/long ton.

Investment: 50 additional tank washing machines $150,000/5 years. Capital cost of additional piping $150,000. Maintenance cost of added system $7,000/year. Discount rate 15 percent.

for the sunk investment in equipment might be like that shown in table 11.8, which indicates that, for the assumptions employed in the table, use of COW should be self-enforcing. Assuring proper installation is an aspect that should be no less enforceable with COW than with SBT and certainly more enforceable than LOT.

The economic consequences from a societal viewpoint of mandating the fitting of COW on tankers, as estimated on a per tanker basis, would be similar to that of the integrated oil company's calculation (table 11.7). If the assumptions used in preparing that table are broadly representative of all vessel sizes and operating circumstances, it would be economically beneficial from a societal viewpoint to mandate that COW be fitted on all tankers. Note that COW is environmentally beneficial also, further enhancing its attractiveness.

Given its apparent social, economic, and environmental benefits, and the availability since about 1971 of almost all the essential technology used in the crude oil washing process, one must ask why it has not been developed more quickly and used more widely. The reasons are several. The lower value of retained oil prior to the 1973 quadrupling of oil prices and the focus of innovation on large vessel and power plant fabrication in recent years

TABLE 11.8

CRUDE WASHING ECONOMICS FOR INDEPENDENT TANKER OWNER

| Source | Savings/Loss ($1000/year) |
|---|---|
| Additional capacity gained (sludge) | $ 31 |
| Additional capacity gained (clingage) | 91 |
| Vessel time saved prior to dry-dock | 81 |
| Reduced cleaning cost | 25 |
| Extended discharge time | (68) |
| Increased energy used crude wash | ( 8) |
| Net savings | 152 |

Source: Oil Companies International Marine Forum, *Crude Oil Washing*, MEC/MEPC, Informal 17, 1977.
*Assumptions*

Same as table 11.7, except that any oil saved is valueless to the vessel owner, and that investment costs are sunk, since international law requires the investment.

have contributed to the slow development and diffusion of crude oil washing technology through the industry. Furthermore, independents, given the choice of fitting or not fitting COW, in doing their investment analysis will subtract $75,000 from the net saving estimate shown in table 11.8 due to amortization and maintenance costs they must bear. The appeal of COW is thereby seen to be less to them. The COW capability must be added to an existing vessel at slightly higher cost than if it had been built on as original equipment. During a depressed charter market, with rates much less than the long-run average Worldscale 60 assumed in tables 11.7 and 11.8, new investments are resisted. Thus, the economic attractiveness of COW implied by those tables cannot be assumed to be sufficient to cause an early general investment in COW capability by the industry. Nevertheless, it is probably true that in the absence of governmentally imposed requirements that COW be used, eventually COW will be practiced by most of the larger tankers operating on the long-haul trades from the Middle East to Western Europe, Japan, Virgin Islands, and the U.S. West Coast, and perhaps by smaller tankers operating on other routes such as Middle East and Caribbean to the U.S. East Coast.

To summarize, if crude oil washing were practiced by the world fleet of ships over 20,000 dwt in size with an average performance close to that indicated above, and if LOT were practiced on any oil and water mixtures created aboard the vessel to the standards assumed by the National Academy of Sciences in their preparation of table 11.1, the following effects could be expected: (1) oil discharge from sludge disposal from crude carriers prior to dry-docking could be reduced by about 90 percent, or by .225 million tons annually; (2) oil discharges from routine tanker operations (LOT and non-LOT tankers) could be reduced by 65 percent or by .706 million metric tons annually;[51] and (3) reductions in accidental spills of oil from fires and explosions in cargo tanks (following installation of IGS on the world fleet) of 80 percent, or a reduction of 15,840 metric tons annually.[52] This leads to a total reduction of oil discharges to the sea of .945 million metric tons, or 15.4

percent of the estimated total annual oil discharges to the seas. Some additional discharges would result from increased atmospheric rainout of hydrocarbon vapors. Socioeconomic benefits are not estimated but would evidently be net positive.

## Double Bottoms

Tanker accidents are thought to contribute about 200,000 metric tons of oil to the seas annually. Of this, the U.S. Coast Guard has estimated that 23 percent, or 47,000 metric tons, of oil spills result annually worldwide from the grounding of tankers and subsequent rupture of tanker bottoms.[53]

Groundings of tankers such as the *Argo Merchant* and the *Amoco Cadiz* have spurred national action to limit oil spills in coastal regions, and raised interest in the United States for the requirement that tankers be fitted with double bottoms.

A double bottom is created by installing steel plating above the bottom skin of the vessel along its cargo-carrying length. This plating acts as the cargo tank bottom. Thus a space between the cargo tank and the vessel's bottom skin is created, usually 6 to 10 feet deep, which may be used for ballast water but would not be used for oil, either cargo or fuel (see figure 11.4).

The widely cited work of Porricelli et al. probably marks the popular launching of the idea of fitting double bottoms as a means of reducing oil spills from tanker groundings.[54] Shortly after its publication and the passage of the Ports and Waterways Safety Act of 1972, a movement of U.S. environmental groups to require the fitting of double bottoms on all tankers was launched.[55]

Porricelli et al. based their recommendation on data indicating that 26 percent of the accidents in which oil was known to have been spilled were grounding incidents. Data on actual oil volume outflow were too sparse to be employed. Ramming and collisions accounted for 39 percent of spill incidents but were thought to be avoidable by use of better vessel traffic systems in crowded harbors and port entrances. This latter expectation had not

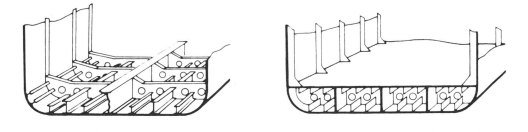

**Single bottom**
*Tough to stow cargo*

**Double bottom**
*Smooth top-Messy below*

Fig. 11.4. *Tanker Bottom Construction*. Source: American Institute of Merchant Shipping, *Tanker Double Bottoms: Yes or No?* (Washington, D.C.: American Institute of Merchant Shipping, July 1974).

yet been borne out by 1973, when the second and most recent analysis was prepared by the Coast Guard of the volume of oil spilled in various kinds of tanker accidents such as fires, explosions, and groundings.[56]

While recognizing that a ruptured double bottom could cause tankers to settle more firmly on the ocean bottom, Porricelli et al. emphasized a catalogue of advantages of double bottoms: (1) they can be used for segregated ballast, (2) they would probably prevent inner cargo tank bottoms from being pierced in many of the cases where groundings occurred in harbors at low speed, and (3) the added bottom structure would make the tanker stronger. The recommendation for fitting double bottoms assumes that their presence would either have no effect on, or would reduce the probability of, complete loss of the ship and cargo once grounded.

More studies followed on the heels of Porricelli et al. A study by Card[57] has influenced opinions in the United States that double-bottomed tankers would be of significant benefit in reducing the incidence of spillage in the event of a grounding accident.[58] Card estimates that roughly 87 percent of the oil outflow from 30 tanker groundings in U.S. waters in the period 1969–1973 could have been prevented if the tankers had been fitted with double bottoms to a depth equal to 1/15th the tanker's width (beam). However, Card employed a simple methodology and somewhat more sophisticated studies have since been undertaken that indicate that double bottoms would be less effective than he estimated. United States Secretary of Transportation Brock Adams cited a refinement of a 1970 Intergovernmental Maritime Consultative Organization study as the most authoritative on double bottoms. It indicates that a double bottom of height above the tanker bottom skin equal to 1/15th the vessel's beam would prevent roughly 50 percent of the oil spillage that would otherwise occur if a single bottom tanker stranded at low speed—such as might occur in a harbor or ship channel.[59] The result of this study implies that about 24,000 metric tons of oil pollution worldwide could be avoided annually if all tankers were fitted with double bottoms. According to Secretary Adams, it was this finding that convinced U.S. President Jimmy Carter to issue a directive to the Coast Guard to publish proposed regulations requiring the fitting of double bottoms on all tankers entering U.S. waters.[60] While directed at a fairly small amount of oil spillage relative to the totals of table 11.1, the protection provided by double bottoms was expected to be economically and environmentally significant, given the high value of the resources threatened by oil spills from grounded tankers in shallow coastal regions.

Achieving a reduction in spillage greater than 50 percent from low-speed grounding accidents appears to be possible only by also establishing national regulations that would require raising the structural strength requirements for tankers. At present, structural standards for all vessel types including tankers are set by private organizations called *classification societies*. So far these societies have established structural standards for double bottom tankers that are roughly equivalent in overall strength to single bottom tankers. For example, since a double bottom tanker has an extra layer of steel in its bottom structure, the societies permit them to be constructed with an 11 percent thinner center keelson girder (a main structural component of a vessel's keel) than is permitted on a single-bottomed tanker.[61] The significance of this difference was overlooked by Card.

Determining the effectiveness of the double bottom requirement for all types of grounding accidents is not without considerable controversy. This is due to the deficiencies of the statistical studies of the question, and to the different interpretations of the physical mechanism involved in the grounding and leakage of oil from a grounded tanker.

The physical mechanisms argument focuses on the events that occur during a grounding. In a single bottom tanker, the vessel's bottom skin and the bottom of the cargo tanks are the same. When a loaded single skin tanker grounds and ruptures the bottom of a cargo tank that is completely full of oil (the normal case) more oil leaks out than is replaced by water, slightly lightening the vessel's load.[62] It has been argued that this oil spillage is useful since it lightens the ship and may decrease the likelihood that the vessel will be totally lost before salvage operations can save it.[63] For a fully loaded double bottom tanker, rupturing the outer bottom leaves the inner bottom intact and causes the vessel to lose buoyancy due to flooding of the double bottom space, and the vessel to settle more firmly on the object it grounded on. This may possibly increase the difficulty of a salvage operation. The emphasis of this argument is on saving the ship and most of its cargo, noting that vessels that are totally lost constitute 60 percent of the oil spilled from grounding accidents.[64] Proponents of double bottoms have countered that rupturing an empty space leads to firmer settling of the vessel which may aid in salvage because the vessel cannot swing around after the initial impact and rupture more cargo tanks, as did the *Metula*.[65] Presumably, a segregated ballast tank could be flooded to achieve the same effect if firmer settling were deemed desirable. Also, when double bottom tankers happen to rupture both the outer and inner skins, an entrapment effect in the double bottom's space has been reported; this is caused by the presence of the double layers of containment wall (which act as a baffle) at the point of rupture. This entrapment effect is said to reduce oil outflow rates.[66]

The Coast Guard has long known that a technical analysis of oil spill from grounded tankers from a physical mechanisms viewpoint is lacking. This is mentioned by Kimon et al.[67] and Card.[68] The latter notes that consultants retained by the Coast Guard found ''the grounding and stranding problem to be significantly more complex than the collision problem, which itself was going to require a larger effort [to analyze] than originally anticipated. Therefore, the Coast Guard decided to omit grounding from the [research] project.''

The only research that has addressed the advantages and disadvantages of double-bottomed (and double-sided) ships is by N. Jones:

> It was also observed in reference [48] that the total plastic energy absorption in a hull is approximately proportional to the shell plate thickness. Thus, a similar energy absorbing capacity was found for single-hull and double-hull ships with the same overall sideplating thickness. However, a double hull is superior to a single shell when punching or tearing action with little energy absorption occurs, since the inner shell may remain intact and prevent leakage of the cargo after rupture of the outer shell . . . The work was theoretical and provides a useful framework for

the future study of minor ship collisions. . . . In contrast to the extensive literature on ship collisions, very few articles appear to have been published on the local structural damage of ships sustained in grounding accidents.[69]

Given that the debate on the physical mechanisms argument is unresolved, the above quote seems to supply some encouragement for the use of double bottoms, but the encouragement is certainly not strong.

Lacking a rigorous engineering analysis of the problem, it seems that statistical studies of spill histories of double and single bottom tankers might be used to resolve the issue. The study cited by Secretary Adams is not definitive, however, because it is not based on actual double bottom crude oil tanker experience, and does not account for changes that the fitting of double bottoms to tankers could cause in accidents due to other causes—especially accidents due to fires and explosions in tanks. These have accounted for 10 percent, or 19,800 metric tons, of all oil spilled from tanker accidents annually.[70] Tanker industry spokesmen have pointed out that empty spaces in tankers (such as would be created by the addition of double bottoms) may trap hydrocarbon gases, which contributed to these accidents.[71] If inert gas from inert gas generating systems (IGS) were introduced to the empty double bottoms, the explosive hazard would be eliminated. At least three tankers that were fitted with IGS (that were malfunctioning) have been lost due to cargo tank explosions.[72] As experience with IGS is gained, these lapses in functioning should be avoidable. Double bottom tanks are difficult and dangerous to inspect during regular safety surveys because the tanks are so remote from the vessel's upper levels.[73] Three crew members are reported to have asphyxiated while inspecting double bottom tanks in an inerted vessel.[74] Correction of these deficiencies should be possible with greater diligence on the part of vessel operators, and perhaps changes in the design of double bottom access ways.

The "fire and explosion in deep tanks" debate will remain academic until actual experience with double bottom crude carriers has been thoroughly documented. By 1975, only 8 double bottom crude carriers had been built, and none existed prior to 1969.[75] Mobil Oil Company is believed to have acquired double-bottomed tankers because it felt the additional cost might be recovered through better tank draining of cargo during unloading. Furthermore, Sun Shipbuilding and National Steel Shipbuilding had laid plans to build DB tankers as a result of observing the strong sentiments for such ships running in the U.S. Senate; the shipyards felt that requirements for the use of DB tankers might be forthcoming.[76]

The statistical study referred to by Secretary Adams was based on experience with noncrude carriers such as general cargo carriers, combination oil and dry bulk carriers, and chemical carriers that fit double bottoms to provide a flat cargo space bottom to improve dry cargo handling and storage or to facilitate tank cleaning when changing the type of liquid cargo being carried. For vessels that typically carry dry cargo, the presence of a double bottom in the event of grounding and rupture of the outer skin aids vessel survivability, since a smaller volume of vessel space is flooded.

The nearly nonexistent experience with double bottom crude oil carriers has become an issue because of concerns that placement of double bottoms in crude carriers might decrease the probability of salvaging grounded tankers. If even a minor decrease in the salvageability of loaded crude oil carriers is caused by the presence of double bottoms, average annual oil outflows from groundings would be increased. Rare large spills from total losses of vessels account for most of the oil entering the oceans from tanker groundings. Since such spills are rare, statistical studies based on slightly different ship types or on short time periods are not adequate to determine the consequences of the construction change.[77] Average spill volume is emphasized here. However, average spill volume from groundings may be a deceptive parameter for decision making. Since spill size can vary by eight orders of magnitude, the variance of the spill distribution should also be considered. If double bottoms had *no net effect* on the average annual volume of oil spilled, but adding double bottoms changed the pattern of spills so some small spills were avoided but an additional very large spill occurred, it could be a significant environmental change. The opposite change in spill incidence is also possible—more small spills and fewer large ones with unknown but possibly important effects for the environment.

The use of historical spill data in decision making implicitly assumes that future developments will employ present technology operated to recent-past standards. Neither of these assumptions would apply in the case of spill incidents from tankers. The average vessel size of the crude carrier fleet was 47,000 dwt in 1970, but by 1974 the average size of crude carrier on order was 200,000 dwt. Recent-past vessel operation standards may be altered by the creation of new international standards for crew training and certification. Should efforts at upgrading crew performances succeed, the tankship industry may experience a reduction in accidents, including groundings, which would reduce the benefits created by fitting double bottoms. In other words, whatever benefit-cost ratio now describes the double bottom question, it will become less favorable in relation to the success of other measures now being advocated to reduce the probability of future tankship grounding accidents.

Considering the complexity of the double bottom issue, it is understandable that the U.S. Coast Guard has been cautious in stating its judgment. According to M'Gonigle and Zacher, the Coast Guard delegation to the 1973 IMCO Convention on tanker pollution was divided in its opinion on double bottoms. By late 1975, the Coast Guard shifted the emphasis of its proposals to IMCO away from requiring double bottoms on all crude carriers and toward protective location of segregated ballast tanks.[78]

Other nations have not supported an international requirement that DBs be fitted on tankers. United States-sponsored proposals put forward at the 1973 IMCO International Convention for the Prevention of Pollution from Ships (MARPOL) that double bottoms be required on crude carriers were defeated by votes of 5−21 and 9−22. Delegations that voted with the U.S. are reported to have done so for reasons of diplomacy. Votes against the proposition were motivated by concerns that double bottoms might be environmentally counterproductive as well as adding significantly to the cost of imported oil. Of the North Pacific nations whose positions are known, the Soviet Union, Japan, and Canada opposed the proposals.[79]

The additional capital costs of fitting double bottoms to tankers ranges from 8 to 11 percent.[80] Minor improvements in cargo discharge capability would increase tanker operating efficiency and slightly offset these added costs, but the belief that fitting double bottoms would result in increased freight bills is undisputed.

In October, 1971, the IMCO Assembly adopted the Code for Construction and Equipment of Ships Carrying Dangerous Chemicals in Bulk. The Code recommends that chemical tankers conform to certain design standards. These standards, which include the fitting of double bottoms among other things, were formulated to promote the protection of the ships, their crews, and human populations in port areas. Prevention of pollution in the event of a collision or grounding was also thought to be an advantage of the Code. Thus, in accepting the Code, but resisting the application of DBs to tankers, a double standard appears to apply. In order to be issued an International Pollution Prevention Certificate for the Carriage of Noxious Liquid Substances in Bulk (Regulation 11 and 13, Annex II of MARPOL), a chemical tanker's design must conform to the standards established in the 1971 Code.[81] MARPOL 73 has received little support from the international tanker shipping industry, in part because the provisions of Annex II have been thought to be too costly.

In summary, the debate over the utility of using double bottoms is formally unresolved. As described below, a new IMCO convention adopts double bottoms indirectly and support of this step is widespread. The adoption involves melding double bottoms to restrictions on cargo tank size and using segregated ballast tanks.

## Restriction of Cargo Tank Size

Following the grounding of the *Torrey Canyon* in 1967, public concern for the consequences of pollution from tanker accidents rose. Furthermore, the size of tankers was growing rapidly during this period and as tanker sizes grew so did the size of the cargo tanks in the larger tankers. If an accident occurred and a cargo tank was breeched, the outflow of oil from the larger tanks would be greater, and so would the ensuing environmental damage. In response to this, it was proposed at IMCO that the size of cargo tanks be limited, so as tanker size grew the cargo space must be subdivided into a larger number of smaller tanks.

These suggestions were incorporated in a 1971 amendment to the 1954 International Convention for the Prevention of Pollution of the Sea by Oil. They were later incorporated into the 1973 International Convention for the Prevention of Pollution from Ships (MARPOL 73). The restriction was to be achieved by hypothesizing a set of serious cargo tank penetrations from collisions and strandings, and stipulating maximum permissible amounts of oil that could be expected to leak from the ruptured tanks. The allowed oil-outflow quantities were designated $O_s$ for strandings and $O_c$ for collisions. Larger ships were permitted larger outflow limits.

Figures 11.5 and 11.6 show the damage assumptions for collisions and strandings respectively. These damages are compared to the vessel's compartmentation plan using certain formulae to determine if the vessel could spill more than its allowed maximum outflow. The logic underlying the formulae goes as follows: Not all of the oil in a ruptured tank will necessarily leak out. The expected percentage of cargo tank contents that will

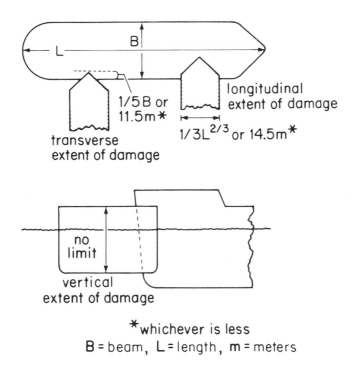

Fig. 11.5. *Hypothetical Damage Following Collision.* Source: G. Victory, "The Load on Top System, Present and Future," *Symposium on Marine Pollution* (London: Royal Institution of Naval Architects, 1973).

escape upon rupture is assumed to be a function of the location of the cargo tank on the vessel and the kind of accident suffered. Tanks located next to the vessel's outer side skin are assumed to spill 100 percent of their contents in the event of a collision. Groundings are assumed to result in the loss of only one-third of a ruptured tank's contents. Tanks located within the ship are assumed to spill a lesser percentage of their cargo when ruptured, the percentage of spill depending on the distance of the cargo tank wall from the ship's outer skin.

As the size of the allowed outflow is reduced for a given size vessel, more compartmentation of the vessel is required. The outflow levels should not be made too low, however. The additional cargo tank surface created by subdividing cargo tanks with bulkheads would be counterproductive, since oil tank clingage would be increased and result in more oil discharges to the sea during routine LOT operations.

According to MARPOL 73, cargo tanks need not be specially subdivided if the tanks are placed further inside the vessel and separated from the skin by SBTs. Thus, the rules created an incentive to place SBTs between cargo tanks and the vessel's skin, since finer cargo tank compartmentation is expensive in terms of added steel, increased cargo discharge times and complications in tank cleaning operations. The MARPOL 73 permissible outflows are shown in figure 11.7.

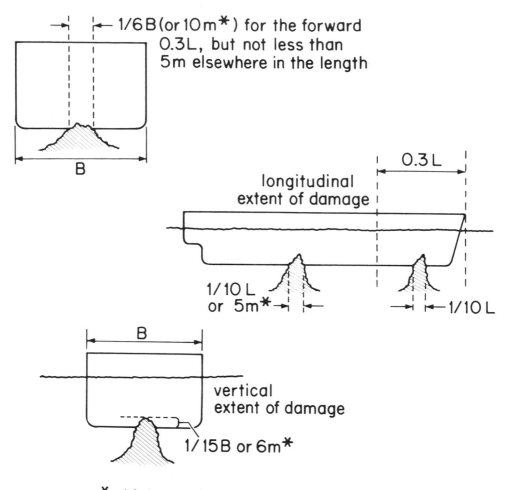

Fig. 11.6. *Hypothetical Damage Following Grounding.* Source: G. Victory, "The Load on Top System, Present and Future," *Symposium on Marine Pollution* (London: Royal Institution of Naval Architects, 1973).

We have found no estimate of the expected consequences of these provisions on worldwide oil spills from tankers. Hood has reported costs to be on the order of 2 percent of total transportation costs for a 300,000 dwt tanker.[82]

## INTERNATIONAL EFFORTS TO CONTROL OIL DISCHARGES FROM TANKERS

The Intergovernmental Maritime Consultation Organization is the depository for four conventions and protocols that pertain to the technological alternatives described above.[83]

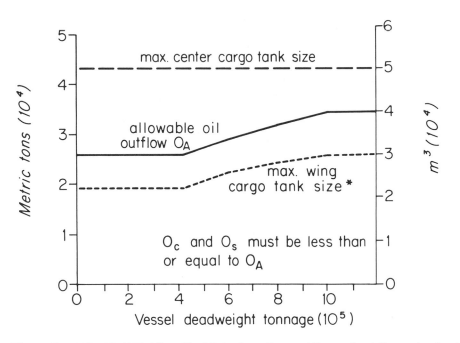

Fig. 11.7. *MARPOL 1973 Allowable Oil Outflows*. Source: "International Convention for the Prevention of Pollution from Ships," *International Legal Materials*, 12:1319. To convert from cubic meters, as employed in the regulation, to metric tons, a conversion factor of 1 metric ton = 1.16 kilo-liters (1 kiloliter = 1 cubic meter) of oil was used. This is a typical value for crude oil. (*)Maximum wing cargo tank size in a segregated ballast tank (SBT) tanker may equal the oil outflow limit if the SBT wing tanks are placed on each side (fore and aft) of the wing cargo tanks, if each SBT occupies a sufficient length along the vessel side so that wing cargo tanks are too far apart for an assumed damage from a collision to rupture more than one cargo tank, and if the center tank sides are placed too deeply inside the vessel to be ruptured by the assumed collision penetration.

The 1954 Oil Pollution Convention, as modified by amendments in 1962, 1969, and 1971 (the 1962 and 1969 amendments have come into force), constitutes present international law for controlling oil pollution from tankers.[84] The 1969 amendments stipulate, among other things, that a tanker that is underway and in a ballast condition may not discharge more oil than 1/15,000th of the cargo it carried prior to taking on ballast, and that LOT may be used to achieve this standard.

Due to post-1969 perceptions that LOT would prove unenforceable, the United States, with the support of Canada, initiated new efforts to obtain international regulations through IMCO that would result in early reduction of oil discharges from tankers.[85] The U.S. effort was accompanied by a strong signal in the form of the U.S. Ports and Waterways Safety Act of 1972 that the U.S. was prepared to impose stringent design standards unilaterally on all vessels entering U.S. waters if the international community did not act expeditiously.[86] As a consequence of the U.S. initiative and with the help of numerous like-minded allies, an IMCO conference of October and November, 1973, passed the Convention for the Prevention of Pollution from Ships (MARPOL 73).[87]

A segregated ballast capacity that achieves 30 to 35 percent, on average, of vessel deadweight tonnage is required by MARPOL 73 to be built into "new" tankers over 70,000 dwt capacity, where newness is defined in the Convention as certain calendar dates, any vessel built thereafter being a "new" vessel. Use of the LOT system is required and cargo tank arrangement and size limitations were established to increase the probability of the vessel surviving an accident and to reduce the volume of oil outflow from groundings and collisions.[88]

MARPOL stipulates that the moulded draft amidships (dm) shall not be less than 2.0 + .02L m, where L is vessel length measured in meters (m) when the vessel is empty of cargo (lightweight) but segregated ballast tanks are full. Table 11.9 tabulates the consequences of this rule for two hypothetical ships, showing how this rule sets the level of SBT required for various ship sizes.

TABLE 11.9

SEGREGATED BALLAST TANK CAPACITY

| Tanker | Measurement |
| --- | --- |
| *Vessel #1* (world fleet average vessel) | |
| Deadweight (dwt) | 250,000 long tons |
| Loaded draft | 19.9 meters |
| Length (L) | 330 meters |
| dm= 2.0 + 6.6= | 8.6 meters |

Therefore, when ballasted, this vessel will achieve $8.6/19.9 \times 100 = 43.2$ percent of full-load displacement. This displacement corresponds to 33 percent of deadweight, which is adequate for good weather sailing.

| | |
| --- | --- |
| *Vessel #2* | |
| Deadweight (dwt) | 120,000 long tons |
| Loaded draft | 15.8 meters |
| Length (L) | 259 meters |
| dm= 2.0 + 5.2= | 7.2 meters |

Therefore, when ballasted, this vessel will achieve $7.2/15.8 \times 100 = 45.6$ percent of full-load displacement. This displacement corresponds to 34 percent of deadweight, which is adequate for good weather sailing.

Source: Compiled by author of this chapter. See also J. J. Creighton and I. E. Telfer, "Segregated Ballast Tankers," *Symposium on Marine Pollution*, pp. 30–59. This shows how to relate vessel displacement to deadweight.

The United States delegation to the 1973 IMCO Convention proposed initially that 20,000 dwt be the cutoff size for application of the SBT rule, thinking that SBT on vessels below this size would be too costly relative to the benefits produced. A secondary position developed by the U.S. negotiators, in light of strong opposition by other delegations to the first, was for a 70,000 dwt cutoff. It was asserted that this was the approximate breakpoint between the size of most crude and petroleum product carriers on order or under construction at the time.[89]

The 1973 Convention does not apply to heavy oils and refined petroleum products. The establishment of calendar dates to define "new" vessels has threatened investors in "new" vessels; if their vessels do not comply with MARPOL 73 standards they will be declared illegal, should MARPOL 73 ever come into force.[90] As of February, 1978, when a new

Conference was held (discussed below), only Jordan, Kenya, and Tunisia had ratified. The prospects for further ratifications were dim, primarily because the requirements set forth in Annex II dealing with nonoil chemical pollutants could not be reasonably met using available technology. Nevertheless, the U.S. Coast Guard published rules in October 1975, under the authority of the Ports and Waterways Safety Act, that implemented the SBT and cargo tank-size limit provisions of MARPOL 73 for U.S. flag tankers operating in domestic trades.[91]

## The Tanker Safety and Pollution Prevention Conference of 1978

Although MARPOL 73 is a step forward, it is not considered sufficient by U.S. authorities. Its shortcomings are that despite the more stringent discharge standards for new tankers, experience shows that such standards are largely meaningless due to the unenforceability of LOT. While the SBT requirement might be enforceable, it would not begin to have an important effect on routine slop oil discharges until after the vessels built during the 1971–1974 tanker-building boom were scrapped, regardless of how early the Convention might come into force; and tankers usually operate for about 15 years.

Furthermore, major accidents from tankers, such as the explosion of the *Sansinena* in Los Angeles Harbor, on December 17, 1976, which resulted in 6 deaths, 3 missing and presumed dead, 58 injuries, and 64 tons of bunker oil spilled, would not have been prevented if MARPOL 73 were in force. The *Sansinena* was 71,763 dwt but did not have an IGS.[92] The explosion was thought to have been the result of a spark igniting explosive gas vapors vented onto the vessel deck during ballast water loading operations. The flames spread to the cargo tanks where a massive explosion ensued.[93]

President Jimmy Carter's message of March, 1977, was in response to this and to the sinking of the *Argo Merchant*. He warned the international shipping community that if more were not done on a multilateral basis to reduce oil spills from accidents and routine vessel operations, the U.S. would unilaterally establish more stringent standards for vessels entering its ports under the Ports and Waterways Safety Act.[94] In February, 1978, an IMCO conference was held in response to the Carter warning.

The 1978 Conference produced two protocols and a set of related recommendations. One protocol modified the 1974 Safety of Life at Sea Convention (SOLAS) and is of interest here because of its provisions regarding the fitting of inert gas systems to crude oil and oil product tankers.[95] The second protocol modifies and incorporates portions of MARPOL 73 and includes the following: "New" crude-carrying tank vessels greater than 20,000 dwt, and new product carriers greater than 30,000 dwt, are required to fit segregated ballast tanks according to the formula employed in MARPOL 73.[96] These tanks are to be "protectively located" (PL) on the vessel. Furthermore, "new" crude carriers greater than 20,000 dwt must also be fitted with COW capability and IGS. In order to achieve an early reduction in routine oil discharges, and recognizing that crude oil washing could contribute to this goal at substantially less cost than retrofitting segregated ballast capability on existing ships, the MARPOL 73 Protocol mandates that on the date it enters into force, either COW capability or SBT capacity, as spelled out in MARPOL 73, be fitted to all crude oil carriers greater than

40,000 dwt then in existence. Existing petroleum product carriers over 40,000 dwt are required to be retrofitted with SBTs.

The upper size limit of the existing fleet of product tankers is about 40,000 dwt, so virtually no product tankers are affected by this rule.[97]

In all cases where SBT on existing crude and petroleum product tank vessels is referred to, Clean Ballast Tanks (CBT) are permitted as a substitute for a period of time. However, since CBT do not involve as extensive a redesign of the vessel as SBT, it is thought to provide a less enforceable means of securing nonpolluting tankship activity. Therefore, the MARPOL 73 Protocol stipulates that CBT must be replaced on crude carriers with either SBT or COW within two years of the coming into force of the Protocol if the vessel is 70,000 dwt or above, and within 4 years for crude carriers falling in the range of 40,000 dwt to 70,000 dwt. Existing petroleum product carriers may use CBT indefinitely.

A ''new'' vessel is defined by the MARPOL 73 Protocol to be one that is contracted for construction or major conversion after June 1, 1979; whose keel is laid or conversion begun after January 1, 1980; or that is delivered from construction or conversion after January 1, 1982. Vessels of 70,000 dwt or greater that are ''new'' according to MARPOL 73 (the equivalent dates were December 31, 1975; June 30, 1976; and December 31, 1979) must still satisfy the Protocol's stipulations for SBT and cargo tank size limits, making the Protocol consistent with the MARPOL 73 provisions. This removes the option of using COW in place of SBT for these ships, but is not discriminatory since ships falling in this category would have had to fit SBT anyway if the 1973 Convention ever came into force. The MARPOL Protocol requires that any tankship fitted with COW must also be fitted with IGS, and refers to the IGS standards listed in the 1974 Safety of Life at Sea (SOLAS) Convention and in its amending Protocol.

The SOLAS 1974 Convention and its amending Protocol stipulate that IGSs be applied to tankers of 100,000 dwt and over and to combination carriers of 50,000 dwt and over. The rule applies only to ships built after the Convention enters into force. SOLAS 74 comes into force in May 1980. The proximity of its coming into force was the principal reason for not merging the SOLAS 74 Convention with the SOLAS Protocol.[98]

The SOLAS 74 Protocol extends the 1974 Convention and stipulates that ''new'' crude oil and combination carriers of 20,000 dwt or greater or ''new'' crude oil carriers of any size using COW must be fitted with IGSs within two years of the date on which the SOLAS 74 Protocol comes into force. Existing crude oil tankers between 20,000 and 40,000 dwt that are not fitted with COW may be exempted from fitting IGSs by the Administration (government of the state whose flag the ship is entitled to fly) if fitting an IGS to these vessels is deemed unreasonable or impractical. Existing product carriers greater than 40,000 dwt must be fitted with IGSs within 4 years of the coming into force of the SOLAS 74 Protocol. Table 11.10 shows a summary of the provisions of the two Protocols.

## Comments on the Protocols and Plans for Implementation

The SOLAS 74 Protocol requirement that IGS be fitted to existing product carriers greater than 40,000 dwt is largely nonfunctional since few products carriers in the world

## TABLE 11.10

### TANKER SAFETY AND POLLUTION PREVENTION CONFERENCE RESULTS

| Tank Vessel | | Requirement (Construction feature, vessel tonnage, date required) |
|---|---|---|
| **New vessels** | | |
| Determining dates | | |
| 6/79 Contract date | | |
| 1/80 Keel laying | | |
| 6/82 Delivery | | |
| Crude oil | PL and SBT | 20,000 dwt and over[a] |
| | COW | |
| | IGS | |
| Petroleum products | PL and SBT | 30,000 dwt and over |
| | IGS | 20,000 dwt and over |
| | CBT | 40,000 dwt and over    then    SBT 70,000 dwt and over at HM + 2 (6/83) |
| | SBT | at HM (6/81)                      COW 40,000 to 70,000 dwt at HM + 4 (6/85) |
| | COW | |
| **Existing vessels** | | |
| Crude oil | IGS | 70,000 dwt and over at HS + -2 (6/81) |
| | | 20,000 to 70,000 dwt at HS + 4 (6/83)[b] |
| | CBT | 40,000 dwt and over at HM (6/81) |
| | SBT | |
| Petroleum products | IGS | 70,000 dwt and over at HS + 2 (6/81) |
| | | 40,000 to 70,000 dwt at HS + 4 (6/83)[c] |

Source: *Federal Register*, 43, 77 (April 20, 1978), 16885–16891.

Note: Dates in ( ) are dates by which Resolutions 1 and 2 adopted by the Conference recommended putting these requirements into effect, without waiting for entry into force of the Protocols.

[a]An inert gas system (IGS) is required whenever a tanker uses crude oil washing.

[b]Between 20,000 and 40,000 dwt the Administration of a Flag State may grant an exemption to the requirements for IGS if high capacity washing machines (i.e., tank washing machines with an individual throughput of greater than 60 cubic meters per hour) are not fitted and the ship's design characteristics make it impracticable to fit IGS.

[c]Tonnage limit for IGS is to be reduced to 20,000 dwt if tank washing machines with an individual throughput of greater than 60 cubic meters per hour are fitted.

Key:
PL — Protection Location
SBT — Segregated Ballast Tanks
COW — Crude Oil Washing
IGS — Inert Gas System
CBT — Clean Ballast Tanks
HM — Target date of entry into force of MARPOL Protocol (which incorporates the MARPOL 73 Convention) of June, 1981.
HS — Target date of entry into force of Solas Protocol. Date of June 1979 was established by Resolution 2. Dates in parentheses in table are dates by which Resolutions 1 and 2 recommend putting these requirements into effect, without waiting for entry into force of the Protocols.

fleet exceed 40,000 dwt.[99] The requirement that IGS be fitted on new product carriers greater than 20,000 dwt will probably result in the reduction or cessation of the construction of product carriers in the 20,000 dwt to 25,000 dwt range, with owners preferring smaller or larger size vessels depending on their calculation of the relative costs. No estimate is known to this author of the cost of implementing the IGS provisions, but the U.S. Coast Guard estimated that the benefits of the SOLAS 74 Protocol provisions (which affect only vessels under 100,000 dwt since IGS was already required by the 1974 SOLAS Convention on larger vessels) will reduce by three the average number of cargo tank fires and explosions, and will save 20 lives per year worldwide.[100] The requirement for COW capability on existing and new tankers is entirely new, and as a substitute for either LOT or retrofit SBT is undoubtedly desirable. Estimates have been made that SBT retrofit would cost oil consumers on the order of $3.2 to $7.4 billion, while reducing oil outflows 490 to 540 thousand metric tons annually. Alternatively, COW with IGSs would be economically beneficial to oil consumers (a net economic saving) and result in an outflow reduction of 945 thousand metric tons.

An interesting provision approved at the 1978 Conference pertained to the protective location (PL) of SBT. This concept first surfaced in October, 1975, when the Coast Guard issued proposed rules for the location of segregated ballast tanks that mandated that segregated ballast spaces be placed protectively on the sides and bottom of U.S. flag vessels operating in domestic trades.[101]

The U.S. placement formula was developed by a technical study group and was based on an examination of the records of a large number of tanker accidents in which the location of damage to the vessel was known.[102] The study group confirmed results of the spill volume analysis that had been published elsewhere, that roughly equal quantities of oil are lost from cargo tank penetrations on the vessel's side as from on the bottom, and that the turn on the bilge keel (where the ship bottom and side meet) is the most injury-prone area of the ship.[103]

The Coast Guard proposed rule was changed and simplified in January, 1976, when it was put into effect for U.S. tank vessels operating in domestic trades.[104] The January, 1976, rule stipulated that 45 percent of the bottom and side surfaces of "new" ships be double-sided with SBTs that are at least 2 meters in depth, and that the allowable hypothetical oil outflow be reduced at least 20 percent from that specified in MARPOL 73. In December of 1976, the 1973 MARPOL SBT rules and the protective location rule were proposed for application to U.S. and foreign flag ships that entered U.S. ports while operating in foreign trades.[105] This resulted in eight letters of protest from foreign governments, mainly because the protective location and outflow limits were original to the U.S. and were deemed as unilateral acts that were not consistent with customary law as then embodied in MARPOL 73.[106] President Carter's March, 1977, statement signaled that enforcement would be forestalled until the outcome of IMCO's 1978 deliberations was known but, as noted above, he did not foreswear unilateral action.

The MARPOL 73 Protocol provision for the protective location of SBT mandates that segregated ballast tanks be at least two meters in depth and be placed next to the ship's skin such that between 30 and 45 percent of its shell is covered with the protective tank space.

Figure 11.8 depicts the rule. Note that a trade-off is permitted designers for vessels over 200,000 dwt. These vessels may have as little as 20 percent of their side shell area covered with SBT if they achieve greater reductions in hypothetical oil outflows than is otherwise required by further subdividing their cargo tanks.

The trade-off shown is between having less vessel skin surface double-sided but smaller tank subdivisions with smaller outflows in the event of a cargo tank penetration, or having more skin surface double-sided but larger potential outflows when a cargo tank penetration occurs. In order to protect as little as 20 percent of the shell area, a 300,000 dwt tanker must be designed such that $O_c$ and $O_s$ are each reduced to only 60 percent of the standard hypothetical outflow (see example in legend of figure 11.8).

The protection outflow standard becomes less onerous as vessel size grows to 200,000 dwt because construction costs for additional tank subdivisions are more significant on the larger vessels. The Coast Guard published no quantitative estimate prior to February, 1978, of the effect of SBT and PL regulations on accidental oil outflows.

A review of the process of conceptualization and implementation of protectively located segregated ballast tanks reveals that it is closely related to the concept of double bottoms, that it grew out of efforts to accomplish what double bottoms might accomplish and that an analysis of costs and benefits is based on the same methods as have been applied to analysis of double bottoms.

In summary, the U.S. delegation to the 1973 IMCO Conference was instructed to press for a Convention mandating the use of double bottoms on tankers. However, the resistance to this by international tanker owners and by government delegates, together with the Coast Guard's growing perception that outflows from collisions were important to control, too, led the Coast Guard in 1975 to propose regulations requiring protective location of SBT on U.S. flag tankers operating in domestic trades. In late 1976, the Coast Guard proposed extending these requirements to all vessels calling at U.S. ports. The Coast Guard judged that the international acceptance of protective location of SBT might be less negative than it had been for double bottoms.[107]

The study report written by Gray, Kiss, and Sutherland described the technical analysis upon which the Coast Guard founded its advocacy of SBT and PL.[108] Twelve SBT tanker designs with SBT located in various side, double bottom, and center tanks were examined; all designs met the MARPOL 73 SBT regulations. The group's purpose was to ascertain how best to utilize segregated ballast capacity as a defensive mechanism against oil pollution from tanker accidents. The group concluded "that segregated ballast capacity should be placed adjacent to the shell and that at the bottom it should preferably be outboard." Their criteria were (1) undamaged vessel stability, (2) damaged vessel stability, (3) hypothetical oil outflow from groundings and collisions, (4) salvageability considerations after grounding, (5) susceptibility to fire and explosion, and (6) personnel safety. The group concluded that stability requirements (1) and (2), as set out by various IMCO load-line and safety-of-life-at-sea formulas, could be met (at some economic cost) and thus that SBT and PL need not be a source of hazard for vessel survivability if injured in deep water. Criterion (3) was analyzed using IMCO's 1973 hypothetical oil outflow regulations. "The

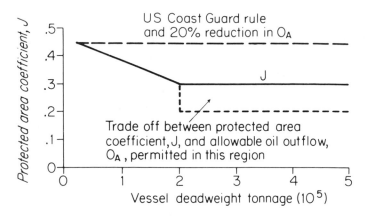

Fig. 11.8. *Area of Vessel Side and Bottom Protected by Segregated Ballast Tanks.*
Source: U.S. Congress, Senate, Committee on Commerce, Science and Transportation, *1978 IMCO Protocols*, 95th Congress, 2d Sess., Serial No. 95-80 (April 5, 1978),
pp. 97–108.

Note: J is the fraction of the side and bottom area that is protected by segregated ballast tanks. The
value of J is determined as follows for tankers 200,000 dwt and above:

$$J = .3 = - a + \frac{0_c + 0_s}{4 \, 0_A}, \text{ or } J = .2, \text{ whichever is greater}$$

$$
\begin{aligned}
\text{where: } a &= .25 \text{ for oil tankers of } && 200,000 \text{ dwt and above} \\
a &= .40 \text{ for oil tankers of } && 300,000 \text{ dwt and above} \\
a &= .50 \text{ for oil tankers greater than } && 420,000 \text{ dwt}
\end{aligned}
$$

For intermediate values of dwt, "a" will be obtained by interpolation. $0_A$ allowable oil outflow, is
defined as shown in Fig. 11.7 and $0_s$ is the allowable oil outflow from a standing or bottom rupture,
while $0_c$ is the allowable oil outflow from a collision or side rupture.

Example calculation: For a 300,000 dwt tanker,

$$J = .3 - .4 \frac{0_c + 0_s}{4 \, 0_A}.$$

For a minimum allowable side shell protected area of 20 percent, $J = .2$. Therefore, with simpli-
fication,

$$.2 - .3 + .4 = \frac{0_c + 0_s}{4 \, 0_A} \text{ or } 1.2 \, 0_A = 0_c + 0_s.$$

This says that the sum of $0_c$ and $0_s$ need be no more than 1.2 times the maximum allowable cargo
outflow limit. For a 300,000 dwt tanker, the $0_A$ limit is 30,000 cubic meters (from Fig. 11.7).
Therefore, one feasible arrangement would be for $0_s$ to equal $0_c$ and for each to be .6 $0_A$, i.e., 60
percent of the allowed limit. In that case, the two parameters become 18,000 cubic meters each. Thus,
if 20 percent of the side shell is protected, it must be that the cargo tanks are small enough so that if the
hypothetical design grounding or ramming accident occurs, only 18,000 cubic meters of cargo is
"allowed" to spill out. (The volume of cargo space penetrated may be larger than 18,000 cubic meters,
since only a portion of the oil in protected tanks is assumed to leak out. A description of the values of the
leakage factors has not been provided in this chapter.)

Fig. 11.8. (Continued)

Should a naval architect wish to employ a larger value for J by designing more of the SBT side shell to be underlain and thus protected, by SBTs, the formula works such that larger design outflows are allowed ($0_c$ and $0_s$) and thus cargo tanks need not be as finely compartmentalized. For example, for J = .25 for 300,000 dwt in the trade-off region of fig. 11.8, the sum of the outflow limits equals $1.40_A$ or $0_c$ and $0_s$ may each be $.7\ 0_A$.

The protective location rules for tankers larger than 200,000 dwt therefore permit the naval architect to choose to design a tanker that has a low probability of suffering a cargo tank penetration in an accident because the cargo tanks are more fully protected by overlying SBTs, but that also has relatively low cargo tank compartmentalization, or to choose to design a tanker with fewer SBTs and thus a higher chance of rupturing a cargo tank if an accident should occur but with more cargo tank compartmentalization so that the resulting spillage will be less than would have been the case otherwise. Combinations of intermediate characteristics are also possible. Regardless of the trade-off made by the architect, however, the rules constrain tanker design and are expected to have the effect of reducing the frequency and magnitude of oil spillage in the event of a tanker collision or grounding accident.

analyses of items 4−6 were necessarily of a more subjective nature but were reached as a group conclusion." The continued use of judgment as opposed to statistical proof or engineering calculation in analyzing the consequences of groundings is notable. A tanker industry spokesman has observed that the 1978 IMCO regulations requiring protectively located SBT are troublesome for the industry but since only a limited portion of the shell is required to be protected, tanker owners still harboring concerns were able to accept the provision.[109] In short, SBT and PL are a compromise in which some of the benefits of fitting tankers with DBs, as estimated by Card and others, will be achieved and less will be spent by tanker owners than would have been the case had DBs been mandated.

It has been reported that the U.S. does not plan any further initiatives in the foreseeable future of the kind that led to the February, 1978, meeting, and that the effect of the Protocols will be monitored as they take effect.[110] The provisions of the two protocols are essentially implemented in the U.S. by the Port and Tanker Safety Acts of 1978.[111]

Resolutions 1 and 2 of the February 1978 IMCO Conference recommend that states that contemplate becoming parties to the Protocols adopt target dates of June 1981 for the MARPOL Protocol and June 1979 for the SOLAS Protocol for their entry into force, and to ensure that the provisions of the Protocols that contain a specific implementation date referring to "new" ships are applied. The U.S. Coast Guard has chosen to adhere scrupulously to the recommended schedule of implementation and application of requirements.[112] Whether foreign governments will also choose the route of early implementation, with or without the Protocol's entering into force, is unknown. One commentator has speculated that the U.S. will lead the way by a considerable margin and that other governments may not accept the U.S. plan with equanimity.[113]

Nevertheless, some tanker owners feel that the new conventions will probably become at least customary law, as evidenced by their rush to place orders for new tankers in May 1979 to beat the June 1, 1979 deadline for defining old and new tankers under the Protocols.[114]

## CONSEQUENCES FOR THE NORTH PACIFIC

The preponderance of petroleum tanker shipping in the North Pacific is the crude oil trade from the Middle East to Japan. Since the vessels that operate in the Japanese trade are too large to enter U.S. ports, early U.S. implementation of the 1978 Protocols will have virtually no effect on these vessels. An oil industry spokesman has opined that Japanese tanker owners will support the new laws since they tend to operate the most up-to-date and efficient vessels in the world fleet.[115] Incidents such as the *Sansinena* explosion should be less probable in U.S. waters in the future.

Japan, the Soviet Union, and Canada will probably elect to ratify the Protocols. M'Gonigle and Zacher report that the Canadians indicated in their oral and written arguments at the 1978 meeting that they favored the requirement for use of COW on existing and new tankers as compared to other alternatives. While the Soviet Union was silent on the matter, Soviet Bloc states—Poland, Romania, and the German Democratic Republic—favored COW over refitting tankers with SBTs. Japan made no public declaration, probably because its shipbuilding industry favored refitting existing tankers with SBT since this would provide work for its shipyards. Since refitting existing tankers with SBT is now unlikely to be considered again, it is probable that the Japanese government will no longer be reluctant to take a stand but rather will support and ratify the Protocols. Japanese controlled tankers are already refitting with COW.[116] The Japanese generally control the most significant tanker tonnage operating on the North Pacific. If the published data are correct, most of the oil outflow in the North Pacific from tanker operations impacts initially on waters near the Japanese islands.[117]

## CONCLUSIONS

It appears that the recently agreed-to Protocols represent progress in controlling oil pollution from tankers and should be ratified by the United States. Nevertheless, significant questions remain. Why was it that the U.S. Coast Guard and other representatives to the IMCO conferences did not fully appreciate the economic disincentives for adherence to the 1969 IMCO LOT regulations, and why has virtually nothing appeared in the Coast Guard's studies on the economic relationship between tanker owners and charterers? What are the incentives for tanker owners and charterers to employ LOT, SBT and PL, COW, and IGS? A fuller appreciation of how economic incentives are perceived by the various industry actors would be very desirable, since international enforcement of IMCO regulations pertaining to vessel operations is indifferent at best.

Since the earliest efforts to control oil pollution from ships it has been standard practice to treat outflows from accidents as equivalent to outflows from tankship operations. This was done implicitly by adding the two together, as in table 11.1. However, this was done because the state of scientific understanding of the damage caused by the two different categories of oil discharge to the sea was too imperfect to warrant separate treatment. This comment also applies to oil inputs from river runoff, atmospheric fallout, and natural seepage. Nevertheless, there is reason to think that the damages caused by each oil outflow source are different, due to the effects of oil toxicity of weathering and dispersion in the sea and the differences in ecological characteristics of the areas in which oil is spilled. As research on the effect of oil pollution in the oceans proceeds, it will become less reasonable to lump spill categories together, and it will become evident whether too much or too little importance has been attached to limiting outflows from the various sources. Finally, it would be good to bear in mind the fairly tenuous nature of the engineering and statistical studies that have been used to justify PL requirements for cargo tank location. Should tankers equipped with PL suffer casualties and oil be spilled, it may indicate the desirability of reexamining the protective location rules.

# PART III

# Marine Scientific Research in the North Pacific

# 12

# International Arrangements Affecting Marine Scientific Research

In order to consider the need for a new international organization concerned with the scientific investigation of the North Pacific (with the objectives, structure, and other characteristics of such an organization, and the problems that must be dealt with in bringing about its establishment) it is helpful to examine relevant existing international arrangements, both in the North Pacific and elsewhere. The purpose of this examination is to see if the activities proposed for the new organization are already being carried out adequately by existing organizations and, if not, to learn how such matters have been dealt with in other bodies. Inquiry is limited to governmental arrangements, hence we have omitted discussion of the Scientific Committee on Oceanic Research (SCOR) (a nongovernmental organization) and other private mechanisms.[1]

Relevant international arrangements fall into three categories and are discussed in the following sections of this chapter:

International Fishery Agreements
Other Regional and Global Marine Research Mechanisms
Bilateral Agreements on Research

Although this is not an exhaustive study of these arrangements, enough information is available to draw some conclusions about their contributions to the goals proposed for the new organization described in chapter 13;[2] these conclusions are set forth in the last section of this chapter.

As a preliminary matter the discussion is weighted heavily toward fishery organizations as coordinating mechanisms for research. This reflects the nature of organized cooperation in marine science in the North Pacific; most of the experience there is in fishery-related research. It is not intended to suggest that a new scientific organization for the North Pacific would be primarily concerned with fisheries research.

## INTERNATIONAL FISHERY AGREEMENTS

International agreements concerning *fisheries research* are of two major types: long-term arrangements that establish institutional mechanisms to carry out certain functions, including research;[3] and short-term agreements that may be most important as supplements to the longer-term institutional agreements.[4] The short-term agreements also relate to research. The organizational arrangements have already been described in chapter 3. In this chapter, we focus only on provisions affecting research. The discussion to follow looks first at agreements in the eastern Pacific, then those in the western, and finally, to agreements that pertain to the world ocean, or a major part thereof, including the North Pacific. In the third section, we discuss both fisheries and oceanographic multilateral arrangements focusing on other parts of the world. The agreements bearing on oceanography include the bilaterals between the U.S. and the USSR and between the U.S. and Japan. These are discussed in the context of other U.S. bilateral arrangements.

## Long-Term Agreements

The long-term agreements in the Northeast Pacific region concern the fur seals, halibut, Fraser River salmon, and other salmon of North American origin, as well as certain other specific species.[5] It is worth recalling that most of the commercial marine fisheries in the North Pacific (east or west) were not, until recently, subject to any authority except that exercised by flag states.[6] The recent extensions of national jurisdiction, and the acceptance of same, have changed this situation dramatically.

In commenting upon the long-term institutional arrangements, observations are organized in terms of their major characteristics: scope of participation, objectives and specific methods of achieving them, the resources devoted to pursuit of these objectives, the strategies by which these means are managed, and the outcomes achieved. Emphasis throughout is on the *research function* of the organization.

### *Participation*

For present purposes, the most important characteristic of participation in fisheries bodies in the North Pacific is its selective nature. With limited exceptions, no international commission involves, even remotely, all of the nations with an interest in the subject matter, or that participate in a relevant fishery.[7] This is not difficult to explain. Fisheries disputes and difficulties that are responsible for the creation of the treaty bodies are either specialized to a particular species or localized to a particular region. The effect of these factors is that the mechanisms to resolve controversies were designed to include only those nations directly involved.[8]

The possible exception is the Fur Seal Commission which involves four of the major North Pacific nations. But this Commission has an extremely narrow mandate, both in terms of species coverage and of the extent of the research undertaken to implement the agreement.

The situation in the western North Pacific is not different and the various fisheries bodies have limited memberships. As noted in chapter 3, Japan and Korea finally resolved their postwar fishery problem by the creation of a joint commission, as did Japan and the USSR. A somewhat broader but still not all inclusive arrangement is seen in the 1956 Convention for Fisheries Research in the Western Pacific. Here the cooperating nations included the USSR, China, Outer Mongolia, North Korea, and North Vietnam.[9]

In all instances in the North Pacific, actual membership in fisheries organizations is limited to nation-states, although, as noted below, other entities participate through other forms of relationship.

## Research Objectives

No previous international mechanism in the North Pacific was created, or sought, to deal with marine research in a comprehensive sense. None of the fishery bodies, with one somewhat obscure exception,[10] was established solely for the purpose of doing fisheries or other marine research, although their terms of reference demonstrate that this function was regarded as an indispensable step to the major objectives of the parties involved. The halibut and salmon treaties between the U.S. and Canada both emphasize the importance of scientific investigation as the essential precondition to recommending conservation measures. In the latter instance, a main purpose of the new commission was to conduct an investigation to determine the cause of the precipitous decline in salmon from the Fraser River,[11] while the halibut agreement specifies that in achieving the objective of securing the maximum sustained yield Commission recommendations of action must be shown to be necessary by investigation.[12] The manner for discharging the research function by means of independent research staffs, discussed below, serves to underline the special emphasis on research in these two bodies.

In the original INPFC also, the various provisions for research were highly significant for the operational goals specified and, although mostly carried out by national agencies, research triggered action by the Commission to allocate salmon and other stocks (via the abstention principle and line) and to recommend conservation measures.[13] The 1978 Protocol replacing the 1952 Convention continues to place emphasis on research and its coordination while maintaining the objective of allocating salmon, and adding significant consideration of marine mammal issues.[14]

The Fur Seal Agreement is no less significant in terms of the central role of research in Commission activities. After Article I defines terms, Article II immediately links research activities to the parties' objectives: "In order to realize the objectives of this Convention, the Parties agree to coordinate necessary scientific research programs and to cooperate in investigating the fur seal resources of the North Pacific Ocean. . . ." The Convention differs from the other agreements in the degree of its specification of the subjects of research; Article II lists a half dozen projects along with a catch-all category to allow the Commission to determine "other subjects involved in achieving the objectives of the Convention. . . ."[15]

In the western North Pacific, all known past long-term agreements also mention scientific research in connection with their objectives. In the Convention on the High Seas

Fisheries of the Northwest Pacific Ocean, Japan and the USSR aim at regulating fisheries in this area, and recognize in the preamble that "it is highly desirable to promote and co-ordinate the scientific studies of the Contracting Parties, the purpose of which is to maintain the maximum sustained productivity of fisheries of interest to the two Contracting Parties."[16] Amongst the Commission's functions, the regulation of fishing, including setting the amount of catch, is supposed to be "determined on the basis of scientific findings,"[17] but the Convention does not say whose findings. In addition, the Commission is to "prepare and adjust co-ordinated scientific programs and recommend them to the contracting parties."[18] It is not known how the parties have implemented these provisions.[19]

The Commission for Fisheries Research in the Western Pacific, established by a 1956 treaty among the PRC, USSR, Mongolia (joined in 1958), North Korea, and North Vietnam, differs from all others because it appears to be aimed solely at research.[20] The Commission is supposed to plan joint research and exploration, to exchange information, and to elaborate measures necessary for conservation based on research data. One study of the North Pacific stated: "Although little is known of the operations of this Commission, its activities appear very limited."[21] In 1966, the agreement was terminated by the People's Republic of China, the Korean People's Democratic Republic, and the Democratic Republic of Vietnam.

The Japan−Republic of Korea agreement concerning fisheries (June 22, 1965) mentions research but it is never made clear how it is to be done and whether or how the parties are to coordinate their activities.[22] Conservation measures are to be based, says Article III, "on the basis of exhaustive scientific research." Article IV declares the functions of the Japan−Korea Joint Fisheries Commission to include making "recommendations to the High Contracting Parties concerning scientific research for the purpose of studying the fishery resources in the sea areas of mutual interest and concerning control measures within the joint control zones to be carried out on the basis of the results of such research and study." It is not known how the parties have implemented these provisions.

## Resources

Commitments to research take the form of funding (direct and indirect), people, and technology. On all counts, the amounts allocated to most North Pacific fishery bodies for research (as distinguished from national research) are not great and, in relation to the value of the resources of the area, can be fairly described as minuscule.

The largest direct commitments of funding and people are made for the commissions with independent research staffs, as might be expected. The Halibut Commission is the most relevant for present purposes, and its budget, largely for research, over the past several years is shown in table 12.1.[23] The Commission employs a total staff of twenty-three persons, of whom thirteen are classified biologists.

The directly budgeted funds of the other fishery bodies are small, and, for the most part, are not for research. Amounts for the INPFC and Fur Seal Commission, for example, were

TABLE 12.1

INTERNATIONAL PACIFIC HALIBUT COMMISSION BUDGET
1970—1978

| Fiscal Year (April, March) | Amount (U.S. $) |
|---|---|
| 1970—1971 | $492,000 |
| 1971—1972 | 492,000 |
| 1972—1973 | 546,000 |
| 1973—1974 | 587,000 |
| 1974—1975 | 643,000 |
| 1975—1976 | 695,000 |
| 1976—1977 | 762,000 |
| 1977—1978 | 890,000 |

U.S. $180,000 and $22,000 respectively. For comparative purposes, a Food and Agriculture Organization (FAO) report of June 1978[24] gave the following annual budgets for other commissions as shown in table 12.2.

More important than direct funds, of course, are those expended by national agencies for associated research activities. We do not have much exact data on this, but have some informed estimates for the most important of the Northeast Pacific multilateral fishery bodies, the INPFC.

The INPFC Executive Director, Roy Jackson, observed in a report published in 1963:

> The work of the Commission has been on a large scale. As many as fifteen or sixteen research vessels have operated on the high seas in most years. Because the Commission's research program is executed by the research agencies of the various countries, it is difficult to make a precise assessment of its total cost. However, it may be estimated that approximately $2,000,000 per year has been spent on this investigation by the three countries combined. By far, the major portion of this amount has been required for the operation of research vessels on the high seas.[25]

TABLE 12.2

ANNUAL BUDGETS OF SELECTED FISHERIES COMMISSIONS

| Commission | Amount (U.S. $) |
|---|---|
| International Commission for the Southeast Atlantic Fisheries (ICSEAF) | $ 253,000 |
| International Council for the Exploration of the Sea (ICES) | 500,000 |
| International Whaling Commission (IWC) | 134,000 |
| Inter-American Tropical Tuna Commission (IATTC) (with an independent research staff) | 1,250,000 |
| International Commission for the Northwest Atlantic Fisheries (ICNAF) | 400,000 |
| International Commission for the Conservation of Atlantic Tunas (ICCAT) | 300,000 |

Some observers interviewed for this report believe this estimate to be excessively low when a larger time period is taken into account, and indicate that in some years U.S. funding alone reached $5,000,000.[26]

Although resources devoted to research under any of the specific entities mentioned above might be adequate for the immediate purpose, allocations determined only, or primarily, on a separate and independent basis do not necessarily serve comprehensive objectives and needs. Furthermore, the selection of research program priorities in such circumstances seems certain to be suboptimal because no genuine overall perspective can be achieved within which the identification of overall priorities can proceed. For this reason, the aggregation of total research dollars spent by the various separate agencies may be less significant than it seems. The aggregate, in actual fact, is less than the sum of its parts.

## Strategies

The three principal mechanisms employed by generating research and scientific advice for an established international fishery body are the use of an independent research staff as part of the functions of the body, the creation of a committee of scientists drawn wholly (or almost so) from the scientific ranks of member nations, and the designation of a completely independent group of scientists as the entity from which scientific advice is to be expected. The former two mechanisms predominate in the North Pacific, although, as noted in later discussion, the IWC, with global responsibilities that include North Pacific fishing operations, employed a variation of the independent entity approach.

The use of a research staff as part of an international fishery commission first occurred in the North Pacific with the establishment of the International Pacific Halibut Commission, which was followed some years later by the International Pacific Salmon Fisheries Commission. Both entities continue to manage these fisheries (although the Halibut Commission now operates under a new 1979 agreement), and the research operations are widely considered to be highly successful in providing the scientific basis of management.

The commission approach is exemplified in the North Pacific by the International North Pacific Fishery Commission and the International North Pacific Fur Seal Commission. In these arrangements, the parties conduct research on a national basis and use the annual commission meeting to plan, coordinate, interpret and report on their work.

Within the specific management contexts involved, including the shared experiences of two neighboring and culturally similar nations, the research staff approach has had undeniable advantages for the parties, as evidenced in part by their willingness to continue support for so many years. Such an arrangement facilitates the development and implementation of a sustained research program directed at meeting needs identified as important for realizing management goals. The independent staff also avoids the sometimes substantial transaction costs involved in arranging for the continual series of meetings of groups of scientists that are necessary to meet management needs.

But even in this favorable situation, the staff approach may have problems. It has been suggested that there is a tendency for research staffs to become ingrown and lose communication with other scientists.[27] Staff attitudes about the correctness of their methodology and analyses may occasionally discourage further research and lead to discounting responsible external criticism.[28]

Other aspects of strategy in employment of resources have to do with communications among those involved, relations with other entities, and techniques for coordination. Following are some observations on these matters.

The fact that current or recently existing North Pacific fishery bodies have, or had, management and allocation responsibilities affects the process of communication among scientists who are involved as participants appointed by national administrations. As is common in any intergovernmental body, the official utterances of policy and position are made solely by government representatives. Such policies and positions are sometimes highly political and reflect many factors in a nation's total political position, in contrast to factors reflecting only scientific understanding. The adoption and promulgation of national positions can therefore be regarded as a constraint upon scientific communications and conceivably can (at times) limit and perhaps distort that communication.

Relationships with other entities are particularly important for bodies having a significant research function. The North Pacific Commissions, old and new, have varying connections with each other, and with other entities. The INPFC over its quarter-century history has interacted with various external groups, including other nations (such as the USSR with its extensive fishery in the Bering Sea and eastern North Pacific) and several other international organizations. Perhaps its closest connection has been with the Halibut Commission representatives, some of which have been listed as consultants to the Commission for many years. By means of the advisory groups affiliated with the member nations, the INPFC maintained connections with the various private groups and entities with special interests in marine resources in the North Pacific. A similar long-standing arrangement is employed by the Halibut and Salmon Commissions.

The new INPFC specifically contemplates the establishment of a new international entity for scientific research in the North Pacific, and the transfer of research responsibility for nonanadromous species to the new organization.[29] In the light of the interrelationship between nonanadromous and anadromous species, the INPFC will have to maintain communications with the new entity.

Mechanisms for coordinating research are a special concern. In this connection, we focus on the INPFC.

According to the original INPFC Agreement, scientific investigations are a fundamental component of the decision making to be carried out by the Commission. The major tasks of the Commission are[30] (1) to study certain stocks of fish to determine whether they meet certain conditions that require one or two of the parties to abstain from exploitation; (2) to study certain stocks to determine whether there is need for joint conservation measures; (3) to "investigate the waters of the Convention area to determine if there are areas in which salmon originating in the rivers of Canada and of the United States of America intermingle with salmon originating in the rivers of Asia"; (4) to conduct further studies for the purpose of recommending new areas for abstention from salmon fishing; and (5) to compile and study records obtained from parties. The main question is how the parties sought to execute these tasks through cooperative action.

The major instrument of cooperation has been the annual meeting of the Commission, when policymakers and scientists come together to carry out the Commission's functions. In a sense, this session provides the skeleton or basic framework for coordination and cooperation; the sinew, muscles, and nerves are composed of the numerous ancillary devices by which research is planned, discussed, coordinated, debated, interpreted, and communicated. The following account, based on experience under the original agreement, calls attention to the overall mechanism and as many of its detailed workings as can be gleaned from an outsider's perspective.

The Commission is composed of national sections representing each member and makes its decisions by unanimous vote (i.e., each member has a veto). The principal decision function is to make recommendations to the contracting parties on the matters delegated by the basic treaty, which were mainly summarized above in the outline of the Commission's tasks. The focus of the Commission's work and the direction of research has changed over the life of the Commission in accordance with both its explicit unambiguous terms and the parties' interpretation of more subjective provisions.

Initially, the major effort was on investigating the offshore distribution of salmon, and areas of intermingling of salmon of Asian and North American origin. The treaty calls for the establishment of a line, the abstention line, east of which the Japanese agreed to abstain from fishing for salmon. The provisional abstention line was established by the Convention at 175° W longitude. A little later the principal effort focused on studies pertinent to determining whether particular stocks continued to qualify for abstention under the conditions established in the treaty. In the final several years of its existence under the 1952 agreement, the research effort expanded a great deal to include groundfish in the Bering Sea and the Gulf of Alaska, and continued to examine the conditions of the king and tanner crab fishery in the Bering Sea. As this shift occurred, there was a corresponding shift from preoccupation with the abstention principle and line to the problem of joint conservation measures and limits on fishing effort for the very large groundfishery in the eastern North Pacific and Bering Sea.

As a result of its concern for offshore salmon distribution of both Asian and American salmon, the Commission was interested not only in research into distinguishing these separate groups but also research into oceanographic conditions in the North Pacific that might bear upon the extent and variability of intermingling.

Within the Commission, the main coordinating mechanism for these various research operations by national sections was centered in the Committee on Biology and Research (CBR), which was divided into subcommittees dealing with various aspects of the salmon question, king and tanner crab, groundfish, oceanographic research, and research plans. From its beginning the CBR paid considerable attention to the needs and means for coordination of research among the three member nations.[31] The parties were expected to present their plans for research in the forthcoming year as well as to report on progress made in the previous year. Specific details of anticipated operations were disclosed and specific attempts were made to mesh the independent programs.[32] It was explicitly recognized that coordination of research was necessary in light of available resources for achieving the purposes of the Convention. These activities took place mainly during the annual meetings and occasionally at special meetings convened for coordination of research projects.

Although the Commission had no independent staff, its executive director and assistant director (both scientists) were active at various times at and between meetings in efforts to facilitate coordination of research.

The question of publishing scientific reports by the Commission itself was given special consideration and a procedure was established for use within national sections by which scientific papers were validated for their pertinence to the Commission's work and their scientific content.[33] Publication by the Commission required approval of the editorial referees for each national section; this permitted one national section to veto Commission publication of a paper.

## Outcomes

The important outcomes of the research activities involving North Pacific fishery bodies consist of management recommendations and research results. Publications pertaining to management and research can be found in the official papers of the various bodies, especially the Halibut, Salmon, and North Pacific Commissions, and in independent publications as well.[34]

The major difficulty in using research results and data produced in the North Pacific area arises because of the differences in the statistical areas employed by the various research bodies and governmental units (including the component states of the United States) in the region. The problem is illustrated in figure 12.1, where the conflicting IPHC and INPFC groundfish areas are shown; further details are given in Erhardt and Bledsoe.[35]

## Conditions

The most important current conditions relevant to international agreements in the North Pacific include the extensions of national jurisdiction which totally alter the distribution of legal authority over some marine activities, certain changes in the process of use of this area, and the general political situation among Pacific rim nations.

An overriding condition affecting research mechanisms in the North Pacific is the extension of national jurisdiction to 200 miles.[36] The effect of this extension has been to require the renegotiation of several international agreements[37] and the conclusion of numerous new such agreements, mainly bilateral.[38] Previous arrangements regarding fisheries are no longer authoritative and some accompanying arrangements for cooperation in gathering and disseminating knowledge are likewise no longer effective. The result is that new arrangements for science are required for fisheries.

Another overriding condition is the increase in uses of the North Pacific and some intensification of prior use. In the Northeast Pacific, fisheries activity is still high but may have fallen off somewhat with the advent of the 200-mile limit.[39] The level of future activity

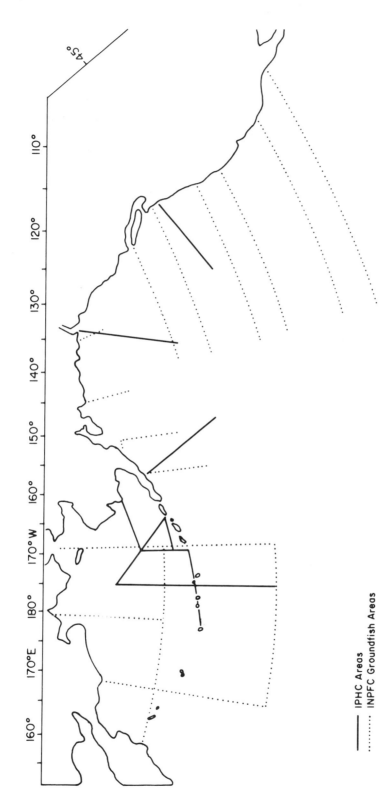

Fig. 12.1. *Conflicts Between International Pacific Halibut Commission (IPHC) and International North Pacific Fisheries Commission (INPFC) for Groundfish in the Northeast Pacific.* Source: N. M. Erhardt and L. J. Bledsoe, "A Comparative Study of the Statistical Areas in the North Pacific Fisheries," NORFISH Technical Report no. 60 (Seattle: Center for Quantitative Sciences in Forestry, Fisheries and Wildlife, University of Washington, May 1975). Solid lines indicate IPHC areas; dotted lines INPFC areas. Other statistical areas in this region are the INPFC salmon areas, the Pacific Marine Fisheries Commission (a U.S. body) groundfish areas, FAO statistical areas, and U.S.–USSR bilateral statistical areas. Each of the sets of areas differs from the others, and all differ from those set out in this figure.

is unclear at this time. Shipping in the North Pacific has increased exponentially, and this trend continues.[40] Movement of oil is substantially greater because of the recent completion of the Alaska pipeline and the shipping of oil to the West Coast and to the Panama Canal for transshipment eastward.[41] Associated with increased oil movement is an increased concern about pollution in an area which, until now, has been little affected by oil spills.

With respect to marine scientific research in the North Pacific, cooperative activity spans about a quarter-century, and pertinent political conditions have varied a great deal over such a time period. From the early 1950s to the 1970s, political relationships among North Pacific rim nations obviously have been subject to considerable change. The range has been from deep hostility and violent conflict to the deliberate pursuit of cooperative programs aimed at improving communications and promoting friendly relations. Prospects for a more receptive political climate, permitting, if not fostering, cooperative scientific activities, are difficult to estimate and to predict. Presently, some countries do not maintain diplomatic relations, and this is likely to affect future participation in new or improved international agencies until the political situation becomes more amicable.

On the eastern side of the Pacific, the traditions of friendship and cooperation between Canada and the United States, based on similar cultures, political perspectives, and economic systems, clearly have influenced development of regional fishery management institutions and associated research. The recent radical transformation in the extent of national fishery jurisdiction has not disrupted political ties between the two countries, but it has placed such strains on fishery relationships that continuation of previous cooperative mechanisms has been imperiled in more than one instance.

Domestic political considerations in both Canada and the United States influence the development of cooperation on marine-related issues between each other and with other nations. Particularly in the United States, the decentralization of authority over fishery management, coupled with the continuing influence of state officials on federal decisions, can be expected to play some role in U.S. participation in future international cooperation in marine science research. The significance of domestic conditions in other Pacific rim nations is not discussed here.


## OTHER REGIONAL AND GLOBAL
## MARINE RESEARCH MECHANISMS

Other mechanisms for coordinating research are considered because they may provide useful guidance about elements of a Pacific International Council for the Exploration of the Sea (PICES) or because they are now being considered for establishment elsewhere and could illustrate possible restraints on creation of new mechanisms. For this purpose, the following discussion concerns, in order, ICES, IWC, the Northwest Atlantic Fisheries Organization (NAFO), the proposed Antarctic agency, and the Intergovernmental Oceanographic Commission Working Group for the Western Pacific and adjacent waters (IOC/WESTPAC).

## International Council for the Exploration of the Sea (ICES)

The International Council for the Exploration of the Sea (ICES)[42] provides a model for the design and function of the proposed organization in the North Pacific. While the experience of international scientific cooperation in ICES during more than 75 years can be drawn upon, it is important to recognize that there are significant political and geographic differences between the North Atlantic and North Pacific, and that ICES itself is in the process of transformation in response to the same maritime jurisdictional changes that occasion consideration of the establishment of a North Pacific organization.[43]

The major characteristics of ICES are discussed in the following sections.

### Participation

Present membership of ICES includes the following countries: Belgium, Canada, Denmark, Finland, France, German Democratic Republic (G.D.R.), Federal Republic of Germany (F.R.G.), Iceland, Ireland, Netherlands, Norway, Poland, Portugal, Spain, Sweden, United Kingdom (U.K.), U.S., and USSR. (Italy withdrew in 1974, the U.S. joined in 1973, and the G.D.R. in 1975). Fourteen of these countries are coastal states in the North Atlantic; seven are members of the EEC.

Despite its title, ICES is a regional organization with principal interest in the Northeast Atlantic, and the North and the Baltic seas. Two members (Canada and the U.S.) do not fish in the region, and other members who do (USSR, Poland, France, G.D.R.) also operate important distant-water fisheries outside the region.

Some measure of the interest of various countries in the work of the Council is reflected in the magnitude of their contribution to the Council's income (the size of the country also affects this ranking indirectly). Of 52 half-shares, countries contribute the following fractions:

4 shares:  France, Federal Republic of Germany, United
       Kingdom, USSR.

3 shares:  Canada, Denmark, German Democratic Republic,
       Netherlands, Norway, Poland, Spain, Sweden, U.S.

2 and less shares: Belgium, Finland (1½), Iceland,
       Ireland, Portugal.

Although election of officers of the Council (President, First Vice-President, five Vice-Presidents), Chairmen of the Consultative Committee, Standing Committee, and Advisory Committee (and hence membership on the Consultative Committee) is open to all countries, a few countries tend to dominate the positions. This is illustrated in their allocation as of the 1977 Statutory Meeting, shown in table 12.3.

Table 12.3 shows the strong positions of the U.K. and F.R.G. and the minor role played at that time by Belgium, Finland, G.D.R., Netherlands, Poland, Spain, and U.S. (although the USSR had one vice-presidency, its role continued to be small). In view of its position as host country and its fisheries in both the North Sea and the Baltic, Denmark could be

TABLE 12.3

NATIONAL DISTRIBUTION OF ICES OFFICERS, 1977

| Country | Bureau | Standing committee | Consultative advisory committees |
|---|---|---|---|
| Belgium | | | |
| Canada | 1 | 2 | |
| Denmark | 1 | 2 | |
| Finland | | | |
| France | | 2 | |
| G.D.R. | | | |
| F.R.G. | 1 | 2 | 1 |
| Iceland | | 1 | |
| Ireland | | 1 | |
| Netherlands | | | |
| Norway | | | 1 |
| Poland | | | |
| Portugal | 1 | | |
| Spain | | | |
| Sweden | 1 | | |
| U.K. | 1 | 2 | 1 |
| U.S. | | | |
| USSR | 1 | | |

expected to be well-represented in the official positions of the Council; the strong position of Canada is more surprising.

In general, it can be said that elections to these various posts depends on both the quality of the candidates and the desire of their countries to have them elected; the question of equitable geographical representation appears to be of less importance (on occasion, special efforts are made to ensure representation of the "Eastern" and "Latin" countries, while other "blocs" seem better able to take care of themselves).

In summary, participation is complete for the region of principal concern to ICES, including two countries (Canada and U.S.) whose fishing interests lie mainly outside of that region. The recent joining of G.D.R. completes coverage of the Baltic Sea. With the withdrawal of Italy, the interests of ICES no longer relate to the Mediterranean (in ICES, Spain and France are concerned with Atlantic questions). Although ICES cooperated with the Intergovernmental Oceanographic Commission in coordinating the CINECA (Cooperative Investigation of the Northeast Central Atlantic) off the northern coast of West Africa, there is no indication that ICES interests will extend south on any permanent basis.

## Objectives

The duties of the Council (Article I of the Convention) are as follows: (1) to promote and encourage research and investigations for the study of the sea, particularly those related to the living resources thereof; (2) to draw up programmes required for this purpose and to organize, in agreement with the contracting parties, such research and investigation as may appear necessary; and (3) to publish or otherwise disseminate the results of research and investigations carried out under its auspices or to encourage the publication thereof.

As can be seen, ICES objectives do not explicitly involve the provision of advice to other bodies. In practice, however, advisory work has become a major element in the Council's activities in the fields of fishery management and politics. As noted below, the advisory activities are carried out in special committees established for this purpose.

### Resources

For fiscal year (FY) 1978–1979, the Council's income is estimated at 4,012,000 DKr (approximately $800,000), of which 3,515,925 DKr (nearly 90 percent) is contributed by Member Countries according to a system of shares. Other sources of income include contributions of fishery and pollution commissions totalling 272,000 DKr, and interest, sale of publications, and miscellaneous sources amounting to 236,000 DKr. Major expenses include salaries and pensions (2,604,000 DKr), office expenses (386,000 DKr), travel and meetings (340,000 DKr) and publications (600,000 DKr).

Although the ICES staff consists of 21 persons, there are relatively few professional scientists (General Secretary, Hydrographer, Statistician, Environmental Officer, System Analyst) whose functions are to support and assist the work of the Standing and Advisory Committees rather than to conduct scientific work themselves. Headquarters facilities are supplied rent-free by the host government, and participation in most meetings (except for the Bureau and mid-term meetings of the Advisory Committees) is paid by Member Governments. Furthermore, the expenses of cooperative scientific projects are met by participating governments, so that the Council's budget represents only a small fraction of the total cost of activities sponsored by the Council.[44]

### Strategies

Scientific activities of the Council arise in its standing committees.[45] A review of contributed scientific papers reveals a need for a concerted joint effort on a certain problem. The Committee decides to develop a project which is then designed by an ad hoc working group. Members (countries) determine the extent of their interest and the nature and magnitude of their contribution by ships and personnel. A working group of the Standing Committee coordinates the development and implementation of the project and the analysis of its results. The final step may be a symposium and the publication of a symposium volume and/or an atlas of the results. At any given time, there may be two or more projects in various stages of development, all reflected in the papers submitted to the Standing Committee. As a formality, committee recommendations are reviewed by the Consultative Committee and approved by the Delegates. It is rare that programs agreed to by interested scientists are significantly modified by this process.

Advisory activities proceed in a different way. Under its present rules of procedure, the Council has two advisory committees, the Advisory Committee on Fishery Management (ACFM) and the Advisory Committee on Marine Pollution (ACMP). In both cases, the chairman is elected by the Consultative Committee, the choice thus being scientific rather than political.[46]

The ACFM includes the chairman of three standing committees (Demersal Fish, Pelagic Fish, and Baltic Fish) together with a number of scientists nominated by national delegations (one each) and appointed by the Council. ACFM, on behalf of the Council, formulates advice on management given to member governments and to the North East Atlantic Fisheries Commission (NEAFC), and the International Baltic Sea Fisheries Commission (IBSFC). Both of these Commissions formally recognize ICES as a statutory advisory body and contribute to its income in recognition of services rendered.

The ACMP also includes the chairman of three statutory committees (Marine Environmental Quality, Hydrography, and Biological Oceanography), plus a number of co-opted members (ten in 1977–1978) selected to provide disciplinary and geographical representatives. ACMP, on behalf of the Council, formulates advice on marine pollution and its effects on living resources, and their exploitation to Member Governments and to the Oslo,[47] Helsinki,[48] and Paris Commissions.[49] During the fiscal year 1978–1979, the Oslo and Interim Paris Commissions contributed to the Council's income.

Matters needing advice are usually identified by the body being advised, although requests for advice may reflect the influence of the Advisory Committee. In the case of ACFM, mutual agreement has developed on the fisheries requiring management, and the ACFM has established some 25 working groups concerned with monitoring and assessing various fish stocks.[50] Recommendations of these working groups are reviewed and sometimes modified by the ACFM, which then passes its assessments and recommendations for TACs to the NEAFC and IBSFB. The requirements for advice on marine pollution are less standard, and the ACMP is not supported by such a network of working groups. Otherwise, the advisory process works in much the same way.

While advice is passed directly to fishery and pollution commissions by the advisory committees, all other actions pass through the Consultative Committee to the Delegates for approval, or are initiated by the Delegates. Delegate initiatives are confined, as a matter of practice, to policy or organizational matters (e.g., consideration of the impact of UNCLOS III on ICES activities, or the restructuring of its subsidiary bodies). Scientific initiatives are developed through the Standing Committees rather than at the Delegate level.

Timely and comprehensive data exchange is central to both stock assessment and to the conduct of joint scientific activities. In the case of physicochemical oceanography and fisheries, the exchange is coordinated and supported by the Staff Hydrographer and the Statistician of the Commission, respectively. Inventories of oceanographic data are published regularly by the Hydrographer, as are various data summaries and other products; data are made available to those requiring it. Fisheries statistics that are provided to stock-assessment working groups and to the ACFM, have been regularly published in the *Bulletin Statistique* and *Statistical Newsletters*, and are now becoming available in computer-compatible form. The Council not only serves as a mechanism for exchange but through its various committees promotes the exchange of new types of data; it also sets data standards and formats. The utility of pooled and exchanged data depends on its quality, and the Council has provided an extensive series of intercalibration exercises at the request of its scientists. The Council has also promoted a series of internationally coordinated hydroacoustic and egg and larvae surveys to augment the fisheries statistics and biological data used by its stock-assessment working groups.

*Outcomes*

An important outcome of the Council's work is its series of publications, which include, (in addition to those already referred to) the following:

*Procès-Verbal* (reports of annual meetings)
*Rapports et Procès-Verbaux* (collections of symposia papers)
*Journal du Conseil* (scientific papers)
*Cooperative Research Reports*
*Annales Biologiques* (annual assessments of research activities)

There are also a large number of less formal documents, including the reports of various stock-assessment working groups, and myriad manuscript papers presented at the annual meetings.[51]

Another major outcome consists of the reports of the advisory committees presented to the fishery and pollution commissions. The impact of this advice is recorded in the reports of those bodies and reflected in their requests for further advice.

*Conditions*

There are a number of reasons for the success of ICES as a regional marine scientific organization. Most of its members have advanced scientific and technical capabilities. There is a long tradition of scientific cooperation and information exchange between the countries of the region. The relatively large number of countries involved lends stability to the organization. Most members are bound together by a common interest in the rational management of shared living resources and by the need to protect a shared marine environment. Members find that scientific objectives can be more readily achieved by pooling their resources than by trying to go it alone.

There are also some problems. The United States, in particular, and Canada to a lesser extent, are more concerned with the western North Atlantic and have yet to find their proper role in Council activities. In many countries, only the fishery institutions are involved, leaving important oceanographic activities outside the purview of the Council. This problem is particularly apparent in the Soviet Union, where major programs of the Academy of Sciences and the Hydrometeorological Service do not enter into ICES activities. The changing situations for fishery jurisdiction with extensions of national jurisdictions and the pooling of EEC member fishery interests have confused the Council's traditional role of fishery advice.[52] The Council is responding slowly to the new challenges and opportunities it faces, and has yet to modernize fully its methods for dealing with a new emphasis on more fundamental scientific problems.

## International Whaling Commission (IWC)

Over the past decade numerous observers have written about the IWC,[53] and it is not proposed here to make a substantial addition to this literature. But it is evident that the IWC as a scientific coordinating mechanism on a global level is relevant to the consideration of PICES, particularly because in recent years the largest catches of whales have been made in the North Pacific,[54] and because there are continuing problems with large and small cetaceans in this region.[55] The controversy surrounding the deliberations of the IWC and the role of scientific advice in whale management direct that this experience be taken into account. Only some highlights are mentioned here.

## Participation

Membership in the IWC has fluctuated over nearly thirty years of its existence (partially because withdrawal was a device for escaping unwanted regulations recommended by the Commission), but has never included all nations whose flag vessels take significant numbers of whales. The major Antarctic whaling nations have long been members of the IWC, but other nations such as Peru and Chile remained outside and were unbound by any restrictions on whaling originated by the IWC.[56] Other nonmember nations also have allowed whaling ships to sail under their flags and thus escape application either of the whaling treaty or of the law of any nation.[57]

## Objectives

Observers have noted that the objectives of the IWC are internally contradictory because they include both the goal of conservation and the goal of promoting the development of the whaling industry.[58] (Some also stress that this duality is not unique to this Convention but is common.) Perhaps a better way to put it is that the Convention sought to balance diverse interests. For many years, emphasis in the IWC was placed squarely on the short-run economic health of the industry, with the status of stocks receiving little, if any, consideration. During this period, the IWC Scientific Committee was unable to reach complete agreement among its members, although there was near unanimity, on the need for conservation actions. It later became evident that even if the Scientific Committee had registered complete unanimity on scientific judgments, the results would not have been different because the Commission gave priority to other factors.

In recent years, beginning in 1965, far more weight attached to conservation, and it is now accurate to say that this goal dominates Commission deliberations. The views of the Scientific Committee are now given decisive weight.[59] This appears somewhat anomalous at a time when fisheries management otherwise is tending toward management for multiple objectives. Some commentators suggest a need to remedy the excessive deference now accorded scientific considerations.[60] The long dominance of short-run economic factors is now wholly ended and is replaced by a primary concern for the long-run status of the stocks, but observers (and participants) remain who believe management is required by the Convention to consider economic, or industrial, constraints as well.

## Resources

To say that the financial support by nations for the work of the IWC has been penurious is gross understatement. But this, too, has changed, at least relatively, and both support for the IWC and national efforts concerned with whale conservation are now much greater than previously. In 1974, the Commission adopted a new approach[61] in support of national activities and employed a scientist as executive secretary who could work directly with scientists serving member governments. The IWC budget is still not large at $134,000, but this is several times that in earlier years.

A special additional source of support for the IWC comes from Norway, which largely finances the Bureau of International Whaling Statistics; the Bureau services the IWC with detailed information about annual whaling operations. Dr. J. L. McHugh summarizes the Bureau's contributions and emphasizes their importance:

> This unique and valuable service to the whaling industry and governments is still funded entirely by Norway, except for a small contribution by the Commission in each of the last few years to cover the extra cost of providing data for stock assessments. The Bureau provided the basic data, going back to 1920, on which the Scientific Committee of the Commission, the Committees of Three and Four, and the FAO Stock Assessment Group drew for stock assessment and other studies. Estimates of the condition of the whale stocks, sustainable yields, and quotas needed to restore or maintain maximum sustainable yields would have been impossible without the help given by the Bureau.[62]

It is extremely difficult to determine what levels of national effort are devoted to whale research and management other than to say that in recent years they are very likely several orders of magnitude larger than in earlier days. In addition to national efforts by governments, private organizations and groups have been active in providing resources by which such research can be furthered. On the international level, UN family units have devoted significant effort to improving understanding of the whale problem. The FAO Whale Consultation involved several years of study and activity by many persons and culminated in substantial written documentation concerning the future of whales and whale research.[63] Major funding for this activity came from the UN Environment Program.

## Strategies

In the past the IWC has not been permitted by its member governments to undertake whaling research independently, although it is authorized to do so. Article IV of the Convention provides that the Commission may "encourage, recommend or, if necessary, organize" studies and investigations "either in collaboration with or through independent agencies of the Contracting Governments or other public or private agencies, establishments, or organizations, or independently. . . ." Instead, the Commission has gotten its scientific advice primarily from scientists acting through the committee structure under the Commission. In one well-known and pivotal instance, the Commission set up a special group, the Committee of Three, to examine evidence and data and to report on the level of sustainable yield that could be supported by Antarctic whale stocks.[64] It is revealing of the orientation of the IWC during the earlier and middle years of its existence that the advice and recommendations from the Committee of Three were initially disregarded despite explicit statements by the IWC that it intended to take action by a fixed time.[65]

The record shows that the Commission for years routinely ignored the recommendation of its own Scientific Committee as well as later independent inputs from external sources. This situation began to change in 1965, and in subsequent years the recommendations of the Scientific Committee were given greater (and eventually decisive) weight, as noted further below.

The North Pacific region became the focus of particular attention in the IWC. Beginning in the early 1960s, a North Pacific Working Group met annually to make assessments and recommendations concerning the stocks in the region. The Working Group consisted of Canada, the U.S., Japan, and the USSR. In addition, the commissioners representing these four nations met separately from the Commission at intervals between IWC meetings.[66]

There have been marked differences of view within the Scientific Committee of the IWC. Thus, the Scientific Committee has at times refrained from making recommendations that had very strong and wide support within the Committee when one or two members expressed the view that the evidence for such action was not conclusive. It is not possible here to document that this insistence upon a very high standard of proof is linked to the national policies of the members involved, but it is generally assumed that IWC delegates do reflect national policies.

Scarff has called attention to the problem of biological uncertainty concerning whales and its effects upon the decisions of the IWC and its Scientific Committee.[67] One means chosen to persuade others of the substance and credibility of a recommendation was to secure unanimous support by the Committee. But this, in turn, affected the actions of the Committee in choosing among various pieces of evidence on which to base judgment.

> The following process of resolving ambiguity was used until the 1975 meeting of the IWC. The Scientific Committee would review the catch statistics, CPUE data, sighting accords, and the population estimates derived from this data. Often there would be two or more estimates of population size and sustainable yield for the same stock presented by the same or different scientists. The Committee would debate the merits of the various population estimates and come up with its own "best estimate." The criteria used to determine this "best estimate" were rarely articulated in print or verbally and often the figure chosen represented a political compromise designed to achieve unanimity or to avoid the withdrawal of one or more members of the Commission.[68]

When these estimates were discussed by the Commission, Scarff reports, they would either be compromised again due to political reasons or action would be delayed pending availability of further research.

Recognition of this situation produced some reforms in the operation of the Scientific Committee, including the use of majority and minority estimates in Committee reports; improvements in communication between scientists inside and outside the Committee with external groups; increase in staff size; and "more precise articulation of management guidelines in the New Management Procedure and the resulting minimization of input by the full Commission."[69]

Scarff also notes that adoption of the New Management Procedure in the IWC reverses the previous position of the Scientific Committee. From a position of little influence on Commission decisions, its recommendations are now decisive.

> The determination by the Scientific Committee on weak and ambiguous data that a stock is more or less than 10 percent below its theoretical MSY level determines whether any exploitation of that stock will be allowed. Even if only a few hundred whales are involved, this decision may involve many millions of dollars in gross revenue.
>
> Total management responsibility should not be given to the scientists, but the division of responsibility for management between the scientists and the Commission needs to be clearly articulated. In the past, when the Commission ignored the Scientific Committee recommendations, it did so on the pretense that the scientific conclusions were not clear enough. In reality, the Commissioners apparently believed that the scientists had not adequately considered industrial or political problems. Having no particular expertise in economic or political areas, the scientists were not in a position to consider these aspects of the problem. In contrast, under the present scheme, the whaling nations have been backed into the position of declaring that economic and political criteria are irrelevant to the management decisions.[70]

### Outcomes

As is common with virtually all international fishery bodies, the IWC decisions take the form of recommendations to members, which they can accept or reject or otherwise avoid by withdrawal from the Commission. For many years, the effect of the Commission on the external world was virtually nil because the Commission recommendations fit well with continued nearly unlimited harvesting. As noted above, this situation is now changed insofar as members are concerned, but the IWC still has little or no impact on whaling by nonmembers.

In early years, the IWC role in coordinating research concerning whales was minimal, but beginning with the Committee of Three in 1960 its efforts in this direction took on greater importance. Most recently, major efforts at making authoritative assessments of the state of research have been made under the auspices of FAO with the financial support of the UN Environment Program. These activities have been undertaken in coordination with the IWC.

### Conditions

It is not clear what the future is for the IWC. Drafts of a new convention have been proposed by members and studies of a new mechanism are being pursued outside the Commission as well. Possible new arrangements for dealing with the scientific advisory function are part of this examination, including the possible imposition of a duty on the IWC to undertake independent scientific investigation.

### The Northwest Atlantic Fisheries Organization (NAFO)

The International Commission for Northwest Atlantic Fisheries (ICNAF) was created in 1950 to consider conservation measures in the Northwest Atlantic off the U.S., Canada, and Greenland. With the advent of 200-mile fishing limits extending to most of the fisheries in this region, it was necessary to reconsider the structure and function of ICNAF. Interested states met in Canada in 1977 to seek agreement on a new international arrangement. This resulted in the recently drafted Convention on Northwest Atlantic Fisheries creating the Northwest Atlantic Fisheries Organization (NAFO),[71] which makes new and interesting provisions concerning scientific research and the fisheries in the area to which the Convention will be applicable.

The NAFO Convention Area is specifically delimited by latitude and longitude and extends beyond the fisheries jurisdiction areas of adjacent coastal states. The area outside coastal jurisdiction is called the "Regulatory Area." The purpose of the new organization is "to contribute through consultation and cooperation to the optimum utilization, rational management, and conservation of the fishery resources of the Convention Area." To this end, the organization consists of a General Council, a Scientific Council, a Fisheries Commission, and a Secretariat. Each contracting party is a member of the former two Councils, while membership in the Fisheries Commission depends upon participation (or expected participation according to "evidence satisfactory to the General Council") in the fisheries of the Regulatory Area. The function of the Commission is to be responsible for the management and conservation of the fishery resources of the Regulatory Area and particularly to secure consistency between measures adopted by coastal states and those adopted for the Regulatory Area.

The functions of the Scientific Council (SC) include two very different elements. The first is the more or less conventional one of serving as a "forum for consultation and cooperation among the Contracting Parties with respect to the study, appraisal, and exchange of scientific information and views relating to the fisheries of the Convention Area," and also encouraging and promoting "cooperation among the Contracting Parties in scientific research designed to fill gaps in knowledge pertaining to these matters."

The other function is to act as a scientific advisory body to (1) coastal states and (2) the NAFO Fisheries Commission (i.e., to states participating in fisheries within the Convention Area beyond coastal jurisdiction). In both capacities, the SC may be asked to "consider and report on any question pertaining to the scientific basis for the management and conservation of fishery resources" within the relevant area. Although the subject matter is the same in both instances, the procedures for such consideration vary—perhaps significantly.

With respect to coastal states, the SC is obliged to respond to its request and cannot volunteer advice, but for the Fisheries Commission it may provide advice on its own initiative while also being required to respond to requests for same.

The procedures for addressing questions also differ. When a coastal state seeks advice on a question, it "shall, in consultation with the Scientific Council, specify terms of reference for" such question. These terms of reference shall include anything deemed appropriate, but the Convention specifically lists some that may be applicable:

    (a)   a statement of the question referred, including a description of the fisheries and area to be considered,

(b)  where scientific estimates or predictions are sought, a description of any relevant factors or
     assumptions to be taken into account, and

(c)  where applicable, a description of any objectives the coastal State is seeking to attain and an
     indication of whether specific advice or a range of options should be provided.

When the Fisheries Commission requests advice, it, too, may specify terms of reference, but the Council is required only to take them into account. This could mean, and probably does in view of the SC's capacity to act on its initiative, that the SC need not respond in the form or manner suggested by the Commission and may otherwise act at its discretion. The SC does not have such authority regarding coastal states, although it still must be consulted about the terms of reference.

In exercising its advisory function, the Council is to make determinations by a consensus and, if this cannot be achieved, report "all views advanced on the matter under consideration."

## Draft Antarctic Convention on Living Marine Resources

The March 1978 Draft Convention on the Conservation of Antarctic Marine Living Resources[72] makes provision for only two constituent bodies, a Commission and a Scientific Committee, both of which have functions pertaining to scientific research. The Commission's prime function is to give effect to the objective of conserving Antarctic marine living resources and to the principles of conservation to be established by the Convention. In doing so, it is inter alia to (a) "facilitate research into and comprehensive studies of Antarctic marine living resources and of the Antarctic marine ecosystem"; (b) compile data on the population of such resources and on factors affecting distribution, abundance, and productivity of harvested and dependent or related species or populations; (c) acquire catch-effort statistics on harvested populations; (d) analyze, disseminate, and publish information mentioned in subparagraphs (b) and (c) and reports of the Scientific Committee; (e) identify conservation needs and analyze effectiveness of conservation measures; and (f) formulate, adopt, and revise conservation measures on the basis of the best scientific evidence available.

The Scientific Committee is to be a forum for consultation and discussion among the contracting parties concerning the collection, study, and exchange of information that concerns resources covered by the Convention. It is also to encourage and promote cooperation among the same states in scientific research to add to knowledge of the living resources in the Antarctic marine ecosystem. The Scientific Committee has such specific functions as to (a) establish criteria and methods to be used for determinations that concern conservation measures; (b) regularly assess the status and trends of the populations of Antarctic marine living resources; (c) analyze data concerning the effects of harvesting on populations; (d) assess effects of proposed changes in methods of harvesting and proposed conservation measures; (e) transmit assessments, analyses, reports, and recommendations as requested or on its own initiative regarding measures and research to implement the conservation objective; and (f) formulate proposals for the conduct of international and national research programs into Antarctic living marine resources.

The Draft Convention does not presently provide for voting in the SC except to require that any Committee rule of procedure shall include procedures for presentation of minority reports.

The Commission is to have a secretariat whose head would be an Executive Secretary with a staff appointed on such terms and conditions as the Commission determines.

Under the present Draft Convention, the SC's determinations concerning conservation measures are only advisory and the Antarctic Commission is not obliged to accept the scientific judgments of the Convention.

The Draft Convention specifies that the Commission and the Scientific Committee shall cooperate with other governmental and nongovernmental bodies including the Antarctic Treaty Consultative Parties, FAO, and other specialized agencies, the Scientific Committee on Antarctic Research, the Scientific Committee on Oceanic Research, and the International Whaling Commission. In a somewhat unusual provision, the Commission is authorized to enter into agreements with the above-named organizations and with others as may be appropriate.

## Proposed Intergovernmental Oceanographic Commission (IOC) Working Group for the Western Pacific and Adjacent Waters (WESPAC)

### Background

With the winding down of the Cooperative Studies of the Kuroshio and Adjacent Regions (CSK), an IOC program that began in 1965, Japan and other participating countries began to look for a mechanism under which scientific cooperation in oceanographic programs could be continued. In response to proposals from the International Coordinating Group (ICG) for CSK, the IOC Executive Council established an ad hoc task team for WESTPAC to identify relevant marine scientific problems and to recommend ways whereby national and cooperative programs could be developed and coordinated. The task group met in June 1977, and its recommendations were endorsed in a July meeting of the ICG. In late 1977, the IOC Tenth Assembly approved the reports of these meetings and decided to establish the Working Group for the Western Pacific (WESTPAC).[73]

### Participation

Countries involved in the 1977 discussion included France, Indonesia, Japan, Korea, USSR and U.S. (observer). It was proposed that WESTPAC would consist initially of countries in the ICG for CSK but that membership should be open to all interested IOC members.[74]

The Western Pacific region would include all of the Bering Sea, and the Pacific south of the Aleutians to 40° S and west of 170° W.

### Objectives

The ultimate objectives of WESTPAC are the prediction of variability in ocean climate and ocean food resources and improved understanding of geological processes with economic impact upon the countries of the region. Attainment of these objectives requires fundamental research in dynamics of ocean circulation and their relation to the distribution of productivity and ocean food resources, and in the geology of the region. The program would presumably include elements related to marine pollution, and to training, education, and cooperation with other IOC bodies specifically concerned with these topics.

### Resources

The IOC Assembly, in establishing WESTPAC, invited member states and international organizations ''to provide personnel and/or financial support for the establishment of a full-time Secretariat to be located within the region.'' This follows IOC practices in the analogous body, IOCARIBE.[75] IOC would provide some limited financial support to the proposed Secretariat and to training, educating, and mutual assistance programs, to the extent they are supported by member states. Expenses of scientific programs would be met by participating members.

### Strategies and Outcomes

The IOC Working Group for the Western Pacific (WESTPAC) held its first meeting on February 21–24, 1979, and adopted a scientific program based on recommendations of a preceding workshop. Task teams were established on (1) marine pollution research and monitoring using commercially exploited shellfish as determinants, and on (2) ocean monitoring in the WESTPAC region. It was also agreed to convene workshops on (1) geosciences in the Northwest Pacific, (2) geosciences in the Southwest Pacific, (3) biological methods, and (4) coastal transport of pollutants.

Subsequently, the IOC Executive Council at its Eleventh Session (Mexico City, February–March, 1979, Resolution EC-XI.7) approved in principle the Executive Summary of the WESTPAC meeting and its 20 resolutions, instructed the Secretary to implement the resolutions as soon as possible, asked the Assembly to consider establishing a regional secretariat, approved a meeting of the first task team, and asked SCOR to advise on the proposals of the physical oceanography subgroup of the workshop. Approval of these steps by the IOC Assembly was obtained at its meeting in late 1979.

## BILATERAL AGREEMENTS ON RESEARCH

Formal bilateral agreements directly concerning marine research are relatively recent, apart from agreements establishing bilateral fishery commissions with independent staffs. Formal bilateral agreements in oceanography (in contrast either to ad hoc, one-time, or private arrangements) are even more recent, beginning essentially in the 1970s and involving primarily the most advanced researching nations. Prior to this decade, the U.S. has had bilateral arrangements with neighboring Canada and Mexico, but these were informal understandings regarding the mechanics of conducting research.

### Agreements Concerning Fisheries Research

Bilateral agreements regarding fisheries research seem essentially a function of extended jurisdiction. Prior to the intially modest, but widespread, extensions beginning in

1958, there appear to have been no such agreements. But as coastal nations began to claim wider area controls, even as modest as the extension from 3 to 12 miles, research in this area came to be seen as valuable, and arrangements for access and coordination with other nations became increasingly important. Thus, cooperative fisheries research increased as the awareness of the value of living marine resources increased.

In the case of the North Pacific, the earliest agreements relating to research were those between the neighboring states of the U.S. and Canada as they struggled with common fisheries problems affecting halibut and salmon.[76] These difficulties led to the earliest fishery commissions and to the development of independent research staffs to carry out the necessary research. Other commissions were formed around the world, but very few bilateral agreements are found for the coordination of fisheries research until after 1960, when fisheries zones began to be common. In the North Pacific, the first bilaterals dealing with fisheries zones were those concluded by the U.S. and Canada with the Soviet Union and Japan. In the mid-1970s, on the eve of establishing 200-mile fishing zones, there were nine ad hoc bilateral agreements in force in the eastern North Pacific, some providing for cooperation in fisheries research in addition to several other matters.

Three bilaterals between the U.S. and the USSR emphasized scientific research. The most important one concerned the northeastern part of the Pacific Ocean off the Pacific Coast of the United States. This Agreement came into effect February 13, 1967, and in Paragraph 9 provided:

> Both Governments consider it desirable to expand fishery research in the northeastern part of the Pacific Ocean on species of common interest, both on a national basis and in the form of joint investigations. The competent agencies of the two Governments will arrange for the exchange of scientific data and results of research on the fisheries, for meetings of scientists and, when appropriate, for participation by scientists of each Government in investigations carried out on board research vessels of the other Government. Each Government will, within the scope of its domestic laws and regulations, facilitate entry into appropriate ports for research vessels of the other Government engaged in such joint research.[77]

Pursuant to this arrangement, the two states have held annual (later biennial) meetings of scientists, alternating between Moscow and Seattle, to exchange views on the fisheries in the area. In addition, Soviet research vessels have been permitted access to the U.S. exclusive fishing zone. These research arrangements sometimes pose difficulties in implementation and on one occasion, because of misunderstandings, Soviet research vessels were not permitted to enter the U.S. fishing zone.

The 1971 agreement, which replaces the 1967 agreement as amended and extended, repeats the substance of Paragraph 9, now elevated to Paragraph 1, and adds detail. It states:

> The competent agencies of both Governments shall ensure the following, at least on an annual basis.
>
> a.   An exchange of scientific and statistical data, published works and the results of fishery research;

b.    Meetings of scientists and, in appropriate cases, the participation of the scientists of each
      Government in fishery research conducted on the research vessels of the other
      Government.[78]


The record of accomplishment under these agreements is mixed. Participants in the
U.S. do not believe much was accomplished from the scientific perspective, although some
joint work was done and there were some positive scientific results.[79] A main benefit was
some improvement in Soviet fishery statistics, although even in this instance the improvement was relative. Some believe a major gain was the opportunity to discover how the Soviet
system of scientific inquiry operated and to learn of the problems involved in working with
each other. The latter include bureaucratic delays, inability to meet commitments such as
scheduled cruises, exchanges of personnel, production of data, and production of inadequate data.[80]

Other scientific meetings pursuant to bilateral agreements were very productive. Both
the Japanese and Polish arrangements involved joint efforts that worked well and produced
more adequate data. These bilaterals, including the Soviet one, had an impact on U.S.
scientific activity in the sense that the U.S. redesigned its survey activities and altered its
methodology.

Beginning in 1975, bilateral agreements concerning fisheries began to increase notice-
ably around the world and a number of them contain provisions on research cooperation. It
seems probable that this increase in fisheries bilaterals is directly associated with the
accepted widespread extension of national fishery jurisdiction to 200 miles. A recent FAO
publication explicitly makes this connection in listing about ninety "selected bilateral
fishery agreements concluded as a result of the new regime of the ocean."[81] While most of
these agreements probably deal only with conditions of access to fishery zones, the
obligations of flag states, enforcement, and dispute settlement matters, twenty of them
contain provisions concerning research. The United States is listed as party to two of these
agreements but, in fact, is a party to twelve others that contain provisions on research,
making a total of at least thirty-three such agreements out of one hundred.[82] Probably others
exist that have not come to attention.

Interestingly, nine developing states are in the group of approximately twenty-six that
have concluded bilaterals that deal with research.[83] In terms of substance, the agreements
provide for such activities as joint scientific programs, meetings and consultations, planning, exchange or submission of data, and training programs, the precise nature depending
on the specific agreement. The FAO study contrasts agreements between developed states
with those between a developed and developing state.[84] The former call for mutual
obligations, while "Agreements providing for joint research activities between a developed
and a developing country usually describe in detail the contribution that will be made by the
developed country."[85] Several Soviet agreements are cited in this connection;[86] others do
not fit this mold.

The bilateral agreements by the United States (called "GIFAs" for "governing international fishery agreement," a term employed in the U.S. legislation extending its fishery

jurisdiction) are perhaps anomalous because they are concluded by a developed state whose major (but not sole) interest is in its own coastal fisheries. Each agreement makes nearly identical provision for coordination of research efforts and for consultation about setting up a new multilateral institution for scientific research.[87] The provisions for research concern stocks within the U.S. fishery zone and are especially significant because under U.S. legislation the U.S. must make key catch determinations under the Act in accordance with the best available scientific evidence concerning such stocks.[88]

Actions by the United States to implement the GIFA provisions have included separate meetings of U.S. scientists with those from Korea and Japan, indirect communications with Polish scientists, and a meeting with Soviet scientists in December, 1978. But convening a series of separate meetings is not an improvement over previous bilateral arrangements. Invitations have been issued to all GIFA nations to meet as a group, but it has not yet been possible to find acceptable dates.

## Agreements on Oceanographic Research

U.S. arrangements for coordinating oceanography research are embodied in broad agreements or understandings addressed to science and technology (with one exception). Sometimes, as with the U.S. and France, the arrangements do not even take the form of formal agreements but are entered into by exchange of letters between executive agencies of the two governments. At the moment, the U.S. is party to about 21 agreements on science and technology.[89]

The two main bilateral relationships in the North Pacific concerning marine science, apart from the numerous fishery agreements, involve the U.S.−USSR and U.S.−Japan. The former agreement deals only with the ocean, and the latter is an umbrella accord for science and technology.

The U.S.−USSR Agreement on Cooperation in Studies of the World Ocean was concluded and entered into force in June, 1973, for a five-year period; in 1978 it was renewed for a three-year period.[90] The initial agreement was reached in pursuance of two agreements of a year earlier concerning cooperation in scientific matters. In substance, the 1973 Agreement enumerates some scientific areas in which cooperation is to occur, some of the specific forms of cooperation, provision for cooperation, direct contact between entities within the two countries, the creation of a Joint Committee on Cooperation in World Ocean Studies to implement the Agreement, and designation of an Executive Agent for each party to carry out the Agreement.

After the Agreement was in place for five years, the record of cooperation and relative benefits and costs were such that the United States' Executive Branch decided to agree to its extension. It seems apparent, however, from the available assessments, that the balance of benefits, although positive from the U.S. perspective, has not been so pronounced that there is great enthusiasm for continuation.[91]

The major advantages to the U.S. appear to be (1) some increase in the capability to do "big science," primarily because of the usefulness of the added platforms (ships) made available by the Soviets, (2) the opportunity to become informed about the structure and operation of the Soviet scientific establishment, and (3) some contribution to specific projects, especially Polymode, the study of eddies and currents in the North Atlantic.

The difficulties of an operation in marine science with the USSR are identified by all concerned, but as frustrating as these are, they are usually not offered as sufficient reason to terminate the cooperative ocean study agreement. The problems identified are much like those previously experienced in the much smaller-scale cooperative activities involved under the U.S.−USSR fisheries bilaterals, mentioned above. They include a wholly different structure and approach to research in the two countries, most especially the severe difficulties caused by the centralization of decision making in the USSR compared to the more dispersed authority and flexibility in the U.S. system. Other difficulties are differences in technological capability, problems of logistics and communication (again due to the Soviet system of decision making, which fetters the individual scientists), restrictions on travel and publications, and a general unwillingness to interact outside formal arrangements (as indicated by refusals to permit the participation of third-country scientists).

United States−Japan relations in marine science cooperation take place pursuant to various programs initiated originally in the early 1960s.[92] Activities with at least some science content, albeit mostly applied in connection with resource problems, occur under a variety of programs including the United States−Japan Conference on Natural Resources Development (UJNER), the United States−Japan Committee on Scientific Cooperation, and the United States−Japan Environment Agreement. Forms of cooperation include exchange of information, research, and experts of various kinds; and a variety of joint activities, presentation of papers, and other methods.

The United States−French arrangement is noteworthy as an illustration of an arrangement concluded by agencies of these and other countries in a considerable variety of subject areas.

## IMPLICATIONS OF REVIEW AND ANALYSIS

### Participation

The prospect of increasingly widespread participation in various activities in the North Pacific by various nations and their nationals suggests that interest in an intergovernmental mechanism for the coordination of marine science research may also become more widely shared than in the past. Over the medium- to long-term, therefore, a new mechanism for marine science should contain flexible and open-ended membership provisions to allow adherence by any concerned nation.

In the near term, however, it is plain that wide participation is not probable, and perhaps not feasible, on political grounds alone, if not others. Strained or nonexistent political relations between several Pacific rim nations make it unlikely that the pressures of scientific need are great enough to induce states to join in a new coordinating mechanism. This is not a crippling condition by any means because the major participants (the U.S., USSR, Japan, and Canada) are accustomed to joint marine activities and can undoubtedly create a viable structure among themselves. Furthermore, other organizational considerations could alleviate the disadvantages of a mechanism that is not inclusive in membership.

In considering the success of the previous multilateral coordinating mechanism in the Atlantic Ocean, a prime contributing factor appears to have been the emphasis on participation by other international organizations, groups, and individual scientists. Thus, although ICES is fundamentally organized as an intergovernmental entity, and delegates and experts come from member governments, participation in its working level activities includes nongovernmental scientists. It would be a sustaining factor of no small strength if the new PICES were to be structured to also enlist the active participation of scientists whose affiliations were not necessarily governmental in nature. Insofar as the United States is concerned, the effect would very likely be salutary and result in an increase in the scientific effort devoted to important problems. Moreover, the enlistment of the nongovernmental scientific sector might also result in different, and perhaps improved, assessments of scientific priorities in the area concerned. Also, other international organizations and private associations should be permitted to participate in the scientific effort when they have the necessary scientific expertise to make a contribution.

In reviewing previous mechanisms in the North Pacific, it is evident that the sometimes narrow limits on participation arose from the need to structure organizations to deal with immediate problems of identifiable participants. The fisheries bodies were established to deal with such difficulties and it made sense to limit participation for such purpose. An organization aimed at facilitating scientific inquiry as such can be more flexibly arranged to secure the benefits of more open participation, namely, the contribution of scientific expertise.

## Objectives

Previous international mechanisms for coordinating scientific research have been concerned primarily with issues directly related to management, and their objectives have been aimed in the same direction. Accordingly, the subject areas of research have been determined by management or allocation considerations, leading to fragmented and partial conceptions of research.

Within the constraints of available resources, the objectives of PICES should be broadly formulated so the new structure can be concerned with marine scientific research in the broadest sense. The operational significance attached to a broad statement of research objectives can be made to vary through time as interest, priorities, finances, and other considerations suggest or dictate.

## Resources

Examination of budgets of North Pacific international bodies indicates that only minor sums have been made available for coordinated research in the North Pacific. Individual nations may have sometimes devoted substantial resources to particular projects but this generally has not been the case for projects involving more than one nation. The advent of a PICES does not necessarily mean great increases in research budgets across the board, but would facilitate better use of such facilities and resources as are made available by member states. To the extent PICES were able to identify opportunities for cooperative research, there might be a demand for increased budget support. This process might well justify such increase. In any event, the merits of a particular proposal should be decisive in its acquiring support, and not the character of the sponsoring organization.

One of the major lessons of the past in the North Pacific is that it is most undesirable to establish a series of bilateral agreements concerning research. To do so requires very high transaction costs in the form of a continuous series of meetings involving constant preparations and discussions that seriously reduce the time available for actual research and planning.

## Strategies and Outcomes

The primary question in this connection concerns the structure to be established for coordinating and doing science. Previous mechanisms varied from the independent research staff, delegation of the scientific advisory function to another body permanently or temporarily, and primary reliance on national research agencies and institutions.

With the exception of ICES, most of the previous experience is inapplicable to the proposed North Pacific agency. As noted elsewhere, the ICES experience in the North Pacific was mainly focused on fisheries research and further aimed more sharply at research in aid of management. PICES might rather be conceived as an organization for facilitating marine science across the board, including problems only remotely, if at all, relevant to management concerns. While management functions might be aided by PICES investigations, and perhaps a scientific function related to management might evolve, the major purpose is more comprehensive. Considering the potential breadth of the research activities and interests for participating nations and scientists, the notion of a separate research staff is impractical. At the same time, however, there is value in the creation of a secretariat with sufficient scientific expertise to provide a significantly higher level of knowledgeable assistance than would be obtainable in the absence of such skills.

The prime result of a new scientific coordinating mechanism ought to be an enlarged, improved, and generally more effective process of scientific communication with respect to the North Pacific region. This, in turn, would provide an improved base of knowledge for decisions with respect to the rational use of the North Pacific Ocean and its resources.

# 13

# The Need for a North Pacific Science Organization

The changing legal regime of the ocean and its resources has led to consideration of the need for a new international organization for dealing with scientific questions in the North Pacific. National jurisdictions are rapidly being extended over all fishery resources within 200 miles of the coasts of countries bounding the North Pacific. It has therefore become necessary to modify or replace existing international arrangements for consultation on fishery matters. Only limited mechanisms for scientific cooperation in the region are now in place, and these could be further weakened as extended jurisdiction continues. At the same time, augmented and more varied usage of the ocean and its resources, the presence and growth of threats to the quality of the marine environment, and the ever-increasing need for scientific information as a basis for rational resource utilization further substantiate the requirement for improved arrangements for exchange of information, and for cooperation in the conduct of scientific research among nations bordering the North Pacific.

## REASONS FOR ESTABLISHING A NEW SCIENTIFIC ORGANIZATION

The case for improved arrangements for scientific coordination in the North Pacific is based on the following considerations:

1. Management decisions on the multiple use of the ocean and its resources should be based on adequate scientific understanding of oceanic processes and phenomena in the region.
2. Despite the extensions of national jurisdiction now taking place, or likely to take place, in the North Pacific, conflicts in the use of living resources, both within and beyond the limits of national jurisdiction, are bound to increase.
3. Although several international bodies exist for the management of specific fishery resources in the region, there is no overall mechanism for the exchange and evaluation of data and information on the status of stocks, on which national and international decisions on resource management can be based.

419

4. Increasing uses of ocean resources, the transport of petroleum and other potentially toxic products, and industrial activities around the margins of the North Pacific represent intensifying threats to the health of the marine environment. No mechanism exists for pooling efforts to understand and monitor these threats.

5. The role of the ocean in modulating weather and climate is now evident. An improved mechanism is required for the development and coordination of investigations of ocean-atmosphere interaction that will enhance the possibility of predicting weather and climate.

6. Scientific investigations are conducted in the North Pacific under the auspices of several governments, including those of the U.S., USSR, Canada, and Japan. These investigations fall within all fields of marine science and its applications. Some are multiinstitutional and include arrangements for interinstitutional coordination; others are the efforts of single institutions. No general mechanism exists for the initiation, planning, and coordination of multinational oceanographic and fishery research programs in the region.

7. Data resulting from these investigations, in part at least, eventually find their way into the world data exchange system. However, there is no mechanism for the orderly and timely exchange of data and information between governments and institutions engaged in the research, for improving the quality and intercomparability of measurements, or for selecting common statistical areas and bases.

## Purpose and Activities

If a new organization were established, it might have the following purpose:

To promote the development of cooperative research activities and the exchange of information concerning (1) the North Pacific marine environment and its interactions with land and atmosphere; (2) uses of the North Pacific and its living and nonliving resources; and (3) the effects of man's activities on the quality of the marine environment.

To achieve this purpose, the organization would engage in activities related to marine science, fisheries, quality of the marine environment, and other marine fields as appropriate, such as the following: (1) exchange of data and information; (2) review of research plans, programs, and progress; (3) identification of critical research problems and of methods appropriate for their solution; (4) planning, development, and coordination of cooperative investigations of problems of common interest; and (5) evaluation and interpretation of available data and information from the scientific point of view.

## Informal Discussions of Proposal

Two informal meetings have been held to discuss this proposal. At the first, on March 21, 1978, 20 participants from the United States and Canada examined in considerable detail the need for the organization and the manner in which it might be established and might operate. A summary of those discussions is attached (Appendix I).

The second meeting, on January 17–18, 1979, involved 38 participants, this time from Japan and the USSR as well as Canada and the United States. There was general agreement on a number of specific activities that could benefit from improved cooperation in the North

Pacific. Although existing fishery arrangements were considered inadequate mechanisms for promoting such activities, it was agreed that whatever organization is established should not have responsibilities that directly pertain to resource management. The need for a new organization is more apparent in fisheries than in oceanography. Participants agreed that an acceptable organization should be informal, flexible, and scientific, but there was disagreement on whether these characteristics could be achieved in an intergovernmental organization, even though such an organization might appear necessary if funding and authorization for full exchange of data were to be provided. It was suggested that this question be explored within and between the governments concerned. Meanwhile, informal arrangements could be initiated through convening a steering committee to organize scientific discussions. An agreed summary of views on these matters is attached (Appendix I).

## Analysis of Issues

### Scientific Issues

Areas of scientific agreement among participants in discussions to date include the following:

1. A number of existing functions related to scientific investigations of the North Pacific are of common interest both to scientists and to managers of ocean uses; these functions would benefit from improved cooperation between the countries of the region.
2. Existing international organizations have partially carried out some, but not all, of these functions.
3. Extensions of national jurisdiction and the developing law of the sea have decreased the likelihood that existing organizations can carry out these functions effectively in the future.
4. A new organization could improve the likelihood of these functions being conducted effectively in the future.

There are differences of opinion on the extent to which institutionalized international cooperation is required for carrying out one or another of the identified functions, and on the form and degree of formality required in an organization dedicated to promoting the desired joint action.

The desirable functions can be discussed within the framework of the purposes and activities listed above. The major areas of impact appear to be fisheries, oceanography, and pollution.

1. *Exchange of data and information*. The principal problem is the exchange of fishery statistics. This has normally been accomplished through INPFC, IPHC, and other specialized fishery commissions and bilateral agreements. Since most of the resources, apart from high-seas salmon, albacore, and marine mammals, are now exploited within areas of national jurisdiction, the role of existing international arrangements in data exchange may well decay. The achievement of a comprehensive and normalized data base arising from the application of agreed methods will thus become even more remote than it is at present. The

lack of such a data base becomes increasingly serious as the ecological basis for multispecies management of fisheries is developed.

Oceanographic data are exchanged informally among scientists, and formally through the system of national and international data centers. The World Data Centers are organized by the International Council of Scientific Unions; in oceanography, the Intergovernmental Oceanographic Commission and its Working Committee on International Oceanographic Data Exchange provide both authority and guidelines for this exchange. There are also some effective regional data centers (e.g., that operated by the International Council for the Exploration of the Sea). These data exchange arrangements, although not very prompt, are reasonably effective, especially for the more classical measurements of water properties such as temperature, salinity, and dissolved chemical substances. They are much less effective for biological data or for more modern physical measurements, such as those of velocity or the fine structure of temperature and salinity distributions. Only recently have attempts been made to exchange bathythermograph data internationally in real time and on an operational basis; these exchanges were arranged through the IOC–WMO program known as IGOSS (Integrated Global Ocean Station System). In general, it can be said that although the international exchange of oceanographic data is incomplete and imperfect, these inadequacies have not seriously hampered research in the North Pacific, perhaps because they are not required for operational purposes. However, the data exchange system is inadequate for studies of large-scale variability in the ocean, and its interactions with the atmosphere, which are required for understanding climate changes.

The regional exchange of data on concentrations and effects of pollutants in the marine environment and in marine organisms is fairly rudimentary for several reasons. There is no widespread monitoring system for pollutants, and most measurements are experimental and local. The impact of pollutants on the open ocean and its living resources is not yet established. As pollution studies proceed, and the impact becomes clearer, the need for general monitoring and exchange of data will become more pressing.

In all data exchange, there is a requirement that measurements be made by recognized methods, so that data from different sources can be successfully fitted together. The January, 1979, meeting identified the development and intercomparison of observational and analytical methods in all fields as an important cooperative activity.

2. *Review of research plans, programs, and progress.* Even in the absence of a demonstrated need for cooperative investigations in the region, there is benefit in an exchange of information on ongoing research, particularly when it is of large-scale and general interest. Without international arrangements, research activities of one country are seldom known in any detail in another. Yet an awareness of such activities can reveal opportunities for cooperation and can facilitate national research planning. To the extent that common problems are identified (see below), ongoing programs provide a basis for the development of joint actions of mutual benefit. The utility of this activity does not seem to be an issue, although alone it might not justify creation of a new organization.

3. *Identification of critical research problems.* Marine research in the North Pacific is, for the most part, conducted on a national basis, often in local waters. Some cooperative

studies on fishery problems have been developed, and a large-scale United States study of ocean anomalies that may affect climate has elicited some support from other countries in the North Pacific. In the western Pacific, problems of common interest have been identified by a number of countries participating in the Cooperative Studies of the Kuroshio and Adjacent Regions (CSK). Experience in other regions, notably in the North Atlantic and adjacent seas, has shown the occasional emergence of cooperative efforts to investigate problems identified by scientists in several countries. The International Council for the Exploration of the Sea has provided a forum for the identification of such problems by the scientists concerned.

Participants in the January, 1979, meeting listed examples of subject areas within which critical research problems appeared to exist: (a) regional studies such as those of the Bering Sea, studies of migratory species (such as albacore), studies of the methodology of stock assessment, and development of an ecosystem approach to fishery management; (b) studies of interactions between species, and between species and their environment as affecting the abundance and distribution of stocks; (c) marine pollution studies of the assimilative capacity of coastal waters and the effects of particular pollutants on the population dynamics of stocks; and (d) studies of the interaction between the atmosphere and the sea within the North Pacific and adjacent waters.

Opinions differ on how many problems of this sort are likely to gain enough widespread support that limited national resources will be allocated to cooperative studies for their solution. The fear has been expressed that agreement on critical problems within an intergovernmental organization will tend to distort national research priorities, particularly if diplomats rather than scientists are making the decisions. However, it should be noted that with ICES, an intergovernmental organization that has served as a model for the proposed North Pacific organization, problems and priorities have been established by the scientists involved and have reflected, rather than distorted, national priorities.

4. *Cooperative investigations*. The issues discussed above apply equally to the investigations that might arise to tackle the identified research problems. Countries differ in the extent to which they conduct research in regions beyond those of local interest. Even countries with extensive distant-water operations, such as the United States, devote the majority of their efforts to their own investigations. Because of the growing limitations in national funding for ocean research, there is some tendency for the balance of research effort to shift away from distant-water operations. Yet international cooperative investigations continue to be organized, either within the framework of international organizations or formal bilateral arrangements, or on a more informal and ad hoc basis. There are significant scientific problems that cannot be effectively attacked with the resources of a single country. There are also problems, particularly in fisheries and possibly concerning marine pollution, where international studies are needed to produce results of widespread acceptance. Thus, one can anticipate that scientists will continue to propose large-scale projects of international interest and that the development and prosecution of such projects can be facilitated by appropriately functioning international organizations.

5. *Scientific evaluation of data*. The utility of a comprehensive data base of high quality

in fisheries and oceanography has already been discussed. While the research of individual scientists can benefit from the availability of such a data base, there are also cases where collective review and evaluation of available data is desirable. This is particularly true in fisheries where an agreed assessment of the status of stocks is required for the international management of fisheries. Of course, with the extension of national jurisdiction, most living resources occur and are harvested under national jurisdiction. However, there are still some high-seas stocks of commercially important species, and even within 200 miles of the coast some stocks cross international boundaries. Some scientists feel that even with most of the harvest occurring within national jurisdiction, it is important periodically to examine the status of stocks on a widespread regional basis. This is particularly important when the interspecific interactions are taken into account, as must be the case in the development of an ecological basis for fishery management.

While the utility of an occasional region-wide evaluation of fishery data was widely accepted, some participants in the discussions were obviously nervous about the possibility of such an evaluation leading to an intervention in national fishery management. It was generally agreed that, at least with regard to stocks that are harvested within exclusive economic zones, any new organization should have no specific advisory responsibility that directly pertains to fishery management.

In the case of marine pollution, there is, as noted earlier, no large-scale monitoring program and no extensive collection of relevant data. Even with existing data, however, and with the expectation that the data base will grow, there seems to be utility in an occasional look at the overall health of the marine environment in the North Pacific. Such an assessment should reveal potential problems before they become critical, and should suggest opportunities for further research and observation programs, in some cases of a cooperative nature.

Oceanographic data will be examined en masse by scientists concerned with large-scale processes (e.g., those related to climate). This examination does not normally require any sort of joint evaluation among scientists of different countries. However, since interannual variations in the circulation and in the physical, chemical, and biological conditions of the ocean can have a profound effect on the distribution and abundance of living resources as well as reflecting the evolution of climate, a case can be made for an annual review of oceanographic conditions in the North Pacific that could be conducted within the framework of an appropriate international organization.

## General Issues

Other issues that arose during the informal discussions include the following:

1. *Subject areas*. Without doubt, the principal justifications for a new organization are found in fisheries, where it is generally agreed that existing arrangements are too highly specialized and piecemeal to permit any comprehensive examination of problems. While oceanography as it relates to fisheries is recognized as important, there is less agreement on the contribution that a new organization could make to the prosecution of oceanographic research per se. In part, this is because the percentage of effort applied to large-scale, data-intensive studies has been relatively small. As studies of the ocean's role in climate are intensified, it is possible that the potential contribution of a new organization will be more

widely recognized. The same may be true for the subject of marine pollution as present studies develop beyond very local and specialized problems. It is agreed that at least initially the economic, social, and other applied aspects, including ocean engineering, would be of secondary importance.

2. *Membership*. Discussions to date have involved participants from Canada, Japan, the Soviet Union, and the United States. It is generally accepted that these countries must be represented if a new organization is to be effective. In order for the data base to be comprehensive, it is desirable that other countries bordering the region or operating therein, particularly those fishing in the North Pacific and Bering Sea, be included. However, because of political problems, it seems desirable to start with the four countries already involved and to defer consideration of a further expansion until a later date.

3. *Structure*. The principal issue that dominated the January, 1979, discussions was whether or not any new organization should directly involve governments. It was agreed that the organization should focus on scientific rather than management problems and should deal with them in a flexible and informal way. Some level of governmental involvement will be required for the identified functions to be carried out. Governmental action will be required to obtain full cooperation in providing desired data, information, and financial support necessary for participation in the organization's activities. Yet, intergovernmental organizations tend to develop rigid attitudes and methods and to be dominated by nonscientific considerations.

## CONCLUSIONS

Experience with ICES has shown that a regional intergovernmental organization comprising members with common interests and scientific capabilities can effectively promote scientific activities. This has been accomplished by the structure of meetings, where scientific discussions occupy the central position, and by the structure of decision making, where proposals for action arise in the scientific committees and are supported before the Delegates by the chairman of the scientific body (the Consultative Committee). Those familiar with the operation of ICES are confident that a similar structure would be effective in the North Pacific.

Others feel that the objectives of a new organization could be better achieved through a nongovernmental organization or through periodic regional scientific discussions (congresses). Proponents of this view have not elaborated on the structure of such an organization (or nonorganization) or on how it would obtain the necessary support and cooperation of the governments concerned.

At the conclusion of the January, 1979 meeting, two approaches were recommended. First, discussions should be held within and between the governments concerned to explore organizational alternatives, including a nongovernmental organization, a governmental organization similar to ICES, and a continuation of more focused informal discussions under governmental auspices. Second, a steering committee of representatives from the participating countries should be convened to organize and initiate scientific discussions of problems such as those described above. Thus, despite the general conclusion that it was premature to proceed directly to establishment of an intergovernmental organization, the door is open to further exploration of both the governmental and nongovernmental options.

## EPILOGUE

Subsequent to the completion of this chapter, a number of actions have taken place relating to the further development of institutional arrangements for cooperation in North Pacific marine science.

Discussions within the United States led to the conclusion that while a new organization analogous to the International Council for the Exploration of the Sea (ICES, hence the designation Pacific ICES, or PICES) would serve a variety of purposes, its creation would require a strong justification from the fisheries point of view. Therefore, a third meeting, this time of U.S. fishery experts, was convened, in January 1981, as a result of which three papers were prepared and distributed by the Institute for Marine Studies:

a. Fishery justification for a Pacific ICES: A report on discussions in January 1981, by Warren S. Wooster
b. Notes on the promotion of PICES, by Warren S. Wooster
c. On the fishery science role of PICES, by William F. Royce

The International North Pacific Fisheries Commission, at its 27th Annual Meeting in 1980, decided to invite scientists from both member and nonmember countries fishing in the Convention area (e.g., the USSR), to participate in a 1981 symposium on scientific problems related to Pacific cod and other groundfish fisheries. Thus, INPFC has moved to provide a forum with broader than usual participation for the discussion of regional scientific problems of mutual interest.

The Program Group for Project WESTPAC held two meetings (WESTPAC I, February 19–20, 1979; WESTPAC II, October 19–24, 1981) and took a number of actions, some of which have substantial implications for the design of PICES.

WESTPAC I created three disciplinary subgroups on Physical Oceanography, Marine Biology and Pollution and Marine Geology and Geophysics. These subgroups were given the task of identifying potential programs of investigation, using criteria restricting the search to problems that could not be solved nationally or individually and were not already being carried out.[1] Following this work, WESTPAC sponsored a series of task teams, three of which met in workshops and one worked by correspondence to produce detailed assessments and specifications for research programs and projects.[2]

From the range of programs and projects identified, WESTPAC II met in Jakarta in October 1981 to determine priorities. Its recommendations are as follows:[3]

*Ocean Monitoring*

1. Volunteer Observing Ship Program
2. Island and Coastal Station Program

3. Hydrographic Program
4. Drift Buoy Program

*Coastal Transport of Pollutants*

1. Survey of currents and tides in the nearshore waters of the WESTPAC region.
2. Exchange processes and circulation in coral reefs.

*Marine Biology and Living Resources*

1. On marine biology, choose for study in the region communities of major importance to human utilization.
2. Offer to coordinate the UNESCO program of studies on mangroves and coral reefs in the region and evaluate the effects of pollution on coastal resources.
3. On marine pollution research and monitoring, continue the work of the Task Team using Commercially Exploited Shellfish as Determinants (i.e., the "mussel watch" program) and offer to collaborate with UNEP in implementing the Action Plan for S.E. Asian seas.

*Geology and Geophysics*

No specific priority decisions were taken. The meeting merely recommended that each of the projects identified at the previous workshop should be regarded by member states as a portfolio of priority research tasks from which to select. The future of marine geology and geophysics within WESTPAC remains unclear.

Given these actions taken by WESTPAC II, there appear to be two issues of importance for the design of PICES. The first concerns the difficult problem of finding the most efficient approach for coordinating the work on monitoring of physical oceanographic parameters in relation to climate as envisaged by WESTPAC, planned by the IOC's IGOSS program, already undertaken by NORPAX (North Pacific Climate Study) and planned in several research projects aimed at the Equatorial and South Pacific. The second issue concerns coordination of the intercalibration and standardization of measurement work in relation to planned investigations of the fates and effects of pollutants in the marine environment. These issues will receive more detailed evaluation in a later volume.

# PART IV

# Multiple Use Conditions and Conflicts of the North Pacific

# 14

# Management of Multiple Use Conflicts—Offshore Oil Development, Marine Pollution, and Other Uses

Previous chapters in this volume analyzed the development of fisheries, marine transportation, and marine scientific research in the North Pacific. These single use discussions described the patterns of use, delineated trends, and examined problems that have arisen in each major marine use of the area. This chapter attempts to determine the extent to which management of multiple use conflicts is necessary in the North Pacific. Special attention is given to a description of offshore oil and gas development activities and to marine pollution because of the potential they may have for impacting other ocean uses, particularly fishing.

There are several important reasons for considering the management of multiple use conflicts. First, increased and more diverse use of marine areas increases the potential for conflict. Second, it appears that the relationships between those who study or regulate one use and those who study or regulate other uses are generally weak or nonexistent. Increased diversity of use combined with no reliable means of resolving conflicts may produce a chaotic situation under which multiple use conflicts, actual or perceived, may unnecessarily interfere with some uses, resulting in a loss of benefits to society. If these interactions are not systematically studied, little will be known about the dimensions of the problem and the possible costs to society.

The conflicts between different uses of the resources and space in the North Pacific region have been largely ignored in ocean studies, although there is an increasing recognition of the need to examine them more thoroughly. Our study uncovers more gaps in the knowledge of multiple use conflicts than it fills. It explores what is known and provides a basis for preliminary evaluation of the need for study, and design of a management scheme. We begin with some methodological considerations, proceed with a description of trends in offshore oil development, marine pollution, and other currently lesser known uses of the North Pacific, and conclude with an evaluation of priorities for regional consideration of multiple use conflicts in the area.

## METHODOLOGICAL CONSIDERATIONS

Implicit in most discussions of multiple use conflict is the assumption that more intense use of marine resources and marine space results in a greater degree of conflict between separately managed uses, thereby increasing the need for resolving them in order to increase benefits.[1] While this assumption is intuitively rational, it has not been rigorously examined for a variety of reasons, the foremost among them being the lack of an adequate paradigm and the lack of adequate data. In this study we use the above assumption as a general hypothesis, which we test using empirical data from the North Pacific.

In order to test the hypothesis that multiple use conflicts increase with increases in separately managed uses, it is necessary, first, to document the trend in levels of use for individual uses; second, to define what constitutes a multiple use conflict; third, to identify multiple use conflicts in the North Pacific region; and, fourth, to examine the scale and trends in multiple use conflicts in the area. After these steps have been taken, it is possible to make some observations on the question of whether or not a regional approach is required for resolving multiple use conflicts in the North Pacific in the near term (5–10 years). For the most part, we have simplified the analysis by excluding multiple use conflicts that occur largely within the limits of territorial waters, where they are under coastal state jurisdiction. However, it is desirable that consistent practices be adopted by coastal states with respect to regulations that affect such activities as international shipping in territorial waters.

As the first step in testing the hypothesis, it is necessary to show that various uses of the North Pacific have increased in recent times. This increase has already been documented in preceding chapters on fishing and marine transportation. The evidence is less complete for marine scientific research. The chapters on fisheries and transportation assess the complexity and vast increases in these activities and need not be summarized in this chapter. Offshore oil development and marine pollution—two uses of the North Pacific that have considerable potential for both increased use and the creation of multiple use conflicts— receive extensive treatment here. A number of lesser known uses of the area are examined with respect to specific multiple use conflicts, but do not justify extensive treatment in this study.

The second step in evaluating our hypothesis is to define what we mean by multiple use conflicts. Multiple use conflicts arise when more than one use of a resource or marine area precludes or adversely impinges upon the use of other resources (or the same space) by other users. Multiple use interactions that result in no detrimental impacts or in benefits are not further considered. The range of multiple use conflicts may include actual physical damage done to the resource or the equipment for one use by another use, increased costs of operation caused by changes in patterns and timing of operations to avoid or accommodate other uses, and other constraints on one use imposed by another.

The third step in testing the hypothesis is identification of multiple use conflicts in the North Pacific. This has been done in an iterative fashion. Lists of multiple use conflicts were prepared on the basis of two-dimensional impact matrices typified by the Economic and

Social Council of the United Nations (ECOSOC) matrix entitled Potential Interactions of Marine Activities in Close Proximity, figure 14.1. We noted multiple use interactions where there was some evidence in the North Pacific of conflicts and sought information on others. Multiple use conflicts were identified in the search process, and in research on other topics. We do not claim that the multiple use interactions identified in this study are the only ones that exist in the North Pacific, but are confident that they are representative of the problems that exist in the region.

Using our definition, multiple use conflicts that have been identified in the North Pacific

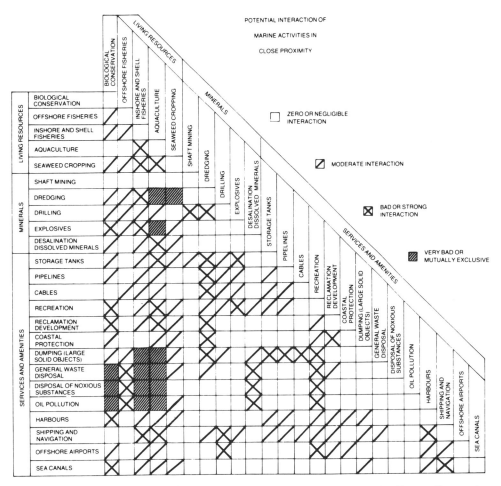

Fig. 14.1. *Potential Interactions of Marine Activities in Close Proximity*. Source: Economic and Social Council, United Nations (ECOSOC), *Uses of the Sea*, Doc. E/5120 (New York: ECOSOC, April 25, 1972), p. 55. The degree of interaction represented in each cell of this matrix is as reported in the original source. These are not our determinations for the North Pacific, since the matrix was used only in preliminary study.

involve offshore oil development, marine pollution, fishing, marine transportation, marine cables, military uses of the ocean, ocean mining, energy production, protection of the marine environment, seaweed farming, and marine science. The first two of these conflicts are treated more extensively than are the others.

Discussion of multiple use conflicts in this study is confined to examples where there is empirical evidence of a multiple use conflict in the North Pacific. We do not discuss potential conflicts, conflicts found in other ocean areas, or the results of laboratory experiments that relate to possible impacts.[2] This is not to imply that evidence of interactions and conflicts in other areas is not important in orienting our thinking about similar situations in the North Pacific. It indicates, however, that evaluation of multiple use conflicts in the North Pacific and elsewhere must proceed directly from analysis of region-specific information.

Examination of the scale and trends in multiple use conflicts is the last step required to test the hypothesis, and it is at once the most important and most difficult aspect of this study. Ideally, it would be desirable to be able to present the following categories of information: (1) the direction of conflict (i.e., which use interferes with or imposes cost on another use); (2) the geographical location and extent of impacts; (3) the number and frequency of conflicts; (4) the conditions under which conflict occurs; and (5) the value of damages imposed on one use by other uses, and the relationship of these values to the total value of the two or more uses involved. In order to assess trends in multiple use conflicts, it is necessary to know if there is a change over time in the following parameters: (1) the direction of conflict and the number of uses that are in conflict; (2) the number and frequency of conflicts; (3) the number of locations, or size of area, where conflicts occur; (4) the conditions under which conflicts occur; and (5) the value of the damages. With respect to each conflict, it is necessary to know whether or not the participants in the conflict are from one or several nations, and if conflict takes place over international marine boundaries.

For the North Pacific, each of these categories of information is incompletely known, or known for a specific area and period. Our assessment of the availability of data showed that it is possible to identify the directions of the conflicts. Geographical location and extent of conflicts are generally known but insufficiently documented because of the difficulty of drawing boundaries around multiple use interactions like marine pollution. We found there was partial data on the number of incidents and frequency of conflict, but seldom adequate data to establish a trend. The conditions under which conflicts occur are not well documented, and data on the value of damages imposed in relation to total value of marine uses is probably the least well known.

Based on our preliminary survey of multiple use conflict data, we considered using multidimensional matrices, multiple objective analysis, and other paradigms for orienting the analysis.[3] All were found to be more sophisticated techniques than the data base permitted us to use. This finding forced us to consider whether it was useful to pursue the analysis of multiple use conflicts further with only partial data and with a paradigm that would not permit other than a fairly subjective determination of outcomes. We decided that a presentation of the assembled empirical data, and our interpretations of it for the North

Pacific, would serve several useful purposes. First, it would summarize what is presently known about multiple use conflicts in the North Pacific. Second, it would identify areas for useful research on multiple use conflicts in the region. Third, it would move comprehensive study of multiple use conflicts away from the hypothetical realm where it has languished for some time because of the difficulty of performing the empirical work. Fourth, it could perhaps assist others by providing a base on which to improve. We intend to continue to pursue management of multiple use conflicts, with increased assistance from colleagues in Canada, Japan, and other North Pacific nations.

We turn now to an examination of multiple use conflicts in the North Pacific through the consideration of offshore oil development, marine pollution, and other uses subject to multiple use conflicts in that area. For each multiple use conflict area, we provide as much information according to the previously outlined categories as we are able, given the limits of the data. To avoid burdening the reader with an avalanche of seemingly unrelated data, we provide interpretations of the interrelationships as we see them. The concluding observations are our best assessment of the nature of multiple use conflicts in the North Pacific at the present time.

## OFFSHORE OIL DEVELOPMENT

Although there has been considerable speculation about the potential for offshore oil production from the continental shelf areas of nations surrounding the North Pacific, not much development has occurred. The earliest commercial oil production from offshore areas in the region took place in the United States off the southern California coast in 1896. Since 1964, Cook Inlet in Alaska has produced commercial quantities of oil.[4] Japan has had offshore production from a number of small fields since the mid-1950s, and production from the Aga-Oki field offshore from Niigata began in 1976. The People's Republic of China (PRC) began producing offshore oil in 1975 from the Gulf of Po Hai. In each case, this production is basically an extension offshore of preexisting onshore production activity. The limited areas of current production belie the intensive exploration that has in fact taken place in the area.

The modern era of exploration for offshore oil deposits began in earnest in the early 1960s in most areas of the North Pacific. For nations with onshore production, the move offshore in the 1960s was in response to scarce domestic reserves, the increasing political and economic sensitivity to oil supply worldwide, and the rapidly improving technical capability to exploit deep-water offshore areas. Continued increases in price on the world market also provided greater incentive to discover offshore deposits.[5]

The following section describes the attempts to develop offshore oil resources in the North Pacific on a nation-by-nation basis and examines the existing and potential conflicts with other uses in the area. Conflicts arising from competition for marine space are presented here; conflicts associated with oil-generated pollution of marine areas are examined in another section of this chapter.

## Canada

Canada's continental shelf off British Columbia extends an average of only 20 miles offshore, and the maximum width of the continental margin in that area is 120 miles.[6] The sedimentary basins that could contain oil deposits on the west coast of Canada are small and geologically complex, making exploration difficult.[7] With respect to environmental conditions affecting offshore oil operations, some of the area is protected from storms by Vancouver Island and the Queen Charlotte Islands, but much of it is exposed to severe wind and sea conditions. The coastline of British Columbia remains ice-free all year.

Seismic exploration of the offshore areas in British Columbia began in 1960, and fourteen wells were drilled off that coast between 1967 and 1969 by Royal Dutch Shell. The drilling rigs were placed in water depths ranging from 25 to 185 meters and holes were drilled to depths varying between 2,550 and 5,220 meters.[8] None of the test holes showed evidence of oil in commercial quantities. Gas shows were noted in the Georgia Basin area but they were not of commercial significance.[9] All of the holes were plugged and abandoned by the end of 1969.[10] Richfield Oil Corporation has drilled six test wells on the Queen Charlotte Islands but they, too, showed little promise.[11]

Most of the Canadian oil exploration efforts have taken place on the East Coast and in the Canadian Arctic instead of the North Pacific, as is apparent in table 14.1. A moratorium on exploration for oil on the west coast of Canada was imposed by the federal government in 1972.[12] The leases held by Royal Dutch Shell were purchased by Chevron, and it appears that the company would like to drill in the area on the basis of new geologic information and interpretations. There are some indications of interest in resuming oil exploration on the

TABLE 14.1

CANADIAN GOVERNMENT OFFSHORE HYDROCARBON EXPLORATION

| | West Coast | | All Canada | |
|---|---|---|---|---|
| Year | Permits issued | Leased area (km$^2$) | Permits issued | Leased area (km$^2$) |
| 1960 | 20 | 4,602 | 32 | 9,242 |
| 1961 | 171 | 51,100 | 171 | 51,100 |
| 1962 | 2 | 180 | 34 | 7,727 |
| 1963 | 10 | 2,696 | 255 | 91,751 |
| 1964 | 77 | 17,077 | 1,317 | 391,347 |
| 1965 | 30 | 4,030 | 351 | 109,590 |
| 1966 | 9 | 1,662 | 547 | 155,780 |
| 1967 | 13 | 2,259 | 385 | 110,054 |
| 1968 | 23 | 3,624 | 1,500 | 400,542 |
| 1969 | 5 | 1,325 | 1,275 | 351,774 |
| 1970 | 0 | - | 395 | 90,434 |
| 1971 | 40 | 11,405 | 525 | 162,030 |
| 1972 | Moratorium on West Coast lease sales. | | | |

Source: After Barry G. Buzan and Danford W. Middlemiss, "Canadian Foreign Policy and the Exploitation of the Seabed," in Barbara Johnson and Mark W. Zacher, eds., *Canadian Foreign Policy and the Law of the Sea* (Vancouver B.C.: University of British Columbia Press, 1977), p. 53, quoting, Resource and Conservation Branch, Dept. of Energy, Mines and Resources.

West Coast by the Provincial government, but most of the Canadian drilling and exploration activity has now shifted to the Labrador shelf, the Arctic Islands, and the Mackenzie Delta.[13] Thus, the future of new offshore exploration in British Columbia appears uncertain.

No references to multiple use conflicts between oil exploration and fishing or marine transportation interests have been found for the short period of activity on the British Columbia shelf. From currently available information, the likelihood of multiple use conflicts from future exploration and production is rather low.

Negotiations on the marine boundaries between Canada and the United States, in the Dixon Entrance area and the Strait of Juan de Fuca, do not involve oil questions, although these boundary areas are indirectly affected by the negotiations taking place on the East Coast of the continent and in the Arctic.[14]

## Democratic People's Republic of Korea (DPRK)

No production of oil, either onshore or offshore, is known in DPRK. Until late 1977, that country had not indicated an interest in obtaining access to oil development technology through purchase or joint operations with foreign companies. In December 1977, DPRK departed from its policy of self-reliance and signed a protocol with Asia Exploration Consultants of Singapore for an offshore oil exploration package, ranging from seismic surveys to eventual oil drilling operations. The most likely area for beginning operations would be in the Gulf of Korea on the DPRK west coast, adjacent to where the People's Republic of China (PRC) has identified promising geological formations.[15]

## Japan

The continental shelf on the eastern or Pacific coast of Japan is quite narrow. Although the western shelf, in the Sea of Japan, is somewhat broader, it still offers only a limited area for petroleum-bearing strata. In the southeast, along the Ryukyu Island arc and Okinawa prefecture, as well as between Japan and the Republic of Korea, there is a broad continental shelf.[16] Major sedimentary basins are found off Hokkaido, east and west coasts of northern Honshu Island, and southwest of Kyushu Island. The continental shelf and margin to a depth of 3,000 meters surrounding Japan encompasses 440,000 nm$^2$; most of it has been leased by Japanese oil companies on a first-come, first-served basis.[17]

Japanese offshore development takes place under severe weather conditions, since typhoons rake the southern parts of the islands, and sea swell and fog hamper the installation of platforms and pipelines. Earthquakes are a direct design consideration for all offshore facilities, and their side effects (submarine landslides and tsunami) also require special planning. Sea ice and drifting ice in the waters around the island of Hokkaido pose a serious problem for oil rigs and pipelines in shallow waters.[18]

In 1880, an artificial island was used in Amaze, Niigata Prefecture, to test for oil offshore but apparently did not lead to production. Cable drilling was tried at Michikawa, Akita Prefecture, in 1952 but extensive offshore surveys did not begin until the first five-year plan of the Ministry of International Trade and Industry was implemented in 1956. A total of 51 wells were drilled off Akita and Niigata prefectures in 1958 but the lack of significant results prompted a move toward overseas development rather than domestic development. Small amounts of oil were produced from offshore wells in the Kubiki, Tsuchizaki-Oki, Fukura, Higashi-Niigata, and Sarukawa fields in the mid-to-late 1950s. Exploration of the Japanese continental shelf resumed in the mid-1960s. After the construction of a new semisubmersible drilling rig in 1971, some 43 wells were drilled and, of these wildcat wells, 9 found oil in commercial quantities. Drilling took place off Niigata (16 wells), Akita (6 wells), Yamagata (1 well), Aga (9 wells), San'in and Goto (8 wells), Joban (9 wells), Kyushu (2 wells), and Okinawa (1 well).[19]

The Aga-Oki field, 11 kilometers offshore from Niigata in 80 meters of water, was discovered in 1972. In 1976, it went into production of oil and natural gas at a rate of 2,200 metric tons per day of oil,[20] with estimated reserves of 1.3 million metric tons of ultimately recoverable resources.[21] In 1977, the Hidaka field south of Hokkaido on the Pacific side showed evidence of gas and oil and constituted the first positive indication that commercial quantities of hydrocarbon resources may exist off Hokkaido.[22] The Joban field, 25 miles off the Pacific side of Honshu Island, near Sendai, showed oil but was not considered to be of commercial significance.[23]

The most promising area for new offshore production appears to be in the shelf area south of Japan and the Republic of Korea (ROK). This area was largely unassessed, except possibly by private oil firms, until the Committee for Coordination of Joint Prospecting for Mineral Resources in Asian Offshore Areas (CCOP) initiated a study of the area in 1968. The report of the CCOP study, published in 1969, touched off a rush of claims to the continental shelf of the area by coastal nations.[24]

Conflicting claims for the seabed in the East China Sea exist between Japan and ROK, Japan and Taiwan, and all three of these claimants and the PRC. The PRC claim, which overlaps the claims of other nations in the area, has never been officially specified geographically but is based on the natural prolongation of the continental shelf eastward of the PRC. Japan and ROK agreed on a joint development plan for part of the disputed area in 1974, but Japan delayed its ratification until 1978. Exploratory activities commenced in that area in 1979 and two test holes are expected to be drilled in April 1980.[25] The most recent estimate of the oil potential in the joint exploitation area are 170–260 (Japan), and 320 (ROK) million metric tons of recoverable crude oil.[26] A Japan–USSR joint venture off Sakhalin Island is discussed below.

Overall, the present contribution of domestically produced offshore oil to national consumption in Japan is negligible and prospects for offshore oil on the continental shelves of Honshu and Hokkaido islands do not appear to promise substantial reserves of oil, but could yield several small fields. The joint ROK–Japan development area appears to offer a high probability of finding oil but production is unlikely before the mid-1980s.

Fisheries and aquaculture interests in Japan are extremely suspicious of efforts to develop offshore oil production. Their considerable political influence, organization in local and national federations, and possession of virtual property rights in fisheries in specified areas make fisheries a potent adversary of offshore oil development. Despite the fact that the areas occupied by offshore production facilities at the present time are small and will remain small (even if substantial finds are made), compensation paid to fishing interests by oil companies is substantial. There have been many cases where drilling plans were delayed or cancelled because of the problems of negotiating satisfactory compensation with fishing interests.[27]

## People's Republic of China (PRC)

Considerable hydrocarbon reserves exist in the People's Republic of China. Total proved reserves are estimated to be 2,730 million metric tons,[28] although estimates as high as 13,700 million metric tons of oil have been made.[29] Offshore ultimately recoverable reserves are estimated to total 4,100 million metric tons for all PRC coastal areas, and a substantial portion of these areas are north of 30° N latitude.[30] The continental shelf claimed by the PRC in the North Pacific area, encompassing the Po Hai, Yellow Sea, Wenchow, and Taiwan basins is thought to contain considerable amounts of recoverable reserves of oil. The political boundaries in those areas, except the Po Hai Gulf, are under dispute at the present time and preclude development on the outer areas of the shelf. Still, the consensus appears to be that "these areas collectively constitute one of the most promising of the unexplored offshore regions of the world."[31] Offshore drilling in the East China Sea area is restricted to the April–July period due to heavy winter gales and summer typhoons.[32] Wave heights in the Yellow Sea and Gulf of Po Hai areas indicate that environmental conditions are relatively good for drilling activities.[33]

The incentive for the PRC to develop offshore oil rather than onshore reserves is related to the fact that (1) its continental shelf area offers a fairly shallow, easily worked area; (2) offshore oil basins are close to domestic demand centers and transportation for export; and (3) offshore areas are distant from the disputed Soviet–PRC boundary.[34] PRC exploration for oil in the offshore areas began in the late 1950s. In 1968, the first offshore oil strike was made from a drilling barge station in the Gulf of Po Hai in 100 ft of water. Japan is reported to have supplied technical advice and equipment.[35] Exploratory drilling was started in 1973 about 15 miles off Tientsin and oil was discovered in 1974, using a jack-up type drilling rig purchased from Japan. By 1974, PRC, under its "self-reliance" policy, claimed the construction and operation of its own drilling rig. A catamaran-type drill ship was constructed and used to drill a well in the southern part of the Yellow Sea in 1974. As of 1977, the PRC did not possess any semisubmersibles suitable for the kind of weather and sea conditions prevailing in areas outside the Gulf of Po Hai. In the Gulf of Po Hai, 82 wells had been drilled as of 1978, of which 22 were declared to be of commercial quality, yielding an average of 548 metric tons of oil per day.[36]

The policy of the Four Modernizations, which supplanted the policy of self-reliance about 1977, has led to an encouragement of foreign participation in the development of offshore areas in China.[37] The Japan National Oil Corporation reached basic agreement with the PRC on exploration and development of oil in the southern part of the Gulf of Po Hai in August 1979. The agreement provided for Japan to invest an estimated $200 million in oil development in the PRC, to be repaid in crude oil in the event of a discovery of commercial oil deposits.[38] Contracts for seismic surveys of the Yellow Sea as far south as Shanghai have been signed with French, American, and British companies.[39] West Germany signed agreements concerning scientific cooperation with the PRC, including joint prospecting for hydrocarbons.[40] It appears that the foreign firms will operate under the following general conditions: the foreign company will bear the costs and risks of seismic and geophysical surveys, promising areas will be offered to the highest bidder, those winning contracts for exploitation will likely receive a 49 percent interest in a joint venture with the Chinese government, and China will do much of the less complex development work to cut costs.[41] In addition, China plans to send thousands of students abroad for technical education, and some of the students will study offshore oil exploration and development technology.[42]

Despite the increase of oil exploration and development in the PRC in the 1970s, no actual reports of multiple use conflicts have surfaced. Multiple use conflicts could increase, for example, if large amounts of oil were exported from the Po Hai Gulf and Yellow Sea regions, depending on the location of the production areas relative to tanker and other shipping routes and fishing areas. With the increased cooperation between the PRC and western oil companies, it is possible that more information on multiple use impacts in that area may become available.

## Republic of Korea (ROK)

The ROK has oil potential in the basins on the continental shelf surrounding the peninsula but little development has taken place. The shelf is fairly shallow and wide except in the strait between the ROK and Japan and along the east coast, where the shelf is narrow. Prospecting for oil began in 1967 under the programs of the Committee for Coordination of Joint Prospecting for Mineral Resources in Asian Offshore Areas (CCOP).[43] Promising areas on the ROK continental shelf were leased to various western oil companies beginning in 1969. Oil shows in the drilling area off Pohang were found in 1975 but are apparently not of commercial quantity.[44] Test holes near the shore in the Yellow Sea off the ROK have been dry.[45]

The outward boundaries of all the ROK leases in the Yellow and East China seas are disputed by the PRC. The boundaries between the ROK and the DPRK are also extremely sensitive. The overlap between the ROK and Japanese claims is subject to the joint development agreement previously mentioned. Evidence of the PRC opposition to ROK claims can be seen in two examples. Exploration of lease sites off the ROK in the Yellow Sea in 1971 was interrupted by fishing vessels from the PRC which reportedly cut the floating tracer cables used in seismic tests.[46] When ROK-authorized exploratory drilling operations took place in 1973, PRC gunboats appeared in the vicinity of the operations, and the PRC officially denounced the drilling activity. The American oil companies that were involved in the incidents were cautioned by the United States government not to force the issue.

Coastal fisheries operations and shipping are important to the ROK, but it is not known to what extent fishing interests have been affected by offshore oil exploration activities. At the present stage, there appears to be little concern over fisheries except in the joint development area with Japan. There, the fisheries relationships with Japan have been extremely sensitive, although they have been considerably better since the signing of the fishing agreement for the East China Sea by the two countries in 1965. Certainly, the value of fisheries and the estimated value of oil production are both significant. The use of the area by both fisheries and oil development would not be expected to be impossible, based on experience in other areas outside the region where oil development and fishing coexist. So far, fisheries and oil development discussions appear to have occurred in separate forums, and no obvious mechanism exists whereby the interests of the two can be expressed and negotiated. On the Japanese domestic front, oil and fishing interests are virtually in adversary positions and there was significant opposition to Japanese ratification of the joint ROK−Japan development agreement by fishing interests.[47] Without knowing more about where prospective exploration and production platforms will be located, it is unrealistic to attempt to assess the impact of oil development on fishing and ship routing in the East China Sea.

## USSR

The Soviet Union has extensive areas of continental shelf in the western Bering Sea, Okhotsk Sea, and northern Sea of Japan. Potential offshore oil-bearing stratigraphic basins include Sakhalin Island, the northeastern Okhotsk Sea, and the western Bering Sea. While some parts of these areas are relatively shallow, they are subject to severe winter weather; icing conditions exist as much as six months of the year in certain areas. Exploration of onshore areas in the Soviet Far East has yielded small amounts of oil in the northern Sakhalin Island area, where production began in 1929. The production from the Far East represents only a small proportion of the total Soviet Union production and none of it is from offshore areas.[48]

The Soviet Union lags somewhat behind other developed nations in terms of offshore oil production technology. Only 1.6 percent of the total Soviet oil production and 3 percent of its natural gas production is derived offshore compared with a world average of 20 percent from offshore areas.[49] The failure of the Soviet's offshore effort to accomplish its technological goals has been subject to internal criticism, the latest round of controversy coming over delays in the Soviet jack-up rig program. By 1979, no Soviet semisubmersible drilling rigs were in service.[50]

The move offshore in the Northwest Pacific by the Soviet Union began in 1971, when slant drilling from onshore areas of the northern Sakhalin Basin tapped offshore deposits. Japan and the Soviet Union entered into an agreement at that time for a joint offshore development project using Japanese equipment and financing.[51] The agreement provides that Japan receive a half-share of any oil production in repayment of the loan, and a similar amount of oil on favorable terms of purchase for several years after repayment. The other half-share is retained by the Soviet Union.[52]

On October 12, 1977, participants in the joint project announced the discovery of four oil reservoirs at a depth of from 1,400−2,200 meters six kilometers offshore from the town of Okha. Drilling was suspended at that time due to the severe climatic conditions accompanying the onslaught of winter. Drilling resumed in June 1978 to determine the commercial feasibility of the discovery.[53] A major oil discovery was reported for the northern Sakhalin offshore area in September 1979.[54]

It is difficult to predict the Soviet interest in developing the offshore oil resources of the

Far East, since there are already considerable reserves in areas closer to markets, areas with vastly greater potential, and areas where environmental conditions are not such barriers to operations. In the event that the Sakhalin reserves prove to be substantial, Japan may have a greater interest in further cooperation to develop these resources, since the Soviet Sakhalin area is considerably closer to the Japanese market than current sources of supply in the Middle East and Indonesia. Japan's willingness to cooperate financially and technically will be prejudiced by other opportunities for obtaining oil, such as from PRC, the Japan−ROK joint development area, and the world market. A general worsening of the political climate between the Soviet Union and Japan over the PRC−Japan Treaty, the continued conflict over the return of the Northern Territories, and the dispute over handling of a defecting Soviet pilot and aircraft in 1977 all make short-term prospects for expansion of cooperation in petroleum development improbable. In addition, if the reports of the late 1970s predicting short falls in Soviet petroleum production are accurate, the Soviet Union may be increasingly reluctant to sell oil to Japan.[55]

Present multiple use conflicts involving offshore oil development in the Soviet Union are probably minor because of the limited extent of the activity. Future development of offshore oil appears to be somewhat distant, given the remoteness of the Far East from consumption centers, the difficult operating conditions in the area, and the relatively slow pace of development of offshore oil technology by the Soviet Union. The active offshore development sites are distant from the major marine transportation routes and fishing areas, which would tend to indicate that multiple use conflicts are unlikely between shipping and oil developments.

## United States

Continental shelf areas off the states of Washington, Oregon, and California are generally quite narrow, except in southern California where the shelf extends approximately 170 kilometers offshore. In the state of Alaska, the continental shelf areas are broad in the Gulf of Alaska, along the Alaska Peninsula, and in the eastern Bering Sea. Stratigraphic basins with hydrocarbon potential exist off Washington, Oregon, and northern California, but the only commercially significant areas so far developed are found off southern California. The major stratigraphic basins offshore from Alaska include Cook Inlet, Kodiak Shelf, St. George, Bristol, Norton, Aleutian Shelf, St. Matthew, Navarin, and Zhemchug basins.[56]

Drilling operations in the northern areas, especially in Alaska, are exposed to extreme weather conditions during the fall, winter, and spring. In general, the environmental conditions affecting offshore oil development in the southern California area are relatively favorable, but storms and seismic activity can present problems. The areas in the Gulf of Alaska and the Aleutians are subject to high seismic activity, but those in the Bering Sea appear to be less affected.[57] Sea ice covers the northern Bering Sea and many coastal areas for as much as half of the year. Cook Inlet operations, for example, must contend with nearly 10 meter tides, strong currents, and a hard seabottom—all of which interfere with positioning and anchoring drilling platforms. There is even a continuous hazard from volcanic activities.[58] Extensive surveys of the operating conditions, geology, and biological features of the continental shelf areas of the United States under consideration for leasing have been carried out under the Bureau of Land Management's Outer Continental Shelf (OCS) leasing program.[59]

Production of oil from southern California prior to 1968 was derived from lease sales on state-controlled waters within three miles of shore. The state of Alaska leased areas in Upper Cook Inlet in the late 1950s, which began producing oil and gas offshore in 1964. Since these areas lie within the territorial sea of the United States and are subject therefore to its jurisdiction, they are not further considered in this assessment. In 1963, the area offshore from Santa Barbara, California, became the first West Coast area opened for oil drilling under the OCS Lands Act (1953) governing oil, gas, and other mineral leasing in the waters under federal jurisdiction. Table 14.2 shows the lease history for West Coast areas under the OCS program.

TABLE 14.2

OCS Oil and Gas Lease Sales on the West Coast of the U.S. 1954 − 1979

| Sale date | Adjacent state | No. of leases | Lease area ($km^2$) |
|---|---|---|---|
| 5/14/63 | California | 57 | 1,267 |
| 10/1/64 | Oregon | 74 | 1,722 |
| 10/1/64 | Washington | 27 | 629 |
| 12/15/66 | California | 1 | 8 |
| 2/6/68 | California | 71 | 1,470 |
| 12/11/75 | California | 56 | 1,255 |
| 4/13/77 | Alaska | 75 | 1,656 |
| 10/27/77 | Alaska | 87 | 2,005 |
| 6/29/79 | California | 55 | 1,666 |

Source: Prior to 1975: M. V. Adams, C. B. John, R. F. Kelly, A. E. LaPointe, and R. W. Meurer, *Mineral Resource Management of the Outer Continental Shelf*, Geological Survey Circular 720 (Washington, D.C.: U.S. Geological Survey, 1975), p. 3; 1975 and following: personal communication, OCS Program Office.

In 1964, leases were offered on the continental shelves of Washington and Oregon, but no discoveries of commercial importance were made. Leases were offered off California again in 1966 and 1968. Production of oil and gas from the Santa Barbara field began in 1968. A blowout in that field in January 1969 brought a 7-year moratorium on federal and state drilling in that area.[60] By the late 1970s, drilling in California had resumed in areas such as the Hondo Field and the San Pedro Field, and production is anticipated in 1980 from Santa Ynez, Port Hueneme, Santa Clara, Pitas Point, and the San Pedro Beta fields.[61] In 1977, the Lower Cook Inlet OCS lease sales were carried out, and another area was let in California in 1979.

Oil and gas production statistics from the Alaskan and Californian continental shelves are shown in table 14.3. All offshore production in Alaska and about 90 percent of the California production came from state-lease areas. Both Alaska and California showed peak production in the early 1970s, with a gradual decline in production of both oil and gas thereafter.

TABLE 14.3

U.S. Offshore Production of Oil and Gas in the North Pacific

| | Offshore oil | | | | | | Offshore gas | | | | | |
| | Alaska | | | California | | | Alaska | | | California | | |
| | Production (mt) | Percent state | Percent OCS | Production (mt) | Percent state | Percent OCS | Production | Percent state | Percent OCS | Production | Percent state | Percent OCS |
|---|---|---|---|---|---|---|---|---|---|---|---|---|
| Prior to 1969 | 9,096 | 100 | — | 139,322 | 100[a] | — | 954 | 100 | — | 8,486 | 100[a] | — |
| 1969 | 8,149 | 100 | — | 13,081 | 90 | 10 | 1,247 | 100 | — | 2,303 | 94 | 6 |
| 1970 | 9,333 | 100 | — | 14,188 | 76 | 24 | 2,982 | 100 | — | 2,017 | 83 | 17 |
| 1971 | 9,047 | 100 | — | 13,839 | 69 | 31 | 3,542 | 100 | — | 1,713 | 74 | 26 |
| 1972 | 8,596 | 100 | — | 12,982 | 76 | 24 | 3,188 | 100 | — | 1,269 | 78 | 22 |
| 1973 | 8,425 | 100 | — | 12,139 | 79 | 21 | 3,104 | 100 | — | 1,064 | 81 | 19 |
| 1974 | 8,142 | 100 | — | 11,426 | 80 | 20 | 3,167 | 100 | — | 1,024 | 80 | 20 |
| 1975 | 8,127 | 100 | — | 10,845 | 81 | 19 | 3,208 | 100 | — | 830 | 80 | 20 |
| 1976 | 7,547 | 100 | — | 9,612 | 80 | 20 | 3,168 | 100 | — | 679 | 80 | 20 |
| 1977 | 6,901 | 100 | — | 8,235 | 80 | 20 | 3,204 | 100 | — | 751 | 72 | 28 |
| 1978 | 6,250 | 100 | — | 7,762 | 80 | 20 | 3,147 | 100 | — | 522 | 72 | 28 |

Source: Production values for Alaska from Alaska Oil and Gas Conservation Commission, personal communication, August 2, 1979; all percentage values for oil and gas and production values for California prior to 1974 from M. V. Adams, C. B. John, R. F. Kelly, A. E. LaPointe, and R. Meurer, *Mineral Research Management of the Outer Continental Shelf*, Geological Survey Circular 720 (Washington, D.C.: U.S. Geological Survey, 1975); and values 1974–1978 from California Dept. of Conservation, personal communications.

Note: Conversion factors used in preparing this table are: 7.3 barrels equal one metric ton and 35.3147 cubic feet equal one cubic meter. Data for the United States west coast offshore in this table differ slightly from table 14.5 due to use of different sources.

[a]Two percent of the 1968 California offshore oil production and one percent of the 1968 California offshore gas production came from the federal OCS area.

Federal OCS lease sales are scheduled for the Gulf of Alaska (1980), Cook Inlet (1981), central and northern California (1981), St. George Basin (1982), Norton Basin (1982), Kodiak Shelf (1983), southern California (1983), northern Aleutian Shelf (1983), central and northern California (1984), and Navarin Basin (1985). Leasing programs for other basins are not scheduled at this date. A 1979 Bureau of Land Management survey of the oil industry, designed to obtain industry evaluations of the offshore areas that showed the greatest potential oil resources, yielded the results shown in table 14.4.

The singular lack of success in exploratory drilling in the Gulf of Alaska (since the lease sale in 1977) has dampened industry enthusiasm for that area, which was ranked first in 1975.[62] The St. George Basin, not separately identified in 1975, was ranked high in 1979. Santa Barbara was rated slightly higher in 1979 than in 1975, and Cook Inlet dropped slightly lower; the areas off Washington, Oregon, and northern California remained at the bottom of the rankings. The ranking of northern California may change in light of the USGS report of high concentrations of hydrocarbons in that area found during prelease drilling.[63] Production from the Santa Barbara and Upper Cook Inlet areas will probably increase with the addition of platforms in new areas.

TABLE 14.4

RANKING OF UNITED STATES OCS AREAS BY PETROLEUM RESOURCE POTENTIAL

| Resource Potential | | Interest in Exploration |
|---|---|---|
| Industry | Geological Survey | Industry |
| 1. Central & West Gulf | Central & West Gulf | Central & West Gulf |
| 2. Beaufort Sea | Chukchi | *Santa Barbara |
| *3. Santa Barbara | Beaufort | Beaufort Sea |
| 4. Mid-Atlantic | Mid-Atlantic | *Bristol Basin |
| *5. St. George Basin | *St. George Basin | North Atlantic |
| *6. Bristol Basin | *Santa Barbara | Mid-Atlantic |
| *7. Southern California | *Eastern Gulf of Alaska | *Central & Northern California |
| 8. North Atlantic | North Atlantic | *Southern California |
| *9. Norton Basin | *Cook Inlet | *St. George |
| 10. Chukchi Sea | *Southern California | *Norton |
| *11. Navarin Basin | Eastern Gulf of Mexico | Eastern Gulf of Mexico |
| *12. Central & Northern California | *Bristol Bay Basin | *Navarin |
| 13. Blake Plateau | *Norton | *Cook Inlet |
| 14. Hope Basin | *Navarin | Hope Basin |
| 15. Eastern Gulf of Mexico | South Atlantic | Blake Plateau |
| *16. Cook Inlet | *Northern California | *Gulf of Alaska |
| *17. Gulf of Alaska | Blake Plateau | Chukchi Sea |
| 18. South Atlantic | *Kodiak | South Atlantic |
| *19. Kodiak | Hope | *Washington-Oregon |
| *20. Washington-Oregon | *Washington-Oregon | Florida Straits |
| *21. Southern Aleutian | *Aleutian Shelf | *Kodiak Shelf |
| 22. Florida Straits | Florida Straits | *South Aleutian |

Source: Bureau of Land Management, Federal OCS Program Coordinator for the Five-Year Leasing Program, November 1979.

*Northeast Pacific OCS Areas

Since it generally takes from 1.5 to 4.5 years after a lease sale is made until oil is discovered, it can be estimated that it would take from 4 to 11 years after the sale to attain initial production in the proposed lease sales in Alaska.[64] This suggests that new production would not be expected (at the earliest) until the mid-1980s from Lower Cook Inlet, assuming that discoveries of commercial quantities of oil are made. Production from other scheduled areas would occur commensurately later. No discoveries were made in Lower Cook Inlet in 1977 or 1978,[65] and the Gulf of Alaska is beginning to look less promising.[66] It appears, therefore, that new exploration and production in offshore areas on the west coast of the United States will not lead to a dramatic increase in multiple use interactions in the near future.

Fishing interests in the Prince William Sound area (through which the tankers from the Port of Valdez must pass carrying crude oil from the North Slope pipeline) have attempted to assure that tanker traffic is made as safe as possible in that area by advocating double hulls for the tankers and full radar coverage of their movements. Other fishing interests in Alaska have opposed the Gulf of Alaska lease sale and were partially responsible for the delay of the sale from the original date in 1976 to 1977, as well as the deletion of some biologically sensitive tracts. The Kodiak Island lease sale scheduled for 1980 poses an extremely sensitive question for fisheries, since high-value fisheries for crab and shrimp are located in that area. In addition to concern for the hazard to fixed gear (like crab pots) due to movements of rig tenders, tankers, and tug boats, there is concern that the semisubmersible drilling rigs that will be used in the area will cause a loss of space and interference with fishing, since each rig and its anchor system occupies an area two miles in diameter.[67]

Some conflicts have already surfaced between the salmon fishing interests in Lower Cook Inlet and the OCS leasing program; prior to that there were conflicts over oil leasing and fishing in Kachemak Bay, in state waters.[68] In 1977 Alaska was forced to buy back 17 state lease tracts in Kachemak Bay because that area is considered a prime spawning area for crab and shrimp.[69] The Lower Cook Inlet sale was delayed and finally modified to adjust to salmon fishing interests, who contended that the presence of oil rigs near the traditional routes followed by migrating salmon would confuse the fish or deter them from entering into the area entirely and result in the loss of an important commercial and recreational fishery.

On the basis of mere proximity to fish stock migrations and major fishing areas, all the main sedimentary basins off Alaska, with the possible exception of Norton Basin, are sites of important domestic and foreign fisheries. Comparison of a computer graphic representation of the distribution of the total fish catch in the eastern Bering Sea (figure 14.2) with the location of sedimentary basins, indicates that the potential for interactions will be great, especially for Bristol Basin and St. George Basin. This raises important questions of how to accommodate fishing interests, which have traditionally used the area and have a considerable stake in the maintenance of a healthy fishery, with offshore oil development.

This is exactly the question being asked with respect to the St. George Basin lease sale. In 1979, the St. George Basin lease sale in the eastern Bering Sea west of Unimak Island, which had been scheduled for 1985, was rescheduled to 1982, which meant that the OCS studies, which were to be completed in 1983, had to be speeded up or not completed. This is

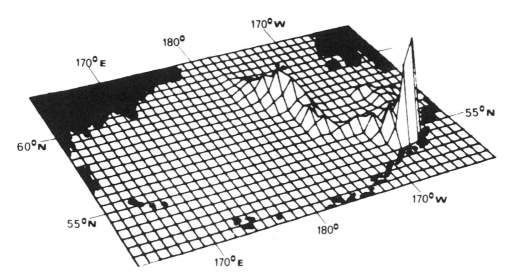

Fig. 14.2. *General Catch Distribution of Groundfish in the Eastern Bering Sea.* Source: Low Lee Low, *Status of Major Demersal Fishing Resources of the Northwestern Pacific: Bering Sea and Aleutian Islands,* processed report (Seattle: Northwest and Alaska Fisheries Center, April 1976), p. 101.

of concern to fishing interests since it is a highly productive crab, halibut, and groundfish fishing area. In addition, the proposed tract includes fur seal and seabird habitats on the Pribilof Islands, a potential shrimp fishery, the wintering grounds for Bering Sea herring, and an area through which the Bristol Bay salmon migrates. The North Pacific Fishery Management Council staff has recommended that the St. George lease sale be postponed indefinitely or considerably modified.[70]

Based on the experience from other areas in the United States and elsewhere, obstructions to navigation, loss of fishing space, subsurface obstructions and debris, installation of pipelines, and onshore impacts associated with offshore oil development do not totally exclude fisheries operations.[71] They do, however, pose some constraints on fisheries operations but these do not appear to impose extreme costs to fishermen under normal circumstances. Past and present levels of interaction between offshore exploration and production and fisheries interests have been relatively minor, primarily due to the limited extent of offshore operations and fishing in those areas, but also due (in many cases) to the ability of fisheries to adjust to oil industry activities. To the extent that costs have been imposed by one use in adjusting to another, it is reasonable to consider some form of compensation for the use that is required to adjust.

Such a compensatory system has been partially provided for in legislation amending the OCS Lands Act in 1978. This Act includes provision of a one million dollar fund to be administered by the Secretary of Commerce to compensate fishermen for any loss of income, or to compensate for damages to vessels or gear resulting from offshore oil development when it is not possible to identify the party, such as an oil company, that is responsible for the damage. The fund will be established by imposing a fee of up to $5,000 on each lessee or permittee in the OCS lease area. In addition, a three-cent per barrel tax on OCS oil production provides revenue for another fund, which would be used for compensating oil spill damages.[72] The compensation scheme is not entirely satisfactory to the fishing industry because, under circumstances where the financially liable party can be identified, the fisherman will have to resort to expensive and time-consuming litigation to recover damages.[73]

Oil exploration activity has conflicted with fishing activity in Alaskan coastal waters where king and tanner crab fishing pots are numerous. In some of these areas, seismic exploration using special cables as much as four inches thick and 1½ miles long has resulted in the displacement of pots and damage to (and loss of) marker buoys. In addition, in some areas crab pot lines and buoys have been damaged by tugs and workboats attending oil development operations.[74] No records concerning the number of such incidents have been discovered, so it is difficult to assess the significance of this reported conflict.

Off southern California, some 20 abandoned wellheads present obstacles to trawlers operating in the area.[75] One wellhead, which projected about 7 meters above the seafloor, was identified by fishermen in the area as causing gear losses for at least as many as five fishing vessels. Oil companies, in cooperation with Sea Grant extension agents and the Bureau of Land Management, removed the offending wellhead using a self-propelled, semisubmersible drilling rig at a cost estimated to be nearly one-half million dollars. The locations of the 19 other wellheads have been marked on charts and made available to fishermen, but reports of problems with three wellheads off Point Hueneme have been made, which suggests that information on wellhead location is insufficient as a means of eliminating conflict. Current OCS regulations do not require that wellheads be kept on leased areas retained by oil companies, so it does not appear that the number of these obstructions will increase. Where it is possible to identify the financially-liable company, a procedure has been established for processing damage claims by fishermen in federal offshore waters.

The Hondo platform in the Santa Ynez area of the Santa Barbara region is facing strict regulations with respect to southern California air quality standards and a requirement that a permit be obtained from the U.S. Environmental Protection Agency certifying compliance with federal air quality standards in OCS areas.[76] Local environmental and civic groups in northern California have requested that the U.S. Department of Interior halt preparation for the sale scheduled in that area in 1981 because in their opinion the low undiscovered recoverable reserve estimates (68.5 million metric tons worth $6.5 billion) do not justify the expense of an environmental impact statement.[77] These examples point to the need for developing some means of fact finding and conflict resolution on a national basis that takes into consideration the concern placed on perceived and actual environmental impacts of offshore oil development.

It appears that the northbound and southbound shipping lanes largely avoid the currently leased areas in the Santa Barbara area. Shipping lanes do not directly traverse areas of present production in the southern California area, although the designated lanes are relatively close to oil leasing activity.[78] It is not inconceivable that vessels that suffer navigation problems, or that lose control of steering or power, could collide with plaforms in the southern California area. Existing sources reviewing the impacts of oil development on other uses in the area do not cite any such incidents.[79]

## Summary of Oil Development

Table 14.5 summarizes production statistics for offshore areas in the North Pacific and compares them with world production, both in terms of total and offshore production. In 1979, only Japan, PRC, and the United States had offshore production of oil in the North Pacific; the vast majority of the production came from the United States. Offshore production from the North Pacific declined by about one-third between 1970 and 1978 and accounted for only one-half of one percent of the total world production, and 2.7 percent of the total world offshore production in 1977. At the price of $25 per barrel, this production was worth approximately 2.8 billion dollars at the 1977 level of production. Thus, offshore oil can be seen to be an extremely valuable resource extracted from several extremely limited areas. While specific data on the value of fisheries are not available for each area of offshore production, it is certain that the value of oil exceeds the annual value of fish caught in those areas. Price trends in both fisheries and oil are upward but not adequately known for predictive purposes. Estimates of oil reserves by offshore area in the North Pacific are not comparable and do not provide a sufficient basis for any observations on the total value of the oil resource.[80]

The short-term potential for increased offshore exploration and development activity is greatest in the areas off the northern coast of PRC, the joint Japan–ROK development area, and coastal areas of Alaska and southern California. Some potential conflicts may exist for the joint Japan–USSR development site in northern Sakhalin. The coastlines of British Columbia, Washington, Oregon, and northern California appear to hold slight promise of offshore activity in the foreseeable future. Similarly, the basins far offshore in the eastern and western Bering Sea will probably not be developed due to their remoteness from shore, depth of water, and environmental constraints, such as heavy sea ice. The disputes over jurisdiction in the Yellow Sea preclude developments in the central part of that area at the present time. Offshore areas of the ROK have been explored without significant success.

The economics of offshore oil development in the North Pacific region are extremely sensitive to alternative sources of supply and other developments on the world market. No drilling or exploration project will likely be attempted unless anticipated results compare favorably with other opportunities elsewhere in the world. In terms of deep-water offshore areas, none in the North Pacific has been designated as significant compared to other available areas worldwide.[81]

Interactions between offshore oil development and fisheries have surfaced in Japan and the United States. To a large extent, it might be argued that the conflicts are largely due to the failure of offshore oil development interests to adequately consider fishing interests in the areas in which they are operating or propose to operate, and to the perception by fishing interests that any oil developments would have major adverse consequences for them. When

## TABLE 14.5

## PRODUCTION OF OFFSHORE OIL AND GAS IN THE NORTH PACIFIC

### OIL (10³ MT) GAS (10⁶ M³)

| | Prior to 1969 | 1969 | 1970 | 1971 | 1972 | 1973 | 1974 | 1975 | 1976 | 1977 | 1978 |
|---|---|---|---|---|---|---|---|---|---|---|---|
| **World production[1] (Total)** | | | | | | | | | | | |
| Oil | 30,801,000[1,b] | 2,147,400 | 2,359,100 | 2,486,500 | 2,623,800 | 2,858,500 | 2,870,400 | 2,725,500 | 2,949,000 | 3,062,900 | 3,084,000[2,c] |
| Gas | 8,980,430[3,d] | 1,055,460 | 1,155,700 | 1,234,300 | 1,229,400 | 1,281,200 | 1,322,600 | 1,270,000 | 1,333,000 | 1,255,000 | 1,302,000[4] |
| **World production (offshore)** | | | | | | | | | | | |
| Oil | 5,047,000[5,e] | 309,750 | 376,615 | 411,228 | 443,924 | 497,806 | 466,525 | 436,557 | 482,897 | 568,823[3] | 513,465[4] |
| Gas | — | — | 146,650 | 171,735 | 180,866[f] | 179,088 | 176,525[3] | 177,169 | 307,308 | 188,993 | 269,264[6] |
| **North Pacific (offshore)** | | | | | | | | | | | |
| Oil | 148,700 | 21,641 | 23,586 | 22,944 | 21,686 | 20,606 | 19,565 | 18,992 | 17,199 | 15,251 | 14,056[g] |
| Gas | 44,755 | 3,382 | 4,086 | 4,065 | 3,337 | 2,998 | 2,816 | 2,626 | 2,600 | 3,030 | 3,073–3,173[g] |
| **Canada** | | | | | | | | | | | |
| Oil | no production | | | | | | | | | | |
| Gas | | | | | | | | | | | |
| **Democratic People's Republic of Korea** | | | | | | | | | | | |
| Oil | no production | | | | | | | | | | |
| Gas | | | | | | | | | | | |
| **Japan** | | | | | | | | | | | |
| Oil | 756 | 81 | 75 | 55 | 39 | 37 | 35 | 28 | 50 | 123 | 118[7,h] |
| Gas | 1,827 | 82 | 67 | 53 | 36 | 20 | 11 | 7 | 148 | 624 | 566[7,h] |
| **People's Republic of China (PRC)** | | | | | | | | | | | |
| Oil | no production | | | | | | | production started | | | 100–200 |
| Gas | | | | | | | | | | | |
| **Republic of Korea** | | | | | | | | | | | |
| Oil | no production | | | | | | | | | | |
| Gas | | | | | | | | | | | |
| **USSR** | | | | | | | | | | | |
| Oil | no production | | | | | | | | | | |
| Gas | | | | | | | | | | | |
| **USA** | | | | | | | | | | | |
| Oil | 147,984 | 21,560 | 23,511 | 22,889 | 21,647 | 20,569 | 19,530 | 18,964 | 17,149 | 15,128 | 13,938[9,i] |
| Gas | 42,298 | 3,300 | 4,019 | 4,012 | 3,301 | 2,978 | 2,805 | 2,619 | 2,452 | 2,406 | 2,407[9,i] |

Sources:

[1]British Petroleum Co., *Our Industry Petroleum* (London: British Petroleum Co., 1977).

[2]British Petroleum Co. *BP Statistical Review of the World Oil Industry, 1978* (London: British Petroleum Co., 1979), various pages.

[3]American Petroleum Institute. *Basic Petroleum Data Book: Petroleum Industry Statistics* (Washington, D.C.: American Petroleum Institute, 1978).

[4]United Nations. *World Energy Supplies 1973–1978* (New York: United Nations, 1979).

[5]Henry L. Berryhill, Jr., *The Worldwide Search for Petroleum Offshore—A Status Report for the Quarter Century 1947–1972*. U.S. Geological Survey Circular NO. 694 (Washington, D.C.: U.S. Geological Survey, U.S. Department of the Interior, 1974).

[6]*Offshore* (June 20, 1957, June 20, 1979).

[7]Japax and Teihoku Oil Co., quoted in personal communication by Dr. Yasufumi Ishiwada. Executive Director. Japan National Oil Corp., March 11 and April 21, 1980.

[8]A. A. Myerhoff and J. O. Willums, "Petroleum Geology and Industry of the People's Republic of China," *CCOP Technical Bulletin* (December 1976) pp. 101, 103–208; *World Oil* (December 1978). p. 49.

[9]Alaska Oil and Conservation Commission, special computer listing, August 2, 1979; Division of Oil and Gas. Department of Conservation. State of California Resources Agency. *Summary of Operations California Oil Fields*. Annual Report of the State Oil and Gas Supervisor, Sacramento, California. 1968–1977. 1978 (preliminary); personal communication, Tom Dunnaway, Bureau of Land Management. Los Angeles, April 4, 1980.

Notes:

[a]The specific gravity of oil varies from field to field. For this reason, the conversion factors used when converting from barrels to metric tons differs from country to country. The following conversion factors are used in this table: 1) World, Canada, Japan, Republic of Korea, and People's Republic of China production and consumption figures—7.3 barrels per metric ton; 2) USSR production and consumption figures—7.33 barrels per metric ton; 3) USA production and consumption figures—7.35 barrels per metric ton. The 7.3 conversion factor was chosen by the authors. All other conversion factors were suggested in British Petroleum Co., Ltd., *Our Industry Petroleum*. (London: British Petroleum Co., Ltd., 1977). p. 584. Only production from offshore towers, platforms or artificial islands is tabulated here unless otherwise stated.

[b]Excludes natural gas liquids.

[c]Includes natural gas liquids.

[d]Data sources commence in 1950.

[e]Cumulative to the end of 1972.

[f]Data for communist countries not available.

[g]Sum of all succeeding entries in this table.

[h]Produced only from offshore platforms.

[i]Produced from offshore platforms, offshore islands and, in the case of southern California, from shore-based operations using directional drilling.

the Ministry of International Trade and Industry granted oil concessions to Japanese oil companies that covered nearly all the continental shelf in 1972, fishing interests were upset at not having had a voice in the process.[82] A similar situation seems to be developing in an international context in the East China Sea because of the lack of any mechanism for the fishing interests of Japan and ROK to participate in the development of plans for the joint Japan—ROK oil development area. This conclusion may be premature, but no signs point to an emerging consensus on how to adjust these issues at the present time.

Further development of offshore oil is surely going to take place in the next 5—20 years in the North Pacific region in many areas where fisheries exist. This points to the need for governments to seek, at both national and international levels, different means of resolving conflicts or ordering policies to reduce the potential for conflict.

At the present scale and location of offshore development, there does not appear to be significant interference with navigation. In fact, some industry claims are made that the presence of platforms assists in navigation by providing more fixed points of reference. In the Santa Barbara Channel, for instance, the platform support vessels and platforms have "several hundred times" provided communications and other assistance, including rescue service, to commercial and recreational boats.[83]

## MARINE POLLUTION

This section summarizes the main pathways by which pollutants enter the North Pacific, describes the known effects of pollution in the area, and attempts to discern trends regarding levels of pollution. The purpose is to specify what is known about pollution in the North Pacific and to assess the multiple use conflicts caused by pollution. Seven categories of marine pollution are examined: (1) synthetic organic compounds, including DDT and PCB; (2) heavy metals like mercury and cadmium; (3) petroleum; (4) dumping and dredge spoils; (5) radionuclides; (6) nutrients; and (7) litter—plastic in particular.[84] Pollution from thermal effluents, chlorination products like chloroform and bromoform, and microorganisms such as viruses and bacteria are not examined here because their impacts as presently known are local, or sufficient information on their impact in the North Pacific is unavailable.

The use of North Pacific waters as a recipient for deliberate and accidental disposal of waste materials in theory presents a classic case of conflicts among users, since by definition pollution implies that unwanted (and perhaps dangerous) side effects produced by one use are passed on to other uses, especially living resources.[85] The scale of pollution impacts in the North Pacific can conceivably range from effects on global energy, climate, and chemical cycles to the effects of low levels of pollution on the metabolism or reproduction of a specific organism in the limited environment of a tide pool. Unfortunately, very little is known about effects of pollution in the North Pacific as a whole. Even though it is suspected that the oceans play a vital role in climate regulation, which is of enormous importance for terrestrial agriculture, transportation, and other human activities, the linkages, if any, between pollution-induced changes of the ocean and changes in climate have not been elucidated. Similarly, at the organism level, minuscule doses of pollutants have been shown to have lethal effects on marine flora and fauna but little is known about long-term exposure to chronic low levels of pollution.[86]

The generalized impacts of pollution on marine life have been summarized in the following manner:

> Marine life may be damaged by pollution and the consequences of other activities of man in a number of ways: (1) destruction of habitat; (2) acute poisoning by toxic wastes; (3) adverse alteration of water quality; (4) sub-lethal effects of pollutants causing impairment of feeding, growth, migration, resistance to disease and parasites, and interference with reproduction; (5) bacteriological and viral contamination; (6) bio-accumulation of toxic metals and organic substances; and (7) tainting and/or discoloration of the flesh by organic and/or metallic substances.[87]

The environmental conditions that affect pollution impacts in the North Pacific Ocean are extremely diverse. Some generalizations assist in understanding the nature of potential pollution impacts on the marine ecosystems in that area.

1. The great size and volume of the oceanic region suggests that the North Pacific has a large capacity to dilute pollutants. Pollutant inputs, however, are neither evenly distributed nor instantaneously dispersed. Pollution can occur and persist in specific areas near the point of origin, and the otherwise large capacity of the North Pacific to dilute pollution may not be utilized.

2. The complex network of surface currents in the North Pacific transports enormous quantities of water throughout the region and this suggests that pollution could also be carried by the current systems. Plastic litter and, to a lesser extent, tarballs entrained in the Kuroshio Current off Japan can be carried to the west coast of North America. Similarly, surface litter caught in the California Current off the west coast of North America can reach Asia. The time it takes for water to make a complete circuit of the North Pacific is four to six years, and during this time pollutants may be metabolized, settled out, or otherwise removed from the water column. Deep ocean sediments may become the final resting place for many forms of marine pollution.[88]

3. The North Pacific region, as defined in this study, stretches from the near-tropics to the subarctic, and pollution impacts and decomposition rates vary considerably over this range. The impact of an oil spill under winter conditions in the Bering Sea, for instance, can be expected to be significantly different from one in the near-tropical waters off southern Japan.

4. Specific information on site, organism, and environmental conditions based on continuous pollution monitoring programs is necessary for policy decisions, given the diversity of the North Pacific region.

The impacts of various forms of pollution and the environmental conditions under which they occur must be observed and documented if progress is to be made on assessing the need for regional management of pollution problems in the North Pacific. This requires that the ''natural'' or background levels of various polluting substances be monitored over a long period of time and that an understanding be reached concerning the concentration that can be safely present in the marine environment under diverse conditions. Monitoring schemes, however, are not adequate for rapid detection of harmful substances since biological effects often show up only after considerable periods of time have elapsed. Therefore, monitoring schemes must be combined with physiological, biochemical, and chemical studies.[89] In the North Pacific, most available data do not satisfy these criteria and there is a continuing vigorous debate over a variety of pollution problems, like the impact of oil pollution.[90]

Nearly all the monitoring of marine pollution that has been done in the North Pacific has occurred on or near waters over the continental shelf. Deep ocean areas comprising the bulk of the region are underrepresented in monitoring programs. This is hardly surprising, since most of the pollutants enter the marine ecosystem from land-based sources by such media as river runoff, industrial and sewage outfalls, dumping, wind transfer; any associated pollution problems would likely be most acute in the coastal areas. For the North Pacific, a limited amount of information is available from Canada, Japan, and the United States; but data on marine pollution in the DRPK, PRC, ROK, and the Soviet Union are not available at the present time. The low population density of the Soviet Far East and Siberia, and the concomitantly small amount of industrial and agricultural activity in the area, would suggest that pollution inputs would be minor except on a local scale.[91] The Amur River, which drains from the inland industrial region of the Soviet Far East, may carry industrial pollutants into the northern Sea of Japan and southern Okhotsk Sea. The large coastal populations and rapid industrialization of the other countries suggest that the potential is increasing for marine pollution problems, at least in coastal waters.

Pollution monitoring efforts have been established in Japan since the early 1970s and are carried out by the Environmental Agency, the Meteorology Agency, and the Maritime Safety Agency.[92] Japan completed a survey of the distribution of 78 chemicals in waters in and around Japan in 1977 and found that 39 of the chemicals constituted potential risks in some areas.[93] On the basis of these findings, the Environment Agency announced that it would establish a marine environment assessment system in fiscal 1979. Neither Canada nor the United States has a comprehensive pollution monitoring program for marine areas, although both nations have specific monitoring programs for limited coastal and harbor areas where pollution has posed actual problems, and the United States is developing a monitoring plan pursuant to the National Ocean Pollution Research and Development and Monitoring Planning Act of 1978.[94] The U.S. National Marine Fisheries Service, for instance, has established a monitoring system for coastal hydrocarbon levels on the route of the Alaskan oil tankers in the Northeast Pacific.[95] The Bureau of Land Management program to assess the environmental impacts of potential offshore oil developments is providing substantial baseline data on marine ecosystems in prospective lease areas. Other programs by states and local governments, as well as research projects of universities, are providing data on marine pollution in specific areas.

## Synthetic Organic Compounds

Synthetic organics such as PCB and DDT reach the waters of the North Pacific in river runoff as a result of agricultural and silvicultural applications, direct dumping of wastes, and airborne particulates from various sources. The number of compounds that fit into this category is quite large and rapidly increasing. Not all of these compounds reach the marine environment or cause environmental damage. Two that have received the greatest attention are DDT (dichlorodiphenyl trichloroethane) and its metabolites and PCBs (polychlorinated biphenyls). Both are extremely toxic and persistent in the marine environment, and are accumulated in the meat, fatty tissues, and internal organs of filter feeders and predatory fish.

Japan has made the most extensive survey of PCBs in coastal waters of any of the North Pacific nations. Standards have been established in Japan with respect to PCB concentrations in fish for human consumption (3 parts per million [ppm]), in effluent water (less than 0.1 ppm), and in bottom sediments (less than 100 ppm). Osaka Bay, Harima Sound, the Iwakuni waterfront, Beppu Bay, and Aita Bay, all of which are confined bays or nearshore areas, exceeded these amounts.[96] Sale of fish from these areas for human consumption has been prohibited and the industries identified as responsible for the pollution held liable for compensating the fishermen for their foregone catches. Table 14.6 shows the concentrations of PCB in various tissues taken from several species of fish in Tokyo Bay and Seto Inland Sea. The fish taken from industrialized nearshore regions possessed higher concentrations of pollutants than fish taken from the open sea.[97] Still, tuna caught in the Kuroshio Current offshore from Japan were found to have a high PCB content in 1970.[98]

PCB in Canadian commercial fish catches (from both west and east coasts) showed a mean value of 0.07 ppm for groundfish, 0.39 ppm for pelagic-estuarial species, and

TABLE 14.6

PCB Residues in Fish from Tokyo Bay and Seto Inland Sea

| Fish | PCB residues (ppm, wet weight) | | | | |
|---|---|---|---|---|---|
| | Meat | | | | |
| | (dorsal) | | (abdominal) | Liver | Fatty tissue |
| *Tokyo Bay* | | | | | |
| young seabass[a] | 3.4 | | 1.7 | 17 | 120 |
| plaice | 0.1 | | 0.3 | 4.5 | nd |
| goby | — | 0.2 | — | — | 5.6 | — |
| *Seto Inland Sea* | | | | | |
| grey mullet[b] | 1.1 | | 3.9 | 0.7 | 18 |
| young yellowtail[c] | | | | | |
| dead | 6.6 | | 16 | 8.4 | 26 |
| alive | 0.1 | | 0.5 | 0.1 | nd |
| sardine[d] (dead) | — | 1.3 | — | — | 3.7 | — |

Source: R. Watanuki, "PCB Residues in Japan," in Jun Ui, ed., *Polluted Japan (Tokyo, 1972)*, p. 27, quoting the work of Dr. R. Tatsukawa et al., Dept. of Agriculture Chemistry, Ehime University, Matsuyama, Ehime.

[a]*Lateolabrax japonica*

[b]*Mugil cephalus*

[c]*Seriola quinqueradiata*

[d]*Engraulis japonicus*

0.12 ppm for molluscs and crustaceans.[99] In the Northeast Pacific, PCB mean values for euphausiids were 9.2 parts per billion (ppb), for pink shrimp 23 ppb, and for flatfish 23 ppb.[100] The USFDA tolerance level for PCB in fish is 5 ppm and it appears that PCB levels in commercial fish species in the Pacific are substantially below that level.[101]

Monitoring of sewage outfalls in marine areas off southern California showed that municipal waste water was the single largest source contributing PCB to coastal waters in that area. Bottom sediments in the vicinity of the outfalls contained as much as 100 ppm PCB. Marine organisms in the vicinity of the outfalls showed appreciably higher concentrations of PCB than did others farther away, and concentrations in Dover sole sometimes exceeded the allowable standard for food in interstate commerce. Reductions in the estimated amount of PCB discharge by sewage outfalls between 1972 and 1975 did not produce corresponding reductions in PCB concentrations in Dover sole by 1976.[102]

It has been shown that DDT residues in marine phytoplankton in Monterey Bay increased markedly between 1955 and 1969.[103] Monterey Bay values cannot be assumed to reflect the situation for all of southern California, yet it is likely that there was a general increase in the DDT content of marine ecosystems in that area during the same period. Few studies, however, are available to substantiate the trend, although other indicators—such as the declining populations of seabirds like the brown pelican in southern California because of eggshell thinning due to DDT pollution—would support the case.[104] In addition, the relatively high concentrations of DDT found in shearwaters (*Puffinus griseus* and *P. tenuirostrus*), which are normally distributed far offshore from coastal areas, suggests that DDT is widespread in the marine environment.[105]

A study in 1968 of DDT residues in fish in the northeastern Pacific showed values for all fish (0.013−0.223 ppm) which were low relative to the standard of 5 ppm established for fish for human consumption set by the Food and Drug Administration in the United States. Mean values for DDT in Northeast Pacific fish species were 2.7 ppb for euphausiids, 2.4 ppb for pink shrimp, and 10.8 ppb for flatfish—all of which seem to be below the level at which damage is evidenced.[106] Values for fish from areas near the mouth of the Columbia River were considerably higher than the values found further north or south of it, which suggests that runoff from agricultural pesticide applications in the states of Washington and Oregon were responsible.[107] Measurement of DDT concentrations in whole seawater off the mouth of the Columbia and along the west coast of the United States did not show a similar increase, however. Greater concentrations of DDT were observed in waters off southern California than off Washington and Oregon.[108] This discrepancy cannot be explained with available data. The difference serves to point out the complexity of the chemical and biological processes that must be understood to adequately monitor pollution impacts on marine organisms and to promulgate effective regulations.

Harbor seals in southern Puget Sound in Washington State were examined in 1977 and found to contain higher levels of DDT and PCBs in body tissues than harbor seals in northern Puget Sound. Furthermore, PCB levels in the southern area of Puget Sound were among the highest reported for harbor seals worldwide. These levels exceeded those known to influence reproductive success in harbor seal populations in other areas.[109] Study of the

California sea lion (*Zalophus californianus californianus*) in southern California has linked chlorinated hydrocarbons to premature births of sea lion pups.[110]

Photosynthesis and cell division in marine phytoplankton have been observed to suffer deleterious effects at PCB concentrations that exist in some coastal and estuarine areas in the North Pacific, but not at levels found in the open ocean.[111] PCBs in concentrations as low as 1 − 10 ppm may reduce phytoplankton biomass and size, which could lead to interruption of normal marine food webs, increase the number of trophic levels in the ecosystem, and favor jellyfish and similar predators over commercially harvestable species of fish.[112]

The use of synthetic organic compounds like DDT and PCB increased rapidly after World War II, and by the middle 1960s the dangerous side effects of their use was recognized in human and animal populations. Voluntary restrictions on the use of PCBs to enclosed systems were instituted in both Japan and the United States in 1971, and a complete ban on manufacture and use of PCB became effective in the United States in January 1979.[113] DDT was banned for most uses in 1971 by Japan and in 1972 by the United States. Use of substances like eldrin or dieldrin and chlordane or heptachlor have been subjected to regulatory scrutiny in both countries.

It has been concluded that DDT concentrations in estuaries in the United States reached a peak in 1968 and have been declining markedly since 1970.[114] Brown pelicans seem to have recovered their reproductive capacity on the west coast of the United States following the reduction of DDE and other DDT compounds in the marine environment.[115] PCB levels in osprey eggs in the Connecticut−Long Island estuary area on the east coast of the United States have not significantly changed despite the decline in use of DDT products. This suggests that PCB may be more persistent than DDT in the marine environment.[116] In addition, PCB concentrations appear to be unrelated to proximity to land, whereas DDT concentrations seem to decrease with distance from shore.[117]

## Heavy Metals

Heavy metals are borne into the marine environment in the effluent of industrial plants, sewage outfalls, river runoff, and by airborne transport. The heavy metals that have received the greatest amount of attention as pollutants are mercury and cadmium, because of known incidents of human poisoning due to their use. A major study of microconstituents in marine fish populations along the coastline of the United States examined 13 other trace metals (arsenic, selenium, silver, chromium, copper, zinc, nickel, molybdenum, vanadium, manganese, antimony, lead, and tin), in addition to the two named above, as being of potential importance to fisheries.[118] Each of these metals exists naturally in a variety of compounds in the marine environment. This fact complicates analysis of the impacts of metals and compounds that are introduced anthropogenically.

Mean values of mercury, cadmium, and lead for 15 species of Northeast Pacific fish, shellfish and crustacea are presented in table 14.7. The U.S. federal action level for mercury in fish is 1 ppm and it appears that all mean values for mercury in fish species from the Northeast Pacific are considerably below that standard.[119] United States' federal action levels for other heavy metals have not been set. On the basis of the data presented here, it

TABLE 14.7

RANGES OF MEAN HEAVY METAL CONTENT IN NORTHEAST PACIFIC FISH AND SHELLFISH
(PPM)

| Fish or shellfish | | Mercury | | Lead | | Cadmium |
|---|---|---|---|---|---|---|
| Anchovy, N | W | <0.1 | W | 1.0−2.0 | W | 0.3−0.4 |
| Pacific cod | M | 0.1−0.2 | M | 0.3−0.4 | M | <0.1 |
| | L | <0.1 | L | 0.3−0.4 | L | 0.2−0.3 |
| Pacific hake | M | 0.1−0.2 | M | 0.5−0.6 | M | <0.1 |
| | L | <0.1 | L | 0.7−0.8 | L | 0.1−0.2 |
| Pollock | W | <0.1 | M | 0.4−0.5 | M | <0.1 |
| | M | 0.1−0.2 | L | 0.2−0.3 | L | 0.2−0.3 |
| Petrale sole | M | 0.1−0.2 | M | 0.5−0.6 | M | <0.1 |
| | L | 0.1 | L | 0.2−0.3 | L | 0.7−0.8 |
| Pacific halibut | M | 0.2−0.3 | M | 0.4−0.5 | M | <0.1 |
| | L | 0.3−0.4 | L | 0.5−0.6 | L | 1.0−2.0 |
| Petrale sole | M | 0.2−0.3 | M | 0.4−0.5 | M | <0.1 |
| | L | 0.3−0.4 | L | 0.5−0.6 | L | 1.0−2.0 |
| Petrale sole | M | 0.2−0.3 | M | 0.4−0.5 | M | <0.1 |
| | L | 0.3−0.4 | L | 0.5−0.6 | L | 1.0−2.0 |
| Sablefish | M | 0.2−0.3 | M | 0.4−0.5 | M | <0.1 |
| | L | 0.5−0.6 | L | 0.3−0.4 | L | 2.0−3.0 |
| Pacific ocean perch | M | <0.1 | M | 0.4−0.5 | M | <0.1 |
| | L | <0.1 | L | 0.3−0.4 | L | 1.0−2.0 |
| Chinook salmon | M | <0.1 | M | 0.4−0.5 | M | <0.1 |
| | L | <0.1 | L | 0.5−0.6 | L | 0.4−0.5 |
| Squid | W | <0.1 | W | 0.6−0.7 | W | 0.7−0.8 |
| Oyster | S | <0.1 | S | 0.6−0.7 | S | 1.0−2.0 |
| Shrimp, Alaska (sidestripe) | P | 0.1−0.2 | P | 0.6−0.7 | P | 0.1−0.2 |
| King crab | U | <0.1 | D | 0.7−0.8 | U | 0.1−0.2 |
| | D | 0.1−0.2 | U | 0.7−0.8 | D | 0.2−0.3 |
| Tanner crab | U | 0.1−0.2 | U | 0.4−0.5 | U | 0.2−0.3 |
| Razor clam | S | <0.1 | S | 0.5−0.6 | S | 0.1−0.2 |

Source: R. A. Hall, E. G. Zook & G. M. Meaburn, *National Marine Fisheries Service Survey of Trace Elements in the Fishery Resource*, NOAA Technical Report, NMFC, SSRF-721, March 1978.

Note: Original source contains data on sample size, range of values, and other data necessary for interpretation of these data. The values presented in this table are only indications of what is presently known and require more refinement.

Key: W = whole; M = muscle; L = liver; S = shucked; U = meat; P = tail; D = claw & body meat; and < = less than

does not appear that any species of fish in the Northeast Pacific presents a health risk to consumers, although the study does not analyze fish from all areas for effects of long-term chronic exposure to low levels of heavy metals.

More comprehensive studies of mercury in halibut,[120] sablefish (blackcod),[121] spiny dogfish,[122] and Pacific hake[123] show interesting geographic patterns. Sablefish and halibut show declining mean concentrations of mercury with increasing latitude. Mean concentration of mercury in halibut, for instance, declines from 0.45 ppm off Washington and Oregon to 0.15 ppm in the Bering Sea. If concentration of mercury in halibut is assumed to reflect the ambient level in the water column, it might be expected that waters of the Bering Sea contain less mercury than waters off Washington and Oregon, and this should be reflected in similar geographic distribution in other species of fish. Pacific hake (Pacific whiting), however, shows an opposite trend. Mean mercury content increases from less than 0.1 ppm off southern California to almost 0.4 ppm off the northern coast of Washington. This difference in the concentration of mercury in species of fish in the North Pacific at varying latitude points to the need to know the metabolism and food habits of each species investigated, in addition to measuring concentrations of trace metals in the water and sediments, if levels of pollution are to be fully understood.[124]

Vitamin pills made from the livers of northern fur seals killed on the Pribilof Islands were found to contain excessive levels of mercury in 1964 and became the first product withdrawn from the public market in the United States because of the human health risk from mercury.[125] Charges have been made that the meat of dolphins caught off the coasts of Japan for human consumption contains mercury levels as high as 4 ppm (the Japanese maximum allowable level in marketed fish is 0.4 ppm).[126] High levels of mercury have also been reported in sperm whale meat, which is presumably due to bioaccumulation throughout the long life of the species, despite its open ocean existence.[127] It has not been shown that these high levels are necessarily due to man-induced pollution.

The effects of trace metals on phytoplankton has been subject to research in Saanich Inlet on the east coast of Vancouver Island, British Columbia. Large-scale experiments using huge seawater-filled test tubes of polyethylene suspended in a marine environment are part of the Controlled Ecosystem Pollution Experiment (CEPEX), in which copper, mercury, and hydrocarbons are introduced in varying minute quantities into "captured" marine environments.[128] When these elements are added in the parts per billion range, "All appear to produce the same basic effect: first, the bacterial population explodes, then returns to normal levels within a few days. But at the same time, the large diatoms begin to disappear, while the number of smaller diatoms increases."[129] Thus fundamental change in size and species composition of the phytoplankton community may have effects on the feeding behavior and survival rates of zooplankton, fish larvae, and young fish. Similar effects have been noted in a freshwater environment for the heavy metals selenium, vanadium and chromium.[130]

Mercury poisoning from eating contaminated fish is known from Minimata Bay and Niigata in Japan.[131] Cadmium poisoning as a result of the use of mine waste water to irrigate rice and other crops is known from several areas of Japan, although no cases attributable to consumption of fish from marine areas that are near the mouths of contaminated rivers have been reported.[132] Most of the research on mercury and cadmium in fish has been aimed at averting human health risks from consumption of contaminated fish; relatively little is known about the impact of low levels of mercury and cadmium on the behavior, health, and reproduction of fish.

Since the relative contributions of anthropogenic versus natural sources of heavy metal pollution have not been defined, it is difficult to know whether or not control measures are indicated in open ocean areas. In 1957, Japan prohibited all fishing in Minimata Bay, and in 1966 it required that all industrial operations with mercury as an effluent must be monitored.[133] It appears that government regulations of effluents discharged into the coastal marine environment in the United States and Japan will have a positive effect on reducing heavy metal pollution, although these substances stored in sediments still pose problems since they can be disturbed by storms and dredging operations and can again resume the role of active pollutants in the water column. Studies by the Hydrographic Department of the Maritime Safety Agency of Japan show considerable differences for many areas between the amount of heavy metals in the water column and the amount lodged in the sediments.[134] Japan is engaged in a project to dredge mercury-laden sediments from affected areas like Minimata Bay, in order to restore the mercury content of the sediments to safer levels.[135]

## Petroleum

Trends in oil pollution in the North Pacific are equally as hard to discern as those for heavy metals and synthetic organic substances. This is due to the facts that (1) natural seepage of oil occurs in many areas of the North Pacific, such as Santa Barbara, Gulf of Alaska, and off the Kamchatka Peninsula; (2) little is known about the background levels, either natural or man-induced, of oil in the waters of the North Pacific; and (3) no systematic sampling of oil content of surface or other waters of the North Pacific has been done, either over a period of time or space, that would permit comparison of levels of oil pollution by region or by time trends.[136] There is considerable uncertainty, as well, over what to attempt to measure as hydrocarbon pollution, since crude oil products and their various decomposed forms are extremely complex substances. Review of available information on occurrence in surface waters of the North Pacific, polluting incidents, oil pollution damage, and shipping casualties and operations, gives an indication of the extent to which oil poses a multiple use problem.

Available data show the concentration of nonvolatile hydrocarbons in the surface waters of the North Pacific to vary from less than 10 parts per billion to as much as 50 to 100 parts per billion.[137] Although the study that produced data represents the most comprehensive presentation of levels of petroleum hydrocarbon in North Pacific surface waters, it contains less than 40 observations for the whole North Pacific, and the values are presumably based on a single sample from each site. No pattern of concentration can be seen from the reported data with respect to coastal or high-seas areas. Levels reported for coastal areas of Japan were on the order of 0.02 ppm in 1973, which is slightly higher than values reported for the open ocean.[138] Since the levels appear to be generally low, the implication that the North Pacific has little ambient petroleum pollution in surface waters is probably warranted. With only single measurements from various sites at one point in time, it is, of course, impossible to abstract a trend from the data.

Since direct measurements of petroleum hydrocarbons in the waters of the North Pacific are not available, it is necessary to try to assess petroleum pollution trends using surrogate methods. In chapter 11 of this volume, it was suggested that discharge levels of hydrocarbons from tankers in the North Pacific are relatively low compared with the expected values, given the total volume of oil shipped into the area, for the following reasons: (1) the bulk of the oil transported in the region travels only a short distance within the region, (2) no major tanker accidents on the scale of the *Torrey Canyon* have occurred within the area, and (3) normal tank washing and deballasting activities probably do not occur in the North Pacific for operational reasons. This leads to the conclusion that hydrocarbon pollution of the open waters of the Pacific Ocean should be relatively less than other ocean areas, like the North Atlantic.

To a certain extent, the above observations are borne out by examination of the number of polluting incidents and amount of oil and other substances spilled in the Northeast Pacific off the United States, as shown in table 14.8. The number of polluting incidents has averaged about 2,300 per year between 1971 and 1978, which amounts to approximately 20 percent of the total number of polluting incidents in United States waters. Most of the incidents in the North Pacific involve oil pollution. In terms of volume, there is considerable variation depending on whether large spills occurred off the Pacific Coast or other coasts of the United States. In years without a large spill on the Pacific Coast of the United States, the volume spilled is less than five percent of the total spills in United States waters. In other years, the volume spilled on the Pacific Coast may reach over 50 percent of total spillage. Still, this amount is small relative to the amounts spilled in a single large tanker accident like

TABLE 14.8

POLLUTING INCIDENTS IN AND AROUND U.S. NORTHEAST PACIFIC WATERS, OIL AND OTHER SUBSTANCES

| Year | Number of Incidents | % Total U.S. | Volume in Gallons | Amount (metric tons) | % Total U.S. |
|---|---|---|---|---|---|
| 1971 | 1,609 | 18.4 | 2,178,621 | 7,060 | 24.6 |
| 1972 | 1,996 | 20.1 | 317,138 | 1,030 | 1.7 |
| 1973 | 3,173 | 23.8 | 8,541,228 | 27,670 | 35.1 |
| 1974 | 2,715 | 19.4 | 493,454 | 1,600 | 3.0 |
| 1975 | 1,768 | 17.4 | 440,923 | 1,430 | 3.0 |
| 1976 | 2,237 (1,842) | 17.7 (17.3) | 1,443,161 (1,219,079) | 4,675 (3,950) | 4.3 (5.3) |
| 1977 | 2,326 (1,861) | 18.1 (17.5) | 9,988,902 (9,965,875)[a] | 32,360 (32,280)[a] | 50.2 (56.5) |
| 1978 | 2,610 (2,155) | 18.2 (18.2) | 306,739 (248,013) | 994 (803) | 1.8 (1.7) |

Source: U. S. Coast Guard, *Polluting Incidents In and Around U. S. Waters* (Washington, D. C.: Department of Transportation, Calendar Years 1971–1978).

Note: Since most of the volume of polluting substances consists of oil, the approximate amount of material by weight is obtained by dividing 308.7 (42 gallons per barrel of oil × 7.35 barrels of oil per metric ton) into total gallons and rounding.

[a]Numbers in ( ) indicate oil only. Includes 31,100 metric tons oil spill from *Irene's Challenge* near Hawaii. Another source lists this spill at 36,000 metric tons. See A.R.V. Bertrand, "Les principaux accidents de déversements pétroliers en mer et la banque de données de l'Institut Francais Du Pétrole sur les accidents de navires (1955–1979)," *Revue de l'Institut Francais du Pétrole* (May–June 1979), pp. 483–541.

the *Amoco Cadiz* (200,000 dwt). Since table 14.8 does not indicate the relative proportion of total volume of oil traffic in each of the regions of the United States, it is not possible to assess whether or not oil transportation activities in the Northeast Pacific are any safer per unit volume transported than other areas simply because the number of incidents and volume of spills is lower. Northeast Pacific values are probably lower because the quantity of petroleum transported there is lower, but more detailed study is necessary to support this view.

Examination of the locations where polluting incidents occurred, shown in table 14.9, is useful in evaluating the extent to which marine pollution can be characterized as a regional problem in the North Pacific, assuming that the distribution of incidents in Japan and Canada are similar to those in the United States. Approximately 80 percent of all polluting incidents on the Pacific Coast of the United States were reported from internal waters such as rivers,

TABLE 14.9

LOCATION OF POLLUTING INCIDENTS IN AND AROUND U.S. NORTH PACIFIC WATERS,
OIL AND OTHER SUBSTANCES

| Location | 1976 | 1977 | 1978 |
|---|---|---|---|
| Internal Waters (rivers, harbors, estuaries) | | | |
| Number | 1,847 | 1,740 | 2,578 |
| % Total U.S. | 82.6 | 74.8 | 98.8 |
| Volume in gallons | 1,219,724 | 209,407 | 305,343 |
| Amount (in MT) | 3,950 | 1,000 | 989 |
| % Total U.S. | 84.5 | 3.1 | 99.5 |
| Territorial Sea and Contiguous Zone (0–12 nautical miles) | | | |
| Number | 373 | 565 | 18 |
| % Total U.S. | 16.6 | 24.3 | 0.7 |
| Volume in gallons | 219,178 | 78,958 | 631 |
| Amount (in MT) | 710 | 260 | 2 |
| % Total U.S. | 15.2 | 0.8 | 0.2 |
| High Seas (beyond 12 nautical miles) | | | |
| Number | 17 | 21 | 14 |
| % Total U.S. | 0.7 | 0.9 | 0.5 |
| Volume in gallons | 4,259 | 9,600,537* | 765 |
| Amount (in MT) | 15 | 31,100* | 3 |
| % Total U.S. | 0.3 | 96.1 | 0.25 |
| All Areas | | | |
| Number | 2,237 | 2,326 | 2,610 |
| % Total U.S. | 100 | 100 | 100 |
| Volume in gallons | 1,443,161 | 9,988,902[a] | 306,739 |
| Amount (in MT) | 4,675 | 32,360[a] | 994 |
| % Total U.S. | 100 | 100 | 100 |

Source: U. S. Coast Guard, *Polluting Incidents In and Around U.S. Waters* (Washington, D. C.: Department of Transportation, Calendar Years 1971–1978).

Note: Since most of the volume of polluting substances is comprised of oil, the approximate amount of material by weight is obtained by dividing 308.7 (42 gallons per barrel of oil × 7.35 barrels of oil per metric ton) into total gallons and rounding.

[a]Includes 31,100 metric tons oil spill from *Irene's Challenge* near Hawaii.

harbors, and estuaries between 1976 and 1978. About 20 percent of the incidents were noted in the contiguous zone less than 12 nautical miles from shore. Less than 1 percent of polluting incidents were reported from high-seas areas along the West Coast of the United States for that same time period. To some extent, this concentration of reports from nearshore areas may be an artifact of the reporting procedure and the greater likelihood of a spill being reported where there is more human activity. Still the pattern of nearshore distribution of polluting incidents seems clear. It has not been possible to determine the source of most of the spills or to ascertain whether they are caused by coastal state or foreign sources. The fact that they occur within the territorial sea suggests that coastal states have jurisdiction and can implement measures to reduce levels of pollution, and that the coastal state is probably the most effective locus for regulation and enforcement over coastal pollution.

While the levels of oil pollution are low in the North Pacific, the risk of a major spill in a coastal area or harbor cannot be totally discounted and efforts should be made to reduce the risk of such an event. Examples of oil spills are known in marine areas of the North Pacific from offshore production, tanker and other vessel accidents, and from spillage from onshore storage facilities. During an approximately 100-day period in 1969, some 10,500 metric tons of oil erupted from an oil well blowout in the Santa Barbara Channel area of the United States.[139] Despite the fact that the discharge of oil was rather small compared to a large tanker accident,[140] the impacts on marine life and the coastal environment were highly visible and expensive to clean up. One estimate of the economic cost of the Santa Barbara blowout assigns it a value of $16.4 million.[141] Table 14.10 gives a breakdown of the estimated costs by sector.

The greatest costs were related to efforts to contain and clean up the leaking oil. Loss of recreational values and property values in the high population density Santa Barbara Channel area were next in order of magnitude. Damage to the commercial fishery was estimated as being substantial, but damage to fish life was considered negligible. The costs of programs administered by the U.S. Department of the Interior, the state of California, and Santa Barbara County to deal with the spilled oil were also considerable. Impact on tourism, seals and sea lions, bird life, and intertidal plants and animals was estimated to be either negligible or relatively low. It should be noted that the contemporary dollar value of the oil lost was relatively small compared with the cost of cleaning it up.*

Costs of a similar blowout in the same area in current dollar terms would undoubtedly be considerably greater. It should also be noted that roughly $6 million of the costs estimated were not recoverable in the form of compensation paid to the injured parties by the use that had inflicted the damage. It has been pointed out that had no attempts been made to clean up the spill, the estimates of the economic cost of the Santa Barbara spill would have been substantially less.[142] This suggests that other methodologies and assumptions used to assess the economic cost of the blowout might have yielded somewhat different results. Still, the procedures used in making the estimates cited here are documented, defensible, and useful in evaluating the economic cost of a major oil spill.

In Japan, the number of incidents and amount of damage caused by oil pollution to fisheries activities is shown in table 14.11.

TABLE 14.10

ESTIMATE OF THE ECONOMIC COST OF THE SANTA BARBARA OIL SPILL

| Item | | Estimated costs (in U.S. $) |
|---|---|---|
| Union Oil Co. on behalf of itself and three partners-Gulf, Mobil and Texaco: | | $10,487,000 |
| Beach cleanup | $4,887,000 | |
| Oil well control efforts | 3,600,000 | |
| Oil collection efforts | 2,000,000 | |
| U.S. Department of the Interior | | 382,000 |
| State of California | | 200,000 |
| County of Santa Barbara | | 57,200 |
| City of Santa Barbara | | negligible |
| Damage to tourism | | negligible |
| Damage to commercial fishing industry | | 804,250 |
| Property value loss | | 1,197,000 |
| Fish life damage | | negligible |
| Bird life damage | | 7,400 |
| Seal and sea lion damage | | negligible |
| Intertidal plant and animal damage | | |
| Low estimate | | 1,000 |
| High estimate | | 25,000 |
| Value of lost oil | | 130,000 |
| Recreational value lost | | 3,150,000 |
| Low estimate | | $16,415,850 |
| High estimate | | $16,439,850 |

Source: W. J. Mead and P. E. Sorensen, "The Economic Cost of the Santa Barbara Oil Spill," in *Santa Barbara Oil Symposium*, December 17, 1970, p. 225.

TABLE 14.11

ACCIDENTAL DAMAGE TO FISHERIES BY OIL POLLUTION IN JAPAN
(1969—1976)

| Years | Incidents | Damages ($ U.S. equivalents) |
|---|---|---|
| 1969[a] | 24 | 1,700,000 |
| 1971—1972[b] | 74 | 6,440,000 |
| 1972—1973[b] | 57 | 7,300,000 |
| 1973—1974[b] | 58 | 5,890,000 |
| 1974—1975[b] | 91 | 86,090,000 |
| 1975—1976[b] | 77 | 8,990,000 |

Sources:

[a]Masaaki Sato, "Prospects for Fisheries in the 200-mile Fishery Zone of Japan," Special Volume, Research Institute of the North Pacific Fisheries, Faculty of Fisheries, Hokkaido University (December 1977), p. 44.

[b]Teruji Sakiyama. "Cost of Japanese Fisheries Under Expanding Environmental Pollution," preliminary draft, Institute for Developing Economies (Tokyo, Japan: no date), p. 7.

*For example, the value of 10,500 MT (76,650 bbls.) of crude oil at 1968 prices of $3.00—$4.00 per barrel falls in the range of $230,000—$307,000.

The high value in the 1974–1975 period was due to the loss of approximately 8,500 tons of heavy oil from the Mizushima Petrochemical Complex in Okayama Prefecture on the Seto Inland Sea. Compensation on the order of 14,839 billion yen (approx. $53 million at Y-280=$1) was paid to four prefectural federations and one national federation of fishermen from this single incident. No distinct trend in either the number of incidents or the amount of damages can be discerned from these figures. One important role is that the figures specify only damages to fisheries. It might be expected that the total damages to property, recreation, etc. would be considerably greater if the estimates from Santa Barbara were used as a guide; and, certainly, the costs incurred in attempts to clean up the oil would be substantial.

Marine pollution incidents from all sources reported to, and confirmed by, the Maritime Safety Agency of Japan are shown for the years 1969–1975 in table 14.12. By far, the largest category of reports are concerned with oil discharged from vessels, but the extent to which this has caused damages, or the quantity and type of spillage, is not reported. Land-based discharges of large quantities of oil are small in number, and nonoil sources of pollution are a small proportion of total reports. This may be due to the fact that such discharges are less easily discerned than oil floating on the surface of the water and washing up on beaches.

TABLE 14.12

MARINE POLLUTION INCIDENTS REPORTED TO THE MARITIME SAFETY AGENCY OF JAPAN

| Cause of incident | 1970 | 1971 | 1972 | 1973 | 1974 | 1975 |
|---|---|---|---|---|---|---|
| Nonoil sources | 12 | 185 | 136 | 190 | 83 | 144 |
| Oil, sources unknown | 118 | 324 | 795 | 752 | 708 | 513 |
| Oil, land discharge | 40 | 97 | 98 | 97 | 106 | 84 |
| Oil, vessel discharge | 191 | 879 | 1,090 | 1,211 | 1,171 | 987 |
| Total No. of polluting incidents | 361 | 1,485 | 2,119 | 2,250 | 2,068 | 1,728 |

Source: Maritime Safety Agency of Japan, *White Paper on Maritime Safety 1976* (Tokyo, 1976) and Environment Agency, *Annual Report on Present Situations of Pollution* (Tokyo, 1977).

Data on oil spills from shipping casualties in the North Pacific were presented in chapter 8. (See also *Atlas of Marine Use in the North Pacific Region*). Of 332 documented casualties in the area, approximately 45 percent involved tankers, 47 percent involved other vessels, and 8 percent were related to drilling, pipelines, storage, and other causes. Almost all of the casualties have occurred in coastal waters. In general, the spills in the North Pacific have been small in comparison to the major tanker accidents in other areas, but this is no guarantee that a large spill could not occur, or that the damage from the reported spills has been inconsequential. No trends in either the number of incidents or the frequency of incidents can be discerned.

Since normal operation of tankers can lead to oil pollution from deballasting and tank washing, it is useful to study trends in tanker movements in the North Pacific as a possible index to potential increase in oil pollution. The trends in oil tanker traffic in the Northeast

Pacific show a large increase over what previously had been very small levels of activity; this is due to the activation of a tanker route between Valdez, Alaska and West Coast United States ports and the Panama Canal. (See chapter 8.) It is projected that foreign imports to the west coast of the United States will decrease or, at most, remain the same, while (between 1978 and 1985) the total demand for tanker tonnage on the Valdez routes will rise by about 15 percent.[143] If substantial discoveries are made in the Gulf of Alaska, Bering Sea, Beaufort Sea, and on the North Slope, it is conceivable that this traffic could continue to increase after the middle 1980s but probably will not increase before that time. A tanker route could be initiated from Alaska to Japan in the late 1980s, which could carry oil from areas not covered by the U.S. Congress-imposed moratorium on shipment of crude oil from the North Slope. Statistical studies by the state of Alaska predict that during the 25-year expected lifetime of the Alaska pipeline operation, 20 major spills totalling approximately 10,200 metric tons of oil will occur as a result of tanker accidents.[144] This estimate of potential spills assumes that no catastrophic spills will occur.

In terms of shipping traffic conflicts with oil development, the problems in the North Pacific at the present time appear to be relatively minor. For the southern California area, most of the large-vessel traffic (estimated at 5–12 vessels per day, depending on the particular route and ports entered) moves in vessel traffic lanes. Much of the small boat traffic and recreational boating traffic, however, does not follow a pattern and adds to the congestion. Fog can be a problem for shipping in the areas off southern California since it hampers visual navigation and increases the possibility of collisions, but most large vessels are equipped with radar. Some 20 of the 65 active leases in 1977 in the Santa Barbara Channel were intersected by the shipping lanes, and 7 out of 13 OCS leases in San Pedro Bay were in shipping lanes, or the surrounding buffer zone.[145] Unless drilling actually occurs within the part of the leased areas overlapping the vessel traffic lanes or directly adjacent to them, conflicts should not arise. Shipping interests using those areas have expressed their view that the lanes need to be kept clear of oil drilling structures.[146] Obviously, this conflict between drilling and shipping is a symptom of government agencies acting independently to regulate single use activities and ignoring the need to integrate management.

Since British Columbia is largely supplied by pipeline from sources in the Province of Alberta, there should not be any major increase in tanker traffic to that area, unless the much discussed Kitimat pipeline connection becomes a reality. The Kitimat connection would permit oil from Alaska or other areas to be transported via the Canadian network of pipelines. Politically, at least, this has not been feasible.

The use of a Canadian pipeline route has perhaps been obviated by the recent U.S. decision to consider a Northern Tier proposal to build a pipeline from the Strait of Juan de Fuca and Puget Sound across the northern states to the Midwest. Prior to this decision, a pipeline across the southern states originating in Long Beach, California, was a much discussed proposal.[147] Any of these prospects carries with it the possibility of increased tanker traffic and potential oil spills in certain coastal areas.

A few examples of spill reports from the North Pacific give a flavor of the types of problems from shipping casualties that exist in the Northeast Pacific. In 1972, the Canadian destroyer, *Gastineau*, spilled 3 tons of Bunker C fuel, which washed up on beaches near Nanaimo, B.C. In the same year, the Panamanian-registered freighter, *Vanlene*, went aground near Barclay Sound and spilled about 120 tons of heavy bunker fuel onto beaches in that area.[148] In 1973, the American tanker, *Hillyer Brown*, struck a rock entering Cold Bay, Alaska, and spilled 650 tons of gasoline and diesel oil. And, in 1976 the United States Navy tanker *USNS Sealift Pacific* ran aground in Cook Inlet and lost 1,195 tons of jet fuel.[149]

Operation of large factory trawlers and motherships in North Pacific fisheries present the potential for losing large volumes of fuel oil in accidents. The *Ruyuo Maru #2* grounded on St. Paul Island in 1979 and spilled 710 tons of fuel oil into fur seal and seabird habitats in the vicinity.[150] Similarly, other large transport vessels in North Pacific trades are occasionally lost at sea.

Oiled seabirds are often a visible casualty of oil spills, and deserve some attention in this study. No systematic reports on numbers of oiled seabirds are available for the North Pacific. Reports of seabird mortalities associated with oil spills in the North Pacific indicate that several thousand birds have been killed in single incidents. Weather conditions, the location of the oil spill, and the time of year are all factors that may influence seabird mortality. On the basis of actual and estimated bird mortality, the Santa Barbara spill killed approximately 7,400 seabirds.[151] Another instance of recorded seabird mortality occurred when the freighter *Seagate* crashed on the rocks off Washington State and fuel oil spilled along the coastline in September 1956. A few days later, white-winged scooters (*Melanitta deglandi*) and common murres (*Uria aalge*) washed onto the beach in a dead or dying condition; mortalities were estimated at 2,120 and 904 birds, respectively.[152] Considerably more work needs to be done by ornithologists to determine the impacts of oil pollution-caused mortalities of seabirds on total species population structure and seabirds as part of an ecosystem.

Japan is almost totally dependent for domestic oil consumption upon oil imports carried by tankers, mostly from the Middle East and Indonesia. Some small increment to domestic production from offshore areas of Japan, estimated at a maximum of 2 percent of Japan crude oil demand in fiscal 1976,[153] may displace a small amount of the imports, but the probable increasing demand for oil will result in overall increased imports. Part of the potential production from the northeastern Sakhalin operations in collaboration with the Soviet Union would be shipped to Japan, although it is unclear if and when tanker movements might begin. There have also been discussions in recent years of Japanese imports from the Tumen field in Siberia via rail or pipeline to Nakhodka, but this linkage is rather unlikely, given the alternative sources of supply and the reluctance of Japan to be reliant upon the Soviet Union for important shares of its energy resource supply.[154] Some oil is presently imported via Nakhodka for use in forestry in Hokkaido.[155] The most likely development, in addition to continued reliance on the Middle East and Indonesia, is increased imports from PRC. Present and planned imports from PRC are shown in table 14.13. Japan may import as much as 15 million metric tons of oil from PRC by 1985, according to a long-term trade agreement negotiated in 1977.[156]

The rapidly growing economy of the ROK will demand increased oil imports but the

TABLE 14.13

JAPANESE IMPORTS OF PRC CRUDE OIL 1973–1977 AND PROPOSED IMPORTS 1978–1985
(1,000 MT)

| Year | Through Kokusai Sekiyu | Through Importer's Conference | Total |
|------|------------------------|-------------------------------|-------|
| 1973[a] | 1,002 | – | 1,002 |
| 1974 | 2,994 | 1,002 | 3,996 |
| 1975 | 5,741 | 2,420 | 8,161 |
| 1976 | 3,799 | 2,322 | 6,121 |
| 1977 (scheduled) | 4,000 | 2,530 | 6,530 |
| | For refining | For burning | Total |
| 1978[b] | 3,900 | 2,840 | 6,740 |
| 1979 | 4,375 | 3,270 | 7,645 |
| 1980 | 4,590 | 3,350 | 7,940 |
| 1981 | 5,205 | 4,200 | 9,405 |
| 1982[c] | | | 15,000 |
| 1985[b] | | | 12,000–15,000 |

Source:

[a]*Japan Petroleum News* (October 21, 1977).

[b]*Japan Petroleum News* (November 30, 1977).

[c]*Japan Petroleum News* (December 2, 1977).

level of tanker traffic will remain relatively small compared with Japan. Some PRC crude is reaching ROK via trade agreements with major Western oil companies in sufficient quantities to make Seoul examine the feasibility of expanding its Yosu refinery.[157] The DPRK is supplied with oil by pipeline from PRC at a rate that amounted to approximately 1.2 million tons per year in 1974.[158] This import occurs under an agreement for mutual supply of goods signed in 1964.[159] The DPRK also imports oil from the Soviet Union, presumably by tanker, at a rate of 544 thousand tons per year as of 1974.[160] Another source placed DPRK imports from the Soviet Union at 1.1 million tons in 1976.[161]

Increased trade in oil cargoes across the East China Sea, Yellow Sea, and the Sea of Japan carries with it the potential for increased pollution in those areas from cargo tank washing and deballasting, unless facilities are provided in ports or other steps taken to avoid operational oil discharges. The possibility also exists that a large spill from a casualty could damage marine life and interfere with fishing in the shallow, relatively confined waters of those areas.

Several recent developments in domestic oil politics related to multiple use of marine areas around Japan have sparked controversy. When it was proposed to replace the Seto Inland Sea Environment Preservation Emergency Measures Law in 1978 by legislation that more stringently regulated the navigation of very large crude carriers (VLCCs) in that area, the Petroleum Association of Japan warned the Ministry of International Trade and Industry that new restrictions would severely affect distribution of oil products in the area.[162]

The second controversy concerns the use of some of Japan's idle tanker fleet to serve as floating storage facilities. Japan employed a fleet of 20 idle tankers in the 200,000 to

250,000 dwt VLCC class as floating storage for about 4.3 million metric tons of Middle Eastern crude oil, starting in September 1978. After a careful study of environmental conditions, it was decided to attempt to anchor 10 of the vessels in Tachibana Bay, Nagasaki Prefecture, and to permit the other 10 to drift in a designated zone in the Pacific Ocean west of Iwo Jima and Okinawa. Both of these floating oil storage areas have brought protests from Japanese fishing interests. Nagasaki prefectural officials are helping the Japan National Oil Co. (JNOC) to negotiate a settlement with the 15 fisheries cooperatives in Tachibana Bay, whereby JNOC will pay about $5 million annually (roughly equal to one-seventh of the value of the annual catch from the area) to the cooperatives and $2.5 million to local authorities as grants-in-aid as compensation for use of the Bay. Bonito and tuna fishing interests in the designated drifting sea claimed that the tankers would disturb the bonito fishing grounds. A settlement is also being negotiated there. If the negotiations with the Tachibana Bay interests prove intractable, the 10 tankers scheduled to be anchored there will join the drifting tanker fleet.[163]

In the short run, there is little likelihood of large increases in oil pollution from increased offshore production of oil or increased tanker traffic. Over 7,000 wells had been drilled offshore on the west coast of the United States without a large spill prior to 1969. Since 1969, federal and state regulations have been strengthened, drilling operations have become better supervised, and blowout prevention technology and equipment have been improved.[164]

The long-run prospects for oil pollution from offshore developments and tanker traffic in the North Pacific indicate that there will probably be a gradually increasing use of the area for oil-related activities over the next 5–15 years. These uses are not necessarily fated to impinge upon other interests through the generation of more pollution, although some increase in oil pollution can be anticipated unless there is a parallel development of arrangements for regulating polluting activities. Certainly, the offshore oil drilling and production platforms will occupy space and preclude use of limited areas for extended periods of time, but these are quite local problems. Careful national anticipatory planning can accommodate the conflicts between uses via compensation, safety regulations, and other measures.

## Ocean Dumping

The use of the assimilative capacity of the marine environment for disposal of wastes is an important use of the North Pacific. Deliberate disposal of a variety of waste materials ranging from industrial residuals to explosives has taken place in the region, usually on the continental shelf or deep waters adjacent to it. The disposal of dredge spoils from clearing shipping lanes, harbors, and other areas also represents a significant quantity of material dumped in the ocean, and some of this material contains pollutants. Regulation of ocean dumping is the subject of an increasing body of national law and international agreements that seek to mitigate the adverse consequences of waste disposal in the oceans, yet permit use of the ocean's capacity to disperse, break down, or store wastes and thus reduce the costs of land-based waste disposal.

Ocean dumping is only one of the means by which wastes enter the North Pacific, but as a deliberate activity subject to extensive legislation, it is necessary to discuss it as a separate topic. Here, we discuss national ocean dumping practice among North Pacific nations with respect to the location of ocean dumping sites and the materials that are dumped. Data are available from only Canada, Japan, and the United States. Ocean dumping of radionuclides, litter, nutrients, and heavy metals receive separate treatment elsewhere.

Canada regulates ocean dumping under the Ocean Dumping Control Act.[165] The main dumping site designated under this Act, based on the number of permits issued for dumping and the quantities allowed, is located in the Strait of Georgia off Point Grey (49° 15' N, 123° 22' W).[166] Many smaller sites are designated for dumping dredge spills.[167] Overall, from 1976 to 1978, Canada issued approximately 100 permits to dump a total of 8.7 million cubic meters of dredge spoils along the British Columbia coastline at 36 separate sites. (See table 14.14.) It appears that the only material permitted to be dumped in west coast waters off Canada is dredge spoils, although the ocean dumping legislation refers to a wide variety of other wastes. The historical record for Canadian ocean dumping is not well documented; therefore, no data on prior dumping are presented here. Improvements in waste disposal practices and reduction in the amounts dumped may have lessened the severity of marine waste disposal practices in recent years.[168]

Ocean dumping in Japan is regulated primarily by the Marine Pollution Prevention Act of 1970. Under this regulation, Japan has allocated six sites for ocean dumping in waters off the Japanese archipelago.[169] One is located about 100 km west of northern Honshu on the Sea of Japan and a second is located between Japan and the ROK. The third site is found east of Okinawa, and the other three are located beyond the edge of the continental shelf south, southeast, and east, respectively, of Honshu.

Japan has five categories of sea areas where wastes of various types may be legally dumped.[170] Harmful wastes encased in cement or other containers may be dumped in special designated areas within each of the six sites for ocean dumping. Wastes like those from demolition of structures, noncombustible domestic wastes, glass and ceramics may be disposed of in the ocean dumping sites. Dumping of other materials is permitted outside designated sites. For example, excrement, liquid noncombustible wastes and acids or alkalis may be dumped from moving vessels beyond 80 km from land. Organic animal and other wastes may not be discharged within 10 km of the low water line in harbors, the Seto Inland Sea, the Bay of Ise, or other areas reserved from dumping by the Director General of the Environmental Agency. No reference to the annual amounts of various categories of wastes dumped has been found. There are approximately 70 sampling stations where pollution levels are monitored in the waters around Japan.[171] Some of these monitoring sites are in the vicinity of the dumping sites.

Because the dumping sites in the North Pacific east of Japan are located in the path of the Kuroshio Current, dispersion and mixing of the wastes in surface waters is probably good. The ocean dumping sites are beyond the range of most Japanese coastal fisheries, except for the tuna and bonito fisheries. No reference has been found to fishing interest protests over ocean dumping regulations or the location of the sites.

TABLE 14.14

CANADA'S OCEAN DUMPING IN THE NORTH PACIFIC 1976–1978

| | 1976 BC | 1976 Canada | 1977 BC | 1977 Canada | 1978 BC | 1978 Canada |
|---|---|---|---|---|---|---|
| *Number of permits*[1] | 56 | 163 | 45 | 168[a] | 52 | 204[b] |
| *Dredge spoils*[1] | $3.5 \times 10^6 m^3$ | $5.7 \times 10^6 m^3$ | $3.0 \times 10^6 m^3$ | $5.1 \times 10^6 m^3$ | $2.2 \times 10^6 m^3$ | $11.0 \times 10^6 m^3$ |
| *Industrial wastes*[2] | | | — | — | — | — |
| Sludges | 907 MT | 907 MT | — | — | — | |
| Caustic wastes | — | — | — | — | — | 2,000 MT |
| Fish processing | — | — | — | 335 MT | — | 1,575 MT and 1,100 m³ |
| Liquids | $182 \times 10^4 MT$ | $182 \times 10^4 MT$ | — | — | — | — |
| *Ships*[1] | — | 7 ships | — | 4 ships | — | 3 ships |
| *Excavation materials*[2] | $9.95 \times 10^4 m^3$ | $9.95 \times 10^4 m^3$ | $5.4 \times 10^4 m^3$ | $5.4 \times 10^4 m^3$ | — | — |

*Scientific experiments*[2]

| 1976 BC | Material | 1976 Canada | 1977 BC | 1977 Canada | 1978 BC | 1978 Canada |
|---|---|---|---|---|---|---|
| | Crude oil | — | — | — | 820 l | — |
| 13,195 l | Agrifoam | — | — | — | 46 l | — |
| — | Coal dust | — | — | — | 4.5 MT | — |
| 321 MT | Seed oil | — | — | — | 410 l | — |
| 90 m³ | Mud | — | — | — | 10 MT | — |
| — | Salt | — | — | — | — | — |
| 196 MT | | | | | | |

Sources:

[1]Department of Fisheries and the Environment, *A Summary of Permits Issued Under the Ocean Dumping Control Act*, Ottawa, 1978.

[2]International Maritime Consultative Organization, *Convention on the Prevention of Marine Pollution by Dumping of Wastes and Other Matter, 1972*, Report of Permits Issued for Dumping (Annual 1976–1978), LDC 2/Circ. 31, March 19, 1979; LDC 2/Circ. 33, and LDC 2/Circ. 47 (Paris: IMCO, April 10, 1979 and February 12, 1980).

Note: Nearly all permits issued are for disposal of dredge spoils.

[a]Canada issued one permit to use 2 kg of the radioactive tracer Nd[147] in scientific experiments in the Atlantic region.

[b]Canada issued one permit to dump 18,500 cubic meters (m³) of ammunition in the Atlantic region.

Ocean dumping on the U.S. Pacific coast, including Hawaii, is used for such materials as explosives, solid wastes, sewage sludge, industrial wastes, and dredge spoils. Compared to other areas in the United States, the Pacific Coast has a low level of ocean dumping on a weight basis.[172] Between 1949 and 1953, ocean dumping in the Pacific, exclusive of dredge spoils, radioactive wastes, and military explosives, amounted to approximately 50,000 MT per year.[173] The trend in ocean dumping on the Pacific Coast was upward with the annual average increasing to about 85,000 MT for the period 1954–1958, 94,000 MT for the period 1959–1963, and 340,000 MT for 1964–1968.

Alarmed at this rapid increase in pollution from ocean dumping, the United States adopted the Marine Protection, Research, and Sanctuaries Act of 1972.[174] The Act establishes a permit system to control ocean dumping, and about 40 sites have been designated for dredge spoil disposal off the U.S. west coast. Not all of these sites are in current use.[175] Table 14.15 summarizes the amounts of various dumped materials off the Pacific Coast in comparison with total ocean dumping for the United States. Prior to 1973, industrial wastes and solid wastes were dumped into the Pacific. After 1973, these activities virtually stopped. The largest quantity of waste disposed currently in the waters off the United States comes from dredge spoils. It has been estimated that about one-fifth of the dredge spoils on the Pacific Coast are polluted on the basis of measurements of chlorine, biological oxygen demand, chemical oxygen demand, volatile solids, oil and grease, phosphorus, nitrogen, iron, silica, color, and odor.[176]

National legislation by Canada, Japan, and the United States seems consistent with the general restrictions on ocean dumping embodied in the global London Convention on Ocean Dumping.[177] It appears that each of these nations has made a concerted effort to reduce the levels of dumping of highly toxic materials in the North Pacific and has sought to reduce the impact of other wastes on the marine ecosystem by specifying the sites, conditions, and methods for disposal of many other categories of pollutants. From the evidence available from the west coast of the United States, pollution from ocean dumping has decreased markedly over the levels in the late 1960s. Without further data, it is not possible to adequately ascertain the levels of ocean dumping in the North Pacific or to gain an accurate impression of the trends in that activity.

## Radionuclides

Artificially produced radioactive wastes have entered the North Pacific as the result of weapons testing, ocean dumping of radioactive wastes, leaks from nuclear-powered electricity generation, operation of nuclear-powered vessels, nuclear-powered satellite disintegration, and leaks from nuclear waste storage facilities. Increased transport of radioactive wastes and spent fuel rods for reprocessing may also add to the amounts of wastes entering the oceans. Radionuclides were the first marine pollutants to receive international scientific recognition and are important because of their potential threats to human health.[178] The effects of radionuclides in concentrations that do not appreciably alter what are considered to be background levels normally present in the sea are not thought to cause any harm to humans.[179] Concern has been expressed over the possibility of an accident with a nuclear-powered vessel or nuclear-generated facility that might result in the release of large amounts of radioactive materials.[180] Table 14.16 shows the levels of some of the more widely studied nuclides in North Pacific waters. Low levels of radioactivity in sea waters can be concentrated in marine organisms, although there is quite a variation in the uptake by different species and trophic levels. It appears that radionuclide bioaccumulation does not increase up the food chain but that highest levels are found at relatively low trophic levels.[181] According to what is presently known, these levels do not appear to constitute a threat to human health.

Atmospheric nuclear weapons testing has produced the greatest amounts of artificially introduced radioactivity in marine areas.[182] France, India, People's Republic of China, USSR, United Kingdom, and the United States have exploded atmospheric nuclear devices.

## TABLE 14.15

## U.S. Ocean Dumping in the North Pacific 1968–1978

| Waste | 1968 N. Pac. | 1968 Total U.S. | 1973 N. Pac. | 1973 Total U.S. | 1974 N. Pac. | 1974 Total U.S. | 1975 N. Pac. | 1975 Total U.S. | 1976 N. Pac. | 1976 Total U.S. | 1977 N. Pac. | 1977 Total U.S. | 1978 N. Pac. | 1978 Total U.S. |
|---|---|---|---|---|---|---|---|---|---|---|---|---|---|---|
| Dredge spoils | 8.32[1] | 52.20[1] | N.A. | 96.1 | 17.3[2] | 118.4[2] | N.A. | 125.5 | 16.31[3] | 93.78[3] | 19.75[3] | 60.02[3] | 15.20[3] | 74.48[3] |
| Industrial waste | .98[1] | 4.70[1] | 0[4] | 5.05[4] | 0[4] | 4.58[4] | 0[4] | 3.44[4] | 0[4] | 2.73[4] | 0[4] | 1.84[4] | 0[4] | 2.55[4] |
| Sewage sludge | 0[1] | 4.48[1] | 0[4] | 4.80[4] | 0[4] | 5.01[4] | 0[4] | 5.04[4] | 0[4] | 5.27[4] | 0[4] | 5.13[4] | 0[4] | 5.53[4] |
| Construction & demolition debris | 0[1] | .57[1] | 0[4] | .97[4] | 0[4] | .77[4] | 0[4] | .39[4] | 0[4] | .31[4] | 0[4] | .38[4] | 0[4] | .24[4] |
| Solid waste | .03[1] | .03[1] | neg.[4] | neg.[4] | neg.[4] | neg.[4] | 0[4] | 0[4] | 0[4] | 0[4] | 0[4] | neg.[4] | 0[4] | 0[4] |
| Explosives | 0[1] | .01[1] | 0[4] | 0[4] | 0[4] | 0[4] | 0[4] | 0[4] | 0[4] | 0[4] | 0[4] | 0[4] | 0[4] | 0[4] |
| Incinerated chemicals | 0[1] | 0[1] | 0[4] | 0[4] | 0[4] | .01[4] | 0[4] | neg.[4] | 0[4] | 0[4] | .01[4] | .03[4] | 0[4] | 0[4] |
| TOTAL[a] | 1.00 | 9.78 | – | 10.93 | – | 10.39 | 0 | 8.89 | 0 | 8.33 | .01 | 7.4 | 0 | 8.10 |

Sources:

[1] Ocean Disposal Study Steering Committee, *Disposal in the Marine Environment, An Oceanographic Assessment* (Washington, D.C.: National Academy of Sciences, 1976). Also cited in Alexander W. Reed, *Ocean Waste Disposal Practices* (Park Ridge, N.J.: Noyes Data Corporation, 1975).

[2] Committee on Commerce, U.S. Senate, *Ocean Dumping Regulation: An Appraisal of Implementation* (Washington, D.C.: U.S. Government Printing Office, April 1976).

[3] U.S. Army Corps of Engineers, *1978 Report to Congress on Administration of Ocean Dumping Activities* (Washington, D.C.: Department of the Army, June 1979).

[4] Office of Water Programs, U.S. Environmental Protection Agency, *Annual Report to Congress Jan.–Dec. 1978: on Administration of the Marine Protection, Research and Sanctuaries Act (PL 92–532) and Implementing the International Ocean Dumping Convention* (Washington, D.C.: U.S. Government Printing Office, June 1979). Also cited in Council on Environmental Quality, *The Tenth Annual Report of the CEQ* (Washington, D.C.: U.S. Government Printing Office, December 1979).

Note: Dredge spoil tonnages for 1973 and 1975 are obtained by multiplying the spoil volume, measured in cubic yards, by the conversion factor 1.43 short tons per cubic yard. This factor is estimated from the U.S. experience reported in reference 3, and spoil volumes are from the 1976 version of that reference. N.A., Data not available. Neg., Negligible or values less than .01X10$^6$ tons.

[a]Totals do not include dredge spoils and may not add correctly owing to rounding.

TABLE 14.16

LEVELS OF MAJOR FALLOUT RADIONUCLIDES IN SURFACE SEA WATER

(AVG. CONCENTRATION AND/OR RANGE MEASURED IN PICO CURIES PER LITER pCi/L)

| Location | Strontium-90 | Cesium-137[a] | Tritium | Carbon-14 | Plutonium-239 |
|---|---|---|---|---|---|
| NE Pacific Ocean | 0.54(0.07−3.1) | 0.86(0.11−5.0) | 29(6−70) | 0.03(0.02−0.03) | $(0.1−1.3)×10−3$ |
| NW Pacific Ocean | 0.27(0.05−0.58) | 0.43(0.08−0.93) | 44(10−240) | 0.03(0−0.04) | $(0.1−1.3)×10−3$ |

Source: Adapted from Edward D. Goldberg, *The Health of the Oceans* (Paris: The UNESCO Press, 1976), p. 84.

[a]Calculated from the strontium-90 values on the assumption that the activity ratio of cesium-137/ strontium-90 = 1.6.

Nuclear weapons testing in the Pacific closed off large areas to the fishing fleets of Japan and other nations and is reported to have caused widespread short-term damage to marine life in some areas.[183] The Soviet Union, United Kingdom, and the United States no longer test nuclear weapons in the atmosphere, although France and People's Republic of China have not ceased infrequent testing.

Ocean dumping of low-level radioactive wastes has taken place in waters off the Pacific coast of the United States and probably off the coasts of other nations, although these activities are not well known. Several sites off the coast of California were used by the United States prior to 1970 for dumping of low-level radioactive wastes.[184] Between 1946 and 1970, the United States Atomic Energy Commission (AEC) licensed a total of over 14,000 curies of low-level radioactive wastes to be dumped in that area.[185] Under AEC license, 52,538 containers (usually 55 gallon drums filled with concrete) of radioactive wastes were dumped in the area southwest of the Farallon Islands between 1946 and 1968 as shown in table 14.17.[186]

Both the United States and the Soviet Union operate nuclear-powered submarines and other vessels in the North Pacific. Japan has also had brief experience with a nuclear-powered vessel, the *Mutsu*, which, unfortunately, leaked small amounts of radioactive material.[187] This accidental release from the *Mutsu* prompted great concern from the Japanese fishing industry and others about the safety not only of nuclear vessels but of nuclear-powered thermal electric plants.[188] Nuclear-powered vessels are prohibited from operating in Japanese territorial waters.

Nuclear-powered thermal electric generating plants have been placed in coastal areas by Japan and the United States, and the Republic of Korea has plants under construction and on order.[189] Under normal conditions these plants discharge small but relatively continuous low-level radionuclides into the marine environment due to the cycling of cooling waters. Consequences of a major accident at a coastal nuclear power plant are difficult to predict but could have important consequences for pollution by radioactive wastes, at least within the coastal and nearshore waters.

Drainage of leaks from waste storage and nuclear research facilities, such as the one at Hanford, Washington, on the Columbia River, may also add some usually small amounts of radioactive wastes to the Pacific Ocean.[190] Studies of the impact on aquatic living resources

# TABLE 14.17

## U.S. Disposal of Radioactive Wastes in the North Pacific 1946–1967

| Place | Coordinates | Depth (m) | Distance from Continental Coastline (km) | Years Dumpsites Used | Estimated Number of Dumped Containers[a] | Estimated Activity in Containers at Time of Packing in Curies (Ci) |
|---|---|---|---|---|---|---|
| Farallon Island[1] (subsite A) | 37° 38' N 123° 08' W | 900 | 60 | 1951–1953 | 3,500 | 1,100 |
| Farallon Island[1] (subsite B) | 37° 37' N 123° 17' W | 1,700 | 77 | 1946–1950 1954–1965 | 44,000 | 13,400 |
| Other[2] | | greater than 2,000 | greater than 240 | no dates (11 instances) | – | – |
| Total Pacific U.S.[3] | n.a. | n.a. | n.a. | n.a. | 52,538[b] | 14,708[b] |
| Total U.S.[3] | n.a. | n.a. | n.a. | n.a. | 86,537 | 94,202 |

Sources:

[1]Council on Environmental Quality. *Environmental Quality: The Tenth Annual Report of the CEQ* (Washington, D.C.: U.S. Government Printing Office, December 1979). pp. 624–626.

[2]Council on Environmental Quality, *Ocean Dumping: A National Policy*. **Report** to the President (Washington, D.C.: U.S. Government Printing Office, October 1970), pp. 6–8.

[3]Alexander W. Reed. *Ocean Waste Disposal Practices* (Park Ridge. New Jersey: Noyes Data Corporation, 1975). p. 21.

Note: No radioactive wastes were dumped by the United States in 1968. For 1969 and 1970 a total of 29 curies of radioactive wastes were dumped.[2] United States ceased ocean dumping of radioactive wastes in 1970.[1] Comparable data are **not** available for other North Pacific nations.

[a]Containers were generally 55 gallon (US) drums filled with concrete.

[b]Columns do not add due to use of different sources.

by discharges of low-level radioactive wastes from the Hanford site indicate that impacts at the mouth of the Columbia River have been minimal.[191]

Research is currently going on to evaluate the potential for disposal of high-level radioactive wastes in the sediments of the seafloor in deep-ocean areas.[192] Sites under consideration are those in the middle of the oceanic gyres and in the middle of the lithospheric plates. The midplate, midgyre area in the North Pacific at a depth of over 4,000 meters north of the Hawaiian Islands has been viewed at the present time as the best area for such purposes because of its remoteness from land and the stability of the deep-ocean sediments there.[193]

Disposal of high-level radioactive wastes in the seabed of the mid-North Pacific area as a prospective use of the ocean poses some difficult questions. The activity itself is specifically prohibited by the 1973 International Convention on Prevention of Marine Pollution by Dumping of Wastes and Other Matter (London Dumping Convention), although the text might be construed to apply only to sea bottom disposal—not emplacement in the seabed. Canada, USSR, and the United States have ratified this convention. The Soviet Union has expressed its opposition to the disposal of low- and medium-level radioactive wastes by European countries in the North Atlantic under the auspices of the Nuclear Energy Agency of the Organization for Economic Cooperation and Development.[194] The Soviet Union would presumably be consistent in opposing disposal of high-level radioactive wastes in the North Pacific. Japan, which has only limited capacity for land-based storage of such wastes would probably view deep seabed disposal in the North Pacific with some interest.

Disposal of radioactive wastes by emplacement in the ocean bottom is considered by some "to be an extremely risky scheme, one with far more dangers to man than land-based disposal. Considering the potentially rapid dispersal rate and the irretrievability of such wastes if dispersed in the ocean, this concept has much against it."[195] Others are more sanguine about the prospects of seabed disposal and argue that, despite the technical problems that must be overcome, and the gaps in knowledge that must be filled by research, the deep ocean sediments may offer the safest long-term disposal site.[196]

In terms of a regional approach to control of the disposal of radioactive wastes in the North Pacific, the most promising area for regional cooperation is investigation of seabed emplacement of high-level radioactive wastes. Doubtless, there is a broader international interest in this question, and it may be more appropriate to deal with this topic on a worldwide basis. Nuclear weapons testing in the atmosphere is already subject to global agreement and concern, while the siting of nuclear power plants, land storage facilities, and regulations for disposal of low-level radioactive wastes may be most effectively accomplished by the coastal state.

## Nutrient Pollution

Nutrients can be defined as any substance, organic or inorganic, that can be used by marine organisms to support life, growth, and reproduction. Addition of nutrients to marine areas as a result of human activities like sewage discharge, ocean dumping, and runoff from agricultural fertilizers can alter food chains, alter the species composition of the ecosystem, influence fish catches, and change the distribution of marine organisms. Nutrient pollution can probably be said to occur when these effects can be noted and increased levels of nutrients documented.

Human input of nutrients in the oceanic North Pacific has not produced identifiable ocean-wide effects at present levels, but it has seriously affected some confined inlets, harbors, and coastal areas. Since the impacts of nutrient pollution in the North Pacific are primarily coastal and not region-wide, this type of pollution is not treated as extensively as others.

Increased consciousness of the impacts of excess nutrients on marine ecosystems, particularly in relatively confined areas, has led to a greater concern on the part of the governments of Japan, Canada, and the United States; vigorous attempts are being made to reduce the dumping of raw sewage wastes in coastal waters and to reduce agricultural runoff and industrial waste discharges into coastal waters.

Japan, for example, has taken special emergency measures to speed the recovery of Seto Inland Sea from excessive nutrient pollution, and to protect it from further degradation because of its value as a fish producer, site for aquaculture, and as a popular center for tourism. The Port of Nagoya in Japan is able to show preliminary evidence that nutrient pollution levels are decreasing in the Port area.[197] Another assessment claims that since 1972, due to the enactment of the Environmental Protection Law, environmental pollution in Japanese marine areas has been gradually decreasing.[198]

In the United States and Canada efforts have been made to reduce the amount of sewage sludge discharged through pipelines, wood, and fish processing wastes in coastal waters.[199] In the southern California bight, studies of the open ocean waters in the vicinity of sewage outfalls show that approximately 160 km² of the 64,500 km² in the bight have been to some degree affected by human inputs. While trends in levels of heavy metal pollutants and DDT have been decreasing in the area, the levels of organic matter appear to be fairly stable.[200]

One of the more interesting aspects of nutrient pollution is that it is suspected of contributing to the incidence of red tides in the coastal waters of Japan.[201] This observation is based on the fact that as nutrient pollution in coastal waters increased, the incidence (and possibly the severity) of red tides also increased. However, no specific linkage has been established that scientifically validates this connection. Still, most reports on pollution in Japan make reference to red tides because of the considerable circumstantial evidence that correlates them with nutrient pollution, and because of the importance of red tide impacts on coastal aquaculture and fisheries.[202] Occurrence of red tide in the Seto Inland Sea, one of the most heavily impacted areas in Japan, has been monitored for over a decade in a systematic fashion. Table 14.18 shows that red tide occurrences there have steadily increased from 48 (reported in 1967) to 326 (reported in 1976). Red tides that have damaged fisheries resources, however, increased from 8 cases in 1967 to a high of 39 cases in 1971, and then declined somewhat. This contradictory relationship between registered cases of red tide and damage by red tide to fisheries may be due to an improved red tide information monitoring system, which increases the number of cases reported, or to the fact that red tide-sensitive organisms have previously been reduced in population due to earlier incidents, or possibly to

TABLE 14.18

REGISTERED CASES OF RED TIDE IN SETO INLAND SEA

|  | 1967 | 1968 | 1969 | 1970 | 1971 | 1972 | 1973 | 1974 | 1975 | 1976 |
|---|---|---|---|---|---|---|---|---|---|---|
| Cases causing damage to fisheries | 8 | 12 | 18 | 35 | 39 | 23 | 18 | 17 | 29 | 18 |
| Total number of registered cases | 48 | 61 | 67 | 79 | 136 | 164 | 210 | 298 | 300 | 326 |

Source: Fisheries Agency of Japan, *Red Tide of Seto Inland Sea* (Japan: Seto Naikai Gyogyo Chosei Jimkyoku, March 1977), p. 2. (in Japanese)

other yet unrecognized interactions.[203] Damages to fisheries believed to be caused by red tide outbreaks fluctuated from a low of $350,000 (1974–1975) to a high of $26,620,000 (1972–1973).[204]

While the data available are not comprehensive, it appears that nutrient pollution levels in some areas in the coastal North Pacific have stabilized (or possibly declined) under marine pollution control efforts. Since the effects of nutrient pollution are not detectable in the open ocean in the North Pacific, it does not appear that this form of pollution requires regional cooperation to devise methods of reducing current levels. Further investigation of the relationship, if any, between nutrient pollution and the red tide is probably worthwhile, and exchange of information between scientists in North Pacific nations might be facilitated by more regional cooperation.

## Litter

Litter in the form of plastic bottles, glass, rubber, nylon nets, and other materials is becoming a problem for fishing interests whose nets are increasingly fouled by such foreign matter floating in the North Pacific. In addition, the large quantities of these materials that wash up on beaches are a threat to aesthetic appreciation of coastal and marine areas. Litter has been lightly studied in a quantified manner.[205] Cundell, in a general study, has discussed plastic in the marine environment with respect to ocean dumping of plastics, the types of plastics manufactured, and the susceptibility of these products to biodegradation.[206] Some observations from the Central North Pacific Ocean have been published, but they are scarcely more than anecdotal.[207] Goldberg makes reference to a National Marine Fisheries Service study of a remote 60-mile stretch of beach near Amchitka, Alaska, on which it was estimated that 24,000 plastic items, 12 tons of polypropalene gill nets, and 7,000 gill-net floats washed up during a six-month period.[208] Two studies of litter caught in benthic trawl surveys showed that 49 percent of the trawls contained man-made debris in the Bering Sea in 1976, and that 57 percent of the trawls made in the Gulf of Alaska in 1975 contained litter. From the types of materials recovered and the location of the trawl surveys, it was thought that much of the litter was due to fishing activities.[209]

Some research has been done on pelagic tar and plastic distribution in the North Pacific.[210] The results show that the pelagic tar has its origins in tropical waters of the western Pacific, an area that corresponds to the tanker route southwest of Japan. Pelagic tar moves into the North Pacific through the Kuroshio system. Microparticles of plastic are more widely spread than pelagic tar and seem relatively more abundant in the Northeast

Pacific than in the Northwest Pacific, which may be a consequence of the longer lifetime of plastic than tar in seawater.[211] Adverse effects from plastic rubbish have been observed in Japanese waters.[212]

Discarded fishing nets interfere with fishing operations and are known to have contributed to seabird and marine mammal mortalities.[213] In 1977, it was estimated that as many as 8,000 northern fur seals were affected by plastic debris entangled on their bodies, and many were expected either to starve, strangle, drown, or die of infections caused by the binding materials.[214] The proportion of harvested males entangled in plastic debris increased steadily from 0.1 percent in 1967 to 1.15 percent in 1977. In addition, there were probably a substantial number of male fur seals that did not survive the entanglement.[215]

An unusual form of litter that impacts on coastal shipping off British Columbia is logs. About 31 percent of the wood debris in Canadian west coast waters was attributable to losses in booming, transporting, handling and storing logs in the British Columbia forest products industry. Another 32 percent could be judged to have originated from human activities, and the remainder came from natural causes. It has been estimated that this debris causes about $1 million of damage to coastal navigation and presents a hazard, especially to small boats.[216]

Since litter has been given a low research priority, no trends can be established. The increased reference to litter as a threat to amenity values on beaches suggests, however, that litter is becoming more of a problem. Plastic, in particular, with its resistance to biodegradation, can become an increasing problem. In certain respects, seaborne litter is a regional problem in that it tends to circulate in the regional system of currents, but the extent to which regional action to regulate pollution from litter is necessary or possible is not clear.[217]

## OTHER MULTIPLE USE CONFLICTS

There are a number of conflicts among uses of the North Pacific that are of such a limited coastal extent that they will not be treated in this discussion. These include interactions between fishing interests and thermal effluents from coastal industry or power generation; land use practices and their impact on anadromous fish stocks, like salmon; and the effects of land reclamation on fisheries. Still other uses of a greater international interest appear to conflict, but relatively little data are available to interpret the scale of interaction. This latter category includes interactions between (1) fishing vessels with other marine transport; (2) marine cables with fishing and shipping; (3) military uses of the sea with other uses; (4) ocean mining with other uses; (5) production of energy from marine biomass with transportation; (6) the rising demands for protection and/or preservation of animal and plant species and marine habitats with their impacts on other uses; and (7) marine science with other uses.

### Fishing with Marine Transport

Frequently, there are complaints in the fisheries press on the United States Pacific Coast that large commercial cargo ships in coastwise traffic run through areas where fishing vessels are operating or where fishing gear is set. Few reports of damage to gear, vessels, or crew are noted, however, and it is likely that casualties are rare. Claims of damage can be settled via both informal and formal legal processes in coastal states. The claims procedure whereby fishing vessels from the United States, Poland, and the Soviet Union can settle damage claims is noted in earlier chapters on fishing in this volume. It appears that the main problem is the psychological impact of a large vessel looming up out of the fog (or night) in the vicinity of small fishing vessels, and the threat this poses. From the perspective of larger vessels, the small fishing and recreational boat traffic interferes with coastwise navigation. Fishing operations that do not conform to the normal directional orientation of coastwise trade result in the need to alter course. Sometimes the fishing gear is inadequately marked or difficult to see under prevailing weather conditions.

Areas where such conflicts are thought to be most severe are in the entry to channels and harbors and within the confines of ports. Vessel separation schemes in harbors, both voluntary and mandatory, have probably relieved some of the problems. One somewhat perverse mitigating factor in some ports is that pollution levels have resulted in reduced fishing potential to the point that conflicts are less severe than they otherwise might be. In some cases, fishing rights to certain areas have been purchased by port authorities in order to develop port facilities and/or to provide unimpeded access.[218] Discussions in earlier chapters have emphasized that shipping and fishing activities are considerably greater in the coastal areas of Japan than on the west coast of the United States, and one would expect vessel conflicts to be greater there. Adequate data do not exist, however, to help make that comparison.

## Marine Communication Cables with Other Uses

Conflicts between marine communication cables and fishing and shipping interests are a nuisance, but of large economic importance to cable owners. The International Cable Protection Committee was established in 1958 to promote protection of undersea cables, and Canada, Japan, and the United States are members.

There are relatively few undersea communication cables in the North Pacific area. Frequent cable breaks from fishing activities and the cost of repairing the Port Angeles–Ketchikan cable system were prime reasons that American Telephone & Telegraph Co. decided to discontinue that cable in 1977.[219] Despite the fact that cable companies supply charts of cable locations free to fishermen and vessel captains, this public relations effort does not seem to reduce the incidence of breaks appreciably. Between February 1971 and October 1974, there were seven recorded interruptions of the British Commonwealth Teleglobe cable between Vancouver and the island of Oahu. Three of these interruptions were caused by ships dragging their anchors in the Georgia Strait area of British Columbia, and four were caused by fishing activity on La Perouse Bank off British Columbia. Between July 1969 and September 1975, compensation totalling approximately $4,000 was paid in ten separate incidents where fishing gear or anchors were sacrificed to protect cables.[220] Geostationary satellites are now used in trans-Pacific telecommunications, and it is unlikely that the number of undersea cables will increase. In recent years, cable owners have buried cables in the seabed or rerouted the cable track to avoid conflicts with fishing interests. These measures have reduced damage to cables and reduced claims from fishermen and others in the North Pacific area.

## Military Uses with Other Uses

Military uses of the marine environment of the North Pacific are understandably not well known, even though they are of major and continuing importance. This study is not designed to examine military strategic interests in the sea, but it should be noted that in coastal areas military operations do conflict with recreation, commercial fishing, offshore oil production, and shipping. In addition, large areas of the high seas are occasionally reserved by the military for maneuvers.[221]

Extensive military zones have been established by North Korea in the Sea of Japan, and by China in the Po Hai Gulf and other coastal areas. The United States Navy uses large areas off the coast of southern California and northern Washington for training, testing, local security operations, and as a missile firing range. A study of interference between military operations and other activities in the southern California area showed only a slight increase in the level of interference between the 1960s and early 1970s. The most serious conflicts were with fishing, merchant marine traffic, and recreational boating.[222] Oil drilling in the Santa Barbara area poses a significant constraint on military uses of that area, and the military is reluctant to see lease sales further offshore.[223] On the other side of the issue, oil drilling towers near Long Beach, California, help local Naval minesweeping training operations by providing outstanding day and night navigational landmarks. The Navy has attempted to reduce interference with other uses by scheduling its activities to avoid others, by coordinating with them, and by changing the locations of some of its maneuvers. In most cases of reported interference, it is asserted that nondefense activities allowed priority over defense-related activities.[224]

## Ocean Mining with Other Uses

Offshore production of solid minerals from the continental shelf is a relatively minor activity in the North Pacific and is likely to remain that way.[225] The most promising areas for seabed mining of manganese nodules is south of the boundary defined for this project, although manganese nodules are found throughout the study area. Some interest is reported for mining nodules off the coast of British Columbia but that is unlikely.[226]

Barite sands are being mined on the seabed in Alaska and the presence of gold in bore holes indicates that marine deposits of placer gold off Nome in Norton Sound may have commercial significance. In 1968, three companies had permits to explore a total of 340 km$^2$ of the seabed in Norton Sound for placer gold.[227] The unfavorable winter weather in that area allows only a short operating period and the high estimated costs (five times) of marine mining versus land operations make development unlikely. Surveys of mineral sands in other areas of Alaska show some areas of concentration, but the commercial feasibility of development has not been addressed.[228]

In Japan, silica stone was dredged in Omura Bay, in Nagasaki Prefecture, between 1960 and 1969. Iron sand deposits have been worked in coastal areas of Japan since 1956 and the record of this production is noted in table 14.19. Recently, contracts with Australia and New Zealand, respectively, for iron ore at low prices have reduced the level of iron sand mining in Japan.[229]

The Soviet Union has found gold off the west coast of the Kamchatka Peninsula in the Sea of Okhotsk, in the Gulf of Sakhalin, and in the northern Sea of Japan. Offshore from Irurup Island in the southern Kurils, there was experimental mining of titanomagnetite sands in 1969. Casserite and ilmenite-rutile-zircon sands have been discovered on the eastern shelf of Sakhalin Island.[230] It does not appear that there is commercial production from any of these deposits at the present time.

Phosphorite deposits exist on the continental shelf of southern California and west of central Honshu in Japan.[231] Production from California marine deposits was attempted at a site leased from the federal government in 1961.[232] During the initial phases of the dredging activity in 1962−1963, unexploded naval shells from a firing range and dumping ground were discovered and work was halted. Enough dredging had occurred, however, to indicate that both the quality and quantity of phosphorite available in the area were less than expected. Eventually, the project was abandoned and the lease bonus repaid. Another deposit on the 30-mile bank west of San Diego was evaluated in the early 1960s but it, too, was found uneconomic under existing conditions. Phosphorites are used in the manufacture of fertilizers and the increased demand for agricultural fertilizers worldwide may require increased production, although it appears that land deposits are quite extensive and more easily worked.[233]

It appears that offshore mineral production is uneconomic compared with onshore development, and ocean mining for hard minerals in the North Pacific is, therefore, unlikely on any significant scale in the near future.

TABLE 14.19

PRODUCTION OF IRON SANDS IN JAPAN

| Year | Iron sand[a] production (x 1,000 tonnes) | Offshore iron sand production (x 1,000 tonnes) | % Offshore sand to total production | No. of offshore operations |
|---|---|---|---|---|
| 1956 | 967 | 0.5 | 0.05 | 1 |
| 1957 | 1,142 | 0.7 | 0.06 | 1 |
| 1958 | 955 | 4 | 0.4 | 1 |
| 1959 | 1,357 | 8 | 0.6 | 1 |
| 1960 | 1,751 | 2 | 0.1 | 2 |
| 1961 | 1,712 | 32 | 1.9 | 4 |
| 1962 | 1,443 | 40 | 2.8 | 4 |
| 1963 | 1,295 | 33 | 2.5 | 3 |
| 1964 | 1,425 | 39 | 2.7 | 4 |
| 1965 | 1,389 | 47 | 3.4 | 4 |
| 1966 | 1,289 | 41 | 3.2 | 3 |

Source: A. A. Archer, "Economics of Offshore Exploration and Production of Solid Minerals on the Continental Shelf," *Ocean Management* (1973), 1:33.

[a]Concentrates

## Offshore Energy and Biomass Production with Other Uses

Various proposals to utilize tidal energy, wave energy, and temperature and salinity differences of the sea to generate electrical power have been put forth. The most likely form of energy production from the marine environment of the North Pacific, however, may prove to be energy conversion from marine biomass. In 1978, General Electric began testing the concept of an underwater seaweed farm in deep water five miles off Laguna Beach, California to produce giant California kelp for conversion into methane gas.[234] General Electric will attempt to install farms of up to 100,000 acres off the coast of California by 1985 if the test proves successful. Kelp in the farm will be supplied nutrients piped from deeper waters in the area of the farms, and this addition may make surface and surrounding waters somewhat richer, increasing primary and secondary productivity. It is projected that kelp harvests from a farm of that size could generate 3.45 billion cubic meters of methane gas in a one-year period.[235] A prototype study carried out by scientists from the California Institute of Technology was badly damaged by being run over by a large vessel, which points to the potential interference of this activity with coastwise navigation.

Farming of seaweed in coastal waters is traditional in Asia and is coming under greater scrutiny on the coasts of North America. In Japan, China, and ROK, the commercial harvest of seaweed (nori, kombu, wakame, etc.) for industrial and culinary purposes is well known and represents an important economic activity. Seaweed farms in shallow bays are a part of the traditional seascape. Conflicts occur when seaweed farming is damaged by industrial pollutants and oil, or when it occupies space desired for port expansion or land reclamation for industrial sites.

Because of the increasing conflicts between nori culture and marine pollution and land reclamation in the shallow coastal areas where it has traditionally been done, nori culture in Japan is rapidly moving offshore to waters of 30−40 meters in depth using floating nets. This has had some interesting effects. Productivity of nori culture offshore is higher than in the areas previously used, and it appears that oil slicks float through the nets and do less damage than similar incidents inshore, where the oil tends to accumulate. Oily residue from land-based sources is also less of a threat. The large offshore areas required for the floating nori farms could pose problems for marine transportation, but licensing by prefectural officials ensures that the anchoring sites are not in conflict with shipping lanes. Conflicts over space with fishing groups are normally not a problem, since nori farmers and members of their families are often members of the fisheries cooperatives and placement of the culture sites is negotiated.[236]

Some seaweed, particularly kelp, is harvested commercially along the coasts of North America, and since 1974 the provincial government of British Columbia has spent over $400,000 in grants to investigate the potential for a seaweed industry based on kelp. Salmon fishermen fear development of large-scale kelp harvests, since salmon are often found in kelp beds.[237]

## Protection of Marine Habitats and Animals with Other Uses

The demand for protection of marine habitats and species of marine animals has injected a new use into the North Pacific (i.e., the reservation of areas and particular species of animals from consumptive uses). These changes have somewhat altered the character of domestic activities in coastal states and have had international ramifications. In many respects, the impacts of the new regulations are not yet known, but it is useful to review some of the changes and to discuss their implications.

The concept of reserving marine areas for scientific study and recreational and aesthetic purposes has been applied by Japan and the United States. Japan has established 43 underwater marine parks spaced throughout the archipelago.[238] These parks are viewed with suspicion by fishing interests who fear loss of fishing rights and interference with operations due to expansion of the parks, and conflicts with recreational interests.[239]

The Marine Protection, Research, and Sanctuaries Act and the Coastal Zone Management Act in the United States provide for establishment of marine sanctuaries in near- and offshore waters. As of early 1980, no marine sanctuaries had been established on the west coast of the United States. A large no-lease area has been proposed by municipalities in southern California between Santa Barbara Island and San Diego because of environmental concerns about offshore drilling.[240] This proposal has received the greatest amount of attention, although six areas each in California and Washington, and eleven in Alaska, have been recommended for marine sanctuary status. Of these, only three off California are under active consideration, including the Santa Barbara-San Diego area.[241] Precisely what form these recommendations will later take is hard to predict, yet surely the intent will be to limit or prohibit competing uses of specific marine areas in order to protect other significant or particularly valuable portions of the marine environment.

Protection of species of marine animals and their habitats has altered the management of these species in Canadian and U.S. waters, and some of the changes have affected the operations of foreign fishing and whaling fleets in the Northeast Pacific. The conflicts involve a variety of conflicts including harvest of whales versus protection, marine mammals versus damage to fishing gear, marine mammals versus taking of commercial fishermen's catch, and the more complex question of competition between seabirds and marine mammals versus fish for food within the ecosystem.

Harvest of whales in the Northeast Pacific by Soviet and Japanese fleets is somewhat circumscribed by United States and Canadian prohibition of taking of marine mammals within their 200-mile fisheries zones. Prior to the extension of coastal state jurisdiction, whale stocks in that area were under the management of the International Whaling Commission, which set quotas for taking whales in the North Pacific, and prohibited the taking of species that were considered to be overharvested on the basis of available scientific information. Under U.S. jurisdiction, foreign whaling fleets are not permitted to operate, and fishing fleets must obtain a permit for their incidental catches of whales and other marine mammals. Japan and the Soviet Union argue that prohibition of whaling in the Northeast Pacific is not necessary for several of the harvested stocks. Under a protocol to the renegotiated International North Pacific Convention, Japan has agreed to joint investigations of the status of Dall porpoise (*Phocoenoides dalli*) and northern fur seals (*Callorhinus ursinus*) in their high-seas salmon drift-net fishery.

Conflicts involving gear damage and the taking of catch are known from the following fisheries: gill net fisheries for salmon are affected by Stellar and California sea lions

(*Eumetopias jubatus* and *Zalophus californianus*), harbor seals (*Phoca vitulina*), and beluga whales (*Delphinapterus leucas*); longline fisheries for halibut and sablefish are affected by Stellar sea lions; purse seine fisheries for anchovy and herring are affected by harbor seals and Stellar and California sea lions; and trolled gear for salmon are affected by sea lions.[242]

For the most part, the damage to gear or loss of fish has not been well documented and it is therefore difficult to obtain an idea of the magnitude of this sort of multiple use conflict. Estimates indicate that the costs to fishermen from marine mammal interactions are not trivial. In the Copper River Delta salmon gill-net fishery, for example, the estimated value of fish loss was \$230,122 and the cost of damaged gear was \$72,000 during the 1977 fishing season. The incidental catch of porpoise in tuna purse seines has attracted national attention to marine mammal conflicts. Sea otters (*Enhydra lutris*) competing with divers for abalones off California are another instance of such conflicts.

British Columbia and the states on the west coast of the United States each instituted bounty systems and control programs to harass or eradicate marine mammals that were interfering with fisheries, beginning in the early part of the twentieth century. By the late 1960s and early 1970s, the programs of control or eradication had been reversed and converted into management programs to protect stocks of marine mammals. Protection of marine mammals, including whales, became national policy in the United States with the passage of the 1972 Marine Mammal Protection Act (PL 92−522) and the 1973 Endangered Species Act (PL 93−205). The extension of Canadian and United States jurisdiction over fisheries to 200 nm in 1976 also applied to protection of marine mammals within the zone. Under protection, local and national, some stocks of marine mammals could show a growth in population and could result in an increasing nuisance to commercial fisheries.

With the protection of marine mammals under national legislation and seabirds under bilateral agreements between the United States and Canada and Japan, respectively,[243] and the increasing interest in maximizing the production of fish from the Northeast Pacific, there is speculation on the competition between marine animals and fish for food. Study of the ecosystemic relationships between fish and other marine animals is taking place to determine the extent of competitive interaction between these species.[244]

Some interesting aspects of the marine animal protection controversy are the conflicts generated by these animals vis-à-vis other uses. One instance of this interaction is the loss of fishing gear to a grey whale migrating along the coast of Washington. The animal became entangled in the gear and swam off with it.[245] Thus, valuable gear was lost and the animal possibly injured. Another example is the case where crested auklets landed on a crab fishing vessel transiting Kupreanof Strait in such numbers in windy weather that the boat nearly capsized.[246] While such interactions are decidedly rare, they do raise the question of what should be done to adjust the conflicting objectives of various pieces of federal legislation if protection of marine mammals is shown to seriously impact the development of national interests in fishing.

## Marine Science with Other Uses

Marine science as a use of the North Pacific is probably only minimally affected by multiple use conflicts.[247] Increased use of the oceans by different activities requires a concomitant increase in scientific activity to assist with development. Marine science is used to ascertain the dimensions of multiple use conflicts and to help determine means to mitigate them. In that sense, marine science can be seen to benefit from multiple use conflicts. Not much information is available on documented conflicts between marine scientific research and other uses in the North Pacific. As an example of such conflict, dense fishing activity can make it difficult to perform experiments where it is necessary to use fixed buoys for radar positioning, since it is sometimes hard to discriminate between the target buoy and the fishing vessels. Fishing vessels towing nets have been known to disturb and damage fixed scientific instrumentation; when possible, marine scientists avoid areas where intensive fishing is known to occur. Basic research on seafloor sediments using deep-sea drilling techniques, as in the international cooperative research with the deep-sea drilling ship *Glomar Challenger*, has sought to exclude potentially petroliferous areas.[248] Penetration of oil-bearing strata without the proper equipment to contain the oil could cause serious pollution problems, to say nothing of the political ramifications. Polluted coastal areas and munitions dumping areas preclude some types of marine science from defined areas, and military operations can restrict or exclude scientific research at some times. These conflicts do not appear to be major impediments to marine science at the present time.

The potential list of uses of the sea—airports, underwater cities, nuclear power plant siting, and others—is virtually endless. New uses of the sea will probably always be viewed with suspicion by existing uses, whether or not any conflicts are evidenced. How these and other problems of increased multiple use are to be resolved is not clear but the complicated, fragmented, and post hoc means by which marine uses are presently managed does not recommend itself as a satisfactory alternative. We turn now to an assessment of the original hypothesis concerning the need for arrangements to deal with multiple use conflicts in the North Pacific.

## OBSERVATIONS CONCERNING MULTIPLE USE CONFLICTS IN THE NORTH PACIFIC

We have examined our hypothesis that increased use and increased diversity of use have resulted in a rising level of conflict between uses of the North Pacific. The following observations can be made with respect to the specific data categories required to test our hypothesis. The direction of conflict has been fairly easily identified in the process of defining multiple use conflicts, but it has not been possible to show that over time more uses are affected by multiple use conflicts. The geographical location and extent of multiple use conflicts appears to be largely near shore and usually under the territorial jurisdiction of coastal states; or, with respect to oil development, it involves continental shelf areas over which claims to national jurisdiction have been made. With the emergence of 200-mile exclusive economic zones, virtually all marine activities, except high-seas shipping in the North Pacific, will probably fall under some form of national jurisdiction. Pollution by litter, synthetic organic compounds, oil, and radionuclides has been detected at low levels in the open ocean areas, but most of the demonstrable pollution impacts have been from heavy metals, oil, and nutrients polluting confined coastal areas and bays. Evidence of transboundary pollution impacts has not been found, although the potential for oil pollution from oil tanker traffic is of concern to Canada and the United States, especially in the Straits of Juan de Fuca and northern Puget Sound. Data are inadequate to assess systematically the trends in the number and frequency of multiple use conflicts, the conditions under which such conflicts occur, and the value of the damages caused by multiple use conflicts in relation to the total value of the activities.

In a broader sense, our study of multiple use conflicts in the North Pacific permits us to make the following observations.

First, there is a distinct lack of information on multiple use conflicts in the North Pacific. Most of what we have learned is based on the use of surrogate rather than direct measures. This lack of data is not as important, however, as the question of why such information is not collected. We ascribe this failure to collect the data on multiple use conflicts to a combination of factors, not the least of which are (1) fragmented single use oriented management authorities at national and international levels, and (2) lack of perception of the importance of such data by persons in a position to collect and evaluate them.

Second, with respect to the rate at which offshore oil developments are now taking place, we have observed that the number of areas under consideration for development is fairly small, and the expected rate of successful exploration leading to offshore production is even lower. Even if oil is discovered in the proposed sale areas in Alaska or in the joint Japan–ROK development area in 1980, it will be on the order of 5–10 years before production can begin if normal patterns are followed. This allows adequate time to begin to develop ways of coordinating oil development and fisheries operations. Limited prior experience in the North Pacific has shown that oil development is not necessarily preemptive of fishing operations, even when the Santa Barbara blowout is considered. Coastal aquaculture in Japan has, however, experienced severe impacts from oil pollution from land-based sources and shipping accidents. Given the small scale of current and projected developments and their limited geographic scope, oil developments have not thus far been seen to be a problem for marine navigation in the North Pacific.

Third, regulatory actions by the governments of Canada, Japan, and the United States in the late 1960s and early 1970s have probably led to either a reduction in the levels of pollution of most types in coastal, and thereby offshore, waters of the North Pacific or a slowing of the rate of increase in pollution levels. This is a somewhat startling observation to most who have only recently been apprised of the hazards of PCB and DDT, and who have been convinced by a barrage of media information that pollution levels are inexorably increasing. The fact that the pollution peak with respect to heavy metals and synthetic organic compounds may have come and gone by the mid-1970s is not grounds for complacency, since "safe" levels of pollution in marine environments are still not known. Furthermore, considerably more effort is required to gain an understanding of how to use the capacity of the marine environment effectively to absorb pollutants.

Fourth, the potential impacts of some new developments in marine use, such as creation of marine sanctuaries, preservation of marine mammals and their habitat, and biomass energy conversion from kelp farming, offer examples of uses that will probably need to be accommodated by existing uses. In some areas, like off southern California, marine sanctuary proposals have already stirred up considerable concern on the part of offshore oil interests. It is unlikely that other uses like hard mineral mining of the seabed, emplacement of submarine cables, and military uses of the sea will increase above present levels, and it is conceivable that each of them could actually decline in importance in the North Pacific due to changing market conditions and use of alternative technologies or strategies to accomplish desired aims. The interaction between fishing vessels and other vessels in marine transportation and recreational activities needs to be studied to determine to what extent there are harmful interactions.

Fifth, rather than trade-offs between mutually exclusive uses arbitrated by governmental decision makers, the process of multiple use interaction is often one of interuse accommodation involving changes in levels of use, operating patterns, technologies, and sequencing of uses. Sometimes this process is initiated by the affected users and sometimes effected through the implementation of policies determined by the government policy makers. The resolution of conflicts arising from interaction between multiple uses of a particular area can be an extremely complex interplay between private and public responses, and considerable care must be accorded to determining the appropriate level for intervention by governments at a local or national level, and by government participation in other international arrangements.

Sixth, no mechanism exists at national or international levels that is capable (or specifically assigned the task) of assisting in the accommodation of marine multiple use conflicts on a continuing basis. While some of the previously made observations may be interpreted to mean that multiple use interactions in the North Pacific do not warrant serious consideration because they appear to be moderate, rather than severe in nature, this is not a valid conclusion. Even at moderate or low levels of conflict, there is a need to develop a predictable process of multiple use accommodation, since the failure to provide such a mediation service can lead to costly delays and possible damages, and contribute to the creation of an adversary rather than consensus-oriented conflict-resolution process. Furthermore, some of the multiple use conflicts involve millions of dollars worth of damage, as seen in the case of the Santa Barbara blowout and the Mizushima oil spill.

The accommodation of user interests in multiple use conflicts is basically a problem of providing assurance to all interested users that they will be participants in the resolution of conflicts involving them, and in planning processes that permit activities that may result in impacts on their particular use. New users must anticipate that established users will be concerned about possible impacts on their use of resources or their activities in an area and should be prepared to discuss those concerns. Changes in the scale or operating patterns of existing users vis-à-vis each other can also be expected to engender concern among potentially affected parties. Consultation among users is necessary before actions are taken and general agreement on how to settle damage claims arising out of conflicts between uses is desirable. Where it is impossible to know the impacts prior to developing a use, agreement is also desirable on how to proceed under conditions of uncertainty. Continued discussion and study of the effects of multiple use interactions must take place after a new use is initiated or existing uses alter the character of their operations. All of these points lead to the conclusion that it is crucial to create a conflict-resolution environment receptive to analysis of information, assessment of impact and, when necessary, payment of compensation.

The general picture that emerges from this study is that multiple use conflicts in the North Pacific do not register as important issues requiring immediate regional attempts to resolve them. Multiple use conflicts, however, can be locally important and involve considerable costs and benefits. This leads to the conclusion that multiple use conflicts can best be dealt with on a national or subnational basis in the North Pacific, except where the desirability of global standard-setting removes the focus of decision making from even a regional focus, as in the case of ship-generated pollution. There are potentially a few instances like transboundary pollution and disposal of high-level radioactive wastes in the seabed where common regional or subregional interests indicate the need for coordination of national approaches on a bilateral or multilateral basis. None of this precludes the exchange of information between nations on how to solve multiple use conflicts in coastal and offshore waters.

# 15

# Legacy of the Past and Directions for Future Marine Policy in the North Pacific

The perspective chosen to analyze the marine policy problems of the North Pacific region emphasizes the patterns of interaction between the seven nation-states bordering the North Pacific Ocean. Our aims are to describe trends in patterns of ocean use, to explain the conflicts that have arisen within and between uses, and to assess the extent to which technological advance and jurisdictional change have altered the contexts of marine policy problems and the process of ocean management.

Quite clearly, fisheries are *the* major regional issue though they have never been handled comprehensively on a regional basis. Patterns of use in marine transportation, including both trade and regulations designed to reduce the level of ship-generated oil pollution in the ocean, have significant regional implications though they are driven by different global dynamics. Marine scientific research, especially as it relates to problems of management affecting living resources, climate change, and marine pollution, would clearly benefit from a more systematic regional approach, which would also strengthen the links between research output and management decisions. However, this area of use also suffers from fragmentation and uncoordinated approaches adopted historically by the participants. The evidence shows that neither marine pollution nor multiple use conflicts are significant *regional* problems in the North Pacific; they are primarily local problems. The more significant multiple use conflicts involve the incompatibilities of fish production versus hydrocarbon exploitation, and the transport of petroleum versus fishing, but these are unlikely to become major problems in the region as a whole, given the relatively restricted hydrocarbon development potential of the North Pacific. However, significant areas in the Bering and East China seas may be exploited for oil. Since the former is heavily fished and the latter is used widely for more marine transportation, important multiple use conflicts may emerge there in the future.

When one attempts to assess the ways in which countries in the North Pacific appear to deal with marine policy problems, the overwhelming impression is the consistent haphazardness that reflects the absence of thought and action in pursuit of deliberately formulated policy objectives and, therefore, results in "dynamic ad hocery." It is very difficult to find clear attempts to calculate benefits, costs, and defined priorities among the national participants. National marine policy seems to be pushed and pulled by the dynamics of each issue plus the occasional contamination by external considerations of high politics. Marine policy is therefore still in a fairly primitive stage in the countries of the North Pacific and exhibits the following characteristics:

1. National policy is the aggregation of haphazard responses to external demands and is primarily reactive.
2. The national decision process is highly fragmented and suffers from a large number of internal, competing jurisdictions with no clear sense of national or regional priorities. Not surprisingly, this fragmentation is refracted regionally as well.
3. There are only weak or, in most cases, no links between decisions and policies that affect different patterns of ocean use.
4. Little formal attention is paid to formulating objectives and identifying and evaluating alternative strategies for pursuing policy objectives.[1]
5. There is no official perception of the need to calculate net benefit, given expanded national jurisdiction over a wide range of resources and activities in the areas of the ocean recently coming under national control.

Let us therefore consider what the major future policy problems seem to be for fisheries, marine transportation, and marine scientific research, since these patterns of use are most affected by the change in the world ocean regime combined with the vector of technological advance.

## LIVING RESOURCES

Fisheries are the major regional issue in spite of the absence of a comprehensive regional approach because there are organic links between fish stocks and fishing patterns across the entire North Pacific. Even where there is no intermingling of stocks, policy decisions have substantial regional effects because Japan, the USSR, and the Republic of Korea are the major participants in the fisheries of the Northeast, as well as the Northwest Pacific.

Prior to the emergence of extended national jurisdiction in 1976–1977, the largest catches of the North Pacific were not under the management of any party. Though a significant number of regional commissions with wide geographic scope were in existence, they were generally weak and had jurisdiction over only a few stocks. Given voluntary participation in these management schemes, the normal deficiencies of open-access regimes for fisheries were clearly evident. The decision systems were cumbersome, decision times were protracted, and there were serious constraints on enforcement actions so that compliance with regulations was commensurately low. In these conditions, biological and economic waste is likely to be high, and conflict is also likely to be high. The transaction costs of this approach are also high since negotiations are continuous, and scientific information is inadequate and primarily reflects national positions.

The phenomenon of extended coastal state jurisdiction rapidly swept away the open-access regimes of the past in most cases and theoretically solved the problem of control. This change in authority leads to the assumption of control by the coastal state over all stocks that fall completely within its extended zone, and generates concern within national fishing communities for formulating coordinated fisheries policy affecting all stocks in the area. The bilateral and trilateral approach has been retained as well but its nature has been much changed, since in most cases it is the coastal state that defines and enforces the terms of participation in the fishery. The only exceptions to this occur when particular stocks are significantly shared between adjacent states (eg., the salmon interception convention being negotiated between Canada and the United States); these arrangements then seek to specify the conditions of sharing in the catch as well as in the research and the development of conservation regulations. In fact, a significant increase in the amount and quality of information available on the status of the stocks in the Northeast Pacific has been a welcome consequence of extended jurisdiction.

The nature of the stakes has also been changed considerably. Access to markets and forms of international cooperation in fisheries have become major issues in the new regime precisely because they have been linked by the coastal states to access to raw material. This approach, combined with more extensive national legislation, observation, and enforcement of distant-water fishing operations, has generated significant changes in the patterns of deployment and operation of distant-water fleets, especially in the Northeast Pacific.

The major policy problems of the future for fisheries in the North Pacific seem to be the following:

1. An evaluation of the need for and, where necessary, the design of policies to facilitate the development of coastal state harvesting and processing capabilities and their effects on the foreign fishing states. This implies further questions relative to (a) the role of international cooperation (i.e., joint ventures and other modalities), and (b) access to and control over markets (especially for the U.S. and Japan).

2. The impacts of coastal state regulations on the operations of the fishing fleets in the Northeast and Northwest Pacific.

3. The impacts of coastal state regulations on short- and long-term trends in resource utilization in the North Pacific as a whole.[2]

4. The impacts of nonfisheries politico-strategic issues and boundary conflicts in the Northwest Pacific on the fisheries policies and relationships of the USSR, Japan, the Republic of Korea, and the People's Republic of China.

5. The impacts of the issues mentioned above and other external political events (e.g., the Soviet invasion of Afghanistan in 1980) on the fisheries policies of the United States in the Northeast Pacific.

The first set of problems exists on both sides of the North Pacific but in a more acute form in the Northeast Pacific. In chapters 6 and 7 we described the conflicts that occurred in

1978 involving the United States, Japan, and the Republic of Korea over the issues of joint ventures and removal of import restrictions on surimi in Japanese and Korean markets. Not surprisingly, these issues have now become linked both to the general question of facilitating development of U.S. harvesting and processing capabilities and to division of the surplus yield in fisheries occurring in the extended zone of the United States.

Section 201 of the FCMA specifies the criteria that are to be used by the Secretary of State, in cooperation with the Secretary of Commerce, in determining the allocation among foreign nations of the total allowable level of foreign fishing (TALFF). These criteria are: (1) whether and to what extent the fishing vessels of such nations have traditionally engaged in fishing in such fishery; (2) whether such nations have cooperated with the United States in, and made substantial contributions to, fishery research and the identification of fishery resources; (3) whether such nations have cooperated with the United States in enforcement and with respect to the conservation and management of fishery resources; and (4) such other matters as the Secretary of State in cooperation with the Secretary [of Commerce] deems appropriate.

The North Pacific Fishery Management Council, however, and components of the harvesting and processing industries in the states of Alaska, Washington, and Oregon give a high priority to developing U.S. harvesting and processing capabilities relative to species currently unutilized or underutilized by them, and increasingly phasing out the foreign fishermen. At the same time, the countries traditionally fishing in the Northeast Pacific and eastern Bering Sea face increasing competition from new entrants like the Republic of Korea, Poland, Bulgaria, German Democratic Republic, Federal Republic of Germany, Taiwan, and Mexico, who themselves (except for Mexico) are seeking access to new sources of raw materials as a result of being excluded elsewhere by the global implementation of extended fisheries zones. Consequently, the U.S. industry and their representatives have begun to suggest that allocations of TALFF, which already take third place after domestic allocations and allocations to joint ventures, should be guided by what each recipient is prepared to do to foster the development of U.S. harvesting and processing capabilities.[3]

The linking of these issues is potentially severely destabilizing in the short run for the historic pattern of fishing in the Northeast Pacific and eastern Bering Sea, and increases the competition among the distant-water fleets operating in the area. This is probably inevitable anyway and not necessarily bad in itself, though care must be taken to accommodate links made previously in arrangements for different fisheries (e.g., Bering Sea pollock and the high-seas salmon fishery of Japan). At the same time, it behooves the coastal state to determine its own priorities for development and management of various fish stocks and to choose carefully among alternative paths for pursuing these objectives. If neither priorities nor policies are clearly stated, actions will be taken willy-nilly without regard for inconsistencies, balancing of short-term gains against long-term costs, and the like.

There are in fact many modalities of international cooperation in fisheries and they are not all equally appropriate in all circumstances. Joint ventures, for example, take many forms[4] and combinations including as many as six major components: domestic fishing effort, foreign fishing effort, domestic processing, foreign processing, domestic marketing, and foreign marketing. Before the coastal state launches a massive program in one direction or another, several questions need to be analyzed. The basic policy questions are: (1) Whose benefits are we attempting to maximize and how are ''benefits'' to be defined? (2) Under what conditions would it be advantageous for the coastal state to encourage foreign participation in any or all of the combinations identified above? (3) After combinations are chosen, what are their operational characteristics, costs, and benefits in the near- and long-term? (4) What policies, organizational arrangements, and procedures seem to be most appropriate in the circumstances? These questions urgently need to be tackled in future studies.

Another line of investigation for the future deals with the impacts of coastal state regulation on patterns of fleet deployment and operations by distant-water nations in the North Pacific. The process of adjustment has not yet been concluded; it should be monitored carefully in the future because it is contributing to a major restructuring in the composition and patterns of operation of the major distant-water fleets of the world, and to substantial shifts in the patterns of resource utilization. Consequently, these trends will have substantial impacts on the actual levels of fish production from the North Pacific over the long term.

As a result of decreased quota allocations for the Soviet Union (since 1978) and Poland (only in 1978), mainly for Pacific hake and Alaska pollock, both nations have had to reduce the number of fishing vessels sent to Washington, Oregon, and California waters, as well as to the Gulf of Alaska, the Bering Sea and the Aleutians. According to the NMFS and Coast Guard data, Russian and Polish fishing capacities were reduced in 1978 to 60−70 percent of their fleet's potential in the beginning of 1977.[5] However, since 1979, Poland has benefited from reductions in the Soviet quota for pollock in the eastern Bering Sea as a result of increasing conflict between the U.S. and USSR.

East German and Bulgarian fleets engaged in harvesting Pacific hake in Washington, Oregon, and California coastal waters have been totally withdrawn from these fisheries, as those two nations did not receive national quotas from the U.S. government. On the other hand, Mexican flag trawlers were allowed a quota in the same area and in the Gulf of Alaska, and Mexico has been allowed to develop these fisheries as a newcomer within reciprocity arrangements established between the Mexican and U.S. governments.

One clear result of the U.S. quota allocation policy in 1977 and 1978 is that Soviet Bloc fleets had to sharply curtail their catches in the Northeast Pacific and Bering Sea, while Japan maintained her catch volumes with only relatively small (10%−15%) reductions from the previous levels. However, Japan has been seriously affected by two developments: first, the reductions in fleet capacity necessitated by declining quotas in the Soviet zone; and, second, reductions in the high-seas salmon fleet as a result of new and more stringent restrictions imposed in the renegotiated International North Pacific Fisheries Convention. The restrictions on the Japanese fleets in the Northwest Pacific have led to increasing competition between their trawlers and longliners for access to fishing grounds in the Northeast Pacific. The Republic of Korea has received increased allocations to mitigate the impact of losses incurred by implementation of the Soviet exclusive fisheries zone. Since 1979, Poland has also benefitted from drastic declines in the Soviet allocations.

Since all foreign fleets in U.S. waters have been allowed to take their quotas only during reduced fishing seasons, and only in certain strictly determined fishing areas, many distant-water operators began to send only the most modern, efficient, and seaworthy vessels to assure full utilization of the quota. However, strict by-catch regulations have contributed to underutilization of the quotas by some fleets (mainly by the USSR, Poland, and Taiwan) operating in the U.S. zone, since they were not able successfully to apply more selective fishing gear to harvest only their target species.

Utilization of quotas by some foreign fleets was surprisingly low; for example, according to NMFS data for 1977, the USSR took only 55 percent of its U.S. quota, Poland 69 percent; Taiwan 20 percent.[6] In 1978, the USSR caught 73 percent, Poland 55 percent, and Taiwan 51 percent.[7] In fact, not all foreign fleets were able quickly to adjust their patterns of operation, fleet composition, fishing gear, and other capacities to obstacles produced by coastal state restrictions. The target fisheries were consequently less fully utilized than the coastal state intended.

Fisheries relationships and policies in the Northwest Pacific are hostage to external politico-strategic issues to a much greater extent than they are in the Northeast Pacific.[8] Japan has succeeded in coming to terms on fisheries with all her neighbors: China, ROK, DPRK, and the USSR. However, these arrangements are not necessarily stable in the long run because they depend on the pattern of settlement to be achieved with China, ROK, and the USSR on the outstanding boundary conflicts that have existed for some time in that area. These are made more difficult to solve in some cases by the hydrocarbon potential of the continental shelves, and the high salience now attributed to oil in world politics.[9]

In the Northeast Pacific, fisheries relationships between North Pacific countries are also affected by external politico-strategic concerns, but in a fairly limited way. When a major event occurs, as in the U.S. response to the Soviet invasion of Afghanistan in January 1980, the trade-offs that are proposed nationally may be quite different from those that are seen to be desirable from a regional or subnational perspective.[10] This does not always lead to conflict, but it can. These events give participants in the North Pacific and Pacific Fishery Management Councils levers used to make lasting changes in the patterns of foreign fishing in the Gulf of Alaska, eastern Bering Sea, and waters off Washington, Oregon, and California.

## MARINE TRANSPORTATION

Marine transportation policy problems continue to be divided between the problems of commercial shipping and the special problems of regulating tankers as generators of oil pollution. Chapter 8 in this volume provides, for the first time, an integrated description of cargo flows in the North Pacific. The analysis is based on a consistent matrix of import and export figures for 1976 by eight commodity categories. The pattern of trade shows that petroleum, containerized, and noncontainerizable general cargoes are the three most important commodity groups moving on the North Pacific. Japan is by far the predominant shipping country. Trade movement by ships, therefore, is not spread uniformly but is concentrated around Japan, extending south and east. The density of international shipping traffic in the Northeast Pacific, however, is low, except for the Los Angeles and Long Beach area. The dominant shipping link in the North Pacific is between Japan and the U.S.

Recent studies by Immer[11] and by Gibbs and Meyer[12] indicate that U.S. general cargo trades with Pacific nations are growing faster than trades with any other foreign area. This trade growth is accompanied by a shift of cargo movements away from using the Panama Canal and U.S. East Coast ports, and toward intermodal transportation systems involving U.S. transcontinental railroads and U.S. West Coast ports. As we have seen, the U.S.–Japan trade link is the most significant in the North Pacific region, so any important revision in overall U.S. ocean shipping policy will have an impact on the patterns of trade in the North Pacific region.

The major determinants affecting future trends in commercial shipping in the North Pacific are the policies adopted by the Soviet Union, particularly with respect to the Far East Shipping Co. (FESCO), and those being considered by the United States. We note again, however, that these policies do not have their origin in the North Pacific. Since the dynamics of commercial shipping policy are global in nature, these policies have been developed and are being considered in a global context. It is undeniable, however, that the pursuit of these policies will have major impacts on commercial shipping in the North Pacific.

Claims have been made in Canada, the U.S., and Japan that the competitive practices of Soviet shipping are unfair because the cost bases and commercial objectives of the Soviet fleet are radically different from those of Western (capitalist) countries. In the North Pacific, these questions have been addressed specifically to the operations of FESCO. These claims need to be tested in some detail and an assessment made whether, in fact, Soviet commercial shipping practices represent an unfair competitive threat. A major issue in such a study will be the comparability of Soviet and Western accounting bases and what they reveal about corporate objectives in the operation of their shipping industries. After this has been accomplished, Canadian, U.S., and Japanese shipping policies will have to be evaluated in a coordinated fashion in the light of the conclusions reached on the comparability of Soviet and Western shipping enterprises.

On the U.S. side, the issues raised by the debate on U.S. shipping policies have an additional dimension.

The U.S. Congress (House Merchant Marine and Fisheries Committee), in reaction to anti-trust action taken by the U.S. Department of Justice against U.S. and foreign cartelized shipping lines, has proposed sweeping revisions of the 1920, and 1936, and 1970 ocean shipping acts and amendments (H.R. 4769, the Murphy Bill). These proposals, if implemented, would bring U.S. ocean shipping policy into conformity with all other nations (closed conferences and endorsement of shipper's associations), as well as reducing construction differential subsidies. These changes would affect (1) the freight tariffs charged in international trade, and thus result in balance of payments and national income gains and losses; (2) the flag makeup of liner conferences calling at U.S. ports and its trade partners, which will, in turn, affect U.S. and foreign business and labor interests; (3) U.S. (and foreign) national security via changes in the numbers of U.S. flagged and crewed ships and U.S. shipyards. The policy change would thus have ramifications in the first instance for the U.S.; in the second, for U.S. trade partners; and in the third, for all U.S. nationals engaged in ocean shipping. It is likely that the second and third effects will be overlooked in the domestic public debate on the new policy; these two effects, especially the effects on United States trade partners in the North Pacific, will require evaluation.

With respect to oil pollution generated by shipping, the evidence available shows that the North Pacific Ocean as a whole is not much affected by oil pollution generated by tankers. There are, however, localized problems, around Japan especially and off the states of California and Washington. As a result of oil production in Prudhoe Bay, Alaska, and the export of oil through the port of Valdez, Alaska, there is growing concern in British Columbia and the state of Washington over the possibilities of increasing pollution associated with increasing density of tanker traffic. Additional issues revolve around the location of a terminal in Washington or British Columbia for transshipment of such oil, and the imposition of a prohibition on supertankers in Puget Sound.

Chapters 9 and 10 of this book describe in detail the global regime affecting tankers with respect to oil pollution controls. The regulatory system is perhaps more complex than is desirable, with some Conventions being in force and others not. The problem at the global level revolves around the standards to be adopted and their relative cost-effectiveness on one hand, and the system of enforcement on the other, in particular the rights and duties of flag, coastal, and port states. Again, as in the case of commercial shipping, while the level of action on this issue has thus far been primarily global, the results of policies pursued will be felt regionally. Moreover, since regional effects may often differ widely from the global average, tension will be inevitable. This, in part, explains why several important conventions have not yet come into force.

Future policy problems affecting the North Pacific will be of five kinds. First, since Japan has by far the largest commercial fleet operating in the North Pacific, there is a need to assess the domestic implications for the Japanese-controlled tanker fleet of the new policies on ship-generated pollution contained in recent IMCO Conventions (especially the 1973 and 1978 Conventions) and the regulations and enforcement provisions of the Draft Convention. Second, chapter 9 assesses in detail the dynamics of technological advance that affect controls over tanker-generated pollution. Since in the North Pacific the major impacts will be experienced by the Japanese fleet, there is a need to assess the economic incentives and disincentives posed by these new technologies for the fleet owners. Third, in some parts of the world there is a tension between the perceived gaps in the comprehensiveness and effectiveness of global action and the perceived increasingly urgent requirements of unilateral action to protect port and coastal states. This trend has in fact resulted in both a new Convention (1978) and an assertion by the U.S. that it will begin enforcing the 1973 and 1978 IMCO Conventions even before they have received the necessary ratifications to enter into force. This action is meant to preempt even more strident demands for increasingly stringent regulation made by some U.S. groups. Domestic demands for stringent controls on tanker design and operation are also strong in Canada. Furthermore, the enforcement problems of national and international standards will be complicated for all coastal states by the expansion of territorial control to twelve miles and the potential differences of regulation to be applied therein as opposed to the economic zone. This trend is again most significant in the North Pacific for the Japanese tanker fleet, since Japan has by far the largest seaborne imports of oil in the region.

The fourth policy problem that requires investigation concerns the patterns of tanker traffic in the Northeast Pacific between Valdez, Alaska and some point or points in British Columbia and/or Washington, and regulations affecting them. The U.S. Trans-Alaska Pipeline Act of 1974 foresaw the early marine shipment of Alaskan oil in the Northeast Pacific from Valdez to Cherry Point, Washington, or to a terminal to be built at Kitimat, British Columbia. This assumption was invalidated by resistance from environmentalist groups documented in the "Thompson Hearings" sponsored by the Canadian federal government in 1977–1978. However, the possibility of Alaskan, and perhaps even Arctic Canadian, oil coming into British Columbia on tankers from Alaska is not foreclosed. The whole issue, therefore, requires some systematic reassessment. This is true, too, of the fifth and last issue, which deals with the consequences of removing the Congressional prohibition of the export of Alaskan oil to Japan. Clearly, if this prohibition is removed, the pattern of tanker traffic on the North Pacific will change significantly. Unlike the case of fisheries, in which questions of total nutritional supply were not seen to be significant in U.S. policy, Alaskan oil tends to be seen as one component of the total U.S. oil supply problem, and is thus strongly linked to "external" considerations of a more strategic nature.

## MARINE SCIENTIFIC RESEARCH

The marine scientific research issue in the region as a whole is multifaceted and of major significance for resource use and management. The central question on marine scientific research, which we address in chapters 12 and 13 of this book, concerns the need for and approaches to the design of a new, comprehensive regional scientific organization called PICES. Briefly, the arguments in favor of creating such an organization are restated in the following paragraphs.

Although several international bodies exist for the management of specific fishery resources in the region, there is no overall mechanism for the exchange and evaluation of data and information on the status of stocks on which national and international decisions on resource management can be based. Moreover, increasing uses of ocean resources, the transport of petroleum and other potentially toxic products, and industrial activities around the margins of the North Pacific can, in the future, represent intensifying threats to the health of the marine environment. No formal mechanism exists for pooling efforts to understand and monitor these potential threats.

The role of the ocean in modulating weather and climate is now evident. An improved mechanism is required for the development and coordination of investigations of ocean-atmosphere interaction that will enhance the possibility of predicting weather and climate. Scientific investigations are conducted in the North Pacific under the auspices of several governments, including those of the U.S., USSR, Canada, and Japan. These investigations include all fields of marine science and its applications. Some are multiinstitutional and include arrangements for interinstitutional coordination; others are the efforts of single institutions. No general mechanism exists for the initiation, planning and coordination of multinational oceanographic and fishery research programs in the region.

Data resulting from these investigations, in part at least, eventually find their way into the world data exchange system. However, there is no mechanism for an orderly and timely exchange of data and information between governments and institutions engaged in the research, for improving the quality and intercomparability of measurements, or for selecting common statistical areas and bases.

Having identified the tasks to be done, we proceed now to an evaluation of the political process within which the decision to create or not to create such an organization will be taken. This process will be primarily intergovernmental involving appropriate agencies in Canada, the U.S., USSR, and Japan. In reaching such a decision, governments at one level will undoubtedly wish to assess the level of support expressed by different components of national marine science constituencies, the scale of financial commitments required to engage in such an undertaking, and the possibility of alternative arrangements for meeting needs that might be less costly and yet, at the same time, be at least as efficient and effective as creating a new intergovernmental organization. At another level these specific issues will be seen in a more general context shaped by the political relationships of the four countries. The questions raised by the latter dimension will undoubtedly be more salient to the leadership in each country and will probably be more intractable since they relate to general issues of conflict and cooperation between Canada, the U.S., Japan, and the USSR. It will be in the interest of those in support of creating a new organization, therefore, to attempt to encapsulate the proposals and seek to have them considered on their own merits. Linking these issues to larger questions of political relationships will at best delay substantially, or at worst prevent, moving ahead on the creation of PICES, for which there is a demonstrable need.

It is not difficult to see why the idea of PICES is attractive to the three countries in the North Pacific with the largest interests in fisheries issues. The costs of the ad hoc approach to investigations are high, since neither a common data base nor a comprehensive understanding of common problems currently exists. Piecemeal approaches produce high transaction costs through a variety of bilateral and multilateral arrangements. These approaches strain existing budgets and governments could more easily ensure increased efficiency by eliminating the ad hoc individual arrangements. A comprehensive approach would also be able to produce a common data base. While the new organization would specifically be prohibited from involving itself in questions of resource management, the direct connection between the scientific data and benefits for government agencies with operational responsibilities would yield high priority for this set of tasks, though some qualifications appropriate to each country need to be taken into account.

For example, in Japan two systems of budgeting for fisheries research exist in an uncoordinated fashion. University scientists are linked to the Ministry of Education, while government research laboratories are linked, through the Japan Fisheries Agency, to the Ministry of Agriculture, Forestry, and Fisheries. The interests of academic scientists are more varied and not as clearly focused as those of the government scientists. Support for PICES from the academic group might be mixed at best. From government scientists, however, support would be very high, since their operational responsibilities are closely tied to new bilateral agreements that Japan has entered into with the U.S., Canada, and the USSR.

In the USSR, a different division exists. Fisheries scientists with the most direct interests are found in the Pacific laboratory (TINRO) of the Ministry of Fisheries in Vladivostok. Presumably, also, those in the central laboratory (VNIRO) in Moscow would also have a strong interest. The academic oceanographers are organized separately in the Academy of Sciences of the USSR, but it happens that these scientists also have a strong interest in creating PICES. Significantly, at the 1977 task group meeting for Project WESTPAC in 1977, the USSR representatives sought to broaden the terms of reference for the Project in a way that would have made the expanded Project WESTPAC almost identical to PICES as currently envisaged. The geographic scope of WESTPAC, as currently defined, is broader than that envisaged for PICES, since the Southwest Pacific is also included. However, WESTPAC excludes the Northeast Pacific.

In the United States, the situation is somewhat similar to that in Japan. The government scientists have the clearest, most focused need for creating PICES, but only if it replaces the large number of bilateral meetings which the ad hoc approach has created. If this efficiency is not specifically provided for, interest in PICES will drop off sharply. University fisheries scientists would share these views, if not with the same intensity, and biological oceanographers would be equally in favor because they see a need to develop a data bank on a pan-oceanic basis, and it would be more difficult to cooperate with scientists in the USSR and Japan without such a mechanism as PICES.

From the fisheries point of view as well, there would be great serendipitous utility to approaching fisheries problems in a wider context of international and interdisciplinary collaboration. The argument from this perspective is that it is neither accurate nor useful to make a strict differentiation between fisheries and nonfisheries activities in PICES because, if prediction of stock size is an objective, physical oceanography is a critical component. Fisheries science by itself cannot adequately answer questions relating to the causes of fluctuations or the absence of fluctuations in fish stocks. The only distinction that makes sense in practice is between research that is required for the routine preparation of fishery management plans and research that is oriented to problems like variability in stocks, species interrelationships, and interaction between various species and their ocean environment. Only the latter would be appropriate for the PICES framework.[13]

In addition, a comprehensive approach could more effectively facilitate the development of an ecosystem approach to the management of fisheries. This would be of particular significance to the Bering Sea, and would help to identify the key factors that influence the distribution of major biota. PICES could also facilitate the building of a common data base by fostering assessments on the same species in different locations, or on different assessments of the same species in the same location. In this manner, therefore, PICES could contribute to a step-level change in the direction and scale of fisheries science in the North Pacific. The serendipitous effect would be enhanced by providing a forum for problem formulation on issues that cannot adequately be tackled under existing fragmentary arrangements.

Perceptions of the utility of PICES become more diffuse as we move from fisheries research to oceanography and the monitoring of the ocean environment. Oceanographers as a group have more varied views than fisheries scientists and, in an organizational sense, there is less coherence in the community, perhaps because the links to operational responsibilities are not substantial. Some Canadian oceanographers, in particular, fear that a new organization would lead to governmental commitments that would skew their own research priorities in unwelcome directions. They see little utility in creating a mechanism for coordination of research when they claim there is little to coordinate and when the costs of meaningful cooperation in oceanography between the four countries will be quite high. Finally, they argue that whenever collaboration is necessary, there are alternative, less costly, and more effective informal ways of doing so.

Similar differences of view affect the proposed monitoring function. Fisheries scientists, biological oceanographers, physical oceanographers interested in ocean and atmosphere coupling, atmospheric scientists, and chemical oceanographers interested in the fate and effects of pollutants in the ocean environment would have the greatest interests in developing a region-wide monitoring capability. On the other hand, oceanographers who are not primarily interested in long-term changes, and those who do not have operating responsibilities, are much less convinced of the need for spending resources on developing such a capability.

Understanding the role of the ocean in climate change requires very large-scale monitoring of sea surface temperatures. A number of piecemeal arrangements have been made with ships of opportunity in the context of the North Pacific Climate Study (NORPAX). While the use of Japanese, U.S., and Canadian commercial shipping and fishing vessels can be arranged without formal involvement of the Soviet government, Soviet ships and facilities cannot be used extensively, if at all. This results in lost opportunities and less than uniform or complete coverage of the North Pacific. The scale of the logistic problem therefore currently exceeds the capacity of the existing research mechanism. Assuming Soviet membership in PICES, major advances in the capabilities of the observing network could be arranged. However, some oceanographers who are not interested primarily in long-term changes argue that for them there is a lack of consistent alignment between the scale of effort required in establishing monitoring arrangements and interest in analyzing the data collected. This, they claim, is a recalcitrant problem that cannot be solved with present technology, and they fear being forced into such monitoring arrangements by fiat (i.e., governmental commitment) because they think the arrangements will not lead to productive results.

Given this distribution of views, let us raise the major questions. Are the benefits to be derived from participation in PICES sufficiently great and applicable to a sufficiently large group of scientists in each country to make it work? What are the likely costs of PICES? Are there alternative arrangements for deriving these benefits at less cost?

The answer to the first question is clearly yes for Japanese, Soviet, and American fisheries scientists, oceanographers interested in primarily long-term changes, and oceanographers with operating responsibilities. In each case, a mechanism like PICES can produce utilities that cannot be derived from piecemeal approaches; each country has an agenda of very specific research problems they want to pursue.

We cannot answer the second question at this time because those assessments have not been made. That is the next step in this series of investigations. The third question also requires further investigation, especially after the cost estimates have been produced. There is one alternative, however, that has been suggested and can be evaluated at this time. It has been suggested that the recently renegotiated INPFC can easily be broadened to include the tasks outlined above. Article IV of the new Protocol reads:

> The Contracting Parties shall work towards the establishment of an international organization with broader membership dealing with species of the Convention area other than anadromous species. . . . When such an international organization becomes functional, discussions of scientific research relating to non-anadromous species under this Convention shall be terminated and transferred to the new organization.

Given the wording of this Article, the signatories clearly did not intend the INPFC to assume these broadened tasks indefinitely and they specifically foresaw that expanded membership (i.e., the USSR) in such additional arrangements would be necessary. The reason for this lies primarily in the Japanese desire to avoid being caught in the same organization (which deals with the management of the high-seas salmon fishery of Japan) between the major states of origin in the Northeast and Northwest Pacific. It is difficult to foresee a change in the Japanese position in the short run unless the Japanese high-seas salmon fishery were phased out entirely. This is, therefore, not a viable option in the immediate future (i.e., one to two years), though it may become so later and recent events already indicate some tentative shifts in that direction.

Given Soviet interests in expanding the focus of Project WESTPAC, it seems useful to provide an in-depth analysis of that alternative in terms of assessing its potential for future cooperative research efforts in the North Pacific. Similarly, given the importance of the monitoring function for air and sea interaction studies, it would be useful to analyze the present monitoring of physical oceanographic conditions in the North Pacific as they relate to weather and climate. This would require a detailed inventory of capabilities defined in terms of ships of opportunity, buoys, remote sensing equipment, coastal stations, light ships, etc. This inventory could then be used for development of a system of future monitoring of the North Pacific, with emphasis on the dimension of organizational arrangements.

Future work on policy problems relating to marine scientific research in the North Pacific will revolve around several major issues. There is a certain urgency attached to producing the cost estimates for PICES and identifying and evaluating possible alternatives for deriving the same benefits at less cost. It is also important to provide a more comprehensive picture of the scale and locus of marine scientific research activities in the North Pacific by compiling a profile of the nature and magnitude of the research effort undertaken by the United States, Canada, USSR, and Japan with emphasis on work conducted at sea. This research will be tied to an evaluation of the existing data exchange system and to an assessment of the links between the research output and management decisions in the four areas of fisheries, oceanography, climate, and marine pollution.

## SEABED DISPOSAL OF HIGH-LEVEL RADIOACTIVE WASTE

The last major *potential* regional problem of the North Pacific that requires some assessment concerns the question of seabed disposal of high-level radioactive nuclear waste. This is an entirely new possibility in the use of the North Pacific Ocean.

Most of the reported work so far on this problem has dealt with either the environmental or geological aspects of seabed disposal, or with the global policy issues posed by the problem.[14] The latter have been couched primarily in terms of the London (Dumping) Convention of 1972 and the International Atomic Energy Agency's (IAEA) inspection standards and procedures. Some attention has also been given to internal (U.S.) governmental organizational arrangements and procedures. However, since the North Pacific is the most likely location for such disposal efforts by the U.S., Japan, and possibly others in the foreseeable future, explicitly regional concerns must be built into the primarily global and national scenarios described so far.

Given the potential multiplicity of acceptable sites, it is easy to foresee that standard-setting, monitoring, and inspection of operations would be centralized at the global level in an organization like the IAEA, but it is unlikely that control over the actual operations would be vested there. Indeed, even at this early exploratory state, the Nuclear Energy Agency of the Organization for Economic Cooperation and Development (OECD) is an operating consortium that has a role clearly competitive to the IAEA. The reason for this is that the OECD includes a much smaller group of advanced industrial countries (the U.S., Canada, Western Europe, and Japan) as members. However, the fact that the USSR is not a member of OECD severely restricts the utility of this organization vis-à-vis the North Pacific potential site.

The proposed assessment should assume that a decision has been made to utilize the midplate, midgyre site in the North Pacific based on the criteria identified by the Sandia Laboratories study[15] for the subseabed disposal of high-level radioactive nuclear waste. It should assume further that the IAEA's role will be restricted along the lines described in the previous paragraph. As such, most of the global effort will actually be focused on standard-setting with respect to (1) the chemical properties of the vitrified waste (leach resistance and the probabilities of fracturing), (2) container characteristics (in particular, lifetimes), (3) criteria governing choice of sites, (4) the actual method of disposal, (5) final location of the containers, and (6) safeguards in the event of leakage.

The proposed assessment should assume, finally, that the actual operations relative to any specific site will involve only a relatively small group of countries acting as some sort of consortium, even though wider regional consultations would probably precede the operations.

The intent of the proposed study is therefore to describe and assess, specifically and in detail, the range of operations, organizational arrangements, and resources required for disposal of high-level radioactive waste in the North Pacific, to assess probable costs, and to estimate the probable consequences of alternative approaches. In doing so, it would be fruitful to follow the line of argument developed by Todd Laporte[16] and we expect that the results of such a study would be useful both for other regions of the world ocean and for comparing the utility of subseabed disposal with other choices.

The specific questions which should be addressed are:

1. How might a consortium of states in the North Pacific, concerned primarily with operating systems of subseabed disposal of high-level nuclear wastes, be created? This would include criteria for membership, terms of reference, structure, and problems of negotiating its creation.
2. With respect to actual operations:
   a. What activities are required for subseabed disposal?
   b. What resources (i.e., people, funds, and support facilities) are required?
3. What scale of organizational systems and capabilities are required?
   a. What problems of size (number of employees and range of geographic dispersion) are involved?
   b. What problems of complexity (vertical and horizontal differentiation of units, number of occupational specialties, differences of national procedures, etc.) are generated?
   c. Is the level of complexity manageable with respect to the need for coordination and management? If no, what alternatives are available for reducing complexity? If yes, what are the points of probable breakdown and what safeguards are available?
4. What are the probable social, economic, and political consequences, for other marine and nonmarine-related activities in the North Pacific, of operating such a consortium in the foreseeable future?

## WHAT CAN BE LEARNED FROM THE NORTH PACIFIC EXPERIENCE

We contend that the dominant impression one takes away from studying marine policies in the North Pacific is one of fragmentation and haphazard approaches in all uses, and especially with respect to interactions between uses. This fragmentation stems from severe decentralization in the organization and process of policy formulation at the *national* level. However, it must be remembered that these countries are among the most advanced maritime countries in the world, so we would expect similar disarray in most marine regions of the world because national systems are everywhere inadequately organized and developed.

With respect to fisheries policy in the North Pacific, the open-access era was characterized inter alia by excessive decentralization of authority and lack of control over the stocks in question. The major global contribution of extended fisheries zones has been to resolve the problem of control over stocks, but this phenomenon has not led to a reduction in the degree of decentralization in the organization and process of fisheries management. It has simply shifted the focus of concern to the level of the coastal state where the management system is still inadequate to the task. We do not know what will happen to fish production and fishing in the North Pacific over the long term because it will depend upon the specific policies to be followed by the respective coastal states of the region. There are many alternative courses of action available and it is not yet clear which choices will be made, or even ought to be made. Since international jurisdictional issues have virtually disappeared from the agenda, major concern has now shifted to questions of national organization, objectives, the management of domestic and foreign fleet operations, policies determining the allocation of surplus production among foreign fleets, policies affecting patterns of international cooperation in fisheries, and international trade in fish products for human consumption. We expect that this picture will be replicated in most other marine regions except the Northeast Atlantic, where there already exists a much higher level of regional integration than exists anywhere else in the world. In that region, the institutional authority, arrangements, and machinery for developing *regional* policy are already in place.

In the North Pacific, on the other hand, where the regional infrastructure is relatively rudimentary, problems of national objectives, policies, and so on are not developed on an exclusively regional basis, even though they have very significant regional *effects*. The region, per se, is not the operative context in actual management except for salmon on the high seas and fur seals, so that fragmented approaches to fisheries management continue, albeit of a different kind.

In the category of marine transportation, the most important activity for regional policy is the Japan–U.S. trade connection, especially since the annual rate of increase of U.S. West Coast trade (primarily with Japan) is growing faster than U.S. East Coast trade with Western Europe. This trade link, as we have pointed out before, is driven primarily by global dynamics, but is sensitive to changes in policies deliberately or inadvertently followed by the respective states. In this connection, U.S. merchant shipping policies and practices are especially important. The effects of the recent growth and practices of the Soviet flag fleet in the North Pacific maritime trades are also quite important.

The evidence shows that there is no cause yet for regional concern about oil pollution from ships. This is a problem primarily of local impacts, principally around Japan (where the political impact of environmentalist groups is weak) and, to a lesser extent, on the U.S. and Canadian west coasts (where environmental concerns tend to be strongly articulated). Over time, a regional problem may arise if trans-Pacific transport of oil is significantly increased via Alaska to Japan and the Malacca Straits to the U.S. Concerns about marine transportation problems at the regional level, therefore, turn primarily on the effects of policy changes implemented at the national and global levels on regional patterns. These effects should be systematically evaluated and weighted as part of the general policy formulation process leading to the initiation of change.

With respect to marine scientific research, regionalization requires creating something that was not there before. This should be attempted only after there are clear, positive answers to the question of whether there are tangible and intangible benefits of sufficiently high priority to be derived from such an approach at cost levels the participants are willing to bear. The first part of the question is much more important than the second part, since there are many more alternatives available in the design of organizational arrangements for minimizing costs to governments.

The other crucial question to be raised after clear benefits of high priority have been established is what links are likely to be made by the participants between the proposed creation of PICES and other, often unrelated, issues already in contention between them. From the point of view of those pushing for a regional initiative in marine science, therefore, we repeat that the preferred strategy would be, first, to make a powerful case on the benefits to be derived and, second, to try to design organizational alternatives to minimize cost. The objective here is to make the case for the new initiative so attractive as to induce the governments in question to treat the issue on its own terms and to refrain from linking concessions on this issue to concessions on other issues.

The general point that is worth making about marine policy for attempts to extrapolate from the experience of the North Pacific to other parts of the world is that self-consciously regional orientations exist with respect only to fisheries and, in the cases of the Mediterranean and the Baltic, with respect to pollution as well. Regional concern with pollution is likely to spread to all governments abutting enclosed or semienclosed seas. Regional concern with fisheries derives from the history of fisheries management under open-access regimes and actual patterns of fishing, though the infrastructure remains very weak. In the North Pacific, for instance, we repeat that a definite regional orientation exists primarily among those who fish throughout the region and this means only Japan, the USSR, and the ROK. Two other coastal states, Canada and the U.S., have fully regional concerns only with respect to two species, though they have secondary interest in questions of regional fisheries development as well.

The immediate dilemma highlighted by our study of the North Pacific is that marine policies pursued haphazardly by governments have clear regional impacts on fishing, shipping, and scientific research, even though the governments in question do not act on that basis. Moreover, since marine policy generally is still in a primitive stage of development and national approaches remain highly fragmented, it is very difficult to get systematic evaluation of alternative possibilities at *any* level. This lack of maturity to the marine policy process will affect all proposals for new initiatives in the near future, but it is hoped that over time analyses like those undertaken in this project will help to transform governmental approaches to the identification and evaluation of alternative marine policy choices in the North Pacific and elsewhere.

**Appendixes**

# APPENDIX A

## Maps of Fisheries Convention Boundaries in the North Pacific

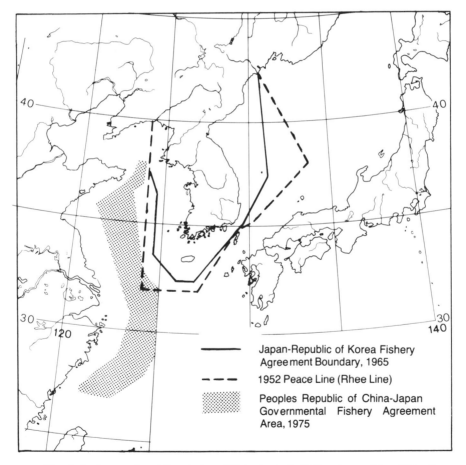

Fig. A.1. *International Regulation of Fisheries in the Yellow Sea and East China Sea.* Source: Choon-ho Park, ''Fishing Under Troubled Waters,'' *Ocean Development and International Law Journal*, 2, 2 (1974), pp. 112, 113. (See *Atlas of Marine Use in the North Pacific Region*, p. 6, accompanying this volume, for a more detailed map.)

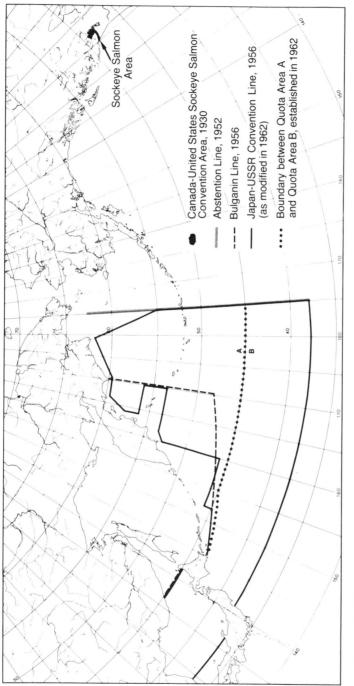

Fig. A.2. *Salmon Regulatory Areas in the North Pacific Prior to Extended Jurisdiction.* Sources: *Canada–U.S. Sockeye Salmon Convention Area*—Drawn on the basis of Article 1, "Convention for the Protection, Preservation and Extension of the Sockeye Salmon Fishery of the Fraser River System 1930," available in *League of Nations Treaty Series*, Vol. 184, pp. 305 ff. *Abstention Line*—Drawn on the basis of Annex, to "International Convention for the High Seas Fisheries of the North Pacific Ocean 1952," available in the *United Nations Treaty Series*, Vol. 205, pp. 81 ff. *Bulganin Line*—Hiroshi Kasahara, "Japanese Distant-Water Fisheries: A Review," *Fishery Bulletin*, 70, 1 (1973), p. 240. *Japan–USSR Convention Line (as modified 1962)*—R. A. Fredin, et al. *Pacific Salmon and the High Seas Salmon Fisheries of Japan*, processed report (Seattle: Northwest and Alaska Fisheries Center, December 1977), p. 73. (See *Atlas of Marine Use in the North Pacific Region*, p. 6, accompanying this volume, for a more detailed map.)

# APPENDIX B

## List of International Agreements for North Pacific Fisheries

**INTERNATIONAL AGREEMENTS RELATED TO LIVING RESOURCES IN THE NORTHEAST PACIFIC OCEAN\***

Key:

ILM    International Legal Materials

LNTS   League of Nations Treaty Series

TIAS   United States—Treaties and International Agreements Series (post-1945)

TS     Treaty Series—U.S. State Department, Pamphlet Series (pre-1945)

UNLS   United Nations Legislative Series (ST/LEG/B/16 and B/18)

UNTS   United Nations Treaty Series

---

\*Denotes treaties in force prior to extension of jurisdiction. Earlier agreements are provided to illustrate the development of the international regime for fisheries in the Northeast Pacific Ocean. Agreements related to shellfish sanitation, natural resources in general, and cooperation in environmental protection are excluded.

## I. Multilateral Agreements

| Title | Year signed | Signatories | Reference |
|---|---|---|---|
| 1. Convention for the Preservation of Fur Seals | 1911 | Canada, Japan, USSR, U.S. | TS 564 |

(Japan notified the other nations of intent to withdraw from the convention in 1940. Canada and the United States concluded a separate agreement on a bilateral basis in 1942.)

| Title | Year signed | Signatories | Reference |
|---|---|---|---|
| Interim Convention on Conservation of North Pacific Fur Seals | 1956* | Canada, Japan, USSR, U.S. | UNTS 314:105 |
| Amended by Protocol | 1963* | | UNTS 494:303 |
| Extended by an Exchange of Notes | 1969* | | UNTS 719:313 |
| Amended and Extended | 1976* | | TIAS 8368 |
| Amended | 1978 | | TIAS 9842 |
| 2. International Convention for the Regulation of Whaling | 1937 | Canada, Japan, USSR, U.S.[a] | LNTS 190:79 |
| Replaced by: International Convention for the Regulation of Whaling | 1946* | | UNTS 161:73 |
| Amended by Protocol (Numerous other amendments to whaling schedules) | 1956* | | UNTS 338:336 |
| 3. International Convention for High Sea Fisheries in the North Pacific Ocean | 1952[b] | Canada, Japan, U.S. | UNTS 205:81 |
| Amended | 1962* | | TIAS 5385 |
| Amended | 1978 | | TIAS 9242 |
| 4. Convention on Fishing and Conservation of Living Resources on the High Seas | 1958* | United States (subject to an understanding)[a] | UNTS 559:285 |
| 5. Convention on the Continental Shelf | 1958* | Canada (with a declaration), USSR, U.S.[a] | UNTS 499:311 |

[a]North Pacific nations which are signatories.

[b]This treaty follows the provisions of the Treaty of Peace with Japan 1951 signed by the Allied Powers (TIAS-2490). Article 9 of that treaty requires that Japan negotiate agreements regulating fishing on the high seas.

## II. Canada—United States Bilateral Agreements

| Title | Year signed | Signatories | Reference |
|---|---|---|---|
| 1. Convention Respecting Fisheries, Boundary, and the Restoration of Slaves | 1818 | Canada, U.S. | TS 112 |
| Agreement on Boundaries | 1827* | | TS 116 |
| 2. Convention on Fur Seal Fishing | 1894 | Canada, U.S. | TS 307 |
| (Replaced by multilateral agreement) | 1911 | | |
| 3. Convention for the Protection of Migratory Birds | 1916 | Canada, U.S. | TS 628 |
| 4. Convention for the Preservation of the Halibut Fishery of the Northern Pacific Ocean and Bering Sea | 1923 | Canada, U.S. | TS 701 |
| Supplanted by Agreement | 1930 | Canada, U.S. | TS 837 |
| Replaced by Agreement | 1937 | Canada, U.S. | TS 917 |
| Replaced by Agreement | 1953* | Canada, U.S. | UNTS 222:77 |
| Amended | 1979 | | TIAS 9855 |
| 5. Convention for the Protection, Preservation, and Extension of the Sockeye Salmon Fisheries in the Fraser River System | 1930* | Canada, U.S. | LNTS 184:305 |
| Exchange of Notes Constituting an Agreement to Facilitate the Ascent of Salmon in Hell's Gate Canyon and elsewhere in the Fraser River System. | 1944* | Canada, U.S. | UNTS 121:300 |
| Protocol Amending the Convention to include Pink Salmon in the Fraser River System. | 1956* | Canada, U.S. | UNTS 290:103 |

## II. Canada–United States Bilateral Agreements (Cont.)

| Title | Year signed | Signatories | Reference |
|---|---|---|---|
| 6. Convention Concerning Fur Seals | 1942 | Canada, U.S. | a |
| Amended | 1947 | Canada, U.S. | TIAS 1686 |
| (Replaced by multilateral agreement 1956) | | | |
| 7. Convention for the Extension to Halibut Fishing Vessels of Port Privileges on the Pacific Coasts of USA and Canada | 1950* | Canada, U.S. | UNTS 200:212 |
| 8. Agreement between the Government of the USA and the Government of Canada on Reciprocal Fishing Privileges in Certain Areas of their Coasts | 1970 | Canada, U.S. | UNTS 752:3 |
| Extended | 1972 | Canada, U.S. | TIAS 7323 |
| Reciprocal Fishing Privileges | 1973 | Canada, U.S. | TIAS 7606 & 7676 |
| Reciprocal Fishing Privileges | 1974 | Canada, U.S. | TIAS 7818 |
| Reciprocal Fishing Privileges | 1975 | Canada, U.S. | TIAS 8057 |
| Reciprocal Fishing Privileges | 1976* | Canada, U.S. | TIAS 8251 |
| Amended | 1977 | | TIAS 8648 |

[a]No. 415 in the U.S. State Department, Executive Agreement Series.

## III. Canada–Bilateral Agreements with Countries Other Than the United States

| Title | Year signed | Signatories | Reference |
|---|---|---|---|
| 1. Agreement between the Government of Canada and the Government of USSR on Cooperation in Fisheries in the Northeastern Pacific Ocean off the Coast of Canada | 1971* | Canada, USSR | UNLS B16:546 |

## III. Canada—Bilateral Agreements with Countries Other Than the United States (Cont.)

| Title | Year signed | Signatories | Reference |
|---|---|---|---|
| 2. Agreement between the Government of Canada and the Government of USSR on Provisional Rules of Navigation and Fisheries Safety in the Northeastern Pacific Ocean off the Coast of Canada | 1971* | Canada, USSR | UNLS B16:543 |

## IV. United States—Bilateral Agreements with Countries Other Than Canada

| Title | Year signed | Signatories | Reference |
|---|---|---|---|
| A. Japan | | | |
| 1. *Crabs* | | | |
| Exchange of Notes Constituting an Agreement between USA and Japan Relating to the King Crab Fishery in the Eastern Bering Sea | 1964 | Japan, U.S. | UNTS 533:30 |
| Amended | 1966 | | UNTS 680:382 |
| Amended | 1968 | | UNTS 714:286 |
| Replaced by: Exchange of Notes Constituting an Agreement between the U.S. and Japan Regarding the King and Tanner Crab Fisheries in the Eastern Bering Sea | 1970 | Japan, U.S. | UNTS 776:239 |
| Extended | 1972 | | TIAS 7527 |
| Replaced by: Agreement Concerning Fisheries: Certain Fisheries off the United States Coast, Salmon Fisheries, King and Tanner Crabs | 1974* | Japan, U.S. | TIAS 7986 |

## IV. United States—Bilateral Agreements with Countries Other Than Canada (Cont.)

| Title | Year signed | Signatories | Reference |
|---|---|---|---|
| 2. *Certain Fisheries* | | | |
| Exchange of Notes Constituting an Agreement Concerning Certain Fisheries off the Coast of the United States | 1967 | Japan, U.S. | UNTS 685:268 |
| Amended and Extended | 1968 | | UNTS 714:330 |
| Replaced by: Exchange of Notes Constituting an Agreement between Japan and U.S. Concerning Certain Fisheries off the U.S. Coast and Salmon Fisheries | 1970 | Japan, U.S. | UNTS 776:197 |
| Amended and Extended | 1972 | | TIAS 7528 |
| Replaced by: Agreement Concerning Fisheries: Certain Fisheries off the United States Coast, Salmon Fisheries, King and Tanner Crabs | 1974* | Japan, U.S. | TIAS 7986 |
| 3. *Whale Observers* | | | |
| Agreement Concerning an International Observer Scheme for Whaling Operations from Land Stations in the North Pacific Ocean | 1972 | Japan, U.S. | TIAS 7315 |
| Extended | 1973 | | TIAS 7647 |
| Extended | 1974 | | TIAS 7823 |
| Extended | 1975 | | TIAS 8088 |
| Extended | 1976* | | TIAS 8399 |

## IV. United States—Bilateral Agreements with Countries Other Than Canada (Cont.)

| Title | Year signed | Signatories | Reference |
|-------|-------------|-------------|-----------|
| 4. *Migratory Birds* | | | |
| Convention for the Protection of Migratory Birds and Birds in Danger of Extinction, and their Environment | 1972* | Japan, U.S. | TIAS 7900 |
| Amendment to Annex | 1974* | | TIAS 7990 |
| B. Poland | | | |
| 1. Agreement between the two Governments regarding Fisheries in the Northeastern Pacific Ocean off the Coast of the USA | 1975* | Poland, U.S. | TIAS 8100 |
| (Settlement of Claims in the Northeastern Pacific Ocean is dealt with under the procedures established in Agreement Regarding Fisheries in the Western Region of the Middle Atlantic Ocean, 1973 TIAS 7659, extended 1975 TIAS 8099.) | | | |
| C. Republic of Korea | | | |
| 1. Agreement Concerning Cooperation in Fisheries with Agreed Minutes | 1972 | ROK, U.S. | TIAS 7517 |
| Terminated | 1977 | | TIAS 8525 |
| D. Soviet Union (USSR) | | | |
| 1. Convention Regarding Navigation, Fishing and Trading on the Pacific Ocean and along the Northwest Coast of America | 1824* | USSR, U.S. | TS 298 |
| 2. Agreement on Fur Seal Fisheries | 1894 | USSR, U.S. | TS 307 |
| (Replaced by Multilateral Convention) | 1911 | | |

## IV.  United States—Bilateral Agreements with Countries Other Than Canada (Cont.)

| Title | Year signed | Signatories | Reference |
|---|---|---|---|
| 3. *Fishing Operations* | | | |
| Agreement between USSR and U.S. Relating to Fishing Operations in the Northeastern Pacific Ocean | 1964 | USSR, U.S. | UNTS 531:214 |
| Amended and Extended | 1967 | | UNTS 697:318 |
| Amended and Extended | 1969 | | UNTS 714:281 |
| Replaced by: Agreement between USSR and U.S. Relating to Fishing Operations in the Northeastern Pacific Ocean | 1971 | USSR, U.S. | UNTS 777:41 |
| Extended | 1972 | | TIAS 7541 |
| Replaced by: Agreement between the two Governments Relating to Fishing Operations in the Northeastern Pacific Ocean | 1973 | USSR, U.S. | TIAS 7572 |
| Extended | 1974 | | TIAS 7981 |
| Extended | 1975 | | TIAS 8020 |
| Replaced by: Agreement between the two Governments Regarding Fisheries in the Northeastern Pacific Ocean off the Coast of the U.S. | 1975* | USSR, U.S. | TIAS 8207 |
| 4. *Crabs* | | | |
| Agreement between the Government of the U.S. and the Government of the USSR Relating to Fishing for King Crab | 1965 | USSR, U.S. | UNTS 541:97 |
| Amended and Extended | 1967 | | UNTS 688:428 |
| Amended and Extended | 1969 | | UNTS 714:292 |

## IV.  United States—Bilateral Agreements with Countries Other Than Canada (Cont.)

| Title | Year signed | Signatories | Reference |
|-------|-------------|-------------|-----------|
| Replaced by: Agreement between the Government of the U.S. and the Government of the USSR Relating to Fishing for King and Tanner Crab | 1971 | USSR, U.S. | UNTS 781:203 |
| Extended | 1972 | | TIAS 7541 |
| Replaced by: Agreement between the Governments of the USA and the USSR Relating to Fishing for King and Tanner Crab | 1973 | USSR, U.S. | TIAS 7571 |
| Extended | 1974 | | TIAS 7981 |
| Extended | 1974 | | TIAS 8020 |
| Replaced by: Agreement between the two Governments Relating to Fishing for King and Tanner Crab | 1975* | USSR, U.S. | TIAS 8160 |
| 5. *Certain Fisheries* Agreement between USSR and U.S. on Certain Fishery Problems in the Northeastern Part of the Pacific Ocean off the Coast of the U.S. | 1967 | USSR, U.S. | UNTS 688:158 |
| Extended | 1968 | | UNTS 697:362 |
| Amended and Extended | 1969 | | UNTS 714:352 |
| Replaced by: Agreement between USSR and U.S. on Certain Fishery Problems in the Northeastern Part of the Pacific Ocean off the Coast of the U.S. | 1971 | USSR, U.S. | UNTS 777:18 |
| Amended | 1972 | | TIAS 7328 |
| Extended | 1972 | | TIAS 7541 |

## IV. United States—Bilateral Agreements with Countries Other Than Canada (Cont.)

| Title | Year signed | Signatories | Reference |
|---|---|---|---|
| Replaced by: |  |  |  |
| Agreement on Certain Fisheries Problems in the Northeastern Part of the Pacific Ocean off the Coast of the U.S. | 1973 | USSR, U.S. | TIAS 7573 |
| Extended | 1974 |  | TIAS 7981 |
| Replaced by: |  |  |  |
| Agreement between the two Governments Regarding Fisheries in the Northeastern Pacific Ocean off the Coast of the U.S. | 1975* | USSR, U.S. | TIAS 8207 |
| 6. *Settlement of Claims* |  |  |  |
| Agreement Relating to the Consideration of the Claims Resulting from Damage to Fishing Vessels or Gear and to Measures to Prevent Fishing Conflicts | 1973* | USSR, U.S. | TIAS 7575 |
| Amended | 1974* |  | TIAS 7663 |
| Amended | 1975* |  | TIAS 8022 |

## V. Fisheries Regime in the Northeastern Pacific Ocean Following Unilateral Extension of Fishery Zones to 200 Miles

A. *National Acts Extending Jurisdiction*

| Nation | Title | Date | Reference |
|---|---|---|---|
| Canada | Act Amending the Law on Territorial Sea and Fishing Zones | 1970 | ILM 9:543 |
|  | Proposed Fishing Zones | 1976 | ILM 15:1372 |
| DPRK | Economic Zone | 1977 | Foreign Broadcast Information Service, vol. 4, July 1, 1977, DZ |

## V. Fisheries Regime in the Northeastern Pacific Ocean Following Unilateral Extension of Fishery Zones to 200 Miles (Cont.)

| Title | | Year signed | Signatories | Reference |
|---|---|---|---|---|
| Japan | Law on Provisional Measures Relating to the Fishing Zone | 1977 | | Unofficial translation. U.S. Natl. Marine Fisheries Service |
| USSR | Edict on Provisional Measures for the Preservation of Living Resources and the Regulation of Fishing in Marine Areas | 1976 | | ILM 15:1381 |
| United States | Fisheries Conservation and Management Act of 1976 | 1976 | | ILM 15:634 |

B. *Fisheries Agreements Relating to 200-Mile Fishing Zones in the Northeastern Pacific*

| Nation | Title | Date | Reference |
|---|---|---|---|
| Canada—USSR | Agreement for Fisheries within the Canadian 200-mile Fishery Zone | 1976 | ILM 15:1267 |
| Canada—Japan | Agreement for Fisheries within the Canadian 200-mile Fishery Zone | 1976 | No published reference available. Similar to Canada—USSR. |
| Canada—Poland | Agreement for Fisheries within the Canadian 200-mile Fishery Zone | 1976 | No published reference available. Similar to Canada—USSR. |
| U.S.—Japan | Governing International Fisheries Agreement | 1977 | TIAS 8728/8728 |
| U.S.—GDR | Governing International Fisheries Agreement | 1976 | TIAS 8527 |
| U.S.—ROK | Governing International Fisheries Agreement | 1976 | TIAS 8526 |
| U.S.—Poland | Governing International Fisheries Agreement | 1976 | TIAS 8524 |
| U.S.—Taiwan | Governing International Fisheries Agreement | 1976 | TIAS 8529 |

## V. Fisheries Regime in the Northeastern Pacific Ocean Following Unilateral Extension of Fishery Zones to 200 Miles (Cont.)

|  | Title | Year signed | Signatories | Reference |
|---|---|---|---|---|
| U.S.–USSR | Governing International Fisheries Agreement | 1976 | TIAS 8528 |
| U.S.–Canada | Interim Agreement on Reciprocal Fisheries | 1977 | TIAS 8648 |

Note: Agreements that are under active renegotiation include:
  Canada–U.S. Halibut Convention
  Canada–U.S. Agreement on Management of Shared Salmon Stocks
  Canada–U.S. Agreement on Reciprocal Fisheries
  Canada–Japan–U.S. International North Pacific Fisheries Convention

# INTERNATIONAL AGREEMENTS RELATED TO LIVING RESOURCES IN THE NORTHWEST PACIFIC OCEAN

| | Year signed | Signatories | Reference |
|---|---|---|---|
| **Multilateral Agreements** | | | |
| West Pacific Fisheries, Oceanology and Limnology Research Cooperation Agreement | 1956 | DPRK, N. Vietnam, PRC, USSR (1958, Outer Mongolia joined, and 1967, PRC, withdrew) | (1) |
| **Bilateral Agreements** | | | |
| *China–Korea* | | | |
| Sino–Korea Trade Agreement—Includes Reciprocal Fishery Clause | 1882 | China, Korea | (1) |
| *Japan–Korea* | | | |
| Agreement to Permit Japanese Fishermen to Live in Three Korean Ports | 1426 | Japan, Korea | (1) |
| Agreement to Regulate Japanese Fishing in Waters Near Korea | 1442 | Japan, Korea | (1) |
| Trade Agreement—Includes Reciprocal Fishery Clause | 1883 | Japan, Korea | (1) |
| Fishery Treaty | 1889 | Japan, Korea | (1) |
| Superseded | 1908 | Japan, Korea | (1) |
| *PRC–DPRK* | | | |
| Fishery Agreement for the Yellow Sea | 1959* | PRC, DPRK | (1) |
| Agreement Regarding Fishery Cooperation | 1972* | PRC, DPRK | (2) |

## INTERNATIONAL AGREEMENTS RELATED TO LIVING RESOURCES IN THE NORTHWEST PACIFIC OCEAN (Continued)

| | Year signed | Signatories | Reference |
|---|---|---|---|
| **Japan–ROK** | | | |
| Agreement on Fisheries Between Japan and the Republic of Korea | 1965* | Japan, ROK | *International Legal Materials*, vol. 4, p. 1128. |
| Agreement on Increased Fisheries Claims Compensation. nongovernmental | 1979* | | *Latest Developments in World Fisheries*, NMFS, Part II (January 1980). For mention of earlier nongovernmental arrangements see (3). |
| **Japan–PRC** | | | |
| Nongovernmental Agreement on Japanese Fisheries in Waters Near PRC | 1955 | | (1) |
| Extended | 1956 | | (1) |
| Extended | 1957 | | (1) |
| Lapsed | 1958 | | (1) |
| Second Nongovernmental Agreement on Japanesee Fisheries in Waters Near PRC | 1963 | | (1) |
| Third Nongovernmental Agreement on Fisheries in Waters Near PRC | 1965 | | (1) |
| Extended six times through 1975 | | | |

| Agreement | Year | Parties | Reference | Note |
|---|---|---|---|---|
| Nongovernmental Seine Fishing Regulation | 1970 | | | (1) |
| Agreement on Fisheries Concluded Between the Governments of Japan and the People's Republic of China | 1975* | Japan, PRC | *Japanese Annual of International Law*, vol. 20 (1976). | |
| Extended | 1978* | Japan, PRC | *Latest Developments in World Fisheries*, Part II, NMFS (December 1978). | |

## Japan–DPRK

| Agreement | Year | Parties | Reference | Note |
|---|---|---|---|---|
| Nongovernmental Agreement on Japanese Fisheries in the Exclusive Zone of DPRK | 1977* | | | (2) |
| Extended for two years | 1978 | | | (2) |
| Extended for two years | 1980* | | *Latest Developments in World Fisheries*, Part II, NMFS (May 1980). | |

## DPRK–USSR

| Agreement | Year | Parties | Reference | Note |
|---|---|---|---|---|
| Meeting Regarding Fishing in Respective Zones of Extended Jurisdiction | 1977 | DPRK, USSR | | (2) |
| Protocol for Scientific and Technical Cooperation in Fisheries | 1980* | DPRK, USSR | *Latest Developments in World Fisheries*, NMFS (November 1978). | |
| Protocol for Expanded Fisheries Cooperation | 1980* | DPRK, USSR | *Latest Developments in World Fisheries*, NMFS (March 1980). | |

## INTERNATIONAL AGREEMENTS RELATED TO LIVING RESOURCES IN THE NORTHWEST PACIFIC OCEAN (Continued)

| | Year signed | Signatories | Reference |
|---|---|---|---|
| *Japan–Russia* | | | |
| Poutiatine's Treaty | 1855 | Japan, Russia | (4) |
| Treaty of Exchange of Sakhalin and the Kurile Islands | 1875 | Japan, Russia | (4) |
| Russo–Japanese Peace Treaty (Portsmouth Treaty) | 1905 | Japan, Russia | (4) |
| Russo–Japanese Fishery Convention | 1907 | Japan, Russia | (4) |
| *Russia–Great Britain* | | | |
| Treaty of 1825 | 1825 | Russia, Great Britain | Jozo Tomasevich, *International Agreements on Conservation of Marine Resources* (Palo Alto: Stanford University, 1943). |
| Fur Seals Northwest Pacific | 1893 | Russia, Great Britain | (5) |
| *Russia–U.S.* | | | |
| Fur Seals Northwest Pacific | 1894 | Russia, United States | (5) |
| *Japan–USSR* | | | |
| Convention Embodying Basic Rules of the Relations Between Japan and USSR | 1925 | Japan, USSR | (4) |
| Fishery Convention Between Japan and USSR | 1928 | Japan, USSR | (4) |

| Agreement | Year | Parties | Reference | |
|---|---|---|---|---|
| Extended Annually Until World War II | | Japan, USSR | | (4) |
| Protocol Extending for Five Years the Japan—USSR Fishery Convention | 1944 | Japan, USSR | | (4) |
| Convention Between Japan and the USSR Concerning the High Seas Fisheries of the Northwest Pacific Ocean | 1956 | Japan, USSR | | (4) |
| Denounced by the USSR | 1978 | | | (6) |
| Replaced by: | | | | |
| Japan—USSR Interim Fishery Agreement (Japanese Access to the Soviet Zone) | 1977* | Japan, USSR | *Government Gazette* (Japan), Extra no. 43 (June 10, 1977). | |
| Japan—USSR Interim Fishery Agreement (Soviet Access to the Japanese Zone) | 1977* | Japan, USSR | *Japanese Annual of International Law*, no. 22 (1978). | |
| Both Agreements Extended | 1978* | Japan, USSR | | (6) |
| Agreement Between the Great Japan Fisheries Association and the National Commission of Fisheries of the Soviet Socialist Republics Pertaining to Collection of Tangle in the Area round Kaigara Islands (Sigalnui Is.) by Japanese Fisheries, nongovernmental | 1963 | | Shigeo Sugiyama, "The Japanese—Soviet Tangle Collection Agreement of 1963," *Japanese Annual of International Law*, no. 9 (1964). | |
| Extended for 1964 and Lapsed | 1964 | | Sugiyama, "Tangle Collection Agreement." | |
| Exchange of Notes Concerning the Crab Fisheries | 1970 | Japan, USSR | *Japanese Annual of International Law*, no. 14 (1970). | |
| Agreement Between Japan and the USSR on the Regulation of North Pacific Whaling | 1974 | Japan, USSR | *Japanese Annual of International Law*, no. 19 (1975). | |

## INTERNATIONAL AGREEMENTS RELATED TO LIVING RESOURCES IN THE NORTHWEST PACIFIC OCEAN (Continued)

| | Year signed | Signatories | Reference |
|---|---|---|---|
| Replaced by: | | | |
| Agreement Between Japan and the USSR on the Regulation of North Pacific Whaling | 1975 | Japan, USSR | *Japanese Annual of International Law*, no. 20 (1976). |
| Agreement Between Japan and the USSR on Whaling | 1979* | Japan, USSR | *Latest Developments in World Fisheries*, Part I, NMFS (December 1979). |
| Agreement on Bilateral Claims Settlement | 1975 | Japan, USSR | (3) *Japanese Annual of International Law*, no. 20 (1976). |

Notes: The discussion presented here is interpreted from available sources of information on international agreements related to living resources. Dates followed by an asterisk indicate agreements in effect January 1, 1980. References cited more than once are indicated by numbers in parentheses and listed below.

(1) Choo-ho Park, "Fishing Under Troubled Waters: the Northeast Asia Fisheries Controversy," *Ocean Development and International Law Journal*, 2, 2 (January 1979).

(2) *Ocean Development and Law of the Sea Newsletter*, no. 2 (January 1979).

(3) Shoichi Tanaka, "Japanese Fisheries in the Northwest Pacific," *Ocean Development and International Law Journal*, vol. 6, Pacific Rim Issue (1979).

(4) Zengo Ohira, "Fishery Problems Between Soviet Russia and Japan," *The Japanese Annual of International Law*, vol. 2, 1958.

(5) Stefan A. Reisenfeld, *Protection of Coastal Fisheries Under International Law*, Monograph Series of the Carnegie Endowment for International Peace, Division of International Law (Washington, D.C.: 1942).

(6) *Ocean Development and Law of the Sea Newsletter*, no. 3 (June 1979).

# APPENDIX C

## Allocation Arrangements for the North Pacific

TABLE C.1

Japanese Salmon Quotas Under the Northwest Pacific
Fisheries Convention, 1956 (1955–1961)

(metric tons)

| Date | Quota | Description |
|------|-------|-------------|
| 1955 | 170,000 | Japanese high-seas salmon catch[a] |
| (1956) | 50,000 | Proposed quota for Soviet and foreign fishing under the Bulganin Line[b] |
| 1956 | 65,000 | Quota set for Japanese provisional operations in the area established by the Bulganin Line[a] |
| 1957 | 120,000 | Japanese quota set by the Northwest Pacific Fisheries Commission[c,d] |
| 1958 | 110,000 | Restricted Japanese catch in Okhotsk Sea (6,500)[e] and closed areas on east coast of Kamchatka |
| 1959 | 85,000 | Okhotsk Sea and North Pacific W. of 162° E closed to Japanese salmon fishing |
| 1960 | 67,500 | |
| 1961 | 65,000 | |

[a]Shoichi Tanaka, ``Fisheries in the Northwestern Pacific and Fishery Resources—Mainly on the Japanese Fisheries and International Problems Surrounding Them,'' in Christine L. Dawson, ed., *The North Pacific Project* (Seattle: Institute for Marine Studies, University of Washington, 1977), pp. 217–311.

[b]Zengo Ohira, ``Fishery Problems Between Soviet Russia and Japan,'' *Japanese Annual of International Law*, no. 2 (1958), pp. 1–19.

[c]Hiroshi Kasahara, ``Japanese Distant-Water Fisheries: A Review,'' *Fishery Bulletin* 70,1 (1973), 229–290.

[d]Quotas applied to the area west of 175° W and north of 45° N. The quotas did not apply to Japanese harvests south of 45° N where the catches were 61,500 (1957), 72,000 (1958), and 85,000 (1959).

[e]Shigeru Oda, ``Japan and International Fisheries,'' *Japanese Annual of International Law*, no. 4 (1960), 52.

## TABLE C.2

QUOTA AND CATCH IN THE JAPANESE AND USSR SALMON FISHERIES, 1962–1976
(UNIT = 1000 MT)

| Date | Japan Quota | Japan Catch | Japan Coastal | Japan Total | USSR Planned | (USSR high seas) | USSR Catch |
|------|-------------|-------------|---------------|-------------|--------------|------------------|------------|
| 1962 | 115.0 | 95.7 | 17.2 | 112.9 | 70.0 | | 60.6 |
| 1963 | 120.0 | 120.4 | 24.6 | 145.0 | 78.0 | | 81.1 |
| 1964 | 110.0 | 99.4 | 15.6 | 114.9 | 65.0 | | 45.3 |
| 1965 | 115.0 | 119.7 | 22.3 | 142.0 | 85.0 | | 87.6 |
| 1966 | 96.0 | 101.2 | 22.1 | 123.3 | 65.0 | | 56.2 |
| 1967 | 108.0 | 114.9 | 26.6 | 141.5 | 83.0 | | 78.9 |
| 1968 | 93.0 | 92.0 | 17.1 | 109.1 | 60.0 | | 36.2 |
| 1969 | 105.0 | 109.8 | 26.8 | 136.6 | 80.0 | | 75.5 |
| 1970 | 90.0 | 90.9 | 23.7 | 114.5 | 40.0 | | 39.1 |
| 1971 | 95.0 | 99.3 | 34.6 | 133.9 | 83.0 | (10.0) | 77.6 |
| 1972 | 87.0 | 90.5 | 25.7 | 116.2 | 40.0 | (10.0) | 30.6 |
| 1973 | 91.0 | 95.3 | 36.3 | 131.6 | 80.0 | (10.0) | 77.7 |
| 1974 | 83.0 | 86.9 | 42.3 | 129.2 | 35.0 | (3.0 | 47.2 |
| 1975 | 87.0 | 91.0 | 64.0 | 155.1 | 73.5 | (10.0) | 82.9 |
| 1976 | 80.0 | | | | 46.0 | (5.0) | |

Source: Shoichi Tanaka, "Fisheries in the Northwestern Pacific and Fishery Resources—Mainly on the Japanese Fisheries and International Problems Surrounding Them," in Christine L. Dawson, ed., *The North Pacific Project* (Seattle: Institute for Marine Studies, University of Washington, 1977), pp. 217–311.

# TABLE C.3

## West Kamchatka King Crab Quotas 1958–1976

### (1000 cases)

| Date | Japan | Soviet Union | Ratio |
|------|-------|--------------|-------|
| 1958 | 320 | 480 | 2:3 |
| 1959 | 280 | 420 | 2:3 |
| 1960 | 260 | 390 | 2:3 |
| 1961 | 260 | 390 | 2:3 |
| 1962 | 252 | 378 | 2:3 |
| 1963 | 252 | 378 | 2:3 |
| 1964 | 252 | 378 | 2:3 |
| 1965 | 240 | 420 | 4:7 |
| 1966 | 240 | 420 | 4:7 |
| 1967 | 232 | 406 | 4:7 |
| 1968 | 224 | 432 | — |
| 1969 | 216 | 432 | 1:2 |
| 1970 | 183 | 286 | |
| 1971 | 119 | 272 | |
| 1972 | 105 | na | |
| 1973 | 60 | na | |
| 1974 | 30 | na | |
| 1975 | 0 | na | |
| 1976 | 0 | na | |

Source: *1958–1969* Shigeru Oda, "Japan and International Conventions Relating to North Pacific Fisheries," *Washington Law Review*, 43, 1 (1967). *1970–1976* Shoichi Tanaka, "Fisheries in the Northwestern Pacific and Fishery Resources—Mainly on the Japanese Fisheries and Problems Surrounding Them," in Christine L. Dawson, ed., *The North Pacific Project* (Seattle: Institute for Marine Studies, University of Washington, IMS-UW-77-1, 1977), quoting Japan Fisheries Agency.

Note: One case is equal to 48 cans of crab of 1/2 lb each. For frozen crab meat, Japan considers 29.3 lbs of meat to be equivalent to one case. Other crab fishing areas open to Japan in Soviet waters are subject to allocation arrangements affecting both catch and fishing effort. The Japanese king crab annual quota in the four-island area was 600,000 crabs between 1969 and 1976. Blue king crab fishery in the East Sakhalin area had a quota of 600,000 crabs in 1969, but this was gradually reduced to 105,000 crabs by 1976. Tanner crab stocks in the East Sakhalin area allowed a 1,082,000 crab limit in 1963 but this increased rapidly to 26,950,000 by 1967 and declined to 14,189,000 in 1971. The Japanese annual quota for the western Bering Sea tanner crab fishery began at 2,427,000 crabs in 1967, rose to 16,433,000 in the next year, and declined to 4,500,000 crabs in 1976. Other crab species—*ibaragani*, *aturagani-kegani* and *hanasagani*—are also subject to quotas.

## TABLE C.4

QUOTAS UNDER BILATERAL CRAB AGREEMENTS BY JAPAN AND USSR WITH U.S.,
1965–1976

| | Japan | | USSR | |
|---|---|---|---|---|
| Years | King crab cases[a] | Tanner crab number | King crab cases | Tanner crab cases |
| 1965–1966 | 185,000 | | 185,000 | |
| 1967–1968 | 163,000 | | 100,000 | |
| 1969–1970 | 85,000 | 16,000,000[b] | 53,000 | 40,000 |
| 1971–1972 | 37,500 | 15,000,000[c] | 23,000 | 35,000 |
| | Number | Number | Number | Number |
| 1973–1974 (Area A) | 270,000 | 6,000,000 | 100,000 | 1,800,000 |
| 1973–1974 (Area B) | 430,000 | 8,000,000 | 160,000 | 2,400,000 |
| | MT | MT | MT | MT |
| 1975–1976 (Area A) | 0 | 2,500 | 0 | 750 |
| 1975–1976 (Area B) | 953 | 7,700 | 256 | 2,310 |

Source: National Marine Fisheries Service, *Demersal Fish and Shellfish Resources of the Eastern Bering Sea in the Baseline Year 1975*, Processed Report, Northwest and Alaska Fisheries Center (Seattle, Washington: 1977), p. 543.

[a]One case is equal to 48 ½-pound cans. In producing frozen meat Japan considers 29.3 pounds of crab meat equivalent to one case.

[b]Plus an allowance of 15 percent.

[c]Plus an allowance of 10 percent.

TABLE C.5

CATCH QUOTAS FOR FOREIGN FISHERIES IN THE EASTERN BERING SEA AND ALEUTIAN ISLANDS REGIONS

| Nation | Area | Fisheries | Species | 1973 | 1974 | 1975–1976 |
|---|---|---|---|---|---|---|
| Japan | Eastern Bering Sea | Mothership-North Pacific trawl | Pollock | 1,500,000 | 1,300,000 | 1,100,000 |
| | | | Other groundfish | — | — | 160,000 |
| | | North Pacific longline-gillnet | Herring[a] | 33,000 | 33,000 | 15,000 |
| | | | Herring[b] | 4,600 | 4,600 | 3,000 |
| | | Land-based dragnet | All groundfish | — | — | 35,000 |
| | Aleutian Region | Mothership-North Pacific trawl and longline-gillnet | Pacific ocean perch | — | — | 9,600 |
| | | | Sablefish | — | — | 1,200 |
| | | Land-based dragnet | All groundfish | — | — | 8,500 |
| USSR | Eastern Bering Sea | — | Flatfish | 100,000 | 100,000 | (Included in other species) |
| | | | Pollock | — | — | 210,000 |
| | | | Herring | — | — | 30,000 |
| | | | Other Species | — | — | 120,000 |
| | Aleutian Region | | Rockfish | — | — | 12,000 |
| | | | Other Species | — | — | 16,000 |
| ROK | No quota restrictions apply to ROK except that they refrain from fishing for halibut east of 175° W. | | | | | |

Source: National Marine Fisheries Service, *Demersal Fish and Shellfish Resources of the Eastern Bering Sea in the Baseline Year 1975. Processed Report*, Northwest and Alaska Fisheries Center (Seattle, Washington: 1977), p. 24.

Note: A catch quota for Pacific halibut of 5,000 MT was established for Canada, the United States, and Japan in 1963 in the triangular area shown in figure 6.4. Except for 1963, reported catches in this area have fallen far below this quota due to the low abundance of halibut in the eastern Bering Sea.

[a]The 33,000 MT quota was in effect from 1969.

[b]The 4,600 MT quota was in effect from 1971.

# APPENDIX D

## Articles from the Draft Convention on the Law of the Sea, Dealing with Living Resources in the Exclusive Economic Zone

### Article 61

#### Conservation of Living Resources

1. The coastal State shall determine the allowable catch of the living resources in its exclusive economic zone.

2. The coastal State, taking into account the best scientific evidence available to it, shall ensure through proper conservation and management measures that the maintenance of the living resources in the exclusive economic zone is not endangered by over-exploitation. As appropriate, the coastal State and relevant subregional, regional and global organizations shall cooperate to this end.

3. Such measures shall also be designed to maintain or restore populations of harvested species at levels which can produce the maximum sustainable yield, as qualified by relevant environmental and economic factors, including the economic needs of coastal fishing communities and the special requirements of developing States, and taking into account fishing patterns, the interdependence of stocks and any generally recommended international minimum standards, whether subregional, regional or global.

4. In taking such measures, the coastal State shall take into consideration the effects on species associated with or dependent upon harvested species with a view to maintaining or restoring populations of such associated or dependent species above levels at which their reproduction may become seriously threatened.

5. Available scientific information, catch and fishing effort statistics, any other data relevant to the conservation of fish stocks shall be contributed and exchanged on a regular basis through competent international organizations, whether subregional, regional or global, where appropriate and with participation by all States concerned, including States whose nationals are allowed to fish in the exclusive economic zone.

## Article 62

### Utilization of the Living Resources

1. The coastal State shall promote the objective of optimum utilization of the living resources in the exclusive economic zone without prejudice to Article 61.

2. The coastal State shall determine its capacity to harvest the living resources of the exclusive economic zone. Where the coastal State does not have the capacity to harvest the entire allowable catch, it shall, through agreements or other arrangements and pursuant to the terms, conditions, laws and regulations referred to in paragraph 4, give other States access to the surplus of the allowable catch, having particular regard to the provisions of Articles 69 and 70, especially in relation to the developing States mentioned therein.

3. In giving access to other States to its exclusive economic zone under this Article, the coastal State shall take into account all relevant factors, including *inter alia*, the significance of the living resources of the area to the economy of the coastal State concerned and its other national interests, the provisions of Articles 69 and 70, the requirements of developing countries in the subregion or region in harvesting part of the surplus and the need to minimize economic dislocation in States whose nationals have habitually fished in the zone or which have substantial efforts in research and identification of stocks.

4. Nationals of other States fishing in the exclusive economic zone shall comply with the conservation measures and with the other terms and conditions established in the laws and regulations of the coastal State. These regulations shall be consistent with the present Convention and may relate, *inter alia*, to the following:

   (a) licensing of fishermen, fishing vessels and equipment, including payment of fees and other forms of remuneration, which in the case of developing coastal states, may consist of adequate compensation in the field of financing, equipment and technology relating to the fishing industry;

   (b) determining the species which may be caught and fixing quotas of catch, whether in relation to particular stocks or groups of stocks or catch per vessel over a period of time or to the catch by nationals of any State during a specified period;

   (c) regulating seasons and areas of fishing, the types, sizes and amount of gear, and the types, sizes and number of fishing vessels that may be used;

   (d) fixing the age and size of fish and other species that may be caught;

   (e) specifying information required of fishing vessels, including catch and effort statistics and vessel position reports;

   (f) requiring, under the authorization and control of the coastal state, the conduct of specified fisheries research programmes and regulating the conduct of such research, including the sampling of catches, disposition of samples and reporting of associated scientific data;

(g) the placing of observers or trainees on board such vessels by the coastal state;

(h) the landing of all or any part of the catch by such vessels in the ports of the coastal state;

(i) terms and conditions relating to joint ventures or other cooperative arrangements;

(j) requirements for training personnel and transfer of fisheries technology, including enhancement of the coastal state's capability of undertaking fisheries research;

(k) enforcement procedures.

5. Coastal States shall give due notice of conservation and management laws and regulations.

## Article 63

### Stocks occurring within the exclusive economic zones of two or more coastal States or both within the exclusive economic zone and in an area beyond and adjacent to it

1. Where the same stock or stocks of associated species occur within the exclusive economic zones of two or more coastal States, these States shall seek, either directly or through appropriate subregional or regional organizations, to agree upon the measures necessary to coordinate and ensure the conservation and development of such stocks without prejudice to the other provisions of this Part.

2. Where the same stock or stocks of associated species occur both within the exclusive economic zone and in an area beyond and adjacent to the zone, the coastal State and the States fishing for such stocks in the adjacent area shall seek, either directly or through appropriate subregional or regional organizations, to agree upon the measures necessary for the conservation of these stocks in the adjacent area.

## Article 64

### Highly Migratory Species

1. The coastal State and other States whose nationals fish in the region for the highly migratory species listed in Annex I shall cooperate directly or through appropriate international organizations with a view to ensuring conservation and promoting the objective of optimum utilization of such species throughout the region, both within and beyond the exclusive economic zone. In regions for which no appropriate international organization exists, the coastal State and other States whose nationals harvest these

species in the region shall cooperate to establish such an organization and participate in its work.

2. The provisions of paragraph 1 apply in addition to the other provisions of this Part.

## Article 65

### Marine Mammals

Nothing in this Part restricts the right of a coastal State or the competence of an international organization, as appropriate, to prohibit, limit or regulate the exploitation of marine mammals more strictly than provided for in this Part. States shall cooperate with a view to conservation of marine mammals and, in the case of cetaceans, shall in particular work through the appropriate international organizations for their conservation, management and study.

## Article 66

### Anadramous Stocks

1. States in whose rivers anadromous stocks originate shall have the primary interest in and responsibility for such stocks.

2. The State of origin of anadromous stocks shall ensure their conservation by the establishment of appropriate regulatory measures for fishing in all waters landward of the outer limits of its exclusive economic zone and for fishing provided for in paragraph 3(b). The State of origin may, after consultation with the other states referred to in Paragraphs 3 and 4 fishing these stocks, establish total allowable catches for stocks originating in its rivers.

3. (a) Fisheries for anadromous stocks shall be conducted only in waters landward of the outer limits of exclusive economic zones, except in cases where this provision would result in economic dislocation for a State other than the State of origin. With respect to such fishing beyond the outer limits of the exclusive economic zone, States concerned shall maintain consultations with a view to achieving agreement on terms and conditions of such fishing giving due regard to the conservation requirements and needs of the State of origin in respect of these stocks.

   (b) The State of origin shall cooperate in minimizing economic dislocation in such other States fishing these stocks, taking into account the normal catch and the mode of operations of such States, and all the areas in which such fishing has occurred.

   (c) States referred to in sub-paragraph (b), participating by agreement with the State of origin in measures to renew anadromous stocks, particularly by expenditures for that purpose, shall be given special consideration by the State of origin in the harvesting of stocks originating in its rivers.

(d) Enforcement of regulations regarding anadromous stocks beyond the exclusive economic zone shall be by agreement between the State of origin and the other States concerned.

4. In cases where anadromous stocks migrate into or through the waters landward of the outer limits of the exclusive economic zone of a State other than the State of origin, such State shall cooperate with the State of origin with regard to the conservation and management of such stocks.

5. The State of origin of anadromous stocks and other States fishing these stocks shall make arrangements for the implementation of the provisions of this article, where appropriate, through regional organizations.

## Article 67

### Catadromous Species

1. A coastal State in whose waters catadromous species spend the greater part of their life cycle shall have responsibility for the management of these species and shall ensure the ingress and egress of migrating fish.

2. Harvesting of catadromous species shall be conducted only in waters landward of the outer limits of exclusive economic zones. When conducted in exclusive economic zones, harvesting shall be subject to this article and the other provisions of the present Convention concerning fishing in these zones.

3. In cases where catadromous fish migrate through the waters of another State, whether as juvenile or maturing fish, the management, including harvesting, of such fish shall be regulated by agreement between the State mentioned in paragraph 1 and the other State concerned. Such agreement shall ensure the rational management of the species and take into account the responsibilities of the State mentioned in paragraph 1 for the maintenance of these species.

## Article 68

### Sedentary Species

This Part does not apply to sedentary species as defined in Article 77, paragraph 4.

## Article 69

### Right of Land-locked States

1. Land-locked states shall have the right to participate, on an equitable basis, in the exploitation of an appropriate part of the surplus of the living resources of the exclusive economic zones of coastal States of the same subregion or region, taking into account the relevant economic and geographical circumstances of all the States concerned and in conformity with the provisions of this article and of Articles 61 and 62.

2. The terms and modalities of such participation shall be established by the States concerned through bilateral, subregional or regional agreements taking into account *inter alia*:

    (a) the need to avoid effects detrimental to fishing communities or fishing industries of the coastal State;

    (b) the extent to which the land-locked State, in accordance with the provisions of this article, is participating or is entitled to participate under existing bilateral, subregional or regional agreements in the exploitation of living resources of the exclusive economic zones of other coastal States;

    (c) the extent to which other land-locked States and States with special geographical characteristics are participating in the exploitation of the living resources of the exclusive economic zone of the coastal State and the consequent need to avoid a particular burden for any single coastal State or a part of it;

    (d) the nutritional needs of the populations of the respective States.

3. When the harvesting capacity of a coastal State approaches a point which would enable it to harvest the entire allowable catch of the living resources in its exclusive economic zone, the coastal State and other States concerned shall co-operate in the establishment of equitable arrangements on bilateral, subregional or regional bases to allow for participation of developing land-locked States of the same subregion or region in the exploitation of the living resources of the exclusive economic zones of coastal States of the subregion or region, as may be appropriate in the circumstances and on terms satisfactory to all parties. In the implementation of this provision, the factors mentioned in paragraph 2 shall also be taken into account.

4. Developed land-locked States shall, under the provisions of this article, be entitled to participate in the exploitation of living resources only in the exclusive economic zones of developed coastal States of the same subregion or region having regard to the extent to which the coastal State in giving access to other States to the living resources of its exclusive economic zone has taken into account the need to minimize detrimental effects on fishing communities and economic dislocation in States whose nationals have habitually fished in the zone.

5. The above provisions are without prejudice to arrangements agreed upon in subregions or regions where the coastal States may grant to land-locked States of the same subregion or region equal or preferential rights for the exploitation of the living resources in the exclusive economic zones.

## Article 70

### Right of States with Special Geographical Characteristics

1. States with special geographical characteristics shall have the right to participate, on an equitable basis, in the exploitation of an appropriate part of the surplus of the living

resources of the exclusive economic zones of coastal States of the same subregion or region, taking into account the relevant economic and geographical circumstances of all the States concerned and in conformity with the provisions of this article and of Articles 61 and 62.

2. For the purposes of this Convention, "States with special geographical characteristics" means coastal States, including States bordering enclosed or semi-enclosed seas, whose geographical situation makes them dependent upon the exploitation of the living resources of the exclusive economic zones of other States in the subregion or region, for adequate supplies of fish for the nutritional purposes of their populations or parts thereof, and coastal States which can claim no exclusive economic zones of their own.

3. The terms and modalities of such participation shall be established by the States concerned through bilateral, subregional or regional agreements taking into account *inter alia*:

   (a) the need to avoid effects detrimental to fishing communities or fishing industries of the coastal State;

   (b) the extent to which the State with special geographical characteristics, in accordance with the provisions of this article, is participating or is entitled to participate under existing bilateral, subregional or regional agreements in the exploitation of living resources of the exclusive economic zones of other coastal States;

   (c) the extent to which other States with special geographical characteristics and land-locked States are participating in the exploitation of the living resources of the exclusive economic zone of the coastal State and the consequent need to avoid a particular burden for any single coastal State or a part of it;

   (d) the nutritional needs of the populations of the respective States.

4. When the harvesting capacity of a coastal State approaches a point which would enable it to harvest the entire allowable catch of the living resources in its exclusive economic zone, the coastal State and other States concerned shall co-operate in the establishment of equitable arrangements on bilateral, subregional or regional bases to allow for participation of developing States with special geographical characteristics of the same subregion or region in the exploitation of the living resources of the exclusive economic zones of coastal States of the subregion or region as may be appropriate in the circumstances and on terms satisfactory to all parties. In the implementation of this provision, the factors mentioned in paragraph 3 shall also be taken into account.

5. Developed States with special geographical characteristics shall, under the provisions of this article, be entitled to participate in the exploitation of living resources only in the exclusive economic zones of developed coastal States of the same subregion or region having regard to the extent to which the coastal State, in giving access to other States to the living resources of its exclusive economic zone, has taken into account the need to minimize detrimental effects on fishing communities and economic dislocation in States whose nationals have habitually fished in the zone.

6. The above provisions are without prejudice to arrangements agreed upon in the sub-regions or regions where the coastal States may grant to States with special geographical characteristics of the same subregion or region equal or preferential rights for the exploitation of the living resources in the exclusive economic zones.

## Article 71

### Non-applicability of Articles 69 and 70

The provisions of Articles 69 and 70 do not apply in the case of a coastal State whose economy is overwhelmingly dependent on the exploitation of the living resource of its exclusive economic zone.

## Article 72

### Restrictions on Transfer of Rights

1. Rights provided under Articles 69 and 70 to exploit living resources shall not be directly or indirectly transferred to third States or their nationals by lease or license, by establishing joint collaboration ventures or in any other manner which has the effect of such transfer unless otherwise agreed upon by the States concerned.

2. The foregoing provision does not preclude the States concerned from obtaining technical or financial assistance from third States or international organizations in order to facilitate the exercise of the rights pursuant to Articles 69 and 70, provided that it does not have the effect referred to in paragraph 1.

## Article 73

### Enforcement of Laws and Regulations of the Coastal State

1. The coastal State may, in the exercise of its sovereign rights to explore, exploit, conserve and manage the living resources in the exclusive economic zone, take such measures, including boarding, inspection, arrest and judicial proceedings, as may be necessary to ensure compliance with the laws and regulations enacted by it in conformity with the present Convention.

2. Arrested vessels and their crews shall be promptly released upon the posting of reasonable bond or other security.

3. Coastal State penalties for violations of fisheries regulations in the exclusive economic zone may not include imprisonment, in the absence of agreement to the contrary by the States concerned, or any other form of corporal punishment.

4. In cases of arrest or detention of foreign vessels, the coastal State shall promptly notify the flag State, through appropriate channels, of the action taken and of any penalties subsequently imposed.

# APPENDIX E

## Law on Provisional Measures Relating to the Fishing Zone (Japan) (Law No. 31 of 2 May 1977)

(Purposes)

Article 1

This Law, in line with factors such as the recent rapid developments in the international community toward a new order of the sea and other significant changes in the international environment relating to fisheries, and to ensure proper conservation and management of fishery resources, shall prescribe provisional measures necessary for the exercise of jurisdiction over fisheries and similar activities within the fishing zone.

(Jurisdiction within the Fishing Zone)

Article 2

1. Japan has jurisdiction over fisheries (The term ''fisheries'' means the undertaking involving the catching and taking or culturing of marine animals and plants. The same shall apply hereinafter.) within the fishing zone.

2. Japan also has jurisdiction over the catching and taking of marine animals and plants (other than that which falls under ''fisheries.'' The same shall apply hereinafter.) within the fishing zone.

3. In exercising its jurisdiction provided for in the preceding two paragraphs, Japan shall respect the recommendations relating to the conservation and management of fishery resources of international organizations of which Japan is a member.

(Definitions)

Article 3

1. In this Law, the term ''the baseline of Japan'' means the baseline provided for in Article 2, Paragraph 1, of the Law on the Territorial Sea (Law No. 30 of 1977).

2. In this Law, the term "median line" means the line every point of which is equidistant from the nearest point of the baseline of Japan and the nearest point on the baseline from which the breadth of the territorial sea pertaining to the foreign coast which is opposite the coast of Japan is measured.

3. In this Law, the term "fishing zone" means the areas of the sea (excluding the territorial sea and such areas of the sea as prescribed by Cabinet Order) which extend from the baseline of Japan to the line every point of which is two hundred nautical miles from the nearest point on the baseline of Japan. Provided that, where any part of that line as measured from the baseline of Japan lies beyond the median line, the median line (or the line which may be agreed upon between Japan and a foreign country as a substitute for the median line) shall be substituted for that part of the line.

4. In this Law, the term "foreigner" means the following:

    (1) Persons who are not Japanese nationals, with the exception of persons lawfully resident in Japan and designated by the Minister of Agriculture and Forestry;

    (2) Foreign countries, public organizations of a foreign country or similar organizations, or juridical persons and other organizations established under foreign laws.

(Application of Laws and Regulations within the Fishing Zone)

Article 4

The Laws and Regulations of Japan shall apply, as prescribed by Cabinet Order, with respect to the fisheries and the catching and taking of marine animals and plants in which foreigners engage within the fishing zone. The technical modification necessary for the application of these Laws and Regulations shall be prescribed by Cabinet Order.

(Prohibition of Fisheries, etc.)

Article 5

Foreigners shall not engage in fisheries or in the catching and taking of marine animals and plants in the following areas of the sea within the fishing zone, except insofar as such catching and taking of marine animals and plants is of insignificant nature as prescribed by Ministry of Agriculture and Forestry Ordinance.

    (1) Areas of the sea within the designated areas provided for in Paragraph 2 of the Supplementary Provisions of the Law on the Territorial Sea but limited to that part of the sea which extends from the baseline of Japan to the line every point of which is twelve nautical miles from the baseline of Japan;

    (2) Areas of the sea designated by the Minister of Agriculture and Forestry as necessary for the protection of fishery resources and for fisheries adjustment.

(Permission to Engage in Fisheries, etc.)

## Article 6

1. Foreigners shall not engage in fisheries or in the catching and taking of marine animals and plants within the fishing zone (The areas prescribed in each of the sub-paragraphs in the preceding Article are excluded therefrom. The same shall apply in the next Article and in Article 9, Paragraph 1.), without obtaining permission from the Minister of Agriculture and Forestry as prescribed by Ministry of Agriculture and Forestry Ordinance, except insofar as the case falls under one of the following sub-paragraphs:

   (1) Where the fisheries or the catching and taking of marine animals and plants pertain to highly migratory species prescribed by Cabinet Order;

   (2) Where the catching and taking of marine animals and plants is conducted with the approval provided for in Article 9, Paragraph 1;

   (3) Where the catching and taking of marine animals and plants is of insignificant nature as prescribed by the Ministry of Agriculture and Forestry Ordinance referred to in the proviso of the preceding Article.

2. Where the Minister of Agriculture and Forestry grants the permission provided for in the preceding paragraph, the Minister shall issue a permit to the foreigner concerned, as prescribed by Ministry of Agriculture and Forestry Ordinance.

3. The foreigner, having obtained the permission provided for in Paragraph 1, shall display a prominent sign to that effect on the vessel pertaining to the fisheries or the catching and taking of marine animals and plants in which he engages and shall keep the permit provided for in the preceding paragraph on the vessel, as prescribed by Ministry of Agriculture and Forestry Ordinance.


(Criteria for Permission, etc.)

## Article 7

1. When an application for the permission provided for in the first paragraph of the preceding article is made, the Minister of Agriculture and Forestry shall not grant the permission of the aforesaid paragraph unless it is considered certain that the fisheries or the catching and taking of marine animals and plants pertaining to the application will be conducted properly in accordance with an international agreement or other arrangements, that such activities will not exceed the limit of catch laid down by the Minister of Agriculture and Forestry for each of the classifications prescribed by Ministry of Agriculture and Forestry Ordinance for the fisheries or the catching and taking of marine animals and plants in which foreigners engage within the fishing zone, and that such activities will be in conformity with other criteria prescribed by Cabinet Order.

2. Decisions on the limit of catch pursuant to the provisions of the preceding paragraph shall be made, as prescribed by Cabinet Order, on the basis of fishery resources trends supported by scientific evidence and of the actual situation with respect to fishing by Japanese fishermen within the fishing zone, and with overall consideration of factors such as the actual situation with respect to fishing by foreigners within the fishing zone and the situation with respect to Japanese fisheries in the waters adjacent to a foreign country.

(Fishing Fees)

Article 8

1. Where a foreigner is granted a permit pursuant to the provisions of Article 6, paragraph 2, he shall pay to the State fishing fees the amount of which shall be prescribed by Cabinet Order.

2. Where a special reason justifies it, the fishing fees provided for in the preceding paragraph may be reduced or remitted, as prescribed by Cabinet Order.

3. In addition to what is prescribed in the preceding two paragraphs, other necessary matters relating to fishing fees shall be prescribed by Cabinet Order.

(Approval Relating to the Catching and Taking of Marine Animals and
Plants for the Purpose of Experiment, Research, etc.)

Article 9

1. A foreigner who wishes to engage in the catching and taking of marine animals and plants within the fishing zone for the purposes of experiment or research, or for other purposes prescribed by Ministry of Agriculture and Forestry Ordinance, shall obtain approval from the Minister of Agriculture and Forestry as prescribed by Ministry of Agriculture and Forestry Ordinance, except insofar as the catching and taking of marine animals and plants pertains to highly migratory species prescribed by the Cabinet Order referred to in Article 6, Paragraph 1, sub-paragraph 1, or is of insignificant nature as prescribed by the Ministry of Agriculture and Forestry Ordinance referred to in the proviso of Article 5.

2. A foreigner who applies for the approval provided for in the preceding paragraph shall, as prescribed by Cabinet Order, pay to the state fees the amount of which shall be prescribed by Cabinet Order.

3. The provisions of Paragraph 2 and Paragraph 3 of Article 6 shall apply mutatis mutandis to the approval provided for in Paragraph 1, and the provisions of Paragraph 2 of the preceding Article shall apply mutatis mutandis to the fees provided for in the preceding paragraph.

(Conditions and Restrictions)

### Article 10

The permission provided for in Article 6, Paragraph 1, or the approval provided for in Paragraph 1 of the preceding Article may be made subject to conditions or restrictions, which may be subsequently altered.

(Revocation, etc. of Permission and Approval)

### Article 11

1. Where a foreigner who has obtained the permission provided for in Article 6, Paragraph 1, contravenes Laws and Regulations, or conditions or restrictions provided for in the preceding Article, the Minister of Agriculture and Forestry may order the suspension of fisheries or of the catching and taking of marine animals and plants for a fixed period of time or may revoke the permission provided for in the aforesaid paragraph.

2. Where a foreigner who has obtained the approval provided for in Article 9, Paragraph 1, contravenes Laws and Regulations, or conditions or restrictions provided for in the preceding article, the Minister of Agriculture and Forestry may revoke the approval provided for in the aforesaid paragraph.

(Conservation and Management of Anadromous Species)

### Article 12

From the standpoint that in areas of the sea beyond the fishing zone also (excluding the internal waters, the territorial sea and the areas of the sea equivalent to the fishing zone of a foreign country) Japan has jurisdiction over the anadromous species which spawn in fresh waters of Japan, Japan shall endeavor to achieve, through international cooperation, proper conservation and management of anadromous species in the aforesaid areas of the sea.

(Delegation of Powers to Cabinet Orders, etc.)

### Article 13

Where Cabinet Orders or Ministry of Agriculture and Forestry Ordinances are enacted, amended or abrogated in accordance with the provisions of this Law, such Orders or Ordinances may prescribe necessary transitional measures (including transitional measures relating to penal provisions), insofar as they are considered reasonably necessary for such enactment, amendment or abrogation.

### Article 14

Exemption from the provisions of Article 5 to 11 may be granted by a Cabinet Order to the foreigner and for the areas of the sea designated by that Order with respect to one or more of the aforesaid provisions.

## Article 15

Unless otherwise provided for in this Law, procedures necessary for the implementation of this law and other matters necessary therefor shall be prescribed by Ministry of Agriculture and Forestry Ordinance.

### (Effect of Treaties)

## Article 16

Where a treaty provides otherwise for matters provided for in this law, the provisions of the treaty shall apply.

### (Penal Provisions)

## Article 17

A person who falls under one of the following sub-paragraphs shall be liable to a fine not exceeding ten million yen.

(1) A person who has contravened the provisions of Article 5 or of Article 6, Paragraph 1;

(2) A person who has contravened conditions and restrictions to which the permission provided for in Article 6, Paragraph 1, is made subject pursuant to the provisions of Article 10, including those altered pursuant to the provisions of Article 10;

(3) A person who has contravened an order issued pursuant to the provisions of Article 11, Paragraph 1.

## Article 18

A person who has contravened the conditions and restrictions to which the approval provided for in Article 9, Paragraph 1, is made subject pursuant to the provisions of Article 10, including those altered pursuant to the provisions of Article 20, shall be liable to a fine not exceeding five hundred thousand yen.

## Article 19

In cases which fall under the two preceding articles, any catch and its products, any vessel or any fishing gear or other objects which may be used for fisheries or for the catching and taking of marine animals and plants owned or possessed by the offender may be forfeited. Provided that, where the forfeiture of the whole or part of the aforesaid objects owned by the offender is impracticable, the monetary value thereof may be forfeited.

## Article 20

A person who has contravened the provisions of Article 6, Paragraph 3, (including cases where the paragraph shall apply mutatis mutandis under Article 9, Paragraph 3) shall be liable to a fine not exceeding two hundred thousand yen.

## Article 21

Where a representative of a juridical person or an agent, employee or other worker of a juridical person or of a person has acted, with respect to the business activities or properties of the juridical person or the person, in contravention of Article 17, Article 18, or the preceding Article, not only shall such offender be liable, but the juridical person or the person shall also be liable to the penalty provided for in whichever Article is relevant.

(Exception Relating to the Jurisdiction of the First Instance)

## Article 22

The jurisdiction of the first instance with respect to legal proceedings pertaining to offenses under the provision of this Law shall also be conferred upon District Courts.

## SUPPLEMENTARY PROVISIONS
(Date of entry into force)

1. This Law shall enter into force on the date prescribed by Cabinet Order, which shall be within two months of the date of its promulgation.

(Partial Amendment of the Law on Regulation of Fisheries of Foreigners)

2. The Law on Regulation of Fisheries of Foreigners (Law No. 60 of 1967) shall be partially amended as follows:

The heading of Article 3 shall be amended to read "Prohibition of fisheries, etc.," and in the same Article the words "shall not engage in fisheries" shall be amended to read "shall not engage in fisheries or in the catching and taking of marine animals and plants (Other than that which falls under "fisheries." The same shall apply hereinafter.), except insofar as such catching and taking of marine animals and plants is of insignificant nature as prescribed by Ministry of Agriculture and Forestry Ordinance."

Sub-paragraph 2 of the same Article shall be amended to read as follows:

(2) Foreign countries, public organizations of a foreign country or similar organizations, or juridical persons and other organizations established under foreign laws.

The following Article shall follow Article 6:

(Transitional Measures)

Article 6 — 2

Where Cabinet Orders or Ministry of Agriculture and Forestry Ordinances are enacted, amended or abrogated in accordance with the provisions of this Law, such Orders or Ordinances may prescribe necessary transitional measures relating to penal provisions, insofar as they are considered reasonably necessary for such enactment, amendment or abrogation.

The words ''or the catching and taking of marine animals and plants'' shall follow the words ''fisheries'' in Article 9, Paragraph 2.

# APPENDIX F

## Union of Soviet Socialist Republics: Edict on Provisional Measures for the Preservation of Living Resources and the Regulation of Fishing in Marine Areas Adjacent to the Coast of the USSR

Edict of the Presidium of the USSR Supreme Soviet, December 10, 1976

The presidium of the USSR Supreme Soviet notes that recently an ever greater number of States, including those neighboring the USSR, are establishing off their coasts economic or fishing zones with a breadth of up to 200 nautical miles, without waiting for the conclusion of the international convention being worked out at the III United Nations Conference on the Law of the Sea.

The Soviet Union will also work in the future for the regulation of the pressing problems of the legal regime of the World Ocean on an international basis and for the conclusion to this end of a convention in which such problems, and in particular the questions of using the living resources of coastal sea waters, would be resolved in an integrated and interrelated manner, taking into account the legal interests of all states.

Having in view that until the conclusion of such a convention it is necessary to take measures without delay for the protection of the interests of the Soviet state with respect to the preservation, reproduction, and also the optimal utilization of the living resources of marine areas adjacent to the coasts of the USSR, the Presidium of the USSR Supreme Soviet decrees:

### Article 1

In marine areas, adjacent to the coast of the USSR, of a breadth up to 200 nautical miles computed from the same baselines as the territorial waters of the USSR there shall be introduced in accordance with the provisions of the present Edict provisional measures for the preservation of living resources and for the regulation of fishing.

The establishment of such provisional measures shall not affect the regime of territorial waters of the USSR.

## Article 2

The USSR, within the limits of marine areas provided for in Article 1 of the present Edict, shall exercise sovereign rights over fish and other living resources for the purpose of exploring, exploiting, and preserving them. These rights of the USSR also shall extend to migratory species of fish within the migratory areas of such species except for the period when they may be within the limits of the territorial waters or the economic or fishing zones of other States which are recognized by the USSR.

## Article 3

The commercial catching of fish and other living resources as well as exploratory and other operations connected with such commercial fishing, hereinafter "commercial fishing" may be carried on by foreign juridical and physical persons within the limits of the areas provided in Article 1 of the present Edict only on the basis of agreements or other arrangements between the USSR and foreign States.

## Article 4

Within the areas provided for by Article 1 of the present Edict, the optimal utilization of fish and other living resources will be effectuated on the basis of the respective scientific data and, in appropriate instances, taking into account the recommendation of competent international organizations. In particular, there shall be established for this purpose:

(a) a total annual permissible catch for each species of fish and other living resources;

(b) a portion of the annual permissible catch of fish or other living resources which may be taken by foreign fishing vessels, if the amount of the total permissible catch of any stock of a commercial species exceeds the production capacities of the Soviet commercial industry;

(c) measures to ensure the rational conduct of fishing and the preservation and reproduction of living resources.

## Article 5

While observing the provisions of Articles 2, 3 and 4 of the present Edict, a catch quota may be established for foreign states, and in accordance with such quotas, foreign fishing vessels shall be issued permits for commercial fishing, without which commercial fishing shall not be permitted.

## Article 6

The conditions and periods for introducing the provisional measures for the preservation of living resources and for the regulation of fishing applicable to specific marine areas adjacent to the coast of the USSR, the establishment of measures for control over the observance of the provisions of the present Edict, and also the procedure for the application of Articles 2, 3, 4, and 5, shall be determined by the USSR Council of Ministers.

## Article 7

For a violation of the provisions of the present Edict or the rules promulgated in the execution thereof, the guilty persons shall be subject to punishment in the form of a fine. The amount of the fine imposed in an administrative procedure shall be established as not exceeding 10,000 rubles.

If the said violations caused material harm or entailed other grave consequences or were twice committed, the guilty persons shall be brought to judicial responsibility. The fine exacted in a judicial procedure shall be established in an amount not exceeding 100,000 rubles. A court may, upon the petition of agencies responsible for the conservation of fish and other living resources in the areas provided for in Article 1 of the present Edict, confiscate the vessel, equipment, and gear used by the offenders, as well as everything taken illegally.

In the event of the arrest or detention of a foreign vessel, the respective Soviet competent agencies shall immediately notify the flag State concerning measures taken and any consequent measures of punishment. The detained vessel and its crew shall be released immediately after submitting a reasonable pledge or other security.

## Article 8

The provisions of the present Edict will remain in force until the adoption, taking into account the work of the III United Nations Conference on the Law of the Sea, of another legislative act of the USSR defining the regime of the marine areas provided in Article 1 of the present Edict.

Chairman of the Presidium of the USSR Supreme Soviet
N. Podgornyi
Secretary of the Presidium of the USSR Supreme Soviet

# APPENDIX G

## Highly Migratory Species

1. Albacore tuna: *Thunnus alalunga*

2. Bluefin tuna: *Thunnus thynnus*

3. Bigeye tuna: *Thunnus obesus*

4. Skipjack tuna: *Katsuwonus pelamis*

5. Yellowfin tuna: *Thunnas albacares*

6. Blackfin tuna: *Thunnus atlanticus*

7. Little tuna: *Euthynnus alletteratus*; *Euthynnus affinis*

8. Frigate mackerel: *Auxis thazard*; *Auxis rochei*

9. Pomfrets: Family Bramidae

10. Marlins: *Tetrapturus angustirostris*; *Tetrapturus belone*; *Tetrapturus pfluegeri*; *Tetrapturus albidus*; *Tetrapturus audax*; *Tetrapturus georgei*; *Makaira mazara*; *Makaira indica*; *Makaira nigricans*.

11. Sailfishes: *Istiophorus platypterus*; *Istiophorus albicans*

12. Swordfish: *Xiphias gladius*

13. Sauries: *Scomberesox saurus*; *Cololabis saira*; *Cololabis adocetus*; *Scomberesox saurus scombroides*

14. Dolphin: *Coryphaena hippurus*; *Coryphaena equiselis*

15. Oceanic sharks; *Hexanchus griseus*; *Cetorhinus maximus*; Family Alopiidae; *Rhincodon typus*; Family Carcharhinidae; Family Sphyrnidae; Family Isurida

16. Cetaceans: Family Physeteridae; Family Balaenopteridae; Family Balaenidae; Family Eschrichtiidae; Family Monodontidae; Family Ziphiidae; Family Delphinidae

17. Southern bluefin tuna: *Thunnus maccoyii*

# APPENDIX H

## International Fishery Commissions

| Organization | Inter-American Tropical Tuna Commission | International North Pacific Fisheries Commission | International Pacific Halibut Commission |
|---|---|---|---|
| Members as of 1978 | Canada, Costa Rica, France, Japan, Nicaragua, Panama, and the United States | Canada, Japan, and the United States | Canada and the United States |
| Date established and auspices | Mar. 3, 1950 under auspices of 1949 International Convention | June 12, 1953 under auspices of 1952 International Convention | Under auspices of 1923 Convention as amended |
| Resource Covered | Yellowfin and skipjack tuna, bait fish, and other fish taken by tuna vessels | All, with particular emphasis on halibut, herring, and salmon | Pacific halibut |
| Area of Competence | Eastern Tropical Pacific Ocean | All waters of the North Pacific and adjacent seas excluding territorial waters | Territorial sea and high seas off Western Coast of Canada and the United States |
| Objectives | Maintaining the populations of yellowfin and skipjack and other kinds of fish taken by tuna vessels at a level that will permit maximum sustained catches year after year | Securing the maximum sustained productivity of fisheries of joint interest | Developing the stocks of halibut at levels that will permit the maximum sustained yields and maintaining the stocks at those levels |

558

| International Pacific Salmon Fisheries Commission | International Whaling Commission | North Pacific Fur Seal Commission | International Council for the Exploration of the Sea |
|---|---|---|---|
| Canada and the United States | Argentina, Australia, Brazil, Canada, Denmark, France, Iceland, Japan, Mexico, Netherlands, New Zealand, Norway, Panama, S. Africa, U.S.S.R., U.K., and the United States | Canada, Japan, U.S.S.R., and the United States | Belgium, Canada, Denmark, Finland, France, West and East Germany, Iceland, Ireland, Netherlands, Norway, Poland, Portugal, Spain, Sweden, U.K., the United States, and U.S.S.R. |
| June 28, 1937 under auspices of 1930 International Convention as amended | Dec. 2, 1946 under auspices of 1946 International Convention as amended | Jan. 1958 under auspices of 1957 International Interim Convention as amended; original treaty concluded in 1910 | 1902 under auspices of 1899 and 1901 Conferences; constitution replaced by 1968 International Convention |
| Sockeye and pink salmon | Most whale stocks, status of small cetaceans controversial | Fur seals | All |
| Fraser River and its tributaries, territorial sea and high seas off the estuary | All waters in which whaling is prosecuted by factory ships, land stations, and whale catchers | North Pacific Ocean | Atlantic Ocean and its adjacent seas, primarily the North Atlantic |
| Protecting, preserving, and extending the sockeye and pink salmon fisheries | Achieving the optimum level of whale stocks as rapidly as possible without causing widespread economic and nutritional distress | Achieving the maximum sustainable productivity of the fur seal resources so that the population can be brought to and maintained at levels that will provide the greatest harvest year after year with due regard to their relation to the productivity of other living resources in the area | Investigating the sea |

## International Fishery Commissions (Continued)

| Organization | Inter-American Tropical Tuna Commission | International North Pacific Fisheries Commission | International Pacific Halibut Commission |
|---|---|---|---|
| Functions | To carry out research on tuna and porpoises by own research staff; to recommend conservation measures; to disseminate its findings | To promote and coordinate studies; to recommend conservation measures; to administer the abstention system | To study halibut stocks; to recommend conservation measures such as catch regulation, size control, open or closed seasons, vessel and gear control, and licensing |
| Assets | | | |
| Vessels, computers, hardware | Charters vessels; arranges for use of computer and research facilities of SIO, and satellite services of NESS and NOAA | Charters vessels | Charters vessels; owns computers; owns research facilities and gear |
| Personnel | Up to 4 commissioners per member party; advisory committee for each member party; independent research and support staff | One national section per member party consisting of not more than 4 members, accompanied by advisors and experts; advisory committee for each national section; committees—biology and research, financial and administrative; secretariat—executive director, assistant director, administrative assistant, clerical and interpretive staff | Three commissioners per member party; independent research and support staff |

| Budget | FY | US$ | FY | US$ | FY | US$ |
|---|---|---|---|---|---|---|
| | 1970–1971 | 479,898 | 1970–1971 | 75,061 | 1970–1971 | 492,000 |
| | 1971–1972 | 491,898 | 1970–1971 | 97,813 | 1971–1972 | 492,000 |
| | 1972–1973 | 535,114 | 1972–1973 | 109,132 | 1972–1973 | 546,000 |
| | 1973–1974 | (739,048) | 1973–1974 | 96,699 | 1973–1974 | 587,000 |
| | 1974–1975 | 789,947 | 1974–1975 | 148,901 | 1974–1975 | 643,000 |
| | 1975–1976 | 896,332 | 1975–1976 | (179,700) | 1975–1976 | 695,000 |
| | 1976–1977 | 1,128,950 | | | 1976–1977 | 762,000 |
| | 1977–1978 | 1,725,498 | | | 1977–1978 | 890,000 |
| | 1978–1979 | (1,870,651) | | | | |

| International Pacific Salmon Fisheries Commission | International Whaling Commission | North Pacific Fur Seal Commission | International Council for the Exploration of the Sea |
|---|---|---|---|
| To carry out investigations; to recommend conservation measures such as gear control, catch regulations, and construction projects; to apportion the catch | To promote research; to collect and analyze statistical information; to publish and disseminate information; to recommend conservation measures such as open and closed seasons or areas, size limitations, and catch limits | To formulate, coordinate, and recommend research programs; to recommend conservation measures in respect to size, sex, and age composition of the seasonal commercial kill from a herd; to make recommendations regarding methods of sealing | To promote research and investigation for the study of the sea particularly those related to living resources; to draw up programs for this purpose; to disseminate the findings |
| Charters vessels; owns research facilities and gear | Charters vessels; access to computers; member parties utilize own resources to conduct research | Member parties utilize own resources to conduct research | Rents computers; working groups utilize resources of member parties to conduct research |
| Three commissioners per member party; independent research and support staff | One commissioner per member party accompanied by advisors and experts; committees—scientific, technical, and financial and administrative; secretariat—secretary, assistant secretary, executive officer, clerk, audio typist | One commissioner per member party accompanied by advisors and experts; committees—scientific, finance and administration, and press; secretariat—executive, technical, and assistant technical secretaries, interpreters, translators, typists, and calligraphers | Two delegates per member party; bureau; committees—consultative, finance, publications, advisory, and standing; working groups; secretariat—20 full-time and 3 part-time posts including a general secretary, environment officer, system analyst, hydrographer, statistician and assistants, librarian, administrative officers, assistants and secretaries, technical editor, publications assistant, and a printer and assistant |

| | FY | Pounds | FY | US$ | FY | D.Kr. |
|---|---|---|---|---|---|---|
| | 1970–1971 | 6,537 | 1970–1971 | 26,149 | 1970–1971 | 1,266,709 |
| | 1971–1972 | 5,775 | 1971–1972 | 23,201 | 1971–1972 | 1,382,000 |
| | 1972–1973 | 7,084 | 1972–1973 | 22,923 | 1972–1973 | 1,577,000 |
| | 1973–1974 | 7,699 | 1973–1974 | 32,193 | 1973–1974 | 1,826,000 |
| | 1974–1975 | 29,590 | 1974–1975 | 26,191 | 1974–1975 | 2,060,000 |
| | 1975–1976 | 32,372 | 1975–1976 | 29,053 | 1975–1976 | 2,405,500 |
| | 1976–1977 | 65,498 | 1976–1977 | 33,054 | 1976–1977 | 2,904,000 |
| | | | 1977–1978 | 37,398 | 1977–1978 | 3,360,000 |
| | | | 1978–1979 | (32,000) | 1978–1979 | 4,024,000 |

International Fishery Commissions (Continued)

| Organization | Inter-American Tropical Tuna Commission | International North Pacific Fisheries Commission | International Pacific Halibut Commission |
|---|---|---|---|
| Methods of Operation | | | |
| Meetings | At least annually; meetings may be public | At least annually | At least annually |
| Independent research staff | Director, subdirector, 24 scientists, 14 technicians, and 5 administrative staff located at its headquarters and several important tuna fishing centers | None; research conducted by member parties | Director, assistant director, 13 biologists, and 10 administrative, clerical and technical personnel, including a programmer, card punch operators, and a librarian at its headquarters |
| Relations with other international organizations (io) | Participates in international scientific meetings; serves on working parties and advisory groups, works closely with ICCAT, Commission Permanente del Pacifico Sur, South Pacific Commission, FAO, and other international organizations and similar institutions in Asia, Europe, Latin America, and the Pacific Islands; invites observers to its meetings; sends observers to other io meetings | IPHC serves as consultant-observer; invites observers to its meetings (e.g., IPSFC ICNAF, IATTC, FAO, ICCAT, IOC (1976); sends observers to other io meetings (e.g., FAO, ICNAF ICCAT, IATTC, IPHC, BBIMFC 1974) | Serves as consultant-observer to the INPFC |
| Relations with national agencies | Works closely with national fishery agencies of the member parties | | |

| International Pacific Salmon Fisheries Commission | International Whaling Commission | North Pacific Fur Seal Commission | International Council for the Exploration of the Sea |
|---|---|---|---|
| Very frequently, formally and by telephone | At least annually | Normally annually | Normally annually |
| 56 members: director, assistant director, administrative officer, chiefs of engineering, operations, environmental conservation, and other researchers, and support staff members at its headquarters, laboratory, and field stations | None; research conducted by member parties | None; research conducted by member parties | None; research conducted by member parties |
|  | Contributes data to other io's (e.g., ACMRR Working Party on Marine Mammals, 1976, 1977); invites io and other observers to its general meetings, including members of international and national research and conservation organizations, interested nonmember whaling nations, and the press; and scientifically qualified representatives to its scientific committee meetings; sends observers to other io meetings (e.g., ICES, 1976) |  | Advisor to NEAFC and IBSFC; cooperates in research with other io's (e.g., Baltic Open Sea experiment with SCOR, 1977); co-sponsors symposiums and workshops (e.g., CINECA symposium, 1978); invites io and other observers and guests to its meetings (e.g., C.E.C., EUROSTAT, EIFAC, FAO, IAPSO, ICNAF, Interim Baltic Marine Environment Protection Commission, IOC, IPHC, IWC, New Zealand High Commission, OECD, World Data Center A, ICSEAF, WHO, Inland Fisheries Commission, and Nordic Council of Ministers, 1978); sends observers to other io meetings |
| Works closely with U.S. national and state agencies and Canadian provincial governmental entities, particularly the Canadian Department of Fisheries for data collection |  | Addressed letters to governments of noncontracting parties whose nationals fish in the North Pacific urging their cooperation in controlling the discard of fishing nets and other debris (1977, 1978) | Works closely with national research agencies of member parties to coordinate and implement research |

## International Fishery Commissions (Continued)

| Organization | Inter-American Tropical Tuna Commission | International North Pacific Fisheries Commission | International Pacific Halibut Commission |
|---|---|---|---|
| Relations with other participants | Maintains contacts with university and governmental research institutions | | |
| Relations with fishing industry | Advisory committee | Advisory committee; as advisors and experts to Commissioners | Conference board, consisting of fishermen and vessel owners representatives, recommends conservation measures; Advisory group, consisting of fishermen, vessel owners, and processor representatives, observes sessions when regulatory decisions are made |
| Strategies | | | |
| Voting | One vote per national section; decisions by unanimous vote | One vote per national section; decisions by unanimous vote of three except under art. II, sec. 1(c)(ii) when only two participate | One vote per commissioner; decisions only by concurrence of at least two commissioners of each member party |
| Special arrangements | | | |
| Coordinators of research | Director | Committee on Biology and Research, aided by Director | Director |
| Other arrangements | | Editorial referees: 1 referee per national section, reviews reports submitted from national sections for publication in bulletin series; unanimity required | |
| Expeditions and scientific projects | Spacecraft-oceanography studies with SIO, NESS, NOAA (1975); FROMSAT cruise with NMFS (1976); JOINT-II with INPE; tuna workshops with Hubbs-Sea World Research Institute and NMFS (1977); tuna investigations with Central National por l'Exploration des Oceans, Office de la Recherche Scientifique et Technique Outre-Mer, Service de la Peche de la Polynesie Francaise (1977) | | Tagging research with U.S.S.R. (1974, 1975) |

| International Pacific Salmon Fisheries Commission | International Whaling Commission | North Pacific Fur Seal Commission | International Council for the Exploration of the Sea |
|---|---|---|---|
| Works closely with non-fishing interests (e.g., lumber and hydroelectric companies to monitor and control water quality) | | | Works closely with other research organizations to coordinate and implement research |
| Advisory committee, consisting of representatives of commercial and sport fishermen and salmon processors, invited to participate at all nonexecutive meetings | As advisors and experts to Commissioners | As advisors and experts to Commissioners | |
| One vote per commissioner; decisions only by concurrence of at least two commissioners of each member party | One vote per member party; decisions by simple majority of those voting except art. V, three-fourths required | One vote per member party; decisions by unanimous vote | |
| Director | Scientific Committee and its subcommittees | Standing Scientific Committee | Standing Scientific Committees |
| Joint research and monitoring projects with industry (e.g., detoxification with the Prince George Pulp and Paper Co. Ltd., 1973), municipalities (e.g., sewage toxicity and treatment with the Greater Vancouver Sewage and Drainage District and the Department of the Environment, 1973), and national and provincial entities (e.g., data collection with the Canadian Department of Fisheries, 1973) | Proposed international decade of cetacean research; joint research projects with UNEP, FAO, and FAO-ACMRR | | Expeditions among member parties: working groups and cooperative research, and with other io's (e.g., JONSDAP-76 exercise with the JONSIS group, 1976, Baltic Open Sea experiment with SCOR, 1977, and CINECA operations with IOC and FAO, 1978) |

International Fishery Commissions (Continued)

| Organization | Inter-American Tropical Tuna Commission | International North Pacific Fisheries Commission | International Pacific Halibut Commission |
|---|---|---|---|
| Outcomes | | | |
| Intelligence gathering | | | |
| Data collection, storage, and dissemination | Commission staff collects and analyzes data; publishes summaries of its staff and cooperating scientists research in its bulletins and annual reports; world-wide dissemination | Member parties collect, analyze, and report data; CBR compiles; Commission publishes summaries of member parties research in its annual reports and bulletins, and statistics of the fishery in its yearbook; library | Commission staff collects data from commercial fishermen, processors, and own research, analyzes, and publishes summaries of its research in its annual, scientific, and technical reports; computer storage, library |
| Publications | Annual Reports and Bulletins | Annual Reports, Bulletins, and Statistical Yearbooks | Annual, Scientific, and Technical Reports |
| Recommendations | Conservation measures | Research, conservation measures, abstention determinations, and penalties | Conservation measures |
| Enforcement | No enforcement authority | No enforcement authority | No enforcement authority |

| International Pacific Salmon Fisheries Commission | International Whaling Commission | North Pacific Fur Seal Commission | International Council for the Exploration of the Sea |
|---|---|---|---|
| Commission staff collects data, e.g., with cooperation of the Canadian Department of Fisheries, analyzes, and publishes summaries of its research in its annual and progress reports | Member parties collect, analyze, and report data; SC and BIWS compile; Commission publishes summaries of member parties research in its annual reports; BIWS publishes statistics of the fishery | Member parties collect, analyze, and report data; SSC compiles; Commission publishes summaries of member parties' research in its proceedings and report on investigations | Working groups collect, analyze, and report data; Commission publishes summaries of working groups' research in its various publications; magnetic tape storage and library; data available to public |
| Annual, Progress, and Administrative Reports, Bulletins, and miscellaneous booklets and pamphlets | Annual Reports | Proceedings and Report on Investigations | Annales Biologiques, Bulletin Statistique, Cooperative Research Reports, Fiches d'Identification du Zooplancton, ICES Oceanographic Data Lists and Inventories, Journal du Conseil, Proces-Verbal de la Reunion, Rapports et Proces-Verbaux, and Statistical News Letter |
| Conservation measures including construction projects for the removal of obstructions to the ascent of salmon | Research and conservation measures | Research and conservation measures | Research and conservation measures |
| No enforcement authority | International observer program; no enforcement authority | No enforcement authority | No enforcement authority |

# APPENDIX I

## Discussion of Questions Concerning the Proposed International Council for Scientific Investigation of the North Pacific

1. What international arrangements for consultation on fishery matters are likely to survive, and to what extent are they likely to carry out the functions of the proposed organization?

Discussion is limited to two fishery organizations, the International North Pacific Fishery Commission (INPFC) and the International Pacific Halibut Commission (IPHC). INPFC is the fishery organization with the broadest responsibility and membership in the North Pacific. However, the organization is unlikely to be able to carry out the proposed tasks of the new scientific organization, the Pacific International Council for the Exploration of the Sea (hereafter referred to as PICES), because of its present limited membership (the USSR is not a member) and because its focus is restricted to the management of fisheries outside the limits of national jurisdiction (principally the high-seas salmon fishery).

Because of changes in national jurisdiction over fisheries, the present INPFC treaty is being renegotiated. The new draft treaty provides for the possible transfer of some responsibilities to other organizations, such as PICES, where appropriate.

The future of IPHC is also undetermined. Its responsibilities might be extended to other groundfish, or it might be replaced by a less formal U.S.–Canada bilateral agreement, with separate panels for each coast.

A major problem is that the surviving organizations may not be able to provide a comprehensive and credible information base. No single existing body includes all of the major states as members, except the Fur Seal Commission whose mandate is limited. None of the present regional bodies are concerned with the exchange of data other than those relating to certain specific fisheries. It is noteworthy that the information exchange between IPHC and the subcommittees of INPFC has been limited. PICES committees might be able to arrange agreements on statistical areas and other aspects of fishery data exchange, thus facilitating the maintenance of comparable fishery statistics.

2. Are there other international organizations that could contribute significantly to the functions of the proposed organization?

In convincing governments of the desirability of establishing a new organization, it will be important to demonstrate that existing intergovernmental and international nongovernmental organizations cannot perform the tasks envisaged for PICES. Three intergovernmental bodies are discussed, the Food and Agriculture Organization (FAO), the World Meteorological Organization (WMO), and the Intergovernmental Oceanographic Commission (IOC).

With regard to FAO, it should be noted that the PICES concept is inherently broader than the charter of FAO in that it includes elements related to programs of WMO and IOC in addition to fishery matters. The limited resources of FAO are principally devoted to problems of developing countries rather than to those of the proposed charter members of PICES, Canada, Japan, U.S. and USSR. It is not certain that a new FAO-sponsored regional fisheries organization would be acceptable to all of the major countries of the region (note that the USSR is not a member of FAO).

Although WMO has regional bodies, they tend to be land-oriented and delineated. WMO will continue to have the leading international role in the global collection of weather information, but its interests coincide only to a limited, but still important, degree with those proposed for PICES.

The IOC has also increasingly turned its attention to problems of developing countries. Where a strong regional organization exists (e.g., ICES), IOC has tended to work through that organization; this could be expected to happen if PICES were established. The IOC is establishing a new body for scientific cooperation in the Western Pacific (WESTPAC); objectives of WESTPAC are ''the prediction or forecast of ocean climate variability and of ocean food resources variability and the improved understanding of geological processes which have economic impact upon the countries comprising the Western Pacific community.'' Although the geographical coverage of this organization differs markedly from that proposed for PICES—WESTPAC is concerned with the region west of 170° W extending south to 40° S—there is a possibility for overlap that requires further consideration.

There do not seem to be nongovernmental bodies that systematically engage in activities such as those proposed for PICES in the North Pacific. For example, the Pacific Science Association is a nongovernmental organization with much broader geographical and intellectual interests than those proposed for PICES. However, its principal activity seems to be the organization of general meetings at four-year intervals.

Bilateral arrangements will continue and possibly increase in importance. In the field of scientific cooperation, they have been particularly effective between the U.S. and Canada. It is also reported that there has been some success in the Japan–USSR bilateral in fishery oceanography. In general, the transaction costs of bilateral arrangements appear to be high. However, such arrangements can facilitate the exchange of fishery statistics. For example, information provided under the Governing International Fishery Agreements (GIFAs) might be aggregated to give a broader body of fishery data than has generally been available.

3. Who are the major and minor players in marine scientific research in the North Pacific, and how do they interact politically and scientifically? To what extent does each treat scientific cooperation as separate from other marine issues?

Most marine scientific research in the North Pacific is done by scientists and institutions of Canada, Japan, U.S., and USSR. Yet, despite the advanced capabilities of these countries, the coverage of scientific observations, particularly those that are repeated systematically (to provide information on variability) and those beyond the coastal region, is very sparse. Minor players include Poland, China, and both Koreas.

Scientific cooperation in most countries tends to be linked with other marine issues. Furthermore, the practice of fitting science to national positions is fairly common; this is unlikely to be changed by the existence of a multilateral forum. To the extent that PICES emphasizes fishery matters, decoupling from political issues will be particularly difficult. Yet the experience in ICES has shown that this can be done, at least in the areas of periodic review of scientific progress, joint planning, and the promotion of mutually agreed-upon investigations.

It is clear that there is a delicate line between science and politics in the interests of coastal states. On the one hand, it is important that the proposed organization deal with problems of direct interest to governments. On the other, it is important to avoid politicizing desirable scientific studies.

4. Should membership in the proposed organization be restricted to countries bordering the region? Which countries must be members for the organization to be effective? How should the geographical region of interest be defined?

It is essential that the four major countries of the region—Canada, Japan, U.S., and USSR—be members. Whether to include other members, including those from outside the region, is of secondary importance at this time. Such membership is certain to have political implications. Yet, membership of all countries engaged in scientific research and other relevant marine activities in the region is important to the collection of a comprehensive data set. In view of the potential political problems, it is probably realistic to start with the key members and to consider additional membership after the organization is established.

The geographical region of PICES interest should extend from the coasts of Japan and the USSR to those of Canada and the U.S. It should include the Bering Sea and the Pacific Ocean south of 30° N and should be extended farther south only for special purposes.

5. What objectives (benefits) are at stake for each player in seeking cooperation and/or coordination of marine scientific research in the region? What loss is incurred by each if cooperation or coordination is ineffective?

Participants in the proposed organization would have some or all of the following objectives:

1. A more effective organization for pooling information on various marine activities in the region.
2. A mechanism for facilitating the systematic collection of needed information.
3. A broadened and credible data base for fisheries and marine science.
4. A mechanism for coordination and cooperation in research related to fisheries.

5. Establishment and/or replacement of the peer review procedures in fisheries that may be lost in the process of reorganizing INPFC and IPHC.

6. Greater efficiency and reduced cost in cooperative activities.

7. Greater international cooperation in the acquisition and exchange of information on the ocean environment and on ocean uses.

While all coastal countries are concerned to some extent with the long-range and large-scale aspects of such objectives, their interest in specific problems appears to fall off exponentially with the distance of these problems from the coast. In the region beyond the limits of their exclusive economic zones, the interests of coastal states pertain mainly to high-seas fisheries, marine scientific research and pollution (to some extent), and weather and climate.

To establish a permanent organization without specific project responsibilities is seen by some as dangerous. In the absence of very specific terms of reference, such an organization could create work to keep its staff occupied. From that point of view, ad hoc arrangements for specific projects would be preferable. Therefore, in considering the activities of the proposed organization, it is important to identify the specific functions that it is to carry out as well as the benefits that will be derived therefrom. Because of the interactions among all of the various marine activities and the environment in which they are carried out, the organization should focus not only on science per se, but also on appropriate applications of the scientific findings.

6. What criteria should be applied to the specific functions of the proposed scientific organization?

Specific functions with minimal political implications include the following:

1. Data exchange—especially important in fisheries and marine science, less so with other marine uses (ports, oil, shipping) because these are not heavily science-related.

2. Planning—cases should be emphasized where common interests overlap. Attention should also be paid to specific projects of interest to one or more members. Details of project design should be elaborated by working groups.

3. Collective assessment—problems related to fisheries, climate, pollution, and marine science.

Criteria that should be applied to these functions include (1) clearly identified benefits that cannot otherwise be obtained, and (2) increased efficiency through replacement of existing activities. The aim should be to start with a limited mechanism and a small number of functions of circumscribed scope, but to provide an opportunity to expand functions as needed.

Assessment and planning should be narrowly defined and should include review of the nature and quality of the data base and of the methods of interpretation. In dealing with assessment, it is important to avoid the implication of independent conclusions that impinge on management of national resources. Nevertheless, a scientific organization should be able to discuss and evaluate questions from a scientific point of view. Evaluation by peers is generally recognized as valuable. An international peer body that evaluates scientific issues can make an important contribution to the development of both national and international positions.

An independent international scientific staff might contribute to the credibility of the proposed activities and evaluations. Initially, however, it may only be practicable to provide an administrative staff. The need for an independent staff might then be established after experience with the activities of the organization has been gained.

7. Is it more fruitful from the scientific perspective, as well as more effective from a political standpoint, to deal with all marine scientific problems of the North Pacific in a single mechanism, or should such problems be broken down by subregion, discipline, or subject matter?

It is conceivable that fisheries, marine scientific research, marine pollution, and other topics could be treated separately, on either a permanent or on an ad hoc basis. However, a principal disadvantage of this approach is that it ignores the interactions between uses and the need for information and ideas to be exchanged across disciplines and uses. An important virtue of a multidisciplinary organization would be a closer integration of appropriate fisheries and oceanographic studies.

Yet some separation of functions is necessary. An organization that deals directly either with conflicts and their resolution or with management and the allocation of resources should be separate and distinct from one that is concerned with the development of a credible data base and with the scientific evaluation of information. The latter functions are proposed for PICES.

The principal management problems, apart from those of fisheries, concern marine pollution and its monitoring, and the management of multiple uses. Management problems, which should be handled by fishery or pollution commissions or other such bodies, require scientific information and evaluation of a multidisciplinary nature that could be supplied through the efforts of PICES and its members. The basic scientific work would be done at the national level; PICES would assist in its development and coordination and would facilitate the compilation and interpretation of results. Adequate monitoring for either pollution or weather and climate purposes will be extensive and expensive, and the design of an appropriate monitoring system must be based on adequate scientific understanding. National data systems are inadequate in scale for the required regional coverage, and data from several national sources may not be comparable without agreement on sampling and standards.

While PICES could provide a useful service to national and international fishery management in the region, its focus should be broader than fisheries. Its general interests should be the collection, evaluation, and production of knowledge. But these general interests should be achieved through projects and activities designed to answer specific questions and needs. The means and mechanisms for carrying out these activities should be specified carefully. At the same time, it is important that the projects and activities not be too narrowly defined and that provision be made for future expansion of responsibilities should that prove desirable. A continuing mechanism, such as PICES, could facilitate the accomplishment of a series of specific regional investigations with limited objectives. But a periodic overview of these investigations on a broader basis is required if more general and coordinated scientific responses to practical problems are to be developed.

At present, there are numerous bilateral and multilateral arrangements and meetings in the region. A single annual meeting of PICES could simplify arrangements and save funds and time of those concerned. This annual meeting would stress planning and review of activities, but it should also include top-level scientific exchanges. To stimulate the participation of scientists, meetings must be designed to attract their interest.

8. How will member governments respond to organization proposals for cooperative scientific programs that require significant funding?

Where proposals arise for large-scale and expensive international projects through the activities of the secretariats of international organizations, governments tend to react negatively. On the other hand, where scientific proposals have originated with scientists, the response has been more favorable. For example, ICES proposals for Overflow Experiments, WMO and ICSU proposals for large meteorological experiments, and SCOR proposals for the International Indian Ocean Expedition have had favorable impacts on national support of both national and international programs. In such cases, the implementation of desirable projects has resulted from scientific agreement rather than from the power of the international organization involved.

Yet, there is some concern that identification of scientific gaps and the assessment of research priorities by international organizations could impinge on the intranational competition for scarce resources. Such harmful effects could be mitigated if projects arose from discussions among active scientists in the countries concerned. In such cases, the support of the international body might have the beneficial effect of stimulating national support for desirable activities.

The role of international organizations has been to encourage rather than to pressure governments to change their priorities. Proposals commonly arise from scientists in the major countries, and such leadership is essential if the projects are to implemented.

9. Should there be a separate category of membership for scientific institutions to ensure their full participation in the scientific activities of the organization? Is there a special role for laboratory directors, as middle-level decision makers?

The involvement of scientific institutions and communications among them are vital because resources are deployed at that level. Such institutions are often more active in nongovernmental than in intergovernmental organizations. ICES has been remarkably successful in assuming many of the characteristics of nongovernmental bodies, despite its intergovernmental charter.

In the United States, there is some experience with organizations of laboratory directors, but neither the Joint Oceanographic Institutions nor the Council of Oceanographic Laboratory Directors appears to be as relevant a model as the Canadian Committee on

Oceanography, which includes senior members from both government and academic laboratories.

In ICES, directors of the important scientific institutions are involved although their participation has not been institutionalized. Rather, it has arisen because of the interest and importance of ICES programs to their laboratories. A similar evolution would be desirable for PICES. Certainly, consideration of any formal arrangements for the participation of laboratory directors should be deferred until after PICES has been established and gained experience.

10. Does the proposed structure facilitate scientific decisions and recommendations that are responsive to the collective requirements of member governments and yet are effectively insulated from political influence?

An important structural question is whether PICES should be intergovernmental. While some of the proposed tasks might be more easily accomplished if the organization were nongovernmental, there appear to be important reasons for it to be intergovernmental. Major functions that have been identified require governmental action, for example, the provision of policy commitment and resources along with cooperation in providing desired information and data on fisheries, pollution, and other ocean uses. Government support will be required to meet operating expenses, which include funding for a secretariat, travel, and publications. Some costs, such as those of participation, would be paid directly by governments in the case of an intergovernmental organization. That objective scientific recommendations can be produced by an intergovernmental organization has been demonstrated by ICES, where scientists collectively contribute and evaluate data.

11. If there were orderly and timely exchange of data, how would the organization handle, use, and disseminate it? What factors affect the usefulness for management purposes of the exchange of data and information on the status of stocks and on the quality of the marine environment?

Data exchange should not be promoted for its own sake. Not all data are worth exchanging, and some principles and guidelines are required to determine those that are. If PICES were to restrict itself merely to the exchange of selected data, it would be functioning as a data sink. An alternative is for PICES to be involved in evaluating the exchanged data and in preparing recommendations based on such evaluations.

In the case of ICES, fisheries data are exchanged and evaluated in the various stock assessment groups; recommendations are considered in the relevant Advisory Committee. As a consequence, reliable information is made uniformly available, both to members and to nonmembers.

Comparable fisheries data are lacking for the North Pacific, and a need has been expressed for a single, agreed-upon source document. A computer-based system is desirable, with a clear organizing concept to deal with problems of selection and aggregation. It might be modeled after the ICES system, with agreed-upon collection and reporting schemes and with close attention to sampling requirements. It would apply not only to fisheries data but also to hydrography and pollution.

Utilization of data that might be collected could be limited by available computer capacity. Details of the system for data exchange are a matter for specialists to discuss after the general principles and guidelines have been established.

To be useful for management purposes, the data set should be comprehensive. This will require that the membership include at least all of the major players in the region. At present the USSR is not a member of INPFC and thus does not participate fully in the exchange of fisheries data. Countries not included in PICES membership may be unwilling to provide desired data.

Initially, the new organization could focus on data exchange related to a few problems of common interest; for example, scientific investigations in the region both within and beyond the 200-mile zone.

12. What should be the role of the proposed organization with regard to the formulation of advice to member governments or to appropriate regional organizations?

Use of the term ''Advisory Committee'' and the question of the advisory role of the proposed organization require careful examination. It must be clear that the focus of the organization is on scientific rather than management questions. Thus, it will be appropriate to deal with questions of data base, methodology, and models. The assessment function should be carefully delimited and, at least initially, the advisory function should be avoided. While the organization might deal with the status of stocks, it should avoid fishery quota issues.

At the very least, assessment should be concerned with what data are available. There could also be an assessment of the nature and level of national scientific activities in the region. Assessment of the state of the marine environment in the region may also be of general interest. Initially, such assessments could be based on national statements, the examination of which could reveal the need for additional data and studies.

Within areas of extended national jurisdiction, other countries are unlikely to have a say about total allowable catches unless the stocks in question are shared across jurisdictional boundaries. In the United States, however, the Fishery Conservation and Management Act requires the use of the best scientific data in determining TACs. Thus, international data and assessments are to be taken into account.

In the view of some, PICES should undertake a stock-by-stock review of the status of fishery resources and their current sustainable (biological) yields. It should promote the exchange of scientific information through, for example, the organization of symposia on the biology of fish stocks, sampling methodology, methods for age determination, standardization of fishing effort, and techniques of stock assessment. It should review research programs and progress, and it should plan cooperative and coordinated investigations where they are deemed essential. In the case of stocks that occur at least temporarily outside of national jurisdiction, PICES should have a committee to assess the stocks, and in this case to recommend management requirements to governments.

The PICES role as a data center requires critical examination from the fishery point of view. PICES could try to arrange for agreement on a body of data and could discuss techniques of its interpretation. While the organization should avoid consideration of national fishery decisions, it could promote a dialogue and could even comment on scientific information relating to stocks allocated to countries and to the possibility of overfishing. For example, PICES might organize a symposium on the situation in the pollock fishery.

The problem of relating exchanged data to management is not unique to fisheries. There is also international interest in oil, pollution, and other technical developments. It will be difficult to avoid discussion of scientific information that relates to matters of coastal state interest. Peer review and discussion of data can benefit all participants. It should be noted that even in the Draft Convention on the Law of the Sea the coastal state is not completely sovereign in the exclusive economic zone. For example, provisions on endangered stocks obligate coastal states to consider information from other sources.

## Summary of Views on Specific Questions

The views summarized below do not represent the unanimous position of all participants in the discussion of questions considered here, but can be considered a common basis for continuation of the dialogue.

A general conclusion was that while there were a number of important scientific activities that would benefit from improved international arrangements in the North Pacific, it was premature to establish now an intergovernmental organization to coordinate and support these activities. The preferred approach was to continue informal discussions in a more organized fashion and to allow the informal arrangements to evolve towards a more permanent and formal institution as required by developing circumstances.

1. What marine scientific activities in the North Pacific could benefit from enhanced international cooperative research and exchange of information?

It was agreed that fisheries, biological oceanography, and oceanography more generally would be the central interests of a new organization. At least initially, the economic, social and other applied aspects, including ocean engineering, would be of secondary importance. It was generally agreed that whatever form of organization is eventually selected, it should have no specific advisory responsibility that directly pertains to resource management.

Despite the general agreement that the organization should not provide direct advice on management and allocation of stocks, the view was expressed that a useful function could be served by periodic general assessments of the living resources of the North Pacific. There is a general recognition of the need for the development of common data bases of high quality resulting from the use of understood methods, particularly in the field of fisheries, but also in other scientific fields where specific needs have been identified.

Examples of specific activities that could benefit from improved cooperation in the North Pacific include:

1. The development and intercomparison of observational and analytical methods in all fields.

2. Regional studies such as those of the Bering Sea, studies of migratory species such as albacore, studies of the methodology of stock assessment and development of an ecosystem approach to fishery management.

3. Studies of interactions among species and between species and their environment as affecting the abundance and distribution of stocks.

4. Marine pollution studies of the assimilative capacity of coastal waters and the effects of particular pollutants on the population dynamics of stocks.

5. Studies of the interaction between the atmosphere and the sea within the North Pacific and adjacent waters.

2. To what extent are these activities being handled through existing national and international arrangements?

Most participants considered that the existing arrangements in fisheries were piecemeal in nature and were highly specialized with regard to problems and participation. Not even the bilateral arrangements are comprehensive, and they involve different national laboratories in different problems. The characteristics of the present fishery arrangements are often incompatible with the development of approaches that require contributions from several disciplines.

These problems have been exacerbated by the changes in national jurisdiction resulting from the developments in the law of the sea.

In the field of oceanography, existing informal and ad hoc arrangements, together with the international oceanographic data exchange system, are satisfactory for some problems but are far from adequate for dealing with many others.

Marine pollution is a subject of widespread concern and is addressed by various national programs. Some participants thought, however, that an occasional look, perhaps at 5 to 10 year intervals, at the overall health of the ocean environment in the North Pacific is necessary. This is not provided for in any existing arrangements and would require serious scientific discussion of both the need and the methodology by which it might be approached.

3. How could the proposed organization improve the carrying out and support of such activities?

It was agreed that an organization concerned with ocean sciences in the North Pacific could improve the conduct of marine scientific activities by:

a. Facilitating systematic communication between scientists of different countries and disciplines.

b. Providing a forum for identification of scientific problems of common interest and for formulation of approaches to their solution.

c. Developing cooperative research programs of mutual interest.

d. Providing a forum for international review of marine science conducted in the North Pacific.

e. Providing a mechanism for the systematic exchange of data and information.

f. Reducing redundancy and improving efficiency in the mechanisms of international cooperation in relevant areas.

g. Facilitating interactions among international organizations involved in marine scientific work in the region.

4. What should be the relationship between governmental decision making and scientific evaluation and recommendation?

As already discussed in question 1, there was general agreement that the organization should be concerned with scientific questions, including the scientific evaluation of available data, within the context of national prerogatives in these mattters.

5. What structure would be most effective for the proposed organization?

Participants desired a flexible, informal, and scientific organization. Some participants expressed the view that assuring adequate financial support for the activities identified would require an organization at least sponsored by governments. Several approaches were proposed, including a nongovernmental organization, a governmental organization similar to ICES, and a continuation of more focused informal discussions under governmental auspices. Discussions within and among the governments concerned could explore these approaches. Meanwhile, it was proposed that steps be taken promptly to initiate informal arrangements. It was generally agreed that initial membership should be from Canada, Japan, U.S. and USSR.

6. What procedures would be appropriate?

It was proposed that a steering committee be convened to organize and initiate scientific discussions of the character described above. The steering committee should consist of not more than three members from each of the participating countries. In establishing its arrangements, it should take into account the agreement of participants that meetings every two years should be appropriate, with the location and chairmanship rotating among the members. Subsidiary activities, including the development of a common data base, might require more frequent meetings.

**Notes**

# Notes

## 1. Introduction

1. Doc. #A/CONF. 62/L.78, 28 August 1981. Third United Nations Conference on the Law of the Sea (UNCLOS III).

2. There are separate provisions for archipelagoes affecting the baseline from which the territorial sea is measured, Articles 46–54.

3. See, for example, Bruce Russett, *International Regions and the International System* (Chicago: Rand McNally, 1967); Karl Deutsch et al., *France, Germany and the Western Alliance* (New York: Scribner's, 1967); Leon N. Lindberg and Stuart A. Scheingold, *Europe's Would-Be Polity* (Englewood Cliffs, N.J.: Prentice Hall, 1970); Leon N. Lindberg and Stuart A. Scheingold, eds., "Regional Integration: Theory and Research," *International Organization*, 24, 4 (Autumn 1970); Joseph S. Nye, *Peace in Parts* (Boston: Little, Brown, 1971).

4. A similar definition of the North Pacific region is found in Hiroshi Kasahara and William T. Burke, *North Pacific Fisheries Management*, Resources for the Future (RFF), Program of International Studies of Fisheries Arrangements, Paper 2 (Washington, D.C.: RFF, 1973), p. 1.

5. Ibid., pp. 39–50. See also: N. M. Erhardt and L. J. Bledsoe, *A Comparative Study of the Statistical Areas in the North Pacific Fisheries* (Seattle: Division of Marine Resources, University of Washington NORFISH ND07, Technical Report #60, May 1975).

6. Masao Oda, "Marine Transportation of Japanese Seaborne Trade and Related Laws and Regulations," in Christine L. Dawson, ed., *The North Pacific Project* (Seattle: Institute for Marine Studies, University of Washington, 1977), table 18, pp. 528–530. This has also been published in *Ocean Development and International Law Journal*, 6 (1979), 237–304.

7. Ibid., table 19, p. 532.

8. The oil pollution problem is treated at length in chap. 9, this volume.

9. Warren S. Wooster and Nona R. Henderson, "Marine Scientific Activities in the North Pacific," in Christine L. Dawson, op. cit., p. 568.

10. See, for example, several valuable, pioneering efforts: M. M. Sibthorp, ed., *The North Sea: Challenge and Opportunity* (London: Europa Publications, 1975), especially chap. 3, "Competing Uses and Interests in the North Sea"; Woods Hole Oceanographic Institution, Marine Policy and Ocean Management Program, *Effects on Commercial Fishing of Petroleum Development Off The Northeastern United States*, Report #WH01-76-66, April 1976, especially chap. 1, "Statement of the Problem. Analysis and Summary of Findings"; M. M. Sibthorp, ed., *Oceanic Management: Conflicting Uses of the Celtic Sea and Other Western U.K Waters* (London: Europa Publications, 1977); and Lee G. Anderson, "The Economics of Marine Resource Management," in Douglas M. Johnston, ed., *Marine Policy and the Coastal Community* (London: Croom Helm, 1976), pp. 65–84.

## 2. Development of Living Resources Under the Regime of the High Seas

1. Jan J. Solecki, *Economic Aspects of the Fishing Industry of Mainland China* (Vancouver: Institute of Fisheries, University of British Columbia, Spring 1966), p. 74.

2. Hiroshi Kasahara, *Fisheries Resources of the North Pacific Ocean*, Parts I and II, F. R. McMillan Lectures in Fisheries, Norman J. Wilimovsky, ed. (Vancouver: University of British Columbia, 1964), p. 12.

3. Dayton L. Alverson, "Fishery Resources in the Northeast Pacific Ocean," in Dewitt Gilbert, ed., *The Future of the Fishery Industry of the United States*, University of Washington Publications in Fisheries, New Series (Seattle: College of Fisheries, 1968), 4:89.

4. Richard Fleming, *Review of the Oceanography of the Northern Pacific*, Bull. no. 2 (Vancouver: International North Pacific Fisheries Commission, 1955), p. 11.

5. Kasahara, op. cit., p. 9.

6. Mikhail Chernyshov, "Resources of the Oceans Must Not Be Depleted," *Western Fisheries*, 95, 3 (December 1977), 42, 44—45.

7. Kasahara, op. cit., p. 9.

8. Ibid., p. 9.

9. Felix Favorite, A. J. Dodimead, and K. Nasu, *Oceanography of the Subarctic Pacific Region 1960—1971*, Bull. no. 33 (Vancouver: International North Pacific Fisheries Commission, 1976); and Felix Favorite, Taivo Laevastu, and Richard Straty, *Oceanography of the Northeastern Pacific Ocean and Bering Sea and Relations to Various Living Marine Resources*, Processed Report (Seattle: Northwest and Alaska Fisheries Center, June 1977).

10. Favorite et al., Oceanography of the Subarctic Pacific, pp. 76—81.

11. L. A. Zenkevitch, *Biology of the Seas of the USSR* (New York: Interscience Publishers, 1963), pp. 688—697.

12. Clinton E. Atkinson, *Northeast Asian Fisheries*. Unpublished draft of lecture presented at the Institute for Marine Studies, University of Washington, November 16, 1976, p. 3.

13. Alverson, op. cit., p. 87.

14. See, for example, Alverson, op. cit.; Shoichi Tanaka, "Fisheries in the Northwestern Pacific and Fishery Resources—Mainly on the Japanese Fisheries and International Problems Surrounding Them," in Christine L. Dawson, ed., *The North Pacific Project* (Seattle: Institute for Marine Studies, University of Washington, 1977), pp. 217—311; National Marine Fisheries Service (NMFS), *Pacific Salmon and the High Seas Salmon Fisheries of Japan* (Seattle: Processed Report, Northwest and Alaska Fisheries Center, December 1977), 324 pp.; NMFS, *Demersal Fish and Shellfish Resources of the Eastern Bering Sea in the Baseline Year 1970* (Seattle: Processed Report, Northwest and Alaska Fisheries Center, December 1977), 619 pp.; North Pacific Fisheries Management Council, *Fishery Management Plans for Pacific Salmon, Herring, Tanner Crab, King Crab, Groundfish and Shrimp*; North Pacific Fisheries Management Council, *Fishery Management Plans for Pacific Salmon, Northern Anchovy, Squid, and Groundfish*; and John L. Hart, *Pacific Fishes of Canada* (Ottawa: Fisheries Research Board of Canada, 1973).

15. North Pacific Fisheries Management Council, *Fisheries Management Plan and Draft Environmental Impact Statement for the Groundfish Fishery in the Bering Sea/Aleutian Island Area* (Anchorage, Alaska, March 23, 1979), p. 116.

16. Kasahara, op. cit., p. 66.

17. North Pacific Fisheries Management Council, "Report of the Working Group on Halibut," unpublished manuscript, 1977.

18. Kasahara, op. cit., p. 91.

19. Ibid., p. 92.

20. Ibid., p. 84.

21. NMFS, *Demersal Fish and Shellfish*, p. 440.

22. Kasahara, op. cit., p. 86.

23. Alverson, op. cit., p. 89.

24. M. Tillman, "Tentative Recommendations for Management of the Coastal Fishery for Pacific Hake (*Merluccius productus* [Ayres]) Based on a Simulation Study of the Effects of Fishing on a Virgin Population," Master of Science thesis, College of Fisheries, University of Washington, Seattle, 1968, p. 24.

25. Elbert H. Ahlstrom, "Fishery Resources Available to California Fishermen," in Dewitt Gilbert, ed., *The Future of the Fishery Industry of the United States*, University of Washington Publications in Fisheries, New Series (Seattle: College of Fisheries, 1968), 4:73.

26. Kasahara, op. cit., p. 98.

27. NMFS, *Demersal Fish and Shellfish*, p. 436.

28. Alverson, op. cit., p. 29.

29. Tanaka, op. cit., pp. 236–238.

30. Kasahara, op. cit., p. 57.

31. Ibid., p. 119.

32. Tanaka, op. cit., p. 227.

33. Kasahara, op. cit., p. 113.

34. Ibid., p. 105.

35. Ahlstrom, op. cit., p. 71.

36. NMFS, *Pacific Salmon*, pp. 5–7.

37. Ibid., p. 17.

38. Kasahara, op. cit., p. 33.

39. NMFS, *Demersal Fish and Shellfish*, pp. 531, 532.

40. Kasahara, op. cit., p. 189.

41. NMFS, *Demersal Fish and Shellfish*, p. 545.

42. North Pacific Fisheries Management Council. *Draft Fishery Management Plan and Draft Environmental Impact Statement for the Pribilof Area Shrimp Fishery in the Bering Sea* (Anchorage, January 8, 1979), p. 2.

43. Office of Fisheries, Republic of Korea, *Fisheries of Korea* (Seoul: Hong Won Printing, 1966), p. 85.

44. Richard A. MacIntosh, "Alaska's Snail Resource," *Alaska Seas and Coasts*, 6, 5 (December 1978–January 1979), 1–4.

45. T. Okutani, *Stock Assessment of Cephalopod Resources Fished by Japan*, Fisheries Technical Paper No. 173, FIRST 173 (Rome: Food and Agriculture Organization, 1977), p. 4.

46. Shoichi Tanaka, personal communication.

47. Okutani, op. cit., p. 48.

48. International Union for the Conservation of Nature, *IUCN Bulletin*, 9, 1–2 (1978).

49. R. H. Lander and H. Kajimura, *Status of Northern Fur Seals*, Scientific Consultation on Marine Mammals, Advisory Committee on Marine Resources Research, Bergen, Norway, August 31–September 9, 1976, ACMRR/MM/SC/34 (Rome: Food and Agriculture Organization, April 1976), p. 29.

50. A. W. Erikson, "Marine Mammology Notebook" (course materials), College of Fisheries, University of Washington, 1978, p. 48.

51. A. A. Berzin, *The Sperm Whale* (Jerusalem: Israel Program for Scientific Translations, 1972) p. 190.

52. Gerald A. Sanger, "Preliminary Standing Stock and Biomass Estimates of Seabirds in the Subarctic Pacific Region," in D. W. Hood and E. J. Kelley, eds., *Oceanography of the Bering Sea: Proceedings of an International Symposium for Bering Sea Study*, Occasional Publication no. 2, (Fairbanks: Institute of Marine Science, University of Alaska, 1974), pp. 589–611.

53. Göran Michanek, *Seaweed Resources of the Ocean*, Fisheries Technical Paper No. 138,

FIRST 138 (Rome: Food and Agriculture Organization, 1975), pp. 79–104.

54. Georg Borgström, *Revolutionen i Världsfisket* (The Revolution in World Fisheries) (Halmstad, Sweden: Hallandspostensboktryckeri, 1966), p. 57.

55. Royal Commission on Canada's Economic Prospects, *The Commercial Fisheries of Canada* (Ottawa: Department of Fisheries of Canada and the Fisheries Research Board, 1956), p. 7; see also W. A. Carrothers, *The British Columbia Fisheries* (Toronto: The University of Toronto Press, 1941), 136 pp.; and Anne D. Forester and Joseph E. Forester, *Fishing: British Columbia's Commercial Fishing History* (Saanichton, British Columbia: Hancock House, 1975), 224 pp.

56. Takashi Ino, President, Shimonoseki University of Fisheries, discussion November 4, 1977.

57. Georg Borgström, *Japan's World Success in Fishing* (London: Fishing News [Books], 1964), p. 29.

58. Ibid., p. 31.

59. NMFS, *Demersal Fish and Shellfish*, p. 455.

60. Hiroshi Kasahara, "Japanese Distant Water Fisheries: A Review," *Fishery Bulletin*, 70, 2:261.

61. See chaps. 3 and 4, this volume, for more detailed treatment.

62. Kasahara, "Japanese Distant Water Fisheries," p. 231.

63. Ibid, p. 233.

64. Philip E. Chitwood, *Japanese, Soviet and South Korean Fisheries Off Alaska: Development and History Through 1966*, Circular No. 310 (Washington, D.C.: U. S. Fish and Wildlife Service, 1969).

65. NMFS, *Pacific Salmon*.

66. *Korea: Past and Present* (Seoul: Kwangmyong Publishing Co., 1972), p. 206.

67. Ibid., p. 210.

68. Chitwood, op. cit.

69. See discussion in chap. 3 of this volume.

70. A. N. Lavrishchev, *The Economic Geography of the USSR* (Moscow: Progress Publishers, 1969), p. 254.

71. U.S. Senate Committee on Commerce, *Soviet Oceans Development* (Washington, D.C.: U.S. Government Printing Office, 1976), p. 382.

72. L. G. Vinogradov et al., "Fisheries Resources," in I. P. Gerasimov et al., eds., *Natural Resources of the Soviet Union: Their Use and Renewal*, translated by Jacek I. Romanowski, English editor, W. A. Douglas Jackson (San Francisco: W. H. Freeman, 1971), p. 327.

73. N. P. Sysoev, *Economics of the Soviet Fishing Industry* (Jerusalem: Israel Program for Scientific Translations, 1974), p. 28.

74. Borgström, op. cit., p. 27.

75. Sysoev. op. cit., pp. 1–6.

76. A. T. Pruter, "Soviet Fisheries for Bottomfish and Herring of the Pacific and Bering Sea Coasts of the United States," *Marine Fisheries Review*, Paper 1225, December 1976, p. 14.

77. U.S. Senate Committee on Commerce, op. cit., p. 388.

78. Paul Dibb, *Siberia and the Pacific: A Study of Economic Development and Trade Prospects*, Praeger Special Studies Program (New York: Prager, 1972), p. 96.

79. Pruter, op. cit., pp. 9, 11.

80. Ibid., p. 2.

81. Tanaka, op. cit., p. 252.

82. Ibid., p. 251.

83. John N. Cobb, *Pacific Cod Fisheries*, Bureau of Fisheries Document No. 830 (Washington, D.C.: U.S. Department of Commerce, 1916), p. 24 ff.

84. Robert S. Browning, *North Pacific Fisheries* (London: Fishing News [Books], 1974), pp. 7–58.

85. P. A. Larkin, "Management of Pacific Salmon of North America," in Norman G. Benson, ed., *A Century of Fisheries in America* (Washington, D.C.: American Fisheries Society, 1970), Special Publication No. 7, p. 232.

86. NMFS, *Demersal Fish and Shellfish*, p. 27.

87. North Pacific Fisheries Management Council, *Draft Fishery Management Plan for Tanner Crab Off Alaska* (Anchorage, Alaska: July 1977).

88. John Wiese, "Alaska's Shrimp Industry," in Tussing et al., eds., *Alaska Fisheries Policy*, Institute of Social, Economic and Government Research (Fairbanks: University of Alaska, 1972), p. 179.

89. Solecki, op. cit., p. 68.

90. Ibid., p. 73.

91. Atkinson, op. cit., p. 15, referring to FAO estimates.

92. Ibid., p. 27.

93. Michanek, op. cit., p. 79.

94. Food and Agriculture Organization, *Review of the State of Exploitation of the World Fish Resources*, Committee on Fisheries, Eleventh Session, April 19–26, 1977 (Rome: COFI/77/5, November 1976), p. 5.

95. U.S. Senate Committee on Commerce, op. cit., p. 377.

96. Dibb, op. cit., p. 97.

97. Atkinson, op. cit., p. 12.

98. This situation may change as North Korea was admitted to the Food and Agriculture Organization in 1977.

99. U.S. Senate Committee on Commerce, op. cit., p. 426; Pruter, op. cit., pp. 7–8, urges caution in making such gross comparisons.

100. Fisheries Agency of Japan, *Fisheries Statistics of Japan*, Statistics and Information Dept., Ministry of Agriculture and Forestry (Tokyo, 1976), p. 8.

101. Fisheries and Marine Service, *Annual Statistical Review of Canadian Fisheries*, vol. 6 (1973).

102. Office of Fisheries, *Yearbook of Fisheries Statistics 1977* (Seoul, October 1977), p. 210.

103. Organization for Economic Cooperation and Development, *Report on Fisheries of Member Countries 1977* (Paris, 1977).

104. Atkinson, op. cit., p. 5.

105. Interview with Prof. Yutaka Hirasawa, Tokyo Fisheries University, December 15, 1977.

106. Teruji Sakiyama, "Policies in Pollution, Aquaculture and Coastal Management in Japan," *Marine Policy*, 3, 1 (January 1979), 25.

107. Syosoev, op. cit.

108. Wlodzimierz Kaczynski, "Alternatives Facing Distant-Water Fishing States in the Northeast Pacific Ocean," *Ocean Development and International Law Journal* (1979), 6:74.

109. National Marine Fisheries Service, *Report for the Year 1976* (Washington, D.C., 1977).

## 3. Traditional Regime for Fisheries Management

1. Hiroshi Kasahara and William T. Burke, *North Pacific Fisheries Management*, Resources for the Future Program of International Studies of Fisheries Arrangements (Washington, D.C.: RFF, 1973), chap. 3.

2. See Myres S. McDougal and William T. Burke, *The Public Order of the Oceans* (New Haven and London: Yale University Press, 1962), pp. 89–97, 155–156, 173, 305–318, 453–563 and

642–704; and Douglas M. Johnston, *The International Law of Fisheries* (New Haven and London: Yale University Press, 1965), chap. 5, pp. 157–252.

3. Data on limits are taken from Department of State, Limits in the Seas Series, *National Claims to Maritime Jurisdictions*, #36, Rev. 2, April 1, 1974; and FAO, *Limits and Status of the Territorial Sea, Exclusive Fishing Zones, Fishery Conservation Zones and the Continental Shelf*, Doc. #FID/C/ 127, Rev. 2, 1975.

4. The Revised Territorial Sea and Fishing Zone Act of December 26, 1970.

5. Kasahara and Burke, op. cit. (MS), p. 43. This citation, and those which follow, are from the original, mostly unpublished, manuscript version of chap. 2, pp. 41–103.

6. United Nations, Convention on the Continental Shelf, April 25, 1958, Doc. #A/CONF. 13/L.55.

7. See the *American Journal of International Law*, 53, 3 (July 1959), 763–768, for the text of this Convention.

8. Kasahara and Burke, op. cit., p. 96.

9. Ibid., and figure 18, p. 221.

10. Ibid., p. 101.

11. Ibid., and figure 17, p. 220.

12. The categories for bilateral short-term agreements are taken from Ibid., p. 89.

13. While the International Whaling Commission (IWC) Convention, of course, applies to the North Pacific, it is global in its scope.

14. Kasahara and Burke, op. cit., p. 86.

15. Choon-ho Park, "Fishing Under Troubled Waters: The Northeast Asia Fisheries Controversy," *Ocean Development and International Law Journal (ODILJ)*, 2, 2 (1974), 123.

16. Interim Convention on the Conservation of North Pacific Seas, February 9, 1957, in U.S. Senate, Committee on Commerce, *Treaties and Other International Agreements on Fisheries, Oceanographic Resources, and Wildlife to which the United States is Party*, 93d Congress, 2d Session, December 31, 1974, pp. 374–392.

17. Preamble.

18. Preamble.

19. Article III.

20. Article V.

21. Article VIII (2).

22. Article IX.

23. International Convention for the High Seas Fisheries of the North Pacific Ocean, with Annex and Protocol, May 9, 1952, U.S. Senate, op. cit., pp. 231–243.

24. Preamble.

25. Preamble.

26. Article III (1a).

27. Article III (1b).

28. Article III (1c & d).

29. Protocol to the International Convention for the High Seas Fisheries of the North Pacific Ocean, in U.S. Senate, op. cit., p. 239.

30. Choon-ho Park, "Fishing Under Troubled Waters."

31. See William T. Burke, Richard Legatski, and William W. Woodhead, *National and International Law Enforcement in the Ocean* (Seattle: University of Washington Press, 1975), pp. 10–27.

32. U.S. Senate, op. cit., pp. 283–386, see especially Article III.

33. No general summary of the work of the Commission is available. Pages 12–18 have therefore been written by Dr. George Harry, then Acting Director, National Marine Mammal Laboratory, National Marine Fisheries Service. We are grateful to Dr. Harry for his invaluable assistance.

34. G. Y. Harry, Jr., Fur Seal Population Numbers, U. S. Dept. of Commerce, NOAA, National Marine Fisheries Service (Seattle, July 3, 1974), unpublished memorandum, 2 pp.

35. Marine Mammal Division, *Fur Seal Investigations, 1975*, U.S. Dept. of Commerce, NOAA, National Marine Fisheries Service (Seattle, 1975), processed report, 115 pp.

36. Marine Mammal Division, *Fur Seal Investigations, 1978*, U.S. Department of Commerce, NOAA, National Marine Fisheries Service (Seattle, 1979), processed report, 115 pp.

37. North Pacific Fur Seal Commission, *North Pacific Fur Seal Commission Report on Investigation from 1958 to 1961* (Tokyo: Kenkyusha, 1964), 183 pp.

38. Marine Mammal Division, *Fur Seal Investigations, 1973*, U.S. Dept. of Commerce, NOAA, National Marine Fisheries Services (Seattle, 1974), processed report, 96 pp.

39. Marine Mammal Division, *Fur Seal Investigations, 1978* (1979).

40. National Marine Fisheries Service, *Draft Environmental Impact Statement for the Interim Convention on Conservation of North Pacific Fur Seals*, U.S. Department of Commerce, NOAA/NMFS (1979).

41. Ibid.

42. P. G. Nikulin, ''Present condition and growth perspectives of the Commander Islands fur seal population.'' Trans. Vses, Nauchno-iss, ed., Inst. Movsk Rybn. Zhoz. Okeanogr. 68, in Russian (1968). Trans. by Israel Prog. Sci. Trans., in V. A. Arsenev and K. I. Panin, eds., *Pinnipeds of the North Pacific*, avail. Natl. Tech. Inf. Serv., Springfield, VA. as TT 70-54020 (1971) pp. 28–38.

43. F. G. Chelnokov, Pacific Scientific Research Institute of Fisheries and Oceanography, Petropavlovsk, Kamchatka, USSR. Personal communication.

44. R. H. Lander and H. Kajimura, ''Status of Northern Fur Seals,'' ACMRR/MM/SC 34. Scientific consultation on marine mammals (Bergen, Norway, 31 August–9 September 1976), 50 pp.

45. Kasahara and Burke, *International Fishery Management in the North Pacific: Present and Future* (Seattle: University of Washington, 1972), mimeo, p. 71.

46. Ibid., p. 72; and Ralph W. Johnson, ''The Japan–United States Salmon Conflict,'' in *Washington Law Review*, 43,1 (October 1967), 6.

47. Loh Lee Low, *Status of Major Demersal Fishery Resources of the Northeastern Pacific, Bering Sea, and Aleutian Islands*, NMFS, Northwest and Alaska Fisheries Research Center, Processed Report (April 1976), p. 53 and table 19, p. 90.

48. Kasahara and Burke, *International Fishery Management*, pp. 75–76.

49. Choon-ho Park, op. cit., p. 123.

50. Office of International Fisheries, NMFS, NOAA, *People's Republic of China–Japan Fisheries Agreement*, Analysis and Text, F41/MB, #186 (September 15, 1975).

51. Halibut Convention, Article 1, U.S. Senate, op. cit., pp. 679–682.

52. Bernard Einar Skud, *Jurisdictional and Administrative Limitations Affecting Management of the Halibut Fishery*, IPHC Scientific Report no. 59 (Seattle, Washington, 1976), p. 9; see also James Crutchfield and Arnold Zellner, *Economic Aspects of the Pacific Halibut Fishery*, U.S. Dept. of the Interior, Bureau of Commercial Fisheries, Fishery Industrial Research, 1,1 (1962).

53. Preamble to the Salmon Convention, U.S. Senate, op. cit., p. 654.

54. Protocol Amending the Convention, to include Pink Salmon in the Fraser River System (December 28, 1956), U.S. Senate, op. cit., pp. 662–665.

55. Salmon Convention, Article VII, U.S. Senate, op. cit.

56. Choon-ho Park, op. cit., pp. 110 ff. The sources for the texts of the various agreements are provided by Park in notes 60, 62, 64, 68, 70, 71 and 72 on pp. 132–134. Indications of English translations where available are also provided.

57. Ibid., p. 118.

58. Office of International Fisheries, NMFS. Text of the Agreement on Fisheries Concluded Between the Government of Japan and the Government of the People's Republic of China, Preamble.

59. *AJIL*, 53, 3 (July 1959), pp. 763–768.

60. An English translation of the Treaty is available in the *Japanese Annual of International Law*, #110 (1966), pp. 264–283. For description and analysis of Treaty provisions, see Park, op. cit., pp. 106–107, and Shigeru Oda, "Japan and International Conventions Relating to North Pacific Fisheries," *Washington Law Review*, 43, 1 (October 1967), 70–73.

61. Park, op. cit., p. 123.

62. Article I.

63. Article V.

64. Article XI.

65. Article VIII.

66. Park, op. cit., p. 108.

67. Halibut Convention, op cit., Article III (1).

68. Article III (1).

69. Article III (1).

70. Donald L. McKernan, personal communication, February 6, 1975.

71. Article III (2).

72. Skud, op cit.

73. Article II.

74. Skud, op. cit., pp. 11, 12.

75. Stephen H. Hoag and Robert R. French, *The Incidental Catch of Halibut by Foreign Trawlers*. International Pacific Halibut Commission, Scientific Report #60, (1976), table 8, p. 21. All figures in this paragraph are from Hoag and French.

76. Bernard Einar Skud, "Management of the Pacific Halibut Fishery," *Journal of the Fisheries Research Board of Canada*, 30, 12, Part 2 (1973), 2393–2398.

77. Stephen H. Hoag, *The Effect of Trawling on the Setline Fishery for Halibut*, IPHC Scientific Report #61 (1976).

78. Ibid., p. 10.

79. Salmon Convention, Article III, U.S. Senate, op. cit.

80. Article IV.

81. Article V.

82. Article III of the Protocol.

83. Kasahara and Burke, *International Fishery Management*, p. 67.

84. Article III.

85. Shigeru Oda, op. cit., pp. 71, 72.

86. Article VI.

87. Article VI.

88. Bernard Einar Skud, *Regulations of the Pacific Halibut Fishery, 1924–1976*, IPHC Technical Report #15 (1977). A brief history of the Commission's experience can also be found in F. Heward Bell, "Management of Pacific Halibut," in Norman G. Benson, ed., *A Century of Fisheries in North America* (Washington, D.C.: American Fisheries Society, 1970), pp. 209–221.

89. Bernard Einar Skud, *Jurisdictional and Administrative Limitations*.

90. Ibid., p. 9.

91. Ibid., p. 13.

92. Hoag, *The Effect of Trawling*, p. 15.

93. Ibid., p. 16.

94. U.S. Senate, op cit., Protocol of Exchange, Convention for the Protection, Preservation, and Extension of the Sockeye Salmon Fishery of the Fraser River System, July 28, 1937, pp. 660, 661.

95. U.S. Senate, op. cit., Agreement to Facilitate the Ascent of Salmon in Hell's Gate Canyon and Elsewhere in the Fraser River System (July 21 and August 5, 1944); and Recommendation of

International Pacific Salmon Fisheries Commission for Overcoming Obstructions to the Ascent of Sockeye Salmon, Pursuant to Terms of a Treaty Between Canada and the United States, pp. 666–675.

96. James A. Crutchfield and Giulio Pontecorvo. *The Pacific Salmon Fisheries* (Washington, D.C.: The John Hopkins University Press for Resources for the Future, 1969), p. 143.

97. Ibid., p. 143.

98. Ibid.

99. Ibid., p. 144.

100. For a concise but comprehensive discussion of the problem of salmon management in the Pacific Northwest, see P. A. Larkin, "Management of Pacific Salmon of North America," in Benson, op. cit., pp. 223–236. See also W. F. Royce, "Salmon Management in the United States," FAO Technical Conference on Fishery Management and Development (Vancouver, Canada, February 1973), Doc. #FI: FMO/73/S-24, 13–23.

101. Kashara and Burke. *International Fishery Management*, p. 81.

102. Ibid., p. 82; see also Shigeru Oda, op. cit., p. 68.

103. Article IV (a & b).

104. Kasahara and Burke. *International Fishery Management*, p. 84.

105. Shigeru Oda, op. cit., p. 68. This citation is the source for all figures in this paragraph.

106. Ibid., p. 69.

107. Shoichi Tanaka, "Fisheries in the Northwest Pacific and Fishery Resources—Mainly on the Japanese Fisheries and International Problems Surrounding Them," in Christine L. Dawson, ed., *The North Pacific Project* (Seattle: Institute for Marine Studies, University of Washington, IMS-UW-77-1, 1977), p. 247, see also *ODILJ* (1979), 6:163–236.

108. Ibid., table 11, p. 297.

109. Ibid, pp. 248, 249.

110. Oda, op. cit., pp. 69, 70.

111. Park, op. cit., p. 108.

112. Tanaka, op. cit., pp. 254, 255.

113. Ibid., p. 257.

114. Ibid., p. 258.

115. This section was written by Professor William T. Burke. It is a previously unpublished portion of chap. 2 in Kasahara and Burke. *International Fishery Management*, pp. 87–101.

116. Hiroshi Kasahara, "Management of Fisheries in the North Pacific," *Journal of the Fisheries Research Board of Canada*, 30, 12, part 2 (1973), 2355.

## 4. Conflicts over Living Resources under Traditional Fisheries Regime and Trends Toward Extended Coastal State Jurisdiction

1. Myres S. MacDougal and William T. Burke. *The Public Order of the Oceans* (New Haven: Yale University Press, 1962), p. 156.

2. Kasuomi Ouichi, "A Perspective on Japan's Struggle for Its Territorial Rights on the Oceans," *Ocean Development and International Law Journal*, 5, 1 (1978), 111.

3. Shoichi Tanaka, "Fisheries in the Northwestern Pacific and Fishery Resources—Mainly on the Japanese Fisheries and International Problems Surrounding Them," in Christine L. Dawson, ed., *The North Pacific Project* (Seattle: Institute for Marine Studies, University of Washington, 1977), pp. 217–311. Later published in *ODILJ* (1979), 6:163–236.

4. W. C. Herrington, "Operation of the Japanese Fishery Management System," *Occasional Paper No. 11* (Kingston: Law of the Sea Institute, University of Rhode Island, 1971), p. 11.

5. See, for example, Milan A. Kravanja. "The Soviet Fishing Industry—A Review," in *Soviet Oceans Development* (Washington, D.C.: Committee Print, Committee on Commerce, National

Ocean Policy Study, 94th Congress, 2d Session, October 1976), pp. 377–470.

6. Hiroshi Kasahara. "Japanese Distant-Water Fisheries: A Review," *Fishery Bulletin*, 70, 1 (1973), p. 228.

7. Hiroshi Kasahara and William Burke, *North Pacific Fisheries Management*, Resources for the Future Program of International Studies of Fisheries Arrangements (Washington, D.C.: RFF, 1973) p. 47.

8. Shigeru Oda, "Japan and International Conventions Relating to North Pacific Fisheries," *Washington Law Review*, 43, 1 (1967), 40.

9. Zengo Ohira, "Fishery Problems Between Soviet Russia and Japan," *Japanese Annual of International Law*, no. 2 (1958), pp. 1–19. For a more recent treatment, see William H. McKenzie, "Japan–USSR Negotiations on Safe Fishing and Reversion of Disputed Islands in the North Pacific: 1945–1977," *Marine Affairs Journal*, no. 5, January 1978.

10. James E. Wilen, *Common Property Resources and the Dynamics of Over-Exploitation: The Case of the North Pacific Fur Seal* (Vancouver: Resource Paper no. 3, Programme in Natural Resource Economics, University of British Columbia, September 1976), pp. 6, 7.

11. Walter B. Parker, *International Fisheries Regimes of the North Pacific* (Anchorage: Alaska and the Law of the Sea, Arctic Environmental Information and Data Center, University of Alaska, June 1974), p. 5.

12. Barton W. Everman, "The Northern Fur Seal Problem as a Type of Many Problems of Marine Biology," *Bulletin of the Scripps Institute for Biological Research* no. 9 (December 15, 1919), pp. 21, 22.

13. Shigeru Oda, *International Control of Sea Resources* (Leyden: A. W. Sythoff, 1962), p. 76.

14. Stefan A. Riesenfeld, *Protection of Coastal Fisheries Under International Law* (Washington, D.C.: Monograph Series of the Carnegie Endorsement for International Peace, Division of International Law, no. 5, 1942), p. 277.

15. Ohira, op. cit., p. 3.

16. Convention for the Preservation of Fur Seals, *U. S. Department of State Pamphlet Series*, no. 564.

17. Oda, *International Control*, p. 77.

18. Convention Concerning Fur Seals, U.S. Department of State, *Executive Agreement Series*, no. 415.

19. Interim Convention on Conservation of North Pacific Fur Seals, *United Nations Treaty Series*, 314:105.

20. Exchange of Notes Constituting an Agreement Concerning Certain Fisheries Off the Coast of the United States, *United Nations Treaty Series*, 685:268.

21. Esther C. Wunnicke, "The Legal Framework Governing Alaska Fisheries," in Tussing et al., eds., *Alaska Fisheries Policy* (Fairbanks: Institute of Social Economics and Government Research, University of Alaska, 1972), p. 242.

22. Ohira, op cit., p. 4.

23. Ibid., p. 8.

24. Ibid., p. 4.

25. Georg Borgström, *Japan's World Success in Fishing* (London: Fishing News [Books], 1964), p. 29.

26. Ohira, op. cit., p. 4.

27. Homer E. Gregory and Kathleen Barnes, *North Pacific Fisheries: With Special Reference to Alaska Salmon* (New York: American Council Institute of Pacific Relations, Studies of the Pacific no. 3, 1939), p. 291.

28. Ibid., pp. 285–397, applies to this and the following discussion.

29. Ibid., p. 298.

30. International Convention for High Seas Fisheries in the North Pacific Ocean, *United Nations Treaty Series*, 205:81.

31. Discussed in Ohira, op. cit. For an official translation of the text of this Agreement, see "Convention Between Japan and the USSR Concerning the High Seas Fisheries of the Northwest Pacific Ocean," *The Japanese Annual of International Law*, no. 1 (1957), pp. 119–131.

32. Ralph W. Johnson, "The Japan–United Nations Salmon Conflict," *Washington Law Review*, 43, 1 (1967), 15.

33. Ibid., for a much expanded discussion of these claims.

34. Soji Yamamoto, "The Abstention Principle and Its Relation to the Evolving International Law of the Sea," *Washington Law Review*, 43, 1 (1967), 45–62.

35. Kasahara, op. cit., p. 246.

36. R. A. Fredin, Richard L. Major, Richard G. Bakkala, and George K. Tanonaka, *Pacific Salmon and the Japanese High Seas Salmon Fisheries* (Seattle: Processed Report, Northwest and Alaska Fisheries Center, 1977), pp. 93–140.

37. Shigeru Oda, "Japan and International Fisheries," *Japanese Annual of International Law*, no. 4 (1960), p. 52.

38. Kasahara, op. cit., p. 238.

39. Ohira, op. cit., p. 11.

40. Kasahara, op. cit., p. 239.

41. Ohira, op. cit., p. 11.

42. Ibid., pp. 12, 13.

43. Shigeru Oda and Hisashi Owada, "Annual Review of Japanese Practice in International Law 1961 and 1962," *Japanese Annual of International Law*, no. 8 (1964), p. 124.

44. Ohira, op. cit., p. 13.

45. Kasahara, op. cit., p. 239.

46. Kenzo Kawakami, "Outline of the Japan-Soviet Fishery Talks (1962)," *Japanese Annual of International Law*, no. 7 (1963), pp. 25–29.

47. Convention for the Protection, Preservation and Extension of the Sockeye Salmon Fisheries in the Fraser River System, *League of Nations Treaty Series*, 184:305.

48. Agreement between the Government of the U.S.A. and the Government of Canada on Reciprocal Fishing Privileges in Certain Areas Off Their Coasts, *United Nations Treaty Series*, 752:3.

49. J. V. Minghi, "The Conflict of Salmon Fishing Policy in the North Pacific" (Master's thesis, University of Washington, 1969). See also Ralph Johnson, op. cit., p. 60.

50. In 1978 concern over interception and allocation of stocks between Canada and the United States eclipsed the previous cooperation in importance and led to a breakdown in the relationships. Substantial agreement remains, however, on the desirability of excluding other nations from fishing for North American spawned salmon.

51. R. M. Logan, "Geography and Salmon: The Noyes Island Conflict, 1957–1967," *The Journal of the West*, 8, 3 (1969), 438–446.

52. Clinton E. Atkinson, "Northeast Asian Fisheries," unpublished draft of lecture presented at the Institute for Marine Studies, University of Washington, November 16, 1976.

53. Kasahara, op. cit., p. 250.

54. Ralph Johnson, op. cit., p. 37.

55. Kasahara, op. cit., p. 280.

56. Convention for the Preservation of the Halibut Fishery of the Northern Pacific Ocean and Bering Sea, *U.S. Department of State Pamphlet Series*, no. 701.

57. Gregory and Barnes, op. cit., pp. 283–285.

58. Oda, "Japan and International Conventions," pp. 64–66.

59. F. Heward Bell, "Management of Pacific Halibut," in Norman G. Benson, ed., *A Century of Fisheries in North America* (Washington, D.C.: Special Publication no. 7, American Fisheries Society, 1970), p. 220.

60. See chap. 3, this volume.

61. Stephen H. Hoag and Robert R. French, *The Incidental Catch of Halibut by Foreign Trawlers*, International Pacific Halibut Commission, Scientific Report #60 (1976), p. 21.

62. International North Pacific Fishery Commission, *Statistical Yearbooks* (Vancouver, B.C.: INPFC, various years).

63. Bernard E. Skud, *Jurisdictional and Administrative Limitations Affecting Management of the Halibut Fishery*, IPHC Scientific Report no. 59 (Seattle, 1976), pp. 12−14.

64. International Pacific Halibut Commission, *Annual Report 1976* (Seattle: International Pacific Halibut Commission, 1977), p. 13.

65. Convention on the Continental Shelf, *United Nations Treaty Series*, 499:311.

66. Ibid., Article 2, para. 4.

67. The Bartlett Act, PL 88-38.

68. Ko Nakamura, "The Japan−United States Negotiations Concerning King Crab Fishery in the Eastern Bering Sea," *Japanese Annual of International Law*, no. 9 (1965), p. 43.

69. Parker, op. cit., p. 31.

70. Shigeru Oda and Hisashi Owada, "Annual Review of Japanese Practice in International Law III (1964)," *Japanese Annual of International Law* no. 10 (1966), p. 67.

71. Exchange of Notes Constituting an Agreement Between USA and Japan Relating to the King Crab Fishery in Eastern Bering Sea, *United Nations Treaty Series*, 533:30.

72. Parker, op. cit., p. 31.

73. Tanaka, op. cit., p. 250.

74. Marine Mammal Protection Act, 16 USC, 1361 ff.; Endangered Species Protection Act, 16 USC, 1531 ff.

75. Parker, op. cit., p. 32.

76. William M. Marquette, *The 1976 Catch of Bowhead Whales (Balaena mysticetus) by Alaskan Eskimos, with a Review of the Fishery 1973−1976 and a Biological Summary of the Species* (Seattle: Processed Report, Northwest and Alaska Fisheries Center, May 1977), p. 1.

77. Oda, "Japan and International Conventions," p. 65.

78. Bernard E. Skud, "Management of North American Herring Stocks," in Norman Benson, ed., op. cit., p. 204.

79. Kawakami, op. cit., p. 28.

80. Tanaka, op. cit., p. 249.

81. Office of Fisheries, Republic of Korea, *Fisheries in Korea* (Seoul: Hong Won Printing, 1966), p. 7.

82. Oda, op. cit., p. 27.

83. Guenter Weissberg, *Recent Developments in the Law of the Sea and the Japanese−Korean Fishery Dispute* (The Hague: Martinus Nijhoff, 1966), p. 8.

84. Office of Fisheries, Republic of Korea, op. cit., p. 8.

85. Choon-ho Park, "Fishing Under Troubled Waters: The Northeast Asia Fisheries Controversy," *Ocean Development and International Law Journal*, 2, 2 (1974), 101, 102.

86. Hideo Takabayashi, "Normalization of Relations Between Japan and the Soviet Union," *Japanese Annual of International Law*, no. 11 (1966), pp. 264−283.

87. Ibid., p. 17.

88. See Oda, "Japan and International Fisheries"; Weissberg, op. cit.; and Park, op. cit.

89. Weissberg, op. cit., p. 10.

90. Takabayashi, op. cit., pp. 16, 17.

91. Park, op. cit., p. 130.

92. Tanaka, op. cit., p. 256.

93. Ibid., p. 253.

94. Zengo Ohira and Terumichi Kuwahara, "Fishery Problems Between Japan and the People's Republic of China," *Japanese Annual of International Law*, no. 3 (1959), p. 111.

95. Ibid., p. 111.

96. Ibid., p. 123. This total applied to the period June 13, 1955 to September 30, 1957.

97. Weissberg, op. cit., p. 73.

98. Oda, "Japan and International Fishing," note 33, p. 62.

99. Kasahara and Burke, op. cit., p. 62.

100. Park, op. cit., p. 123.

101. Atkinson, op. cit., p. 28.

102. See Article 14, par. b, Japan–Soviet Agreement 1956.

103. See Annex and Agreed Minutes of the Japan–Republic of Korea Agreement 1965.

104. See Kasahara, op. cit., pp. 252, 253.

105. See Articles III and IV of the INPFC Agreement.

106. Ibid.

107. Jean E. Carroz, "Regional Fishery Bodies and the Apportionment of the Yield from the Living Resources of the Sea" (Kingston: Conference on the Legal Framework and the Continental Shelf, University of Rhode Island, January 30–31, February 1970), (mimeo), p. 29.

108. Gregory and Barnes, op. cit., p. 292.

109. See Appendix C for annual quotas and catches under this Agreement and a map of the areas covered.

110. Tanaka, op. cit., p. 245.

111. Ibid., p. 246.

112. Oda, "Japan and International Conventions," p. 69.

113. Oda, "Japan and International Fisheries," p. 52.

114. Tanaka, op. cit., p. 297; see also discussion in chap. 3, this volume.

115. Oda, "Japan and International Conventions," p. 68.

116. Barbara Johnson, "Canadian Foreign Policy and Fisheries," in Barbara Johnson and Mark Zacher, eds., *Canadian Foreign Policy and the Law of the Sea* (Vancouver: University of British Columbia Press, 1977), p. 58.

117. Parker, op. cit., p. 51.

118. See Appendix C.

119. See Paragraph 1.B-a and b of the U.S.–Japan 1974 Agreement on Crab Fishing, #7986, *Treaties and International Agreement Series*; and Paragraph 2 of the U.S.–USSR 1973 Agreement on Crab Fishing, #7571, *Treaties and International Agreements Series*.

120. See Appendix C for annual allocations for herring.

121. Skud, op. cit., p. 204.

122. Tanaka, op. cit., p. 249.

123. See Appendix C.

124. See Japan–U.S. Agreement Concerning Certain Fisheries, *Treaties and International Agreements Series*, No. 7986 (same as Crab Agreement); and Japan–USSR 1975 Agreement Concerning Certain Fisheries, No. 8207, *Treaties and International Agreements Series*.

125. See Article IX of the Fur Seal Agreement.

126. See Article V, International Convention for the Regulation of Whaling 1946, *United Nations Treaty Series* 161:73.

127. Parker, op. cit., p. 20.

128. Agreement Between Japan and the USSR on the Regulation of North Pacific Whaling, *Japanese Journal of International Law*, no. 19, 1975.

129. Park, op. cit., p. 123.

130. Karl William Kieninger and David A. Reifsnyder, "Fishing Gear Conflict Settlement Under Extended Jurisdiction," *Journal of Maritime Law and Commerce*, 8,1 (1977), 32.

131. Parker, op. cit., p. 31.

132. Barbara Johnson, op. cit., p. 58; see also Barbara Johnson and Frank Langdon, "Two Hundred Mile Zones: The Politics of North Pacific Fisheries," *Public Affairs*, 49,1 (1976), 11.

133. Discussion with Donald L. McKernan, Institute for Marine Studies, University of Washington, July 22, 1977.

134. See, for example, Article 10, Agreement on Certain Fisheries Problems in the Northeastern Part of the Pacific Ocean Off the Coast of the USA (USSR/USA 1973), *Treaties and International Agreements Series*, no. 7553.

135. Kieninger and Reifsnyder, op. cit., p. 137; see Agreement Relating to the Consideration of Claims Resulting from Damage to Fishing Vessels or Gear and Measures to Prevent Fishing Conflicts USSR/USA 1973, *Treaties and International Agreements Series*, No. 7575.

136. U.S. – USSR Fisheries Claims Board, *Report for the Year 1976 of the U.S. – USSR Fisheries Claim Board* (Washington, D. C.: January 1, 1977).

137. Tanaka, op. cit., p. 305.

138. Personal discussions with various Japanese fisheries officials, Fall 1977.

139. Tanaka, op. cit., p. 255.

140. Hoag and French, op. cit., p. 21.

141. Stephen H. Hoag, *The Effect of Trawling on the Setline Fishery for Halibut*, Scientific Report no. 60 (Seattle: International Pacific Halibut Commission, 1976), p. 8.

142. International Pacific Halibut Commission, op. cit., p. 13.

143. International North Pacific Fishery Commission, *Proceedings 1974* (Vancouver, B.C.: INPFC, 1975), p. 263.

144. Ian E. Ellis and Robert French, *Selective Harvesting Gear and Methods: Some Developments Useful for Reduction of Conflicts Including Those Between Fisheries Directed and Different Species* (Seattle: Paper prepared for 8th Session of the Advisory Committee on Marine Resources Research, Processed Report, Northwest and Alaska Fisheries Center, July 1975), p. 16.

145. Bruce Rettig and Richard Johnston, "Anadromous Species and Extended Jurisdiction," (Ann Arbor: Science Publishers, 1977), pp. 133–137.

146. Ellis and French, op. cit., p. 14.

147. Arden E. Schenker, "Foreign Fishing in Pacific Northwest Coastal Waters," *Oregon Law Review* (1966–1967), 46:422–453.

148. U.S. Department of State, *Draft Environmental Impact Statement for the Renegotiation of the International Convention for the High Seas Fisheries of the North Pacific Ocean* (Washington, D.C.: U.S., GPO, May 1978), pp. 107, 108, 126.

149. See Kasahara, op. cit., p. 228; and Philip E. Chitwood, *Japanese, Soviet and South Korean Fisheries Off Alaska: Development and History Through 1966* (Washington, D.C.: Circular 310, U.S. Fish and Wildlife Service, 1969), p. 7.

150. Refer to tables 4.1, 4.2, and 4.3, this chapter.

151. Ohira and Kuwahara, op. cit., p. 123.

152. Weissberg, op. cit., p. 10.

153. Kanae Taijudo, "The Dispute Between Japan and Korea Respecting Sovereignty Over Takeshima," *Japanese Annual of International Law*, no. 11 (1967), p. 16.

154. Kawakami, op. cit., p. 27.

155. Parker, op. cit., p. 6.

156. Ibid., p. 8.

157. Fredin et al., op. cit.

158. A. T. Pruter, "Soviet Fisheries for Bottomfish and Herring Off the Pacific and Bering Sea Coasts of the United States," *Marine Fisheries Review*, paper 1225 (December 1976), p. 12.

159. Ibid., p. 14.

160. Edward Miles, "Technology, Ocean Management and the Law of the Sea: Some Current History," *Denver Law Journal* (1969), 46:245.

161. Ibid., p. 246.

162. Ibid., p. 249.

163. Barbara Johnson, "Canadian Foreign Policy and Fisheries," *Canadian Foreign Policy and the Law of the Sea* (Vancouver: University of British Columbia Press, 1977), pp. 52–99; see also: Parzival Copes, *International Fishery-Resource Management: A Position for Canada*, a background paper for government/industry seminars on fishery policy, prepared for the Fisheries Service, Environment Canada, Revised April 1972; Gordon R. Munro, "Canada and Fisheries Management with Extended Jurisdiction: A Preliminary View," in Lee G. Anderson, ed., *Economic Impacts of Extended Fisheries Jurisdiction* (Ann Arbor: Ann Arbor Science Publishers, 1977), pp. 29–50; and Rodney Snow, "Extended Fishery Jurisdiction in Canada and the United states," *Ocean Development and International Law Journal*, 5,2 and 3 (1978), 291–344.

164. U.S. Senate, Committee on Commerce, *A Legislative History of the Fishery Conservation and Management Act of 1976*, 94th Congress, 2d Session (October 1976), p. 660.

165. Ibid., p. 661.

166. Public Law 88-308; see Eugene R. Fidell, "Ten Years Under the Bartlett Act: A Status Report on the Prohibition on Foreign Fishing," *Boston University Law Review* (1974), 54:703–756.

167. Edward Miles, "The Dynamics of Global Ocean Politics," in Douglas Johnston, ed., *Marine Policy and the Coastal Community* (London: Croom Helm, 1976), pp. 171, 172.

168. Rodney Snow, op. cit., p. 297.

169. *Memorandum by the U.S. Commissioners Requesting Consideration of the Regulation of Fishing Effort at the 1973 Special ICNAF Meeting, January 1973*, October 2, 1972. These innovations are systematically evaluated by Francis Christy, "Northwest Atlantic Fisheries Arrangements: A Test of the Species Approach," *ODILJ*, 1,1 (Spring 1973), 65–92.

170. For an analysis of these and other problems, see Jon Jacobson and Douglas Cameron, "Potential Conflicts Between a Future Law of the Sea Treaty and the Fishery Conservation and Management Act of 1976," in *Washington Law Review*, 52, 3 (July 1977), 451–494.

171. Data released by Japan Fisheries Agency and reported in *Suisan Tsushin*, January 29, 1977, and *Suisan Keizai Shimbun*, January 31, 1977.

172. *The Seattle Times*, November 20, 1976.

173. *The Honolulu Star-Bulletin*, December 10, 1976.

174. *The Mainichi Daily News*, August 2, 1977.

175. Ibid.

176. Informal Translation, U. S. Fisheries Attaché, American Embassy, Tokyo.

177. *The Japan Times* and *Mainichi Daily News*, December 17, 1977.

178. *Ashahi Evening News, Mainichi Daily News*, and the *Japan Times*, October 15, 1977.

## 5. Extended Jurisdiction: A Comparative Analysis of the Acts and Management Regimes

1. Can. Rev. Stat. 1970 c.T-7 as amended by Can. Rev. Stat. 1970, c. 45 (1st supp.).

2. *Fishing Zones of Canada (Zones 4 and 5) Order*, S.O.R./77-62.

3. Japan, *Law on Provisional Measures Relating to the Fishing Zones*, Law No. 31 of 2 May 1977 (see Appendix E for complete text).

4. Union of Soviet Socialist Republics, *Edict on Provisional Measures for the Preservation of Living Resources and the Regulation of Fishing in Marine Areas*. Edict of the Presidium of the USSR Supreme (I.L.M.) Soviet, December 10, 1976, as found in *International Legal Materials* 15:6 trans. William E. Butler, from the official Russian text in *Izvestiia*, December 11, 1976, p. 1381. (See Appendix F for complete text.)

5. *Fishery Management and Conservation Act of 1976*, 16 United States Code (U.S.C.) 1801.

6. DOC. #A/CONF. 62/L.78, Article 3. Relevant portions of the Draft Convention are reproduced as Appendix D to this chapter.

7. Can. Rev. Stat. 1970 c. 45 (list supp.).

8. Japan, *Law on the Territorial Sea*, Law No. 30 of 2 May 1977.

9. DOC. #A/CONF. 62/L.78, Articles 55 and 57.

10. See S. Rep. No. 515, 94th Congress, 1st Session 3 as reprinted in the *Legislative History*, 571 (1976).

11. S.O.R./77–62.

12. 16 U.S.C. 1801.

13. I.L.M. 15:6, p. 1381.

14. Japan, Law No. 30 of 2 May 1977.

15. Japan, Law No. 31 of 2 May 1977.

16. "North Korea Declares Military Boundary," in *Mainichi Daily News* (Japan), August 2, 1977.

17. Seminar by Prof. Victor Li, Stanford Law School, at the University of Washington, March 1978.

18. See Kiofumi Nakauchi, "Problems of Delimitation in the Japan and East China Seas," *The North Pacific Project*, ed. Christine L. Dawson (Seattle: The Institute for Marine Studies Publication Series/IMS-UW-77-1, 1977), p. 360. Published also in ODILJ (1979), 6:305–316.

19. No. 66 Translations in the Law of the Sea, J.P.R.S. 70360 (Washington, D.C., December 20, 1977).

20. People's Republic of China, Mission to the United Nations Press Release No. 49, June 13, 1977.

21. DOC. #A/CONF. 62/WP. 10/Rev. 1, Articles 15 and 74. Art. 74 (1) has now been reformulated and the priority accorded the median line deemphasized in the Draft Convention.

22. Choon-ho Park, "Sino-Japanese-Korean Sea Resources Controversy," 16 *Harvard International Law Journal* 38.

23. Li, seminar, op. cit.

24. *Japan Times*, September 9, 1979.

25. DOC. #A/CONF. 62/L.78, Article 56 (1) (a).

26. Ibid., Article 56 (1) (a).

27. It appears that paragraph (3) of Article 58 modifies the rights of noncoastal states engaging in such activities in economic zones by subjecting them to "laws and regulations established by the coastal state in accordance with this Convention." For example, coastal states have promulgated regulations under fisheries jurisdiction that prohibit or restrict the laying of submarine cables in certain areas. Another modification occurs in the case of fishing vessels transiting exclusive economic or fishery zones. Even though such vessels are required to have their gear secured and are obviously not allowed to engage in fishing operations, the coastal state may perceive a potential for violations. The coastal state may then require that fishing vessels wishing to transit a fishery zone notify the appropriate coastal state authority, thus impinging upon the freedom of navigation.

28. DOC. #A/CONF. 62/L.78, Article 61.

29. Ibid., Article 62.

30. S.O.R./77–62 Preamble.

31. It should be noted that many of the Canadian marine pollution provisions are made expressly applicable in the fishing zones. Thus, it can be argued that by expanding the fishing zones, pollution laws were automatically extended to 200 miles. Canada has claimed extensive pollution control since 1970, when the *Arctic Pollution Prevention Act* came into force. This Act established a 100-mile pollution prevention zone in waters north of the Arctic Circle. Can. Rev. Stat. 1970 c.2 (1st Supp) s.3, as found in Rodney Snow, *Extended Fishery Jurisdiction in Canada and the United States*, Master of Law thesis, University of Washington, 1977, p. 17.

32. Coastal Fisheries Protection Act, S.O.R./76–803.

33. Japan, Law No. 31, Article 1.

34. Ibid., Article 5.

35. Ibid., Article 9 (1).

36. There is no text available at this time. The interpretations given reflect Japanese newspaper reports.

37. *Mainichi Daily News*, August 2, 1977.

38. *Japan Times*, August 11, 1977.

39. I.L.M. 15:6, Article 1, p. 1381.

40. Ibid., Article 2.

41. *Japanese–Soviet Provisional Fisheries Agreement*, May 25, 1977, Article 3.

42. *Japan Times*, August 11, 1977, p. 2.

43. 16 U.S.C. 1801, Sec. 2 (b) (1).

44. 33 U.S.C. 1251–1376.

45. 16 U.S.C. 1812.

46. Article 77 states the rights of the coastal state over the continental shelf: the coastal state exercises sovereign rights for the purpose of exploiting the natural resources of the continental shelf. Natural resources include "living organisms which, at the harvestable stage, either are immobile on or under the seabed or are unable to move except in constant physical contact with the seabed or subsoil." These rights are independent of coastal states rights in the EEZ and allow the coastal state to extend its jurisdiction beyond 200 miles in the case of continental shelf resources—this is not to affect the legal status of the superjacent waters. (DOC. #A/CONF. 62/L.78, Articles 77 and 78).

47. Ibid., Articles 63 and 64 respectively.

48. Ibid., Articles 66 and 69 respectively.

49. Can. Rev. Stat. 119 s.1.

50. Ibid., 119 s.2.

51. Ibid., 119 s. 12–16.

52. Ibid., 119 s. 24 (1).

53. Ibid., 119 s. 26. This article lists the following as marine mammals: porpoises, whales, walruses, and sea lions.

54. Ibid., 119 s. 10–11.

55. Ibid., 119 s. 17–18.

56. Ibid., 119 s. 34.

57. Japan, Law No. 31, Articles 6 and 12.

58. I.L.M. 15:6, p. 1381, Article 2.

59. *Japanese–Soviet Provisional Fisheries Agreement*, Articles 1, 3 (1), and 3 (2).

60. 16 U.S.C. 1802, Sec. 3 (6).

61. Ibid., 1801, Sec. 2 (b) (1).

62. Ibid., 1802, Sec. 3 (4).

63. Ibid., 1802, Sec. 3 (6).

64. DOC. #A/CONF.62/L.78, Article 56 (1) (b) (ii). Jurisdiction over marine scientific research is specifically given in this subsection.

65. Can. Rev. Stat. 119 s. 34 (6).

66. *Marine Fisheries Review*, National Marine Fisheries Service, NOAA, Department of Commerce, 40,1 (January 1978), 36.

67. Japan, Law No. 31, Article 2 (1).

68. I.L.M. 15:6, p. 1381, Article 3.

69. *Japanese–Soviet Provisional Fisheries Agreement*, Article 4.

70. 16 U.S.C. 1802, Sec. 4 (10).

71. Ibid., Sec. 4 (11).

72. PL 95-354, August 28, 1978.

73. 44 F.R. 7708–7711.

74. There has been considerable debate within the various sectors of the fishing industry as to the breadth of the "preference" given to U.S. processors. During a public hearing on the regulations, held in Washington, D.C. on March 3, 1979, members of the processing sector advanced the position that the legislation does not require United States processors to outbid foreign processors. A more rational view was that under the 1978 amendments, domestic processors have a "preference" that is identical in kind and degree to that granted United States fishermen under the FCMA. The U.S. fishing industry should not be subject to the dictates of the fish processing industry as it would be if the former interpretation of the legislation is accepted.

75. DOC. #A/CONF. 62/L.78, Articles 62 (1), 61 respectively.

76. Ibid., Article 61 (2).

77. Professor Donald L. McKernan, personal communication, July 1978.

78. DOC. #A/CONF. 62/L.78, Article 297 (3) (a).

79. See comment "Judicial Review of Fishery Management Regulations Under the Fishery Conservation and Management Act of 1976," Christopher L. Koch, *Washington Law Review* (1977) 52:599.

80. Can. Rev. Stat. 119 s. 34.

81. Snow, op. cit., p. 41.

82. *Canada–USSR Agreement on Fisheries Regulations*, May 19, 1976, I.L.M. 15:6, Article 2 (2) (c), p. 1267.

83. Japan, Law No. 31, Article 7.

84. I.L.M. 15:6 1381, Article 3.

85. Ibid., Article 4.

86. Dr. Wlodzimierz Kaczynski, personal communication, June 1978.

87. 16 U.S.C. 1824, Sec. 204 (2).

88. DOC. #A/CONF. 62/L.78, Articles 61 and 62.

89. Canada has signed bilateral fishery agreements with Bulgaria, Cuba, Japan, Norway, Poland, Portugal, Spain, and the USSR.

90. Japan, Law No. 31, Article 7 (2).

91. *Japan Times*, September 11, 1977.

92. 16 U.S.C. 1821, Sec. 201 (e).

93. Ibid., 1821, Sec. 201 (e), as amended by PL 96-61 signed into law 3/78.

94. Ibid., 1824, Sec. 104 (f).

95. Ibid.

96. PL 96-61, Sec. 3.3.

97. See Senate Committee on Commerce, Science, and Transportation, *Hearings on Pirate Whaling*, June 22, 1979.

98. DOC. #A/CONF. 62/L.78, Article 61 (4) (a).

99. Can. Rev. Stat. 119 s.34 (c).

100. S.O.R./76-803 s.5 (a).

101. J. E. Carroz and M. J. Savini, *Bilateral Fishery Agreements*, FAO Fisheries Circular no. 709, Food and Agriculture Organization of the United Nations, (Rome: FAO, April 1978), p. 5.

102. Japan, Law No. 31, Article 6 (1) and (2).

103. *Provisional Agreed Minutes Concerning Cooperation in Fisheries Between Japan and (North) Korea*, par. 2.

104. I.L.M. 15:6, p. 1381.

105. Ibid., Article 5.

106. 16 U.S.C. 1824.

107. Ibid., 1854.

108. See William T. Burke, "Recapture of Economic Rent Under FCMA: Sections 303–304 on Permits and Fees," *Washington Law Review*, 32, 3 (July 1977), 681.

109. DOC. #A/CONF. 62/L.78, Article 66 (1).

110. I.L.M. 15:6, Article 3, p. 1267.

111. Ibid., Article 2, p. 1381.

112. Japan, Law No. 31, Article 12.

113. 16 U.S.C. 1802, Sec. 3 (1).

114. DOC. #A/CONF. 62/WP.10/Rev. 2, Article 66 (2). The same wording has carried over to the Draft Convention.

115. Letter with attachment from Ambassador Elliot L. Richardson to Governor Jay S. Hammond, May 31, 1978.

116. Parzival Copes, "The Law of the Sea and Management of Anadromous Fish Stocks," Department of Economics and Commerce Discussion Paper Series, Paper 76-11-1, Simon Fraser University, British Columbia, Canada (1976), p. 22.

117. Prof. Donald McKernan, personal communication, July 1978.

118. I.L.M. 15: 6, Article 2, p. 1381; 16 U.S.C. 1812.

119. Japan, Law No. 31, Article 6 (1.1).

120. Ibid., Article 6 (1.1).

121. 16 U.S.C. 1813.

122. I.L.M. 15:6, Article 2, p. 1381.

123. DOC. #A/CONF. 62/L.78, Article 62.1.

124. Ibid., Article 61(3).

125. Ibid., Article 73.

126. Ibid., Article 62 (4) (e)(f)(g)(j).

127. S.O.R./77-50 s. 28 (1).

128. *Marine Fisheries Review*, 40, 1 (January 1978), 36.

129. Can. Rev. Stat. 119 s. 35.

130. S.O.R./76-803.

131. I.L.M. 15:6, Article 2, p. 1381.

132. *Japanese–Soviet Provisional Fisheries Agreement*, Article 7 (1) and (2).

133. 16 U.S.C. 1861, Sec. 311 (b).

134. EIS/PMP, *Trawl and Herring Fishery in the Bering Sea and Aleutian Islands*, National Marine Fisheries Service (January 1977), p. 115.

135. See Lee Morgan, "The Role of Observer Programs in Managing and Enforcing Foreign Fishing Under the Fishery Conservation and Management Act of 1976 (Master of Science thesis, University of Washington, 1978).

136. DOC. #A/CONF. 62/L.78, Article 73 (3).

137. Japan, Law No. 31, Article II (2).

138. Ibid., Articles 17(1), 18 and 20.

139. Ibid., Article 19.

140. I.L.M. 15:6, p. 1381.

141. Can. Rev. Stat. 119 s.61.

142. *Marine Fisheries Review*, 40, 1, 36.

143. *Marine Fisheries Review*, 40, 2 (February 1978), 35.

144. B. Johnson and D. Middlemiss, "Canada's 200-mile Fishing Zone: The Problems of Compliance," *ODILJ*, 4, 1 (1977),67.

145. 16 U.S.C. 1858, Sec. 308 (a).

146. Ibid., 1859, Sec. 309.

147. *A Governing International Fishery Agreement Between the United States and Japan*, pursuant to Sec. 203(a) of PL94-265, Agreed Minutes (3).

148. DOC. #A/CONF. 62/L.78, Articles 61 and 62.

149. *Policy for Canada's Commercial Fisheries*, Fisheries and Marine Service, Environment Canada (Ottawa: 1976), p. 51.

150. Ibid., pp. 60–63.

151. Ibid., p. 69.

152. Snow, op. cit., pp. 45–46.

153. Ibid., p. 41.

154. *Policy for Canada's Commercial Fisheries*, pp. 56, 63.

155. It should be noted that entry controls may take various forms, some do not adequately limit entry into particular fisheries and others perpetuate inefficient fishing methods.

156. See G. Alex Fraser, *License Limitation in the British Columbia Salmon Fishery*, Technical Report Series No. PAC/T-77-13. Economics and Special Industry Services Directorate, Pacific Region, Fisheries and Marine Service, Department of the Environment (July 1977).

157. Ibid., pp. 61, 62. It has been argued that the British Columbia salmon license limitation program has been relatively successful in the short run, but over the long run it will prove to be less than effective.

158. Masaaki Sato, *Prospects for Fisheries in the 200-mile Fishery Zone of Japan*, Coastal Fisheries Ground Development Section, National Federation of Fisheries Cooperative Associations (ZENGYOREN), Tokyo.

159. Zigurds L. Zile, "Soviet Struggle for Environmental Quality," in *Contemporary Soviet Law*, ed. Donald D. Barry et al. (The Hague: Martinus Nijhoff, 1974), p. 137.

160. Dr. Wlodzimierz Kaczynski, personal communication, June 1978.

161. I.L.M. 15:6, Article 4, p. 1381.

162. Wlodzimierz Kaczynski, "Controversies in Strategy of Marine Fisheries Development Between Eastern and Western Countries," internal circulation, Institute for Marine Studies, University of Washington (January 1977), pp. 8, 9. Later published in *ODILJ*, 4, 4 (1977), 399–408.

163. Ibid., p. 11.

164. Mikhail Chernyskov, "Resources of Oceans Must Not Be Depleted," *Western Fisheries*, vol. 95, no. 3 (December 1977).

165. *Soviet–Cuban Fishery Research*, ed. A. S. Bogdanov, trans. from the Russian (Jerusalem: Israel Program for Scientific Translations, 1969).

166. No. 69 Translations in the Law of the Sea, J.P.R.S., 70680, p. 143.

167. Zile, op. cit., p. 151.

168. 16 U.S.C. 1802, Sec. 3 (2).

169. Dayton L. Alverson, "The Role of Conservation and Fishery Science Under the Fishery Conservation and Management Act of 1976," *Washington Law Review*, 52, 3 (July 1977), 726.

170. 16 U.S.C. 1801, Sec. 2 (6)(4).

171. Alverson, op. cit., pp. 738, 739.

172. 16 U.S.C. 1851, Sec. 301 (a).

173. Ibid., 1856.

174. Ibid., 1853, Sec. 302.

175. Ibid., 1853, Sec. 303.

176. Ibid., 1852, Sec. 302 (h)(5).

177. Ibid., 1854, Sec. 304.

178. Ibid., 1852, Sec. 302 (h) (3).

179. Snow, op. cit., p. 44.

180. North Pacific Fishery Management Council Newsletter, March 1978, Issue #8.

181. An excellent example of an overuse of emergency measures can be found in the Atlantic groundfish management. During 1978, there were no less than 12 interim emergency regulations, extensions of and corrections to the emergency regulations published for Atlantic groundfish (cod, haddock and yellowtail flounder); See 43 FR 777 (Feb. 4, 1978); 43 FR 6094 (Feb 13, 1978); 43 FR

13578 (March 31, 1978); 43 FR 14968 (April 10, 1978); 43 FR 17361 (April 24, 1978); 43 FR 19233 (May 4, 1978); 43 FR 20505 (May 12, 1978); 43 FR 31015 (July 19, 1978); 43 FR 39108 (Sept. 1, 1978); 43 FR 42764 (Sept. 21, 1978); 43 FR 53040 (Nov. 15, 1978); 43 FR 55441 (Nov. 28, 1978). This list does not include closures or changes issued under nonemergency procedures.

182. Romeo LeBlanc, response to a letter in *Western Fisheries* (December 1977).

183. Edward L. Miles, "On the Utility of Regional Arrangements in the New Ocean Regime," in Douglas Johnston, ed., *Regionalization of the Law of the Sea* (Cambridge, MA: Ballinger Publishing, 1978), p. 16.

184. M. S. McDougal and F. P. Feliciano, "Law and Minimum World Public Order," in *International Law, Cases and Materials*, ed. Wolfgang Friedmann et al. (St. Paul, Minn.: West Publishing Co., 1969), p. 29.

185. Richard B. Bilder, "The Consequences of Regionalization in the Treaty and Customary Law of the Sea," in Johnston, ed., op. cit., pp. 4, 5.

186. Ibid., pp. 9, 10.

## 6. Assessment of the Implications of Extended Coastal State Jurisdiction

1. This is true of all maritime issues, especially boundary conflicts. See Barry Buzan, "Maritime Issues in Northeast Asia," *Marine Policy* (July 1979), 190–200.

2. This category includes species other than groundfish, such as Atka mackerel and squid.

3. The North Pacific Council defined MSY as "an average over a reasonable length of time of the largest catch which can be taken continuously from a stock under current environmental conditions." *Fishery Management Plan, Gulf of Alaska Groundfish* (April 1978), p. 10.

4. If a stock is incapable of producing MSY, equilibrium yield (EY) is used to determine OY. EY is defined as the "annual or seasonal harvest which allows the stock to be maintained at approximately the same level of abundance in succeeding seasons or years."

5. The North Pacific Fishery Management Council uses Foreign Allowable Catch (FAC) interchangeably with TALFF.

6. FMP, Gulf of Alaska Groundfish (April 1978), p. 2.

7. 16 U.S.C. 1821.

8. Draft FMP Bering Sea and Aleutian Islands Groundfish (July 1978), p. 20.

9. 50 C.F.R. 611.14/611.15.

10. Letter from Rear Admiral J. B. Hayes, USCG, to Jim Branson, Exec. Dir. NPC (January 6), 1978.

11. *Supplement to the EIS/PFMP for Sablefish of the Bering Sea and Northeastern Pacific* (November 1977), p. 10.

12. Draft FMP Bering Sea Groundfish (July 1978), pp. 112–115, 223–224.

13. *Supplement to the EIS/PFMP for Groundfish* (November 1977), p. 13.

14. FMP, Gulf of Alaska Groundfish (April 1978), p. iv.

15. Ibid., p. 203.

16. Ibid., p. 202.

17. Elizabeth R. Mitchell, "Implementing the FCMA: Tanner Crab in the Bering Sea and Groundfish in the Gulf of Alaska: Impact of Fishery Management Plans on Japanese Fishing" (unpublished paper, College of Law, University of Washington, Seattle 1978), p. 41.

18. *Comments by the Delegation from the Japan Fisheries Association on the U.S. Policy for Management of Fishing in the FCZ* (August 1978), p. 21.

19. Ibid., pp. 23–25.

20. Department of State telegram, November 28, 1978.

21. Department of State telegram to American Embassy in Tokyo, November 30, 1978. Subject: Allocation of Gulf of Alaska Resources by Fishing Area.

22. 16 U.S.C. 1851, Sec. 301 (a) (3).

23. *The New York Times*, September 16, 1979.

24. *Comments by the Government of Japan* (September 1977), p. 26. This request was made again in 1978, in conjunction with requests for sablefish in the Gulf of Alaska, see Comments by the Delegation from the Japan Fisheries Association (August 1978), p. 15.

25. *Comments by Government of Japan* (October 1977), p. 16.

26. Ibid. (September 1977), p. 29.

27. *Fishery Management Plan for Bering Sea and Aleutian Islands Groundfish* (July 1978), pp. 114−115.

28. Agenda Item #11, North Pacific Fishery Management Council (July 1978).

29. *First Draft FMP for Tanner Crab Off Alaska* (July 1977), p. 36.

30. Ibid., p. 20.

31. Ibid., p. 307.

32. *Draft FMP for Tanner Crab* (1977), p. 308.

33. See Mitchell, op. cit., for detailed accounting.

34. Ibid., p. 76.

35. North Pacific Council meeting minutes, March 24, 1978.

36. Mitchell, op. cit., pp. 73−75.

37. The Japanese take of tanner crab in 1978 was 14,962 metric tons, approximately 2,500 metric tons more than they harvested in 1977. *Fisheries of the United States*, p. 20.

38. 44 *Federal Register*, 15503 (March 14, 1979).

39. 42 *Federal Register*, 195:54588−89 (November 7), 1977.

40. 16 U.S.C. 1822.

41. *Protocol Amending the International Convention for High Seas Fisheries of the North Pacific Ocean*, Annex.

42. Ibid., Annex (2).

43. Ibid., Annex (1).

44. Ibid., Memorandum of Understanding (Japan−U.S.).

45. NMFS, Southwest Fisheries Center Monthly Report (April 1978), p. 28.

46. For a summary, see L. L. Jones and G. C. Bouchet, "Progress Report on 1981 Research on Dall's Porpoise Incidentally Taken in Japanese Salmon Gillnet Fishery." Document submitted to the Annual Meeting of the INPFC, Vancouver, Canada, October 1981, Northwest and Alaska Fisheries Center, NMFS.

47. *Federal Register*, Friday, May 15, 1981, Part III, "Taking of Marine Mammals Incidental to Commercial Fishing Operations," Department of Commerce, NOAA, pp. 27056−27063.

48. *Joint Report of Ambassador Cadieux and Ambassador Cutler to the Governments of Canada and the United States: Negotiations on Maritime Boundaries and Related Resource Issues*, undated, p. 2.

49. Letter from Ambassador Cadieux to Ambassador Cutler, with attachments (April 10, 1978).

50. Exchange of letters from Ambassador Cutler to Ambassador Cadieux (March 28, 1978); from Ambassador Cadieux to Ambassador Cutler (April 11, 1978).

51. *Comparative Draft: Discussion Draft Agreement*, February 2, 1979. Informal document.

52. Since this section on U.S.−Canada West Coast salmon negotiations was written Christine Dawson joined the U.S. Department of State and has been a participant in these negotiations. In November, 1981, therefore, Edward Miles updated the analysis without consulting Christine Dawson.

53. *Agreed Summary Record of Canada−United States Discussions on a Comprehensive Agreement on the Management and Development of Pacific Salmon Stocks of Mutual Concern*, Lynwood, Washington, October 20−25, 1980, p. 3. Informal document.

54. *FMP for Groundfish of the California, Oregon, and Washington Region* (June 1978), p. 104.

55. Ibid., p. 115.

56. 16 U.S.C. 1861.

57. Ibid., 1856.

58. April 29, 1958, 449 U.N.T.S. 311.

59. 16 U.S.C. 1812.

60. Ibid., 1850.

61. Ibid., 1861.

62. Ibid., 1861.

63. Ibid., 1824.

64. Fidell, Eugene R., "The Policeman's Lot," *Washington Law Review*, 52, 3:456.

65. 16 U.S.C. 1859.

66. Ibid., 1857.

67. DOC. #A/CONF. 63/L.78, Article 73 (3).

68. Enforcement activities reported between 1 March 1977 to 28 February 1978 indicate that for foreign vessels no criminal sanctions were pursued to conclusion. Four vessels were seized, 365 citations issued, and 1,581 boardings were made in the U.S. fishery conservation zone. In the Northwest Pacific and Alaska regions, 885 boardings were made, 80 citations issued, and 2 foreign vessels were seized. (Status of Enforcement Activities, NMFS, March 21, 1978.)

69. GIFA with Japan. Agreed Minutes, par. 2 and 3.

70. 16 U.S.C. 1861.

71. "U.S. Intensifies Patrols Within 200-Mile Limit," *Canadian Fisherman & Ocean Science* (December 1977/January 1978), pp. 18, 19.

72. *Comments by the Japanese Fisheries Association on the Foreign Fishing Regulations of the FCMA* (September 1977), p. 33.

73. 16 U.S.C. 1821.

74. A major government-sponsored conference on U.S. fisheries development was held May 23–25, 1979. At this conference, government and industry representatives indicated their commitment to developing a viable, strong U.S. fishing industry.

75. Department of State telegram September 26, 1977.

76. Ibid., November 28, 1978.

77. Rodney Snow, "Extended Fishery Jurisdiction in Canada and the United States," *Ocean Development and International Law Journal* 5, 2 and 3 (1978), 306.

78. The new limit does not apply to the Strait of Korea, where the limit remains at three miles, *Mainichi Daily News*, April 30, 1978.

79. *Japan Times*, May 12, 1978.

80. Ibid., May 13, 1978.

81. *New York Times*, August 14, 1977.

82. *Japan Times*, May 15, 1977.

83. Ibid., p. 88.

84. *Japan Times*, May 13, 1977, and *Asahi Evening News*, November 21, 1977.

85. Ibid., May 11 and 14, 1978, and *Mainichi Daily News*, May 14, 1978.

86. *Mainichi Daily News*, May 16, 1978.

87. Text of Japanese–Soviet Interim Fisheries Agreement: Japan, Okura Sho, Insatsu Kyoku, *Kampo, Gogai* (Government Gazette, Extra), no. 43 (June 10, 1977), pp. 1–7.

88. In actual fact, the Japanese had to sustain a 30 percent reduction of the 1975 total catch rather than a 46 percent reduction.

89. Additional information, Consulate of Japan, Anchorage, Alaska. Letter to James H. Branson, Executive Director, North Pacific Fishery Management Council, June 20, 1977, Ref. JC77-119.

90. U.S. Dept. of Commerce, *Survey of Foreign Fisheries, Oceanographic and Atmospheric Literature*, Washington, D.C., #C-18 (1977), p. 8. Taken from *Minato Shimbun*, 8902 (March 4, 1977), p. 1.

91. Ibid.

92. Ibid., p. 9.

93. *Japan Times*, May 15, 1977.

94. *Mainichi Daily News*, May 18, 1977.

95. Shoichi Tanaka, "Fisheries in the Northwestern Pacific and Fisheries Resources—Mainly on the Japanese Fisheries and International Problems Surrounding them," in Christine L. Dawson, ed., *The North Pacific Project* (Seattle: Institute for Marine Studies, University of Washington 1979), table 10, p. 296.

96. Takashi Inoguchi and Nobuhara Miyatake, "Negotiating as Quasi-Budgeting: The Salmon Catch Negotiations Between Two World Fishery Powers," *International Organization*, 33, 2 (Spring 1979), figure 1, p. 242.

97. Ibid.

98. Ibid.

99. Advance copy, full Text of Japanese–Soviet Provisional Fisheries Agreement, Appendix and Agreed Minutes on Salmon and Samon-Trout, Office of the Fisheries Attaché, U.S. Embassy, Tokyo, May 25, 1977.

100. U.S. Dept. of Commerce, op. cit., #C-20 (1977), p. 11. Taken from *Minato Shimbun*, no. 8874, June 1, 1977, p. 1.

101. Ibid., #C-18 (1977), p. 6. Taken from *Minato Shimbun*, no. 8889, February 17, 1977, p. 1.

102. Ibid.

103. *Yomiuri Shimbun*, evening, August 4, 1977, p. 2.

104. Japan, Ōkura Shō, Insatsu Kyoku, *Kampō* (Government Gazette), no. 15129 (June 17, 1977), p. 5.

105. Japan, Suisan Chō, Kaiyō Gyogyō Bu, Kokusai Ka, *Nikkan Gyogyō Kyōtei no Gaiyō*, (Summary of the Japan–Korean Fishery Agreement) (April 1977), p. 1.

106. See map in *Tokyo Shimbun*, evening, June 14, 1977, p. 1; Japan, Ōkura Shō, Insatsu Kyoku, *Kampō*, no. 15129 (June 17, 1977), pp. 5, 6.

107. U.S. Dept. of Commerce, NOAA/NMFS. *Foreign Fishery Information Release*, #77-16 (December 8, 1977), p. 1. Taken from *Suisan Keizai Shimbun*, November 30, 1977. However, the catch quotas listed here, 70,000 MT and 37,800 MT, are in error.

108. U.S. Dept. of Commerce, NOAA/NMFS, *Foreign Fishery Information Release*, #78-1 (January 10, 1978), p. 1. Taken from *Suisan Keizai Shimbun*, December 19, 1977.

109. *Japan Times*, March 7, 1978.

110. Ibid.

111. *Suisan Keizai*, January 17, 1979 and February 2, 1979; *Nihon Keizai*, January 17, 1979.

112. *Nihon Keizai Shimbun*, April 6, 1978, p. 1. Translated by the Office of the Regional Fisheries Attaché, U.S. Embassy, Tokyo.

113. Ibid.

114. *Nihon Keizai Shimbun*, April 19, 1978, p. 1. Translated by the Office of the Regional Fisheries Attaché, U.S. Embassy, Tokyo.

115. Ibid.

116. Ibid.

117. *Suisan Keizai Shimbun*, April 20, 1978. Translated by the Office of the Regional Fisheries Attaché, U.S. Embassy, Tokyo.

118. *Nihon Keizai Shimbun*, April 20, 1978. Translated by the Office of the Regional Fisheries Attaché, U.S. Embassy, Tokyo.

119. *Japan Times*, May 20, 1978.

120. Ibid.

121. *Japan Times*, May 19, 1978.

122. Ministry of International Trade and Industry (Japan), *Japanese Markets: The Myth and the Reality* (Tokyo: September 1977). See also the summary appearing in the *Mainichi Daily News* for September 12 and 13, 1977.

123.  U.S. Department of Commerce, NOAA/NMFS. Foreign Fishery Information Release No. 77-16 (December 8, 1977), p. 2.

124.  Japan Marine Products Importers Association, informal communication, May 2, 1979.

125.  Ibid.

126.  *Japan Exports and Imports* (December 1978).

127.  Statistics and Information Department, Ministry of Agriculture, Forestry and Fisheries, *Fisheries Statistics of Japan, 1978* (Tokyo: Government of Japan, 1980), p. 38.

128.  Clinton E. Atkinson, "Northeast Asian Fisheries." Lecture delivered at the Institute for Marine Studies, University of Washington, Seattle (November 16, 1976), p. 20.

129.  Letter of February 28, 1978.

130.  *Congressional Record* (May 9, 1978), pp. 57161, 57162.

131.  Letter of May 30, 1978 to James H. Branson, Executive Director, North Pacific Fishery Management Council.

132.  Undated copy sent to North Pacific Council.

133.  *The Fishermen's News* (Alaska), second issue (April 1978).

134.  *Japan Times*, May 16, 1978, p. 5.

135.  *Yomiuri Shimbun*, May 15, 1978. Translated by the Office of the Regional Fisheries Attaché, U.S. Embassy, Tokyo.

136.  Ibid. See also *Nihon Keizai Shimbun*, May 19, 1978, p. 6.

137.  "JFA Decides Not to Increase Import Quota for Pollock," *Shin Suisan Shimbun*, January 23, 1978, p. 1. Translated by the Office of the Regional Fisheries Attaché, U.S. Embassy, Tokyo.

138.  U.S. Department of Commerce. *Survey of Foreign Fisheries*, no. C-18 (1977), p. 10. Taken from *Minato Shimbun*, no. 8912 (March 16, 1977), p. 1.

139.  James A. Crutchfield, Robert Hamlisch, Gerald Moore, and Cynthia Walker, *Joint Ventures in Fisheries* (Rome: FAO/UNDP, 1975).

140.  For a detailed account of this trend, see Per O. Heggelund. "Japanese Investments in Alaskan Fishing Industry," *Alaska Seas and Coasts*, 5, 4 (October 1977), 1, 2, 8, 9; Per O. Heggelund, "U.S.–Foreign Joint Ventures in the Northeast Pacific," *Alaska Seas and Coasts*, 6, 1 (February 1978), 10–14; Hilary K. Josephs, "Japanese Investment in the U.S. Fishing Industry and Its Relation to the Two-Hundred-Mile Law," *Marine Policy* (October 1978), 255–267; W. P. Dougherty, "Japanese Seafood Investment Climbs," *Alaska Fisherman*, 6, 2 (October 1978), 1, 6, 16–19; and Trevor B. Proverbs, *Foreign Investment in the British Columbia Fish Processing Industry*, Fisheries and Marine Service Industry Report #105 (Vancouver, B.C.: Economics and Statistical Services, Department of Fisheries and the Environment, July 1978).

141.  In 1979, Davenny and Associates withdrew from the joint venture.

142.  See two statements by Dr. Walter T. Pereyra before the Pacific Fisheries Management Council, May 2–3, 1977, and January 12–13, 1978. Dr. Pereyra is Vice President and General Manager for U.S. operations of Marine Resources Co.

143.  Letter of Terry L. Leitzell, Acting Assistant Administrator for Fisheries to Edward J. Piszek, Office of the President, Mrs. Paul's Kitchens (March 27, 1978).

144.  *Kodiak Daily Mirror*, May 4, 1978.

145.  See, for instance, telegram from Governor Hammond to Secretary of Commerce, Juanita Kreps, May 16, 1977; and telegram from Philip Daniel, Exec. Director, United Fishermen of Alaska to Elmer Rasmussen, Chairman, North Pacific Fishery Management Council, May 12, 1977.

146.  Letter from Jay S. Gage, President, Peter Pan Seafoods, to Elmer Rasmussen, Chairman, North Pacific Council, May 24, 1977.

147.  Letter to Governor Hammond and Press Release, October 14, 1977.

148.  See the letter from Walter Pereyra to John W. McKean, Chairman of the Pacific Council, May 19, 1977 and Dr. Pereyra's statement before the Pacific Council, January 12–13, 1978. In both documents, the arguments for and against are conveniently summarized. Another comprehensive summary is available in a memo prepared by Dr. John P. Harville, Executive Director, Pacific Marine

Fisheries Commission, to John W. McKean, Chairman of the Pacific Council, May 6, 1977.

149. Letter from James K. White, Alaska Regional Counsel, NOAA, to James Branson, Executive Director, North Pacific Council, May 23, 1977.

150. Ibid.

151. Ibid.

152. Letter from James K. White, Alaska Regional Counsel, to Thomas Casey, March 17, 1978.

153. Letter from J. P. Tebeau, Director, Carriers, Drawback and Bonds Division, U.S. Customs Service, to Rear Adm. G. H. Patrick Bursely, Chief Counsel, U.S. Coast Guard.

154. Informal, undated document from James K. White, Alaska Regional Counsel, NOAA. On the same issue, Congressman Les AuCoin of Oregon had introduced a Bill (H.R. 2564) jointly with Rep. Gerry Studds of Massachusetts in the U.S. House on January 27, 1977, the intent of which was to limit foreign investment in fishing vessel operation by requiring 75 percent U.S. ownership of such companies. This Bill was in the form of an amendment to the FCMA and in a later revision was expanded to include joint ventures.

155. *Federal Register*, 43, 27 (February 8, 1978).

156. Letter from Gary C. Hufbauer, Deputy Assistant Secretary, Department of the Treasury, to Alfred J. Bilik, Enforcement Division, NMFS, February 23, 1978.

157. Letter from John D. Negroponte, Deputy Assistant Secretary for Oceans and Fisheries Affairs, Department of State, to Richard Frank, Administrator, NOAA, February 23, 1978.

158. Summary of Highlights, NPFMC, Thirteenth Plenary Session, February 23−24, 1978, p. 1.

159. U.S. Department of Commerce, NOAA/NMFS. Council Memorandum, 2, 4, April 1978, pp. 5, 6.

160. *Congressional Record*, no. 3709 (May 9, 1978), p. E 2422.

161. Letter from Douglas J. Bennet, Jr., Assistant Secretary for Congressional Relations, Department of State, to James T. McIntyre, Jr., Director, Office of Management and Budget, undated copy, May 1978.

162. Memorandum for North Pacific Fishery Management Council Members, from James K. White, Alaska Regional Counsel. Subject: Joint Ventures.

163. Ibid., p. 1.

164. We are indebted to Professor James Crutchfield for these points.

165. Text in English and Japanese printed by the Japanese Foreign Ministry. See also Office of the Geographer, U.S. Department of State, *Limits in the Seas*, no. 75, Continental Shelf Boundary and Joint Development Zone: Japan−Republic of Korea, September 2, 1977.

166. See map attached to the Northern Continental Shelf Agreement. Also, Gaimu Shō internal document, "Nik-Kan Tairiku-dana Kyōtei no Sōki Teikestsu no Hitsuyōsei," pp. 9, 10, and Office of the Geographer, U.S. Department of State, op. cit.

167. Northcutt Ely and Robert F. Pietrowski, Jr., "Boundaries of Seabed Jurisdiction Off the Pacific Coast of Asia," *Natural Resources Lawyer*, 8, 4, pp. 611−629.

168. K. O. Emery and H. Niino, "Stratigraphy and Petroleum Prospects of the Korea Strait and East China Sea," *Technical Bulletin* (1968) 1:13−27; and K. O. Emery et al., "Geological Structure and Some Water Characteristics of the East China Sea and the Yellow Sea," *Technical Bulletin* (1969), 2:3−43.

169. Japan, Gaimu Shō, Hokutō Ajia Ka, "Nik-Kan Tairiku-dana Kyōtei ni Tsuite" (January 20, 1977), fifth map; also Choon-Ho Park, *Continenal Shelf Issues in the Yellow Sea and the East China Sea*, Occasional Paper no. 15 (Kingston: Law of the Sea Institute, University of Rhode Island, September 1972), Map no. 5.

170. Japan, Tsūshō Sangyō Shō, Shigen Enerugi Chō, "Nik-Kan Tairiku-dana Kyōdo Kaihatsu ni Tsuite" (February 1976), p. 1; Kokumin Gaikō Kyōkai, *Nik-Kan Tairiku-dana to Nihon no Emerugi*

*Shigen* (Tokyo: December 1976); Kokumin Gaikō, no. 56; Speech of Tetsuya Endo, chief of the Northeast Asia Section of the Asia Bureau of the Foreign Ministry to the Policy Committee of the Petroleum Industry Federation, December 18, 1975, "Nik-Kan Tairiku-dana Kyotei."

171. Text of the agreement, agreed minutes, and exchange of notes printed by the Japanese Foreign Ministry in Japanese and English.

172. 15 Stat. 539, 11 Malloy 1521, 11 Bevans 1216.

173. Lewis Alexander and Virgil Norton, "Maritime Problems Between the U.S. and Canada," *Oceanus*, 20, 3 (Summer 1977), 28, 29.

174. We are indebted to Prof. James A. Crutchfield for this point.

175. Data provided by Regional Fisheries Attaché, U.S. Embassy, Tokyo. Taken from Japan Fisheries Agency, *Fish Catch and Aquaculture by Area, 1975*.

176. *The Japan Times*, February 2, 1978.

177. Japan Fisheries Association, *Fisheries of Japan, 1980*, p. 11.

178. For the 1979 allocations, see "The 1979-Year Russo–Japanese Northwest Pacific Salmon Fishery Negotiations," Ushio Office, in Tokyo, *Ocean Development and the Law of the Sea Newsletter*, 3 (June 1979).

179. These paragraphs on the future of the Fur Seal Convention (pp. 117, 118) were written by Dr. George Harry.

180. This pattern of conflict can be observed in Japanese reactions to U.S. PMPs and FMPs since 1976. See, for example, Japan Fisheries Agency, *Japanese Fisheries in the Eastern Bering Sea and Northeast Pacific Ocean*, October 1976; *Summary of Japanese Comments on the PMP and Related Subjects (excluding the question of salmon)*, November 12, 1976; Japan Fisheries Association, *Comments by the Japan Fisheries Association on the Foreign Fishing Regulations of FCMA*, September 1977.

181. *Japan Times*, May 11, 1977; *The Japan Economic Journal*, October 25, 1977; *Mainichi Daily News*, May 21, 1978.

## 7. Alternatives for Distant-Water Fishing States, Primarily in the Northeast Pacific

1. As, for example, massive sardine catches for fish meal carried out in the 1960s by the Republic of South Africa, and in the beginning of the 1970s by Bermuda in the West African fishing grounds.

2. For example, in Georges Bank (subareas 5 and 6 of ICNAF), the total fishing effort during 1971 was only 31 percent higher in relation to that necessary to obtain maximum sustainable yield of all bottomfish species harvested in these areas. See Memorandum by the U.S. Commission on the Regulation of Fishing Effort, Advance Copy, ICNAF, 14 November 1972, p. 12.

3. Full analysis of the distant-water activities in the Northeast Pacific should also include other nations that exploit the marine resources in this area (i.e., Japan, South Korea, and Taiwan). These problems are discussed in other chapters of this study as they pertain to Japan and South Korea.

4. G. E. Schroeder and B. S. Severein, "Soviet Consumption and Income Policies in Perspective," in *Soviet Economy in a New Perspective* (Washington, D.C., 1976).

5. E. Wisniewski, "Aktualne i przyszlosciowe zadania gospodarki rybnej (The Present and Future Tasks of the Fishing Industry)," *Technika i Gospodarka Morska (Marine Technology Economy)*, no. 3 (309) (Gdansk, March 1977).

6. N. P. Sysoev, *Economics of the Soviet Fishing Industry* (Moskwa, 1970).

7. Ibid.

8. S. V. Mikhailov, *Okeanologia* (Moscow: Academy of Sciences of the USSR, 1962), pp. 385–387.

9. Joseph Jawaorski, Zygmunt Polanski, and Wlodzimierz Kaczynski, *Criteria for Attaining Remunerative Effects by Polish Fisheries with Charges for the Benefit of Coastal Countries*. Publication prepared for UNCLOS III Conference in Caracas, Sea Fisheries Institute (Gdynia, 1974).

10. Interview of Vice Minister for Fisheries, Mr. E. Wisniewski, in *Kultura* (weekly), March 6, 1977, pp. 7, 8.

11. For example, the interrelationship between volume of catch and per capita consumption of fish and fishery products.

12. M. Kravanja, *The Soviet Fishing Industry: A Review*, Foreign Fisheries Leaflet no. 77-2, NMFS (Washington, D.C., 1977). p. 377.

13. Stanislaw Mickiewicz, "Polish Sea-Fisheries in 1976," *Polish Maritime News* (monthly), no. 226, June 1977, p. 17.

14. Poland belongs to the major producers of fishing and transport vessels in the world.

15. Milan Kravanja, *Fisheries of the USSR, 1976*, NMFS, Office of International Fisheries (Washington, D.C., February 1977), p. 425.

16. *Marine Fisheries Review*, NOAA, NMFS, vol. 39, August 1977.

17. Regional Fisheries Attaché Report, American Embassy, Tokyo, 1977; See chap. 6, table 6.10, this volume.

18. Foreign Fishery Information Release, no. 78-1, NOAA, NMFS, January 10, 1978.

19. *Technika i Gospodarka Morska (Maritime Technology and Economy)* (monthly), no. 5.3 (March 1977).

20. F.A.O., *Yearbook of Fishery Statistics* (1971) (Rome, 1972).

21. For 1977, TAC for the Baltic Sea was established at the level of 800,000 MT. The Soviet Union's quota was 305,000 MT; Poland's 180,000; German Democratic Republic (GDR) 153,000; Sweden 89,644; Denmark 87,931; Finland 79,475; and Federal Republic of Germany (FRG) 41,555. For 1978, national quotas were slightly lower. The Baltic Convention was not able to elaborate an effective method of enforcement. This can lead to nonobservance of national quota limits and to the depletion of Baltic fishery resources.

22. Telegram of Department of State to U.S. Embassies, November 20, 1977.

23. The total required by Mexico for Gulf of Alaska was 66,200 MT, and for the Northwest Atlantic, 10,000 MT.

24. Polish research vessel R/V *Profesor Siedlecki* developed in second half of 1977 three months' cooperative research activities in the Northeast Pacific coastal waters.

25. Letter of Executive Director of the Pacific Fishery Management Council to Assistant Secretary for Oceans and Fisheries, Department of State, October 24, 1977.

26. Boris N. Slavinsky, "Siberia and the Soviet Far East Within the Framework of International Trade and Economic Relations," in *Asian Survey* (April 1977), p. 326.

27. *The Japan Economic Journal*, September 20, 1977.

28. *Mainichi Daily News*, Tuesday, September 13, 1977.

29. Paul Dibb, *Siberia and the Pacific, A Study of Economic Development and Trade Prospects* (New York: Praeger, 1972), p. 261.

30. *Polish Maritime News* (monthly), no. 226 (June 1977), p. 18.

31. Mikhail Chernyshov, "Resources of the Ocean Must Not Be Depleted," *Western Fisheries*, 95, 3 (December 1977).

32. For example, the 1977 expedition led by the research vessel *Profesor Siedlecki* was composed of 4 large factory-trawlers specially equipped for catching and processing krill as well as subantarctic fin fishes. Over 400 fishermen and scientists were engaged in this voyage, carried out during the first half of 1977. Another expedition led by the newest Polish commercial-research vessel, *Profesor Boguki*, started on November 5, 1977 and was scheduled to develop survey and large-scale harvesting activities in the antarctic fishing grounds.

33. The data related to the shipbuilding activities of Polish shipyards were taken from the following sources: (1) *Budownictwo Okretowe* (Jan–Feb 1977); (2) *Morska Gospodarka Rybna-Biuletyn* 1, (1977); and (3) *World Fishing* (May 1977).

34. J. Krepa, "Problemy dalszego rozwoju techniki polowow i floty polskiego rybolowstwa morskiego (Problems in the Future Development of Harvesting Techniques and of the Polish Fishing

Fleet)," *Morska Gospodarka RYBNA (Sea Fisheries Economy)*, no. 111 (1977).

35. J. Joseph and J. Greenough, *Alternatives for International Management of Tuna Resources* (Seattle: University of Washington Press, 1978).

36. For example, some fish species, particularly highly valuable *nototenia* characterized by very slow life cycles and reduced concentrations, are heavily exploited by some distant-water fleets around Kerguelen, Cruzet, and South Georgia Islands. Other subantarctic fin fish stocks are actually in threat of decimation by international distant-water vessels shifting here from northern fishing grounds.

37. Except salmon, halibut, and almost all shellfish, which are species totally reserved for the U.S. and Canadian fishermen in the Northeast Pacific.

38. *Federal Register*, October 7, 1977.

39. NOAA, NMFS, *Letter*, 1, 12 (December 1977), 6.

40. Donald Whitaker, "New Fees Proposed for Foreign Vessels," *Washington Bulletin*, 1977.

41. National Marine Fisheries Service, NOAA, *Preliminary Results of an Industry-Government Venture on Alaska Groundfish*, Northwest Fisheries Center, Processed Report, 1974; and *Demersal Fish and Shellfish Resources of the Eastern Bering Sea in the Baseline Year 1975*, Northwest Fisheries Center, October 1976.

42. During 1976 an average exchange rate for $1 was 297 yen.

43. Regional Fisheries Attaché, American Embassy, Tokyo, 1977, based on data released by Japan Deep Sea Trawlers Association and Japan Medium Trawlers Association.

44. Comments by the Government of Japan on the *Federal Register* of June 15, 1977 containing a Proposed Fee Schedule for 1978, July 15, 1977.

45. Augustyn Wos, *Zwiazki rolnictwa z gospodarka narodowa (Relationships of Agriculture with National Economy)* (Warszawa, 1975), p. 23.

46. The importance of these factors was stressed by J. M. Gates et al., in "Economic and Allied Data Needs for Fisheries Management, A Draft Report of the Interdepartmental Committee on Fisheries Management Data," U.S. Department of Commerce, August 1977.

47. *U.S. Imports of Consumption and General Imports, TSUSA, Commodity by Country of Origin*, Department of Commerce, Washington, D.C. 1976.

48. Alaska Dept. of Fish and Game, Report to the North Pacific Fishery Management Council, September 11, 1981.

49. M. Okadu and E. Noguchi, "Trends in the Utilization of Alaska Pollock in Japan," in *Fishery Products*, Rudolph Kreuzer, ed. (Surrey, England: Fishing News [Books], 1974), p. 190.

50. L. J. Bledsoe, K. Mesmer, and P. Katz, "Calculation of Supply Curve for Domestic Groundfish from the North Pacific," in *Report of the National Workshop on the Concept of Optimum Yield in Fisheries Management, Part 1* (Houston, Texas, June 6–10, 1977).

51. L. J. Bledsoe et al., ibid.

52. S. Jaeger, "Foreign Ventures," *The Fishermen's News*, 33, 15 (second issue) (July 1977).

53. National Marine Fisheries Service, NOAA, *Preliminary Results of An Industry-Government Venture On Alaska Groundfish*, Northwest Fisheries Center, Processed Report, November 1974; and *Demersal Fish and Shellfish Resources of the Eastern Bering Sea in the Baseline Year 1975*, Northwest Fisheries Center, October 1976, p. 382.

54. See letter of May 6, 1977, John P. Harville, Executive Director of Pacific Marine Fisheries Commission, to the Chairman of PMFC.

55. National Marine Fisheries Service, *Fishery Market News Report*, B-42 (Friday, April 8, 1977), p. 1.

## 8. International Marine Transportation

1. *Committee of Inquiry into Shipping* (Rochdale Report) (London: Her Majesty's Stationery Office, 1970), p. 13.

2. Preparation of this section benefited greatly from access to unpublished course notes by John

W. Devanney, Massachusetts Institute of Technology, Cambridge, 1976.

3. The U.S. representatives of the London association are Association of Ship Brokers and Agents (Worldscale), 17 Battery Place, New York, N.Y. 10004.

4. See table "Tanker" in *Chartering Annual* (New York: Maritime Research, 1977).

5. Personal communication, Henry Labash of Labash, ship brokers, New York, N.Y., May 1978.

6. See table 19, "International Marine Transportation" in *Atlas of Marine Use in the North Pacific Region*, accompanying this volume.

7. United Nations, Organization for Economic Cooperation and Development (OECD), *Maritime Transport 1976* (Paris: OECD, 1977).

8. Ibid.

9. A. Renouf, "Shipowners, Bankers and Oil Men Talk on Costs and Revenues," *Seatrade* (May 1976), pp. 55–57.

10. Ian Middleton, Anthony Renouf, and David Parton, "Facing the Unacceptable," *Seatrade* (October 1979), pp. 3, 4.

11. 41 Stat. 988 (Merchant Marine Act of 1920).

12. Paul Bartlett, "World Tanker Fleet Trends Reviewed," *Seatrade* (March 1980), pp. 53–55.

13. T. C. Koopmans, *Tanker Freight Rates and Tankship Building* (London: De erven F. Bohn, Haarlem, and P. S. King and Son, 1939); and Z. S. Zannetos, *The Theory of Oil Tankship Rates* (Cambridge: M.I.T. Press, 1966).

14. B. M. Deakin with T. Seward, *Shipping Conferences* (London: Cambridge University Press, 1973); and E. Bennathan and A. A. Walters, "Conferences: An Economic Analysis," *Journal of Maritime Law and Commerce*, 4 (1972).

15. *Shipping Act*, 1916, as amended, 39 Stat. 728, Chapter 451, Sec. 14 a.

16. U.S. Department of Justice, *The Regulated Ocean Shipping Industry* (Washington, D.C.: U.S. Government Printing Office, January 1977), Appendix E.

17. "Latest Rise in Panama Canal Tolls Solidly Opposed by Users," *Seatrade* (December 1976), p. 67.

18. Stephen Gibbs and Brad Meyer, "The Effect of the Panama Canal Treaties on the General Cargo Traffic of U.S. West Coast Ports," unpublished draft, Seattle, Institute for Marine Studies, University of Washington, June 1979.

19. John R. Immer, "Liner Cargo, Changing Patterns," *American Seaport* (December 1978), pp. 11–13, 49.

20. Ibid., p. 11.

21. Walter A. Radius, *United States Shipping in Transpacific Trade, 1922–1938* (Stanford: Stanford University Press, 1944), p. 2. See the vessel ship tracks across the North Pacific in "International Marine Transportation," in *Atlas of Marine Use in the North Pacific Region*, accompanying this volume.

22. U.S. Hydrographic Office, *Distances Between Ports*, Publication 151 (Washington, D.C.: U.S. Government Printing Office, 1965).

23. For illustrations of shipping routes, see maps in the accompanying *Atlas of Marine Use in the North Pacific Region*, p. 58.

24. *Containerizable General Cargo*, consisting of live animals; processed, canned, chilled or frozen foods and beverages; sugar and syrups; tobacco and products; animal skins; silk; wool; plant and man-made fibers; nonferrous metals; lubricating oils; animal and seed oil; chemicals and drugs; plastic and leather goods; articles of rubber; paper and building board; textile fibers and fabric; carpets; tile; glass; china and porcelain articles; ferroalloys; silver, copper, nickel, aluminum, lead, zinc, and tin alloys—wrought and unwrought; fasteners; tools; engines and parts; small machines and appliances; wire and cable; parts of machines and vehicles; clothes; musical instruments; toys; artwork; furniture and wood articles; sporting goods; electronics, and the like. *Non- and Marginally-Containerizable General Cargo*, consisting of natural rubber; wood pulp; cotton; iron or steel ingots, blooms, blanks,

rods, bars, nails, angles, plates, pipes and tubes; boilers; agricultural machinery; heavy machinery; locomotives; cars; aircraft; and logs and lumber. *Petroleum and Products*, consisting of crude oil; light, medium, and heavy liquid petroleum products; natural gas; coal tar; pitch and asphalt. *Other Liquid Bulk*, consisting of molasses; palm oil, coconut oil, and palm kernel oil. *Iron Ore*, consisting of iron ore and iron pellets. *Coal and Coke. Grains*, consisting of wheat; rice; barley; corn; rye and oats. *Other Dry Bulk*, consisting of raw sugar; soy beans; fertilizers; gypsum; sand and gravel; sulfur; salt; copper, nickel, bauxite, lead, zinc and tin ore; ammonia; wood chips; lime; cement; and steel scrap.

25. See tables 12, 15–18, "International Marine Transportation," in *Atlas of Marine Use in the North Pacific Region*, accompanying this volume.

26. Panama Canal Company, *Annual Report of the Panama Canal Company, June 30, 1976* (Balboa Heights, Canal Zone: Panama Canal Company, 1976).

27. United Nations, *United Nations Statistical Yearbook* (New York: United Nations, 1978), table 17.

28. Ibid.

29. Ibid.

30. Ibid., table 149.

31. Ibid.; and U.S. Central Intelligence Agency, *Handbook of Economic Statistics* (Washington, D.C.: U.S. Government Printing Office, 1978).

32. Ibid.

33. Ibid.

34. Ibid., U.N., *Yearbook*, table 17.

35. Kathleen E. Braden assisted in the acquisition of trade data on the Soviet Union and in the development of the analysis of that data presented here.

36. E. S. Kirby, *The Soviet Far East* (London: St. Martin's Press, 1971).

37. E. B. Miller, "The Trans-Siberian Land Bridge," *Soviet Geography* (April 1978).

38. Ministry of Economic Development, *British Columbia Economic Activity, 1977 Review and Outlook* (Victoria, B.C., March 1978); and U.N., *Yearbook*, table 17.

39. Ministry of Economic Development, *British Columbia Economic Activity*; and U.N., *Yearbook*, table 149.

40. U.S. Department of Commerce, Bureau of the Census, foreign trade data tapes *SM305* and *SM705*, run by Port of Seattle, Department of Planning and Research, for special report to the North Pacific Project, 1979; U.S. Department of Commerce, Maritime Administration, *United States Oceanborne Foreign Trade Routes (1975–1976)* (Washington, D.C.: U.S. Government Printing Office, March 1978); and U.N., *Yearbook*, table 149.

41. Office of Customs Administration, *Statistical Yearbook of Foreign Trade 1976* (Seoul: Bureau of Assessment and Clearance, Office of Customs Administration, 1977).

42. Maritime Industry Research Institute, Nikoku-kan bōekiryō yusōryō tōkei Chōsa (Bilateral Trade and Transportation Statistics) (Tokyo: Ministry of Transportation, Maritime Bureau, March 1977).

43. Tao-tai Hsia, "China's Foreign Trade and the 'Gang of Four'," in *Post-Mao China and U.S.–China Trade*, Shoo-chuan Leng, ed. (Charlottesville: University Press of Virginia, 1977), pp. 93–107. Hsia indicates that his source is the Japan External Trade Organization.

44. Nai-ruenn Chen, "The Chinese Economy in the 1970s: Performances, Problems and Prospects," in Leng, ed., *Post-Mao China* (Charlottesville: University Press of Virginia, 1977), pp. 30–51.

45. Newspaper Enterprises Association, Inc., *The World Almanac and Book of Facts, 1978* (New York: Newspaper Enterprises Assn., 1977), p. 551.

46. W. Radius, op. cit., p. 7.

47. Ibid., pp. 7–8.

48. Maritime Trade Research Institute, *Bilateral Trade* (1977).

49. World Bank, *World Development Report 1978* (Washington, D.C.: The World Bank, 1978).

50. Ibid.

51. Panama Canal Company, *Annual Report* (1976).

52. World Bank, *World Development Report*.

53. U.S. Department of Commerce, *SM 305* and *SM 705*.

54. Ibid.

55. Ibid.

56. Ibid.

57. Ibid.

58. Ibid.

59. Ibid.

60. Statistics Canada, *Origin and Destination for Selected Ports*, Shipping Report Part IV (Ottawa: Statistics Canada, 1976).

61. Ibid.

62. L. I. Vasilevski, "Ekonomicheskaja Geograpfia Mirowogo Okeana, Geografia Mirowogo Okeana ("Geography of Marine Transportation," in *Economics Geography of the World Ocean*) ed. K. K. Markov (Leningrad: Nauka, 1979), 1:158–201.

63. Nena Vreeland et al., *Area Handbook of North Korea*, 2d ed. (Washington, D.C.: U.S. Government Printing Office, 1976).

64. Office of Customs Administration, *Statistical Yearbook of Foreign Trade 1976*.

65. Ibid.

66. Ibid.

67. Ibid.

68. Ibid.

69. Ian Middleton, *China, A 'Seatrade' Study* (Colchester Seatrade Publications, December 1979).

70. Ibid., p. 27.

71. *Seatrade*, July 1979, p. 35.

72. Ibid.

73. Maritime Industry Research Institute, *Bilateral Trade* (1977).

74. Henry Romer, "Alaskan Marine Petroleum Transportation, Interim Report," to Department of Environmental Conservation, State of Alaska, April 1978.

75. U.S. Census Bureau, *SM305* and *SM705*.

76. *Japan Petroleum News*, October 21, 1977; November 30, 1977; and December 2, 1977.

77. P. V. Slambrouck, "U.S. Oil Companies Look Forward to China Sales," *Christian Science Monitor*, March 27, 1979.

78. Henry Hyman, "Oil Imports to Japan Falling," *Seatrade*, July 1979, p. 61.

79. *Seatrade*, October 1979, p. 51.

80. British Petroleum Company, *B. P. Statistical Review of the World Oil Industry* (London: British Petroleum Company, 1979).

81. United Nations, *World Energy Supplies 1973–1978* (New York: United Nations, 1979).

82. U.S. Central Intelligence Agency, *Prospects for Soviet Oil Production*, Report ER-77-10270 (Washington, D.C.: U.S. Government Printing Office, April 1977).

83. U.S. Department of Commerce, *SM305* and *SM705*.

84. Ministry of Trade and Commerce, *Shipping Report, Part II* (Ottawa: Statistics Canada, 1976).

## 9. Existing Regulatory Regime Governing Marine Transportation

1. For an excellent study of the development of state positions on the issue of ship-generated marine pollution, see R. Michael M'Gonigle and Mark W. Zacher, *Pollution, Politics and Interna-*

*tional Law: Tankers at Sea* (Berkeley, Los Angeles, and London: University of California Press, 1979).

2. The waters landward from the baselines from which the territorial sea is measured; *Convention on the Territorial Sea and Contiguous Zone* (1958), 516 *United Nations Treaty Series* 205.

3. The U.S. Congress has authorized the denial of entry to foreign vessels guilty of noncompliance (46 U.S.C. Section 391-e) (supp. IV 1974). The 1971 Amendments to the 1954 *Convention for the Prevention of Pollution of the Sea by Oil* (11 *International Legal Materials* 1972) grants similar rights.

4. *Convention on the Territorial Sea*, op. cit., Article 17.

5. Ibid., Article 24.

6. *Convention Relating to Intervention on the High Seas in Cases of Oil Pollution Casualties* (1969), 13 *International Legal Materials* 546 (1974). This Convention entered into force in 1975.

7. *Convention on the High Seas* (1958). 450 *United Nations Treaty Series* 82, Article 6.

8. Flags of convenience are adopted by shipowners to reduce costs and avoid taxation schemes that owners regard as costly.

9. Colin Warbrick, "The Regulation of Navigation," in Robin Churchill, K. R. Simmonds, and Jane Welch, eds., *New Directions in the Law of the Sea* (New York: Oceana Publications, 1973), 3:137.

10. Ibid., p. 138.

11. Ibid., p. 140.

12. For the text of the 1972 Convention of the Rules of the Road, see 33 *CFR*, subchapter DD., p. 262.

13. Warbrick, op. cit., p. 139.

14. 1972 Rules of the Road, op. cit., Rules 6 (b) and 7 (b).

15. Ibid., Rule 3.

16. Ibid., Rule 10.

17. See "Collision Regulation: A 200-Year Quest for Safety," *IMCO News*, no. 2, 1977, pp. 4–8.

18. 536 *United Nations Treaty Series* 27 (1965).

19. Lt. Larry C. Wiese, Statement of Evidence at Kittimat Oil Port hearings, "West Coast Oil Ports Inquiry," Commission Council, September 1977.

20. Ibid., p. 15.

21. Ibid., p. 20.

22. For a description of the Canadian Puget Sound and San Francisco VTSs, see Peter N. Swan, *Vessel Traffic Systems: An Analysis of the Design, Implementation and Legal Implications of Three West Coast Ports*, Oregon State University Sea Grant, Public no. ORESU-T-76-001, May 1976.

23. Eric Wang and Barry Mawhinney, Statement of Evidence, "West Coast Oil Ports Inquiry," Commission Council, August 1977.

24. Swan, op. cit., p. 10.

25. Ibid.

26. See the Oil Spill Prevention Amendments to the *Canadian Shipping Act*, Ch. 27, Section 731.

27. *Japanese Port Regulations Law*, #174, 15 July 1948, with 1971 Amendments, in *Laws and Regulations on Ports and Harbors in Japan*, Ministry of Transport, Bureau of Ports and Harbors, 1976.

28. Masao Oda, "Maritime Transportation of Japanese Seaborne Trade and Related Laws and Regulations," in Christine L. Dawson, ed., *The North Pacific Project* (Seattle: Institute for Marine Studies, University of Washington, 1977), pp. 471–573. This is reprinted in *ODILJ* (1979), 6:237–304.

29. The MSA is similar to the USCG in its function.

30. *Maritime Safety Law* (effective July 1973).

31. Ibid.

32. These figures are based on the best available information. Nevertheless, the data base is very limited. See *Petroleum in the Marine Environment* (Washington, D.C.: National Academy of Science [NAS], 1975), from which this estimate is taken.

33. 600 *United Nations Treaty Series* 332, and 327 *United Nations Treaty Series* 3. Entered into force 8 December 1961 for the U.S. (Deposited at IMCO after it was created in 1958.)

34. Ibid.

35. 1969 Amendments, Article III.

36. 1962 Amendments, Article III.

37. 1962 Amendments, Article III.

38. Ibid., Article VI.

39. Several devices are being developed and tested to measure petroleum outflow from vessel discharges, but the variability of oil and water characteristics and the severe environmental conditions aboard vessels have rendered technical progress slow.

40. The jurisdictional basis for the coastal state in the territorial sea is clear.

41. *International Legal Materials*, 466 (1969).

42. Ibid., Article III.

43. Ibid., Article V.

44. Ibid., Article VI.

45. 9 *International Legal Materials* 45 (1970).

46. Ibid., Article III.

47. Ibid.

48. Ibid., Article V.

49. Ibid., Article VIII.

50. 11 *International Legal Materials* 1291 (1973). Entered into force 30 August 1975.

51. Ibid., Article IV.

52. Ibid., Article I.

53. Annex I covers materials that may not be dumped (mercury, cadmium, oil, and radioactive material); and Annex II regulates matters to be dumped with permit approval (arsenic, lead, zinc, cyanides, fluorides, and pesticides).

54. Ibid., Article VI. Dumping associated with seabed mining is *not* regulated by the Convention, however.

55. There are few nuclear powered submarines and warships. See Philip F. Schuster II, "Nuclear Pollution: National and International Regulation and Liability," *Environmental Law* (1975), 5:203 ff.

56. Entered into force on 26 May 1966.

57. 536 *United Nations Treaty Series* 472.

58. Ibid., Regulation 9.

59. Ibid., Regulation 7a.

60. Ibid., Regulation 1.

61. Ibid., Regulation 9.

62. Chapters 11, 14, 15 of Title 46 U.S. Code.

63. Wiese testimony. op. cit.

64. Ibid., p. 9.

65. Ibid., p. 10.

66. Ibid., p. 14.

67. Ibid., p. 16.

68. 31 U.S.C. Section 1001 (1973).

69. PL 91-224.

70. Ibid., Subsection 311 p.; See Weise, op. cit., p. 29.

71. 43 U.S.C. 165 e (1973).

72. 14 U.S.C. 89.

73. 50 U.S.C. 191; See Weise, op. cit. p. 33.

74. Ibid., p. 34.

75. *Revised Statutes of Canada* (1ST Supp.), C.2, 3 (1970).

76. Ibid.

77. 19 and 20 Elizabeth II, 29th Parliament, 3d Session, C. 27 (1970).

78. Ibid.

79. Ibid.

80. Wang and Mawhinney, op. cit., p. 11.

## 10. Emerging Regulatory Trends and Their Implications for Ocean Commerce

1. See S. A. Lawrence, *International Transport: The Years Ahead* (Lexington, Mass.: Lexington Books, 1972); and chap. 8, this volume.

2. Myres McDougal and William T. Burke, *Public Order of the Oceans* (New Haven: Yale University Press, 1957).

3. Edward L. Miles, "On the Utility of Regional Arrangements in the New Ocean Regime," in Douglas Johnston, ed., *Regionalization of the Law of the Sea* (Cambridge, Mass.: Ballinger, 1978), pp. 255–275.

4. Draft Convention on the Law of the Sea, Doc. A/CONF. 62/L-78, 28 August 1981.

5. November 2, 1973, in 12 *International Legal Materials* (ILM) 1320 (1973), Annex I.

6. Annex II, "Regulations for the Control of Pollution by Noxious Liquid Substances in Bulk," 12 *ILM* 1319.

7. For a discussion of the creation of oil residues and why they must remain on board, see chap. 11.

8. Annexes III, IV and VI, "Regulations for the Prevention of Pollution by Harmful Substances Carried by Sea in Packaged Forms, or in Freight Containers, Portable Tanks, or Road and Rail Wagons," "Regulations for the Prevention of Pollution by Sewage from Ships," and "Regulations for the Prevention of Pollution by Garbage from Ships," respectively.

9. MARPOL, Article 5, par. 2.

10. As of September 7, 1979, only 6 of the 65 required ratifications were present.

11. Luther Carter, "*Amoco Cadiz* Incident Points Up to the Elusive Goal of Tanker Safety," *Science* (May 5, 1978), 200:514–516.

12. *Outcome of the International Conference on Tanker Safety and Pollution Prevention*, IMCO: MSC XXXVIII/4, March 6, 1978.

13. SBT involves the segregation of ballast tanks from the cargo tanks, used instead of pumping out the oil and using cargo tanks to carry ballast water. COW involves the use of cargo oil as a solvent to clean the walls of cargo tanks. The residue is pumped to shore and the cargo tanks may then be used for ballast, if necessary. These issues are discussed in detail in chap. 11, this volume.

14. New tankers are defined as those contracted for after June 1, 1979, those having their keels laid after January 1, 1980, and those delivered after June 1, 1982.

15. Gibbs and Teeter, "Management of Marine Transportation on the Northeast Pacific," in C. Dawson, ed., *The North Pacific Project* (Seattle: Institute for Marine Studies, University of Washington, IMS-UW-77-1, 1977), p. 427.

16. Ibid., p. 462.

17. IMCO, *Draft Convention on the International Organization for a Maritime Satellite System* (IMMARSAT). For a brief discussion of the Conference, see P. K. Menon, "International Maritime Satellite System," in *Journal of Maritime Law and Commerce* (October 1976), 8:95–106.

18. Ibid.

19. Draft Convention, op. cit., Article 3, "Breadth of the Territorial Sea," establishes a 12-mile limit.

20. Article 21 (2). Sovereign immunity is granted to warships.

21. Article 22, par. 1–4. Informal meetings in the Third Committee (protection and preservation of the marine environment) in the Spring 1978 session resulted in some minor changes in Part XII of an earlier version of the Draft Convention. One of the proposed changes required that states that establish various requirements for foreign vessels wishing to gain access to their ports and internal waters must publicize such information. This includes the communication of such information to IMCO. The provision is found in "Results of Negotiations on Part XII During the Seventh Session," UNCLOS III, Third Committee, MP/24 (May 15, 1978). See also, Informal Composite Negotiating Text (ICNT), Doc. #A/CONF. 62/WP.10/Rev. 2, 11 April 1980, Art. 211 (3).

22. See also discussion of coastal state enforcement authority.

23. Article 220, par. 6.

24. On the North Pacific alone, some 1.5 million tons of oil have been spilled in accidents (collisions, strandings) between 1967 and 1976. Taken from Center for Short-Lived Phenomena data.

25. 42 *Federal Register* (May 16, 1977): 24868–24876.

26. U.S. Congress, Senate, Committee on Commerce, Science and Transportation, *The Tanker and Vessel Safety Act of 1977: Report on S. 682*, 95th Congress, 1st Session, May 1977, S. Report 95-176.

27. This is not the place to describe the virtues or vices of the liner conference system. There is ample literature on this. See Daniel Marx, *International Shipping Cartels* (Princeton: Princeton University Press, 1958); B. M. Deakin, *Shipping Conferences* (Cambridge, 1973); Jack Devanney et al., *Conference Rate Making and the West Coast of South America*, MIT Commodity Transportation and Economic Development Laboratory, Technical Report 72-1, 1972; *The Regulated Ocean Shipping Industry* (U.S. Dept. of Justice (DOJ), January 1977) and other sources for a discussion of conferences and conference rate making. The DOJ document contains several appendixes addressing the abusive practices question.

28. See Appendix G of DOJ Study (op. cit.) for a brief rejoinder to this widely made claim and the later 5 (3) July 1978 issue of *Maritime Policy Management*, which is *entirely* devoted to rebutting the DOJ study.

29. U.N. Conference of Plenipotentiaries on a Code of Conduct for Liner Conferences (Vol. II: Final Act, including the Convention and resolutions and tonnage requirements; 1975), hereafter referred to as the *Code*. See William J. Bosies, Jr. and William G. Green, "Comment: The Liner Conference Convention: Launching An International Regulatory Regime," in *Law and Policy in International Business* (1974), 6:533 ff., for a legislative history of the Code.

30. The Code will enter into force when at least 24 states, representing at least 25 percent of the world's general cargo shipping tonnage, have ratified, accepted, or acceded to the Convention. As of late 1977, 14 states had ratified the Code, and 10 others have accepted it. The tonnage represented by these nations was less than 5 percent of the total world tonnage—far from the 25 percent required by the Code.

31. *Code*, chap. II, Article 2, and chap. I (Definitions). A national shipping line is one having its head management office and effective control in the country.

32. B. J. Abrahamsson, "The Marine Environment and Ocean Shipping: Some Implications of a New Law of the Sea," in Edward Miles, ed., *Restructuring Ocean Regimes* 31 (Special issue of *International Organization*) (Spring 1977), p. 291 ff.

33. Ibid.

34. See Gibbs and Teeter, op. cit., for a discussion of this.

35. George Lauriet, "FESCO's Ups and Downs," *Seatrade*, November 1977, p. 19.

36. U.S. Department of Commerce (DOC), Maritime Administration, Office of Policy and Planning, *Expansion of Soviet Merchant Marine into the U.S. Maritime Trades*, pp. 13–32.

37. *Seatrade*, "MARAD Report on Soviet Penetration," November 1977, p. 37.

38. DOC, *Expansion*. The Soviets handle 80 percent and 60 percent respectively, of their trade with the U.S. and Canada.

39. See Timofei Guzhenko, "Soviet Merchant Marine and World Shipping," in *Marine Policy* (April 1977), p. 102 ff., for a discussion of these goals. See also *Seatrade*'s special issue, "Soviet Shipping," February 1976.

40. U.S. Department of Justice, *The Regulated Ocean Shipping Industry*, January 1977.

41. Boris N. Slavinsky, "Siberia and the Soviet Far East Within the Framework of International Trade and Economic Relations," *Asian Survey* (April 1977), p. 311 ff.

42. Ibid.; and Elisa Miller, "The Trans-Siberian Landbridge, The New Trade Route Between Japan and Europe: Issues and Prospects," *Soviet Geography* (April 1978).

43. *The Oil and Gas Journal* carries recent information on the status of the leasing and exploitation of Alaskan oil, as does *World Oil*.

44. A. A. Meyerhoff, in *World Petroleum Report*, 1975, p. 21.

45. Selig Harrison, *China Oil and Asia: Conflict Ahead?* (New York: Columbia University Press, 1977); also Choon-ho Park, "Oil Under Troubled Waters: The Northeast Asia Sea Controversy," *Harvard Journal of International Law* (1973), 14:212 ff.

46. Arthur J. Klinghoffer, *The Soviet Union and International Oil Politics* (New York: Columbia University Press, 1977).

47. Gerald B. Greenwald, "LNG Carrier Safety: A Guide to a System of Federal Regulation," *Journal of Maritime Law and Commerce* (January 1978), 9:155–183.

48. "Keeping Oil from Troubled Waters," *New Scientist*, 77, 1085 (January 12, 1978), 90.

49. Various estimates exist for the causes of major spills. The Coast Guard estimates that 85 percent are caused by human error.

## 11. New Technologies of Transportation and the Problem of Tanker-Originated Pollution

1. P. M. Kimon, R. K. Kiss, and J. D. Porricelli, "Segregated Ballast VLCCs: An Economic and Pollution Abatement Analysis," *Marine Technology* 10, 4 (October 1973), 334–363.

2. T. D. Heaver and W. G. Waters II, "An Economic Analysis of Control of the Discharge of Oil at Sea," *Proceedings: Fifteenth Annual Meeting of the Transportation Research Forum* 15, 1 (1974), 571–581.

3. See "Marine Pollution" in Edward Miles et al., *Atlas of Marine Use in the North Pacific Region*, accompanying this volume. Much more sophisticated analysis of spill probabilities is possible and our calculations are meant to be indicative only. See R. Stewart and J. Devanney, "Estimating Tanker Spill Risks in U.S. Waters," Business and Economics section, *Proceedings of the American Statistical Association, 1978*, pp. 464–469.

4. C. S. Wong, D. R. Green, and W. J. Cretney, "Distribution and Source of Tar on the Pacific Ocean," *Marine Pollution Bulletin* 7, 6 (1976), 102–106.

5. *Petroleum in the Marine Environment* (Washington, D.C.: National Academy of Sciences, 1975), p. 55.

6. "Data Sheet, Ballast Treatment Facilities" (Alyeska Pipeline Service Co., 1975).

7. If Japan's annual oil imports are taken as 254 million metric tons (1978), and if .4 percent of this (or 1.02 million metric tons) becomes tank clingage, and if 60 percent of the cargo tanks are ballasted and cleaned each voyage, and if 80 percent of the clingage in these tanks is entrained in the ballast and wash waters, then the potential spillage of oil to the seas from ballast and wash waters is 488,000 metric tons annually; the amount of oil inferred to be discharged into the seas based on Wong's data (71,500 metric tons) is 14 percent of this.

8. Seibin Arasaki, "Control of Marine Pollution," in *Utilization and Development of the Pacific Ocean*, proceedings of the International Symposium on the Pacific Ocean 1976 (Tokyo: Ocean Association of Japan, 1977), pp. 113–118.

9. See the history of international efforts to control tankship oil pollution in R. Michael M'Gonigle and Mark W. Zacher, *Pollution, Politics and International Law: Tankers at Sea* (Berkeley, Los

Angeles, and London: University of California Press, 1979).

10. *Petroleum*, op. cit., pp. 106–107.

11. U.S. Congress, House Committee on Merchant Marine and Fisheries Subcommittee on Coast Guard and Navigation and the Subcommittee on Merchant Marine, *Coast Guard Miscellaneous*, 95th Congress, 1st session, May–September 1977, p. 185; an excellent review article on the environmental consequences of chronic oil discharges is R. W. Howarth, "Fisher versus Fuel: A Slippery Quandary," *Technology Review* (January 1981), 34:68–77.

12. The legal and political setting in which decisions are made on a national and international level is often a subject of research. The legal and political perspectives do not constitute a human interest in the same sense as the two interests listed here, however.

13. For a discussion of the merits and techniques of multidimensional problem formulation, see David C. Major, "Multiobjective Redesign of the Big Walnut Project," in Richard de Neufville and David H. Marks, eds., *Systems Planning and Design: Case Studies in Modeling, Optimization, and Evaluation* (Englewood Cliffs, N.J.: Prentice-Hall, 1974).

14. See Heaver and Waters, ibid.; and Charles S. Pearson, *International Marine Environmental Policy: The Economic Dimension* (Baltimore: John Hopkins University Press, 1975) for their development of this approach as applied to the Intergovernmental Maritime Consultative Organization (IMCO) 1973, International Convention for the Prevention of Pollution from Ships.

15. Tanker Safety and Pollution Prevention Conference, Information Document No. 17 (IMCO, February 1978).

16. S. M. Wilcox and W. J. Mead, *The Impact of Offshore Oil Production On Santa Barbara County*, NTIS No. COM-74 10264 (February 1973).

17. The possibility for being held to standards of strict liability or vulnerability to adverse public opinion pressure has worked to mitigate this market failure. Certainly not all tanker owners are penurious and callous. Nevertheless, "rogue" tankers such as the *Argo Merchant*, owned by obscure holding companies and operated to minimum or subminimum standards, still exist.

18. For more details on this approach, see A. Myrick Freeman III, R. H. Haveman, and A. V. Kneese, *The Economics of Environmental Policy* (New York: John Wiley and Sons, 1973). The formal statement of this principle is that the marginal cost of pollution abatement be equalized for all vessels. This condition will be achieved at different levels of cost and oil discharge for each vessel in the fleet.

19. Freeman, Haveman, and Kneese, op. cit.

20. Pearson, op. cit.

21. Terry L. Leitzell, "Oil Spills: Issues and Actions," *Marine Technology Society Journal* 11, 1 (June 1977), 26–29; and conversation with William O. Gray, Exxon Corporation, 1978.

22. See statement of Admiral William M. Benkert and Lt. (J.G.) D. H. Williams of March 1974 before the Marine Safety Council, quoted in U.S. Congress, House Committee on Merchant Marine and Fisheries, Subcommittee on Government Activity and Transportation on the Committee on Government Operations, *Coast Guard Efforts to Prevent Oil Pollution Caused by Tanker Accidents*, 95th Congress, 1st session, March 1977, p. 141.

23. U.S. National Archives, *Federal Register* (April 12, 1979), 44:21974–21991.

24. Some have argued strongly for the U.S. to pass special regulations for its foreign and domestic tanker trades. See P. A. Cummins et al., "Oil Tanker Pollution Control: Design Criteria vs. Effective Liability Assessment," *Journal of Maritime Law and Commerce* 7, 1 (October 1975), 170–206. The point has been raised that should the United States act unilaterally to control the character of foreign vessels entering U.S. waters, this might undermine the incentive of other countries to ratify the 1973 IMCO Convention for the Prevention of Oil Pollution from Ships or later conventions. The result might then be to reduce oil spillage on and near U.S. waters but to forestall improvements in global spillage from tankers. See: William Benkert and D. Williams, "The Impact of the 1973 IMCO Convention on the Maritime Industry," *Marine Technology* 11, 1 (January 1974), 1–8.

25. Other alternatives now under discussion, but not involving major design and equipment

features, are the creation of new international standards for crew training and crew certification and requirements that tanker vessels be equipped with modern navigational equipment, such as long-range position fixing equipment, collision avoidance radar, and redundant steering systems, among others. There is only one existing international agreement relating to personnel qualifications, the *Officer Competency Certificates Convention* of 1936, implemented in 46 U.S.C. 224a. Crew training standards were considered at an IMCO conference in June–July 1978. Another concept considered for controlling oily-water discharges from tankers in the early 1970s was the installation of flexible membranes in cargo tanks with ballast water always pumped in and out on one side of the membrane and cargo on the other. This concept was carefully analyzed and then dropped from further consideration. Excessive wear on the membrane and the necessity for complicated pumping sequences made the concept impractical. See Alexander D. Carmichael et al., "The Isolation of Oil and Other Fluids in Tankers from Seawater," Massachusetts Institute of Technology special report to the U.S. Coast Guard (December 1972) NTIS No. AD 759 832.

26. A more detailed description of the LOT operation may be found in G. Victory, "The Load on Top System - Present and Future," *Symposium on Marine Pollution* (London: Royal Institution of Naval Architects, 1973), pp. 10–20. The sea water discharged at sea from the slop tanks and the ballast water discharged in the loading port may both contain oil. The actual amount of oil discharged depends on a large number of variables.

27. Sonia Z. Pritchard, "Load on Top - From the Sublime to the Absurd," *Journal of Maritime Law and Commerce* 9, 2 (January 1978), 185–224. The text of the amendment may be found in 9 *International Legal Materials* (ILM) 1.

28. See P. A. Cummins et al., op. cit.

29. M'Gonigle and Zacher, op. cit., p. 111; and M. P. Holdsworth, "Loading Port Inspection of Cargo Residue Retention by Tankers in Ballast," *Proceedings of the IMCO Symposium on Prevention of Pollution from Ships* (Acapulco: IMCO, March 1976).

30. M'Gonigle and Zacher, op. cit., pp. 102, 108; and Pritchard, op. cit.

31. See the quote of J. H. Kirby, former director of Shell Marine International, in Pritchard, op. cit., p. 214.

32. Pritchard, op. cit., and Toshio Okuhara, "The New Law of the Sea and Prevention of Pollution by Vessels," in *New Trends in Maritime Navigation 1979*, proceedings of the 4th International Ocean Symposium (Tokyo: The Ocean Association of Japan, 1980), pp. 36–39.

33. Holdsworth, op. cit.

34. W. G. Waters II, T. D. Heaver, and T. Verrier, *Tanker Operational Pollution: Causes, Costs, Controls* (Vancouver: University of British Columbia, Centre for Transportation Studies, 1980), Exhibit VI-6.

35. Holdsworth, op. cit.

36. Twenty-five percent of the vessels surveyed in 1975 were owned by major oil companies and presumably practiced LOT with 100 percent effectiveness. The remaining vessels were on long-term charter to the oil companies or were third-party ships, loading oil at an oil terminal for an unidentified customer. These latter groups were largely equivalent in their retention of slops, implying that the captains of the vessels did not feel the same contractual incentives as did captains of vessels owned by major oil companies to retain slops and practice LOT effectively.

37. Kimon, Kiss, and Porricelli, op. cit.

38. When a tanker is fully loaded, depending on the vessel's size, between 10 and 15 percent of its displacement will be due to the weight of steel in the vessel. Thus, when a vessel achieves 50 percent of full displacement when in ballast, about 40 percent of its rated deadweight tonnage is composed of ballast water. See L. J. Creighton and I. E. Telfer, "Segregated Ballast Tankers," *Symposium on Marine Pollution*, pp. 30–59.

39. Tankers built according to the IMCO formula for SBT capacity will have ballast capacity equal to between 30 and 40 percent of vessel deadweight tonnage. It is intended that these tonnages

provide sufficient ballast for most operations, implying that tankers will be expected to operate at lower ballast levels when sailing in foul weather than has been true historically. See William O. Gray, "Segregated Ballast and Related Aspects of Tanker Design," and J. M. Cruikshank and A. C. Landsburg, "Guidelines for Operations at IMCO Segregated Ballast Levels," both in *Proceedings of the IMCO Symposium,* 1976, op. cit.

40. V. X. Lanotee and J. E. Shermaker, "Tanker Sludge Removal and Disposal," Exxon International Co. (June 1976), NTIS No. PB 255 174.

41. *Draft Environmental Impact Statement: International Conference on Tanker Safety and Pollution Prevention* (U.S. Coast Guard, Dept. of Transportation, February 1978).

42. Kimon, Kiss and Porricelli, op. cit., ship design no. 250-E1, table 5.

43. "U.S. Stays Cool Over Tanker Safety Alternatives," *Seatrade,* November 1977, 69–74.

44. William O. Gray, personal correspondence.

45. The description of COW is adapted from Oil Companies International Marine Forum, *Crude Oil Washing,* MEC/MEPC Inf. 17 (prepared for the 1978 IMCO Conference on Marine Oil Pollution), and from "U.S. Coast Guard Implementation of Presidential Initiative for Evaluation of Costs and Benefits of Crude Oil Washing: Executive Summary," in U.S. Congress, Senate, Committee on Commerce, Science and Transportation, *1978 IMCO Protocols,* 95th Cong., 2d session, Serial no. 95-80, April 5, 1978, pp. 97–108.

46. J. D. Porricelli, V. F. Keith, and R. L. Storch, "Tankers and the Ecology," *Transactions of the Society of Naval Architects and Marine Engineers* (1971), 79:169–221.

47. For a description of the possible causes of cargo tank vapor explosions, see, *Safety in Shipping,* a special report prepared by the publishers of *Seatrade,* October 1976.

48. Luther J. Carter, "*Amoco Cadiz* Incident Points up the Elusive Goal of Tanker Safety," *Science* 200, 4341 (May 5, 1978), 514–516; and R. Bavister, "Controlling Hydrocarbon Emissions," *Exxon Marine* 24, 2 (Autumn 1979), 12–17.

49. M'Gonigle and Zacher, op. cit., p. 132.

50. Oil Companies International Marine Forum, *Crude Oil Washing,* op. cit.

51. It is assumed that 20 percent of world oceanborne petroleum is either carried on vessels smaller than 20,000 dwt or the petroleum consists of either petroleum products or of high density, high viscosity crudes. These cargoes would not be subject to a rule requiring the fitting of crude oil washing capacity. Thus, $.8 \times 1.08 = .864$ million metric tons of oil spillage would be affected by a COW capability requirement, and .216 million metric tons would not. Since at least all tanks used to contain water ballast are crude oil washed each round trip, and 35 percent of cargo tanks are used to carry ballast on average (as opposed to 48 percent washed using LOT) then $(48-35)/48$ or 27.1 percent (.234 million metric tons) less oil would come into contact with seawater annually if COW were used. But, even more oil is saved because only 25 percent as much oil clingage remains in the ballast tanks in a COW'd tanker as in a LOT tanker, and thus 75 percent less oil is spilled from the LOT operation performed on the ballast and wash waters. Thus, $.75 (.864 - .234)$ million metric tons, or .472 million metric tons of oil are saved for this reason, for a total savings of .706 million metric tons. This is 65 percent of the 1.08 million metric tons spilled annually by all tankers.

52. Lt. Commander J. C. Card, P. V. Ponce, and Lt. Commander W. D. Snider, "Tankship Accidents and Resulting Oil Outflows, 1969–1973," *American Petroleum Institute Conference on Prevention and Control of Oil Pollution* (Washington, D.C.: American Petroleum Institute, 1975), pp. 205–213. The authors show that of the oil spilled from accidents, 19,800 million metric tons annually is due to fires and explosions, and if 80 percent of the oil carried is on vessels fitted with IGS and practicing COW, this percentage would approximate the percentage of spills avoided.

53. Card, Ponce, and Snider, op. cit.

54. Porricelli, Keith, and Storch, op. cit.

55. Eight environmental groups united and retained Mr. Eldon Greenberg as their spokesman. See Mr. Greenberg's comments in *Final Environmental Impact Statement: Regulations for Tank*

*Vessels Engaged in the Carriage of Oil in Domestic Trade* (U.S. Coast Guard, August 1975: NITS No. AD-A036 719).

56. Card, Ponce, and Snider, op. cit.

57. J. C. Card, "Effectiveness of Double Bottoms in Preventing Oil Outflows from Tanker Bottom Damage Incidents," *Marine Technology* 12, 1 (January 1975), 60–64.

58. U.S. Congress, Senate, Committee on Commerce, Science, and Transportation, *The Tanker and Vessel Safety Act of 1977: Report on S. 682*, 95th Congress, 1st session, May 1977, S. rep. 95-176. The results of Card's study, ibid., are referred to in this report.

59. See testimony of Secretary of Transportation Brock Adams in U.S. Congress, Senate, Committee on Commerce, Science and Transportation, *Recent Tanker Accidents: Legislation for Improved Tanker Safety*, 95th Congress, 1st session, Part II, March 1977, pp. 835–850.

60. Jimmy Carter, "Oil Pollution of the Oceans: The President's Message to the Congress Recommending Measures to Control the Problem," *Weekly Compilation of Presidential Documents* 13, 12 (March 1977), 408–409. The proposed regulations appeared in U.S., National Archives, *Federal Register* (May 16, 1977), 42:24868–24876 (hereafter cited as F.R.).

61. American Bureau of Shipping, *Rules for Building and Classing Steel Vessels* (New York: American Bureau of Shipping, 1977), Section 7.

62. American Institute of Merchant Shipping, *Tanker Double Bottoms: Yes or No?* (New York: American Institute of Merchant Shipping, July 1974), p. 5. It is worth noting that under some circumstances, such as would be the case if an SBT tank is also ruptured in the accident, that loss of oil cargo can result in a further settling of the stricken ship.

63. "Reducing Tanker Accidents," Exxon Background Series 5-9/73, Exxon International Co. 1973. So long as the tanker's segregated ballast tanks are undamaged, rupture of cargo tanks should not be fatal to the tanker's survival. If a segregated ballast tank or partly filled cargo tank, or the engine room is ruptured, buoyancy will be lost and the vessel's survival may be threatened.

64. Card, op. cit.

65. Roy W. Hann, for the U.S. Coast Guard, *VLCC 'Metula' Oil Spill*, Report No. CG-D-54-75, December 1974. The circumstances in which this would be desirable are probably fairly limited. It would not have helped the *Argo Merchant* or the *Amoco Cadiz*, for example.

66. *Netherlands Ship Model Basin Report for Mobil Shipping and Transportation Co.* (January 1972), cited in U.S. Congress, Office of Technology Assessment, *Oil Transportation by Tankers: An Analysis of Marine Pollution and Safety Measures*, July 1975, p. 45.

67. Kimon, Kiss, and Porricelli, op. cit.

68. Card, op. cit.

69. N. Jones, "A Literature Survey on the Collision and Grounding Protection of Ships," for the U.S. Coast Guard, NTIS No. AD A069 032, 1979.

70. Card, Ponce, and Snider, op. cit.

71. U.S. Congress, *Oil Transportation*, p. 46.

72. U.S. Congress, *Coast Guard Miscellaneous*, p. 295.

73. Personal conversation with William O. Gray, Exxon Corporation, June 1978.

74. U.S. Congress, *Recent Tanker Accidents*, p. 785.

75. U.S. Congress, *Oil Transportation*, table IV-1, p. 39. Twenty-six double-bottomed tankers were under construction or contract in 1974. Ten of the 34 double-bottomed tankers existing or under construction were expected to be used to move oil from Alaska to the U.S. domestic market and thus would operate in the North Pacific Ocean.

76. Comments from Dan Roseman, Hydronautics, and William O. Gray, Exxon International, 1978.

77. The author interprets a chart in Card, op. cit., that roughly 5 percent of the tankship groundings that result in an oil spill (or 1 percent of all groundings accidents) contribute 75 percent of the oil spilled from groundings.

78. M'Gonigle and Zacher, op. cit., p 119; and F.R. (October 14, 1975), 40:48289.

79. M'Gonigle and Zacher, op. cit., pp. 118–121.

80. U.S. Congress, *Oil Transportation*, p. 43.

81. For a description of the design standards of the Code, see R. C. Page, "The Prevention of Pollution from Chemical Tankers," *Symposium on Marine Pollution*, pp. 21–29.

82. E. M. Hood, "Ecology, Shipbuilding Prices, and Consumer Cost," *Report on the Sixteenth Annual Tanker Conference* (Washington, D.C.: American Petroleum Institute, Division of Transportation, May 1971), p. 203.

83. This section will focus on the *technological implications* of the existing regime. A comprehensive summary of relevant international conventions and domestic laws can be found in chaps. 9 and 10.

84. The Convention texts can be found in 327 *United Nations Treaty Series* (UNTS) 3; and the amendments are 600 UNTS 332 (1962), 9 *International Legal Materials* (I.L.M.) 1 (1969); 9 I.L.M. 25 (1971).

85. M'Gonigle and Zacher, op. cit., p. 108.

86. Public Law (PL) 29-340, July 10, 1972.

87. 12 I.L.M. 1319 (1973).

88. The provisions with respect to cargo tank size and arrangement first appeared in the 1971 amendments to the 1954 Convention as Resolution A/346 (VII) 9 I.L.M. 25 (1971).

89. U.S. Congress, Senate, Committee on Commerce, Science and Transportation, *1973 IMCO Conference on Marine Pollution*, 93d Congress, 1st Session, Serial no. 93-52, November 1973, p. 16.

90. Resolution 11 of the 1973 Convention notes that almost all tankers built after January 1, 1972 had complied with the 1971 amendments for cargo tank arrangement. This was the first employment of the device of setting calendar dates to encourage early compliance. Evidently, this device worked.

91. F.R. (October 14, 1975), 40:48280.

92. *Draft Environmental Impact Statement*, p. 5.

93. Marine Oil Transportation Task Force, "*S.S. Sansinena*, Synopsis of Explosion and Fire in San Pedro, California, with Loss of Life," U.S. Department of Transportation, January 11, 1977, interim report.

94. J. Carter, op. cit.

95. Intergovernmental Maritime Consultative Organization, *International Convention on Safety of Life at Sea* (London, 1974).

96. The 1978 Conference produced two Protocols and a set of 18 Resolutions. Texts for these have appeared as follows: *Protocol of 1978 Relating to the International Convention for the Safety of Life at Sea, 1974*, TSPP/CONF/10 and TSPP/CONF/10 Add. 1; *Protocol of 1978 Relating to the International Convention for the Prevention of Pollution from Ships*, 1973, TSPP/CONF/11 and TSPP/CONF/11 Add. 1; and *Resolutions Adopted by the Conference*, TSPP/CONF/12. These appeared in February and March of 1978. They may also be found in 17 I.L.M. 546.

97. *Analysis of World Tankship Fleet, December 31, 1976* (Chester, Pennsylvania: Sun Shipbuilding and Dry Dock, 1978), p. 14.

98. The SOLAS 74 provisions first appeared in an amendment to the 1960 SOLAS Convention as a resolution. The resolution was adopted in 1973. These were applied by the U.S. Coast Guard to U.S. vessels and to foreign vessels (that entered U.S. waters), whose keels were laid after January 1, 1975, by a ruling published in F.R. (January 26, 1976), 41:3838, as customary international law even though the resolution had not yet come into force.

99. See the statement of James P. Walsh, U.S. Congress, *1978 IMCO Protocols*, op. cit., p. 113.

100. *Draft Environmental Impact Statement*, p. 56.

101. F.R. (October 14, 1975), 40:48289.

102. William O. Gray, R. K. Kiss, and R. A. Sutherland, "Segregated Ballast Tanker Arrangements for Pollution Abatement Due to Accidents," *Proceedings of the IMCO Symposium*, op. cit.

103. Card, Ponce, and Snider, op. cit.

104. F.R. (January 8, 1976), 41:1479–1482.

105. F.R. (December 13, 1976), 41:54177.

106. Letter of Admiral W. O. Siler to Senator W. G. Magnuson, January 31, 1977, reproduced in U.S. Congress, *Recent Tanker Accidents*, p. 193.

107. M'Gonigle and Zacher, op. cit., p. 129.

108. Gray, Kiss, and Sutherland, op. cit.

109. Personal conversation with William O. Gray, Exxon International Co.

110. Statement of James P. Walsh, *1978 IMCO Protocols*, p. 115.

111. 33 U.S.C.A. sections 1221 ff., and 46 U.S.C.A. section 391a (1978).

112. See the U.S. Coast Guard regulatory implementation plan published in F.R. (September 21, 1978), 43:42833.

113. Trevor Lones, "Tanker Safety Still An Open Issue," *Seatrade*, March 1978, pp. 83–85.

114. *Seatrade*, July 1979, p. 91.

115. William O. Gray, personal communication, 1978.

116. M'Gonigle and Zacher, op. cit., pp. 136–138.

117. Wong, Green, and Cretney, op. cit.

## 12. International Arrangements Affecting Marine Scientific Research

1. For an account of SCOR activities, see W. Wooster, "The Scientific Committee on Oceanic Research," *Ocean Yearbook* (1978), p. 563.

2. Information relevant to International Fishery Commissions is summarized in tabular form in Appendix H.

3. Descriptions and summaries of information about many institutions may be found in *Annotated Directory of Intergovernmental Organizations Concerned With Ocean Affairs*, U.N. Doc. #A/CONF. 62/L.14 (1976).

4. Short-term agreements have not attracted attention until recently. For a review of older agreements in the North Pacific, see H. Kasahara and W. Burke, *International Fishery Management in the North Pacific: Present and Future* (University of Washington, Seattle, Unabridged MS, mimeo 1972). This review is briefly summarized in the monograph by H. Kasahara and W. Burke, *North Pacific Fisheries Management Resources for the Future Program of International Studies of Fisheries Arrangements* (Washington, D.C.: RFF, 1973) and in chap. 3 of this volume. For a review of contemporary bilaterals on a global scale, see J. Carroz and M. Savini, *Bilateral Fishery Agreements*, FAO Doc. FID/C709 (1978).

5. Interim Convention on Conservation of North Pacific Fur Seals, February 9, 1957, 8 U.S.T. 2283, T.I.A.S. no. 3948, 314 U.N.T.S. 105, amended October 8, 1963, 15 U.S.T. 316, T.I.A.S. no. 5558, 494 U.N.T.S. 303, extended on September 3, 1969, 20 U.S.T. 2992, T.I.A.S. no. 6774, 719 U.N.T.S. 313, and amended and extended on May 7, 1976, T.I.A.S. no. 8368 (hereinafter cited as Fur Seal Convention). Convention for the Protection, Preservation, and Extension of the Sockeye Salmon Fishery of the Fraser River System, May 26, 1930, Canada–United States, 50 Stat. 1355, T.S. no. 918, amended on December 28, 1956, 8 U.S.T. 1057, T.I.A.S. no. 386, and on February 24, 1977 (not in force) 76 *Department State Bulletin* 275 (1977) (hereinafter cited as Fraser River Convention). Convention for the Preservation of the Halibut Fishery of the Northern Pacific Ocean and Bering Sea, March 2, 1953, Canada–United States, 5 U.S.T. 5, T.I.A.S. no. 2900, amended on March 29, 1979, 79 *Department State Bulletin*, no. 2026, at 68 (1979) (hereinafter cited as Halibut Convention). International Convention for the High Seas Fisheries of the North Pacific Ocean, May 9, 1952, Canada–Japan–United States, 4 U.S.T. 380, T.I.A.S. no. 2786, 205 U.N.T.S. 65 (hereinafter cited as North Pacific Convention), and amended on April 25, 1978, 79 *Department State Bulletin* no. 2025, at 67 (1979).

6. Kasahara and Burke, *International Fishery Management*, op. cit., pp. 107–109, estimated in 1973 that 90 percent of the North Pacific fisheries were beyond any regulation by agreement or otherwise.

7. International North Pacific Fisheries Commission (hereinafter cited as INPFC) membership includes Canada, Japan, and the U.S.; it could include South Korea and the USSR. North Pacific Fur Seal Commission (hereinafter cited as NPFSC) membership includes Canada, Japan, the U.S., and the USSR; it could include South Korea. International Pacific Halibut Commission (hereinafter cited as IPHC) and International Pacific Salmon Fisheries Commission (hereinafter cited as IPSFC) membership include Canada and the U.S.; both could include Japan and the USSR.

8. For documentation on this point, see Kasahara and Burke, *International Fishery Management*, op. cit., pp. 47ff.

9. Ibid., pp. 81–87, 100–101, for a discussion on these Western Pacific entities. See also chaps. 3 and 4, this volume.

10. Commission for Fisheries Research in the Western Pacific, created by the Convention for Cooperation in the Execution of Fishery, Oceanological, and Limnological Research in the Western Pacific, June 12, 1956, *Chug-hua jen-min kung-ho-kuo t'iao-yuen-chi No. 5* (compilation of treaties of the People's Republic of China 1949–1964), pp. 169–172 (hereinafter cited as the Convention for Fisheries Research in the Western Pacific). For an English translation, see FAO, Convention, Statutes, and Rules of Procedure of the Commission for Fisheries Research in the Western Pacific, FAO Doc. FTb/T50 (1965).

11. Article III of the Fraser River Convention (see note 3 above) provides:

> The Commission shall make a thorough investigation into the natural history of the Fraser River sockeye salmon, into hatchery methods, spawning ground conditions and other related matters . . . to recommend to the Governments . . . removing or otherwise overcoming obstructions to the ascent of sockeye salmon . . . where investigations may show such removal of or other action to overcome obstructions to be desirable.

In 1944, as a result of extensive investigations carried out pursuant to Article III, the Commission recommended remedial measures for overcoming obstructions to the ascent of the salmon in Hell's Gate Canyon, and further investigation and remedial measures for overcoming obstructions elsewhere in the Fraser River watershed. The two governments agreed to provide an estimated two million dollars to implement these recommendations. Agreement to Facilitate the Ascent of Salmon in Hell's Gate Canyon and Elsewhere in the Fraser River System, July 21–August 5, 1944, Canada–United States, 59 Stat. 1614, E.A.S. no. 479. See, for example, "Accommodation of Indian Fishery Rights in An International Fishery: An International Problem Begging for An International Solution," *Washington Law Review*, 54: 403, 408–18; W. Burke, "Aspects of Internal Decision Making Processes in Intergovernmental Fishery Commissions," *Washington Law Review*, (1967), 43:115.

12. Halibut Convention (see note 4 above ), Article III (2).

13. The Commission had established an Ad Hoc Committee on Abstention to help it perform the responsibilities set forth in Article III (1) (a) of the Convention. The Commission's recommendation to the Contracting Parties on abstention are based on this Committee's determinations: removal from the Annex of herring stocks off the coast of Alaska, INPFC, *Proceedings of the Sixth Annual Meeting* (1959), pp. 45–46; removal from the Annex of herring stocks off the coast of the United States mainland, INPFC, *Proceedings of the Eighth Annual Meeting* (1961), pp. 38–39; and removal from the Annex of halibut stocks in the East Bering Sea and herring stocks off the west coast of Queen Charlotte Islands, INPFC, *Proceedings of the Ninth Annual Meeting* (1962), pp. 36–38. Salmon stocks listed in the Annex continue to qualify for abstention due to disagreement within this Committee, INPFC, *Proceedings of the 24th Annual Meeting* (1977), p. 62.

Brief summaries of the abstention determinations are published in INPFC Annual Reports; comprehensive summaries are in INPFC Bulletins.

The Commission also established two committees to help it deal with the problems raised by the Protocol: the Standing Committee on Biology and Research (hereinafter cited as CBR) to conduct scientific investigations, and the Ad Hoc Committee on the Protocol to study the findings of the CBR for the purpose of recommending to the Commission action necessary to perform the responsibilities set forth in the Protocol. Nonetheless, the Protocol has been impossible to implement. An interpretation of the intent of the Protocol was requested of the Contracting Parties in 1959, INPFC, *Proceedings of the Sixth Annual Meeting* (1959), pp. 44–45, but as of 1975, no communication from the Contracting Parties had been received. As a result, no action had been taken on implementing the Protocol, and the provisional dividing lines for salmon fishing remained in effect until implementation of the 1978 Protocol.

Conservation measures are also based on the recommendations of the CBR and its subcommittees and other scientific investigative groups. See INPFC, *Proceedings of the 10th Annual Meeting* (1963), pp. 43, 238.

14. Article X of the 1978 Protocol amending the North Pacific Convention (see note above), S. Exec. Doc. J, 95th Congress, Second Session (1978), provides:

> The Contracting Parties agree that a scientific program is necessary to carry out the provisions of this Convention. To this end, the Contracting Parties agree to establish such a program to coordinate their research activities with respect to anadromous species in the Convention area as well as species of marine mammals incidentally caught in fishing for anadromous species. In this regard, the Contracting Parties agree to exchange scientists in order to carry out scientific observations with respect to the catches and methods of operation. The Contracting Parties shall establish procedures to facilitate such observations.

See Articles III, IV and VIII, Agreed Minutes and Memorandum of Understanding.

15. Comprehensive summaries of the findings of scientific investigations carried out pursuant to the objectives set forth in par. 1 and 2 of Article II have been published in NPFSC, *North Pacific Fur Seal Commission Report of Investigations*, for the years 1958–1961, 1962–1963, 1964–1966, and 1967–1972 (1973–1976 proposed). Brief summaries are published in NPFSC Proceedings of the Annual Meeting Reports.

16. Convention Concerning the High Seas Fisheries of the Northwest Pacific Ocean, May 14, 1956, Japan–USSR, Genko Joyaku Iken no. 1314 (1956). For an English translation, see *American Journal of International Law* (AJIL) (1956), 53:763.

17. Ibid., Article IV (a).

18. Ibid., Article IV (d).

19. See, for example, Kasahara and Burke, *International Fishery Management*, op. cit., p. 86; S. Tanaka, "Fisheries in the Northwest Pacific and Fishery Resources—Mainly on the Japanese Fisheries and International Problems Surrounding Them," in C. Dawson, ed., *The North Pacific Project* (Seattle: Institute for Marine Studies, University of Washington, 1977), pp. 219, 243–252 (hereinafter cited as the North Pacific Project).

20. See A. Koers, *International Regulation of Marine Fisheries* (London: Fishing News [Books], 1973), p. 102.

21. Kasahara and Burke, *International Fishery Management*, op. cit., p. 86.

22. Agreement in Fisheries, June 22, 1965, Japan–Republic of Korea, *Joyuku Shu* 247 (1965), 583 U.N.T.S. 51.

23. See *IPHC Annual Report 1971* at 7 (1972); *IPHC Annual Report 1972* at 7 (1973); *IPHC Annual Report 1973* at 7 (1974); *IPHC Annual Report 1974* at 7 (1975); *IPHC Annual Report 1975* at 5

(1976); *IPHC Annual Report 1976* at 5 (1977); *IPHC Annual Report 1977* at 4 (1978); *IPHC Annual Report 1978* at 4 (1979); expenses of the Commission are shared equally by both governments.

24. FAO, *Future of FAO Regional Fisheries Bodies*, FAO Doc. COFI/78/5 (Rome: FAO, 1963), p. 13.

25. INPFC, *Salmon in the North Pacific* (Part 1), in Bull. no. 12 (1963), pp. 3–4.

26. Based on an interview by the authors with Donald L. McKernan on September 6, 1978.

27. F. Christy, Jr. and A. Scott, *The Common Wealth in Ocean Fisheries* (Baltimore: The Johns Hopkins Press, 1965) p. 207.

28. An account of a possible instance is in B. Skud, "Revised Estimates of Halibut Abundance and the Thompson-Burkenroad Debate," IPHC, *Scientific Report No. 56 (1975)*. See esp. the Epilogue, pp. 30–31.

29. Protocol to the North Pacific Convention (see note 13 above), Articles III and IV.

30. North Pacific Convention (see note 4 above), Article III and Protocol.

31. See, *Interim Report of the Committee on Biology and Research*, in *INPFC, Minutes of the Annual Meeting* (1954), p. 35 (hereinafter cited as *Interim Report*); *First Report of the Committee on Biology and Research*, in *INPFC, Minutes of the Annual Meeting* (1955), pp. 48, 50; *Report of the Committee on Biology and Research*, in *INPFC, Minutes of the Annual Meeting* (1956), p. 65; *Address of the Chairman*, in *INPFC, Minutes of the Annual Meeting* (1957), pp. 35–36.

32. See, *Interim Report* (see note 30 above), pp. 31–35.

33. *Report of the Committee on Biology and Research*, in *INPFC, Proceedings of the Annual Meeting* (1957), p. 67.

34. The IPHC issues information bulletins and publishes annual, scientific, and technical reports. The latter two publications contain the results of scientific studies and statistical records of the fishery. Information bulletins contain summaries of research and are primarily distributed to fishermen and industry members. Annual reports contain brief year-end summaries of the activities of the Commission, including its scientific studies, and the status of the fishery.

The INPFC publishes annual reports, bulletins, and statistical yearbooks that are similar to IPHC publications. Annual reports contain summaries of the Commission's meetings, administrative and fiscal reports, and research findings. Bulletins contain comprehensive summaries of research findings and are published at irregular intervals. Statistical yearbooks contain summaries of fishery statistics of joint interest to the Contracting Parties and distribution is limited to those directly involved with INPFC activities.

The IPSC issues bulletins and publishes annual, progress, and administrative reports that are similar to the IPHC and INPFC publications. A list of each Commission's publications can be found in their respective annual reports.

35. N. Eberhard and L. Bledsoe, *A Comparative Study of the Statistical Areas in the North Pacific Fisheries*, Norfish Technical Report (1975), p. 60.

36. The following North Pacific nations have adopted 200-mile fishing zones: Canada, Japan, N. Korea, S. Korea, the USSR, and the United States. The North Korean legislation establishes an exclusive economic zone. These are analyzed in chap. 5, this volume.

37. Renegotiated agreements include the Protocol to the North Pacific Convention and the Protocol to the Halibut Convention. The Fraser River Convention has not yet been renegotiated and the Fur Seal Convention is up for possible extension in 1979. (The United States Fishery Conservation and Management Act of 1976 expresses the sense of Congress that agreements inconsistent with its terms should be renegotiated within a reasonable time.)

38. Bilateral agreements are discussed later in this chapter. See section on Bilateral Agreements on Research.

39. *The Seattle Times*, August 4, 1979, p. A7, col. 3; National Oceanic and Atmospheric Administration, U.S. Department of Commerce, *1977 Annual Report on the Fishery Conservation and Management Act of 1976* (1978), p. 20 (table 8); National Oceanic and Atmospheric Administration,

U.S. Department of Commerce, *Calendar Year 1978 Report on the Implementation of the Fishery Conservation and Management Act of 1976* (1979), p. 11 (table 3).

40. See S. Gibbs and D. Teeter, "Management of Marine Transportation in the Northeast Pacific," in C. Dawson, ed., *The North Pacific Project*, op. cit., pp. 463–464.

41. Ibid., p. 454.

42. Convention for the International Council for the Exploration of the Sea, Sept. 12, 1964, 24 U.S.T. 1080, T.I.A.S. no. 7628, 652 U.N.T.S. 237, amended on Aug. 13, 1970, 27 U.S.T. 1022, T.I.A.S. no. 8239 (hereinafter cited as ICES Convention).

43. Council Res. 1976/2:1, Conseil International Pour L'Exploration De La Mer (hereinafter cited as ICES), *Procès-Verbal De La Reunion* 125 (1976). See, ICES, *Procès-Verbal De La Reunion* (1977), pp. 15–26.

44. See *Report on the 3d Meeting of the Working Group on the Overflow 1973 Expedition*, in ICES, *Procès-Verbal De La Reunion* (1973), 66 (Annex IV).

45. The following area and subject committees have been established: Gear and Behaviour Committee, Hydrography Committee, Statistics Committee, Fisheries Improvement Committee, Demersal Fish (northern) Committee, Demersal Fish (southern) Committee, Pelagic Fish (northern) Committee, Pelagic Fish (southern) Committee, Baltic Fish Committee, Shellfish and Benthos Committee, Plankton Committee, Anadromous and Catadromous Fish Committee, and the Marine Mammals Committee. However, other committees can be formed by the Council as it deems necessary to discharge its functions. ICES Convention, supra note 41, Article XII.

46. Members of the Consultative Committee are elected chairmen of the various Standing Committees and therefore represent groups of scientists rather than political entities.

47. Convention on the Protection of the Marine Environment of the Baltic Sea Area, March 22, 1974, *Sveriges Overenskommel ser Med Frammande Makter* no. 13 (1974); *International Conventions and Protocols in the Field of the Environment*, U.N. Doc. A/32/156, at 92 (1977) (hereinafter cited as Conventions on the Environment).

48. Convention on the Prevention of Marine Pollution from Land-Based Sources, June 4, 1974, Conventions on the Environment (see note 46 above), p. 93.

49. Convention for the Prevention of Marine Pollution by Dumping from Ships and Aircraft, February 15, 1972, *Bundesgesetzblatt No. 165* (Sec. 11) (1977); Conventions on the Environment (see note 46 above), p. 79.

50. ICES, *Procès-Verbal De La Reunion* XXIX–XXXV (1978).

51. Unfortunately, there is no all-inclusive index to ICES publications. F. Host et Fils, *Index to Publications by the International Council for the Exploration of the Sea* (1899–1939) indexes the following publications: *Bulletin Hydrographique, Bulletin Planctonique, Bulletin Statistique, Bulletin Trimestrial, Journal du Conseil, Publications de Circonstance, Rapports et Procès-Verbaux*, and other special publications for the years 1899 through 1939. This index, however, has not been updated.

52. See A. Koers, "The External Authority of the E.E.C. in Regard to Marine Fisheries," *Common Market Law Review* (1977), 14:269; M. Hardy, "Regional Approaches to the Law of the Sea Problems: The European Community," *International and Comparative Law Quarterly* (1975), 24:336; D. Johnson, ed., *Regionalization of the Law of the Sea* (Cambridge, Mass.: Ballinger, 1978); D. Driscoll and N. McKellar, "The Changing Regime of North Sea Fisheries," in *The Effective Management of Resources—The International Politics of the North Sea*, pp. 125–167.

53. See J. Scarff, "The International Management of Whales, Dolphins, and Porpoises: An Interdisciplinary Assessment," (Parts 1 and 2), *Ecology Law Quarterly* (1977), 6:323,571; S. McVay, "Reflections on the Management of Whaling," in W. Schevill, ed., *The Whale Problem: A Status Report*, (Cambridge: Harvard University Press, 1974), p. 369 (hereinafter cited as *The Whale Problem*); J. McHugh, "The Role and History of the International Whaling Commission" in *The Whale Problem*, op. cit., p. 305; P. Bock, *A Study in International Regulation: The Case of Whaling*, unpublished thesis, University Microfilms, Ann Arbor, Michigan, 1966.

54. Bureau of International Whaling Statistics, 81 *International Whaling Statistics* 12 (table C), Comm. for Whaling Statistics ed. (1978).

55. The best illustrations are the bowhead whale and Dall porpoise. On the former, see Scarff, op. cit., pp. 400–404, 632–633; on the latter, see U.S. Dept. of State, *Environmental Impact Statement for the Renegotiation of the International Convention for the High Seas Fisheries of the North Pacific Ocean* (1978), pp. 100–108. The status of such small cetaceans under the International Whaling Commission (hereinafter cited as IWC) is controversial. See Scarff, op. cit., pp. 373–375.

56. The 28th Report of the IWC (1978) lists the following Commission members: Argentina, Australia, Brazil, Canada, Denmark, France, Iceland, Japan, Mexico, the Netherlands, New Zealand, Norway, Panama, South Africa, USSR, U.K., and the U.S. Other nations, however, are now more interested in the IWC, apparently as a result of United States pressure. Several U.S. laws impose trade sanctions on uncooperative whaling nations. For example, see 1978 (Pelly Amendment) of the Fishermen's Protective Act of 1967, 22 U.S.C. sec. 1971 (1968), grants the President authority to direct the Secretary of Treasury to ban imports of the fish products of a nation when the Secretary of Commerce certifies that the nationals of that nation "directly or indirectly, are conducting fishing operations in a manner or under circumstances which diminish the effectiveness of an international fishery program." It has been the policy of NOAA to invoke the Act, at least in aggravated circumstances, against offending whaling nations that are not signatories to the IWC (Scarff, op. cit., p. 604, n. 703) and President Carter considered invoking the Act against S. Korea, Peru, and Chile. He declined, however, because all three nations subsequently joined or took steps toward joining the IWC. (*Marine Mammal News.* Vol. 5 (1979), p. 2.) See also Marine Mammals Protection Act of 1972, 16 U.S.C. sec. 1361 (1972); Convention on International Trade in Endangered Species of Wild Fauna and Flora, March 4, 1973, 27 U.S.T. 1087, T.I.A.S. no. 8249. At its 29th meeting, the IWC adopted a United States-sponsored resolution to encourage nonmember nations to join the IWC by preventing their whale products from being imported by IWC members. *Chairman's Report of the 29th Meeting*, in IWC, 28th rep. 23 (1978).

57. Scarff, op. cit., p. 598; ibid., n. 662. Until recently, the most prominent nonmember whaling nations were Chile, Peru, Portugal, S. Korea, the Somali Republic, Spain, and Taiwan (Chile and Peru are now members).

58. Ibid., pp. 353–354; McHugh, op. cit., p. 317; Bock, op. cit., p. 135.

59. See the New Management Procedure (see note 60 above); Scarf, op. cit., pp. 371, 421–422.

60. Ibid., pp. 422, 628–631; FAO, *Report of the Advisory Committee on Marine Mammals*, FAO Doc. FIR/R194 (En), (1977), p. 36.

61. The new management procedure refers to the need to preserve and enhance whale stocks as a resource for present and future use but also takes into consideration the interests of consumers of whale products and the whaling industry. It recognizes that the management of whale stocks should be based not only on the concepts of maximum sustainable yield in number of species, but should include such considerations as total weight of whales and interactions between species in the marine ecosystem. All stocks of whales are to be classified into one of three categories according to the advice of the Scientific Committee, the stocks being defined for this purpose as the units that can be most effectively managed individually: (i) *Initial Management stocks*, which may be reduced in a controlled manner to achieve MSY levels or optimum levels as they are determined; (ii) *Sustained Management stocks*, which should be maintained at or near MSY levels and then at optimum levels as they are determined; (iii) *Protection stocks*, which are below the level of sustained management stocks and should be fully protected. Furthermore, the procedure provides that: (a) commercial whaling shall be permitted on initial management stocks subject to the advice of the Scientific Committee as to measures necessary to bring the stocks to their MSY level and then optimum level in an efficient manner and without risk of reducing them below this level; (b) commercial whaling shall be permitted on sustained management stocks subject to the advice of the Scientific Committee; and (c) there shall be no commercial whaling on species or stocks classified as protection stocks, including those species listed for full protection.

Implementation is by the Scientific Committee providing advice, to be updated annually, on the criteria to be used in defining the above categories of whale stocks to be incorporated into the schedule. *Chairman's Report of the 26th Meeting*, in IWC, 26th rep. (1976), pp. 25–26; See IWC, 27th rep. (1977), pp. 6–7.

62. McHugh, op. cit., p. 321.

63. *Report of the Advisory Committee*, supra note 59.

64. Chairman's Report of the 12th Meeting, in IWC 12th rep. (1961), p. 16.

65. "Finally, in setting up this group of scientists, the Commission declared their intention to be that the Antarctic catch limit should be brought into line with the scientific findings not later than 31st July, 1964, having regard to the provisions of Article V(2) of the Convention." *Chairman's Report of the 12th Meeting*, in IWC 12th rep. (1961), p. 16. At the Sixteenth Meeting in June 1964, the resolution to implement the scientific advice of the Committee of Three was rejected. The decisive votes against were justified on the ground of Article V(2) (d) (regulation: "shall take into consideration the interests of the consumers of whale products and the whaling industry"). "Some of the opponents contended that the condition of their whaling industries could not support the catch restrictions recommended." *Chairman's Report of the 16th Meeting*, in IWC 16th rep. (1966), p. 18.

66. IWC 13th rep. (1962), p. 7; *Report of the Ad Hoc Scientific Committee*, ibid., pp. 26–27, for example, *Report of the Working Group on North Pacific Whale Stocks*, in IWC 14th rep. (1963), p. 29.

67. Scarff, op. cit., pp. 417–427.

68. Ibid., pp. 418–419.

69. Ibid., p. 421.

70. Ibid., p. 422.

71. Convention on Future Multilateral Cooperation in the Northwest Atlantic Fisheries, S. Exec. Doc. T, 96th Congress, 1st Session (1979).

72. The September 1978 Draft Convention on the Conservation of Antarctic Marine Living Resources appears in *Environment Policy and Law* (1979), 5:58.

73. IOC Res. X-11, *Intergovernmental Oceanographic Commission (IOC) Summary Report* (10th Assembly), Annex (Agenda Item 8.3) 11, UNESCO Doc. SC/MD/60, (1978), pp. 11–12.

74. IOC, Doc. IOC/WESTPAC ad hoc - 1/3.

75. IOCARIBE is an IOC regional science association for the Caribbean and adjacent regions formed after termination of the CICAR (Cooperative Investigations of the Caribbean and Adjacent Regions) working group. Its tasks are to oversee all IOC projects in the Caribbean areas and to coordinate these activities with those of other U.N. bodies. IOCARIBE is intended to continue for six years after which a review will be held on the question whether or not to continue for a longer period. Current membership includes eighteen states of the regions: Colombia, Costa Rica, Cuba, Dominican Republic, France (Guadeloupe, Martinique, and French Guyana), Guatemala, Guyana, Haiti, Jamaica, Mexico, the Netherlands (Netherlands Antilles), Nicaragua, Panama, Surinam, Trinidad and Tobago, U.K. (Belize, British Virgin Islands, Cayman Islands, Turks and Caicos Islands, and West Indies Associates States), the U.S. (Puerto Rico and U.S. Virgin Islands), and Venezuela, as well as Brazil and the USSR. Its secretariat is currently located in San Jose.

76. All North Pacific Ocean Agreements up to 1972 are reviewed in some detail in Kasahara and Burke, *International Fishery Management*, and in chap. 3, this volume.

77. Agreement on Certain Fishery Problems in the Northeastern Part of the Pacific Ocean Off the Coasts of the United States, February 13, 1967, United States–USSR, 18 U.S.T. 190, T.I.A.S. no. 6218, extended Dec. 18 1967; 18 U.S.T. 3162, T.I.A.S. no. 6409, and amended and extended on January 31, 1969; 18 U.S.T. 340, T.I.A.S. no. 6636, par. 9.

78. Agreement on Certain Fisheries Problems in the Northeastern Part of the Pacific Ocean Off the Coasts of the United States, February 12, 1971, United States–USSR, 22 U.S.T. 143, T.I.A.S. no. 7046, par. 1 (a) and (b).

79. These are general conclusions based on interviews by the authors with several persons

involved with these agreements: Dayton L. Alverson, Donald L. Bevan, and Donald L. McKernan.

80. Appraisal of the North Atlantic experience differs. Accomplishments there are seen to be more substantial and there were fewer operational difficulties. See L. Nakatsu, "United States—U.S.S.R. Cooperation in Fisheries," in *Soviet Oceans Development*, 94th Congress, 2d session, (1976), pp. 463—478; personal communication to the authors from Dr. Robert Edwards, Director, Northeast Fisheries Research Center, NMFS, Woods Hole, Mass.

81. Carroz and Savini, op. cit.

82. As of 1978, twelve Governing International Fishery Agreements (GIFAs) had been concluded since passage of the Fishery Conservation and Management Act of 1976. National Oceanic and Atmospheric Administration, U.S. Department of Commerce, *Calendar Year 1978 Report on the Fishery Conservation and Management Act of 1976* (1979), p. 8:

| *Country* | *Signed* | *Duration* | *Document* |
|---|---|---|---|
| Bulgaria | Dec. 17, 1976 | July 1, 1983 | T.I.A.S. no. 9045 |
| Cuba | Apr. 27, 1977 | 5-year period | T.I.A.S. no. 8689 |
| European Economic Community | Feb. 15, 1977 | July 1, 1984 | T.I.A.S. no. 8589 |
| German Democratic Republic | Oct. 5, 1976 | July 1, 1983 | T.I.A.S. no. 8527 28 U.S.T. 793 |
| Japan | Mar. 18, 1977 | Dec. 31, 1982 | T.I.A.S. no. 8728 28 U.S.T. 7507 |
| Mexico | Aug. 26, 1977 | July 1, 1982 | T.I.A.S. no. 8852 |
| Poland | Aug. 2, 1976 | July 1, 1982 | T.I.A.S. no. 8524 28 U.S.T. 1681 |
| Republic of Korea | Jan. 4, 1977 | July 1, 1982 | T.I.A.S. no. 8526 28 U.S.T. 1753 |
| Romania | Nov. 23, 1976 | July 1, 1982 | T.I.A.S. no. 8825 |
| Spain | Feb. 16, 1977 | July 1, 1982 | T.I.A.S. no. 8523 |
| Taiwan | Sept. 21, 1976 | July 1, 1982 | T.I.A.S. no. 8529 |
| U.S.S.R. | Nov. 26, 1976 | July 1, 1982 | T.I.A.S. no. 8528 28 U.S.T. 1847 |

83. The bilaterals are as follows: Cuba—United States, Mexico—United States, Senegal—Spain, Chile—Spain, Sierra Leone—USSR, the Gambia—USSR, Guinea Bissau—USSR, Mauritania—USSR, and Angola—USSR.

84. Carroz and Savini, op. cit.

85. Ibid., p. 8.

86. For an interesting analysis of Soviet practices in fishing agreements, see L. Powers, *Soviet Fisheries Policy 1956—1974* (1974), unpublished student paper in the University of Washington School of Law Library.

87. See, for example, Article XII of the Agreement Concerning Fisheries Off the Coasts of the United States, November 23, 1976, United States—Romania, T.I.A.S. no. 8825, provides that the United States and Romania:

[U]ndertake to cooperate in the conduct of scientific research required for the purpose of managing and conserving living resources subject to the fishery management authority of the United States, including the compilation of best available information for the management and conservation of stocks of mutual concern. The competent agencies of the two Governments may enter into such arrangements as may be necessary to facilitate such cooperation, including the exchange of information and scientists and regularly scheduled meetings between scientists to prepare research plans and review progress, and shall implement and maintain a standardized information in accordance with the procedures in Annex III.

Furthermore, Article XIII provides that the United States and Romania:

[S]hall carry out periodic bilateral consultations regarding the implementation of this Agreement and the development of further cooperation in the field of fisheries of mutual concern, including the establishment of appropriate multilateral organizations for the collection and analysis of scientific data respecting such fisheries.

88. Fishery Conservation and Management Act of 1976, sec. 1851 (a) (2), 16 U.S.C. sec. 1801 (1976).

89. One of the more recent bilaterals on Cooperation in Science and Technology was signed with the People's Republic of China (Agreement on Cooperation in Science and Technology, January 31, 1979, PRC–United States, T.I.A.S. no. 9179). Bilaterals have also been signed between the United States and the following nations: Argentina, Australia, Brazil, Canada, Egypt, France, Greece, Hungary, India, Israel, Italy, S. Korea, Mexico, New Zealand, Poland, Tunisia, the USSR, Yugoslavia, and Taiwan.

90. Agreement on Cooperation in Studies of the World Oceans, June 19, 1973, United States–USSR, 24 U.S.T. 1452, T.I.A.S. no. 7651 and extended on June 19, 1978, T.I.A.S. no. 9008.

91. Hearings on World Ocean Studies Before the Subcommittee on Oceanography of the House Committee on Merchant Marine and Fisheries, 95th Congress, 380–92 (part 2) (1978) (testimony of Richard A. Frank, Administrator, National Oceanic and Atmospheric Administration, and Chairman of the U.S. Joint Committee Delegation).

92. Most of the U.S.–Japan Cooperative Programs can be traced to a 1961 meeting between President Kennedy and Prime Minister Ikeda, where, to strengthen the partnership between the two nations, they agreed to establish three high-level consultative bodies: The U.S.–Japan Committee on Trade and Economic Affairs, the U.S.–Japan Committee on Scientific Cooperation, and the U.S.–Japan Committee on Cultural and Educational Exchange. White House Press Release, June 22, 1961, 45 *Department of State Bulletin 58* (1961). These committees have met at least annually to execute their ongoing functions; the U.S.–Japan Conference on Natural Resources Development grew out of the third meeting of the Committee on Trade and Economic Affairs. U.S. Department of State Press Release no. 150, June 10, 1965, 52 *Department of State Bulletin* 1052 (1965). The Environmental Agreement, however, is based on a treaty: Agreement on Cooperation in the Field of Environmental Protection, August 5, 1975, U.S.–Japan, 26 U.S.T. 2534, T.I.A.S. no. 8172.

## 13. The Need for a North Pacific Science Organization

1. IOC/UNESCO, Workshop Report no. 16, *Workshop on the Western Pacific*, Tokyo 19–20 February 1979.

2. See: IOC/UNESCO, Workshop Report no. 23, *WESTPAC Workshop on the Marine Geology and Geophysics of the Northwest Pacific*, Tokyo, 27–31, March 1980; IOC/UNESCO, Workshop Report no. 24, *WESTPAC Workshop on Coastal Transport of Pollutants*, Tokyo, 27–31 March 1980; Draft Report, *Proceedings of the WESTPAC Workshop on Marine Biological Methodology*, Tokyo, February 1981; Task Team on Ocean Monitoring, Draft Report, *Ocean Monitoring in WESTPAC*, July 1981.

3. Draft Report, WESTPAC II, Jakarta, October 24, 1981.

## 14. Management of Multiple Use Conflicts—Offshore Oil Development, Marine Pollution, and Other Uses

1. More intense use of marine resources and marine space can result from an increase in activity by existing uses as well as from an increase in the number of different uses that take place in the area. Multiple use conflicts are not necessarily a linear function of increased intensity of use, however, since changes in the technologies used and the patterns and sequencing of operations can alter the impacts of increased use.

2. See the following references for examples of actual and experimental data on marine pollution interactions on living resources: D. L. Alverson and G. J. Paulik, "Objectives and Problems of Managing Aquatic Living Resources," *Journal of the Fisheries Research Board of Canada* 30, 12 (1973), pt 2; Edward D. Goldberg, *The Health of the Oceans* (Paris: UNESCO Press, 1976); Michael Waldichuk, "Coastal Marine Pollution and Fish," *Ocean Management*, 2,2 (1974); A. D. McIntyre and K. J. Whittle, eds., "Petroleum Hydrocarbons in the Marine Environment," Proceedings from ICES Workshop held in Aberdeen, September 9–12, 1975, *Rapports et Procès-Verbaux des Réunions* (August 1977), 171:233 pp.; Food and Agriculture Organization (FAO), "Impact of Oil on the Marine Environment," IMCO/FAO/UNESCO/WMO/WHO/IAEA/UN Joint Group of Experts on the Scientific Aspects of Marine Pollution–GESAMP *Reports and Studies*, no. 6 (Rome, 1977), 250 pp.; "Recovery Potential of Oiled Marine Northern Environments," *Journal of the Fisheries Research Board of Canada*, Special Issue, 35,5 (1978), 499–795; Woods Hole Oceanographic Institution (WHOI), *Effects on Commercial Fishing of Petroleum Development Off the Northeastern United States*, A Report from the Marine Policy and Ocean Management Program, WHOI-76-66 (April 1976), 80 pp.; International Decade for Ocean Exploration (IDOE), *Baseline Studies of Pollutants in the Marine Environment and Research Recommendations: The IDOE Baseline Conference*, May 24–26, 1972 (New York, 1972), 54 pp.

3. David C. Major, *Multiobjective Water Resource Planning*, Water Resources Monograph 4 (Washington, D.C.: American Geophysical Union, 1977), 81 pp.

4. M. V. Adams, C. B. John, R. F. Kelly, A. E. La Pointe, and R. W. Meurer, *Mineral Resources Management of the Outer Continental Shelf*, Geological Survey Circular 720 (Reston, Virginia: U.S.G.S., 1975), p. 27.

5. The United States government ordered a speed-up in its outer continental shelf leasing program in 1979, for example.

6. Barry Buzan and Danford M. Middlemiss, "Canadian Foreign Policy and the Exploitation of the Seabed," in Barbara Johnson and Mark W. Zacher, eds., *Canadian Foreign Policy and the Law of the Sea* (Vancouver: University of British Columbia Press, 1977), p. 3.

7. D. H. Shouldice, "Geology of the Western Canadian Continental Shelf," *Bulletin of Canadian Petroleum Geology* 19,2 (1971), 405–436. Maps of the sedimentary basins, lease areas, drilling and production sites for Canada and other North Pacific nations are found in *Atlas of Marine Use in the North Pacific Region*, accompanying this volume.

8. Department of Energy, Mines and Resources, *Offshore Exploration, Information and Procedures for Offshore Operators*, 6th Issue (Ottawa, January 1977), p. 45.

9. G. L. Bell, "Big Potential Oil Basins Offshore from West Coast," *Oilweek* (June 26, 1967), p. 50. Basin referred to as Comox Basin in this source.

10. Department of Energy, Mines and Resources, op. cit., p. 45.

11. Shouldice, op. cit., p. 405.

12. *Victoria Times*, September 24, 1979.

13. *The Oil and Gas Journal*, April 4, 1977, p. 58.

14. Buzan and Middlemiss, op. cit., p. 43.

15. John Burgess, "North Korea Seeks Help in Offshore Oil Search," *Washington Post*, December 12, 1977.

16. Yasufumi Ishiwada and Katsuro Ogawa, "Petroleum Geology of Offshore Areas Around the Japanese Islands," *United Nations ESCAP, CCOP Technical Bulletin* (1976), 10:24 ff.

17. U.S. Geological Survey, *Summary of 1972 Oil and Gas Statistics for Offshore Areas in 151 Countries*, Geological Survey, Professional Paper 885 (Washington, D.C.: U.S. GPO, 1973).

18. Tomoya Takei, "Problems of Petroleum Development in the Continental Shelf of Japan," in *Marine Technology and Law, Development of Hydrocarbon Resources and Offshore Structures*, Proceedings of the Second International Ocean Symposium, Tokyo, 1977 (Tokyo: Ocean Association of Japan, June 1978), p. 24.

19. Ishiwada and Ogawa, op. cit., p. 24.

20. A. A. Meyerhoff, "Eastern Asian Coasts and Offshore Are Promising Petroleum Frontiers," *The Oil and Gas Journal*, December 27, 1976, p. 220.

21. J. Aiba, "The Geological Factors Controlling the Formation of the Large Oil and Gas Fields in Northwest Japan," in *Professor Kazuo Huzioka Memorial Volume* (Akita, Japan, 1977).

22. U.S. Embassy, Tokyo, February 1, 1977.

23. Selig S. Harrison, *China, Oil, and Asia: Conflict Ahead?* (New York: Columbia University Press, 1977), p. 169.

24. See various articles in *Technical Bulletin*, vol. 1, Economic Commission for Asia and the Far East Committee for Coordination of Joint Prospecting for Mineral Resources in Asian Offshore Areas, June 1968.

25. *Dong-A Ilbo* (Seoul Daily), January 19, 1980, p. 1.

26. Jeffrey Segal, "South Korean Imports—Mounting Insecurity," *Petroleum Economist* (November 1979), p. 450.

27. Wataru Tanaka, Director, Research Institute for Ocean Economics, personal communication, October 1977.

28. Larry Aldridge, "World Oil Flow Gains Slightly, Reserves Dip," *The Oil and Gas Journal*, December 28, 1978, p. 103.

29. *The Oil and Gas Journal*, February 12, 1979, p. 40. For a thorough description of China's oil policy, see: Jerome Alan Cohen and Choon-ho Park, "China's Oil Policy," in Shao-Chuan Leng, ed., *Post-Mao China and U.S. China Trade* (Charlottesville, Virginia: University of Virginia Press, 1979), pp. 108–140.

30. A. A. Meyerhoff and J. O. Willums, "China's Potential Still A Guessing Game," *Offshore* (January 1979), p. 56.

31. Harrison, op. cit., p. 51.

32. Ibid., p. 53.

33. Jan-Olaf Willums, "China's Offshore Petroleum," *The China Business Review* (July–August, 1977), p. 13.

34. Harrison, op. cit., pp. 38–41.

35. Customary English equivalents of Chinese place names are used throughout, despite the recent change in transliteration.

36. *World Oil* (December 1978), p. 50.

37. *China Business Review* (July–August 1979), p. 62.

38. Paul Bartlett and T. M. Burley, "China Takes a Bite at the Offshore Cherry," *Seatrade* (September 1979), p. 49.

39. *China Business Review* (July–August 1979), p. 62.

40. *The Seattle Times*, November 21, 1979.

41. Bartlett and Burley, op. cit., p. 49.

42. *World Oil* (December 1978), p. 52.

43. Committee for Coordination of Joint Prospecting for Mineral Resources in Asian Offshore Areas, *The Offshore Hydrocarbon Potential of East Asia, A Decade of Investigations (1966–1975)*, CCOP/TP 4, The Office for the Project Manager/Coordinator, UNDP Technical Support for Regional

Offshore Prospecting in East Asia, RAS/73/022 (September 1976).

44. Ibid., p. 60.

45. Ibid., p. 14; and Meyerhoff, op. cit., p. 220.

46. Harrison, op. cit., p. 130.

47. There have been extensive and protracted discussions between Japanese oil and fisheries interests over compensation in the joint development area (Yasutumi Ishiwada, Executive Director, Japan National Oil Corporation, personal communication).

48. Harrison, op. cit., pp. 215–221.

49. *The Oil and Gas Journal*, June 25, 1979, pp. 40–41.

50. *The Oil and Gas Journal*, June 25, 1979, p. 40.

51. Ibid.

52. *Petroleum Economist* (November 1977), p. 449; see also, Elliot Marshall, "Gain in Soviet Oil Reserves Doubted," *Science* (December 21, 1979), 206:1379–82.

53. *Nihon Keizai Shimbun*, October 13, 1977.

54. *The Oil and Gas Journal*, September 24, 1979, p. 78.

55. *The Wall Street Journal*, July 6, 1979.

56. Adams et al., op. cit.; see also, A. B. Coury and T. A. Hendricks, *Map of Prospective Hydrocarbon Provinces of the World, North and South America (Map MF-1044A) and East Asia, Australia and the Pacific (Map MF-1044C)* (Reston Virginia: U.S. Geological Survey, U.S. Dept. of Interior, 1978); also *Atlas of Marine Use in the North Pacific Region*, accompanying this volume.

57. National Oceanic & Atmospheric Administration, *Environmental Assessment of the Alaskan Continental Shelf: Annual Reports Summary for the Year Ending March 1976* (Washington, D.C.: NOAA, no date), p. 342.

58. *The Oil and Gas Journal*, June 7, 1976, p. 129.

59. National Oceanic & Atmospheric Administration, *Alaska OCS Principal Investigators Reports* (Washington, D.C.: NOAA, various years).

60. *Offshore* (July 1977), p. 47.

61. Michael P. Fergus, Public Affairs Officer, Pacific Outer Continental Shelf Office, Bureau of Land Management, U.S. Department of Interior, Los Angeles, California, July 10, 1979, personal communication.

62. *World Oil* (December 1, 1975), p. 70.

63. *The Oil and Gas Journal*, January 21, 1980, p. 45.

64. Adams et al., op. cit., p. 31.

65. *The Oil and Gas Journal*, February 13, 1978, p. 38.

66. *The Oil and Gas Journal*, May 8, 1978, p. 142.

67. Stephen Cline, "Oil and Fishermen, Part II," *Alaska Fishermen* (February 1978), p. 3.

68. Ibid., p. 3.

69. *The Oil and Gas Journal*, January 17, 1977, p. 28, and January 24, 1977, pp. 32–33.

70. North Pacific Fishery Management Council, "Comments on St. George Basin Oil Lease Sale," (October 1979).

71. WHOI, op. cit.

72. *The Oil and Gas Journal*, September 25, 1978, p. 69.

73. Mark Miller, "One Man's Opinion: Oil Contingency Fund Act Promises More Than It Is Likely to Deliver," *National Fisherman* (January 1979).

74. See, for example, Library of Congress Congressional Research Service, *Effects of Offshore Oil and Natural Gas Development to Coastal Zone*, Committee Print, Ad Hoc Select Committee on Outer Continental Shelf (Washington, D.C.: U.S. GPO, March 1977), pp. 246, 247.

75. Mark Miller, "Nets Snagged on Well Head Recovered, But Snags Remain," *National Fisherman* (January 1979).

76. *The Oil and Gas Journal*, May 8, 1978, p. 142.

77. *The Oil and Gas Journal*, October 16, 1978, p. 25.

78. Bureau of Land Management, *Final EIS Oil and Gas Development in the Santa Barbara Channel Off California* (Washington, D.C.: U.S. Department of Interior, 1978).

79. Library of Congress, *Effects of Offshore Oil and Natural Gas*, 396 pp.

80. See, *Atlas of Marine Use in the North Pacific Region*, accompanying this volume, for reserve estimates.

81. *The Oil and Gas Journal*, February 13, 1978, p. 23.

82. For a discussion of this problem with respect to Japan, see Masaaki Sato, "Prospects for Fisheries in the 200-mile Fishery Zone of Japan," *Special Volume*, Research Institute of North Pacific Fisheries, Hokkaido University (December 1977), p. 28.

83. *Offshore* (July 1977), p. 47.

84. *Ocean Science News*, September 18, 1978, reported this list as the categorization to be used in the national marine pollution monitoring program being developed in the United States.

85. Pollution of the marine environment can be defined as "the introduction by man, directly or indirectly, of substances or energy into the marine environment (including estuaries) which results, or is likely to result, in such deleterious effects as harm to living resources, hazards to human health, hindrance to marine activities including fishing and other legitimate uses of the sea, impairment of quality for use of sea water, and reduction of amenities." (Document A/CONF. 62/WP. 8/Rev. 1/ Part III).

86. See, for example, Goldberg, op. cit.; Waldichuk, op. cit.; McIntyre and Whittle, op. cit.; FAO, op. cit.; Northwest and Alaska Fisheries Center, *Monthly Report* (March 1977); David A. Salisbury, "A Delicate Balance," *Technology Review*, vol. 70 (July/August 1976); and M. Bernard and A. Zaterra, "Major Pollutants in the Marine Environment," in E. A. Pearson and E. De Farga Frangipane, eds., *Marine Pollution and Marine Waste Disposal*, Proceedings of the Second International Congress, San Remo, December 17–21, 1973 (New York: Pergamon Press, 1975).

87. Waldichuk, op. cit., p. 1.

88. D. L. Elder and Scott W. Fowler, "Polychlorinated Biphenyls: Penetration into the Deep Ocean by Zooplankton Fecal Pellet Transport," *Science* (July 29, 1977), p. 459.

89. Vizitko, "Fifteen Years of Environmental Research," *Marine Pollution Bulletin* (1979), 10:100.

90. See, for example, the discussion on duration of effects from catastrophic oil spills on marine ecosystems in *Science* (October 1, 1978), 201:7; see also J. H. Vandermeulen, A. H. Southward, D. C. Malins, J. W. Farrington, G. R. Hampson, H. L. Sanders, and J. M. Teal, *Science*, vol. 201 (October 8, 1978).

91. Dennis P. Tihansky, "International Scope of Marine Pollution Damage," *Marine Pollution Bulletin* (1973), 4:152.

92. Prof. Makato Shimizu, University of Tokyo, personal communication.

93. Teruji Sakiyama, "Cost of Japanese Fisheries Under Expanding Environmental Pollution," paper presented to the Meeting for the Economics of Fisheries, The Agricultural Economics Society of Southeast Asia, November 3–6, 1977, Iloilo, Philippines.

94. For Canada, see Michael Waldichuk, "Canadian Activities in the Pacific Region," in Christine Dawson, ed., *The North Pacific Project* (Seattle: Institute for Marine Studies, University of Washington, 1977), pp. 544–561. For U.S., see Warren S. Wooster and Nona Henderson, "Marine Scientific Activities in the North Pacific," in ibid., pp. 562–600. The National Ocean Pollution, Research and Development and Monitoring Planning Act of 1978 (Public Law 95-273) requires that a plan be developed, and a first draft was circulated in April 1979.

95. Northwest and Alaska Fisheries Center, *Monthly Report* (June 1977).

96. Food and Agriculture Organization (FAO), "Assessment of the Effects of Pollution on Fisheries and Aquaculture in Japan," FAO Fisheries Technical Paper no. 163, FIR/T163 (Rome, October 1976).

97. R. Watanuki, "PCB Residues in Japan," in Jun Ui, ed., *Polluted Japan*, Reports by members of the Jishu-Koza Citizens Movement (Tokyo: Jishu-Koza, 1972), p. 25.

98. Sakiyama, op. cit., p. 2.

99. John M. Graham, "Levels of PCBs in Canadian Commercial Fish Species," in Franklin A. Ayer, comp., *National Conference on Polychlorinated Biphenyls*, Conference Proceedings, Environmental Protection Agency (Washington, D.C.: Office of Toxic Substances, March 1976), p. 156.

100. IDOE, op. cit., p. 14.

101. Charles F. Jelinek and P. E. Cornelinssen, "Levels of PCBs in the U.S. Food Supply," in Franklin A. Ayer, comp., op. cit., p. 147.

102. David R. Young, Deirdre J. McDermott, and Theodore C. Heesen, "Marine Inputs of Polychlorinated Biphenyls Off Southern California," and Deirdre J. McDermott, David R. Young, and Theodore C. Heesen, "PCB Contamination of Southern California Marine Organisms," both in Franklin A. Ayer, comp., pp. 199–217.

103. James L. Cox, "DDT Residues in Marine Phytoplankton: Increase from 1955 to 1969," in *Science* (October 2, 1970), 170:71–73.

104. Edward D. Goldberg, *The Health of the Oceans* (Paris: UNESCO Press, 1976), p. 63.

105. This was the conclusion in R. W. Risebrough, R. J. Hugget, J. J. Griffen, and E. D. Goldberg, "Pesticides: Transatlantic Movements in the Northeast Trades," *Science* (March 1968), 159:1233. For data on seabirds, see R. J. Risebrough, Daniel B. Menzel, D. James Martin, Jr., and Harold Olcott, "DDT Residues in Pacific Sea Birds: A Persistent Insecticide in Marine Food Chains," *Nature* (November 11, 1967), 216:589–591.

106. IDOE, op. cit., p. 14.

107. Virginia F. Stout, "Pesticide Levels in Fish of the Northeast Pacific," *Bulletin of Environmental Contamination and Toxicology*, 3,4 (1968), 240.

108. James L. Cox, "DDT Residues in Seawater and Particulate Matter in the California Current System," *Fishery Bulletin*, 69, 2 (1971), 445. Values in northern waters were from 2–3 parts per trillion (ppt), and in southern California ranged from 3 to over 5 ppt.

109. John Calambokidis et al., *Chlorinated Hydrocarbon Concentrations and Ecology and Behavior of Harbor Seals in Washington State Waters*, a student-originated study supported by the National Science Foundation, the Evergreen State College, March 28, 1977 to March 28, 1978.

110. R. L. Delong, W. G. Gilmartin, and J. G. Simpson, "Premature Births in California Sea Lions' Association with High Organochlorine Pollutant Residue Levels," *Science* (1973), 181: 1168–70.

111. Lawrence B. Harding, Jr. and John H. Phillips, "Polychlorinated Biphenyls' Transfer from Microparticulates to Marine Phytophankton and Their Effects on Photosynthesis," *Science* (1978), 202:1189–1192.

112. Harold B. O'Connors, Jr., Charles F. Wunster, C. Donald Bowers, Douglas C. Riggs, and Ralph Rowland, "Polychlorinated Biphenyls May Alter Marine Trophic Pathways by Reducing Phytoplankton Size and Production," *Science* (August 25, 1978), 201:737–739.

113. For Japan, see, FAO, op. cit., and for the U.S. see, Council on Environmental Quality, *Environmental Quality 1977*, The Eighth Annual Report of the Council on Environmental Quality (Washington, D.C.: CEQ, 1978).

114. Goldberg, op. cit., p. 59.

115. D. W. Anderson, J. R. Jehl, Jr., R. W. Risebrough, L. A. Woods, Jr., L. R. Deweese, and W. G. Edgecomb, *Science* (November 21, 1975), 190:806.

116. Paul R. Spitzer, Robert W. Risebrough, Wyman Walker II, Robert Hernandez, Allan Poole, Dennis Puleston, and Ian C. T. Nisbet, "Productivity of Ospreys in Connecticut–Long Island Increases as DDT Residues Decline," *Science* (October 20, 1978), 202:333.

117. IDOE, op. cit., p. 11.

118. R. A. Hall, E. G. Zook, and G. M. Meaburn, *National Marine Fisheries Service Survey of*

*Trace Elements in the Fishery Resource*, NOAA Technical Report NMFS SSRF-121 (Washington, D.C.: U.S. Department of Commerce, March 1978), 311 pp.

119. Prior to 1979, the U.S. federal action level for mercury was 0.5 ppm. according to the U.S. Food and Drug Administration, "Action Levels for Poisonous or Deleterious Materials in Human Food and Animal Feed," Industry Guidance Branch, January 6, 1978. Following extensive review and testimony on consumption patterns, this standard was changed to 1 ppm. for fish and fish products, *Western Fisheries*, 97 (November 1978), p. 56.

120. Alice S. Hall, Fuad M. Teeny, Laura G. Lewis, William H. Hardman, and Erich H. Gauglitz, Jr., "Mercury in Fish and Shellfish of the Northeast Pacific, I. Pacific Halibut, *Hippoglossus stenolepis*," *Fishery Bulletin*, 74, 4 (1976).

121. Alice S. Hall, Fuad M. Teeny, Laura G. Lewis, William H. Hardman, and Erich H. Gauglitz, Jr., "Mercury in Fish and Shellfish of the Northeast Pacific, II. Sablefish, *Anoplopoma fimbria*," *Fishery Bulletin*, 74, 4 (1976).

122. Alice S. Hall, Fuad M. Teeny, and Erich H. Gauglitz, Jr., "Mercury in Fish and Shellfish of the Northeast Pacific, III. Spiny Dogfish, *Squalus acanthias*," *Fishery Bulletin*, 75, 3 (1977).

123. Norman H. Cutshall, J. R. Naidu, and W. G. Pearcy, "Mercury Concentrations in Pacific Hake, *Merluccius productus* (Ayers), As A Function of Length and Latitude," *Science* (June 20, 1978), 200:1489.

124. Cutshall, op. cit., p. 1489.

125. F. M. D'Itri, *The Environmental Mercury Problem* (Cleveland: Chemical Rubber Press, 1972), p. 102.

126. David Tharp, "Japan Accused of Hiding Dolphin Meat Poisoning," *Christian Science Monitor*, November 10, 1978. Also, David Tharp, "New Evidence of Contamination in Dolphin Meat," *Christian Science Monitor*, November 13, 1978.

127. John F. Beary III, "Mercury in Sperm Whale Meat," *Science* (December 14, 1979), 206:1260. It should be noted that sperm whale meat is not generally eaten by humans.

128. George D. Grice, "Controlled Ecosystem Pollution Experiment," *Oceanus*, 18, 1 (1974), 24–31.

129. Timothy R. Parsons, "Controlled Aquatic Ecosystem Experiments in Ocean Ecology Research," *Marine Pollution Bulletin* (1977), 8:203–205; and David F. Salisbury, op. cit., p. 8.

130. Ruth Patrick, "Effects of Trace Metals in the Aquatic Ecosystem," *American Scientist* (March–April, 1978), 66:187.

131. K. Okani and Jun Ui, "Minimata Disease," in Jun Ui, ed., *Polluted Japan*, Reports by Members of the Jishu-Koza Citizens Movement (Tokyo: Jishu-Koza, 1972); F. M. D'Itri, op. cit., and Masazumi Harada, "Methyl Mercury Poisoning Due to Environmental Contamination ('Minimata Disease')," in Frederick W. Oehme, ed., *Toxicity of Heavy Metals in the Environment, Part I* (New York: Marcel Dekker, 1978), pp. 261–302.

132. Jun Kobayashi, "Pollution by Cadmium and the Itai-Itai Disease in Japan," in Frederick W. Oehme, ed., op. cit., pp. 199–260.

133. D'Itri, op. cit., p. 88.

134. Hydrographic Department, *Report of Marine Pollution Surveys* (Tokyo: Maritime Safety Agency, various years) in Japanese with English abstract and titles.

135. FAO, op. cit.

136. The most comprehensive survey of hydrocarbons in surface waters is, Edward P. Meyers and Charles G. Gunnarson, *Hydrocarbons in the Ocean*, MESA Special Report (Boulder, Colorado: Maritime Administration and NOAA Environmental Research Laboratories, April 1976), 42 pp; see also, R. A. Brown, T. D. Searle, and C. B. Koons, *Measurement and Interpretation of Hydrocarbons in the Pacific Ocean*, NOAA Data Report ERL MESA-19 (Boulder, Colorado: NOAA, April 1976), 246 pp. (microfiche). Note that these studies do not permit any generalizations to be made about trends of oil pollution in the marine environment.

137. U.S. Department of Commerce, *Report to Congress on Ocean Pollution—Over-Fishing and Offshore Development, July 1973 through June 1974*, PL 92−532, Title II, sec. 202(c). (Washington, D.C.: NOAA, January 1975), p. 21.

138. FAO, op. cit., p. 1.

139. Walter J. Meade and Philip E. Sorensen, "The Economic Cost of the Santa Barbara Oil Spill," in Robert H. Holms and Floyd A. DeWitt, Jr., eds., *Santa Barbara Oil Symposium*, Offshore Oil Production and Environmental Inquiry at the University of California, Santa Barbara, December 16−18, 1970 (Santa Barbara, California: Marine Science Institute, 1971), p. 184. Meade and Sorensen cite the estimate of A. A. Allen of General Research Corp. as being the most thorough.

140. The *Torrey Canyon* lost on the order of 97,200 MT and covered 220 km of British and French beaches, whereas the Santa Barbara blowout spilled an estimated 10,500 metric tons and covered 50 km of beaches. Dispersants used in the Santa Barbara Channel were the low toxicity variety that impacted less severely on marine life than did those used in the English Channel.

141. Mead and Sorensen, op. cit., p. 225.

142. See remarks by Professor Dorfman, in Edward J. Mitchell, ed., *The Question of Offshore Oil* (Washington, D.C.: American Enterprise Institute for Public Policy Research, 1976), p. 90.

143. See chap. 8, table 8.11, this volume.

144. *Petroleum Information*, Section 1 (January 1977), p. 4.

145. *OCS Project Task Force, Offshore Oil and Gas Development: Southern California, Vol. 1* (Sacramento: California Coastal Commission, October 1977), p. 82.

146. Ibid., p. 565.

147. Mark Stevens, "Local Voters OK Oil Terminal for Long Beach," *Christian Science Monitor*, November 10, 1978.

148. William M. Ross, *Oil Pollution As An International Problem: A Study of Puget Sound and the Strait of Georgia* (Seattle: University of Washington Press, 1973), p. 214.

149. Tanker Advisory Center, *Tanker Advisory Center Annual Report 1977* (New York: 1977).

150. *The Seattle Times*, November 16 and 24, 1979.

151. Mead and Sorensen, op. cit., p. 207.

152. Frank Richardson, "Sea Birds Affected by Oil from the Freighter *Seagate*," *The Murrelet* (1956), 37:20.

153. *Seatrade* (August 1978).

154. Harrison, op. cit., pp. 151−153.

155. *Japan Petroleum News*, October 21, 1977.

156. Ibid.; Cohen and Park, op. cit., suggests that imports of as much as 30 million metric tons by 1985 have been contemplated by the government of Japan. Whether or not China would be willing to supply this amount is uncertain, although the capacity to export that amount exists. The estimated import of 15 million MT is approximately 6 percent of Japan's 1978 consumption of crude oil.

157. *Seatrade* (July 1978).

158. Harrison, op. cit., p. 144.

159. Choon-ho Park and Jerome A. Cohen, "The Politics of China's Oil Weapon," *Foreign Policy* (1975), 20:35.

160. Harrison, op. cit., p. 44.

161. *The Oil and Gas Journal*, August 15, 1977, p. 28.

162. *Japan Petroleum News*, October 27, 1977.

163. This discussion is based on Yoshihiko Miwa, "Oil Storage in Laid-Up Tankers: The Japanese Plan," paper presented to the 12th Annual Conference, Law of the Sea Institute, University of Hawaii, October 23−26, 1978, The Hague, Netherlands.

164. William B. Travers and Percy R. Luney, "Drilling, Tankers and Oil Spill on the Atlantic Outer Continental Shelf," *Science* (November 19, 1976), 194:792.

165. Ocean Dumping Control Act (SC. 1974−75, C.55).

166. Marine Sciences and Information Directorate, comp., *A Summary of Permits Issued Under the Ocean Dumping Control Act* (Canada: Ocean and Aquatic Sciences, Dept. of Fisheries and the Environment, Summaries for 1977 and 1978); Waldichuk, op. cit., p. 554.

167. See *Atlas of Marine Use in the North Pacific Region*, accompanying this volume, p. 79, for locations of the nationally designated ocean dumping sites.

168. Waldichuk, op. cit., see discussion of Canadian experience under the various subheadings of this article; see also Michael Waldichuk, "Disposal of Mine Wastes into the Sea," *Marine Pollution Bulletin*, 9,6 (June 1978), pp. 141–143; K. E. Conlan and D. V. Ellis, "Effects of Wood Waste on Sand-Bed Benthos," *Marine Pollution Bulletin* (1979), 10:262–267.

169. Sato, op. cit., pp. 46–47.

170. Ibid.

171. See FAO, op. cit., and Hydrographic Dept., op. cit., for locations of these sites.

172. National Academy of Sciences, *Disposal in the Marine Environment: An Oceanographic Assessment* (Washington, D.C.: Ocean Disposal Steering Committee, Commission on Natural Resources, National Research Council, 1976), p. 6.

173. Council on Environmental Quality (CEQ), *Ocean Dumping: A National Policy*, Report to the President (Washington, D.C.: U.S. GPO, October 1970), p. 8.

174. Marine Protection, Research and Sanctuaries (Ocean Dumping) Act (PL 92–532), October 23, 1972.

175. U.S. Congress, *Federal Register*, 42,7 (January 11, 1977), 2462–2490, and 43,4 (January 6, 1978), 1071–1072; U.S. Army Corps of Engineers, 1978 Report to Congress on Administration of Ocean Dumping Activities, 1979.

176. Council on Environmental Quality, *Ocean Dumping*, p. 3.

177. International Convention on Prevention of Marine Pollution by Dumping of Wastes and Other Matter 1973, *International Legal Materials*, 11:1291 ff.

178. Goldberg, op. cit., p. 79.

179. C. Allday, "The Discharge of Radioactive Effluents from the Nuclear Power Programme into the Western Waters of Britain," in M. M. Sibthorp, ed., *Oceanic Management, Conflicting Uses of the Celtic Sea and Other Western U.K. Waters*, Report of a Conference held at University College of Swansea, September 19–22, 1975 (London: Europa Publishers, 1977), p. 63.

180. Milner B. Shaeffer, "New Research Required in Support of Radioactive Waste Disposal," Reprinted from: *Disposal of Radioactive Wastes* (Vienna: International Atomic Energy Agency, 1960).

181. Charles Osterberg, William G. Pearcy, and Halbert Curl, Jr., "Radioactivity and Its Relationship to Oceanic Food Chains," *Journal of Marine Research*, 22,1 (1964), 10, 11.

182. Goldberg, op. cit., p. 81.

183. William E. Butler, *The Soviet Union and the Law of the Sea* (Baltimore: The Johns Hopkins Press, 1971), p. 190.

184. Council on Environmental Quality, *Ocean Dumping*. This reference contains maps that show dumping sites off the coasts of the United States. At least five sites where radioactive wastes were dumped are shown off the coast of California.

185. David A. Deese, "Seabed Emplacement and Political Reality," *Oceanus*, 20,1 (1977), 51.

186. Alexander W. Reed, *Ocean Waste Disposal Practices* (Park Ridge, New Jersey: Noyes Data Corporation, 1975), p. 324.

187. Yutaka Hirasawa, "Can the Seas Be Resuscitated?," *Japan Echo*, 4,3 (1977), 57.

188. Ibid.

189. Deese, op. cit., pp. 56, 57.

190. Osterberg et al., op. cit., p. 2.

191. A. T. Pruter and D. L. Alverson, eds., *The Columbia River Estuary and Adjacent Ocean Waters—Bioenvironmental Studies* (Seattle: University of Washington Press, 1972), 868 pp.

192. Charles D. Hollister, "The Seabed Option," *Oceanus*, 20,1 (1977), 18–25.

193. *Ocean Science News*, September 18, 1978, p. 3; also, Richard A. Kerr, "Geological Disposal of Nuclear Wastes: Salt's Lead Challenged," *Science* (May 11, 1979), 204:606.

194. Deese, op. cit., pp. 55–59.

195. Ernest E. Angine, "High-Level and Long-Lived Radioactive Waste Disposal," *Science* (December 2, 1977), 199:899.

196. See Hollister, op. cit., and Robert R. Hessler and Peter A. Jumars, "Abyssal Communities and Radioactive Waste Disposal," *Oceanus*, 20,1 (1977), 41–46.

197. Briefing by Port of Nagoya Authority, October 19, 1977.

198. FAO, op. cit., p. ix.

199. See, for example, Gerald Berg, "Regional Problems with Sea Outfall Disposal of Sewage on the Coasts of the United States," in A. L. H. Gameson, ed., *Discharge of Sewage from Sea Outfalls* (New York: Pergamon Press, 1975); D. V. Ellis, "Pollution Control in the Fraser River Estuary," *Marine Pollution Bulletin*, 10:35; Michael Waldichuk, "Effects of Sulfite Wastes in a Partially Enclosed Marine System in British Columbia," *Journal of the Water Pollution Control Federation*, 38:1484–1505; and Donald L. Beyer, Roy E. Nakitani, and Craig P. Staude, "Effects of Salmon Cannery Wastes on Water Quality and Marine Organisms," *Journal of Water Pollution Control Federation*, 47:1857–1869.

200. Southern California Coastal Water Research Project, *Effects of the Ocean Disposal of Municipal Wastes* (El Segundo, Calfornia: Commission of the Coastal Water Research Project, June 1978), p. 20.

201. "Red tide" is the name given to water tinged reddish by the dense concentrations of certain marine dinoflagellates. The cause of the observed sudden increases in the population size of these organisms is unknown, but the toxic effects on marine life are still in fish kills. Shellfish that filter feed on these organisms can become lethal for human consumption.

202. See, for example, FAO, op. cit., p. 97

203. Ibid.

204. Sakiyama, op. cit., p. 7.

205. *Ocean Science News*, September 18, 1978. See also, John B. Coulton, Jr., "Plastics in the Ocean," *Oceanus*, 18,1 (1974), 61–64.

206. A. M. Cundell, "Plastics in the Marine Environment," in R. Gordon Pirie, *Oceanography*, 2d ed. (New York: Oxford University Press, 1977).

207. E. L. Venrick, T. W. Backman, W. C. Bartram, C. J. Platt, M. S. Thornhill, and R. E. Yates, "Man-Made Objects on the Surface of the Central North Pacific Ocean," *Nature* (January 26, 1973), 241:271.

208. Goldberg, op. cit., p. 138.

209. Steven C. Jewett, "Pollutants of the Northeast Gulf of Alaska," *Marine Pollution Bulletin* (1976), 7:169; and Howard M. Feder, Steven C. Jewett, and John R. Hilsinger, "Man-Made Debris on the Bering Sea Floor," *Marine Pollution Bulletin* (1977), 8:52,53.

210. D. G. Shaw and G. A. Mapes, "Surface Circulation and the Distribution of Pelagic Tar and Plastic," *Marine Pollution Bulletin* (1979), 10:160–162.

211. C. S. Wong, David R. Green, and Walter J. Cretney, "Quantitative Tar and Plastic Waste Distributions in the Pacific Ocean," *Nature*, 247, 5435 (January 4, 1974), 32.

212. Kazuo Sumi, "Protection of the Marine Environment in the East Asian Waters," in *Utilization and Develoment of the Pacific Ocean*, Proceedings of the International Pacific Symposium on the Pacific Ocean (Tokyo: Ocean Association of Japan, 1977).

213. Pacific Sea Bird Group, "Pacific Sea Bird Group Policy Statement: Incidental Sea Bird Kills from Salmon Gillnet Fisheries," *Pacific Sea Bird Group Bulletin*, 2, 1 (Spring 1975).

214. Michael Waldichuk, "Plastics and Seals," *Marine Pollution Bulletin*, 2,8 (1978), 197.

215. Ibid.

216. Michael Waldichuk, "Log Pollution," *Marine Pollution Bulletin*, 9, 12 (December 1978), 313.

217. Since much of the plastic debris originates from fishing vessels, it has been suggested that coastal states prohibit foreign fleets from discharging plastic litter as part of the fisheries zone regulations; see Theodore R. Merrell, Jr., "Accumulation of Plastic Litter on Beaches of Amchitka Island, Alaska" (Auke Bay, Alaska: Northwest and Alaska Fisheries Center, Auke Bay Laboratory, no date), p. 17.

218. Briefing by Nagoya Port Authority, October 19, 1977.

219. J. E. Gormley, Overseas Maintenance Manager, Eastern Telephone and Telegraph Co., personal communication, April 18, 1978.

220. T. C. M. Whelan, Secretary, International Cable Protection Committee, London, personal communication, October 7, 1977.

221. Butler, op. cit., p. 173.

222. Norman Breckner, Robert L. Friedheim, Leslie Hesetton, Jr., Lee S. Mason, Stuart G. Schmid and Robert H. Simmons, *The Navy and the Common Sea* (Washington, D.C.: Office of Naval Research, 1972), pp. 14–16.

223. *Coastal Zone Management* (April 6, 1977).

224. Breckner et al., op. cit., p. 18.

225. These activities have been reviewed in an article by A. A. Archer, "Economics of Offshore Exploration and Production of Solid Minerals on the Continental Shelf," *Ocean Management*, 1, 1 (1973), 5–40.

226. *Victoria Times* (September 24, 1979).

227. Archer, op. cit., pp. 25, 26

228. G. D. Sharma, "Marine Placers on the Alaskan Shelf," in *Proceedings of POAC 77*, Fourth International Conference on Port and Ocean Engineering Under Arctic Conditions, St. John's, Newfoundland, Canada, September 26–30, 1977.

229. Archer, op. cit., p. 33.

230. Donald Bakke, "Russia Strengthens Its Mining Program," *Offshore* (November 1971), pp. 38, 39.

231. James W. Adams, Jr., "Unexplored Far Eastern Areas Look Promising," *Ocean Industry* (December 1969), p. 53.

232. Eilif Trondsen and Walter J. Mead, *California Offshore Phosphorite Deposits: An Economic Evaluation*, University of California Sea Grant College Program, La Jolla, California, August 1977, pp. 79–83.

233. Nicholas Wade, "A Dearth of Phosphate," *Science* (January 4, 1980), 207:41.

234. General Electric Co., *Energy from Marine Biomass: A Program for 1978–1985*, GE-RESC Proposal No. N-74601, Reentry and Environmental Systems Division (Philadelphia, May 26, 1978).

235. *Offshore* (November 1977), p. 55.

236. Discussion with Mitsugi Kawakami, Professor of Geography, Tohuku University during his visit at the Institute for Marine Studies, Seattle, Washington, January 30, 1980.

237. *The Seattle Times*, September 21, 1978.

238. Serbin Arasaki, "Biological Aspects of the Protection of the Marine Environment," in *Utilization and Development of the Pacific Ocean*, Proceedings of the International Pacific Symposium on the Pacific Ocean (Tokyo: Ocean Association of Japan, 1976).

239. Discussion with President Ino, Shimonosecki University of Fisheries, November 28, 1977.

240. *The Oil and Gas Journal*, September 5, 1977.

241. *Federal Register*, 44, 212 (October 31, 1979).

242. This discussion is based on, Bruce R. Mate, *Workshop Report for Marine Mammal—Fisheries Interactions in the Eastern Pacific*, Final Report to the U.S. Marine Mammal Commission for Contract MM 8AC-003 (Newport, Oregon: Oregon State University, February 1978).

243. See Convention for the Protection of Migratory Birds 1916 Between Canada and the United States (TS628); and Convention for the Protection of Migratory Birds and Birds in Danger of Extinction and Their Environment 1972 between Japan and the United States (TIAS 7990).

244. Taivo Laevastu, Felix Favorite, and W. Bruce McAllister, *Final Report RU77 Ecosystem Dynamics Birds and Marine Mammals*, Environmental Assessment of the Alaskan Continental Shelf sponsored by the U.S. Department of Interior, Bureau of Land Management (Seattle: Northwest and Alaska Fisheries Center, National Marine Fisheries Service, September 1976).

245. *The Seattle Times*, March 18, 1978.

246. Matthew H. Dick and William Donaldson, "Fishing Vessel Endangered by Crested Auklet Landings," *Condor* (1978), 80:235–236.

247. Discussion with Warren Wooster, Institute for Marine Studies, University of Washington, Seattle, Washington, January 16, 1980.

248. Richard A. Kerr, "Explorer: Can Oil and Science Mix?" *Science* (February 8, 1980), 207:627.

## 15. Legacy of the Past and Directions for Future Marine Policy in the North Pacific

1. A similar complaint has been addressed to U.S. fisheries policy under extended jurisdiction but we think this complaint is justifiably extended to the whole range of marine policy in the North Pacific and elsewhere. See Daniel D. Huppert, "Constraints to Welfare Gains Under Extended Jurisdiction Fisheries Management," *American Journal of Agricultural Economics*, 59, 5 (December 1977), 877–882.

2. These regulations would encompass not only current allocations but also regulations designed to facilitate development of underutilized species as well as coastal state moves to manage entire ecosystems (e.g., the eastern Bering Sea, in an integrated fashion).

3. This issue is treated by Robert L. Stokes, "U.S.-Foreign Cooperation for Fisheries Development: A Preliminary Economic Analysis," unpublished manuscript, Institute for Marine Studies, University of Washington, January 1980.

4. See James A. Crutchfield et al., *Joint Ventures in Fisheries* (Rome: FAO/UNDP, Doc. #10FC/DEV/75/37, April 1975).

5. "Foreign Vessels Under FCMA; 1978 Permits Issued and Vessels Permitted to Fish by Fishery," National Marine Fisheries Service, *Council Memorandum*, 3, 1 (January 1979). Also, circular letter from Robert W. Schoning, Director, National Marine Fisheries Service, "Status of the Applications/Permits Issued," NMFS, April 3, 1977, F35/WPA.

6. Wlodzimierz Kaczynski, "Management of Foreign Fleets in the Northeast Pacific and Bering Sea," unpublished MS, Institute for Marine Studies, University of Washington, January 1980, table 4, p. 30.

7. Kaczynski, op. cit.

8. See Barry Buzan, "Maritime Issues in Northeast Asia," *Marine Policy* (July 1979), pp. 190–200; Choon-ho Park, "Fishing Under Troubled Waters: The Northeast Asia Fisheries Controversy," *Ocean Development and International Law Journal*, 2, 2 (1974), 93–135; Choon-ho Park, "The Sino–Japanese–Korean Sea Resources Controversy and the Hypothesis of a 200-mile Economic Zone," *Harvard International Law Journal* (1975), 16:27–45; Choon-ho Park, "Marine Resource Conflicts in the North Pacific," in Douglas Johnston, ed., *Marine Policy and the Coastal Community* (London: Croom Helm, 1976), pp. 215–232; and Northern Territories Issue Association, *Japan's Northern Territories* (Tokyo, 1974).

9. Selig A. Harrison, *China, Oil and Asia* (New York: Columbia University Press, 1976); Arthur Jay Klinghoffer, *The Soviet Union and International Oil Politics* (New York: Columbia University Press, 1977); Choon-ho Park, "Oil Under Troubled Waters: The Northeast Asia Sea-Bed Controversy," *Harvard International Law Journal* (1973), 14:212–260; Tadashi Kikuchi, "Delimitation of the Continental Shelf of the East China Sea," *Meijo Law Review*, 22, 3–4 (October 1977), 1–51; and Kiyofumi Nakauchi, "Problems of Delimitation in the East China Sea and Sea of Japan," *Ocean Development and International Law Journal* (1979), 6:305–316.

10. See, for instance, Kaczynski, op. cit., pp. 26–43.

11. J. R. Immer, "Liner Cargoes, Changing Patterns," *American Seaport* (December 1978).

12. Stephen R. Gibbs and Bradford Meyer, "The Effect of the Panama Canal Treaties on the General Cargo Traffic of U.S. West Coast Ports," draft, Institute for Marine Studies, University of Washington, June 1979.

13. The emphasis here is on broader, longer term questions. While particular stock assessment efforts would fall into the first category, research on the relative utility and power of different methods of stock assessment would fall into the second category.

14. W. P. Bishop and C. D. Hollister, "Seabed Disposal—Where to Look," *Nuclear Technology* (December 1974), 24:425–443; "High-Level Nuclear Wastes in the Seabed?" *Oceanus*, 20, 1 (Winter 1977); Paul Grimwood and Geoffrey Webb, "Can Nuclear Wastes Be Buried at Sea?" *New Scientist* (24 March 1977), pp. 709–711; David Deese, *Nuclear Power and Radioactive Waste: A Sub-Seabed Disposal Option?* (Cambridge, MA.: Lexington Books, 1978); Gene I. Rochlin, "Nuclear Waste Disposal: Two Social Criteria," *Science*, 195, 4273 (7 January 1977), 23–31; Todd R. LaPorte, "Nuclear Waste: Increasing Scale and Sociopolitical Impacts," *Science* (7 July 1978), 201:22–27.

15. Bishop and Hollister, op. cit. See also statement by D. R. Anderson, "Seabed High Level Waste Assessment Program," Hearings on the Disposal of Nuclear Wastes in the Ocean, Subcommittee on Oceanography, U.S. House Merchant Marine and Fisheries Committee, May 16, 1978, unpublished MS.

16. LaPorte, op. cit.

**Index**

# Index